# Savagery in the Heart of Europe

The Bosnian War (1992-1995)
Context, Perspectives, Personal Experiences,
and Memoirs

By
Raphael Israeli and Albert Benabou

Strategic Book Publishing and Rights Co.

Copyright © 2013 Raphael Israeli, Albert Benabou. All rights reserved.

No part of this book may be reproduced or transmitted in any form or by any means, graphic, electronic, or mechanical, including photocopying, recording, taping, or by any information storage retrieval system, without the permission, in writing, of the publisher.

Strategic Book Publishing and Rights Co.
12620 FM 1960, Suite A4-507
Houston TX 77065
www.sbpra.com

ISBN: 978-1-62857-015-1

Design: Dedicated Book Services, (www.netdbs.com)

# Dedication

*To the innocent victims of the war,
Serbs, Croats, Muslims, and others.
Once again proven:
Savagery is not exclusively
the domain of the savages . . .*

*We are grateful to our spouses
Laeticia Benabou and Margalit Israeli
Who accompanied the discussions and writing
With encouragement and enthusiasm
And bore patiently and selflessly
The burden of the countless hours
of absence and absent-mindedness.*

# Table of Contents

Foreword: Horror in Europe .................................................. vi

Chapter 1  The Dismantling of Yugoslavia and the Setting of the Bosnian War ........................................... 1

Chapter 2  The Deadly Triangle: Serbia-Croatia-Bosnia .................................................. 24

Chapter 3  The UN Mission into the War ........................ 82

Chapter 4  From the Diary of an Israeli in a UN Mission ............................................... 166

Chapter 5  Generals and Bureaucrats in the Service of the United Nations ................................. 225

Chapter 6  The UN Impasse Gets the Conflict Nowhere ................................................. 303

Chapter 7  US Mediation and the Dayton Debacle ........ 369

Chapter 8  Dealing with Domestic and International Islam ..................................... 382

Chapter 9  Collecting the Pieces and Adjudicating War Crimes ........................................... 420

Summing Up: Epilogue and Conclusions ...................... 495

Acronyms and Abbreviations ........................................... 512

List of Officials and Key Functionaries (Local and International) .................................... 519

Bibliography ...................................................................... 538

List of Illustrations ........................................................... 542

Index of Names, Locations, Institutions, Key Words ..................................................... 543

## Foreword: Horror in Europe

When one looks from a distance, and even more so at close range, at the horrifying details of the Bosnian War (1992-1995), one is staggered by the virulence, violence, and cruelty which accompanied it on all sides. The Arab-Israeli conflict and other lingering international disputes, compared to the Bosnian War appear as a children's game. Although internecine wars and orgies of killing among Arabs and Muslims, like those in Darfur, Iraq, Afghanistan, Algeria, Libya, Syria, Yemen and more, are admittedly quite horrifying in themselves. Indeed, it seems that while in the sixty-five-year Arab-Israeli dispute on all four fronts (Egypt, Syria, Lebanon, and Jordan-Palestine), Israel has sustained over twenty-five thousand casualties (military and civilian) and the Arabs many more, the Bosnian War arena has produced a disproportionately larger amount of victims, civilian and military, local and international, mostly concentrated within the three years of the war and within the limited contours of Bosnia. Moreover, while the Arab-Israeli confrontations, save for the foundational war of 1948-1949 which spanned an entire year, lasted a few days or at most several weeks, in Bosnia, the massacres went on without respite for the entire duration of that three-year war.

The estimated numbers are indeed staggering. The death toll after the war was originally estimated at around two hundred thousand by the Bosnian government. It also recorded around one million three hundred and twenty-six thousand refugees and exiles, double the amount of Arab-Palestinian refugees who were uprooted, and equivalent to the general combined numbers of Palestinian refugees (some seven hundred thousand in 1948-1949), and Jewish refugees from Arab lands (an equal amount). Later research has determined

*Savagery in the Heart of Europe*

a figure of one hundred and two thousand deaths and estimated the following breakdown: 55,261 were civilians and 47,360 were soldiers. Of the civilians: sixteen thousand and seven hundred were Serbs while thirty eight thousand were Bosniaks and Croats. Of the soldiers: fourteen thousand were Serbs, six thousand were Croats, and twenty-eight thousand were Bosniaks. It appears that the opportunity for mutual slaughter was so limited in time, that all parties exercised their killing instincts to their highest intensity and rejected any idea of toning down their animus towards their perceived enemies, lest the war was terminated without, or before, the full mission of annihilating the others was completed. It is true that the Bosnian War was conducted in one stroke and terminated (for now), while the Arab-Israeli conflict has been continually festering since 1948, in spite of the peace treaties that Israel has signed with Egypt (1979) and Jordan (1994). While mutual genocidal ideologies were invoked in the Balkan Wars, in the Middle East those sinister intentions were voiced unilaterally by Arabs and Muslims against the Jews. One can hear Arabs (and other Muslim countries like Iran and Turkey), falsely complain about Israel's "genocidal designs" against them, rarely the reverse, except for the open and repeated threats coming from Iran under Ahmadinejad.

The controversy of numbers will persist forever,[1] despite the sober numbers advanced by some historians,[2] as will the relative assessments on the two sides of the divide relating to the intensity and relentlessness of the horrors of the World War II Ustasha regime of Greater Croatia on the one hand,[3]

---

[1] See e.g. Vladimir Zerjavic, *Population Losses in Yugoslavia 1941-5*, Zagreb 1997.
[2] Ivo Goldstein, *Croatia: a History* Montreal: McGill Press, 2001. See also other works by this author on his own or in conjunction with his father, Slavko.
[3] See Chapters 3 and 6 on Jadovno and Jasenovac, in R. Israeli, Death Camps in Croatia: Visions and Revisions, Transaction, 2012.

the contributing mythological motivation of the Serbs to "annihilate the Croats" on the other,[4] and the unexpectedly growing literature on the Croats who had allegedly come to the rescue of the Jews in the Ustasha state in the midst of those dark days.[5] However one twists the data, it is evident that while the Ustasha did commit genocide (of Serbs, Jews, Gypsies, and others), even if we accept the minimal numbers admitted by the Croats at their Jasenovac Memorial record, no such blame could be hurled against the Serbs during World War II, either because they were themselves occupied by the Germans or because the project of genocide against Croats and Muslims had never been within their purview at that time. To project the savageries of the Bosnia War of the 1990s, in which all parties have participated, onto the "national character" "of the Serbs, is not a serious proposition even when wrapped in scholarly dissertations and spelled out in fancy social science jargon. Serbs may or may not have been prone to genocide, just like the Hungarians, Lithuanians, Latvians, Ukrainians, Poles and others who directly aided the Germans in the "final solution" against the Jews, but in World War II they (the Serbs) did not commit one, though Nedic and his adepts, namely the Serbs who were under Nazi occupation, in a softer fashion than the Pavelic Ustasha followers who led and operated their death camps, also collaborated with the Nazis in carrying out their annihilation of Jews and Gypsies.

The adamant and unconscionable hurling of numbers, exaggerated upward or downward, has nevertheless produced over the years a process of leveling off, by force of erosion

---

[4] Branimir Anzulovic, *Heavenly Serbia: From Myth to Genocide* Hurst and Co, London, 1999; see also Boze Covic, ed. *Roots of Serbian Aggression,* Center for Foreign Languages Zagreb, 1993.
[5] Esther Gitman, *When Courage Prevailed: Rescue and Survival of Jews in the Independent State of Croatia, 1941-5*, Paragon House, St Paul, 2011.

or under the hammer of perseverance by serious scholars on both sides. Serbs no longer claim the inflated number of seven hundred thousand murdered Serbs, which was, until recently, proclaimed in the Bosnian Jasenovac, at Donia Gradina, nor the exceedingly low number of just over eighty thousand, including Jews and Gypsies, which has been advertised in a two thousand-page directory of names of all victims for visitors of the Croatian Jasenovac across the Sava River. Indeed, at the April 2012 memorial ceremony in Gradina, which was sponsored by President Dodik of the Republika Srpska, and attended by a large delegation from Israel, the number of five hundred thousand Serbian victims was proclaimed, side by side with the other, unchanged numbers of Gypsy and Jewish victims. Between these two extremes one finds various foundations, memorials, archives, and government and scholarly essays which under the impact of conferences, publications, and joint or separate research have considerably narrowed the gap between the two to the order of a few hundreds of thousands for the Serbs, and around one hundred thousand for the Croats. Both are a far cry from what politicians like the Croatian President Franjo Tudjman, who declared that "only forty thousand Serbs" were killed, or the five hundred thousand or more victims that the descendants of the murdered claim. At any rate, a genocide there was, not because of the numbers, but because it was perpetrated by the Ustasha as part of their ideology to annihilate the Serbs or parts thereof.

There is not even an agreement concerning the meaning of words that each party hurls towards the other. Perhaps, first of all, we have to define, "What is extermination?" Or what is *Sho'a* or holocaust for this or that party, when one accuses others with murder, genocide, or disaster of some sort? For this volume, we shall use a working definition, which we hope will be adopted by world bodies and thus facilitate the creation and acceptance of universal yardsticks that we have determined for ourselves. If a few people, meaning innocent civilians, those not in battles, are killed in this or that operation— then we say, that's murder. If a few dozen are killed, then one might say that's mass murder. If it is a few hundred people who are killed, we say it's a massacre. If more, that is, if thousands of people are killed, its extermination, and only if it's tens of thousands or more, like hundreds of thousands, or millions, then it becomes genocide by the perpetrator and a disaster, or, Sho'a or holocaust for the victims. And it is very important to make these distinctions, because if we define exactly the scope of killings, then we keep terminology from depreciating, as when the Palestinians term every clash where a group of their people is killed by Israelis a "massacre" or "genocide". Unless we hold one yardstick to measure these killings, so as to avoid venturing into exaggerations or other sorts of hyperbole, which detach events from reality, we would be describing accusations, claims, or deliberate libel, not facts.

Other considerations should go into the devising of this terminology, nonetheless. Genocide, or total extermination that is purposely inflicted by one party against others, always has an element of ideology in it, like the Armenian massacre by the Turks during World War I, the German "final solution" against the Jews, or the Ustasha against the Serbs (their Jewish and Roma victims were only appendices), or the Hutu-Tutsi disaster in Africa. Namely, genocide is clearly an act of extermination of one external party against another, while in situations of domestic wars, like the American Civil War, or the present orgies of killings during the Arab Spring (2011-12). In other words, despite the high numbers of casualties, one cannot claim that the American North committed genocide against the South, or that Syria or Libya or Yemen are committing genocide against their own people. However, in the case of a domestic war where different ethnic groups are

*Savagery in the Heart of Europe*

involved, like the Sudanese Janjaweed against the blacks of Darfur, or the American and Spanish settlers in the Americas against the Indian natives, the prevailing conquerors may be said to have committed genocide against the occupied peoples. The Ustasha, like the Nazis, had entertained, though they only partly succeeded, their criminal purpose of annihilating the entire collective of their perceived enemies, and the combination of ideology and praxis had lent to their centralized, directed and executed efforts, by their highest authorities via the instrument of their armed forces, a clearly genocidal design. Other events of mass killing, even if they should surpass in numbers acknowledged genocidal orgies of killings, should not be termed genocide. In other words, genocide, like crime in general, requires a criminal intention, what jurists call a *mens rea*, something that was identifiable in the medieval Mongol mass annihilations of their conquered populations, in the combats of the crusaders against Muslim and Jewish populations in the Middle East, in the Armenian massacre of 1915, in the Wannsee Conference of January 1942, and in the Ustasha government since its inception. Other horrifying acts that resulted accidentally in mass killings, like the collateral damages in modern warfare, are not necessarily genocidal, though their results are as unfortunate and regrettable.

Another issue is the battle over names. The medieval mass killings used to be blanket-termed by chroniclers and historians as "massacres," almost detached from any moral judgment, since that was the vogue of the time. An enemy was there to be annihilated, and the victor found no problem with exterminating the conquered. Spanish conquistadors, General Custer, the Boers in South Africa, the Belgians in Congo, and other western colonizers in the Americas, Africa, Oceania, and Asia massacred entire civilizations, at times to the point of annihilation, in order to replace them with the white settlers. Those intentional killings would definitely come today under the definition of genocide, but the legal and moral niceties of universally condemning genocide emerged only much later, mainly within the Western nations after they had completed their own thorough work of genocide. They now stood as the hypocritical preachers of morality in condemnation of others, who performed much less extermination than what they had themselves done. The Jews had elected to dub the annihilation of one-third of them as a Sho'a (Hebrew for disaster) or a holocaust, so it remains specific and unique to that massive enterprise of a "final solution" that had never been repeated against anyone else. Armenians, Serbs, Indians in the Americas, the aborigines in Australia and New Zealand, the Vietnamese, Ceylonese, Chinese, and others, who have also suffered genocide, mainly under the Japanese occupation, may choose to term their plight as they wish, and what they choose will remain theirs, in their own specific languages, to commemorate for all generations to come, without any obligation to adopt the Jewish term as if there were a competition over victimhood.

At any rate, even according to the Croat definition, which admits that at least eighty thousand Serbs were exterminated in Jasenovac and Jadovno, this comes under all these graduated definitions from murder to genocide, and therefore, call it as you wish, it remains within the most highly criminal act of mass extermination that human history knows, comparable to the German final solution, the Janjaweed orgies of killing, the Spanish, Canadian, Australian, and American extermination of the Maya, Inca, and other native American civilizations, and the more recent attempt by the waning Ottomans to annihilate the Armenians (and the Greeks, if they could). And if we don't agree on these definitions, then everybody and anybody can continue to claim whatever they want to claim, and this will throw us into chaos once we

*Savagery in the Heart of Europe*

lose the standard yardstick by which we all agree to measure the horror of these events. It is similar to the contemporary definition of terrorism, which for lack of an accepted terminology turns Muslim murderers into "martyrs" who cannot engage in terrorism, by nature and definition, and the Americans and Israelis who defend themselves against these horrors, in Afghanistan or Gaza, become the "true terrorists."

Anyone who talks to people in the streets of Zagreb, Belgrade, or Sarajevo these days is stunned by the depth of hatred exhibited towards any of those three contenders by any one of the two others. It sounds as if the war and hostility between them are eternal and existential, that none of them may survive, let alone thrive, unless the others are eliminated. The impression has been that this could only be a zero-sum game, whereby a loser would cause the others to win, and no one can be a winner unless the others lose. The poignant aspect of it all has been the fact that the Bosnian War was not a classic international conflict, but looked rather like a civil war between ethno-religious groups who had intermittently belonged to the same state since 1918. Granted that in some Arab quarters similar sentiments are expressed with regard to Israel, and that occasionally open conflict between the parties generates massive killings, especially on the frontlines of the battlefields, never in the history of the Middle East conflict was there such a dense sequence of massacres perpetrated on all sides, some of which, like Srebrenica, Sarajevo, Mostar, and Vukovar, becoming iconic and world infamous, as during the Bosnian War. Moreover, when the battles were interrupted thanks to the UN peacekeeping forces and the US-imposed Dayton settlements, no process of meaningful reconciliation followed. It was as if the exhausted combatants paused for a while, to devise a new strategy for when the hostilities would resume someday. No party is completely satisfied with what was allocated to it, and the feeling of a ticking bomb is left to linger and persist. It also appears that the Bosnian War has its roots in the relations between Serbs, Croats and Muslims in World War II[6] as will be explained below.

This signifies that beyond the ethnic differences, the historical bitterness, the lingering impact of the ancient encroachment of the Ottomans and of their Muslim faith into the Balkans, the plastered-over controversies between the various nationalities in the times of Yugoslavia, and eventually the dismantlement of the Tito State, there is no sufficient substance to explain the root causes of what seems an unbridgeable gulf which perpetuates the hatred and assures its longevity. This volume will explore these issues and examine whether the present malaise in the Balkans is indeed an Ottoman legacy, i.e. was contingent upon the introduction of Islam into the essentially Christian continent of Europe, and owes its contemporaneous vigor to the injections of Muslim power into the European arena. In brief, is it part of the current Muslim effort to effect its third invasion of Europe, following its first incursion into Spain in the eighth century and a second into the Balkans in the fifteenth century, which had ended in failure? If it is so, the Bosnian War will be recorded as the sole military and violent attempt so far (except for the massive acts of terrorism throughout the West) to pursue the expansion of Islam by force as of old, in the midst of the rather peaceful (for now) waves of Muslim immigration into Europe, which began for the purposes of work, then expanded under the guise of "political refugees" seeking asylum, until it became, as the twenty-first century dawned, an unchecked torrent of transfer of populations, from poor and overpopulated Africa and the Middle East into aging and under reproducing Europe, which cries for manpower to maintain its mode of life.

---
[6] See Raphael Israeli, *The Croatian Death Camps: Visions and Revisions,* op. cit.

To meet these challenges, the present book is presented by a joint effort of two authors: Raphael Israeli, who has written many books on Islam in general, and on Islam in Europe, including the Balkans and Asia, particularly China and Central Asia; and Albert Benabou, a senior Israeli official in the Israeli Ministries of Foreign Affairs, and then of Science and Tourism, who was the first Israeli national to work for the UN peace forces anywhere and served in Bosnia during the crucial years of 1993-1994, when he experienced on the ground many operations of rescue, ceasefire, and negotiations between the parties, met and collaborated very closely with the highest echelons of the local and international actors, and collected firsthand documents and impressions from that arena. Today, eighteen years later, at the closing of the Trials in The Hague against criminals in former Yugoslavia, the coauthors are able to join hands and add their Middle East experience, not only to report what happened during that horrible conflict in the Balkans, but also to warn from its renewed explosive potential, and to suggest some parallels to other unresolved disputes. Amidst war, death, destruction, destitution, and tragedy, some moving episodes of love, care, and devotion will alleviate and humanize this otherwise sad and depressing tale.

Jerusalem, 2012

# Chapter One

# The Dismantling of Yugoslavia and the Setting of the Bosnian War

Wars do not determine who is right; they determine who and what is left. As we are trying to recount the madness of this Bosnian war and the irreparable damage it caused in terms of human loss, destruction, the deepening of hatred, and the unbridgeable intercommunal sense of suspicion, fear, blame, and lingering uncertainty, we are posing the inescapable questions:

what caused it in the first place, why was it conducted in such extreme savagery, unfit of civilized people, and why does it remain so difficult to settle, compared for example, to the three major wars between France and Germany (Prussia in 1870, WW I in 1914-1918 and WW II in 1939-1945). Now France and Germany are growing as the leading partners of the European Union. Their leaders are close associates and intimate counselors before any major policy is adopted, and their interests are very intricately intertwined. Are Bosnia and the components of former Yugoslavia, rather comparable to Iraq, Afghanistan, Pakistan, where domestic ethnic, national, and religious unrest has made Western interference with militant Islam a necessity and a determining factor? We need to go back to the genesis.

After the Arab conquests had exhausted the immense primeval energies released by Islam since its inception in the seventh century and up until the ninth century, the Turks of central Asia who arrived on the scene in the eleventh century gave a new impetus to Islamic expansion, this time from the southeast into the heart of Europe. As Bat Ye'or put it:

The Islamization of the Turks within the Muslim Empire integrated new and unlimited forces. Uncouth and hardy, they had, since the ninth century, supplied contingents of slaves exclusively reserved for the Abbasid Caliph's guard and for military service. Thus, quite naturally, the ideology and tracts of Jihad inflamed the warlike tendencies of their tribes, already roaming the Asiatic borders of the Greek and Armenian lands. They joined the ranks of Islam with the enthusiasm of neophytes, and their ravages facilitated the Islamization and Turkification of Armenia, the Greek territories of Anatolia, and the Balkans. Yet, it is also true that their depredations could not be controlled by the Muslim [Abbasid] state and often harmed its economic interests.[7]

The Ottoman state, which reached Vienna at the pinnacle of its expansion in the seventeenth century, was multiethnic and multireligious, and under its Muslim-majority dominance Christians, Jews, and others lived side by side for many centuries. However, this coexistence was not born out of a modern concept of tolerance of the other on the basis of acceptance of differences and equality to all, but on a sense of superiority which tolerated others in spite of their inherent inferiority. Therefore, even though Muslims, or Turks, as they became universally known in European parlance, may have temporarily constituted the minority in the population in some areas of the occupied empire, they reigned supreme by virtue of their Muslim master status, while the various Christian groups (and Jews for that matter) were relegated to the status of "protected people" or *dhimmis*. Christians and others who had integrated into the Ottoman system, by embracing Islam, speaking Ottoman Turkish, and going into the

---

[7] Bat Ye'or, *The Decline of Eastern Christianity Under Islam: From Jihad to Dhimmitude*, 52.

government service, soon became part and parcel of the Ottoman culture even when they kept their attachment to their ethnic origin and to their mother tongue. The case in point were the Bosnians, many of whom felt privileged to go into the devşirme system of enrolling their boys to the prestigious Janissary Corps, who in the course of time were Islamized, though they preserved their Slavic roots and language.[8]

The Balkans were conquered by the Ottomans from the middle of the fifteenth century on. Serbia fell in 1459, and four years later, Bosnia and Herzegovina succumbed to the conquerors. Caught between the economic interest of milking the tax paying dhimmis, which necessitated maintaining the conquered population in place instead of expelling it or converting it by force, and the military and security needs which required that the Muslim population be numerous enough to ensure loyalty to the Empire, the Ottomans tended to implement the latter choice in the Balkans. They adopted the policy of deporting the native populations and settling their own people, or other conquered people in their stead, thus ensuring that no local minority should envisage any insurgency among a Muslim population. In Bosnia, the process of Islamization was reinforced by the native turncoats who flowed to Islam and became the worst oppressors of their former coreligionists. So much so, that the Bosnians were notorious for their role in the Ottoman administration, the military, and especially the Janissaries. Much of the anti-Christian zeal one could detect during the Bosnian War, centuries later, against Serbs and Croats alike, can be traced back to those early times. As late as 1875, way after the introduction of the modernizing tanzimat reforms in the Ottoman Empire, which were supposed to redress the situation of the non-Muslims throughout the Empire, the British

---

[8] ibid., 63.

Ambassador in Istanbul reported that the Ottoman authorities in Bosnia recognized the impossibility to administer justice in equality between the Muslims and the Christians, inasmuch as the ruling Muslim courts accepted no written or oral evidence from Christians. One 1876 report from Bosnia-Serai (Sarajevo) by the British Consul in town, Mr. Majer, tells the whole story:

> About a month ago, an Austrian subject named Jean Udilak was attacked and robbed between Sarajevo and Visoka by nine Bashi-Bazouks. The act was witnessed by a respectable Musulman of this time named Nouri Aga Varinika, and he was called as a witness when the affair was brought before the Sarajevo Tribunal. His testimony was in favor of the Austrian, and the next day he was sent for by the vice-president and one of the members of the court and threatened with imprisonment for daring to testify against his coreligionists.[9]

As Majer tells us, Muslims, Christians (and Jews for that matter) could keep to themselves in their own communities, with their lifestyles, rituals, and festivals running without hindrance, except in the case of intermarriage. For here, the only allowed combination was Muslim men taking in Christian (or Jewish) wives, which consecrated their joint offspring as full-right Muslims. The result was that while non-Muslim culture merged into the predominant Islam, there was also an outside input into the Muslim culture with material culture (food, dress, habits, language) growing to become common to all. All this was acceptable to the Ottoman authorities, who were reluctant to interfere, but as soon as the dhimmis became wealthy and were conspicuous in

---

[9] Cited by Bat Ye'or, *The Decline of Eastern Christianity Under Islam*. Fairleigh Dickinson University Press, Madison 1996 pp. 176-7 and 421-7.
[10] Majer, 67-8.

their dress and demeanor, that was considered a provocation to the Muslim population and dealt with accordingly. Christians who wanted to improve their lot in Bosnia and Albania could always do so through conversion to Islam or by seeking the protection of their Islamized family members.[10]

Towards the end of the Ottoman rule, as economic problems arose, and the state was no longer able to enforce law and order in the face of the nationalist awakening in the various provinces of the Empire, rule grew more despotic in an attempt to hold on to the territories that were slipping out of the Porte's grip. The notions of equality coming from liberal Europe, which made the maintenance of legal and religious inequities within the empire untenable, were conjugated into national terms and spelled out independence from the Ottoman yoke, since the idea of a ruling empire held together by Islam was no longer operative. It was ironically the Ottoman attempts at modernity, by opening up the system, and by addressing individuals instead of traditional communities, which brought it to its downfall and opened the new vistas of nationalism and independence in the Balkans as elsewhere, a situation not unlike Eastern Europe after the Gorbachev Perestroika in the late 1980s and early 1990s. But in view of the respective Greek and Bulgarian plans for a Balkan Federation under their aegis, to take over from the Ottomans,[11] and the tax repression enforced by the Bosnian Muslims, the Serbs rose up in arms (1875), and many of them ran into hiding, leaving behind to the mercy of the Muslims children, the old, and women, something reminiscent of the horrors of the Bosnian War and then the Kosovo War more than one century later.[12]

---

[11] Vrban Todorov, "The Federalist Idea as a Means for Preserving the Integrity of the Ottoman Empire," in Slavenko Terzic (ed), Islam, the Balkans and the Great Powers, Belgrade, 1997, pp. 293-6.
[12] Jean-Paul Bled, "La Question de Bosnie-Hercegovine", La Revue des Deux Mondes, Paris, 1876, Vol II, No 1 pp. 237-54.

According to reports from the time of the rebellion, the Bosnian Muslims, descendants of converted Slavs who had become the landowners and acceded to the status of aristocracy by virtue of their conversion, now practiced their faith fanatically and ruthlessly towards their Orthodox compatriots, who would rather die in battle than submit to the tax exactions. What made things worse, again like in the recent events in Bosnia, was that the Catholics (later identified as Croats) allied with the Muslims against the Orthodox Serbs. An eyewitness of the time reported:

> United under oppression, it was natural that the Serbs should respond by rebellion. But in the entire northern part of Bosnia and Turkish Croatia, . . . the antagonism between the two [Catholic and Orthodox] denominations is vast enough for us to have eye witnessed Catholics marching on the heels of the Turks against Greek insurgents . . . By an inexplicable aberration, the priests of the two denominations entertain hatred [towards each other] and we could say without exaggerating that, if given the choice, the Catholics would rather be dominated by the Turks than by the Orthodox Serbs.[13]

The reporter concluded that the Muslims of Bosnia maintained their loyalty to the Ottomans, and therefore there was no chance of a fusion between the populations, in view of the fact that those Serbs whose ancestors had embraced Islam as a political expediency were now too imbued with it and too captured by the teachings of their holy book to relent from their intense hatred, which had germinated in their bodies and taken them over completely.[14] But this was to be only a foretaste of things to come, as henceforth the politics of Bosnia would be dominated by the alliance of two

---

[13] ibid., 331-2.
[14] ibid., 332.

*Savagery in the Heart of Europe*

of its major religious groups, and later ethnonational communities, against the third. After the Berlin Congress (1878) and the occupation of Bosnia by the Austro-Hungarian Empire, the Serbs allied with the Muslims against the occupiers, who were supported by the Catholics (Croats) in the province. The Hungarian governor of the province tried valiantly to create a new Bosnian identity merging together its three principal communities, but he failed.[15] But the annexation of Bosnia by the occupiers in 1908 created a new alliance, the Serbs of Bosnia, who wished their merger with Serbia (not for the last time), were pitted against the Croat-Muslim coalition who would rather reconcile to their occupation than allow the Serbs to implement their dream. As a result, repression of the Serbs in Bosnia, coupled with the expulsion of Serbs from Kosovo, brought to a record level the bitterness of the occupied Serbs against their oppressors. Sukrija Kurtovic, a Bosnian Muslim, sought the differentiation between ethno-nationality and religion, and pleaded for the unity of the Bosnians with the Serbs in one single national group by reason of their common Serbian roots, arguing that Islam was a common religion of the Bosnians and the Turks, but that in itself did not make them share any national common ground.[16] The idea of Yugoslavism, a larger entity where all the ethnic and religious groups could find their common identity, came to the fore only after the Balkan wars in the early nineteenth century and precipitated World War I following the Sarajevo murder of the heir to the Austro-Hungarian throne in 1914. That war reinforced the Croat-Muslim alliance in Bosnia, which swore to expel the Serbs from Bosnia altogether, and acted upon its vow by perpetrating large-scale

---

[15] Dusan Batakovic, "La Bosnie-Herzegovine: le System des Alliances," in Terzic, op. cit. pp 335-343.
[16] ibid., 343-4.

massacres of the Serbs, thus demonstrating that the concept of an all-Yugoslavian identity was in vain.[17]

A Yugoslavian state was created in 1918 nevertheless, which once again attempted to fuse its components in the ethnic and linguistic domains and leave, as befits a modern European state, the question of religion to the realm of each individual. However, while the Serbs and the Croats of Bosnia could look up to Belgrade and Zagreb, respectively, in matters of identity, the Muslims were left to vacillate between their Muslim, Ottoman, local, and Slavic roots. At first they allied with the stronger Serbs and turned their eyes on Belgrade where they ensured for themselves some privileges, but wary of the competition between the Croats, who championed their nationalism, and the Serbs, who regarded themselves as the guardians of Yugoslavian unity, they focused more and more on their local and religious identity in the form of a Muslim Party (JMO), while the Serbs and the Croats continued to claim that the Muslims of Bosnia were of their respective origins.[18]

The Yugoslavian Kingdom, which was formed in 1918, integrated into a single state the southern Slavic nations of Croatia, Slovenia, Serbia, Bosnia-Herzegovina, Montenegro, and Macedonia. Each one of these nations dwelling in the Balkans, and being the protégé of conflicting interests and competing religious denominations, triggered more than once total confrontations all over Europe. We all remember the memorable murder of the Austrian Duke in Sarajevo that triggered the Great War and caused the death of twenty million persons, deprived Europe of an entire generation of young lives of workers, intellectuals, artists, creative minds, and who knows who else, and instead paved the way for the larger and more cruel and destructive World War II, when

---
[17] ibid., 346
[18] ibid.

frustrated madmen like Adolf Hitler, who could not accept their country's and personal humiliation, set the world on fire.

But when the first Yugoslavian state was created in consequence of that war, inter alia on the ruins of the Austro-Hungarian and the Ottoman sick and obsolete empires, it was the result of positive western attitudes towards its component parts, which were to shift totally in time so as to permit Western intervention in the Bosnian War in favor of some of them and against the others. For example, while at the onset of the Yugoslavian state, Serbia was favorably regarded by the West as its backbone and center, and the Serbs became in the 1990s a "nation of genocidal rapists" and permitted the massive western intervention against Belgrade, its preponderant federal capital, its territorial integrity, and its role of leadership. How and why did this happen would be the key to comprehend the nature of this shift. A 1923 history of the Balkans describes the situation thus:

> In 1922 the new king, to the great satisfaction of his subjects, married, and at his wedding with a Romanian princess, the Duke of York represented the British Royal family. Never have the ties between Great Britain and the Serbs been so close as since the [Great] War, when they fought side by side. Many Serbs found a refuge in England, many were educated at Oxford, and to Englishmen Serbia is no longer an unknown land.[19]

Exaggerated as this image may have been, its reverse, namely that Serbia and the Serbs have become utterly anti-Western, so much so that they deserved being bombed and destroyed by NATO and the West in the 1990s, is also outrageously inflated and one-sided, when they were described

---

[19] William Miller, *The Balkans*: *Rumania, Bulgaria, Serbia and Montenegro*, Fisher Unwin, London,1923, p. 513.

as a nation of "genocidal rapists." There were many genocidal rapes committed by the Serbs to be sure, but so were they by the other actors in the Bosnian War, that is by Croatia, Bosnia, and outside Muslim Mujahidin, and then by the Muslim-Albanian Kosovars during the war of secession of Kosovo, where the West again supported, against its own interests, the Muslim party in the war. And once again, after the fall of Slobodan Milosevic, the hated Serb nationalist who led his nation into the war, the western media rediscovered the "pro-western tradition of the Serbs." And in the 2010s, after the election of President Tadic, who surrendered to the Hague the military leaders of the Bosnian War, those who have been unilaterally accused of war crimes, Serbia became once again a persona grata in European counsels, to the point of being viewed by the EU Foreign Affairs Commissioner, Katherine Ashton, as a worthy candidate to join the Union. Then, what is the source of all this zigzagging? And why since those sad events have unfolded, could the component states of Yugoslavia no longer ally among themselves to pursue their common interests, but reverted to the common hatred they share towards each other rather than against a common enemy or adversary?

If one studies the major policy shifts of Britain during World War II, from an all-out support to the young Yugoslavian king who fled German occupation to England, to sponsoring the resistance of the Chetniks led by General Mihailovic, the pro-royalty fighter, and then abandoning that group in favor of Tito's Partisans, and eventually forcing the king to dismiss Mihailovic, one is also surprised by the British turnabout, effected by Winston Churchill personally, who even committed his own son, Randolph, to be parachuted over Tito-controlled territory and to channel considerable British aid through him to the Partisans, as recounted in Churchill's war memoirs. Obviously, even though

## Savagery in the Heart of Europe

Tito was Croat in origin, he probably sensed that Serbs, who were rebellious and famously not distinguished for their docility to foreign invaders, since they had resisted Ottoman rule and repulsed on many occasions the Austro-Hungarian forces that tried to quell them on the southern front of World War I, were more reliable than the Croats and the Bosnians, who immediately after the German occupation in 1941 had established the pro-Nazi Ustasha state, which encompassed both Croatia and Bosnia and became by definition hostile to Serbia and the Serbs.

Indeed, it did not take long for that state to establish extermination camps in Croatia, Bosnia, and the island of Pag off the Dalmatian coast, where two major centers of physical elimination of Serbs, Jews, and Gypsies were built, following Nazi inspiration, even before the Nazi camp models of the Final Solution were built in Germany and Eastern Europe. Those camp complexes in Jadovno and Jasenovac were proof of Croatian determination to carry out their widely circulated slogan: kill a third, expel a third, and convert a third. We are talking here about more than a million Serbs who found themselves trapped within the Ustasha state, both within the boundaries of Croatia, and the eastern part of Bosnia and Herzegovina (which became after the Bosnian War Republika Srpska), under the dominion of the Ustasha state. More Serbs, who were captured or expelled from occupied Serbia, shared the same lot. Since no known camps of that sort were established for Croats and Bosniaks by the Serbs, probably due to the fact that the latter had rebelled against the Germans rather than submitted to them, therefore they could not be delegated by the Nazis, like the Croats, to embark on the extermination of their enemies. In any case, unlike the proven mutual hatred between the parties, the act of genocide was at that point monopolized by the Ustasha (Croats and Muslims) against the Serbs, the Gypsies, and the Jews, and also some dissident Croats. It was then to be expected that during the Bosnian War of the 1990s the Serbs, who still lived under that trauma, were scared of its repetition and naturally took their revenge, often excessively, or thwarted what they were afraid would become a replay of past horrors if they did not take preventive measures against their recurrence. In any case, enough murder was done, on all sides, during this latter war to share the blame widely.

The Ustasha and Muslim Croats had indeed embarked during World War II, under German protection, on an orgy of killing which many eyewitnesses describe as surpassing the Nazis in cruelty, with one major difference. While after the Wannsee Conference the extermination of the Jews of Europe was at the top of the Nazi agenda, with the industrialized process of gassing the masses of Jews and then burning their corpses in crematoria to eliminate traces of the crime, in the case of the Ustasha, they directed their main attention to their hated competitors, the Serbs, of whom they exterminated in the hundreds of thousands according to the Serbs, many fewer by the Croatian narrative, while the Jews and Gypsies were a secondary target, and "only" tens of thousands of them perished in that fashion under the Ustasha subcontractors of the Nazis. The industry and mechanization-minded Germans quickly invented their industrial mode of genocide when they realized that shooting every individual Jew or Gypsy was too slow, too expensive, and too risky. The Ustasha killers, who were less developed and knew no sophisticated way to eliminate their enemies beyond using the primitive tools that they were familiar with: hammers, ropes, knives, sickles, and strangulating by hand, or dumping their victims live into territorial pits or maritime killing-by-drowning fields, jubilantly resorted to what they knew, and were overjoyed to carry out freely, without restriction and without fear from any authority, the orgy of murder that had brewed in their minds against their Serbian sworn historical enemies and adversaries, and their millennially-despised Jewish "killers of Jesus." Gypsies were an added "bonus," also inspired by their Nazi masters.

Immediately after the German invasion of Yugoslavia on 10 April, 1941, Croatia declared its "independence," under the instigation of Croatian nationalists, the Ustasha, and following Nazi policy, with which they willingly collaborated. They also announced that the Serbs, along with the "inferior" Jews and Roma, were "enemies of the Croatian people." In that land, which was dubbed by Yugoslav Literature Nobel Prize laureate, Ivo Andric, as "the land where they love to hate," massive persecutions of all three peoples were launched, where many tens of thousands of people were annihilated with the collaboration, silent or active, of the Catholic church and Bosnian Muslims. The Serbian Partisans, mostly Communists and Jews at the outset, and the royalist Chetniks, reacted rapidly and started the resistance to both the occupier and its local collaborators. So tangled were the relations between the competing factions that eventually even the Chetniks and the Partisans, both initially Serbian in essence and united in purpose, would eventually diversify their membership, split, and set out against each other. When Belgrade was liberated by the Red Army in September 1944, with the collapse of the main Nazi fronts in Italy, Normandy, and eastern Europe, Josip Broz Tito seized power and proclaimed the establishment of the People's Republic of Yugoslavia, divided, as in the past, into the six republics corresponding to the six Slavic peoples living in the country. Well prepared towards the end of the war, Tito already formulated in 1943 the federal constitution of the future communist Yugoslavia (meaning, literally, southern Slavic country, save Bulgaria), to differentiate it from the northern Slavs dwelling in northern Europe, i.e., Russia and Poland, and the Central Slavs in Czechoslovakia). His slogan, "*Vidimo se u*

*Beogradu"* (Rendezvous in Belgrade) already indicated the focus of his rule, uniting under his charismatic leadership the partisans from various ethnic groups, to the exclusion of the Royalists, and acting with determination for the liberation and rebuilding of Yugoslavia.

However, upon the creation of the renewed state, the three large religious and ethnic entities, Croat Catholic, Serb Orthodox, and Bosnian Muslims, who were distributed across the lands of the federal state, kept nourishing the rooted hostility existing among them. On the one hand, the regime pursued a program of intensive indoctrination amongst the young generation, advocating unity of the federation and plastering over ethnic and religious differences. On the other hand, wishing to lead his country to political independence, while the grip of the Soviet bloc still fluctuated, Tito split in a flashy rupture from Stalin. At that point, Yugoslavia adopted a foreign policy of "nonalignment," differentiating itself from the rest of eastern Europe's Warsaw Pact countries, and affording certain liberties internally, and a measure of goodwill towards, and on the part of, western Europe externally. Thereby, Marshal Tito was presented as defending the national pride and refusing to submit to Stalin's diktat. This would not uproot the hatred between the ethnic groups and the deep estrangement between the various religious divides internally, nor would it ultimately prevent the doomed process of dismantlement of Yugoslavia, which was to shatter it into pieces by the last decade of the twentieth century—each ethnic and religious group proclaiming its return to square one, namely erasing the amalgamated Yugoslav culture and eliminating the stabilizing good neighborliness that Tito had strived to enforce. Even the accepted common language of the federation, which was for years dubbed Serbo-Croatian, became today an obscenity when mentioned before any member of ex-Yugoslavia, each insisting on the absurdity of the totally independent "Serbian," "Croatian," or "Bosnian," etc., as a "separate and original language since antiquity." In that sense, the year of 1963 represents a turning point. A new constitution was adopted, which seemingly triggered a latent process of democratization, but the various ethnic and religious groups felt suffocated, yearning for more liberties and self-expression, and emphasizing their religious, historical, and cultural differences. Worrying signals were discernible already in 1968, with the riots in Kosovo and the attempts of the "Croatian Spring" in 1971, which were repressed by the central government.

In 1970, well before the collapse of the Yugoslavian order imposed by Tito and the outburst of communal nationalism, which instigated the process of its disintegration, a political manifesto was written by a then unknown Muslim in Bosnia, Alija Izetbegovic (born in 1925), but not immediately released to the public. It was, however, duplicated and made available to individual Muslims who circulated it among their coreligionists, apparently to serve as a guide of a Muslim order to replace the godless communist system in Bosnia. That pamphlet was known as the *Islamska Deklaracija* (The Islamic Declaration). In 1983, after Tito's death, and while the communist state was still held together, a trial took place in Sarajevo where the author and some like-minded individuals were prosecuted for subverting the constitutional order and for acting from the standpoint of Islamic fundamentalism and Muslim nationalism. Significantly, after the fall of communist power, the accused were publicly rehabilitated, and the declaration was then officially published in Sarajevo (1990). Izetbegovic, at the head of his Democratic Action Party (SDA) won the majority of the Muslim votes in the first free elections in Bosnia-Herzegovina (November 1990), and his pamphlet was obscured and not heard of again. However, judging from the wide appeal of his later book, *Islam between East and West*, which was published in English in the USA (1984), then in Turkish in Istanbul (1987), and in Serbian in Belgrade (1988), and from the developments in the Bosnian War in the mid-1990s, one might be well advised to take a look at it.

The declaration, which in many respects sounded and looked like the platforms of Muslim fundamentalists elsewhere (e.g. the Hamas Charter),[20] and assumed that its appeal would be heeded by Muslims around the world, and not only by its immediate constituency, accused the West of wishing to "keep Muslim nations spiritually weak and materially and politically dependent," and called upon the believers to cast aside inertia and passivity in order to embark on the road of action.[21] And like Muslim radicals such as Sayyid Qutb of Egypt (d.1966), who had urged his followers to reject the world of ignorance around them and transform it on the model of the Prophet of Islam, the Declaration of Izetbegovic also called upon the millions to join the efforts of Muslim individuals who had fought against the Jahiliyya (the state of ignorance and godlessness which had preceded the advent of the Prophet),[22] and dedicated the text to the memory of "our brothers who have laid their lives for Islam,"[23] namely the *"shuhada'* [martyrs] of all times and places who had fallen for the cause of Islam."

In the year of 1974, another effort was invested by Tito aiming to level the disparity and settle down the animosities between the various ethno-religious groups. The new constitution strengthened the political self-management of the executive authority in each republic, and Tito was nominated

---

[20] Raphael Israeli, "The Charter of Allah: the Platform of the Hamas," in R. Israeli, Islam and Israel, Unuiversity Press of America, 1993, Lanham, pp. 99-134.
[21] ibid., Introduction to the Pamphlet,1-2.
[22] ibid., 2.
[23] ibid.

president for life. With his death in May 1980, the clock was set up, launching the countdown of the survival of the Federal State of Yugoslavia. The succession was reshaped in a collective presidency, in which the president of every republic became head of state for a year, and none of them was able to run the entire country. Slobodan Milosevic, leader of the Serbian nationalist movement in Serbia, reorganized all the powers under his authority in 1987. Following a general strike and violent clashes in March 1989, he declared a state of emergency and sent the army to Kosovo. One year later, the chauvinistic spirit gained in crescendo—Franjo Tudjman campaigned in May 1990, on the theme of the rehabilitation of the Croatian nation. With his election, a massive race was launched, pushing the federated nations of Yugoslavia to slide into an inevitable civil war. The Serbs were concerned that out of 4.76 million inhabitants in Croatia, 580 thousand were Serbs (twelve percent of the population), dramatically down from their numbers before WW II and the genocidal thinning of their ranks by the Ustasha regime, whose trauma is still lingering. The last count prior to the Bosnian War included 150 thousand Serbs in Krajina, 200 thousand in Slavonia, and the remaining in large cities. In September 1990, the Krajina Serbs decided by referendum on autonomy for their region. Riots broke out in the Lika region and around Knin, and in May the following year the uprising spread into Eastern Slavonia. At the same time, ethnic unrest erupted also in Bosnia-Herzegovina.

Slovenia declared its independence in June 1991. Immediately, the federal government responded by sending in its army, mostly Serb. This war was short (nineteen days) due to pressure from the European community on Belgrade to withdraw its troops. The Serbs of Belgrade did not seem much concerned then about the fate of the Serbs in this republic, which amounted to only a tiny proportion of the population (two percent). Slovenia was recognized by the international community in January 1992 and would become, in 2004, a member of the European Union. Nonetheless, the domino effect had started; in January 1991, the Republic of Macedonia proclaimed its independence. In Croatia, the Krajina Serbs proclaimed their independence and claimed their attachment to the Republic of Serbia. On the 25th of June 1991, Croatia seceded in turn, joining the pattern of Slovenia. This démarche announced in fact the beginning of a war that would engulf the entire Croatia (excluding Istria, which is adjacent to the Italian enclave of Trieste) until January 1992. One third of Croatian territory was occupied by the Serb militias, with the support of tanks of the Yugoslav Federal Army, while all major Croatian cities like Dubrovnik, Split, Sibenik, and Vukovar were bombarded. Two of them, Vukovar and Dubrovnik, suffered a long and stressing siege by Serbian forces. In November 1991, Vukovar fell after three months of Serbian siege. The Croats expectedly brandished the images of devastation of Vukovar as a symbol of resistance defying Serbian vandalism, something of a minor Stalingrad, which helped thenceforth to demonize Serbia as the villain of the war. The momentum of disintegration and the slide into war continued, igniting also the civil war in Bosnia.

During most of its existence, the federation of Yugoslavia, both under the monarchical system up to World War II, and thereafter under Communist rule, was dominated by its Serbian component, which was its most numerous, influential and powerful part, illustrated by the fact that the affairs of the state were managed from Belgrade. The Croats, who constantly aspired to autonomy, often translated it into self-rule, nationalism, and independence, and were perennially bitter about their inability to achieve it, except during the brief World War II experiment with the Ustasha state, which they created in collaboration with the Nazis and in which they incorporated also the Bosnians, who were mostly Muslim and also had been disenchanted with Serbian hegemony. The Bosnians, or Bosniaks under a more recent appellation, who had gained their separate cultural identity under the Ottoman Empire by adopting Islam and enrolling into the public service of the Turks, began crystallizing their separate political identity only under Tito, when they were recognized as one of the six people making up the federation (Serbs, Croats, Bosniaks, Macedonians, Montenegrins, and Slovenians). They controlled a distinct territory, which made their Islamic faith an equivalent of the ethnic groups who derived their peoplehood from their respective distinct territories. The dismantlement of Yugoslavia gave the opportunity to each of its components to assert its territoriality/ peoplehood/ faith/ ethnicity, all in one, and turned the federal partners of yesteryear into bitter rivals and enemies, vying each for its own interests and pitting one against all the rest. That was essentially what the Bosnian War was all about.

At first, the Clinton administration dispatched former Secretary of State, Cyrus Vance, to work out a ceasefire in the incessantly growing open hostility between the belligerents in Bosnia since the opening of the war. The ceasefire was signed on 3 January 1992, which temporarily ended the fighting, while UN troops were deploying throughout Croatia. The new state of Croatia was recognized on 23 December, 1991 by Germany, its partner and sponsor in World War II under the Nazi-Ustasha collaboration. This German step would be misinterpreted by some nationalist Croats, who came to believe that they could now air their territorial aspirations in Bosnia-Herzegovina as of old. On 15 January, 1992, the European community also recognized Croatia, which was then admitted to the UN on 22 May, 1992. After the secession of Slovenia and Croatia in 1991, Bosnia-Herzegovina in turn raised the question of its threatened survival in a Serb dominated future Yugoslav state, if one should reemerge from the ashes of conflict. The tendencies of the various ethnic groups within Bosnia were divided. The Serbs, dominating its northern and eastern parts, though constituting only one third of the Bosnian population, were in favor of leaving the federal union valid, after the secession of three of its components, or alternately attaching themselves to Serbia. Muslims leaned towards independence, while the Croats in Bosnia were torn between the attachment to Croatia and independence in their semi-autonomous area of Herzeg. The Republic of Bosnia and Herzegovina proclaimed its sovereignty on 15 October, 1991, and its independence following a referendum was held, at the request of the European community, on 29 February and 1 March 1992. Serbia and Montenegro formed a new state, the Federal Republic of Yugoslavia (FRY), which was not recognized by the international community. Slobodan Milosevic was reelected as president of Serbia in 1992, and of what was left of FRY. The positions of the presidents of Montenegro and of the FRY, purely honorific, were occupied by his faithful supporters.

This was the genesis of the Bosnian War, when Bosnian Serbs controlled seventy percent of Bosnian territory, and Sarajevo, the capital, was regularly shelled by the surrounding Serbian militias who controlled the high grounds around the city. By the end of April 1992, Belgrade announced that it withdrew the federal (that is Serbian) army from Bosnia. In fact, something different happened. About eighty percent of the troops, consisting mainly of Bosnian-Serbs, joined the ranks of the army of the new Bosnian Serb Republic (later recognized as *Republika Srpska*), supplemented by new soldiers recruited by the militias in Serbia. Belgrade also ensured the provision of food, gasoline, and medicine to the new breakaway entity. The international community reacted;

in May 1992, Milosevic was subject to an embargo nearly on all levels (commerce, oil, air, culture, and sports). Milosevic stood aside when in May 1994 the Croatian army occupied/ liberated Western Slavonia and in August 1995, the Krajina. He did not get involved either when this same army backed the Croatian-Muslim forces in their conquest of Western Bosnia. These operations threw away about three hundred thousand Serbs on the roads, completely emptying the regions where the Serbs had been settled for centuries. This attitude was considered by Serbs living outside the FRY as a real betrayal of pledges done to them regarding their safety. Milosevic, who had previously benefited from the support of most Serbs, saw his popularity tumbling down in 1997. Challenged and beaten by the extreme right, which made a breakthrough in the presidential elections in Serbia in 1997, his election was invalidated, and finally it was Milan Milutinovic, a Milosevic faithful partisan, who became president of Serbia. In Montenegro, Milo Djukanovic, an advocate of liberalization and greater autonomy of his republic from Serbia and the federation, got a landslide victory against Momir Bulatovic, the Milosevic faithful follower.

On 19 March, 1996, Sarajevo was reunited, followed by an exodus of almost all of its Serb inhabitants. On 14 September, 1996, the Muslim Nationalist parties won the elections in Bosnia and Herzegovina. The Muslim, Alija Izetbegovic (SDA), was elected head of the presidency, with the Serb, Momcilo Krajisnik (SDS) and Croat, Kresimir Zubak (HDZ), serving at his side in the Presidency Council, in accordance with the new Washington accords. On 3 October 1996, the presidents of Serbia and Bosnia signed, at the Élysée Palace, an agreement that provided the establishment of diplomatic relations. Serbs also recognized the territorial integrity of Slovenia and Croatia, officially abandoning the claim for Krajina and Eastern Slavonia. In

November-December 1996, the cancellation by the Serbian authorities of municipal elections won by the opposition in a dozen cities, including Belgrade, caused a powerful wave of popular protests and clashes with the forces of order. NATO sent in December 1996 a new force in Bosnia, the Stabilization Force (SFOR), with the participation of the German army. In September 1997, Albanian student demonstrations were repressed by the Serbian police in Kosovo. Clashes erupted in the region of Drenica in February-March 1998. Serbian police and the Yugoslav army caused the destruction of many villages, killing nearly two thousand Muslim victims, and causing the escape of 250 thousand refugees. Kosovo Albanians voted overwhelmingly on the 22 of March 1998, reelecting their "President" Ibrahim Rugova and a parliament where the Democratic League of Kosovo (LDK) had a majority, but they were not recognized by Belgrade.

In order to assure the cohesion of the Federation and curb the separatist aspirations of Montenegro and Kosovo, whose separation from Serbia in the Yugoslav entity could further destabilize the Balkans, leaders from Serbia and Montenegro, in the presence of the representative of the European Union, Javier Solana, signed a tentative agreement (ratified by Parliament on 31 May, 2002) on the formation of the new federal state Serbia and Montenegro. This new state, the successor to the Federal Republic of Yugoslavia (FRY), was scheduled for a period of at least three years, after which "Member states shall be entitled to pursue procedures changing the institutional status of the state, that is to say, withdrawing from the union." It remained a unitary state composed of two entities and governed by a united parliament, which elected the president, who was controlled by a judiciary court and possessed an army. Eventually, that also fell apart and gave way to seven totally independent republics, two of which have become part of the European Union

(Slovenia and Croatia), and the rest are either vying for this privilege (Serbia, Montenegro, Macedonia, Bosnia) or at least for being recognized by the entire international community (Kosovo).

# Chapter Two

## The Deadly Triangle: Serbia-Croatia-Bosnia

How do we describe the outburst of belligerence between those ethnic groups, which constituted former Yugoslavia? Was it the eruption of a dormant volcano, which blew its top with the dismantlement of the Yugoslavian state? Was it a domestic civil war where the international community felt at first that it had no business to meddle? Or, was it a total war with one party aspiring to the annihilation of the other, as openly proclaimed by Mate Boban, the Croatian president of the self-declared independent Herzeg-Bosnia, or as hinted by the hardly more discreet Serbian leaders and practiced in Srebrenica? In spite of their common Slavic bonding, the southern Slavs do not share the same religion, a lingering vestige of the spread of the Greek Orthodox Church into the area since medieval times, of the penetration of the Muslim Ottoman Empire into the Balkans in early modern Europe, and of the conquests of Catholic Austro-Hungary in more recent times. So, are we facing a war of religion between Catholics (the Croats), Orthodox (the Serbs), and Muslims (lately taking up the religious/ethnic identity of Bosniaks)? In this chapter, we will review the position of each one of them, depicting their expectations when they launched their campaign, their prevailing ideology and strategic designs as they pursued their war aims, and their frustration at the final results they were left with, when international diktats forced them to subscribe to what was achieved and finalized by outside powers. It seems, overall, that specific religious and tribal affiliations have predominated over the common Slavic roots of the various groupings.

On a general level, one has to realize that classical, interstate armed conflicts have decreased since the end of the Cold War, while the frequency of civil wars has increased since the disintegration of the Soviet bloc in the Eastern Bloc and the rise of radical Islam on the African and Asian continents. In most of these conflicts, there are no front lines, and the distinction between civilians and combatants is often blurred. Consequently, the rules of conduct to which the international community had become accustomed were not applicable during the war in Bosnia. Indeed, violations of international humanitarian law, human rights, rights of non-combatants, and the rights of refugees became commonplace in all fronts of the war. Most of the victims were civilians, resulting in mutual accusations of "genocide" during the hostilities in the field and after the war in The Hague International Court of war crimes. On the other hand, the UN officers on mission in Bosnia-Herzegovina during the war were constantly reminded that the international community provided fundamental legal tools for the protection of civilian populations in armed conflicts, which primarily consisted of:

(a) An International Humanitarian Law, in particular the Fourth Geneva Convention of 1949 and the two Additional Protocols of 1977, which set basic rules of conduct during hostilities and the requirement for making a distinction between the civilian population and combatants; and

(b) The Convention relating to the Status of Refugees of 1951, granting shelter to those who fled to another country while escaping conflict at home

Defining the series of wars that were fought throughout former Yugoslavia between 1991 and 1995, the international community made use of the term "Yugoslavian wars," precisely when there was no longer a Yugoslavia in existence to justify that epithet. If this armed conflict had been termed "civil war," since it took place within the boundaries of the same previously federated state, it could have been an excuse for nonintervention of the international community, though we have seen such intervention taking place more recently in the Libyan conflict. For, the traditional notion of "sovereignty" would have had to be respected, borders being supposedly untouchable, and each country could do as it pleased within its own boundaries. At the same time, the UN also expected from all armed groups involved, both official armies and local militias, to respect the norms of international law. However, all warring parties were either unable or unwilling to act on this optimistic and unrealistic assumption, for the main sense of the war was for the purpose of brutalizing and removing populations, for the sake of ethnic cleansing, something that is obviously stipulated as illegal, inhuman, and unacceptable in international humanitarian law. The result was that the specific plans and legal norms that were elaborated to protect particularly vulnerable groups, notably women, children, the elderly, the disabled, and displaced persons, became irrelevant on the ground of Bosnia in the state of affairs as it developed. Murder, rape, expulsions, erasing entire villages, cruel sieges, bombardments of cities, and kidnappings were commonly carried out by all sides in the war zone. Fundamental rights such as the right to life and to food and shelter, and the prohibition of torture, expulsion, and ethnic "purification," which emerged in this situation of conflict, were of course disregarded for the most part by all parties. As all belligerents conceived of the war as one of survival, that most primordial of all basic requisites of life naturally took precedence over all other considerations.

Any society perceives out of its own volition that in order to survive, it has to take up arms and go to war against

*Savagery in the Heart of Europe*

any party which threatens its very existence. In so doing, the party concerned willingly takes the risk of exposing its armed and unarmed population to enemy retaliation and counterattacks. But when things turn to its disadvantage, as it often happens in war, the beaten party claims that it fell victim to "massacre" and "genocide," charging the international community with the responsibility and the burden to respond by stopping the carnage and providing aid to the weak and underdog, as the present (2012) situation in the Syrian civil war suggests. During the conflict between the three parties in Bosnia-Herzegovina, namely, Serbs, Croats, and Muslims, the major international policymakers never relented from floating around threats, bombastic statements, promises, and all manner of "necessary steps" and "cures" that were required to put an end to the violence, without fully grasping the context and consequences of their words. In order to avoid a vulgarization and a misleading use of criminal terminology, we have suggested in the foreword a differentiation between a murder, when a few people are killed, a mass murder, when a few dozen are killed, a massacre when a few hundred have been eliminated, an extermination when thousands of people are killed and a genocide[24] when we have tens of thousands or more victims. From the point of view of the victims, who have suffered hundreds of thousands of murdered people, we might be talking of a disaster, a *sho'a* or holocaust. This quantitative gradualism of mass killings permits sustaining a scale of appreciation that introduces an internationally accepted yardstick to measure the scope of killings in any particular conflict. That objective scale was lacking all along in the "Yugoslavian Wars,"

---

[24] A Polish lawyer of Jewish descent, Raphael Lemkin, who lost forty-nine relatives in the Holocaust, coined in 1943 the word genocide. Lemkin presented later a draft resolution, which was served the 12 of January 1951 for the ratification of the UN Convention on the Prevention and Punishment of the Crime of Genocide.

as Muslims were constantly claiming that they were victims of a "holocaust," and, as a result, they lost credibility in international circles. Due to this sort of constant clamoring of "Wolf!" in Mostar, for example, where Benabou was assigned to serve under the UN peace-keeping forces, it was difficult to mobilize the international community when true mass murders or massacres of Muslims were being perpetrated there in reality. This was, by the way, one of the causes of the UN's refusal to include Mostar in the UNPAs (United Nations Protected Areas), which would have included the Muslim hospital in East Mostar that was in dire need of medicine and subjected to the constant shelling and bombardment of the Croats. In this case, the exaggerations of the Muslim leadership, which constantly cried "Wolf!," were counterproductive and did not help Benabou in his relentless appeals to include Mostar in the listing of UNPAs (as we shall see below) or recognize the clinic in the city as a "war hospital" protected under the Geneva Convention.

What remains to be regulated by the international community is the distinction between war and civil war; the first usually waged between two separate political entities, like states and empires, the second customarily referring to an internal strife between the nationals of the same nation within the bounds of the same sovereign state. In this light (or rather obscurity), were the "Yugoslavian Wars" a domestic affair, which we might dub as "internecine war," in par with the American Civil War, which also raged for a few years between the member states of the American Federation and took a heavy toll of casualties; or once Yugoslavia was no more, must its former components be considered as separate independent entities struggling against each other to achieve their own interests? The question is crucial, because if we choose the first option, we cannot perhaps accuse the Northern Union of committing "genocide" against the Confederate South, while if we elect the second definition, we might reach a different conclusion. Yet an additional element of ideology intrudes into our analysis, for it seems that in order to perpetrate genocide there must exist a doctrinal justification to do so. The American North did not pursue any ideological commitment to annihilate Southerners, though the latter fought for the maintenance of slavery while their opponents opposed it. In the Hutu-Tutsi confrontation, as in the Sudanese, Arab-Muslim, Janjaweed annihilation campaign against the black Muslims in Darfur, it was certainly a domestic civil war, but bearing racist ideological characteristics against the "others," who were considered inferior demons, worthy of extinction. The Nazis in Germany and the Ustashas in Croatia had also subscribed to a final solution strategy that was tinged with doctrinal and racist building stones against Jews, Serbs, and Roma.

## The Serbian Vision

Throughout most of the "Yugoslav Wars," the Serbs fought simultaneously against the Muslims and the Croats, cooperating largely with the Croats (faith apparently taking precedence over ethnic and historical resentment) in Bosnia during Muslim-Croat hostilities. However, there were exceptions to this rule of thumb, as Serbian forces were also simultaneously allied with the pro-Yugoslav Muslims in the Autonomous Province of Western Bosnia under Fikret Abdic. Serbian troops also carried out ethnic cleansing operations against non-Serbs living within their territory, the most notorious of which was the Srebrenica massacre in July 1995. The three ethnicities considered the chief yardstick of their success in the battlefield was the expulsion, the "cleansing," that is the deportation of the other ethnic groups, the main objective of each one of them being the creation of demographic homogeneity in the territory they held or claimed. In that context of an all-out war, many Serbs also were targets of atrocities during the war and the victims of the resulting expulsions. During most of the war, the Serb Republic (which was to become the Republika Srpska with Banja Luka at its core), controlled around seventy percent of Bosnia and Herzegovina's soil. Bearing that in mind, for the entire duration of the war they maintained the siege of Sarajevo, the capital and largest city of Bosnia, allegedly in order to tie down the Bosnian Muslim (Bosniak) forces and resources in what the Muslims regarded as their most important, precious, prestigious, and vital objective in the Bosnian-Herzegovinian state, so as to liberate their forces to operate elsewhere on the other fronts. The Serbs maintained close ties with the Republic of Serbia and received volunteers and supplies from the Federal Republic of Yugoslavia (FRY) during the war. The Serb Republic in Bosnia received a large number of Serbian refugees from other Yugoslav war zones, particularly from non-Serbian-held areas in Sarajevo, Herzeg-Bosnia, and Croatia. The 1993 Owen-Stoltenberg peace treaty (see below) was suggested in recognition of that reality and, would have given fifty-two percent of BiH (Bosnia and Herzegovina) to the Serbian side, but it was refused by the Bosniak Muslims as too large a concession. (Eventually, Dayton would assign to them forty-nine percent.)

In 1994, the Federal Republic of Yugoslavia felt the first signs of schism with the Bosnian Serb Republic, as it imposed sanctions on it due to its rejection of the Vance-Owen peace plan (see below) which Serbia had accepted. This rejection by the Bosnian-Serb National Assembly came as the Croatian Army had launched its offensive under General Ante Gotovina[25] to retrieve the territory of Krajina, which

---

[25] General Ante Gotovina was convicted of war crimes by the ICTY and sentenced to twenty-four years imprisonment.

caused some two hundred and fifty thousand Serbs to flee to the Serb Republic and the Serbian side to retreat from the Una (Sava) River to the Sana River. The Croatian Army, supported by the forces of the Muslims of Bosnia and Herzegovina, came within twenty kilometers of the de facto Bosnian Serb capital, Banja Luka. (The capital was still Pale.) The offensive was ultimately halted with the Dayton Peace Agreement, which recognized Republika Srpska, comprising forty-nine percent of the soil of BiH, as one of the two territorial entities of the Republic of Bosnia and Herzegovina. The Serbian side suffered, according to the Demographic Unit at the ICTY (International Criminal Tribunal for former Yugoslavia, located in The Hague), a total of 30,700 casualties—16,700 civilians and fourteen thousand military personnel. Although exact numbers are still disputed, it is generally agreed that the Bosnian War claimed the lives of about two hundred thousand people—Bosniaks, Croats, and Serbs.

The demographics of Bosnia-Herzegovina, as well as Republika Srpska, were tremendously affected by the war. Current estimates indicate that some four hundred thousand Serbs no longer live in the Federation of BiH. By the same token, it is estimated that some four hundred and fifty thousand Bosnian Muslims (Bosniaks) and Bosnian Croats who used to live in Republika Srpska no longer live there. Many Bosnian Serbs immigrated abroad to Canada, the United States, Australia, western Europe, Serbia, and Montenegro. In that sense, the war generated a movement of populations of all parties, as the ethnic groups tried either to assemble their people at the expense of the expelled members of the other groups or to leave the territory when they found themselves outnumbered and migrate to the larger concentrations of their compatriots. Each leader expressly declared or acted for the realization of the same objective, to assure a territorial continuity with at least a consistent majority, if not the totality, of inhabitants from his ethnic group. Even the Muslims, who were fighting for survival in some areas, struggled to hold a Muslim continuity to the Muslim inhabited Sanjak region in southern Serbia. This is why Izetbegovic, the Muslim leader of Bosnia, did not consider Mostar, the shared Muslim-Croatian city on the Croatian border, amongst his first priorities. So, while the Croats conducted there a murderous policy of "all of it at any price," the Muslim priorities turned elsewhere and let their besieged brethren in Mostar beg desperately for UN and international aid. This was the reason for the refusal of the international community to offer any political legitimacy to the Croatian war. On the other hand, the Serbs were primarily concerned with ensuring the survival of and connection to their dispersed communities. Ultimately, the Serbian Republic in Bosnia indeed gained recognition in the Dayton Accords and by the international community, but the autonomous Croat-Herzeg Republic did not, and it had to make do with its inclusion in the Bosnian federation without semi-independent institutions.

Since the establishment of Bosnia and Herzegovina as a state in the 1990s, the Serbs received its citizenship. The Serbs are one of the three constituting nations of this state, predominantly residing in its own political-territorial entity named Republika Srpska, but in other parts of Bosnia, like in Sarajevo the capital, others are residing as minorities since all the rest of their compatriots moved to Srpska or Serbia or other Serbian diasporas. They are frequently referred to as "Bosnian Serbs" regardless of whether they are from Bosnia or Herzegovina. The last 1996 UNHCR population census registered 1,484,530 Serbs or 37.9 percent of the total population of Bosnia and Herzegovina, but the figure was recently slightly reduced to an estimated 37.1 percent (2000) mainly by reason of more migrations of the Serbian minority and by the higher birthrate of the Bosnian Muslims. Those who do not live in the territory of the Republika Srpska are concentrated in West Bosnia and the Una-Sana cantons of the Federation of Bosnia and Herzegovina, but they remain the most territorially widespread, ethnic group of Bosnia and Herzegovina.

The Serbian leadership in Eastern Herzegovina observed and followed with irritation the Washington process (see below) which led to the Dayton Accords, because their military officers lamented the fact that they were not permitted by the political leaders to reach the banks of the Neretva and thus widen their grip on more territory, when it was feasible from their point of view. Thus, the entrance of Belgrade in the Washington process was met by the opposition from:

(a) The Serbian ground forces in Bosnia, who felt that while they sacrificed themselves for the accomplishment of a Serbian national goal, a political settlement was accepted by the leadership of Serbia before that goal was entirely achieved.

(b) The majority of the Serb-Bosnian leadership, primarily from Pale (the temporary capital), who were totally engaged in the war and considered themselves the major decision makers.

(c) The prevailing consensus among the military leaders of the Serbs was that after having endured the battles of the siege around Sarajevo and incurred the condemnations of the international community for it, that city should have remained divided between Muslims and Serbs, just like the inconclusive siege by the Croats against Muslims in East Mostar left that city divided between the two.

Although the Serbs had the most organized and professional army, their performance in the field reflected an absence of flexibility and power of maneuvering. Their deployment was basically defensive, for even their tank units, instead of launching fast moving attacks, were basically used to pound targets and act like barrage artillery (in the Soviet style). Thus, they were not swift enough to take over territory and evict from it undesired populations and forfeited many potential political achievements, which could have shaped the map differently during the negotiations of political settlement. A report of a meeting with General Radovan Grubac, one of the Serbian field commanders, was distributed by Albert Benabou, the UN Civil Affairs Officer of Mostar (see below), which took place on Thursday, 11 November, 1993. Benabou met the Serbian general for close to two hours in Jazina (on the crossing point between Montenegro and the Serbian territory in eastern Herzegovina). Also attending the meeting were Col. Novak Milosevic from the BSA and some UN officials. To understand some of the Serbian moves in the conflict, here are some details excerpted from the UN report:

Concerning the military initiatives, Gen. Grubac specified that the Serbian BSA was not initiating any military action and that his party respected the ceasefire along the confrontation lines. He complained about the infiltration of the Muslim BiH Armija soldiers, who were engaging in provocations and acts of sabotage in the areas of Gorazde, Trvno, and Konjic. He clarified that the Serbs were merely observing the military clashes between the BiH Armija and the Croat HVO in the central zone (Vares, Bugojno, and Vitez). He estimated that Muslim Armija would not give up the battle for Vitez and claimed that the accusations blaming the Serbs for the last brutal shelling of Sarajevo were groundless, stating that he was in possession of the proofs that this was an operation of the Croat HVO using their artillery from Kiseljak. In his opinion this was a revenge conducted by Cmdr. Rajic against the BiH Armija, which had previously dismantled the Croatian Kralij Tvertko Brigade[26] from Sarajevo.

As regards the military prospects for the winter of 1994, Grubac observed that Izetbegovic, the Muslim leader of Bosnia, was concentrating all his efforts and preparing for the winter military offensive. The Serbs considered that the hostilities would continue primarily in the southern part of the country, where the climate conditions permitted such activities. Thus, he called upon the international community to understand that the Serbs, like the Muslims and the Croats, considered the stretch of territory in eastern Herzegovina up to the Neretva River as Serb territory, and they were determined to fight for it. The Serbs considered access to the sea to be their inalienable right; therefore they were ready to exercise that right, possibly through the area of Dubrovnik, where there was a military buildup by both parties, Croat and Serb. He clarified that all the decisions and orders made by the Supreme BSA Army Commander, Radovan Karadzic, were respected and would be obeyed. He ascertained that the Serbian military was a disciplined army, unlike the Muslims and Croats, who were constantly changing their attitudes due to the lack of obedience and coordination between their field commanders and their politicians.

On the political level, Grubac remarked that the Serbs were the only party which had declared clear political goals and had been pursuing them since the beginning of the conflict in BiH. He emphasized that the Muslim government in Sarajevo was considered to be militant and hardliner, especially after the latest promotion of Haris Silajdzic to the post of prime minister. As far as the Serbian side was concerned,

---

[26] HVO Brigade King Tvrtko was disarmed on November 6, 1993. Croatian King Tvrtko Brigade was then formed and operated under the First Corps of the Army of Bosnia and Herzegovina. The brigade was mostly made up of Croats of Sarajevo. It was active until the end of the war in Bosnia and Herzegovina.

he added, Boban, the Croatian-Bosnian Herzeg Chief, was more reasonable and more of a reliable partner for negotiations and for any eventual deal. He thought that Boban had firmer and clearer political positions, but he was significantly restricted by the directives from Zagreb. In that sense, Grubac was expressing a reality that neither the leadership in Zagreb nor the international community grasped. Grubac affirmed that the Serbian interests lay with peace arrangements rather than with the continuation of the war, though his strong determination was evident that in case no agreement was reached, military options remained open. When asked about his preferable partners in peace negotiations, he answered that tripartite negotiations were the most advantageous, and that the prospects of a political solution might include certain local, autonomous arrangements (probably referring to such autonomy as Fikret Abdic's[27]) in the BiH held territories and/or to Mostar, which seemed a possible candidate to achieve certain autonomous features in the future, which at that point the Sarajevo government strenuously rejected.

Grubac also explained that Karadzic rejected the German-French proposals, which ignored the Serbs' cardinal concerns, like the crucial point of the three percent of territory, which the Serbs were required to yield, not so much for its quantity as for the quality of this territory. He reiterated that if the Muslims agreed to cede one percent of a certain area, the Serbs were ready to offer them in exchange up to five percent in other areas. From Grubac's point of view, the Croat-Muslim alliance was unnatural and thus not founded

---

[27] During the Bosnian War, Fikret Abdic declared his opposition to the Bosnian government and founded the small, short-lived, and unrecognized Autonomous Province of Western Bosnia composed of the town of Velika Kladusa and a few nearby villages. The mini-state existed between 1993 and 1995, and it was allied to the army of Republika Srpska.

on solid grounds. That was revealed, he thought, in their latest conflicts in central Bosnia and the Neretva valley. Grubac stated that it was the first time that both Muslims and Croats had experienced genocide on their own populations due to their mutual conflict, which for him proved the religious background of the war. For the first time, a Serbian official insinuated that genocide took place, though not by the Serbs. He noted Croats and Muslims deserved a lesson of history for what they jointly perpetrated during the Second World War to Jews and Serbs.

Colonel Milosevic denied the allegations that there is or there was any military activity coordinated between Serbian forces with the BiH Armija in Mostar. He recognized having met Muslim officials from Mostar; however, he clarified that the only agenda that BSA agreed to talk about was on humanitarian matters. He said, "We made an agreement on POW exchange, and they did not respect it. It is typical of them, they have no central authority, and you cannot rely on them[28]." On the other hand, he himself participated in a military coordination meeting with General Milivoj Petkovic, commander of the Croatian forces. However, since the last meeting, Gen. Grubac and Col. Milosevic expressed a more favorable approach towards the Croats. It seemed that they were getting closer to the Croatian position and distancing themselves from the Muslims, whom they described as unreliable and disrespectful of any agreements.

On humanitarian matters, the meager crops during the summer of 1993 provoked a critical situation in food supply to the local population, which was not receiving any humanitarian relief. Gen. Grubac required the reimbursement of the costs (preferably in fuel), which he faced while exercising humanitarian actions across his territory. The problem of

---

[28] Source: Pronounced at the meeting in Jazina with General Grubac—see Benabou's report to UN headquarters from 11 November 1993.

the Gacko thermal power plant was raised again, and for that matter Benabou was invited to hold a meeting on Tuesday, 16 November , 1993 at 1000h in Gacko with the mayor of Gacko and Col. Milosevic. A proposal for a new humanitarian supply route was made along the axis of Stolac-Gacko-Miljevina-Trvno-Sarajevo. An UNMO team in the area had already collected information concerning humanitarian needs and was forwarding the data to international relief organizations. All along the meeting, Gen. Grubac reflected his determination to implement what he was declaring.[29]

Despite showing a considerable improvement in the spring and summer of 1993, with UNPROFOR's significant help and dedication, the humanitarian situation in Bosnia was again rapidly deteriorating. The Serbs certainly shared much of the blame, but one has to admit that many of their actions were provoked by Bosniak attacks, which were conducted for no ostensible military purpose other than to force a Serbian BSA overreaction, which would have led to further international condemnation. The US policy of nonsupport for UN requests to NATO for airstrikes (requested by the chief of UN forces in Bosnia, General Jean Cot) against any of the warring factions further intensified the Bosnian dilemma. It permitted the Muslims to freely pursue a military option in locations where UNPROFOR did not operate, while they continued to promulgate their status as the "innocent victim" of this civil war in the international press. In fact, the US restrictive policies toward NATO allies and the civil war in Bosnia reflected the political and military realities of the situation, namely the BSA possessed the capability to monitor and control all the major airfields and lines of communication into Bosnia. Any attempt to deliver sophisticated heavy weapons systems to any party necessitated a

---

[29] Report by Albert Benabou on the meeting of November 11, 1993, which he widely distributed to all UN authorities in Bosnia and Croatia.

large commitment of American ground and air forces to secure these areas. Furthermore, Bosnian Muslim troops were incapable of using these weapons without extensive training. Therefore, nobody could guarantee the defense of the Bosniaks under these conditions, for it was ridiculous to believe that the BSA would sit on the sidelines and permit arms deliveries to their enemies and training for their usage to occur.

Under these circumstances, rather than leveling the playing field as some suggested, this US policy could only escalate the fighting and increase both the bloodshed and the stream of refugees attempting to gain entry to western Europe and America. Worse, delivery of arms to Bosnian Muslims logically implied US security guarantees for their protégés. Secretary of Defense Perry had correctly assessed in 1994 that the Bosniaks had no prospect of winning back the seventy percent of the country occupied by the Serbs. It would have been foolish at that point to fall victim to prodigious Bosnian Muslim propaganda efforts seeking sympathy for their victimhood and would have possibly pushed US forces into a futile military quagmire soon after they won the battle against Saddam and ousted him from Kuwait. The United States could gamble on convincing others to provide ground troops in aid to the Muslims, but they knew that only Muslim states and Jihadi movements, who were supportive of the Muslim Bosnian project, like Iran, Saudi Arabia, and Pakistan, would join the effort, at a time when their agents and militias were already deeply involved in the war. Thus, US policymakers had to abandon their inclination to view the civil war in Bosnia-Herzegovina in terms of good guys attacked by bad guys and therefore were deserving of outside support. Such dichotomic distinctions did not exist in Bosnia, as shown above, because ethnic and religious enmity between the major component groups had a long and complicated history, and the inherent problems did not lend themselves to quick and easy solutions.

The main concern of the Serbs was about their brethren in Croatia, where life had never been easy for them, and the lingering memories of incarceration, torture, and genocide during WW II were too recent to forget. Thus, after the proclamation of the Independent Republic of Croatia, the Serbs found themselves once again in a very difficult political and economic position. That is the reason for their determination to organize themselves and fight for their homes and lives, before they took the option to abandon their property and livelihood and run away to safety in Serbian territory. Since separation existed de facto among the three ethnic groups in the course of the war, free exchange of real estate between them could generate a viable solution. But that option required that reason and common interest should prevail in the process of pacification and confidence building between the former Yugoslav peoples for that commonsense course to be adopted. As it happened, the Serbs of Bosnia-Herzegovina, like the other ethno-religious groups, ended up as one of the three constituent nations of this state, predominantly residing in the political-territorial entity of Republika Srpska.

## The Muslim Perspective

In a moment of open and candid talk, in the midst of the siege of Mostar, which was divided between Croats and Muslims, and the general strife of the Bosnian War, a local Muslim leader, Alija Alikadic, confided to Albert Benabou, the Israeli Civil Affairs officer of the UN in the problematic Mostar area, his thoughts about the three main contenders in the Bosnia war: "We were not raised in any distinct military or political tradition from the others, we pray in an unfamiliar language, our past is somehow vague, but in this war, our

Savagery in the Heart of Europe

ethnic consciousness has been asserted—and now, how do we deal with that?!"[30]

The Muslim leaders of Bosnia, who had been (prior to the Ottoman occupation) part and parcel of the Slavic people of their country, hailing from either Croatian or Serbian ethnic origin, had suddenly seen a new nationality (Muslim) thrust upon them by the communist regime. They continued to express, in the thick of the war, their preoccupation with identity and the future character of their political entity. Though their Islamic faith was firmly maintained, more as an identity than as a faith, most of them tended to secularism in their socio-political orientation. However, due to the heavy involvement of Muslim radical movements, mostly from the outside, (like Iran, Saudi Arabia, and even Chechnya), the Muslims of Bosnia, battle-hardened by the Bosnian War and deeply suspicious of their erstwhile Serbian and Croatian compatriots, who grew to become their worst enemies, slowly shifted to the alienating process which defined them as Muslims, different and separate from "the others," who were Christian and by definition hostile. The recently liberated Muslims, who had just been released from communism and Serbian domination, felt embarked on an unknown track without well defined navigation guidelines. They did their utmost to prove that they were part of Western culture, constantly striving to maintain this connection. However, the large presence in Sarajevo of Iranian, Saudi and other Muslim delegations, and Mujahidin, who were zealously engaged in the war already in 1993, helped the Bosniaks, as they had come to be called, discovering and catching up in terms of Muslim religious practice, for they indeed needed some basic training in that primordial domain. When organizing a farewell party for departing Albert Benabou, as he

---

[30] Alija Alikadic, in a private meeting with Albert Benabou in March 1994, prior to the opening negotiations with the Croats in Washington.

41

completed his UN mission in Mostar, they selected the safest available space in Muslim East Mostar—the backyard of a mosque. But in their choice of catering for the event, which included ham and wine (horrible haram in normal Muslim settings), they did not demonstrate much familiarity with Shari'a laws, while the only one who did not consume those outrageously un-kosher (and non-halal) foods, was the Israeli guest of honor, who they dubbed "the Brother from the Orient," for whom the entire event was concocted.

Analyzing post factum the long debates and encounters between UN officials and Muslim leaders in the field during the war, the solid assumption arises that the government in Sarajevo had two immediate goals: first, to ensure that the conflict continued so that more territory was recuperated, since seventy percent of the country was out of their rule, either under Serbian or Croatian control; second, to assemble the largest international support for its long-range objectives, with a view to establishing an Islamic-dominated republic, in par with its official identity. Thus, the Muslim government in Sarajevo led a highly effective propaganda campaign, manipulating with dexterity the international media. The professionalism which the Muslims manifested in managing the press was undertaken by the best US public relations firms based in Washington, D.C. and in New York. Chicago journalist Florence Hamlish Levisohn noted in her book that Muslims and Croats paid thirty thousand dollars a month in fees to the American public relations firm, Ruder Finn, based in Washington, to tell their story to the world.[31] The Croats had taken the initiative, immediately followed by the Bosnian government, which signed on 23 June 1992 a contract to promote a stronger leadership role for the United States in the Balkans. The agency

---

[31] Florence Hamlish Levinsohn, *Belgrade, among the Serbs* 1994, Harold, Washington 1994 pp.312-315 a.

opened a "Bosnia Crisis Communication Center," which permanently updated its audiences on Bosnia-Herzegovina's developments, the involvement of US congressmen, European parliamentarians, and the coverage of events by leading American, British, and French media. Furthermore, they coached and organized for the then Bosnian Foreign Minister, Haris Silajdzic, meetings with influential personalities and decision makers such as Vice President Al Gore in the Clinton administration.

In a meeting in Sarajevo in December 1993, concerning the local UN initiated peace initiative in Mostar (see below), Foreign Minister Silajdzic stated, "The United States is behaving like a young girl, revealing a great reluctance about being drawn into the problems of Bosnia-Herzegovina[32]." He felt that it would be worthwhile to concentrate efforts on Vice President Al Gore, whom he considered a strong and renowned campaigner for human rights. Indeed, in a conversation with Mr. Silajdzic, Mr. Gore had proffered the opinion that this "conflict was both immoral and cowardly treated[33]." Silajdzic felt that many friends in the State Department, in Congress, and in the Senate, would be prepared to lobby as necessary with regard to both the venue and in seeking their support for the negotiations.[34] Realizing that Europe was unwilling to support their cause unilaterally, the Muslims were resolute in their strategy and concentrated their pressure on the US administration in order to convince them to align with Sarajevo. The Muslims kept claiming that "Serbian and Croatian aggression should not be rewarded," and this argument turned out to become an accepted axiom and a fixed

---

[32] Source: Memo No 13 - notes from the meeting in Sarajevo between Albert Benabou and Haris Silajdzic, Bosnian Prime Minister.
[33] ibid.
[34] Memo 14-Mostar Interim Arrangement, 150940 Dec. 93; see following a paragraph on this item. Silajdzic expressed this view in the meeting in Sarajevo with Albert Benabou and the Muslim War leadership from Mostar.

approach, which scuttled any attempt to facilitate a rational debate[35] about the crisis. In April 1993, French television journalist Jacques Merlino asked to interview James Harff, the person in charge of the Balkan contracts at Ruder Finn Global Public Affairs. Harff clarified that the image of both Croats and Bosnian Muslims risked being tarnished by their involvement in the persecution, internment, and annihilation of Jews during World War II.[36] In the first days of August 1992, the Long Island newspaper, *Newsday*, published reports of "atrocious conditions in the Serbian-run internment camps in Bosnia." Without cross verification of the item, Ruder Finn seized upon the potential public relations impact of the emerging comparison with "Nazi death camps." The firm then contacted three major Jewish organizations, the B'nai B'rith Anti-Defamation League, the American Jewish Committee, and the American Jewish Congress, suggesting they publicly protest. The Jewish organizations responded positively. Thus was ignited in the United States the campaign of demonization of the Serbs as the new Nazis in which the Jewish community sided with the Muslims. Capitalizing on his personal openness and intellectual assets, Silajdzic was the main actor in mobilizing the US Jewish community to his cause. In meetings in Sarajevo with Albert Benabou, he manifested his profound knowledge in Jewish history and mentioned more than once his recognition and appreciation for the role played by the Jewish lobby for the Muslim side of the conflict.

In a similar situation, upon his arrival to serve the UN in Mostar, Albert Benabou was invited by UN colleagues to report to the UN headquarters on the "Croatian Nazi acts of

---

[35] David Gompert, formerly Principal Deputy Director of the US National Intelligence, disapproved of the Serbian government controlling the media in its own country, while ignoring the propaganda campaign led by the Bosnian Muslims in Sarajevo and in the US media. See his article, "How to Defeat Serbia" 30-47.
[36] Raphael Israeli, *The Death Camps in Croatia,* especially Chapters 3 and 6, which deal with the incarceration of Jews in Jadovno and Jasenovac

horror" when detaining Muslim civilians in the local heliport of Mostar. Later, when that episode was brought up before the International Tribunal in The Hague, where Benabou was called to present his evidence (see Chapter 9 below), he stated that, "Nobody could access the detention center at the heliport, and no UNPROFOR elements could see the detainees[37]." He thought that the entire story was made up and circulated by irresponsible and unfair journalists, who did not show any pictures nor cite any sources. As a matter of fact, the findings of UNMOs and international military colleagues investigating the story on the ground show that the nature of that story was never confirmed, therefore no indicting report could be issued by the UN peace-keeping forces. Strong on propaganda and firm in imposing its accusations on the West, the Bosnian-Muslim government had accomplished its long-standing goals, prompting President Izetbegovic to argue that the UN "had no right to stand neutral and aside in that conflict[38]" once those stories of atrocities had been spread around and were acknowledged, by default, among western public opinion.

In effect, facts were distorted and blown out of proportion by all sides. The Muslims, for their part, invested considerable efforts in two main tracks:

1. To persuade the western world that, though they were Muslims, they primarily were Europeans and did not pertain to the threatening wave of fanatic Islam that was sweeping the world; and
2. To show, almost at any price, that they were the victims who were exposed and helpless in the face of relentless and brutal Croatian and Serbian military onslaughts that

---
[37] Source: Witness Statement delivered by Albert Benabou to ICTY in the Hague on 5 June 2004 (paragraphs 97-98).
[38] Quoted by Izetbegovic's faithful Political representative, Colonel Safet Orucevic, in the meeting in East Mostar on 10 December 1993 (Benabou's Memoirs).

they could not withstand. At a certain point, those positions, notions, and ideas, which posited the Muslims as the underdogs in this confrontation, just like the Palestinians who pretty much adopted the same strategy, were adopted without questioning, lock, stock and barrel. The very casting of any doubt, or raising the need to verify and inquire before one makes judgments, were considered sacrilegious by the pious western media, which accepted and sanctified Muslim faultless righteousness as an axiom beyond doubt or question.

One of the best examples of this successful Bosnian propaganda unfolded during the battle for Gorazde in April 1994. The Bosnian government in Sarajevo convinced the world that the Serbs demolished the town and inflicted numerous civilian casualties. In fact, most of the damage that was done in the enclave had actually occurred almost two years prior to the battle, when Muslims had conducted their own ethnic cleansing and burned out the Serbs' houses. There was a Muslim radio operator, who was allegedly holed up in a basement and could accurately describe events taking place on the battlefield. But, in fact, no conclusive objective evidence exists that the radio operator was even based in Gorazde. Then, who manipulated whom? Were the journalists who spread the story shackled by their concept of aggressor and victim, and they remorselessly transmitted their distorted reports to their American and European audiences; or was it the public relations firms who maneuvered the western chanceries, or vice versa? Partial answers will come up in the following pages.

The FMSO (Foreign Military Studies Office)[39] issued in 1995 papers reevaluating the American policy in the

---

[39] FMSO, the Foreign Military Studies Office, is a research and analysis center for the United States Army, which does not necessarily represent the official policy or position of the Department of the Army, Department of Defense, or the US Government.

aftermath of the Bosnian civil war. The analyst, Lieutenant Colonel John E. Sray, from the US Army, quoted Henri Louis Mencken, who had commented: "The horrors of war are always exaggerated by sentimentalists[40]." Sray noted that declarations, made by the Department of State and congressional leaders, which indicated that the United States would not participate in military action against the Bosnian-Muslim government in Sarajevo, and that the US Navy would not assist NATO in enforcing the UN arms embargo against the Bosnians, were in fact harmful to US relations with her two key NATO allies, France and Great Britain, who were embroiled up to their ears in that conflict. It appeared as if the United States had chosen sides and no longer wished to seek a mediated solution. Moreover, according to that view, the United States even obstructed the ability of the ground commander of UN forces to remain an impartial player in this conflict. Thus, since no one dared to question the miserable state of affairs of the underdog Muslims, they were encouraged to nourish unrealistic military and political ambitions, which might have contributed, as they had wished, to the prolongation of the hostilities. Therefore, on one hand, the Muslim intransigence grew to accord with the intensive lobby of their campaigners in western capitals, and on the other hand, the Serbs persisted in their refusal to surrender captured land. By the year of 1993, the Bosnian Serbs had occupied much of that land, relegating the Muslim and Croat minorities into isolated urban pockets. Once the Serbs appropriated to themselves the lion's share of the Bosnian territory, the Croats also jumped into the fighting against the Muslims, fearing they would otherwise be discarded when the partition of Bosnia-Herzegovina came up for grabs.

---

[40] The Quotation reflects the events recorded by Albert Benabou in the War Zone and is related to Lieutenant Colonel John Sray on his reevaluation of the U.S. Policy during the War in Bosnia.

In March 1994, most of the Muslim political leadership considered that the framework of a federation/confederation with the Croats might resolve some of the outstanding issues. They were manifestly content with the prospect that the negotiations with the Croats would take place in Washington, where they believed they had an edge over their rivals. That was to be the crowning act of their tremendous effort to involve the United States in the conflict in Bosnia. On the other hand, this political move helped boost the warring enthusiasm of the Muslim Armija commanders on the battlefield. These military minds falsely judged that in order to isolate the Serbs politically it was appropriate to build up their arsenals, recruit and train more troops, and enter a crucial new phase of the war, where they could crush the BSA (Bosnian Serb Army), emerge victorious militarily, and thus reverse the harsh reality whereby they had lost seventy percent of the territory they were supposed to protect. When in October 1994 the State Department declared that the United States would not participate in any military action against the Bosnian Muslim government in Sarajevo, it was countering a warning issued by Lt. Gen. (Sir) Michael Rose, the UN commander in Bosnia, who upbraided the Muslim authorities for their continued deliberate violations of UN negotiated agreements. Christine Shelly, the State Department spokesperson, then proclaimed that the US Navy would no longer assist in the maritime enforcement of the Bosnian arms embargo. She justified those démarches on the grounds that "It's hard to imagine the United States participating in that kind of action against Bosnian government forces when they clearly have been the overwhelming victim in the aggression by the Bosnian Serb forces[41]."

---

[41] Source: WASHINGTON POST quoting the declaration from the State Department on Friday the 7th of May 1994.

That was enough of an indication that the United States had opted to go it alone, totally ignoring N.A.T.O strategy, thus positioning Great Britain and France in an unbearable state of affairs. The latter had contributed significant troops to the peace keeping mission and constantly signaled that only a negotiated solution in Bosnia would be acceptable in the broader Yugoslav context. Indeed, French and British official representatives voiced in various briefings their apprehension that UN and N.A.T.O. disengagement could widen the conflict to the wider Balkan region and from there spill over into all of Europe. Due to these differences in approaches toward the Bosnian problem, the supposedly harmonious strategic alliance between the United States and its European allies was apparently moving towards a collision course. What is more, the Muslim troops often attacked UN convoys or units on duty and blamed that shooting on the Serbs to further discredit their enemies. One of the more notorious of these incidents concerned the preparations for Pope John Paul II's visit to Sarajevo. Muslim troops fired mortar shells at the Danish unit, which was preparing the airfield for the Pope's landing. When confronted with the evidence, Bosnian Vice President Ejup Ganic feigned "surprise and shock" and claimed that UNPROFOR falsely accused a Muslim unit due to its anti-Muslim biased attitude. Subsequent to this incident, the papal visit was cancelled. President Izetbegovic promptly blamed the UN Special Envoy to Bosnia, Yasushi Akashi, for "deceiving the Vatican, by exaggerating security hazards[42]," thus prompting the cancellation of the Pope's visit.

The Clinton administration reprimanded Yasushi Akashi, the chief UN official in Bosnia, for letting Serbian tanks cross

---

[42] Published by Roger Cohen in the New York Times Edition published on 8 September 1994.

a zone near Sarajevo that was prohibited to heavy weapons by UN order.[43] State Department spokesperson, Christine Shelly, called on Yasushi Akashi, the UN special envoy, "to do a better job. We would not like to see him acquiesce in actions which violate the exclusion zone[44]." Secretary General Boutros Boutros-Ghali reiterated his backing for Akashi and ruled out any consideration of firing him. Akashi had indeed been in recurrent situations of outright clashes with the United States and NATO in Bosnia. When a NATO deadline expired on 23 April for the Serbs to pull back their troops from Gorazde, Akashi blocked NATO from launching airstrikes, arguing that the Serbs should be given more time to comply. US Ambassador to the UN, Madeleine Albright, complained to the General Secretary at the beginning of May 1993, after Akashi had said to the media that the United States was "timid" about sending peace keeping troops to Bosnia. Not to lag behind, the Bosnian government accused Akashi of taking the Serbian side in the war and called for his ouster, refusing to deal or have any contact with him.

The Muslims mistakenly believed that due to their significant advantage in military manpower, (they outnumbered the Bosnian Serb Army, approximately two to one), which was boosted by international Mujahidin, they could acquire more land through continued combat operations, rather than by political compromise. The Muslim Armija received and stockpiled significant amounts of small arms and ammunition, as well as produced some of its own war material. Basically the amounts of small arms and light weapons (SALW) were abundant within Bosnia-Herzegovina as a result of historical developments. The remaining military stocks of SALW were leftovers of the former Yugoslav People's Army

---

[43] Source: WASHINGTON POST quoting the declaration from the State Department on Friday the 7th of May 1994.
[44] ibid.

(JNA) and the territorial units' weaponry and ammunition stockpiles. More than fifty thousand people were directly or indirectly employed by the Bosnia-Herzegovina arms factories. As an essential part of the Yugoslav defense doctrine, which was based on the concept of total national defense, the target of the Bosnian defense industry was an enormous output of both small arms and light weapons (below 75mm caliber) and heavy weapons of all types and brands. Moreover, despite the arms embargo, a steady flow of illegal weapons found its way into Bosnia on commercial convoys from Zagreb and via new road links from the Croatian coast through Konjic and Mostar. The Muslim government accumulated small arms and ammunitions to sustain its plans for continued offensive action. The lack of a higher proportion of heavy weapons did not deter the Muslims (or any other army for that matter) from launching attacks. In this type of warfare, light weapons have their own special utility for small-scale operations; they make local successes possible. But the drawback was that at the same time these attacks provoked the BSA (Serbs) or the HVO (Croats) to counterattack with artillery and heavy weapons shelling and bombardment. Consequently, the Muslims were so sapped and worn-out that they surrendered the ground they had controlled before and then complained to the world about criminal acts committed against them, they the poor, miserable victims of the war (very reminiscent of the Palestinian conduct vis-à -vis- Israel in the Middle East).

Much more evidence has been collected in the field indicating that the Muslim Armija was constantly planning and preparing for offensive action. They restricted UNPROFOR access to contested areas along the entire confrontation line, so as to limit UN criticism of their violations of existing agreements. The Bosnian Muslims often took the additional illegal step of painting their aircraft white in an attempt to disguise them as UN helicopters. The commander in chief of the Armija, General Rasim Delic, as well as other senior military leaders, clearly advocated a military solution to the war and openly pledged that they would regain the lost territory through military measures, for they did not desire a permanent ceasefire or an internationally imposed agreement. More specifically, their strategy had been to throw the Serbs and the Croats off-balance while they built and trained an army that could eventually seize some of the land, which they felt belonged to the Muslims. Prior to the winter of 1993, the Armija launched local attacks and made some minor tactical gains in Mostar, Central Bosnia, and around Sarajevo. However, the much exaggerated claims they made to the press and to their own people were designed to create a delusion of success by building false hopes among the population that the continuation of the war would be advantageous to them. However, General Delic's conviction that his forces could succeed in the battlefield stemmed from his incorrect military analysis that time had begun to turn in favor of the Muslims, as if time in itself could favor anybody. The Muslim command also deluded itself that the BSA was overextended and that tactical initiative had definitely been seized by the Muslim Armija. In operational and strategic terms, there was not a single dominating point in the battlefield in existence, which if the Muslims could capture would have generated a victory in the war. In reality, despite their momentary and mediocre field performances, the BSA and the HVO retained the capability to mass sufficient artillery and other heavy weaponry, at the time and place they chose, to deal the Muslims fatal blows, causing them casualties and loss of materiel and territory.

The humanitarian situation in the Muslim controlled areas was permanently on the agenda of the UN, NATO, and the other humanitarian bodies involved. A famous adage in the Jewish Talmud proclaims that: "The cry of the needy is answered by heavens." In this case, the almost only heavens open for the Muslim population, which was caught under siege and manipulated by interested parties, including their own, were mainly the UNPROFOR units and occasionally other NGO's, which acted in collaboration with them. On Friday, 19 November 1993, Benabou sent a report on the humanitarian situation in Muslim East Mostar, which was widely distributed to the UN headquarters in Zagreb as well as to the other UN units and agencies throughout Bosnia. The COS of SPABAT, Lt. Col. Alaman, made an effort to evaluate the needs of Muslim East Mostar by 21 November, 1993 as thirty-five trucks arrived loaded with three hundred and fifty tons, mainly food, blankets, clothes, and sleeping bags (no itemized list was available). There was no confirmation of these figures from any other source. Alikadic, member of the war presidency in East Mostar, maintained permanent contacts with the head of the UNHCR office in Medjugorje, Jerry Hulme, who invested tremendous and relentless efforts to respond to Muslim pleas. Hulme, accompanied by Benabou, paid visits to East Mostar and realized that the basic problem there was that no aid convoys were allowed or prepared to go to either East Mostar, Jablanica, Tarcin, or Konjic, and that only ten trucks were available for all those locations. He also took stock of their warehouses, which were short of protein items of food necessary for the approaching winter. All they could provide, then, was wheat flour, oil, and yeast for bread. However, this situation was supposed to improve shortly.

Karen Koning AbuZayd, the chief of mission for UNHCR in Sarajevo during the Bosnian War, visited East Mostar with Jerry Hulme and was aware of this state of affairs. She counseled that further specific information, concerning the needs and profile of the required supplies, should be collected. The

Muslim authorities in East Mostar repeatedly complained about the mistreatment and discriminatory attitude of the Spanish Battalion towards them, because they viewed the situation in East Mostar as quite critical to them, as reported and verified by the UNMOs. Especially dire was the condition of the children in East Mostar, who were exposed to the constant bombardments of the Croats, for they were victims of that war, not only in terms of causalities and deprivation for those who survived, but also in view of the psychological traumas, which took hold of their young and malleable souls and needed to be addressed urgently. Some of them lost so much of the sense of danger that they were nonchalantly playing in the vicinity of the line of confrontation. Alikadic, a local Muslim leader under siege, was conscious of those risks, and addressed on 21 February 1994, an official request to Albert Benabou, the Israeli head of the Civil Affairs Office of the UN in Mostar, asking to participate in a UNICEF ten-day staff education seminar taking place in Israel. Other participants in that seminar, Professors Nadjija Dzabic and Amela Pedisa, were designated to bring up the life conditions of the children in Mostar.

Part of the Muslim plight in Mostar was attributed to the fundamental gaps that yawned among the Muslim political leadership. On 5 November 1993, Benabou met in Medjugorje with Mr. Alija Alikadic, a member of the East Mostar war presidency. In that two-hour session, consisting of a friendly and open conversation, which Alikadic asked to keep under wraps, he noted that at the beginning of the conflict the political and military leadership in Mostar was neither elected nor designated by Sarajevo. It grew out of the constraints of the local Muslim community in Mostar and received national backing only at a later stage. He even stated that the central Muslim government in Sarajevo had, at a certain point, given up the Neretva Valley and considered

Igman Mountain as the BiH border. He said that they accepted the option of extending the state territory only at a later stage. He affirmed that the local Muslim commanders and representatives of civil authorities in Mostar deserved the credit for establishing and maintaining the Armija presence in the areas of Konjic, Jablanica, and Mostar. Indeed, a difference of interest between Sarajevo and Mostar was manifested then, as, on the one hand, the national leadership was primarily preoccupied by the defense of the eastern corridor between Bosnia and Serbia, but on the other hand, the leadership in Muslim Mostar was constantly focusing on the Neretva Valley border. The conflict of interest was noticeable when the leadership in Sarajevo was looking for rapprochement with the Croats (against the Serbs), while the leadership in Mostar was pushing for contacts with the Serbs (against the Croats). This disparity was due, primarily, to the fact that it was the Croats who acted to destroy and traumatize the Muslim community in Mostar, not the Serbs, while a Croatian alliance was direly needed for the eastern part, which was under the imminent threat of the stronger Serbs.

Sarajevo decided at some point to reshuffle the BiH Armija militarily and the leadership of the City of Mostar politically. General Arif Pasalic, the departing Fourth Corps Commander, who was the most prominent military figure in that zone of operations, was sent to assume the post of Deputy Defense Minister in the new Sarajevo government. Through this promotion, a power struggle was settled, which had lasted for a long time between General Pasalic, the founder of the Armija Fourth Corps defending Mostar, and the Chief of Staff of the Army, General Hallilovic. Pasalic was later killed in an automobile accident near Mostar on 26 April, 1998, at the age of fifty-four. Benabou noted in his memoirs that this courageous man, who expressed more than once his admiration for Israel and the Jewish people, was a living representative of the determination and tenacity of his people. He died in the same manner as General George Patton at the end of the Second World War and deserved an honorable military salute for his dedication to the people of Mostar. Loyal to the values of freedom and democracy, he devoted his life to the attainment of self-determination by his Muslim compatriots, without sinking, however, into religious fanaticism or into messianic delusions. Brigadier General Sulejman Budakovic, who had accumulated power in East Mostar and had served under General Pasalic as the Fourth Corps Deputy Commander, was appointed to succeed him as acting Fourth Corps Commander. Colonel Safet Orucevic, one of the closest of Izetbegovic's associates, was posted in Mostar as the new Fourth Corps Deputy Commander to succeed Budakovic. The respective local commanders of Konjic and Jablanica, Safet Cibo and Zulfikar Alispaho (zuka), who had been acting independently, had been upbraided by General Pasalic before he left his command and asked to choose between obeying the chain of command or facing arrest. Their course of action had indeed been a source of concern among the Muslim leaders in the Mostar area and of terror to the Croats in the region who looked in horror at those freewheeling Muslim officers.

According to Alikadic, in order to reform the nucleus of civil power in East Mostar, a new local civil governmental structure was to cover the area of East Mostar, Jablanica, Konjic, Chaplina, Prozor, Gacko, Nevesinje, and Stolac. Thus, a firm civil administration took control in this zone, the highest authority vested in Smajil Klaric, the actual chairman of the East Mostar War Presidency, and Alija Alikadic was appointed as the chargé d'affaires with the international organizations in the entire region. This civilian government at the county level carried responsibility also for Muslim populations displaced from their homes who were located in territories presently dominated by HVO or BSA. This administration operated in some instances in absentia, i.e., on behalf of refugee populations who had been uprooted from their towns and villages. Alikadic revealed that the essence of the structure of the East Mostar civil administration consisted of encompassing within their jurisdiction Muslim, non-Mostar citizens, such as refugees from Gacko, Nevesinje, Stolac, etc. They were defined as guests of Mostar, who were entitled to temporary shelter from the local structures during the crisis. This status specifically excluded them from the decision making process concerning the future of the town and the community. Alikadic occasionally accused HVO "outsiders" (Croats from Grude, Siroki Brijeg, and other locations) of interfering in (Christian Croatian) West Mostar affairs and systematically taking over leading positions by replacing locals (Croats and Muslims) who were removed. That did not prevent the replacement of Dr. Dragan Milavic, the former head of the East Mostar hospital, by Dr. Setka from Blagaj, who also exercised his much needed skill as anesthesiologist. This swap was justified by the fact that Dr. Milavic had been on duty for too long a term and was exhausted by that tiring and hazardous job. Milavic was also accused of atrophying the war hospital efficiency when employing three hundred and thirty people. Obviously, Dr. Milavic had also dissented from the military and civilian authorities in the city when he publicly expressed his antagonism towards the idea of "a total Muslim state." He repeatedly asserted that the moment he perceived a determined intention to create a Muslim state he would morally face difficulties to continue to act in the hospital of the Mostar enclave.

In terms of the Muslim-Serbian relations in the Mostar area, Alija Alikadic and Dzevad Dziho have conducted intensive negotiations with the BSA (Colonel Milosevic) since

8 August 1993. Apparently, certain understandings have been achieved to allow the Serbian population from the areas of Blagaj and Bijelo Polje (BiH controlled) and the Muslim population of Nevesinje and Gacko (BSA controlled) to return to their original residences. Alikadic even occasionally defended "BSA fairness," specifying that not so many crimes had been committed by the Serbian forces in the area of Mostar in comparison with the events in eastern Bosnia (e.g. Srebrenica). However, that picture was further complicated by the basic disagreement between the Muslim leadership in Mostar and in Sarajevo. The Muslim leaders in Mostar alluded, for example, to the presence of the European (German) administrator in their city with reluctance, clarifying that the authorities in Sarajevo had forced him upon them. Some of them even voiced loudly the ambition to see Mostar demarcated as a Zona Franca, namely free of Sarajevo's control. In fact, they worked out, probably in concert with the local Croats, an arrangement limiting its prerogatives. The friction between Mostar and Sarajevo escalated towards the conclusion of the Washington Agreement in March 1994. As a result of this confrontation, Safet Orucevic took over the rule of Mostar and became the permanent channel of consultations with Sarajevo, and all decisions were made jointly with Safet Orucevic, who was enjoying the political support of President Izetbegovic and of some of the leaders in Mostar. In Sarajevo, tension was discernible between Prime Minister Harris Silajdzic and President Izetbegovic. Apparently, the clash between them was accentuated due to the Washington Agreements between the Muslims and the Croats, which left open two possibilities:

1. Either a tendency (endorsed by Izetbegovic and Ejup Ganic) to enlist the backing of the Muslim countries (such as Iran and Pakistan), with all the cultural and political implications involved, while striving for political support from Europe and the United States; or

2. Adopting another approach (sponsored by Silajdzic) aimed at eliciting the main backing from the United States, while stressing Bosnian differences, as Europeans, from the other Muslim countries.

Concurrently, with the restoration and normalization of their relations with Zagreb and the Croats, the leadership in Sarajevo pursued a line of discrediting the Serbian leadership in Pale and looked instead for direct arrangements with President Milosevic in Belgrade. In this course of action, Sarajevo faced more difficulties in dislodging Karadzic from Pale than Boban from Grude. The Serbs had acted out of a more coherent and ideological standpoint. Karadzic did not carry, apart from his declared leadership of the Bosnian Serbs, any clear function, which he might be required to give up. The intelligence evaluation at the UN headquarters was that a prompt settlement introducing the Serbs into the Bosnian federation/confederation process was required. Muslims (not necessarily from BiH) were already encouraging terrorist activities against Serbs, particularly in Kosovo where the state of affairs was constantly deteriorating and delaying the process of a political solution in Bosnia. The Muslim leaders, who did not accomplish their goal of settling the conflict through military victory over the Serbs, turned to the international arena where they had some achievements. On Wednesday 19 January 1994, Benabou held private and confidential meetings in Muslim East Mostar with Alija Alikadic and in Croatian Grude with Vladislav Pogarcic. It was in the aftermath of the Geneva Conference, and both parties, Muslims and Croats in Mostar, were invited to formulate their intentions and plans. This process was advisedly launched in two separate sessions and locations. Alikadic clarified that the Muslim community of Mostar was represented by Safet Orucevic, who had attended the Geneva Conference with the BiH delegation headed by Izetbegovic. According to Orucevic, no decisions had been adopted there concerning Mostar, and his delegation requested a stronger interference from the United Nations and a decrease of European involvement in the BiH affairs. The Croatian delegate, Vladislav Pogarcic, confirmed that his sources had also assured him that no decisions had been taken about Mostar. The two parties announced to Benabou that by Saturday the 22 they would complete the wording of a letter defining their positions for the future of Mostar. Alikadic emphasized that their document would be prepared in accordance with guidelines from Sarajevo. Pogarcic notified that the same process would be followed by the Croats with Zagreb.

Consequently, at this period of time, the dilemma among the Muslim strategic thinkers was how to obtain weapons without sacrificing the degree of protection offered by UNPROFOR. Their efforts then focused on the willful discrediting of UNPROFOR, combined with a propaganda campaign to persuade the international community that the Serbs (both BSA and rump Yugoslavia) would not cease hostilities or mutual support of each other. UN forces found themselves targeted by Muslim charges ranging from failure to police weapon control check points to permitting the Serbs to besiege Sarajevo. The shadow of guilt and incompetence was cast upon the UN by Muslim propaganda, while their supporters in the United States and elsewhere initiated a lobbying campaign designed to convince the international community that incidents of this nature could come to an end only by strengthening the Muslim army with required heavy weapons. Additionally, the Muslims pressed the UN to redeploy UNPROFOR so as to cease acting as a deterrent to lifting the embargo, while remaining close to the fighting arena to be able once again to stop hostilities if the tide of war did not turn in the Muslims' favor. While the Muslims were currently incapable of launching meaningful, coordinated, large scale offensives at critical points on the battlefield, they continued to initiate fresh local attacks along the confrontation lines wherever local commanders could take the initiative. Were the goodwill of the West and the naiveté of the Bosnian Muslim populace exploited to achieve these tortuous schemes? Apparently, yes. The Muslim leadership hoped to extract the maximum value from their "allies" while manipulating every conceivable advantage of time, space, and opportunity. Concurrently, the Bosnian Muslim troops manning the trenches became exhausted by the war at a time when their political leaders seemed to lack any true interest in their welfare and required them to keep fighting locally even without the benefit of any large, coordinated military campaign other than the ongoing unwinnable war of attrition.

**The Croatian Perspective**

The Croatian involvement in the Bosnian War did not emanate only from their long-dating enmity to the Serbs and their desire to see Serbian dominance of rump Yugoslavia reduced to the minimum, but mainly from the demographic fact that a million and a half Serbs still resided in Bosnia and Croatia in a very widespread pattern that made their eviction totally impractical. Therefore, after the expulsion of many of them from Krajina, Zagreb mobilized all its forces and resources, often in temporary and manipulative collaboration with the Muslims, to contain the remaining Serbs and to protect the Croatian settlements in Bosnia that had become part of the local demography. They did not refrain from collaboration with the Serbs either when they thought that the alliance could bring them more benefits than disadvantages. But during the Bosnian War, much of the confrontation, both in the battlefields and around negotiation tables, was centered on the battles around Mostar against Bosnian Muslims. Much like the Srpska that the Serbs had ascertained for themselves in Bosnia, the Croats of Bosnia, led by Mate

Boban, proclaimed their own Croatian community of Herzeg-Bosnia, which was supported by the Republic of Croatia but contended by Bosnian Muslims. The belligerence between the parties lasted from June 1992 until the Washington Agreement in 23 February, 1994, which was in fact imposed on the Croats by the United States. Considering the involvement and the interference of the National Croatian Leadership from Zagreb in the conflict, the International Criminal Tribunal for former Yugoslavia, later determined, in numerous verdicts against Croatian political and military leaders, that the war's nature was in fact international between Croatia and Bosnia and Herzegovina, not an internecine civil war.

The objectives of the Croatian nationalists who vied for a greater Croatia, as in World War II, were shared by Croatian nationalists in Bosnia and Herzegovina. In fact, the ruling party in the Republic of Croatia, the Croatian Democratic Union (HDZ), also organized and controlled the branch of the party in Bosnia and Herzegovina. By the latter part of 1991, the more extreme elements of the party in Bosnia, under the leadership of Mate Boban, Dario Kordic, Jadranko Prlic, and other local leaders, had taken effective control of the party with the support of Zagreb. In reality, no policy could be adopted, and no decision could be taken without the blessing of Croatia President Franjo Tudjman. Mate Boban was indeed Tudjman's faithful associate and envoy in Bosnia-Herzegovina, representing his interests in the war against the Muslim leadership in Sarajevo, much more so than were the relationships between Milosevic in Belgrade and Karadzic in Pale during the war. Mate Boban, president of the self-declared Independent Herzeg-Bosnia, was born on 12 February 1940 in a large family in the municipality of Grude in Herzegovina, the city where he installed his political and military headquarters in 1991, conducting his daily affairs and leading the war against the Muslims. He was a typical product of the former Communist Yugoslavia, who got implicated in the 1980s in economic frauds and nourished, deep in his heart, Croatian nationalism with a profound hatred to the other ethnicities, particularly towards the Muslims. As a member of the League of Communists of Yugoslavia, he permanently exhibited his Communist Party badge on the dash of his suit. His political associates explained that Boban did not commit any crime and that he was imprisoned because of his fidelity to Croatian nationalism, more precisely after he visited Ante Pavelic's[45] grave in Madrid.

Boban was already retired without any particular ambitions when the war in Bosnia broke out. His most loyal associates were also former Communist party members, and they formed the political and military leadership which accompanied Boban in his war against the Muslims. On 12 November 1991, Mate Boban and Dario Kordic held a joint meeting of the crisis teams of Herzegovina and of the Travnik Regional Communities, which decided that Croats in Bosnia-Herzegovina should institute a policy achieving their own age-old dream of a common Croatian state, which should proclaim a Croatian Banovina[46] in Bosnia and Herzegovina as the initial phase leading towards the permanent settlement of the Croatian question and the creation of a sovereign Croatia within its ethnic and historical borders. On 18 November 1991, Boban proclaimed the existence of the Croatian community of Herzeg-Bosnia, as a separate political, cultural, economic, and territorial entity, on the territory

---

[45] Ante Pavelic was the World War II Croatian nationalist who headed the Ustasha state (including Bosnia), which collaborated with the Nazis and established the death camps where Serbs, Jews, and Gypsies were exterminated in the hundreds of thousands.

[46] Banovina was a province of the Kingdom of Yugoslavia between 1939 and 1941. Its capital was at Zagreb, and it included most of present-day Croatia along with portions of Bosnia and Herzegovina and Serbia.

of Bosnia and Herzegovina. This was in line with the Karadordevo Agreement, previously reached between Croatian President Franjo Tudjman and Serbian President Slobodan Milosevic (then of Yugoslavia) to divide Bosnia and Herzegovina between Croatia and Serbia. Following that track, Boban met with Bosnian Serb President Radovan Karadzic during May 1992 in Graz, Austria, where they agreed on mutual cooperation in the division of Bosnia and Herzegovina that became known as the Graz Agreement. (The pair met again on 2 September, 1993, in Montenegro in order to coordinate their actions after the Bosniaks, who rejected the Vance-Owen Peace Plan. See below.) Boban said that the "Serbs are our brothers in Christ, but the Muslims are nothing to us, apart from the fact that for hundreds of years they raped our mothers and sisters[47]."

The deal called for the Serbs to aid the Croats in defeating the Bosniaks and to carve out a piece of Bosnia and Herzegovina and incorporate it into Croatia. Tensions mounted from June 1992 until early 1993 on the Croatian-Bosnian front. Finally, after many provocations and hostile acts by Croats, open warfare broke out in April 1993 between Croats and Bosniaks. The Croatian militia, the HVO, attacked and expelled Bosniaks all over central and southern Bosnia and Herzegovina. But by early 1994, the tide was turning against the Croats, prompting the United States to impose a peace treaty, known as the Washington Accords, which was signed in March 1994 between Croats and Muslims and would be later consecrated by the Dayton Accord (see below). When the Washington Accords was achieved, Herzeg-Bosnia Boban went into retirement. On 4 July, 1997, Boban had a stroke and died three days later at a hospital in Mostar. His funeral attracted only like minded Croats, such as Gojko

---

[47] Ramet, Sabrina P.; *The three Yugoslavias: state-building and legitimation, 1918-2005*; Indiana University Press, 2006.

Susak and no foreign dignitaries. There were persistent but unproven rumors that his death was faked in order to avoid being tried for war crimes. A memorial plaque in his and Herzeg-Bosnia's honor was placed in a street also named after him in Grude and some other places with a Croatian ethnic majority (such as Kupres, Chaplina, Livno, Posusje, and Lubushki).

Before the postwar settlement, the Croatian Democratic Union of Bosnia and Herzegovina was the leading party of the Bosnian Croats in Bosnia-Herzegovina, and amongst its affirmed objectives figured the statement on the right of the Croats to defend themselves and to secede. The Croatian Defense Council (HVO) became its executive, administrative, and supreme military organ. Dario Kordic held a decisive influence over the objectives and the political and military operations of these structures. Despite the fact that he was not at the top of the political hierarchy, and that he was a civilian unused to the official command structure of the HVO, Dario Kordic made many political and strategic decisions: he negotiated ceasefire agreements, and he issued orders of direct and indirect military significance. Thanks to the high ranking positions he held and due to the power and influence which he wielded, he played a key role in the planning, organization, promotion, and implementation of a politico-military campaign. More than once, Benabou had to face the senseless HVO military actions, which obstructed UNPROFOR movement in the field and which were initiated only due to the competition between Dario Kordic and Bruno Stojic, who was closer to Boban in Grude.

On 27 December 1991, there was a meeting in Zagreb, chaired by President Franjo Tudjman, of the leadership of the ruling party, the Croatian Democratic Union, jointly with its branch in Herzeg-Bosnia. The purpose was, first, to discuss the future of Bosnia-Herzegovina and the differences of opinion on this topic among the leadership in the branch party in Herzeg-Bosnia and then, formulating an overall Croatian political strategy. Some voiced the position in favor of the Croats remaining within Bosnia-Herzegovina. Mate Boban announced that, should Bosnia-Herzegovina disintegrate, Herzeg-Bosnia would be proclaimed as an independent Croatian territory, which would "accede to the state of Croatia, only at such time as the Croatian leadership should decide[48]." Dario Kordic opposed his political partner, Boban, on this issue and declared that the Croatian people of the Travnik region were ready to accede to the Croatian state "at all costs and any other option would be considered treason[49]." But all the participants present at the meeting realized that in due time it would be up to President Tudjman to make the decision. At that time, the policies of the Republic of Croatia and its leader, Franjo Tudjman, towards Bosnia and Herzegovina were never totally transparent, but everyone understood Franjo Tudjman's ultimate aim of expanding Croatia's borders.

In June 1992, the focus of the Croats shifted to Novi Travnik and Gornji Vakuf, where the Croat Defense Council (HVO) efforts to gain control were resisted. On 18 June, 1992, the Bosnian Territorial Defense in Novi Travnik received an ultimatum from the HVO, which included demands to abolish existing Bosnia-Herzegovina institutions, to recognize the authority of the Croatian community of Herzeg-Bosnia and to pledge allegiance to it, to subordinate the Territorial Defense to the HVO, and to expel Muslim refugees, all within twenty-four hours. On 19 June, a violent attack was launched in implementation of the ultimatum, causing damage to the local elementary school and to the post. The

---

[48] Source: ICTY: Kordić and Čerkez verdict". United Nations. 26 February 2001. Page 142.
[49] ibid.

attack was repulsed. At this time, armed incidents started to occur among Croat factions in Bosnia and Herzegovina, which culminated in the summer of 1992 in a confrontation between the HVO (under the leadership of Mate Boban) and the HOS (under the leadership of Blaz Kraljevic). The HVO favored an ethnic partition of the republic, while the HOS fought together with the Muslims for the territorial integrity of the state. Blaz Kraljevic, the primary pro-union Croat leader, understandably supported by Bosnian President Alija Izetbegovic, was killed by HVO soldiers in August 1992. This caused the dissolution of the principal group which supported a Bosniak-Croat alliance. The situation became more serious in October 1992 when Croat forces attacked Bosniak civilian populations in Prozor, burning their homes and killing noncombatants. According to Jadranko Prlic's indictment by The Hague court, HVO forces cleansed most of the Muslims from the town of Prozor and several surrounding villages.

In the latter half of 1992, foreign Mujahidin, hailing mainly from North Africa and the Middle East, began to arrive in central Bosnia and set up camps for combatant training with the intent of helping their "Muslim brothers," as theory dubbed them, against the Serbs. These foreign volunteers were primarily organized into an umbrella detachment of the Seventh Muslim Brigade (made up of native Bosniaks) of the Army of the Republic of Bosnia and Herzegovina in Zenica. Initially, the Mujahidin offered basic necessities, including food to local Muslims. When the Croat-Bosniak conflict began, they joined the BiH Armija in battles against the HVO. By December 1992, much of Central Bosnia was in the hands of the Croats. The Croatian forces had taken control of the municipalities of the Lasva Valley and had only met significant opposition in Novi Travnik and Ahmici. Bosniak authorities forbade Croats from leaving towns such as Bugojno and Zenica and would periodically organize exchanges of local Croats for Muslims. In January 1993, Croatian forces attacked Gornji Vakuf again in order to connect Herzegovina with Central Bosnia. Gornji Vakuf is a town to the south of the Lasva Valley and of strategic importance at a crossroads en route to Central Bosnia. It is forty-eight kilometers from Novi Travnik and about one hour's drive from Vitez in an armored vehicle. For Croats, it was a very important connection between the Lasva Valley and Herzegovina, two territories included in the self-proclaimed Croatian community of Herzeg-Bosnia. The Croatian forces' shelling reduced much of the historical, oriental center of the town of Gornji Vakuf to rubble. On 10 January 1993, just before the outbreak of hostilities in Gornji Vakuf, the Croatian Defense Council (HVO) Commander, Luka Sekerija, sent a military top secret request to Colonels Tihomir Blaskic and Dario Kordic for rounds of mortar shells available at the ammunition factory in Vitez. Sparked by a bomb placed on 11 January, 1993, by Croats in a Bosniak-owned hotel used as a military headquarters, fighting broke out in Gornji Vakuf, followed by heavy shelling of the town by Croatian artillery.

During ceasefire negotiations at the BRITBAT HQ in Gornji Vakuf, Colonel Andric, representing the HVO, demanded that the Bosnian forces lay down their arms and accept HVO control of the town, threatening that if they did not agree he would flatten Gornji Vakuf to the ground. The HVO demands were not accepted by the Bosnian Army, and the attack continued. During the Lasva Valley ethnic cleansing of Muslims, it was surrounded by the Croatian Army and the Croatian Defense Council troops for seven months and attacked with heavy artillery and other weapons (tanks and snipers). The shelling campaign and the attacks during the war resulted in hundreds of killed or injured, mostly Bosnian Muslims. The Lasva Valley ethnic cleansing campaign against Bosniak civilians, which was planned by the Croatian community of Herzeg-Bosnia's political and military leadership, from May 1992 to March 1993, and erupted the following April, was meant to implement objectives set forth by Croat nationalists in November 1991. The Croatian community of Herzeg-Bosnia took control of many municipal governments and services in Herzegovina as well, removing or marginalizing local Bosniak leaders. Herzeg-Bosnia took control of the media and imposed Croatian ideas and propaganda. Croatian symbols and currency were introduced, and Croatian curricula and the Croatian language were introduced in schools.

Mostar was surrounded at that time by Croatian forces for nine months, and much of its historic part of the city was severely destroyed in shelling, including the famous Stari Most Bridge. Slobodan Praljak, the commander of the Croatian Defense Council, was on trial at the ICTY for ordering the destruction of the bridge, among other charges. Mostar was then divided into a western part, which was dominated by the Croatian forces, and an eastern part where the Army of the Republic of Bosnia and Herzegovina was largely concentrated. In the early hours of the ninth of May 1993, the Croatian Defense Council attacked eastern Mostar, using artillery, mortars, heavy weapons, and small arms. The HVO controlled all roads leading into Mostar, and international organizations were denied access. Radio Mostar (in the western part of the city) announced that all Bosnia Muslims should hang a white flag from their windows, which proved that the HVO attack had been well prepared and planned. In June 1993, further fighting broke out in Central Bosnia, some of it caused by the newly revitalized Bosnian Army. Further complications were prompted by the incident between Croats and UNPROFOR known as "The Convoy of Joy Incident." This convoy of aid supplies was made up of several hundred trucks, seven kilometers in length, and was bound for Tuzla. On 7 June, 1993, two members of the UN delegation wrote to the European Community Monitor Mission (ECMM) at Zenica about their fears for the safety of the convoy when it reached the area of Travnik and Vitez, in light of threats made by Mate Boban. As a result, the ECMM decided to monitor the convoy. The convoy then set out and made its way to central Bosnia and the area of Novi Travnik. There it was stopped at a roadblock formed by a large crowd of Croatian women at Rankovici, north of Novi Travnik. Eight of the drivers were shot and killed, vehicles were driven away, and the convoy was looted by civilians and soldiers. Eventually, the convoy was released. In defending the convoy, BRITBAT shot and killed two HVO soldiers.

The series of Muslim counterattacks in central and southern Bosnia culminated in a massive assault between 7 and 13 June 1993 over the municipalities of Kakanj, Travnik, and Zenica. The Armija's Third Corps attacked towns and villages, subjecting Bosnian Croats and Serbs, predominantly civilians, including women, children, the elderly, and the infirm, to willful killings and serious injuries. Furthermore, in the course of, or subsequent to the attacks, at least two hundred Bosnian Croats and Serbs, mainly civilians, were killed, and many more were wounded or harmed while attempting to hide or escape. At this point, the state of affairs in the city of Mostar was at its worse, and each party attempted to prove to the international community that he was the victim. Concerning the military situation, the heaviest fighting took place in the northern part of Mostar (Bijelo Polje area). Artillery, rockets, medium, and light mortars (120mm and 82mm) were used in the exchange of fire between the parties. In the southern part of Mostar, intensive clashes were taking place in the Buna area. Furthermore, along the confrontation line (the "boulevard") in the city, ground, air, and antitank weapons were relentlessly exchanged. Nevertheless, the confrontation line remained relatively stable and no side achieved any noticeable advance on the terrain.

The Croats' first objective was to cut off the road between Mostar and Blagaj. On the opposite side, the Armija in East Mostar was striving to obtain ammunition to pursue its resistance. There exactly lay their Achilles' heel, for in terms of destruction, only the old bridge was still standing in the city (not for too long) while the Tito Bridge was seriously damaged. The living conditions in the east bank of the river continued to deteriorate due to the lack of food, medicines, and potable water, and the humanitarian and sanitary concern was growing because the Muslims were sealed under a tight Croatian siege. Colonel Morales, who commanded the Spanish Battalion near Mostar, tended to take this situation as a fait accompli and accepted the fact that the access to East Mostar was barred by the Croats for more than forty days. Benabou, the Civilian Affairs officer of the UN, learned from radio communications that the situation of the civilian population was catastrophic for fear that eruption of an epidemic disease was imminent. Indeed, the first signs of typhus began to surface. The Muslim population of eastern Mostar counted between thirty and thirty-five thousand, and their only source of water was the Neretva River, which crossed the city. Without potable water and under constant shelling, corpses of killed people were left in open fields in the war zone. Wounded people were not treated, due to the dearth of medical equipment and medicine. Dr. Dragan, the doctor in charge of the war clinic in East Mostar, constantly begged Benabou for medicine.

On 10 August 1993, Cedric Thornberry, a senior UN official (see below) decided to pay a field visit to the region, and Benabou initiated a proposal to include Mostar in his visit. He knew Thornberry was in difficult relations with the military personnel of the UN troops, particularly with General Cot, the UNPROFOR Force Commander. On the other hand, Victor Andreev, another senior civilian officer in the United Nations, insisted that the program should exclude Mostar, explaining that given the importance of Tuzla and the increasing feeling of its population that it had been abandoned, the program should include that city. Another alternative proposed by Andreev was that the visit should include Visoko where the Canadian Battalion (CANBAT) was posted. It appeared his resentment against the Muslims was even stronger than his contempt for the Croats, whom he considered "pure fascists." Therefore, he was in favor of leaving East Mostar to its plight and diverting the visit to Tuzla. Finally, Thornberry opted for Mostar, probably because that was a focal point at the time, and he needed it for his career as a good UN bureaucrat. As an experienced journalist, he knew how to integrate the impact of the press in his visit and to corner those who resisted the plan to reopen Mostar. Benabou, who was familiar with the area of Mostar where he served, took up the negotiations and coordination of the visit, both sides of the conflict being aware that he acted as a fair broker without external interests. Israel was indeed far away from the crisis in former Yugoslavia, and Benabou thought it was time to capitalize on it for a humanitarian benefit to both parties. Thornberry could not foresee the delicate chess game of the Croats and the Muslims in Mostar, so Benabou worked on preventing any faux pas, and he concentrated on planning the visit step-by-step and reaching an agreement between both sides, ignoring the internal power struggle between the UN bureaucrats, at a time when faked UN impartiality became unbearable.

The "humanitarian convoy" to East Mostar entered the besieged city on 26 August. Thornberry required Benabou's participation in the talks with the East Mostar Muslim leaders, with Colonel Morales attending. Thornberry thought that he could cover in his meetings in Mostar the issues of humanitarian access, UNMO presence, humanitarian corridors to central and southern Bosnia-Herzegovina, restoration of power and water supplies, release of civilian captives and full access to them, an exchange of prisoners, and the evacuation of wounded. He would realize later the gap between reality and his wishful thinking. During the preparatory talks with the parties before the visit, both were convened by Benabou and Morales. After some initial verbal fireworks, unsurprising as they had not met for more than two months, the atmosphere between the Croats and the Muslims became friendly and cooperative, and they retired to corners in order to negotiate discreetly with each other. During the night, Morales returned with the Muslim leaders to Mostar, also to try to renegotiate withdrawal of one of his units, held hostage by the Muslims. Before he returned, his superiors in Bosnia, including Lt. General Munoz Grandes, had been trying to find a compromise, which would no longer commit them to a permanent presence in Mostar but would allow them regular access to both sides of the city. To that end, Boban and Foreign Minister Granic were promised that if they allowed access, UNPROFOR would visit Nova Bila hospital in Vitez. These informal stipulations of agreement were transmitted to Thornberry. Thereupon, it was decided that on 31 August a meeting would take place, first with East and then West Mostar authorities, with the purpose to obtain their final agreement for the speedy evacuation of a first group of gravely wounded and sick patients from the Croatian Nova Bila and Muslim East Mostar hospitals.

The idea was to follow this up with standing arrangements through a local mixed committee, providing a regular, as needed process of urgent evacuation of cases requiring treatment outside the war zone enclaves, and in accordance with

UNPROFOR standard operation procedures. Stojic, HVO Minister of Defense, assured that his side would provide the fullest cooperation to the proposed arrangements. During the visit in East Mostar the UN team obtained similar undertakings from the civilian authorities there. Stojic had emphasized during the negotiations that while HVO wanted Mostar as their "capital," they would be interested in a demilitarized and open status for the city. He insisted that the Croats had no desire to push the Muslims out of Mostar. He also cast doubt on the possibility of ever reaching agreement on a map in this area of BiH and wondered aloud if some other options might not have a chance, in which mixed cities and communal enclaves would continue to exist, but with a major UN presence to monitor the peace. In the meantime, however, in order to end the siege of East Mostar and to recapture areas of Herzegovina, which had been encapsulated within the self-proclaimed Croatian Republic of Herzeg-Bosnia, the Bosnian Armija launched, in September 1993, an operation known as "Neretva Ninety-Three" against the Croatian Defense Council and the Croatian Army. But the operation was stopped by Bosnian authorities when they got wind of the massacre perpetrated on Croat civilians in the village of Grabovica. Indeed, during the night between 8 and 9 September, thirty-three Croatian villagers in Grabovica were murdered by members of the Ninth Brigade and other unidentified members of the Bosnian Army.

Unlike the chaos and lack of strict discipline in the Bosnian chain of command, the Croatian officials in Mostar and in Sarajevo were instructed and directly controlled by Zagreb. So, when Zagreb decided that it was time for total confrontation with the Muslims, the Croats in Bosnia-Herzegovina plied to the directives and executed them in the terrain. And when Zagreb decided that it was time for reconciliation, the Croats in Bosnia-Herzegovina conformed and toed the new line. Thus, the Croatian leadership, particularly in Mostar, modulated their expectations, adapting them to the newly imposed reality as dictated by Zagreb. However, realizing more and more that it would not be possible for them to crush and expel the Muslims militarily, some of them did come to consider that they should integrate the Muslim political entity along the Neretva region within their plans. Nonetheless, the moment Zagreb adopted the Washington initiative it became necessary to dismiss from office the "undesired elements" in the Croatian political milieu in Mostar, who took over and persisted despite Zagreb's intentions. In a Croatian gathering in Sarajevo, a Croatian leader pointed his finger at Jadranko Prlic, the Croatian Prime Minister in Herzeg-Bosnia, and declared: "Prlic is to be restrained and removed from position so that other influential radical leaders (such as B. Pusic, the head of the POW release department) will lose their authority and influence in the city[50]."

Those "purges" were applied due to American and European pressures upon President Tudjman as a display of goodwill towards Sarajevo, for they facilitated the process in Washington and permitted the inauguration of a new political process between the Croats and the Muslims. The Croatian leaders in Herzegovina and in Zagreb were satisfied with the ceasefire and the immediate calm installed in Mostar. Benabou evaluated that the Croats would deploy a major effort to reinforce and implant their governmental institutions in the city of Mostar, but as he expected, they did not succeed in the accomplishment of their policy. He had indeed noted in his report: "The Croats are too eager to have it all and therefore they lost it all[51]." They were not keen

---

[50] Benabou noted this in his memoirs of the war, on 26 February 1994, after his meetings at the Assembly of the House of Croat Representatives in Mostar where he attended the crucial session and held series of meetings with the Croat Authorities.
[51] ibid.

on the initiative to obtain a separate arrangement for Mostar, where an agreed modus vivendi could be established at the local level between Muslims and Croats in the city. The Croatian Bosnian War officially ended on 23 February, 1994 when the Commander of HVO, General Ante Roso and the Commander of Bosnian Army, General Rasim Delic, signed a ceasefire agreement in Zagreb. In March 1994, the peace agreement mediated by the United States between the warring Croats (represented by the Republic of Croatia), and Bosnia and Herzegovina was signed in Washington and Vienna, which became known as the Washington Agreement. Under this agreement, the combined territory held by the Croatian and Bosnian government forces was divided into ten autonomous cantons/counties, establishing the Federation of Bosnia-Herzegovina.

At the start of the war, the HVO had controlled more than twenty percent of the territory of Bosnia and Herzegovina, but just before the signing of the Washington Agreement it had dwindled to less than ten percent. The blame was put on the fanatic policies of Boban, who was ousted from control thanks to the pressures of both Pope John Paul II and the US government. Although the Croats were aware of the failure and the weakness of their previous belligerence, they were slow to perceive the concrete benefits of the new policy. The exact definition and status of the cantons vis-à -vis the federation/confederation of all Bosnia remained unclear as yet at that point, but the Croats were looking for the resignation of the actual Muslim leadership in Sarajevo headed by Izetbegovic, and the launching of general elections when the rotating presidency of the federation would be, according to the agreements, in the hands of the Croats (Kresimir Zubak). The Croatian leaders accepted the Washington process, hoping that a rapprochement to the United States would favor and stimulate their deeply troubled economy and prompt the expanding of the acceptance of Zagreb in western capitals, a policy which proved stunningly successful, judging by the admission of new Croatia into the European Union.

As we pointed out for the Muslims, the Croatian government was also vigorously engaged to project a positive image in the United States through public relations campaigns. On 12 August 1991, the Croats hired the American public relations firm, Ruder Finn Global Public Affairs, to "develop and carry out strategies and tactics for communication with members of the US House of Representatives and the Senate as well as with officials of the US government including the State Department, the National Security Council, and other relevant agencies and departments of the US government as well as with American and international news media[52]." Ruder Finn's contract was renewed in 1992 and included lobbying with regard to diplomatic recognition, sanctions, and embargoes, as well as briefings for officials of the first Bush administration. The firm prepared and formulated special background materials, press releases, both reactive and proactive articles, and letters to the editors to appear in major newspapers, and briefings for journalists, columnists, and commentators. In January and February 1992, Ruder Finn organized trips to Croatia for US congressmen. The United States recognized Croatia as an independent state on 7 April, 1992. The Croats wanted to be perceived as the underdog, victims of aggression and discriminated against by the UN representatives. Although this approach seemed to make headway vis-à -vis the Serbs, it did not work with the Muslims, who were champions in victimization.

The Croats constantly complained that UNPROFOR was favoring the Muslims and ignoring the needs of the Croatian community. On 7 March 1994, Andreev addressed Jadranko

---

[52] Source: Belgrade Among the Serbs, Florence Hamlish Levinsohn, Chicago 1994, page 312-314.

Prlic, then acting as prime minister for the self declared republic of Herzeg-Bosnia, in a confidential message clarifying that UNPROFOR was acting fairly and impartially with all parties and that the accusations of favoring the Muslims were unfounded. The message was transmitted as "most urgent " through Albert Benabou, in order to ensure the UN ability to follow up on the terrain and implement UN commitment to assist the Croats as well as the Muslims in Novi Travnik. The concerned units in UNPROFOR, particularly the British engineering corps, were informed of the démarche by IMMARSAT. The main terms of Andreev's response were that he welcomed the opportunity to clarify the existing conditions in the Novi Travnik municipal area and to declare his concern for the welfare of the population of Novi Travnik, regardless of ethnic background or nationality. He said that the UN civil affairs and British representatives had investigated the water and sanitary problems endemic to the area and that they had inspected the pipelines, sewage drains, and refuse disposal, even though they had been fired upon, which was a common situation in the area. Therefore, they were totally aware of the critical health problems faced by the local citizenry. He asserted that the basic problem of water supply was due to a burst water pipe located in the vicinity of Trenica. Bosnian government authorities were cooperative in allowing inspection of the burst pipe and had indicated their willingness to assist in its replacement. Initially, it had claimed that the pipeline was of strategic import, since it might carry strategic materials, for military use and therefore prohibited the shipment of the replacement pipe. But, fortunately the necessary approval and shipment were arranged in Vitez. Unfortunately, however, the pipe brought from UNHCR stocks was plastic instead of cast iron and did not meet the correct dimensions required.

Thereafter, corrective action was taken, and the pipe meeting the correct specifications was ordered, arrived in

Split and was expected to arrive to Vitez soon. Assurance was repeated that within two days of arrival, British engineers, working with government public utilities personnel, would replace the pipe. UNPROFOR would then monitor the operation and ensure that the water was turned on gradually to provide water to the entire population of Novi Travnik. Furthermore, civil affairs also coordinated with the IRC and the ICRC to provide for the delivery and administration of chlorine to purify the water, under UNPROFOR supervision. Also, the imminent delivery of UNHCR/IRC fuel for the entire region would permit the removal of refuse, thereby addressing sanitation and sewage problems. Of course, all of this presupposed the requisite freedom of movement for UNPROFOR and UNHCR to administer the necessary humanitarian assistance. But Andreev's goodwill did not contribute to more cooperation from Prlic or from the interested parties on the terrain. On the contrary, not only was there no cooperation for the repair, but Prlic and his party continued complaining about UNPROFOR "unfairness." Slobodan Bozic, the head of the Croatian office for cooperation with UNPROFOR, requested the transportation of fifty members of the Croatian delegation (including officials and journalists) for the assembly planned in Sarajevo on Monday, 28 March, 1994. A detailed list of members of the delegation was pledged during the weekend, after the assembly of the Croatian parliament in Mostar would elect its delegates. This assembly was also to decide on the constitution of the federation between Muslims and Croats following the Washington Agreement. Bozic suggested departing from Split to Sarajevo on Monday 28 March at 9:00 hours and planned the return from Sarajevo to Split on the thirtieth, unless the developments in the assembly required a longer stay for the delegation. (For the continuation of the negotiations about Mostar, see the following chapter.)

United Nations CAO John Ryan attended a meeting with Pogarcic in Grude on 1 February 1994 with a view to assessing the HVO military strategy with regard to their current and future operations in BiH and to determine their position with regard to political negotiations and other matters. Pogarcic stated that the lack of progress in Geneva was very much due to the "hidden Muslim agenda," according to which the BiH Armija, having realized that taking territory from the Serbs was not a viable course of action, would only have the option for territorial expansion at the expense of the HVO. Their logical targets were in central Bosnia, and Pogarcic predicted a Muslim spring offensive from the Lasva Valley through Kresevo to the Neretva Valley, in order to provide a "living space" for displaced Muslims. In this event, the fate of two hundred thousand people was at risk, and the HVO stood to lose control of central BiH as a political entity. However, General Roso, who had successfully restructured and reorganized HVO forces and gained recent experience from the battlefield, indicated that his troops had become a much more effective and disciplined force. He added that the launching of such an offensive by BiH Armija would draw HVO openly into the conflict. Despite the agreement between Croatia and the union of the republics of Yugoslavia, he suggested that the Serbs and Muslims were natural allies, and he predicted the emergence of an alliance between them in time to achieve their common, long-term objectives—an exit to the Adriatic Sea. The current level of hostilities precluded meaningful negotiations for a peace settlement, and he stated that he had been informed by reliable sources that Safet Orucevic, Deputy Commander Fourth Corps BiH Armija, had received instructions from Sarajevo that peace negotiations at the local level should cease until further notice. President Boban's position was assessed as stable, and as usual, his absence from Geneva was explained as a concession made to appease Izetbegovic. Interestingly, an unsolicited opinion was offered regarding the attention which had recently focused on his association with war crimes, which he thought was not justified. His record on war crimes was stated to be considerably better than the record of many Muslim leaders.

## Chapter Three

## The UN Mission into the War

Since the onset of the process of disintegration of Yugoslavia, the European Union had established a Standing Conference on Former Yugoslavia, which was jointly headed from September 1991 by British Lord Peter Carrington and Portuguese Jorge Cutileiro. Then it was co-chaired in August 1992 by Cyrus Vance, the former US Secretary of State and then UN Special Envoy to Bosnia, and Lord David Owen, a former British Foreign Secretary, and then the appointed EU representative to the troubled Balkans. This American-British team was mandated to negotiate a peace plan for ending the war in Bosnia. Vance, an insightful lawyer and a graduate of the prestigious Yale law school, was a highly skilled negotiator. He had served the US administration in key agreements: SALT II with the Soviets, the Panama Canal Zone, the Camp David Accords between Israel and Egypt, and more. Owen accumulated his experience starting as the youngest British Foreign Minister, who worked out sensitive arrangements in Africa: Rhodesia, Namibia, the confrontation between Tanzania and Uganda and more.

On 2 January 1993, the Vance-Owen Peace Plan (VOPP) for the division of Bosnia-Herzegovina into ten provinces and the demilitarization of Sarajevo under UN control (see map below) was presented to the parties. Bosnian Croats accepted the project. Serbs and Muslims rejected it. Without delay, on 1 April 1993, Cyrus Vance announced his resignation as Special Envoy of the UN Secretary-General. He was replaced by the Norwegian Foreign Minister Thorvald Stoltenberg, and so the Europeans were left to their own game, obstructing each other's proposals, and on 18 June 1993, Lord David Owen declared that his plan was dead. According to America's last ambassador to Yugoslavia, Warren Zimmermann, the Bosnian government was ready to accept the VOPP, but unfortunately the Clinton administration deferred its support, thus perhaps missing a chance to get the plan launched. The VOPP was eventually agreed upon in Athens in May 1993, under intense pressure by all parties, including Bosnian-Serb leader Karadzic, but it was then rejected later by the Bosnian-Serb assembly meeting in Pale, after Karadzic insisted that the assembly had to ratify the agreement. It transpired at that stage that Karadzic had started developing an independent line of conduct vis-à-vis Belgrade and purposely misled all the involved parties by the inconsistent positions he took.

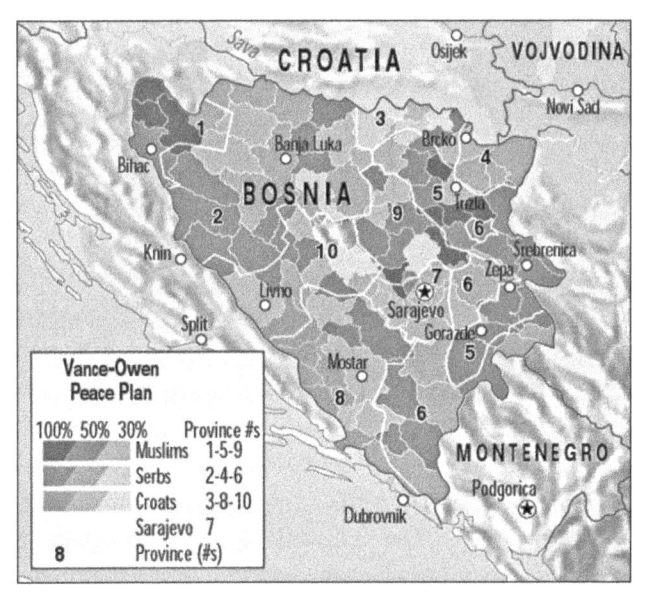

The Vance-Owen Peace Plan, January 1993, (Source: CIA) dividing Bosnia Herzegovina in ten ethnically distinct provinces. Obviously the decentralization of Powers weakened the central Government in Sarajevo and did not respond either to the aspirations of the Nationalists or to the Serbs concern for the protection of their populations. Consequently it was rejected by the main actors in the War and only accepted by the Croats, so all were happy to observe that at the end this option was eliminated.

In the history of this conflict, the United States also appeared to be adopting an ambiguous approach, i.e., encouraging an international collective action up to a certain level and then zigzagging and discontinuing their engagement the moment they were the most needed. In the case of the Vance-Owen démarche, which had been preceded by the 1992 Carrington-Cutileiro Agreement, it was signed on 18 March, 1993 by all three sides: Alija Izetbegovic for the Bosniaks, Radovan Karadzic for the Serbs, and Mate Boban for the Croats. Ten days later, on 28 March, Izetbegovic withdrew his signature and declared his opposition to any type of division of Bosnia. His declaration was made after his meeting the same day with then US Ambassador to Yugoslavia, Warren Zimmermann, in Sarajevo. For the first time, upon the signature of that international agreement, the Americans apparently agreed to a parallel and different "ball game" favoring the Muslims, before even giving a fair chance to "selling" the plan to the parties, in line with their costly and myopic vision of supporting "moderate Islam" along the continuum extending from the Balkans, via Turkey, to central Asia. Lord David Owen did not restrain his frustration and criticized openly the US administration for not giving a chance to the plan. The puzzling question remains: Did the United States indeed promise, in separate discussions, to support Bosnia as an independent state with territorial integrity as it was during the communist regime? The American diplomatic dealings in those days, and later, the conduct of the Clinton administration vis-à -vis the Peace Initiative in Mostar (see below), remain unclear. After Vance's withdrawal, Owen and Thorvald Stoltenberg brokered the EU Action Plan of December 1993. They both helped the Contact Group of the United States, the United Kingdom, France, Germany, and Russia, to present its alternative plan in the summer of 1994 (see map below), which partitioned Bosnia into three republics, leaving the capital in Sarajevo and its surroundings as a neutral zone on the Washington, DC model, which would serve the state institutions common to all three units.

The new plan proposed by the Contact Group on 5 July, 1994 allocated fifty-one percent of the territory to the Croats and Muslims combined and forty-nine percent to the Bosnian Serbs. President Milosevic of Serbia (still, formally, of Yugoslavia) accepted the plan. But the Bosnian Serbs refused, despite the directives they received from Belgrade. This precipitated the break between Belgrade and Pale/Banja Luka and resulted in an embargo on the latter. Milosevic faced a situation in which, as could be depicted in Hebrew, "the monster [Golem][53] turned on its creator." Since then, neither the UN nor Europe would succeed in progressing concretely, unless and until the Americans would come upfront and be seated at the focal power position on the diplomatic scene,

---

[53] *Golem* is one of the mythical "personalities" made out of clay and "life" instilled into him by the famous Rabbi Low in eighteenth century Prague, who walked through its streets. There are countless legends about Golem, mainly that it was made to protect Jews from the anti-Semitic eruptions against them through its extraordinary power. To be an even better protector his master could give him a special necklace. It was made out of deer skin and was decorated with mystic signs. With this ornament Golem became invisible. Because he was a hardworking chap, he also managed to help out in the rabbi's household and in the synagogue. Golem was huge, shapeless, and only vaguely reminiscent of any human being. Nevertheless, according to this legend, he was at first sight undistinguishable from an ordinary human being. The only thing he lacked was the ability to speak and he "lived" only with *a clay tablet* inserted into his mouth, which had to be taken out on Saturday because of the Jewish holy Sabbath. Ultimately, this being grew stronger and stronger. Instead of heroic and helpful deeds, Golem became increasingly uncontrollable and even destructive. One day people found him uprooting trees and destroying Rabbi Low's home when he was in the synagogue. The rabbi rushed to take out the tablet. This was the end of Golem-he was never revitalized. People believed that Rabbi Low hid him in the attic of his synagogue. The entrance into the area was forbidden for hundreds of years, and to make sure the ban was not broken, the stairs to the attic were removed. When the Old-New Synagogue was finally explored, no Golem was found, and the legend thus remains interwoven with mystery to the present day.

Raphael Israeli and Albert Benabou

The Union of Three Republics Plan, September 1993 (Source CIA) Serbian and Croatian nationalists considered this Plan literally as a three way partition, and their respective nationalist leaders, Radovan Karadzic and Mate Boban, felt confidently designated as the presidents of Herceg-Bosna and Republika Srpska. Similarly to the previous peace plans, Bosnia's Muslims were the most deprived and they rejected the fragment republic offered to them.

realizing first, in 1994, the Croatian-Bosnian Agreement in Washington, and in December 1995 the final Dayton Accord. In June 1994, after the NATO bombing of Pale and the kidnapping of "peace-keepers" by the Bosnian Serbs, the Security Council created the multinational Rapid Reaction Force (QRF) to support the emergency troops in place (UNPROFOR), because the pattern of kidnapping peace-keepers had grown profitable to the belligerents and attracted international attention. The Muslims in Mostar, who were under siege, felt abandoned and forgotten by the international community, and in August 1993, they took as hostages the full armored unit of the Spanish Battalion, including the Israeli

Civil Affair Coordinator, Albert Benabou, who had to face the starving crowd of the besieged city.

**The Settlement in Bosnia**

Towards the end of his mission in Bosnia, Benabou, in cooperation with the Armed Forces of the United Nations (Spanish and British Battalions), in consultation with and involvement of Croats, Bosnian Muslims, and UN officials, and accompanied by the international civilian agencies such as UNHCR, ICRC, and IRC, introduced a peace initiative on the local level, with European and American participation. This local peace initiative was worked out in Mostar with the support of Zagreb and Sarajevo and was accurately recorded and described by British Intelligence Officer Captain Peter Loghan, who served as Benabou's military attaché in the war zone. The framework and concept of those talks, which were all documented, served as the draft of final agreement between Croats and Muslims, reached in Washington in February/March 1994. In a meeting in Sarajevo, on 14 December 1993, Harris Silajdzic, the Bosnian Prime Minister, commented that "Benabou had observed fascist tendencies in Mostar[54]," probably meaning to accuse the Croats of those propensities, and added that "being an Israeli, Benabou had the courage to initiate a peace plan, while UN bureaucrats would usually avoid the challenge[55]." Impartial, Benabou replied that he had met such pernicious tendencies in both parts of the city of Mostar (Croatian and Muslim).

On 15 December, Silajdzic stated that "the United States was behaving like a young maiden and was revealing a great

---

[54] Source: Memo No 13—Mostar Interim Agreement—First meeting in Sarajevo with the Prime Minister of Bosnia & Herzegovina, 14 1245 December 93 (paragraph 19-20).
[55] ibid.

Raphael Israeli and Albert Benabou

Accompanied by Mostar Muslim War leadership, the UN Coordinator, Albert Benabou negotiating a peace initiative in a meeting with the Bosnian Prime Minister Harris Silajdzic; East Mostar War Chairman, Smail Klaric on the right side in front.

reluctance about being drawn into the problems of Bosnia-Herzegovina[56]." He felt that it would have been worthwhile for American Vice President Al Gore to concentrate on such efforts as part of his campaign for human rights. Indeed, in a conversation with Silajdzic, Gore had proffered the opinion that this "conflict was both immoral and treated in a cowardly fashion[57]." The Muslims believed that many of their friends in the State Department, in Congress, and in the Senate, would have been prepared to lobby in support for such negotiations in order to transfer the negotiations from the local level in Mostar to the national level of Bosnia-Herzegovina. Silajdzic expressed in the meeting with Benabou on 29 December his skepticism about the EU's participation in

---

[56] Source: Memo No 14—Mostar Interim Agreement—Second Meeting called by the Prime Minister of Bosnia & Herzegovina with delegates from Mostar, 15 0940 Dec 93 (paragraph 11).
[57] ibid.

the process and wished that Europe should stand back in that process, since it "had a tendency to legalize and accept the consequences of ethnic cleansing[58]." For that reason, Silajdzic wished to involve the United States instead in the resolution of the Bosnian conflict. He was eager to obtain the American leadership of that démarche and to ignore all the formulas worded by UN officials, such as Martti Ahtisaari, a former Finnish president, and Thorvald Stoltenberg, a former Norwegian foreign minister. He felt at one point that the United Nations was not standing behind the Mostar initiative, and that was for him a reason for the process to stop. In fact, based upon the approach and parameters of this initiative, Croats and Muslims would have realized their conjectural interest if they agreed, in disregard of their mutual contempt for each other, to form a Muslim-Croat Federation in Bosnia, while Serbs pursued ethnic cleansing in the north. The American diplomat Richard Holbrooke and the Swedish Prime Minister Carl Bildt would later rely on those terms in their negotiations for a truce and for finalizing a peace agreement between all factions in 1995.

In July 1994, a new Serbian offensive was launched against the "security zone" bordering on their held territory. Srebrenica fell to them on 11 July, and Zepa surrendered on 25 July. On 29 August 1994, after the bombing of the Sarajevo market by the Serbs and the carnage it caused, western artillery and aviation attacked Serbian positions. The next day, the Bosnian Serbs designated President Milosevic of Serbia to negotiate on their behalf. On 21 November 1994, the presidents of Serbia, Croatia, and Bosnia assembled for three weeks in the US Air Force base of Dayton, Ohio. They signed an agreement that kept Bosnia and Herzegovina within its internationally recognized borders and endorsed

---

[58] Source: Memo No 21 - Mostar Interim Arrangement Meeting with Mr. Harris Silajdzic in Sarajevo on 29 December 93 (paragraph 3).

the internal partition, which was originally proposed in VOPP with one difference, that the new entity would be composed of only two entities: the Republika Srpska (RS) and the Muslim-Croat Federation (instead of separate entities for the Croats and Muslims, respectively). The economic sanctions against Serbia were lifted in consequence. In December 1994, the Implementation Force (IFOR) took over from UNPROFOR. In February 1996, the Kosovo Liberation Army (KLA, UCK in Albanian acronym), another manifestation of the Muslim belligerency in the Balkans, which had not been taken into account during the peace negotiations, appeared on the scene for the first time, claiming responsibility for several attacks and a series of bombings, which triggered the resumption of the conflict that was thought by its instigators to have been laid to rest.

However, President Milosevic stood aside when in May 1994 the Croatian army occupied western Slavonia and in August 1995 the Krajina region. Nor did he get involved when this same army backed the Croatian-Muslim forces in their conquest of western Bosnia. These operations uprooted about three hundred thousand Serbs and threw them on the roads, completely emptying the regions where the Serbs had been settled for centuries, in other words effecting an ethnic cleansing against the Serbs. This attitude was considered by Serbs living outside the FRY as a real betrayal of the pledges done to them regarding their safety. Milosevic, who had previously benefited from the support of most Serbs, saw his popularity tumble in 1997. Challenged and beaten by the extreme right, which made a breakthrough in the presidential elections in Serbia in 1997, his election was invalidated, and finally it was Milan Milutinovic, a Milosevic faithful partisan, who became president of Serbia. In Montenegro, Milo Djukanovic, an advocate of liberalization and greater autonomy of his republic from Serbia and the federation, won a landslide victory against Momir Bulatovic, the Milosevic faithful follower. On 19 March 1996, Sarajevo was reunited, once again followed by an exodus of almost all of its Serbian inhabitants in a second wave of anti-Serbian ethnic cleansing. On 14 September 1996, the nationalist parties of all sides won the elections in Bosnia and Herzegovina. Muslim Alija Izetbegovic (SDA) was elected head of the presidency, with the Serb Momcilo Krajisnik (SDS) and Croatian Kresimir Zubak (HDZ) serving at his side in the Presidency Council, in accordance with the new accords.

On 3 October 1996, the presidents of Serbia and Bosnia signed, at the Élysée, an agreement that provided the establishment of diplomatic relations between the parties. Serbs recognized the territorial integrity of Slovenia and Croatia, officially abandoning their claims in Krajina and eastern Slavonia, thus handing the Muslim-Croatian alliance a decisive victory. In November-December 1996, the cancellation by the Serbian authorities of municipal elections won by the opposition in a dozen cities, including Belgrade, caused a powerful wave of popular protests and clashes with the forces of order. In December 1996, NATO sent a new force into Bosnia, the Stabilization Force (SFOR), this time with the participation of German troops. In September 1997, Albanian student demonstrations were repressed by the Serbian police in Kosovo. More clashes erupted in the region of Drenica in February-March 1998. Serbian police and the Yugoslavian (that is Serbian) army caused the destruction of many villages, killing nearly two thousand victims and triggering the escape of two hundred and fifty thousand refugees. Kosovo Albanians voted overwhelmingly on 22 March, 1998 to reelect their president, Ibrahim Rugova, and a parliament, in which the Democratic League of Kosovo (LDK) had a majority, but they were not recognized by Belgrade.

Despite various attempts to initiate negotiations and the threat of NATO air maneuvers, clashes continued in

April-August 1998 in Kosovo between Albanian separatists and Yugoslav troops. Following the meeting in May 1998 between the Yugoslavian president, Slobodan Milosevic, and the leader of Kosovo Albanians, Ibrahim Rugova, under the US mediator Richard Holbrooke, Milosevic announced that he was prepared in September to grant Kosovo a degree of autonomy. The international community became impatient, and on 23 September the Security Council called for a ceasefire in Kosovo, the withdrawal of Serbian forces, and the opening of direct negotiations. Agreement was reached in Belgrade on 13 October 1998 between Holbrooke and Milosevic on the withdrawal of Serbian forces, the ceasefire, and the deployment in Kosovo of two thousand "verifiers" from the unarmed OSCE (Organization for Security and Co-operation in Europe). But the fighting between the KLA and Serbian forces resumed. On 6 February 1999, the Contact Group brought together in Rambouillet near Paris representatives from the Belgrade authorities and the main Albanian formations in Kosovo, including those of the KLA. The Albanians were not satisfied by the proposed autonomy for the province, and the Serbs were opposed to the deployment of NATO troops there. After the failure of an ultimate attempt at negotiations between US envoy Richard Holbrooke and Slobodan Milosevic, Javier Solana, the Secretary General of NATO, announced on 23 March 1999 the launching of air operations over the Federal Republic of Yugoslavia.

Louise Arbour, prosecutor of the ICTY, made public on 27 May 1999 the indictment charging Milosevic and four other Yugoslav leaders of "crimes against humanity" and "violation of the laws and morals of war[59]," as if there were any "moral war" in existence in that war. Martti Ahtisaari

---

[59] The UN war crimes tribunal in The Hague (ICTY) formally charged former Yugoslav President Slobodan Milosevic with genocide in connection with the 1992-1995 Bosnian war (Source BBC).

and Viktor Chernomyrdin presented on 2 June 1999, to Milosevic, the requirements of the G8 to end the conflict in Kosovo. This plan included the main objectives of the West for the deployment of an international force, the withdrawal of Serbian forces, and the return of refugees. The plan was accepted by the Serbian parliament meeting in a special session. On 6 June 1999, the foreign ministers of the G8 countries formulated a text on "the effective deployment in Kosovo of international civil and security forces[60]" under the aegis of the UN. On 9 June, a military agreement was attained between NATO and the headquarters of the Yugoslav forces that allowed the Serbs eleven days to leave Kosovo. The next day NATO bombardment stopped, and on 12 June, KFOR, the Kosovo Force, mandated by the Security Council of the United Nations, entered Kosovo. By the end of the month, the Secretary General, Kofi Annan, appointed Bernard Kouchner, administrator for the civil peace in Kosovo.

By the end of the Milosevic decade, on 24 September 2000, his political balance sheet seemed catastrophic: wars, the crowding in Serbian territory of hundreds of thousands of Serbian refugees from Croatia and Bosnia-Herzegovina, the risk of independence of Kosovo and Montenegro, embargo, unemployment, chronic lack of capital, and more. The anti-western sentiment of the population, still traumatized by the air strikes of NATO, probably explains the presidential election victory of Vojislav Kostunica, leader of the Serbian Democratic Party, who opposed the policy of the head of the federation, but he was also a nationalist and hostile to the West. The Milosevic regime recognized the newly elected government on 5 October, 2000. A federal government was set up, headed by Zoran Zizic, a Montenegrin, in

---

[60] Source : NATO Role in Kosovo; Military Technical Agreement, between the International Security Force. ("KFOR") and the Governments of the Federal Republic of Yugoslavia and the Republic of Serbia (9 June 1999).

accordance with the constitution. A member of the Popular Socialist Party, he was seconded by a Deputy Prime Minister, Miroljub Labus, a member of the coalition with Vojislav Kostunica, who also came out winning in the parliamentary elections in Serbia that took place in December the same year. Bowing to international pressure, the new regime decided to imprison former President Slobodan Milosevic and deliver him to the International Criminal Tribunal in June 2001. However, in protest, Prime Minister Zoran Zizic resigned by the end of the month. The Montenegrin Dragisa Pesic, a member of the Socialist People's Party of Montenegro, a former ally of the ex-president, succeeded him as head of government.

In order to assure the cohesion of the federation and curb the separatist aspirations of Montenegro and Kosovo, whose separation from Serbia in the Yugoslav entity could further destabilize the Balkans, leaders from Serbia and Montenegro, in the presence of the representative of the European Union, Javier Solana, signed a tentative agreement (ratified by Parliament on 31 May, 2002) on the formation of a new federal state of Serbia and Montenegro. This new state, the successor to the Federal Republic of Yugoslavia (FRY), was scheduled for a period of at least three years, after which, "Member states shall be entitled to pursue procedures changing the institutional status of the state"[61], that is to say, withdrawing from the Union. It remained a unitary state, composed of two entities, governed by a united parliament, which elected the president, was controlled by a judiciary court, and possessed an army. Before long, however, both Montenegro and Kosovo declared their independence, and Serbia, the center and main engine of Yugoslavia for more

---

[61] Source: Constitution of the FRY - Federal Republic of Yugoslavia. In 2003, it was reconstituted as a state union officially known as the State Union of Serbia and Montenegro.

than eighty years, reverted to its shrunken ethnic perimeter, minus the territory of Kosovo, which had become a major building block in its identity since the Battle of Kosovo where it had been defeated by the Ottoman occupiers in the fifteenth century. Worse, due to the non-Serbian minorities that had been populating parts of Serbia (Muslims in the Sanjak and Hungarians in Voivodina), doubts were raised among many morally beaten and humiliated Serbs, whether the secession of Kosovo from their historical patrimony would also be the last.

## Introducing a Peace Initiative in Mostar

On 20 January 1994, one day after his session with both parties (Croats and Muslims of the Mostar area), Benabou dispatched a message to Alija Alikadic, the Muslim leader of besieged East Mostar, first congratulating him on the wedding of his son and then mentioning that he had paid a visit to the Croatian leadership in Grude, and confirmed that both parties would be sending him a letter of intentions concerning the future of Mostar, in approximately the same terms, endorsing the cessation of hostilities and a joint settlement in the divided city that would ensure the support of Zagreb and Sarajevo. On 4 February 1994, a meeting took place in East Mostar between Benabou and other UN representatives on the one hand, and Smajil Klaric, the chairman of the Muslim War Presidency of Mostar. The purpose of the meeting was to attempt to comprehend Klaric's views on the ongoing peace negotiations and to raise other relevant matters, such as human rights issues and humanitarian aid delivery. Klaric expressed his skepticism regarding the outcome of the forthcoming negotiations in Geneva, planned for 10 February, 1994. He claimed that any proposal for a peace agreement based on "rewarding the aggressor with territorial gains,[62]" would not be acceptable. This attitude was not surprising, since the Muslims were, all along, adamant on drawing the United States, where they had good contacts, to get involved in the conflict and to sponsor the negotiations. They felt that they could not rely on any arrangement produced by the European countries, which had been deeply engaged, up to their necks, in the framework of the UN forces. In fact, Muslims believed that the Europeans had already accepted the principle of territorial redistribution as part of the negotiated federation/confederation. From this point of view, Klaric claimed that the UN forces had failed to implement the various UN Security Council resolutions which had been adopted, and he lamented the fact that the resolution on the arms embargo on the BiH Army had been strictly implemented. He viewed the main stumbling blocks for progress in the peace process as emanating from:

> The Croatian insistence that Mostar should be the capital city of Herzeg-Bosnia, while seventy percent of the population of Mostar (namely the Muslims), would oppose such a proposal.
>
> The demand of the Croats that only the Muslim sector of the city should be placed under European Union administration.
>
> Adequate guarantees securing the rights of citizens in a post agreement phase ought to be put in place[63].

It was suggested to Klaric that such issues would be the substance of negotiations and should be fully provided for in a peace agreement. Klaric condemned what he termed "the lack of a clear-cut policy and resolve[64]" on the part of

---

[62] Source: Meeting in East Mostar held on 4 February 1994 with Smajil Klaric, president, war presidency The purpose of the meeting was to hear Klaric's views on the Geneva peace negotiations.
[63] ibid.
[64] ibid.

the European Union in its attempts to address the conflict in former Yugoslavia. He added that he sometimes wondered whether the European community had embarked on some kind of political adventure or social experiment in former Yugoslavia. The European representatives participating in the meeting attempted to assure Klaric that the European community was guided by the highest motives in its intervention in this crisis. Klaric welcomed the action taken by the UN Security Council on the alleged presence of HVO troops and materiel in central and southern Bosnia and Herzegovina and expressed his hope that the United Nations would continue to insist on their early withdrawal. Turning to human rights issues, he revealed that the expulsions from the Christian West to the Muslim East Mostar continued. A total of twenty persons, including six mental patients, were expelled in the month of January, though the delivery of humanitarian aid continued through the marked increase in the level of hostilities. He expressed satisfaction with the latter, but as usual he could not help repeating his justifiable mantra that "the volume of aid needed to be increased[65]."

When discussing the issue of POW exchange negotiations, it appeared that a stiff position had been adopted by the BiH Armija, due to its genuine conviction that the HVO was seriously maltreating the BiH Armija POWs, and that the seven hundred plus Muslim POWs, who had recently opted to travel to third countries, had not been given any reasonable option to do otherwise. However, Klaric stated that the BiH Armija would be prepared to resume the process if a foolproof agreement for an exchange of all POWs could emerge from the ongoing negotiations, which were due to resume at SPABAT HQ in Medjugorje on 8 February 1994. It was also revealed in those talks that no changes had taken

---

[65] ibid.

place to date in the structure and the new appointments of BiH Armija Sixth Corps. General Budakovic was still commander of the Fourth Corps, and it was now speculated that he might be replaced by Safet Orucevic, deputy commander of the Fourth Corps in the coming days. Though this meeting was conducted in a cordial and pleasant atmosphere, one could not but be impressed by the level of distrust which now existed between the parties, and the deep pessimism which was displayed by both sides in recent days.

At negotiations on the national level between the United Nations and the warring factions, the Bosnian Muslim side was usually represented by hardliner Vice President Ejup Ganic. His appointment, coupled with the traditional intransigence of most Muslim delegations, indicated that the Bosnian Muslim government was not willing to compromise. This attitude probably resulted from their self-delusion that NATO forces would come to their aid in a crisis situation. Unfortunately, the confusing rhetoric emanating from several Western capitals had only aggravated this miscalculation. The truth, as repeated in closed meetings at the UN headquarters, was that the West could simply not bear the military and economic burden of staying indefinitely in former Yugoslavia, and that failure to negotiate a political settlement in the very near future was likely to significantly diminish (if not end) the West's commitment. However, the breakthrough towards a political, negotiated solution to the conflict occurred in practice, only once the Muslims in Sarajevo and in Mostar realized that if they continued to focus on their ephemeral dreams of military victory through constant offensives, they would certainly be ultimately defeated. So, behind the "tranquilizing declarations" they continually emitted to the West, particularly by Prime Minister Silajdzic, the government in Sarajevo based its future strategy on its prospective Islamic allies. Funding was alleged to

*Savagery in the Heart of Europe*

be flowing from wealthy and radical Islamic countries, and foreign Muslims, trained as Mujahedin, were fighting on many instances alongside Bosnian Muslim units, spearheading their attacks, both physically and ideologically. In his numerous meetings with Benabou during the conflict, the President of Herzeg-Bosnia, Mate Boban, was constantly reiterating/threatening that the Muslims were relying for their future on those Muslim states and groups.

At the beginning of the conflict, the Muslims clearly considered the UN forces as playing a vital role in helping them buy time and maintain a low level of violence while they built an army and a state with Muslim aid. Along the same

Mate Boban explaining the Muslim's objective at the negotiating table: "a territorial continuity threatening Europe and the Western World" in his terms. From left to right: Jerry Hulme (UNHCR), Mate Granic (Croat Foreign Minister), Cedric Thornberry (UNPROFOR) , Albert Benabou (UNPROFOR, Leading the dialogue), Edward Joseph (UNPROFOR) Jude Rudman ( Croat Delegation) , Mate Boban ( President of Herzeg-Bosnia), Interpreters.

lines, in April 1994, the Muslims were convinced that the lifting of the arms embargo on Bosnia might actually be achieved. Prime Minister Haris Silajdzic visited Washington, DC to lobby senior congressional leaders to pass legislation unilaterally ending the American participation in the arms embargo. The Muslim decision to dispatch Silajdzic to that mission proved their acute awareness of American politics and policy. He was one of the more popular Muslim politicians among Croats and moderate Muslims, due to his centrist views and promises to work for a secular democracy. Accordingly, he was presented by public relations firms and the media in the United States as one of the personalities who could make the Bosnian Muslim-Croat Federation work. Nonetheless, in the view of some Croats and Muslims, he fell into disfavor when they judged him as compromising those principles after he remained in the more Islamic fundamentalist-dominated Izetbegovic government.

Since positive dynamics were thought to have been kicked off between Croats and Muslims, Benabou considered that it was the appropriate time for initiating confidence-building steps between the two parties. All along 1993, there were many attempts to install a UN Civil Affairs Office in West Mostar (the Croat part). For that whole year, the Spanish Battalion turned a blind eye on the Croatian position and obstructed the process. On the other hand, the Muslims offered a space for the presence of the Civil Affairs Office in the eastern part of the city and were eager to benefit from their positive attitude, at least in terms of public relations. Benabou delayed the establishment of his office in the eastern part of Mostar first in order to maintain an appropriate equilibrium in the UN operation vis-à -vis both sides. On 6 February 1994, he renewed a request to the Croatian authorities and obtained their agreement to search for an appropriate location in West Mostar. From the UN viewpoint, this move was recommended particularly due to:

> The necessity to strengthen the UNPROFOR presence in both sides of Mostar as expressed by all UN officials;
>
> The planned deployment of three SPABAT companies in West Mostar, in addition to their actual permanent presence in East Mostar;
>
> The establishment of the South West brigade of the Armija in Gornji Vakuf (and not in CAPLJINA as previously intended); and
>
> The change of leadership among the Croats who were transferring their political center of action from Grude to West Mostar[66].

An understanding was worked out between Benabou and Lt. Colonel Alaman, the acting SPABAT Commander, who agreed to assist in the transfer of the Civil Affairs Office, which stipulated that:

(a) The new offices in West and East Mostar would be adjacent to the SPABAT HQ on each side;
(b) SPABAT would cover the security of the office operation in the city;
(c) SPABAT's communications system would provide the required connections and extensions to the UNPROFOR; and
(d) The implementation of the project must be coordinated with the concerned parties.

On 10 December 1993, the Muslims issued an official letter addressed to Albert Benabou and signed by Cisic Rusmir, President of the Executive Committee of the Municipality of East Mostar. It stated:

---

[66] Source: Field Report sent by Albert Benabou on 6 February 1994 to UN Headquarters in Sarajevo, Zagreb and New York.

We accept your initiative for organizing the negotiations, which should solve some of the problems in Mostar. Your proposition to work with the three-member commissions, where one member should be military and the other two civilian representatives, is acceptable to us. We consider that HVO should work more intensively regarding the commission for the POW exchange; that they should stop shelling civilian targets; open the corridors for the passage of all humanitarian organizations, whether they are governmental or otherwise; and assure undisturbed medical evacuation of the sick and the wounded, if they are really interested in those negotiations.

We admit the Croatian right to their own political determination in Mostar, as well as we admit that right to the other communities of Serbs, Croats, and Muslims; we also recognize the right of all to live together in Mostar as a multicultural and multinational community. It is completely understandable that for the realization of the stated goals, a political dynamic would be necessary, which should pave the way to the immediate stopping of killing and massacre of the innocent civilians in Mostar.

We will ask for complete discretion regarding further contacts and negotiations. We ask you to transmit this message to Mr. Prlic (Croat) on behalf of the decision-makers in Mostar (Muslim East). We hope that soon you will coordinate the place and the time of the meeting. In this process we would like to avoid, at this stage, the involvement of the Mostar populace. It is obvious that upon the completion of the negotiations, the end results of our work will be ratified by Mr. Silajdzic and Mr. Prlic.[67]

---

[67] Source: Confidential Memo No 6 - Mostar Interim Agreement, Meeting in east Mostar with BiH Armija leadership 10 0935 Dec 93. The Muslim leadership of East Mostar, was clarifying to Albert Benabou, that they did not want Boban as a partner for the interim agreement.

The Muslims in East Mostar offered, in effect, an opportunity to the Croats to obtain the recognition of their political status and rights in Mostar. Moreover, in the minutes of the recorded meeting, the Muslims clearly announced that they would accept the fact that the Croats wanted to consider Mostar as their capital city. The Croats had constantly declared that this was their purpose for the city, but their leaders in Grude did not grasp the enormous dimension of the transmitted Muslim message. The Croats did not explicitly reject the Mostar proposal, for they were divided in their internal approach. Surprisingly, Boban supported the process precisely when Stojic and Prlic were convinced that they could achieve a military breakthrough. Prlic then became the leading voice since Boban was pushed aside at the request of Zagreb (Tudjman, his faithful friend!) and Sarajevo (Izetbegovic). The end result was that the Croats (Stojic & Prlic) paralyzed the process behind their public declaration that they accepted. We have then to assume that Boban adopted his positive approach towards the process in order to gain some political benefit, but it was too late to reverse the negative, practical Croatian attitude to it. Thus, they in fact rejected the deal, which was the best proposal that the Croats would ever receive, for an interim arrangement in Mostar, even compared with the results of the negotiations in Washington and then in Dayton. Apparently, the hidden agenda of Boban was the eviction of the Muslims from the city at any cost. He had indeed repeated frequently that, politically from his point of view, the presence of a Muslim population in Mostar was the most problematic and dangerous obstacle to any settlement. On the same day, 10 December, 1993, the Croatian Defense Council of the municipality of Mostar (West) sent to Benabou a message regarding his proposal to intensify political negotiations in order to achieve a peaceful solution for the conflict in Mostar. They presented their key political guidelines, reflecting the position of the Croatian Democratic Union (HDZ) leadership in the municipality of Mostar:

1. In all preceding peace initiatives, signed and unsigned agreements, under the auspices of the United Nations and the European community, the town of Mostar was considered, beyond any dispute, to be the political, administrative, and territorial center of the Croatian people in Bosnia-Herzegovina, i.e. center of the (self-declared) Croatian Republic of Herzeg-Bosnia, as a component of the Union of the Republics of Bosnia and Herzegovina . . . As you are probably aware, no Muslim delegation, even with Izetbegovic at his head, had any objections concerning this approach, especially since the Muslims have already designated Sarajevo, Zenica, Tuzla, Doboj, and Bihac as their administrative, cultural, and territorial centers.
2. Before and during the war, the Croatian party considered the cessation of hostilities as its primary interest. In that spirit, it always accepted all the initiatives to attain that primary goal. Therefore, we re-affirm our support to your initiative for the town of Mostar.
3. Based upon the previous signed agreements, the Croats view this initiative as useful for the sake of establishing and building up confidence between the Croatian and Muslim people in Mostar. We remind you that our representatives at the peace negotiations constantly honored the rights of all nations and people of Mostar in accordance with the civilized standards guaranteeing all human rights[68].

---

[68] Source: Official Letter sent to Albert Benabou on 10 December 1993 by Cisic Rusmir on behalf of the Croatian Defence Council of the Municipality of West Mostar (Croatian Republic of Herzeg Bosnia (paragraph 3).

In the meantime the Geneva Conference, which was the permanent forum dealing with the dismantlement of former Yugoslavia, kept rolling, at the instigation of the European Community, which undertook to search for a negotiated end to Yugoslavia's dissolution wars in 1991 and set up that Peace Conference for former Yugoslavia. The Carrington-Cutileiro peace plan, named for its authors Lord Carrington and Portuguese ambassador Jorge Cutileiro, resulted from that EC Peace Conference held in February 1992 in an attempt to prevent Bosnia-Herzegovina from sliding into war. After them, the UN Special Envoy Cyrus Vance and EC Representative Lord Owen took up the leadership of the conference, and in early January 1993, began negotiating a peace proposal with the leaders of Bosnia's warring factions, as explained above. The proposal, which became known as the "Vance-Owen Peace Plan," involved the division of Bosnia into ten semi-autonomous regions and received the backing of the United Nations. On 5 May, however, the Bosnian-Serb assembly rejected the Vance-Owen plan, whereupon Vance was out of the game, and the new team, Owen-Stoltenberg, took over. In late July, representatives of Bosnia-Herzegovina's three warring factions entered into a new round of negotiations. On 20 August, the UN mediators, Thorvald Stoltenberg and David Owen, unveiled a map that would partition Bosnia into three ethnic mini-states. Once the proposal for Mostar seemed to acquire a positive turn, and Washington started to pressure the Croats to come to a deal with the Muslims, the Geneva Conference conveners decided to interfere, and they dispatched General Pellnas to take over the Mostar process. But that was too late, too, since Washington had decided to delve into the matter and take the lead.

Following the Geneva Conference, Albert Benabou called for confidential meetings on Wednesday, 19 January, 1994 in East Mostar with Alija Alikadic, and in Grude with Vladislav Pogarcic. His remarks were summed up in his report:

In the aftermath of the Geneva Conference, both parties, Muslims and Croats, in Mostar, were invited to formulate their projections and intentions. This process was initiated in two separate sessions and locations.

Alikadic clarified that the Muslim community in Mostar was represented by Safet Orucevic, who attended the Geneva Conference with BiH delegation headed by Izetbegovic. According to Orucevic, no decisions were adopted concerning Mostar.

Pogarcic confirmed from his sources, that no decisions were taken concerning Mostar. Moreover, the Muslim delegation had requested a stronger interference of the United Nations and a reduced European involvement in the BiH affairs.

Both parties announced that by Saturday, 22 January, they would complete the composition of a letter defining their positions for the future of the city. Alikadic emphasized that their document would be prepared under the guidelines of Sarajevo. Pogarcic notified that the same procedure would be followed by Zagreb[69].

The Croatian lawyer, Ivan Tomic, a fervent nationalist Catholic, dispatched to Benabou on 17 January, 1994 a letter recollecting the highlights of the joint discussions held on 16 January in Medjugorje (the HQ of SPABAT and of the Civilian Affairs Office) between the Croatian and Muslim delegations and the representative of the United Nations in the Geneva conference, General Bo Pellnas. On 19 January 1994, a personal meeting between Tomic and Benabou took place in the former's office in Citluk. Ivan Tomic was a last minute nomination by the Croats, when the representatives from the Geneva Conference started to initiate meetings on a

---

[69] Source: Confidential Memo No 33—Mostar Interim Arrangement, Meetings on Wednesday 19 January 1994 in East Mostar & in Grude, the purpose being evaluation in the aftermath of the Geneva Conference.

solution for Mostar. He was an unknown lawyer from Citluk and did not belong to the milieu which led the war against the Muslims in East Mostar. So, while the Croats replaced the members of their team, probably due to their internal rifts, the Muslims maintained the same group of negotiators. After the talks on 16 January, Tomic had agreed with Benabou that immediately after the meeting with Bo Pellnas he would stay over at the UN base in Medjugorje and discuss with him the prospects of the negotiations. Since Pellnas insisted on dealing with him on maps and frontiers for the new arrangement in Mostar, Tomic left immediately for the base, because he had no mandate to negotiate on maps. His mandate was limited to delivering a statement and leaving. But Pellnas had also not been authorized to discuss matters of maps, for he had been only charged with the mission of hearing statements and reporting them to his superiors, who made the decisions. The situation became awkward due to the overzealousness of Pellnas to roll the ball faster than his authority allowed.

Tomic emphasized that the Croatian delegation must respect the directives of the higher levels (in Zagreb), and at the same time he wanted to represent the position relevant to Mostar as the capital of Croatian Herzeg-Bosnia. If that position were respected, he reflected, it would considerably speed up the solution of any other questions concerning Mostar. But it was too late to bring up this matter, for the momentum was lost when the interim negotiations for Mostar at the local level stopped, and the issue was brought up to the national level where other interests were at stake between Croatia (Zagreb) and Bosnia (Sarajevo). Zagreb did not want to create any friction with the US broker who adopted the Muslim position, according to which Bosnia-Herzegovina was a political entity victim to Serbian and Croatian aggression. At that point, there was no confidence left in the relations between the two communities in Mostar, which had been seriously damaged and were falling in ruins. The Croatian party stated that it was willing to undertake additional measures to rebuild this confidence, and they expected that the European Union administration of Mostar, imposed on them by the international community, would, at least, contribute to that effort. The Croats then named their mission to represent them in the Union of Republics of BiH, whose responsibility would be to protect the overall interests and rights of the Croatian people in the Union of Republics of Bosnia and Herzegovina and to strengthen the relationships between the Croats in the Republic and other parts of the Union. Thus, on 10 November 1993, in accordance with Article Seven of the founding decision on the establishment and declaration of the Croatian Republic of Herzeg-Bosnia, Mate Boban, President of the Croatian Republic of Herzeg-Bosnia, appointed Dr. Jadranko Prlic to the post of Premier as well as the other members of his government. The House of Representatives of the Croatian Republic of Herzeg-Bosnia confirmed these nominations in accordance with the law.

Already on 10 November 1993, a meeting had taken place in Benabou's office in Medjugorje with the participation of Kresimir Zubak (Vice Premier of Herzeg-Bosnia) and Jerry Hulme (HOO of UNHCR Medjugorje). Kresimir Zubak presented an appeal, on behalf of the Croatian authorities, to release urgently the five-hundred-ton food convoy, blocked in Prozor and en route for the area of Vitez-Busovaca. Both UN representatives replied that the solicitation would be forwarded to the attention of the Civil Affairs officers, Thornberry and Morris, in the UN HQ in Zagreb. Also, the question came up of installing UNPROFOR offices in the city of West Mostar, in close proximity to the official Croatian government facilities. Zubak affirmed that he understood the necessity of this presence and that he would transfer his opinion to Prlic. Following Benabou's suggestions, the Croats submitted their request in a written form with additional short explanations. They noted that approximately sixty thousand people were living in the area of Vitez-Busovaca, fifteen thousand of them being children and thirty-nine thousand refugees. Almost all of them survived this far only thanks to the humanitarian relief supplies. The tragic death of the Danish UNHCR employees, while performing their humanitarian assignment of relief supply, had caused the UN decision to suspend humanitarian assistance distribution to central Bosnia, but the Croats emphasized that although these tragic deaths were not caused by the Croatian military units, it was Croatian innocent civilians who were suffering the consequences of such a decision. They warned that the situation regarding humanitarian assistance supply to the population was deteriorating and could result in new tragedies: starvation and deaths, primarily of those who could not stand such duress for a long time, i.e. children, the elderly, the sick, and wounded.

Being sensitive to the plight of civilians, the UN civilian authorities in the area made all the efforts to ensure the supplies for the population as UNPROFOR's assistance was required. Thus local authorities addressed Benabou with a request to ensure the delivery of five hundred tons of food, with the help of humanitarian organizations. The United Nations had transported all the stocks to Prozor and stored them in warehouses, since their delivery to the needy had become impossible in view that the previously given assurances of collaboration to facilitate the transport proved to be nothing more than a vain promise. Accordingly, Benabou once again approached the local authorities and pleaded with them to do their best to provide the transport of the food to Vitez. The United Nations assured that the delivery would be counted as an exception and would not disturb the decision made by the local authorities to suspend the food convoys through central Bosnia. Nevertheless, on 9 November, 1993, the Croatian-Bosnian parliament, which started to call its members to convene in Mostar, resorted to UN logistics to transport them from all parts of western and central Bosnia. The regular session of parliament was scheduled for 20 November, 1993, as the Croats were starting to enlist the political support for a settlement with the Muslims. It now became a complicated process, since they missed the opportunities to reach midterm agreements, which could have ensured some achievements in the city of Mostar. At this point they were pushed, particularly by Washington, to reach a peace agreement with the Muslims, at a time when they could not show any gains to their constituency.

On the same date of 9 November, 1993, as they were striving to assemble their delegates in Mostar for the parliamentary session, where the peace process with the Muslims was on the agenda, the Croats deliberately destroyed the old bridge which symbolized the meeting point and congregation of the city of Mostar. This old bridge, Stari Most, whose construction had started under Suleiman the Magnificent in 1557, crossed the Neretva River and connected the two rival parts of the city of Mostar. The city was named after this bridge, which ranked among the greatest historical monuments in the Balkans. This act of vandalism meant in fact the obliteration of a memory, of a shared cultural heritage and of coexistence, which was thought to be characteristic of Mostar before the war. Once again, what appears on the surface is not necessarily what is under the surface. When the Turks had built the bridge, it was to facilitate their Muslim domination over the dhimmis Croats, something that the latter did not necessarily conserve positive memories of, while for the Muslims, who were left as a minority after the departure of their Ottoman coreligionists, it was convenient to yearn for the old days of their dominion and to talk of a "shared heritage." Alija Alikadic, member of the Muslim war presidency in East Mostar, wrote an official letter, complaining against the Croats and recalling Benabou's warning that the rant and rave violence in the confrontations will end up targeting the old bridge. Clouded minds had succeeded in committing a crime which did not only annihilate the ancient historical structure, but also perpetrated it against all nations of the world. This gesture showed that they (the Croats) did not recognize any multicultural community and what were, in fact, the basic signs of fascism. It was a clear signal from the Croats that they did not intend to accept the hegemony of the Muslims over the city and refused to consider sharing a mode of multicultural administration.

On the days before, 7 and 8 November 1993, the Muslims had launched a massive offensive in central Bosnia, particularly in the area of Vitez generating a large flow of Croatian refugees in critical need of humanitarian aid. Moreover, the Croats were now threatening to blow up the factory of explosives in Vitez, liable to cause an ecological catastrophe in the entire country. Since the Spanish headquarters in Medjugorje were not cooperative that morning, Albert Benabou, assisted by the British Units, had to make his own way through the battle zone in order to reach Mostar West. He noted in his diary that he proceeded *contre vents et marées* (against all odds) and held a meeting on that day in West Mostar with Kresimir Zubak, the deputy prime-minister of the Croatian Republic of Herzeg-Bosnia. Zubak, alarmed and worried, stated without formalities that, in the aftermath of their success in Vares, the BiH Armija launched on 7 November a massive attack south of Vitez with the main objective of taking control of the explosives factory located in Vitez. Zubak warned that HVO troops would not yield possession of the factory to BiH and if necessary "would not withdraw before destroying it first[70]." The Croats also requested that the Muslims be dissuaded, at the highest level in Sarajevo, from pursuing their offensive. Zubak also stated that approximately ten thousand Croatian refugees had fled from Vares to Kiseljak and were accommodated in school buildings, which were inadequate to their needs. He required urgent assistance for them such as food and clothing and intimated that relief convoys were being organized for their evacuation, and he expected UNPROFOR's support and escort in order to protect and enable these convoys to set out.

He reiterated that HVO had already organized and dispatched a convoy containing five hundred tons of humanitarian aid to Vitez and Busovaca, where up to fifty thousand people were expecting those supplies, but the convoy was still blocked in Prozor, and DUTCHBAT had been requested by the Mayor of Vitez, Stipo Valenta, to facilitate access to it. Since no response had been received from DUTCHBAT, he now demanded that UNPROFOR take the necessary measures, as a matter of urgency, to permit the convoy to advance immediately to Vitez and Busovaca. Benabou was not sure that all these logistics were designed only to help the civilians, and he questioned whether there was not a hidden attempt to move supplies and support to the Croatian Units blockaded in central Bosnia. On Sunday, 31 November 1993, in Grude, Albert Benabou held a meeting with Mate Boban, whose comments and proposals were forwarded to the SRGS (Special Representative of the Secretary General) Thorvald Stoltenberg and the headquarters in Zagreb and Kiseljak. Boban lamented the misreading and

---

[70] Source: on the flash report dealing with BiH offensive in Vitez (see paragraph 3) sent by Albert Benabou on the 8th of November at 19h45 to the Civil Affairs Coordinator in Bosnia, Victor Andreev, Brigadier John Reith, Commander of the British Forces, and to Brigadier Ramsey, his Chief of Staff in Central & Southern Bosnia-Herzegovina. The Commander of the Spanish Battalion, Colonel Carvajal, the UN Headquarters in Sarajevo and Kiseljak were also informed.

even the ignoring of the political reality in former Yugoslavia, particularly in Bosnia-Herzegovina, by previous mediators; in his opinion, this was the main cause for not achieving a peace settlement. He recalled that the animosities and the dissension among the people were complex and deeply rooted in history. The only feasible solution, to his mind, was the separation of the three ethnic groups into three political entities (republics) related in a loose union and more specifically:

> In the first stage, the ethnic groups currently living in the other republics should enjoy autonomy within the boundaries of the predominant ruling ethnicity; and
>
> In the second stage, those autonomous communities will have the right, based on free will and agreement, to relocate in the territory of their mother ethnic republic[71].

He clarified that the mediators had not fully grasped the economic and strategic significance of the Neretva Valley, which forms a natural corridor from the Adriatic Sea to central Bosnia, passing by Mostar and Jablanica. He claimed that Muslims and Serbs in this region had a common interest against the Croats and reiterated that both of those parties were making an effort to establish a military alliance in order to wrest control from the HVO. Therefore, the HVO might be compelled to act in self-defense against the BiH Armija and even the BSA (Bosnian Serbian Army). He condemned what he termed as the "uninvited interference of governments participating in UN peace keeping forces[72]" (such as France and Great Britain) and other western states (such as Germany and the United States) in the affairs of the parties in conflict. The mandate of UNPROFOR was outdated to his mind and must be amended, taking into

---

[71] Source: Report on the meeting with Mate Boban requiring the appointment of an expert commission, sent by Albert Benabou on the 2nd of November 1993 to Thorwald Stoltenberg, Special Representative of the Secretary General, with copy to Cedric Thornberry, Head of Civil Affairs and Victor Andreev, the Coordinator.
[72] ibid.

account the political and military situation in the terrain. He stated that the policy of the international community which supported Muslim demands was in fact:

(a) Encouraging them to persevere in the armed conflict;
(b) Nourishing their territorial ambitions;
(c) Strengthening their determination to gain access to the Adriatic Sea;
(d) Perpetuating their belligerence in Mostar and the Neretva Valley; and
(e) Prolonging the war among the three parties[73].

He claimed that this western stance was eroding the foundations for peace and the core of a negotiated arrangement on a territorial basis. In order to inject confidence and life into the peace process, Boban suggested the appointment of a commission of international experts under the United Nations' aegis, to conduct a study on the issues of demography, boundaries, law and order, economics, transport, communications, elections, and religion. He thought that in order to determine the different positions, this commission should enjoy freedom of access and meet with the representatives of the three peoples. This modus operandi and examination of topics would be the most appropriate for the creation of a consensus on the contentious matters. Boban stated that he would welcome a ceasefire and a freeze on troop movement during the working of the commission, whose report would be presented to the representatives of the parties for their remarks and observations prior to ratification. To press in that direction, Vladislav Pogarcic, head of the department for human rights and humanitarian affairs in the Croatian Republic of Herzeg-Bosnia, addressed a letter on 7 November 1993 to General Francis Briquemont, the Commander of

---

[73] ibid.

*Savagery in the Heart of Europe*

UN Forces, where he brought up the concern of the Croatian leadership, which was facing the demands of the Muslim army in Bosnia to integrate all the Croatian military units in Sarajevo and the region into its own structures. He wrote:

> We are deeply disturbed by the recent demands made by the Muslim army, that the HVO brigade (Kralj Tvrtko) of Sarajevo should be placed under their control. As was the case with previous Muslim demands, I urgently request UNPROFOR to immediately deploy its forces in Sarajevo to protect the Croatian people and act as a buffer between the HVO and Muslim forces. Furthermore UNPROFOR forces should be used to protect the HVO Command Center and the commander of the brigade, Slavko Zelic, as his life has been threatened by the Muslim authorities. As we have momentarily lost contact with our brigade in Sarajevo, I kindly request that UNPROFOR provide our office with information of events as they unfold[74].

The second extraordinary session of the Croatian House of Representatives was held on 17 February, 1994, in Mostar, with forty elected representatives of the assembly of BiH, members of the government, representatives of the presidency and other invitees, like ECMM representative and Benabou. The topics brought up in that session were:

Changes and additions to the composition of the House of Representatives of Croatian Herzeg-Bosnia;
The election of the president of the House and his deputy;
The nomination of the members of the presidential council of Croatian Herzeg-Bosnia;
The proposal of a law for the establishment of a Croatian radio and television Herzeg-Bosnia; and

---
[74] ibid.

Presentation of documents from a meeting of the Croats in Sarajevo held on 6 February 1994[75].

Mate Boban had been reconfirmed as the president of the Croatian Republic of Herzeg-Bosnia at the extraordinary session of the House of Representatives held on 8 February 1994, in Livno, and he had transferred his powers to the presidential council. The representatives ratified these appointments by vote. Kresimir Zubak (from Doboj), minister of the administration of justice, was elected president of the presidential council of Croatian Herzeg-Bosnia. Ivan Bender, Pero Markovic, Ivo Zivkovic, Branimir Huterer, Jadranko Prlic, Jozo Martinovic, Valentin Coric, Mile Akmadzic, Ante Roso, and Ivo Lozancic were appointed as members of the presidency council. Vladislav Pogarcic, the faithful companion of Boban, was named secretary of the council. The presidency council carried the responsibility on strategic, political, and defense issues and coordinated the activity of the executive bodies of the Croatian Republic of Herzeg-Bosnia. The representatives ratified also the nomination of Ivan Bender (Neum) as the president of the House of Representatives of Croatian Herzeg-Bosnia, and Dario Kordic (Busovaca), Vlado Santic (Bihac), and Mato Madjarevic (Posavina) as vice presidents. Furthermore, a unilateral ceasefire in the Mostar battlefield was declared by the Croats for the next fifteen days except if they needed to break it in self-defense. The presidential council was put in charge of the implementation of this ceasefire, and the government of Herzeg-Bosnia was called upon to make all efforts to open

---

[75] Source: Report sent by Albert Benabou on 18 February 1994 concerning the second extraordinary session of the Croat House of Representatives which was held on 17 February 1994 in Mostar. At this session were present 40 elected representatives of the assembly of BiH, members of the government, representatives of the presidency and others invitees including. The agenda and decision were transmitted in that report.

offices of Croatian Herzeg-Bosnia in the main cities of Bosnia in Pale, Tuzla, Banja Luka, and Sarajevo.

The intensive negotiations for an interim and separate peace arrangement for the city of Mostar, conducted by Albert Benabou between the Croats and the Muslims, was summed up in a series of confidential memos and correspondence between Croats and Muslims, disclosed here for the first time, which were exchanged in concert with the authorities of Zagreb and Sarajevo and with the participation of international and UN political and military authorities. The process was of significance since it served as a stepping stone, gradually bridging those two fierce enemies, on the way to the agreement achieved under the US umbrella in Washington in March 1994. The negotiations between the parties in East and West Mostar, Grude, Zagreb, Sarajevo, and Geneva lasted for more than three months (November 1993 to January 1994). As we will learn, they was interrupted by the unproductive encounters in Medjugorje in the framework of the Geneva Conference for former Yugoslavia. The conference officers took up the leadership of the initiative, which ended without any concrete results. The issue of Mostar would be treated again only in mid-January 1994, after Alija Izetbegovic and Franjo Tudjman met in Bonn and agreed to resolve the issue.

The war between Croats and Muslims ended officially on 23 February 1994, when the commander of HVO, General Ante Roso, and the commander of the Bosnian Army, General Rasim Delic, signed a ceasefire agreement in Zagreb. The United States convinced the parties to identify and recognize their joint interests in the resolution of the conflict. The wording of the Croatian-Muslim agreement in Washington was signed on 18 March 1994, based on the components and the rapprochement created between the parties in the Mostar Initiative. This was the first concrete move towards the Dayton Agreement, bringing an end to the war in Bosnia-Herzegovina. At the time, when this interim arrangement started, each one of the warring parties had manifested high interest and support for responding positively to the pleas of the inhabitants of both parts of the city, who were utterly exhausted by the bloodshed, siege, deprivation, threats, starvation, and abnormal life. Moreover, as recorded in the first memos of the negotiations, the national leaders, Croats in Zagreb, as well as Muslims in Sarajevo, agreed to prevent any outside interference, thus maintaining distance and respecting the will of the people at its source. They actually encouraged the local leaders, Muslims and Croats, to pursue the negotiations in order to reach an agreement at the local level of the city of Mostar. Nonetheless, as the course of the dialogue developed and progressed, exterior short-term interests blocked the initiative, and the end result was that the agreed benefits were sacrificed and erased and never obtained thereafter, either at the local level or at the national level, not even in the final agreement between Croats and Muslims in Washington.

From the viewpoint of the United Nations in Bosnia, all through the war in Bosnia and Herzegovina a constant movement of population was witnessed, from the rural to the urban agglomerations, as well as an exodus from the cities out of the country. The main regions affected by large influxes of refugees were Sarajevo and Mostar. The rural populations, who had a barely rudimentary education, were easily manipulated and recruited to fundamentalist or extremist ideologies. Benabou lamented in all his reports on his encounters with the various leaders, the flight of the intelligentsia from BiH. He commented that while the presence of this group in any society lends to it the backbone and vitality needed for equilibrium in the urban areas, their replacing groups, flocking from the countryside, tended to be easily persuaded by the present leaders to toe their ideology. This had resulted in mass military conscription to any active faction or to any action required by the leadership. The inbound refugees to the cities were offered access to the abandoned homes, which were mostly furnished, sometimes to high standards. Those rural populations were effectively forced into a sweeping emotional and environmental change, making them dependent on their leaders for almost everything, without the leaders being required to give anything in return. Moreover, aid was delivered from humanitarian relief agencies, via the local leaders, to the population of cities, including the newcomers in its midst. The international community, which was involved in the conflict, particularly Europe, had a merely superficial appreciation of the socio-economic situation of the Balkans, geared to answer immediate and urgent needs, while any attempt of long-term political initiative that was suggested or devised by any outside party, like the United Nations or individuals who served it, encountered disregard and rejection.

The initiative of the UN Civil Affairs Office, in this regard, was built on the assumption that undertaking a micro political process on the local level would induce the parties in conflict to produce ideas and solutions of their own. Obviously, they could be positively encouraged by creative thinking from external actors, but they themselves must be left with bearing the responsibility for the outcome of their implemented policy and with imposing the ultimate overall accountability onto the local leadership, contrary to the more socialist modus operandi, which was more familiar in this region and put the burden of responsibility on the state apparatus while freeing the individuals from any accountability. Two historical examples can be cited to illustrate cases where wars were prolonged due to misguided and misconstrued external interference: one was Vietnam, where the US government did not grasp the complex motivation of the warring rivals (south vs. north). The other was the involvement of the Israelis in the internal conflict in Lebanon in 1982, and both ended up disastrously for the external powers. Throughout the Bosnian conflict, the three warring factions unwittingly contributed to creating and reinforcing their rivals' ethnic identities, ending up in an imposed separation via a cultivated process of martyrdom, which magnified the ethnic gap between those southern Slavic ethnoreligious groups turned enemies. To that, we have to add the characteristics of the mountainous terrain in the arena of the Balkans, which prescribed a military conduct that was inspired more by guerilla and terrorist tactics than by open-field conventional operations and confrontations with the perceived enemies. All parties of that conflict understood that the occupation of a mountain that was viewed as a key terrain or as a dominating feature in its environment, or even of a whole city, could not be defined as a crucial military achievement, unless the undesired ethnic group had been dislodged and expelled from there. Only then was victory considered worth its name.

The war also revealed that new forms of fascism and totalitarianism were in the making; the Muslims were afflicted by Islamic radicalism, whilst the Croats were subject to the intrusion of authoritarianism, both as widely accepted factional ideologies. The Serbs, on their part, were at that point only exposed to extremist politicians, who lent their personal and temperamental twist to the politics of Serbian nationalism that they professed. In West Mostar, General Ante Roso confronted the delicate task of restructuring a fighting Croatian military force from a militia organization. Time did not seem to act in his favor, as a permanent threat loomed in central Bosnia, which if materialized could squeeze the Croats around any negotiating table and curtail their bargaining power. Hence the tough and uncompromising positions they had to adopt, and their perennial attempts to gain time pending the recruiting and training of their new army. They estimated that if a military stalemate were achieved, they would be able to endure a long war of attrition while they were inflicting heavy and untenable losses upon their enemies.

An interesting development unfolded when Boban and Prlic established a new government in Herzeg-Bosnia, as both parties in Mostar perceived a change in the political atmosphere, which might be conducive to a political deal in Mostar. The BiH had recently been enjoying a string of military successes in the arena, after it replicated the experience on the Croatian front with smaller and better trained units that it had learned from its confrontation with the Serbs in other fronts. In Mostar, the major problem for the local leadership was to arrest the flight of the stronger and more influential elements from the city, with a view of reinforcing the capacity of their community to withstand the siege and encourage the weaker elements to sustain the pressures and the losses without yielding or surrendering. We must keep in mind that both the Muslims and the Croats tended to man their troops with soldiers recruited among the newcomers who were alien to their zone of operation. They thought that the European community should encourage the establishment of permanent and responsible local leaderships, which gained legitimacy through a process of local elections, as soon as possible, and was endorsed by a healthy and productive economy as a prerequisite to stabilization. The prevailing mood was that the achievement of an economically stable and credible society would promote the return of the intelligentsia and the other elements who ran away and breathe vitality back into the community. Since the fleeting idea of multiethnic society in Bosnia-Herzegovina had actually expired, the new ambition strove towards the creation of a sensible balance between the various ethnic groups, which would pursue each its own separated, social, and cultural system within the political framework of one state. The interim agreements, such as the one in Mostar, were all geared in that direction.

In the second week of November 1993, Benabou convened in Medjugorje the parties from East and West Mostar, in order to renew the negotiations for the release of detainees and prisoners of war, as a confidence-building measure towards attaining an agreed solution. The already intolerable situation for the civil population was deteriorating in both parts of the city; the citizens (particularly in East Mostar) were constantly targeted by snipers and shelled by medium and heavy artillery, and there was no longer any nucleus of rational people who could question the policy in both parts of the city, for whoever could escape had already run away from the inferno. In all his entrances to the city, Benabou was accompanied by British military escorts, armed with heavy weapons, for neither a military show of force nor the UN flag deterred Croats or Muslims from bombarding each of the visiting UN convoys. Mostar had become a ghetto dominated by incensed militia warriors, who held at their mercy a trapped population, which hardly received any humanitarian assistance, and whatever food distribution there occasionally happened was under the control and consent of the Muslim or Croat leadership on the spot. None of the warring sides was achieving any military progress, for it was a trench war behind the walls of existing buildings, with no substantial movement on the terrain beyond the set borders between the two parts of the city. The strategy of both Croats and Muslims was maintaining the actual line of confrontation and inflicting as many causalities as possible on the enemy, in a hope of rendering the burden or resisting so untenable as to yield and surrender or leave the scene altogether. It therefore

*Savagery in the Heart of Europe*

became crucial to create any sort of communication between the fighting parties in the city. The Croats and the Muslims responded to Benabou's invitation and arrived to the meeting, armed with lists of prisoners and detainees they wished to be released, in addition to the usual recriminations and accusations of the other that both sides hurled against each other around the meeting table. Before the war, the city of Mostar was considered a model of cultural pluralism where Croats and Muslims used to live in harmony. Inaccurate as it was, that image was fading away in the memory of the local population, which was being gradually replaced by the influx of refugees from the outside. The memory of those times appeared far away and blured in the past when in fact it was the very close history of that town.

By the end of November, 1993 the bells of The Hague started to ring, as the International Tribunal collected materials for the indictment of potential war criminals on the battlefields of former Yugoslavia.[76] The local leadership in both parts of Mostar became aware of this development, for those were the times when the worst criminal acts against civil population were perpetrated. Thereupon, Benabou came to the conclusion that the time was ripe for a local initiative in Mostar, bearing in mind that each place in Bosnia required its particular approach, as corroborated by later developments. After he had acted on behalf of the UN Civil Affairs Office for the previous eight months in the region of Mostar, Croats and Muslims came to trust him and offered their joint blessings to his local initiative. On Monday, 29 November 1993, Benabou participated in a UN staff meeting in Medjugorje and informed his colleagues that he had crystallized an approach and concept for an interim arrangement for the city of Mostar, pending the completion of a permanent

---

[76] On 17 November 1993, the International Criminal Tribunal for the former Yugoslavia was inaugurated at the Peace Palace in The Hague, the Netherlands.

settlement. Without further details, he summarized the outline of his plan:

(a) The interim arrangement for the city of Mostar would be uniquely applied to the area of Mostar and not linked to developments anywhere else;
(b) The agreement would consist of the demilitarization of the city and the deployment of UN forces in and around it; and
(c) Free and fair elections for a municipal council of Mostar would be held under the United Nations (or other international) auspices[77].

A week later, on the morning of 7 December 1993, the shuttle negotiations between the two parties were on track and progressed in a strict and tightly synchronized schedule, with a view of introducing the proposed interim arrangement for Mostar. The first to be briefed were the Muslim leaders in East Mostar, attended by the members of the war presidency in East Mostar, among them: Alija Alikadic, Sefkija Dziho, and Zijad Orucevic.[78] The immediate reaction from the Muslims was suspicious and restrained, and they started to raise preconditions. Nevertheless, they delegated Benabou to pursue the project by encountering the Croats and further exploring their take on the new ideas. Benabou introduced the concept of seeking a local interim political solution for Mostar, stressing that time was opportune due to the changes in the HVO leadership and government. The primary confidence building steps would be launched on issues such as POW exchange and power/water supply. Alikadic clarified

---

[77] Source: Confidential Memo No 9—Mostar Interim Agreement, Meeting with BiH Armija leadership East Mostar on 11 December at 13h40 summarizing an overnight brainstorm session about the initiative conducted with the Muslim and Croat local leadership in Mostar.

[78] See the collected correspondence and the series of confidential memos recorded by the British Officer.

right away that the Croats had before started the war in Mostar and that the solution would have to be found in the city of Mostar itself. The member of the Muslim war presidency agreed to Benabou's concept and supported it. However, Alikadic specified that Mostar would not become a Croatian city, as only thirty-four percent of its population was Croatian, and the majority of sixty-two percent were Muslims and others. Beyond that, Alikadic surprisingly endorsed Boban's proposal that the BiH Armija should accept Mostar as a political and cultural center for the Croatian Republic of Herzeg-Bosnia, providing freedom for all communities to practice their own way of life there. This lenient approach, which repeatedly came up all along the negotiations, disappeared nonetheless from the negotiations table in Washington, and this was probably the biggest loss for the Croats, who would not be able to retrieve it at any stage or in any forum.

Benabou emphasized the importance of interim confidence building measures between the parties and reminded the participants that future generations would not look kindly on those who rejected an opportunity for a peace option at that time. He recognized that Croatian Prlic was amenable to a political initiative and that Muslim BiH Armija should support the proposal, too. But Alikadic outlined a number of preconditions for the commencement of negotiations, in particular:

(a) Cessation of the brutal and murderous shelling on civilian targets;
(b) Completion of POW exchange;
(c) Halting the expulsion of Muslims from West Mostar; and
(d) Opening a humanitarian corridor from Ploce to Jablanica through Metkovic and Mostar.

Alikadic also suggested that only after the implementation of those preliminary conditions could infrastructural issues be addressed. Benabou concluded the meeting by adding that the opening of Mostar Airport would be crucial and that the views expressed in that meeting with the Muslims would be presented on the same day to Boban and Prlic on the Croatian side. Indeed, in the late afternoon, the concept of the interim arrangement for the city of Mostar and the hesitant Muslim reaction to the initiative were introduced to the Croats in Grude, to President Mate Boban, and to his close team (Perica Jukic and Vladislav Pogarcic). The Croatian response was firmly positive and urged further contacts on the matter. Benabou informed Boban and his team on the issues brought up at the meeting in Muslim East Mostar and emphasized that in spite of its uncertainty, BiH Armija had a fundamental interest in a political initiative of a local nature for Mostar.

Boban lamented in those discussions the current political vacuum and absence of movement in the deadlocked situation and expressed a keen interest in any new initiative. He stated that the Muslims in East Mostar were acting independently of Sarajevo since the early stage in the conflict, though they might ultimately gain at a later stage an approval from Bosnian President Izetbegovic. Benabou stated that he had informed the BiH Armija leadership that HVO would not give up their desire to retain Mostar as a political and cultural center of the Croats in Bosnia, but that necessitated the joint consent of the decision makers in East and West Mostar, even without approval or assistance from Zagreb or Sarajevo. Boban, adopting the allure of a leader, declared that "when a man of courage was identified[79]" on

---

[79] Source: Confidential Memo No 2 - Mostar Interim Agreement covering the Meeting with Mate Boban, Grude on 7 December 1993 at 18:15; The purpose of this meeting was to introduce the concept of the interim arrangement for the city of Mostar to Boban and present the Muslim reaction to the initiative. The Croat concluding response was firmly positive and called for further contacts on the matter. Attendance: Mate Boban, Albert Benabou, Perica Jukic, Vladislav Pogarcic and John Ryan.

the Muslim side, he, Boban, would be open to dialogue and would be personally available for discussions. However, taking into account the negative sensitivities and antagonism among the Muslims in East Mostar towards Boban, Benabou discouraged his direct involvement in the deal, explaining that his "level would unnecessarily be too high[80]," and he suggested that teams of three persons be appointed from each side to conduct the negotiations. The two teams would be composed of two civilians and one military member and headed by one of the civilians. Benabou emphasized the imperative of secrecy and discretion and warned against any leakage to the media. Boban went on and then spoke of his conviction that Sarajevo would abandon Mostar in pursuit of its interests in East Bosnia and Herzegovina, on the Serbian front, as Izetbegovic would sacrifice much to establish a strong line of communication from Zenica through Sarajevo to the Sandjak (the Muslim-populated part, in addition to Kosovo, of southern Serbia).

In the morning of 9 December, the initiative was presented in West Mostar to Dr. Jadranko Prlic, the prime minister of Herzeg-Bosnia and the second strong man among the Croats, in hidden competition with Mate Boban, the declared president. The goal of this encounter was to brief Prlic on the developments following the launching of the initiative. Prlic offered his full support to the UN initiative and volunteered to assist and cooperate at all levels. He also clarified that it was the proper time for such a proposal. Benabou opened the proceedings by saying that since the new HVO government had come to power, a new understanding and an opportunity presented itself for the creation of a political momentum and for the launching of new initiatives. He stated that he had visited BiH Armija leaders in East Mostar, where the mood for such an initiative was also positive, though accompanied

---

[80] ibid.

with apprehensions. He noted that he received assurances that a Muslim negotiating team would be nominated. Benabou observed that the people in East Mostar had triggered the war for their own town, and that Sarajevo took a free ride on this conflict only at a later stage. Therefore, he felt that the solutions would have to be sought and found in Mostar itself, and Prlic concurred. Benabou also indicated that the BiH Armija leaders had also accepted the concept of Mostar as a capital for the Croats and suggested that Prlic nominate a team of two civilians and one military member to partake of the proposed negotiations. Prlic responded that he would identify appropriate members for such a team and stressed that he needed no approval from Grude for such an initiative, and that, since he was meeting Boban the same day, he would discuss the matter with him at any rate. Prlic also emphasized that it was most important that the BiH Armija team should consist of prominent personalities empowered to make decisions. Benabou underlined the importance of this qualification, for the Muslims of Mostar had gradually surrendered their power to Sarajevo, while it was imperative that the power of decision ought to be retained locally by the Muslims of Mostar.

Before Benabou could deal with the required confidence-building measures to be adopted at the start of the process, Prlic raised that issue and reiterated his position:

(a) That a declaration on the unilateral release of POWs be issued by his party;
(b) That provisions should be made for hospital facilities and public kitchens for Muslims, under the belief that this would create the correct atmosphere for reconciliation.

Prlic also inquired as to the position and status of refugees in East Mostar. He was informed that they did not enjoy any role in determining the fate of the city, but he insisted on being informed as to who held real power in East Mostar before he nominated his own team. Prlic agreed with Benabou's suggestion that a joint council should be created for Mostar, composed of fifty percent Muslim and fifty percent Croatian councilmen, but he also voiced his reservations concerning the ability of the BiH Armija leadership to break away from the influence of Sarajevo.

In order to establish a workable level of coordination between (the temporary Croatian capital of Herzeg) Grude and the Croatian leadership of West Mostar, the UN team led by Benabou again visited Grude in the afternoon of the same day for another round with Vladislav Pogarcic, before Prlic met Boban later that day in order to keep the momentum. The two men decided to review the issues concerning the initiative. Pogarcic emphasized that Boban was the decision maker in such cardinal political matters. Benabou reiterated the importance of the wholehearted support offered by Boban and Prlic to the process and outlined its contours as follows:

(a) The meeting of teams of three persons from each side on the Adriatic Sea aboard the British warship, HMS *Invincible*;
(b) Following three days of negotiations, teams would be appointed by both sides to formulate proposals;
(c) The emerging agreement would be ratified by the Prime Ministers Silajdzic and Prlic (to bypass the severe personal hatred between the presidents Izetbegovic and Boban). Pogarcic then revealed that Boban would shortly depart his post for an "extended recovery period[81]." He

---

[81] Source: Confidential Memo No 4 - Mostar Interim Agreement covering the Meeting with Vladislav Pogarcic, in Grude on 9 December at 14h40; the purpose of this meeting was to establish a level plain field between "Grude and West Mostar." Pogarcic emphasized that in spite of his absence, Boban was the decision-maker in the cardinal political matters.

would be replaced on a temporary basis by a council of which he, Pogarcic, would be the head.

Benabou then outlined his shuttling program among the parties, scheduled for the coming days, in particular his visits to East Mostar, West Mostar, and Sarajevo. There was a feeling that a shift in the center of gravity of power among the HVO Croats was starting to take place, moving from Grude to West Mostar. Apparently, the process would be slow and ostensibly rationalized in democratic terms and façade procedures, but in fact, the "cleaning up the stables[82]," which had begun in the eastern European communist countries in those years, had finally caught up with former Yugoslavia, too. Zagreb was demanding the departure of "undesired elements[83]," first of all Boban himself. The HVO leadership hoped that the sacrifice of Boban could use him as the scapegoat and stop there, for the Muslims considered him responsible for war crimes perpetrated against them with the blessing of his mentor, the president of Croatia in Zagreb, Franjo Tudjman. In any case, the Muslims had developed an intense antagonism towards Boban, except, maybe, for Safet Orucevic, a dedicated young leader in Muslim East Mostar, who actually expressed his readiness to negotiate the fate of the city with Boban. Benabou had learned in a previous meeting from Boban that he intended and planned to eliminate Safet Orucevic. Benabou was startled by this declaration, so when asked where he had met Orucevic, he misinformed Boban by lying that he was actually out of Mostar and that he did not know where he had gone.

In the morning of 10 December, the Muslim leadership from East Mostar arrived to the SPABAT headquarters in Medjugorje and was briefed by Benabou. The present

---
[82] ibid.
[83] ibid.

members of the Muslim war presidency, Alija Alikadic and Zijo Orucevic, were satisfied with the achieved progress and pleased by the Croatian reactions. Benabou briefed the BiH Armija representatives on his meetings with both Boban and Prlic. He stated that it was most important that the people of Mostar, who had the power to do so, should take care of Mostar. The Muslims of Mostar had gained the respect and support of Sarajevo, all right, but it was imperative that Mostar people decided what was important to them before Sarajevo made that decision for them. He also welcomed the response from Prlic, which had been very enthusiastic. However, he made clear that this did not mean that the war would come to an end. He added that what particularly interested Boban was the freedom to define the HVO political identity within Mostar and the opportunity to provide freedom for all communities in Mostar. He reported that Prlic had a special interest in all the people of Mostar, and that he insisted that outsiders had no business in intervening in those local affairs. Benabou concluded that the ongoing war of attrition called the political representatives to act as responsibly as possible and to achieve an agreement as soon as possible.

In the afternoon of 10 December, the meeting with the Muslim leadership, including the military commanders in East Mostar, among them General Suleiman Budakovic and Colonel Safet Orucevic, pursued the talks with the other party. They presented an official letter supporting the project for an interim arrangement in Mostar. The Muslim message alluded explicitly to the political right of the Croats to determine their identity in Mostar and affirmed their full support to the initiative. Benabou announced to the gathering that Boban had responded positively to the initiative and explained that it was necessary to:

(a) Formulate the details of a plan acceptable to both sides;

(b) Nominate the teams representing both parties; and
(c) Obtain proposals and counterproposals from BiH Armija and from HVO to advance the process;
(d) Plan the meeting of delegates in a location to be decided for a period of time of three to four days, produce proposals for an agreement and reach ratification of the agreement by Silajdzic and Prlic; and
(e) Establish the council of Mostar, which would be fifty percent Croat and fifty percent Muslim[84].

For entering the process Alikadic announced that he had a number of preconditions, such as:

(a) Cessation of the shelling of civilian targets;
(b) Opening of humanitarian aid corridors;
(c) Completion of POW exchange; and
(d) HVO should free themselves of Zagreb influence.

Benabou repeated that his objective was to reach an interim agreement for the benefit of the people of Mostar and stressed the importance of discretion as "outside interests" might attempt to jeopardize the process. He spoke of the need for confidentiality, as he feared that the threat posed by contradictory interests in Zagreb and in Sarajevo might scuttle the entire initiative.

General Budakovic accepted the general contours of the proposal, insisting nonetheless that the preconditions had to be met. He clarified that he had the authority to make military decisions in principle and that there was no need to consult with General Delic (BiH Force Commander). However, he would inform General Delic of the initiative and would relay his response.

---

[84] Source: Confidential Memo No 6—Mostar Interim Agreement covering the meeting in East Mostar with BiH Armija leadership on 10 December 1993 at 09h35, concerning the concept of the initiative East Mostar was analyzed with the Muslim leadership; attended: Alija Alikadic, Albert Benabou, General Suleiman Budakovic, Colonel Safet Orucevic and John Ryan

Benabou reacted that this was a political decision, though in a war situation where lines of demarcation between political and military were blurred. He mentioned that UN Civil Affairs officers would travel to Sarajevo to meet Bosnian Prime Minister Harris Silajdzic in order to convince him of the usefulness of the process and to obtain his support. General Budakovic then stated that in principle he accepted the concept of the negotiations and that he would reveal his requests in the course of the meetings. He suggested that Prlic needed support for the process and that he would be prepared to discuss the matter with him. However, emphasized Budakovic, it should be noted that Jadranko Prlic had been member of a government which had committed atrocities, and this fact should not be ignored. Benabou then suggested, in an attempt to heed the conditions and the general thinking of both parties, that the binding terms of an interim agreement should encompass:

(a) A total ceasefire in Mostar and the environment;
(b) A return to normal life in both parts of the city;
(c) Provisions for Croatian rights to establish their identity in Mostar;
(d) The rights of all communities, including Serbs, must be respected, and Muslims, Serbs, and others must live together in the city of Mostar as a multicultural and multi-ethnic community;
(e) No foreign or outside interference should be allowed in the affairs of the city;
(f) POW exchange must be intensified and completed;
(g) The parties must avoid the outside influence of Sarajevo and Zagreb on their respective parties; and
(h) Cessation of targeting civilian objectives as the first prerequisite for any advance.

The UN representative also reiterated that the composition of the negotiating teams should include two civilians and one military on each team, with one of the civilians in charge of his team. He added that meetings would take place in an extraterritorial zone to protect the participants and facilitate ongoing contacts between the negotiating teams. The proposals would have to be ratified by Prlic and Silajdzic. He further stated that the members of the teams could constitute the proposed council of Mostar in the early stages until a permanent council was designated. From what came up in the discussions, Benabou estimated that General Lasic would most likely be the military representative on the HVO side, and General Budakovic would be the representative for the BiH Armija. It was obvious that a proper political ambience was required to realize the above principles, and that the killing and massacre of innocent civilians in Mostar must stop immediately. Benabou was invited to convey this message to Prlic, assuming that the decision on team composition, the date, and the time of the meeting would be agreed shortly, and that Silajdzic and Prlic should be ratifying the results of negotiations.

A reflection of the sense of urgency to pursue the initiative to completion came late that evening on 10 December, when the Muslim letter of agreement to enter in the process was conveyed to Jadranko Prlic in West Mostar. Prlic consented to visit East Mostar if invited, though he knew that Mate Boban would not encourage the idea for domestic political reasons, since he did not want Prlic to gain any political advantage from the initiative. Benabou informed Prlic that he had received the letter of agreement from the BiH Armija leadership in East Mostar, and that once in possession of a similar letter of reference signed by Prlic on behalf of the Croats in Mostar, he would travel to Sarajevo and Zagreb to brief Silajdzic and senior UN officials. He reaffirmed that the BiH Armija leadership recognized the political rights of the Croats in Mostar and stressed the necessity to isolate the Mostar issue from the other problems arising from the Bosnian War, for only the interim arrangement that was being sought could provide the hoped for calm on that front. He suggested the inclusion of the concept of the council of Mostar and added that BiH Armija would welcome Serbian participation in this forum.

On the early morning of 14 December, Benabou and the UNPROFOR negotiating team landed in Sarajevo. Preliminary meetings had taken place with General Rasim Delic, commander of the BiH Armija, who insisted that the first decisive step was to be taken by the politicians in Sarajevo and that the army would follow. Prior to the meeting with the prime minister, a second encounter was set at the presidency with the undersecretary, Sulejman Seljic, and the president's chief of staff, Mugdin Pasic, who were informed in general terms of the initiative and raised doubts about Boban's real intentions. Benabou introduced in general lines the interim initiative for Mostar, stating that, apparently, there was willingness from the parties to realize some progress on the issue. He suggested waiting for the prime minister in order to elaborate on the political dimension of the project. General Delic clarified that he was aware of the initiative and of the blessing of the leaders in Mostar, since a message was passed to him on the matter. Finally, at noon the talks started with Harris Silajdzic, the premier of BiH, and would last for two consecutive days, 14 and 15 December, in interminable sessions. On the first briefing, Silajdzic expressed his positive impression and called for the meeting on the following day with leaders from Mostar, who escaped from the city on horseback riding through the mountains. General Delic participated at both encounters.

Benabou informed Silajdzic that he had spent eight months working in Herzegovina in charge of the Mostar region civil affairs. He was fully familiar with the elements of the conflict in Mostar, and his assessment was that the timing was appropriate to address the political impasse at a local level as an isolated case, with a tacit blessing of the national level. He specified that the previous month was spent in intensive negotiations with both the BiH Armija leaders and HVO leaders in an attempt to identify common grounds of interest for both parties. As a result of those negotiations, he was in possession of position papers, which granted the authorization to initiate full negotiations between the parties at a venue to be decided. He outlined his concept for an interim agreement in which Mostar would be dealt without linkages to any other regions or issues, and any agreement emerging from the talks would not serve as a precedent for any subsequent agreements, which might be reached elsewhere in Bosnia and Herzegovina. Benabou asked Silajdzic for his support, assuming that the city over the Neretva River could be normalized and reopened.

Silajdzic stated that he would be very happy to receive the documents concerning the negotiations, which he would like to study and discuss the following day. He said he would consult with the political leaders of Mostar, who were currently in Sarajevo, and request their attendance at the next day's meeting. Benabou stated that a political vacuum had developed in East Mostar, and that, in effect, it was like a massive concentration camp with a complete lack of freedom of movement for the ordinary citizens. A political solution in Mostar could serve as an example for other areas and open a small window of light in the darkness. He added that the timing was appropriate, since the HVO had now realized that it was useless to pursue the military option in Mostar. Furthermore, some chaos had developed in West Mostar, as the Croats were facing a situation in which on one hand, they themselves became victims of street terror, and on the other hand, they could not justify their sacrifice by any

*Savagery in the Heart of Europe*

concrete achievement in the military domain. It was suggested that Prlic, as head of the new government in Grude, had changed priorities and was now trying to restore some law and order in West Mostar, and it would perhaps be both opportune and beneficial to assist him in this endeavor. Silajdzic asked Benabou whether he was aiming at reversing the ethnic cleansing within the terms of the agreement. He claimed that the Croats had practiced ethnic cleansing in and around Mostar, and that Muslim people had been moved out of Gacko, Stolac, and West Mostar to East Mostar, and that "foreign elements" had been brought in by the HVO to conduct the ethnic cleansing. He stated that it was essential that people who had been displaced should be allowed to return to their homes. He realized that in some cases this would not be possible, as some people would not want to return, and others had been killed in the process. Silajdzic stated that only people from Mostar should decide the destiny of Mostar, as he was worried about the influx of outsiders to Mostar. He feared the risk of destabilization as a result of this influx and compared the situation to Lebanon, where the Palestinian influx in the early 1970s had destabilized the fragile political balance and led to the civil war there.

Silajdzic observed that the Serbs and the Croats were unable at that point to obtain any military victory, their only aim being "killing, killing and killing[85]," as if the Muslims he represented were any different. He stated that the Serbs were recruiting very young boys because they did not possess the one hundred thousand soldiers they needed to be sacrificed

---

[85] Source: Confidential Memo No 13—Mostar Interim Agreement covering the first meeting in Sarajevo with the Prime Minister of Bosnia & Herzegovina, on 14 December at 12h45; The Prime Minister was briefed on the initiative for entering an agreement for Mostar and was invited to extend his support. Silajdzic expressed his positive impression on the project and called for a meeting the following day with leaders from Mostar. Attended: Harris Silajdzic, Albert Benabou and General Delic (see paragraph 21).

for Sarajevo. On the other hand, he said, the Muslims had improved immeasurably their military ability, having one hundred thousand well trained, well armed, and highly motivated combatants. He concluded that this was the main reason for their willingness to negotiate. He noted that the crucial question was the veracity of Croatian commitment and whether the international community would permit the use of force if one side reneged on its obligations. He added that to date he had not seen such willingness on their part. If this scenario were to arise, there would be only two options left, either an intervention by the international community or the intervention by the BiH Armija. He proceeded to compare the situation in Bosnia Herzegovina with the state of affairs in Israel. He erroneously remarked that "Israel had never operated alone, and that it enjoyed the support of two empires, in modern history, first the Ottoman and latterly, the American empire[86]." In his opinion, the Europeans had not matured culturally and politically on the international level, and they were still at the tribal stage. He prophetically reproached them for idealizing a multicultural society, while in fact they neither wanted nor understood it, and congratulated himself for Bosnia remaining "the dream they could not achieve," for "we are the incarnation of the spirit they want to be[87]," added he. He thought that, except the Jews, nobody in Europe had created any religion. Benabou, to whom those complimentary comparisons with Israel were obviously directed, expressed his wish to see Mostar shine and serve as an example of coexistence in this conflict. He concluded by thanking Silajdzic for his remarks and emitted a warm shalom, looking forward to the meeting on the following day.

In the morning of 15 December, the meeting with Silajdzic was renewed with the participation of the leadership of

---

[86] ibid (paragraph 24).
[87] ibid (paragraph 25).

Mostar, among them, Smajil Klaric, Ibrahim Kaluder, and Said Suisjbic. Silajdzic reiterated his total support for the project on Mostar, which he named Mostar Come Home. He stated, however, that it would be very hard to reverse history, and that in his opinion the plan could not be enforced without international military assistance. He added that the return home of the people to Mostar was a very civilized initiative and that it had the added advantage of affording Boban and the HVO an immediate choice between either cooperating with the plan or rejecting it. In this way, it would indicate whether the Croats were serious about it or otherwise. With this in mind, he suggested that it would be a good idea to publicly announce the concept of the return of displaced persons to Mostar. But he expressed doubts about the practicality of the return of the intelligentsia that Benabou had raised, and he feared that they had lost their credibility among common people. He thought that it would be difficult to bring back people who had abandoned their country, leaving it without a vital administrative infrastructure precisely during its most dire period. He stated that he himself had the opportunity to leave the country, but he chose to stay in his homeland and to contribute to its political survival. Nevertheless, he reiterated that he was quite sure that a certain number of the intellectual elite would repatriate, and he said that he could immediately identify at least ten people such as writers and artists who would willingly return. He noted that Benabou too knew of ten individuals who would be willing to return, stressing the importance of this initiative to attain that goal. He nonetheless underlined that Mostar belonged to the people of Mostar, while at present much of the city was inhabited by people from the outside, and he wished that trend to be reversed. He injected a personal note to the talk by adding that he had an intimate knowledge of Mostar and his people, connected to the fact that his wife was a native of Mostar.

Benabou was called to report to the UN HQ in Zagreb for a briefing with Thornberry and Stoltenberg on the progress of the initiative. On the sixteenth, Thornberry and his team were briefed on the proposed interim arrangement for Mostar and in particular on his meetings with Silajdzic in Sarajevo. Thornberry stated that he did not see any particular advantage in using an offshore location for the negotiations, and cities such as Venice or Geneva would be more suitable venues. He was of the opinion that even though the Croats did want to have Mostar as a Croat city, they had now realized that this was not achievable. He thought that what was possible was based on the competing interests of the parties involved and suggested that it was now important to establish what he called, "how far the Croatian cake is baked[88]." He argued that the BiH Croats were subjected to various pressures by Croatia in the first instance, but also to military pressure from both the Muslims and the Serbs. Therefore only a thorough analysis of these various pressures and influences could produce a worthwhile evaluation of the position of the BiH Croats. It was also suggested that the negotiating process should be conducted on varying levels at the same time and that this initiative should not be negotiated at Stoltenberg's level. However, it was recognized that if the Croats did not support the process, they could be pressurized under the threat of moving to Stoltenberg's level. Thornberry remarked that he would be more concerned should Lord David Owen rather than Stoltenberg get involved in this process. The difficulty was that once diplomats got involved at the international conference level, they tended to take over the process, and he thought that the best that could be hoped for would be that Stoltenberg would merely consult with

---

[88] Source: Confidential Memo No 15A—Mostar Interim Agreement covering the Meeting with Thornberry in Zagreb briefing him on the proposed Mostar interim arrangement on 16 December 1993 (see paragraph 6).

and brief Silajdzic and Boban, so as to allow the negotiators to continue with the process at the local level.

Thorvald Stoltenberg, the special representative of the Secretary General of the UN, also wished to be briefed on the proposed interim agreement for Mostar on the same evening, of 15 December, while Benabou was in Zagreb. Stoltenberg thought that the Serbs too should be taken into account in this affair, since this was the first time that any concept was formulated for Mostar. Thornberry then very briefly summarized the plan for Stoltenberg and asked Benabou why he felt that the Croats might be interested in a negotiated agreement at this time. He replied that General Roso now realized that his forces (the HVO) were only a militia and would require considerable training to become a significant fighting force. They had suffered considerable losses in Mostar, and the new HVO government headed by Prlic was anxious to create a new momentum to establish a Croatian political identity in Mostar. He added that the Croatian side had accepted the idea of two constituencies, East and West Mostar, for electoral purposes. Thornberry stated that Mostar would have to be strictly secured in the period between the conclusion of the agreement and the holding of the elections. Benabou agreed and stated that a strong show of force would be required, adding that the utilization of Danish, Nordic, or British units would be desirable. He then briefed the meeting on the concept of repatriating people back home to Mostar and emphasized that Silajdzic regarded this as an essential pillar of any negotiated agreement.

Stoltenberg outlined his schedule over the coming days and stated that he would be meeting with Izetbegovic, Silajdzic, and Boban to discuss the proposals with these people, determine their commitment to the concept and, if possible, elicit their support. Stoltenberg then asked Thornberry for his opinion. He replied that he was not able to fully assess the degree of control exercised by the Croatian government over the Croatian Republic of Herzeg-Bosnia. However, he did believe that a compromise was possible with the Muslims on Mostar. He also found it difficult to assess the Muslim standpoint at present, as he believed that they were firmly on an expansionist drive and that the history of negotiations between the parties had not been positive in former Yugoslavia; however, he did believe that the concept was worth launching at a high level and that if the parties were prepared to compromise, a viable interim agreement could be achieved. On the evening of 16 December, Thornberry initiated a personal meeting with Dr. Granic, the Croatian Minister of Foreign Affairs. He declined the suggestion to be accompanied by Benabou or any member of the negotiating team, for he apparently intended to be briefed by himself and receive guidelines from Zagreb. Granic advised Thornberry to leave the procedures in his hands and avoid unnecessary high level interference. In his report to Stoltenberg, Thornberry remarked that the Croats in Zagreb were not forthcoming on the project. This reversal of the situation was surprising and remained enigmatic, but it bore the suspicion of being connected with that meeting, which Thornberry insisted on holding privately with the high Croatian authorities. Apparently, the UN bureaucrat, Thornberry, who was struggling to renew his contract with the United Nations, attempted to do so by taking over the entire initiative to his credit, and this, far from pushing the program forward, on the contrary, bogged it down. We have seen above that the Croats in Bosnia, and particularly Boban, had agreed to the initiative with the support of Franjo Tudjman, as had been reiterated to Benabou, once and again, by Pogarcic. Once again, a peace initiative from which all the people of Mostar could have drawn benefits would be scuttled by personal struggles between petty bureaucrats and not for the first or last time in the UN's peace keeping missions.

On the morning of 17 December, before returning to his zone of operation in Mostar, Benabou did his best to persuade Thornberry that it was counterproductive to encourage any discussions with the Croatian authorities in Zagreb, for the most promising track to pursue was to permit the Croatian leaders in Grude and Mostar to communicate with Zagreb through their own channels before agreeing or acting on any issue. Since he was unsure of the intentions of his colleague in Zagreb, Benabou was directing his efforts to maintain the Mostar plan at the grassroots level, so as to neutralize any irrelevant interests, while Thornberry seemed more concerned with building up his position in the organization, which often clashed with that of the French UN-PROFOR Commander, General Jean Cot. On 18 December, General Jean Cot, accompanied by Colonel Roger Duburg, was briefed in Zagreb by Benabou about the Mostar interim agreement. The general offered his full assistance and asked Benabou to meet in Sarajevo with UNPROFOR BiH Commander General Briquemont. Gen. Cot instructed Col. Duburg to continue to follow the project and to make the necessary preparations to cover the military aspect of the operation. That meeting, unlike others where Thornberry had participated, took place in a very practical and cordial spirit of goodwill and cooperation.

In the afternoon of that day, after his meeting with General Cot, Benabou responded to an invitation by Vladislav Pogarcic to a private meeting with Dr. Mate Granic, the Croatian minister of foreign affairs, who had met with Thornberry previously. Not surprisingly, and contrary to Thornberry's report to Stoltenberg, Pogarcic announced that Granic expressed a high interest in the initiative, a proposition confirmed by Granic himself during the encounter under the instructions of President Franjo Tudjman, who had instructed the Croatian team in Grude and in Mostar to pursue the project. Later in the day, Pogarcic arrived in Zagreb and accompanied Benabou to the presidential palace for a short courtesy meeting with Tudjman. After noting that he was supporting the process, the main item brought up was the president's desire to visit Jerusalem in his efforts to make up with the Jewish state, as a channel to the United States where he knew Israel had strong links. That issue was to be raised later in 1994 with Foreign Minister Shimon Peres, upon Benabou's return from the UN mission to Israel. On 21 December, a meeting took place between Benabou and HVO representatives at Grude, among them General Milivioj Petkovic, Vladislav Pogarcic, Stojan Vrljic, and others. The purpose was to brief and update the HVO authorities on developments with regard to the progress in the negotiations, to seek their views on those developments, to obtain their renewed commitment after the contradictory declaration in Zagreb quoted by Thornberry, and to elicit their continued support for the process.

Benabou emphasized the extreme importance of maintaining discretion during the negotiations once the key principle of the Muslim acceptance of the Croatian right to self-determination in Mostar was accepted, which gave political, cultural, and administrative status to Croats in Mostar. It was also understood that only native Muslims and Croats who lived in Mostar, and Muslims and Croats who previously lived in Mostar and were now willing to return, would be included in the plan. Thus, it was imperative that no outside interference should occur in the negotiations either from Sarajevo or Zagreb, and that there should be no linkage between Mostar and any other areas or issues to be settled and agreed upon by the parties to the Bosnian War. It was also understood that an absolute cessation of hostilities should be imposed and monitored by an UNPROFOR Battalion. Participation in the negotiations would be restricted to only

Croats and Muslims, but when meaningful progress had been achieved, the Serb delegation would be invited to participate in the process. Once an agreement had been reached which accepted Mostar as enjoying a special political status in the Croatian Republic of Herzeg-Bosnia, the conflict in Mostar would come to an end, since the continued killing of people could no longer be justified by either party.

Interestingly enough, it was Pogarcic who brought up the comparison of the situation with the Middle East, with which Benabou was familiar. Alluding to the situation of his country, he equaled it with that of the Israeli-Arab conflict, in which Israel found itself surrounded by Muslims. He claimed that the HVO had respected all agreements entered into and had only reacted militarily in circumstances of self-defense. He ominously added that experience to date could only leave them skeptical, but he nonetheless reiterated his party's support for the plan, because his primary concern was to reduce the suffering of the people. Mostar's rich academic tradition was also brought up, which stressed how important it was that the University of Mostar should continue to be the source of Croatian academic, political, and cultural values. It was emphasized that people of various ethnic backgrounds had worked at the university prior to the outbreak of hostilities, and that the breakdown, which had occurred among those intellectual elites, had been caused by interference from Muslim Sarajevo, and not by interference of the mixed municipal authority as some believed. For the sake of framing the terms of reference of the negotiations, a definition of the boundaries of Mostar was required, to which Benabou replied that it basically consisted of six neighborhoods, but he predicted difficulties when the time came to delineate boundaries on the ground, due to the military considerations, which would dictate domination of certain high grounds that would be militarily meaningful for defense. That matter too was left to the negotiating process when it was launched.

That meeting was held in a very positive atmosphere. The following morning, 22 December, another meeting was called, this time with the Muslim leadership, which included General Sulejman Budakovic, Colonel Safet Orucevic, and Alija Alikadic. Benabou's team was accompanied by Susan Finch, representing a US Care International Food organization. Although her official field of action was providing food assistance to Mostar, she insisted on participating in the peace initiative briefing with the local Muslim leadership. Benabou agreed reluctantly, for the goal of the meeting was to update the Muslim leaders on the positive response received from the Croatian leadership in Grude and west Mostar, the Muslim leadership in Sarajevo, Stoltenberg and General Jean Cot, so as to encourage the momentum of the initiative. Indeed, the leadership in East Mostar reaffirmed its determination to support the project but urged Benabou to take part with them in a meeting planned for Wednesday, 28 December, with Izetbegovic and Safet Orucevic. In that meeting, the Muslim leaders expressed their disappointment that there had been no indication from HVO regarding the release of four hundred Muslim POWs from the Forty-First Mostar Log Brigade. General Budakovic's current information was that, to date, thirteen hundred and fifty Muslim civilians were released by the HVO, representing only fifteen-twenty percent of the total number of detainees. But given the small amount of released soldiers, the BiH delegates could not consider such a minor gesture of goodwill a valuable one towards a peace process. He stated that while approximately two hundred more civilians would be released shortly, an additional three thousand were being held by the HVO in the Mostar Heliodrom.

Colonel Orucevic agreed to provide the names of the BiH negotiating team in two days' time. He had spoken with

Izetbegovic in Geneva and had been given the mandate to proceed with the talks. But it became evident to Benabou that after so many negotiations and promises, the BiH representatives were becoming intransigent and posing preconditions for launching the actual negotiations. Therefore, he stated that he sensed an impasse in the proceedings, insisting that by linking peripheral issues to the Mostar initiative not under his jurisdiction, the initiative process could not advance forward. He reiterated that he had no immediate interest in those peripheral issues raised by the Muslim delegation and reminded those present that Mostar should be the only focus of the discussion. He thought that when the Muslims suddenly declared that they were not authorized to proceed, he was forced to admit failure. He reminded the delegates that one hundred and forty hours had been invested in the negotiations to date, with the full support of all sides involved, and that the HVO had even provided the names of their delegates to the talks, expecting the Muslims to proceed similarly instead of creating new obstacles by posing new preconditions to an arrangement which was to be launched unconditionally. Alikadic expressed willingness to continue to talk and affirmed that negotiations over the initiative on Mostar were a priority for them as well. His concern was that they did not sense they were equal and could not feel equal as long as the corridors of passage for humanitarian aid to their people were being blocked. He cited the example of a Muslim citizen of Mostar, who was very sick, for whom he had been negotiating evacuation over seven days without success. Alikadic felt that had that individual been a Croat, there would have been no difficulty in arranging an evacuation. As a gesture of good faith, the BiH were willing to arrange for the release of all HVO soldiers originating from Mostar but noted that they comprised less than fifty percent of the prisoners, the remainder being from surrounding areas that fell outside the jurisdiction of the Mostar peace initiative.

Benabou said that he would ask for the corridors of humanitarian aid to be reopened, but Alikadic advised him that the HVO were maintaining their current tactics of deception, and reported that at the Croatian Gabela detention camp four hundred people were being held for prosecution. He also warned that in return the seventy-two prisoners held by the Muslims would be treated in the same way, unless the HVO demonstrated fairness. Benabou noted that denying the release of the seventy-two prisoners would only increase mistrust between the parties, and unless the HVO also released their four hundred prisoners, they would also aggravate the mistrust. Alikadic declared that all prisoners, not just the four hundred detainees, must be released. Benabou redirected the discussion to its originally constructive track. He mentioned that Sarajevo had given the Muslim delegates the mandate to proceed with the Mostar peace initiative, and he believed that success was within reach if two processes could be agreed upon: (1) the demilitarization of the city, and (2) an election process to be held for the joint city council. He stated his intention to respond to the invitation to meet with Silajdzic in Sarajevo on 29 December and then to proceed to Zagreb to inquire whether there was a clear mandate to continue the process. Colonel Orucevic also stated his intentions of meeting with Izetbegovic on 29 December and invited Benabou to accompany him. Following that meeting with his president, he pleaded for UNPROFOR's understanding regarding the BiH requests for fulfillment of their conditions. General Budakovic assured that he would accept any peace proposal that would guarantee the protection of the people of East Mostar, but that any question left open as to their security would cause the process to collapse altogether.

Susan Finch briefly explained the purpose of her presence to assess a Care International Food Kitchen Project in

Mostar. The initiative was born out of a contact with UN-PROFOR Civil Affairs representatives and John Ryan, who had proposed potential sites for the kitchens in the city of Mostar. She mentioned that five kitchens were available by Care International and expressed interest in seeking appropriate sites for their installation on the ground. She emphasized that she was concerned about the safe passage of the kitchens into the Mostar area and the continued safe passage of resupplies of food and fuel must be also be assured. She mentioned that the implementation of the project would be contingent upon ongoing security for any international staff assigned to the project and that UNHCR would have to lend its support to the operation. Alikadic stated that he was in full support of such a project, since the needs in East Mostar were so great, and that, as far as possible, he would support Care International's conditions for the smooth operation of the project. He invited Finch to accompany him to two potential sites in the city for the kitchens at the closure of the meeting. When the meeting was adjourned, Benabou met privately with General Budakovic and Alikadic, inquiring about their genuine intentions regarding the peace initiative, and warned that if he were met by any doubt that could affect the plan, he would immediately withdraw from the process, despite the painstakingly long and laborious investment he had put in it. General Budakovic and Colonel Orucevic affirmed that not only were they in total support of the initiative, but that the timing was most appropriate for the Muslims and Croats.

Sunday, 25 December 1993, the city of Zagreb was covered with a Christmas layer of snow and seemingly immobilized. Benabou had solicited a meeting in Zagreb with Stoltenberg, who was due to inform him about his assessment and the results of his contacts in Geneva and Brussels with the Croats and the Muslims. Ram Sharan, Stoltenberg's assistant, transmitted to him the following disappointing message: "Mr. Stoltenberg is out of town. He notified Lord Owen about the initiative, who at this stage, is deeply involved between Geneva and Brussels and forging ahead with the planned meeting of 15 January, 1994; however, Stoltenberg is interested in any development in this matter[89]." Sharan reaffirmed the interest of the European community in the Mostar negotiations, and a frustrated Benabou could only promise that he would report on the matter. On 29 December, a meeting was called with Harris Silajdzic in Sarajevo, where Benabou was informed that Franjo Tudjman had given instructions to Croatian representatives to abandon the battle in Mostar and instead take care of the deprived people there. Silajdzic expressed his skepticism about EU participation in the process and stated that Europe should stand back, since it had a tendency to "legalize and accept the consequences of ethnic cleansing[90]." He stated that the solution of the Mostar issue and its role in any particular national policy should be established prior to further action and asked who was going to protect the city and enable its people to return to their homes. He then inquired who was backing the project, since it was obviously separate from the Geneva negotiation process. He also expressed his conviction that the people of Mostar must return to their homes, but at the same time expressed skepticism that such a thing could be done unless force was used.

Benabou reassured that although it would not be easy, UN forces, UNCIVPOL, UNMOS, and other UN segments would be there to cope with problems on the ground, and

---

[89] Source: Confidential Memo No 19—Mostar Interim Arrangement; sum up in Zagreb on Sunday, 25 December 1993,(Christmas), recapitulating of course of events.

[90] Source: Confidential Memo No 21—Mostar Interim Arrangement covering a personal meeting between Albert Benabou and Harris Silajdzic in Sarajevo on 29 December 1993; the purpose of the visit was to clarify positions.

furthermore, the European Union would be constantly present and control the operation. Silajdzic reiterated that the European Union and the United Nations were indispensable because only they had troops to facilitate the process, while none of the parties involved had the power to act likewise. As envisaged by the civilian affairs officer, the United Nations and European Union's role in the process would amount to posting forces in the city, clearing it of all criminal elements, and enabling refugees from Mostar to return home. But Silajdzic then expressed his conviction that this concept could be successful only if combined with and included into other current peace programs, based on the "back home" idea. When Benabou pressed for setting a date to launch the program and mentioned January 1994 as the target, Silajdzic surprisingly retorted, "You will be alone on this plan[91]," because he thought that there was no firm support as yet on the part of either the United Nations and the European Union. Benabou, on the contrary, thought that all parties, the Croats with Tudjman, the United Nations, and the European Union, had committed their support. But Silajdzic remained adamant that it was impossible to implement that plan unless it was part of an overall solution for Bosnia and Herzegovina. It was obvious that Silajdzic was seeking a more active role in the affair, being uncertain about United Nations and European Union commitment.

Benabou left the meeting frustrated, and in order to make it to the next round of talks in Mostar, he boarded special flight UN 019 aboard a US Air Force carrier, white-colored with a UN flag. En route, a young US crew officer informed him that the plane was under missile fire. Benabou reacted again with his typical sense of humor: "As long as you are able to report, we are doing fine[92]." After a few minutes the officer returned

---

[91] ibid.
[92] Recorded in Benabou's Personal memoirs of War in Bosnia.

and announced that following instructions from Frankfurt NATO headquarters, the plane must change course and land in Italy. "It would be nice to celebrate New Year in Rome," said Benabou. "No sir," answered the officer. "We will be landing in Ancona, and for safety, you will be transferred to a military base in that area[93]." That was in accordance with American SOP (standard operational procedures) thought Benabou, who felt relieved, but he also remembered that the Croatian military had explained that they were training in firing missiles in the Split area, but neither the control tower of the airport nor the Croatian Army had informed NATO or UN headquarters of these exercises, though adequate channels had been established for this purpose. The only passenger in this flight was Albert Benabou, accompanied by the UNHCR crew, and he was scheduled to arrive to a planned shuttle meeting with the Croats in Mostar. Unsatisfied with the stories he was told, and in view of the urgency of the talks, Benabou decided to ignore the firing and carry on, something that his superiors, Cedric Thornberry and Victor Andreev, characterized in their evaluations of him as "accomplishing his mission at the risk of his life[94]." For him, who never knew anything different, that was one of the vagaries of his job, and he was intent on carrying it out despite the risks.

After some delay and with the dream of a New Year's party in Rome shelved, the meeting took place with East Mostar leaders, with the participation of Alija Alikadic, Smajil Klaric, and Col. Safet Orucevic. Benabou was accompanied by the British officer, Major Peter Loghan, and by J. Valdiness and Philip Watkins representing the ECMM (European Community Monitoring Mission, to be differentiated from the

---

[93] ibid.
[94] UNPROFOR memorandum, 10 September 1993; The Head of the diplomatic Mission with the peace forces in Bosnia praises Benabou's comprehensive vision and his operations in extremely difficult circumstances at the risk of my life.

*Savagery in the Heart of Europe*

UN observers). The ECMM representatives were all dressed in white and gained the title of "ice cream salesmen[95]" in the war in Bosnia. The idea was to reaffirm the commitment of the Muslim side to the Mostar interim arrangement and to smooth out any remaining obstacles. Alikadic complained that the Croats had publicly stated on radio their conditions for the process, and he firmly affirmed that no negotiations would take place until that statement was retracted. Benabou assured his interlocutors that he had the full commitment of the Croats to negotiate, and he reiterated his own belief that negotiations had to proceed before the situation got worse. Therefore, he insisted that what was required was a reaffirmation that the BiH was prepared to press forward. He also asked for the list of names of the BiH negotiating team, as he predicted that the process would start in a matter of days. He stressed his conviction that the aim of these meetings was to achieve results and not to be sidetracked by alien issues to the Mostar affair, which was what the new Croatian statement essentially was. He then introduced the EU representatives to the audience, believing, as did Zagreb, that it was the task of fellow Europeans to monitor the events after the process was set in motion, which was also the request of General Budakovic. This was somehow surprising and contradictory to the policy pursued by Silajdzic, who clarified that Europe was unable to resolve the conflict, and only the United States had to be brought as an honest broker between the parties. This indicated that there might have been a difference of approach between the military and the politicians in Bosnia-Herzegovina.

On the following day, 3 January 1994, another meeting took place between Benabou and Alija Alikadic in Mostar East, in which the UN civil affairs officer was accompanied only by the British officer, Major Peter Loghan. The purpose

---

[95] Recorded in Benabou's Personal memoirs of War in Bosnia. Called so due to the white Uniform they were wearing during the mission in Bosnia-Herzegovina.

of this meeting was to obtain the list of BiH representatives for the forthcoming negotiations and to resolve any minor problems that remained pending. He said that as soon as the convening letter for the talks was signed by the parties, he would go to Zagreb whence he would issue the invitations to launch the negotiations. The format of the negotiating teams would be three residing members of each party, two advisors, and a support team of interpreters and secretaries. Alikadic questioned the idea of using the Mostar airport as a forward headquarters for UNPROFOR, as it was a sensitive location, and much military movement and coordination would have to be undertaken. Both parties agreed to discuss this matter at a later date. Benabou outlined three stages for the whole process:

(a) A preparatory phase, scheduled for 7-10 January, 1994;
(b) A discussion and implementation phase, to take place between 11-24 January, 1994; and
(c) The high political level involvement phase to finalize the agreement on 25 January, 1994.

He added that he would prepare the schedule for the negotiations and issue it with the invitations. He would also prepare a proposal of ground rules to be agreed upon by the parties in the talks. Alikadic stated that cessation of hostilities must be the first stage of the negotiations, with the opening of the roads and restoration of water and electricity supply to follow immediately. At last, a list of the participants for the BiH delegation was delivered, and the concept of the entire plan was clarified and reinforced. The war presidency in East Mostar nominated three members: Alija Alikadic (president), Fatima Leho (member – she was the practical and realistic contributor in all negotiations), and Obren Lozo (member – he was under General Sulejman Budakovic's command).

*Savagery in the Heart of Europe*

Benabou reiterated that if the process were to be scuttled, he would prefer both sides to turn down the negotiations then rather than to back out at a later, more advanced stage. Alikadic stated that the BiH wanted these talks and would not back out. He also advised that the Muslim party was not taking the Vienna talks seriously and then announced that the BiH authorities did not trust Croatian President Boban and that they would prefer dealing directly with his Prime Minister Prlic. Alikadic also said that the Muslim ground conditions were that Mostar was multinational and multicultural and that it could never be totally Croat or divided between Muslims and Croats. At the time, following the fad of multiculturalism that was in vogue in Europe, Benabou also expressed his view that national states were a thing of the past, not knowing that twenty years later the champions of multiculturalism like the British Labor Party, Germany, France, and even Holland would lament that concept of "tolerance," which had brought upon them Muslim unrest and migrant disturbances. They would revert to their originally preponderant respective cultures, which would in effect dictate the integration of the new migrants into the existing cultures and no longer pretend that idealist multiculturalism could work in the real world.

Benabou then outlined the stages of the implementation process:

(a) Cease hostilities on all Mostar fronts;
(b) Move the headquarters of the UNPROFOR Battalion to the Mostar airport;
(c) Hold elections for the Mostar city council;
(d) Make a financial commitment to Mostar by the EEC.

The UNPROFOR team was then taken to a meeting of the local civil, military, and religious authorities, where political statements were made, which created the impression that the Muslim authorities still had reservations about the process due to their mistrust of the Croat, something which set the mood of the forthcoming negotiations. In effect, at the general meeting with the war presidency of East Mostar, Fatima Leho stated that the Muslim attitude was very skeptical to the point that it believed it would take years to restore confidence and trust between the parties. Leho rejected Europe's involvement and its failed initiatives, stressing that the only solution was to keep the project at its local level of a micro plan. Benabou mentioned to his interlocutors that he had complained to Boban about the information leaks and that the latter blamed his Prime Minister Prlic for them, while he manifested his positive attitude towards the plan. In fact, Boban was trying to denigrate Prlic, who was preferred, not only by the Muslims, but also by the Croat decision makers in Zagreb as the leader of the Croatian team. Benabou pleaded that since the Mostar process was detached from all the rest, it was important to demilitarize the city and hold elections within forty-five days for the city council, where seats should be reserved for the Serbs when they joined the talks in later stages. Seats were also to be reserved for the Serb delegates. He said that the UN British and French mixed battalion to be deployed at the airport would protect the city of Mostar and control the movement of the HVO-BiH forces in the area.

Concurrently with these painstaking and lengthy talks mediated by the UN civilian office, the Prime Minister of Bosnia-Herzegovina, Haris Silajdzic, and the Deputy Prime Minister and Foreign Minister of Croatia, Mate Granic, in their capacity as the trusted officials by both Presidents, Franjo Tudjman and Alija Izetbegovic, met in Vienna on 5 January 1994 and discussed the latest developments of the crisis in Bosnia-Herzegovina. In their joint statement, they adopted the framework generated at the local level for the negotiations in Mostar and tackled the specific items identified during the shuttle diplomacy adopted by the UN mediator on the ground. At that point, the Croatian and Muslim national leaders acted according to their respective state prerogative and took total and exclusive control of the Mostar initiative that had been created and devised at the local level in Mostar. They then became the only authoritative instance which set the terms and the mode of action of the negotiations and their implementation. In their released joint document, they confirmed that the immediate ceasefire and the durable cessation of hostilities, as well as the permanent relationship between Croats and Bosniaks in Bosnia-Herzegovina, including the political, territorial, military, humanitarian, and other aspects of it, were in fact of long-term strategic interest of both nations and both states, hence their takeover of the issues involved. They agreed that their superiors, the president of the Republic of Croatia, Franjo Tudjman, and the president of the collective presidency of the Republic of Bosnia-Herzegovina, Alija Izetbegovic, would meet in Bonn on Saturday, 8 January. Both sides confirmed that they would, within the framework of the preparations for the summit meeting of the two presidents, make efforts to prepare a complete plan of ceasefire along all the front lines, to arrest all military activities, establish conditions for a durable cessation of hostilities, the protection of civilians, and the implementation of confidence-building measures.

It was also jointly confirmed that the controversial issues concerning the territorial delimitation of boundaries must be resolved exclusively by peaceful political means without using force, in accordance with the Sarajevo Declaration of November 12, 1993. As regards the humanitarian issues, it was agreed that:

> The Commission for Humanitarian Issues would meet on Friday, 7 January 1994, in order to reach an agreement on the free passage of the humanitarian convoys

and consider the possibilities of opening new routes, as well as discuss the evacuation of the wounded and the permanent medical supply of hospitals;

All necessary guarantees and documentation for the free passage of the mobile hospital for the left bank in Mostar should be provided by Tuesday, 11 January 1994;

The commission for the exchange of detainees would meet on Tuesday, 11 January 1994;

The commission for Mostar, in accordance with the agreements of the last round of negotiations in Brussels, would meet on Friday, 7 January 1994 at the UN-PROFOR Spanish Battalion headquarters in Medjugorje in order to prepare the plan of the renewal of life and the return of citizens of Mostar to the city[96].

The two parties also confirmed their previous agreement on the establishment of a free port zone in the Ploce harbor. Silajdzic and Granic also met with the cochairmen of the peace conference on former Yugoslavia, Lord David Owen and Thorvald Stoltenberg. Moreover, the US ambassador to the United Nations, Madeleine Albright, visited Zagreb on 5 January 1994 and told a press conference that "the United States has supported and will continue to support the territorial integrity of the Republic of Croatia, while urging a peaceful solution for the occupied areas of Croatia, since the aggression and conflict in former Yugoslavia were not justified[97]." Regarding the delivery of relief aid, she said that

---

[96] Source: Confidential Memo No 33—Mostar Interim Arrangement covering the Meetings on Wednesday 19 January in East Mostar & in Grude, the purpose being: evaluation in the aftermath of the Geneva Conference. Attended the meeting with Albert Benabou, respectively in East Mostar: Alija Alikadic and in Vladislav Pogarcic.

[97] Source: Announced at the Press Conference held in Zagreb on 5 January by US Ambassador to the UN Madeleine Albright after her visit in the region and meetings with Croat Officials (covered by the New York Times, Washington Post and Croatian press).

*Savagery in the Heart of Europe*

"Promises that have been made ought to be fulfilled[98]," without however indicting any party, and when asked about Croatia's military involvement in Bosnia-Herzegovina, she said, "the United States had repeatedly warned the Croatian government and its military about these actions[99]." She added that sanctions might be imposed on Croatia if no changes were made in this respect. She also announced that she was going to discuss the issue with President Tudjman.

The US diplomatic bulldozer was activated, pressuring the parties, Croats and Muslims, to stop the hostilities and sit at the negotiating table in Washington. Like the Middle East, where the borders between the warring parties had been the object of endless bickering on each inch of territory for twenty years (1947-1967), and then for another ten years (1967-1977) But when war broke out in 1967, and the peace process in 1977, in one stroke national leadership of the parties reversed the prolonged, indecisive process and made momentous decisions, for war or for peace, which cancelled at once the previous rules of the game and created a new reality that made the previous local negotiations look preposterous. At the same time, there is no doubt that the ultimate decisions could not have been made without the laborious and patient preparatory work that Benabou and his likes persevered in doing against all odds.

On 7 January 1994, Benabou was called to the UNPROFOR headquarters in Zagreb to update Cedric Thornberry and his team, Vladislav Guerassev and Emma Shitaka, on the current status of the proposed interim arrangement for Mostar and to present a complete documented dossier. Thornberry opined that Mostar was primarily a matter for the European Union, and he would favor preparation of a proposal based on the dossier to be transmitted to Stoltenberg through Akashi. He said he was anxious at that time not

---
[98] ibid.
[99] ibid.

to compromise in any way the ongoing negotiations taking place in Geneva, Vienna, and other locations, which were aimed at achieving an overall solution to the Bosnian crisis. In essence, Thornberry seemed anxious to show that the UN staff in Mostar did not stand in competition with the ICFY (International Conference on Former Yugoslavia).

Thornberry then called upon Mr. Guerassev to give an appraisal of the contents of the dossier and then opined that the documents were not yet ripe for action, since certain aspects needed further elaboration and development, especially the military aspect thereof. He articulated his fears of external interference by undisciplined Muslim and Croatian elements in the arena and considered that it was necessary to ensure that the proposals on Mostar were compatible with the terms of the Vance-Owen plan, which had stipulated that Mostar should ultimately be put under EU administration for a transitory period of two years. At that point, Thornberry had not formulated a clear vision of the overall concept contained in the dossier, but from what he understood, he believed it contained many imaginative and worthwhile elements that were certainly worth pursuing. He concluded that assistance would be needed in preparing a comprehensive program of tasks to be assigned to the relevant UNPROFOR role, such as the military, civil, aid relief, supervision of ceasefire, repatriation of refugees, and the like, if and when an agreement was reached. Little did he and others in the UN setup understand that the Mostar process had already died once it was taken over by the national leaders, or perhaps he did understand but found it unbearable to relinquish his role in the process, to which he contributed little but thought he was saving the universe.

Nonetheless, both Croats and Muslims continued their local game in Mostar. They both preferred a British or a US venue for the continuation of their negotiations over Madrid, which was also submitted to their choice, and finally Washington was elected to fill the role of the broker and to lead the negotiations as Silajdzic had wished all the way. The commander of the Spanish Battalion considered that Madrid should have been the city hosting the encounters, particularly since Mostar was under the Spanish UNPROFOR zone of responsibility and did not appreciate the fact that the moment procedures started to firm up the Spanish headquarters in Medjugorje were circumvented and remained outside the procedures. Frustrated, they created confusion through the distribution, on their own initiative, of a letter informing the Muslims of Mostar that Benabou was no longer a UN representative in the area. Not only did the Spanish commander have no mandate to do so, but he also put at risk the personal security of his colleague, who became exposed in the war zone without the UN cover. The issue was immediately dealt with by the Civil Affairs headquarters in Zagreb under Thornberry and in Kiseljak with Andreev. They were very disturbed by the Spanish démarche and informed the entire UNPROFOR chain of command and the warring parties in Mostar to disregard the letter, which was illegal and void. It was also revealed that this embarrassing act was undertaken by the SPABAT commander without consultation with the Spanish authorities.

On 12 January, Benabou was scheduled to meet with the Muslim authorities in East Mostar, Alija Alikadic and Smajil Klaric, to review the position of the BiH authorities and find out how willing they were to proceed with the initiative, after the last high level encounters took place between Croats and Muslims in Vienna, Geneva, and the Bonn summit between Izetbegovic and Tudjman. Alikadic mentioned the mix-up provoked by SPABAT's letter sent to BiH Mostar authorities, and he added that he had sent a protest letter to UNPROFOR HQ in Zagreb, through the BiH Embassy there, and received a clarification that it was a regrettable and irresponsible action. Alikadic expressed high satisfaction about the results of the recent negotiations in Bonn, including Izetbegovic's statement that Mostar must continue to be considered as part of Bosnia-Herzegovina. Klaric announced that a meeting was planned for the following day, Thursday, 13 January, in SPABAT Medjugorje, with the participation of the previously appointed delegations for the Mostar interim arrangement negotiations and said that he had been instructed from Sarajevo to participate in that meeting. Klaric also confirmed his party's determination to go ahead with the local Mostar initiative and that the meeting in Medjugorje should only provide an opportunity to feel the atmosphere, review the issues to be discussed, and find out how serious the intentions of the other side were. However, Klaric did not hide his fears that the Croats might be using the whole démarche just to get some benefit out of it, without really intending to resolve the Mostar conundrum. The meeting concluded with Alikadic and Klaric's statement that the East Mostar authorities were looking forward to the forthcoming invitations for the negotiations.

The meeting of the joint Croat and Muslim Commission for Mostar agreed upon by the Geneva Conference took place in Medjugorje at the headquarters of SPABAT on 13 January 1994, within the framework of the Bonn summit between Izetbegovic and Tudjman, at the same time pretending that the session and its agenda were "an extension of the negotiations held during the previous months at the local level in Mostar[100]." In consultation with Andreev, Benabou

---

[100] Source: Report sent by Albert Benabou on 14 January 1994 to the UNPROFOR Headquarters in Kiseljak and in Zagreb. The brought up subject was the meeting of joint Croat and Muslim Commission for Mostar headed by the Geneva Conference. The meeting took place in Medjugorje, SPABAT unit HQ on 13 January 1994. Albert Benabou was invited to participate. The parties specified to Benabou that this meeting was called within the framework of the Bonn conference between Izetbegovic and Tudjman. This session and its agenda were defined as an extension of the negotiations held during the last month at the local level in Mostar. The meeting was chaired by General Pellnas, acting on behalf of the Geneva Conference.

recommended to offer all assistance to General Bo Pellnas, who was chairing the talks on behalf of the Geneva Conference. Andreev was irritated by the presence of Pellnas, for he too suddenly realized that the International Conference on Former Yugoslavia was appropriating the mandate previously assigned by UNPROFOR to its civil affairs division. In consequence, while the Muslims maintained the same delegation from Mostar, Alija Alikadic, chairman, Fatima Leho, member, and Obren Lozo, member, the Croats shifted gear and replaced their team to a lower political level, Ivan Tomic, chairman, Milan Bodiroga, member and Miso Brajkovic, member. General Pellnas recommended that the negotiations should be conducted between the parties without any UN presence. The head of each delegation made short opening statements, and they were left to direct discussions; all other participants withdrew. The talks were concluded after less than one hour and were adjourned to 16 January 1994.

Following General Bo Pellnas's request, Benabou convened on Monday, 21, February, 1994 a twelve-hour meeting in East Mostar with the participation of the local Muslim leaders in the city, reinforced by the members of the Muslim delegation to the negotiations. Attending among others were Safet Orucevic, Deputy Fourth Corps Commander of the Armija, who had been delegated by Izetbegovic as the plenipotentiary political authority in Mostar; Smajil Klaric, the chairman of the war presidency in Mostar and a key figure in the decision making process; Alija Alikadic, chairman of the Muslim delegation, representing grassroots power in the city. Brigadier Ramiz Drekovic, the new Fourth Corps Commander, was manifestly not solicited to take part. He counted among the senior Muslim military leaders, who clearly advocated a military solution to the war, their incapacity to do so notwithstanding, and openly committed themselves to regaining lost territory through military means. In this regard, they were opposed to a permanent ceasefire or internationally imposed agreement. Those commanders talked openly of defeating the Serbs and clung to the unrealistic perception that the military balance continued to move slowly in their favor. Official documents outlining the Muslim position in Mostar and signed by the War President, Smajil Klaric, were sent at the conclusion of that meeting to the UN headquarters in Zagreb and New York. The main issues brought up again included the Muslim requests:

> To reopen the airport and the heliport of Mostar and put it under the control of the city administration.
> Mostar should neither be part of the Croatian Republic of Herzeg-Bosnia, nor its capital.
> Citizens of Mostar should be permitted to return to their homes from which they had been expelled.
> The European Union should administer Mostar, as a united and open town[101].

Another issue that was brought up in that meeting was the idea of holding an informal meeting in the area of Mostar between Safet Orucevic (the Muslim political authority in Mostar) and Vladislav Pogarcic (secretary of the Croatian presidential council). Zubak (chairman of the Croatian presidential council) and Klaric (the Muslim Mostar War President) might join the meeting. The Muslims were unofficially considering consecrating the status quo in the city of Mostar (i.e. the existing confrontation line) into a permanent "peace line" to be agreed upon, to discuss the political rights of the Croats staying in the city, and the setting of a common council for the separate parts to be monitored by the European Union. Eight days before the signature of the Washington Agreement between Croats and Muslims, on

---

[101] ibid.

10 March 1994, Benabou held another meeting with Alija Alikadic, who stated that the East Mostar authorities were in favor of an EU administration for the whole of Mostar, though he expressed reservations about Germany or Greece taking the leading role in it. He explained that the Bosnian interest in the EU administration stemmed from its need for an international umbrella during the following two years, so as to provide an opportunity for the reestablishment of an equitable legal system. Commenting on Smajil Klaric's recent declaration published in *Oslobobdjenje* (*Liberation*, a popular newspaper in Bosnia-Herzegovina), concerning the East Mostar leadership, Alikadic stated that Klaric identified with Prime Minister Silajdzic's positions, and that he was about to take over a new post in Sarajevo or in the surrounding area. He also mentioned that he would probably be replaced in Mostar by Safet Orucevic (recognized as a close confidant to President Izetbegovic). What was in fact unfolding was that the radicals were taking over the Muslim part of Mostar from the moderates, and Klaric's departure diminished Alikadic's power in the city. Commenting on the new Fourth Corps Commander General Ramiz Drekovic, Alikadic stated that he was considered redundant, since most of the problems in Mostar had been resolved prior to his arrival. He was implying his disapproval of the militant positions expressed by Drekovic, the newcomer from Sarajevo, who aligned with the more militant Izetbegovic. This reversal in the Muslim position, and the upgrading of the talks from local to national, made the noble efforts deployed by Benabou and his colleagues vain at worst, redundant at best. *Sic transit gloria mundi.*

# Chapter Four
## From the Diary of an Israeli in a UN Mission

In September 1992, Israel and the Palestinians were secretly and unofficially maneuvering the signature of the Oslo Accords, which would take place, one year later, on the lawn of the White House. Under those optimistic circumstances, the Secretary General of the United Nations, the Egyptian diplomat Boutros Boutros-Ghali, announced to the Israeli Prime Minister, Yitzhak Rabin, who was visiting New York on the occasion of the General Assembly, that for the first time the United Nations would be offering an opening for an Israeli candidate to serve in a UN peace mission. In consequence, five months after submitting his candidacy, Albert Benabou of the Israeli Foreign Ministry (and the coauthor of this account) was selected from among hundreds of other candidates from all over the world for a post with the UN peace keeping forces in Bosnia. On 8 April 1993, at the height of hostilities in Bosnia and Herzegovina, Benabou was en route for Zagreb as the first Israeli on a peace keeping mission with UNPROFOR (the United Nations Protection Forces in Former Yugoslavia). His defined assignment, as a civil affairs officer, was to help protect peace in the midst of war in Bosnia-Herzegovina. He soon found out that the region of Mostar where he was assigned was located on the Croatian border, and his task was to coordinate matters of peace between the warring parties. But since there was no peace to protect, nor even any serious intention among the parties to establish one, the briefings he received at the UN headquarters in Zagreb, before departing to his mission, presented the Vance-Owen Plan as a fair solution that could stop the bloodshed. That proposal was nonetheless abandoned by all sides, brokers and belligerents. Therefore, it was unthinkable that it could be implemented on the ground.

Who was Albert Benabou, who until then held a quiet, peaceful, unobtrusive Israeli government official job at the Israeli Foreign Ministry as a special assistant and counsel to Foreign Minister David Levy? And where did his motivation to venture into a dangerous combat area emanate from? Maybe his latest positions as a coordinator between Israeli and international scientists in the Ministry of Science, or in charge of initiating academic training programs at the Ministry of Construction and Housing, then as a negotiator for the Ministry of Tourism, followed by his mission as the regional director of the Israeli Ministry of Tourism office in Paris, and then as the Director of Programming at the Israeli Ministry of Tourism, in charge of organizing international events in Israel and abroad, could reveal some aspects of the broad international interests of this unusual man, a native of Morocco, who arrived as a new immigrant to Israel in the 1960s, motivated by Zionist ideals. During his career in Israel, he also developed many projects of cooperation, both on the national and the municipal levels, and between Israel and foreign countries, including the Palestinians, one of which has won him the epithet of "promoter and innovator[102]" by UNESCO. All this vast experience would be put to the test in the enormously complicated task that was assigned to him upon his arrival in Mostar in early 1993 while the war in Bosnia was raging.

Benabou's command of English, Spanish, and French, in addition to his long-time administrative, mediating, and planning experience, together with his flair for public

---

[102] The projects of cooperation initiated by Albert Benabou in 1995 at the municipal level between Morocco and Israel was supported and defined in an official document by the UNESCO delegate in North Africa as promoter and innovator.

relations and sense of humor (quite an innovation for the United Nations), made him a successful civil affairs officer during the year he served there between April 1993 and April 1994. His duties put him in charge of the coordination of civil affairs in the southern and central regions of Bosnia-Herzegovina. It was expected of him to provide political and military analysis of the region to the UN headquarters in the regions of Kiseljak and Zagreb and to the headquarters in New York; to negotiate and generate contacts between the parties in conflict; to assure the movement of food convoys to the besieged civil population; to coordinate and oversee military and humanitarian operations during the conflict between Croats, Muslims, and Serbs in the region; to operate with UN military units (the Spanish and British Battalions) and with civilian agencies such as UNHCR, ICRC, IRC, and others; to mediate between the fighting parties in achieving and managing ceasefires, exchanging POWs, and in evacuating civilian victims and military casualties from the war theater.

Benabou was the first Israeli to serve in the United Nations peace keeping forces in a war zone and to establish and manage the Office of Civil Affairs of UNPROFOR (United Nations Protection Force) in Mostar, Southern Bosnia, and Herzegovina. Already in November 1993, the situation in Mostar was intolerable for the mixed civil population (Muslim and Croatian), which was steadily declining. Civilians were constantly targeted by snipers and subject to regular artillery and mortar bombardments. They were living in no more than a ghetto that was open to limited UN military and humanitarian assistance. After eight months of intensive contacts and service in this area (often at the risk of his life, as acknowledged by his supervisors Victor Andreev and Cedric Thornberry), Benabou formulated, with the contribution of both political and military leaders of the parties in conflict, the outline for a political initiative in Mostar, which obtained the blessing and the support of the Croats, Muslims, and UN authorities. Croatian President Franjo Tudjman and Harris Silajdzic, the prime minister of Bosnia and Herzegovina, commended this initiative, praising the courage it took to confront the realities and to define honestly the state of affairs that existed in reality. Later, the prosecutor in the trial at The Hague International Crime Tribunal for former Yugoslavia referred positively to the contribution of Benabou's numerous field reports to the indictment of war criminals. Upon his request, Benabou appeared at the court from 21st to the 25th of January 2008, fourteen years after he completed his mission, in closed session, and the court thanked Israel for that crucial testimony, stressing that it was entirely acknowledged by the court as valid evidence.

Albert Benabou landed in the midst of the stormy war between ethnic entities struggling for self-determination, deeply loathing each other, and butchering their closest neighbors after having lived side by side with them for generations. He witnessed the vilest conduct of humans before his eyes and often was called to operate in the midst of clashes, rampages, and carnage in the war between Croats, Muslims, and Serbs, and was himself targeted more than once with rockets and machine guns. As observed by Cedric Thornberry, head of civil affairs for the former Yugoslavia, and his direct supervisor, Benabou functioned, in the war zone, constantly risking his life[103]. Lord David Owen, a UN mediator, Mate Boban, the Croatian president of Herzeg in Bosnia-Herzegovina, and other officials who operated for the United Nations occasionally shared with him some of those chaotic and threatening experiences while traveling over land or in the air. Benabou described the

---

[103] See footnote 94.

UN NORMOVCOM (Norwegian Movement Communication—in charge of the air transport from Sarajevo) as Maybe Airlines—when flying a UN plane, everything was always in order, except the destination. Maybe you arrived, maybe you didn't. He recorded a large number of hazardous attacks against him during his travels on duty, and his UN passport was handled by the proper department of the United Nations, the "Stamp Company" as humorously dubbed by his Norwegian colleagues (see the picture below), which became part of the crystallizing local UN folklore.

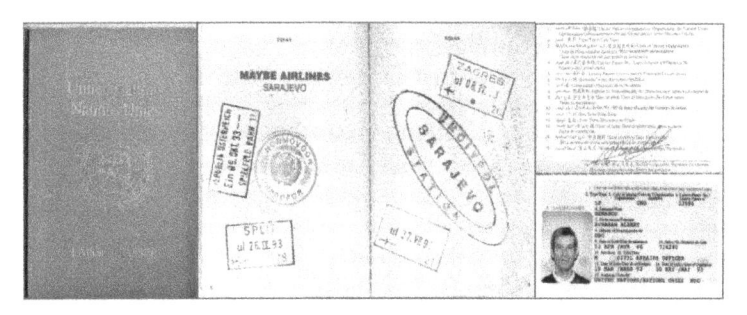

In February 1993, the Security Council of the United Nations passed its Resolution 808, committing the international community to create an International Criminal Tribunal to try those responsible for serious violations of international humanitarian law, perpetrated in the territory of former Yugoslavia since 1991, in a vain attempt to bring to a halt the hostilities between the warring parties, or at least to reduce the intensity of the massacres. Faithful to his culture as an Israeli defense forces officer, and having no axe to grind or interest to satisfy in the Bosnian War, Albert Benabou's reports from the war zone were factual and detailed (at times with attached pictures). Much later, they would provide a key testimony in the trials held behind closed doors, which prosecuted senior Croatian political and military leaders accused of war crimes at the tribunal in The Hague. The attorney general of

*Savagery in the Heart of Europe*

the International Tribunal submitted to the court Benabou's copies of hundreds of his field reports and documents, which he had cautiously and discretely preserved until then. Their content is publicly exposed for the first time in this volume.

Regardless of the combat situation, Benabou established and managed the Civil Affairs Office of UNPROFOR located in Mostar, in southern Bosnia-Herzegovina. Out of the UN headquarters in Medjugorje, where the Spanish Battalion was posted, and Divulje (The British forces base), he coordinated and conducted the humanitarian assistance operations, which also entailed negotiating ceasefires and exchanging prisoners of war. The challenge was beyond dealing with the warring parties, who were plunged to their necks in their constant fighting, each striving and convinced that it would wipe out the other. At times the weaker participants in that all-out confrontation, particularly the Muslims, were solely driven by the thought that they might not survive. Beyond creating the proper setting for negotiations or imposing an agreement, even ad hoc and provisory, Benabou had to consider the competing and conflicting self-interests of the EU member countries participating in the international corps and avoid involvement in the intrigues bubbling underneath the surface of the seemingly correct relationships amongst the UN staff. Under such circumstances, creating a satisfactory formula where everyone was reassured that he and his country were at the core of any crucial démarche was a true tour de force, for otherwise there would have been no chance to move ahead on anything. As he later testified at the court in The Hague, sometimes, in order to execute rescue operations, he had to "dance with the wolves[104]" (the villains who were often criminals) and at other times even show up at the lion's den, at considerable risk to his safety.

---

[104] Noted in the testimony against war criminals in closed court at the Hague in February 2008.

The emergency operations of evacuation from the combat zone were of top importance. On the battleground, Benabou was often called to determine the fate of civilians or military personnel. Shuttling day and night between rival positions, he ran in endless round trips the distances between the belligerents. In view of the recurrent emergency operations, his ability to define the various levels of injuries, minor, moderate, or severe, became irrelevant, since there was no time to prioritize the order of evacuation based on such niceties. He had to act rapidly, exposed to the exchange of fire on the battlefield, and under the constraints of a permanent blockade on Muslim East Mostar, whose unfortunate inhabitants it was his duty to help. The UN headquarters in Zagreb and in New York rejected his application for granting the needed legal "international protection zone" to that war area, required for a war hospital or an infirmary to be installed in the combat zone, because the "medical" building in East Mostar was constantly targeted and bombed. Beyond this, the capacity of teams of UN MEDEVAC (Medical Evacuation) and CASEVAC (Casualties Evacuation) was limited, for hardly were the UN helicopters and ambulances allowed to access the safe perimeter of the combat theater. And then remained the problem of determining who would be evacuated or evacuated first? Upon which criteria should the emergency listings be based? Unlike other UN decisions, which could linger for months, seeking compromises and acceptable formulas, these kinds of decisions had to be made on the spot. Albert Benabou had to live constantly with these difficult dilemmas and make decisions according to his good sense. For example, the Security Council established on 6 May 1993 six "safe areas:" Sarajevo, Bihac, Tuzla, Zepa, Srebrenica, and Gorazde, protected by peace keepers, while the demand of Albert Benabou to include Mostar in the list was rejected by the UN headquarters in Zagreb and in New York. Since it was the Croatian lobby in the United States and the United Nations which prevailed in these pressures and counter pressures, Muslim East Mostar was left to bleed itself to death and destruction for an unimaginably unfair period of time. A sample of this frantic activity, as recorded in Benabou's real time diary, will best illustrate the situation.

**Wednesday, 12 May, 1993 (opening Mostar)**

Late in the night of Wednesday, 12 May, 1993, an agreement on cessation of hostilities was signed between the Croatian and Muslim forces in a pompous ceremony at the military base of SPABAT (Spanish Battalion) stationed in Medjugorje. On the ceremonial stage of official signatures, the UN mediators and the belligerent negotiators, Croats and Muslims, were all visibly exhausted and not only due to the interminable fighting of the warriors. They were concluding a full week of never-ending talks, stretching up to sixteen hours of deliberations per day. Besides, each signatory military chief of staff had to consult for some additional hours with his political superiors: General Safet Hallilovic, Commander of the Armija (Bosnian Army), with Sarajevo, and General Milivoj Petkovic, Commander of the HVO (Croatian Defense Council, the separatist Croatian Forces in Bosnia), with Zagreb. The concluded agreement focused on the battlefield in the Spanish zone of responsibility, where Croats and Muslims were slaughtering each other. The agreement stipulated the steps to be adopted for the "demilitarization of Bosnia and Herzegovina[105]." The document reconfirmed in its declaratory preamble the common will

---

[105] See Agreement on the demilitarization of Bosnia and Herzegovina concluded between General Milivoj Petkovic and General Sefer Hallilovic on the 12th of May 1993 in the presence of Lt. General Philippe Morillon.

"to establish peace within the whole territory[106]," and the commitment "to halt all hostilities and to respect the protocol of the Geneva Convention concerning the protection of victims in International armed conflicts[107]," both of which did not mean much. Many such "agreements" were signed once and again, but only seldom did they mean the end of ethnic cleansing, civilian suffering, killing, destruction of innocent civilians who were not involved in battle operations. In Mostar, which provides one example of such "agreements," the parties also agreed on specific articles trying to apply in practice that declarative preamble.

Freedom of movement, particularly for UNPROFOR personnel, humanitarian aid agencies, and all logistic supply and support convoys of both parties and on all routes, that is to say: Metkovic-Mostar-Tarcin-Kiseljak-Zenica-Tuzla and Jablanica-Prozor-Gornji-Vakuf-Travnik. Those roads were in fact permanently blocked and subject to constant attacks. The civil population living along those roads was in fact sealed off, since the access to it was targeted by the bombardments and sniper fire. They were actually trapped, struggling for survival and depending on the rare openings of traffic for the delivery of basic provisions.

During the withdrawal of armed forces at 1800 hours on the same day, all units would be confined to locations beyond the lines as indicated on an attached map. The implementation of this item was a *sine qua non* for the realization of the former article on freedom of movement.

Prisoners, most of whom were Muslim civilian detainees, were likely to be evacuated from Mostar and the environs in the frame of a planned ethnic cleansing envisaged by the Croats. In order to stop that process

---
[106] ibid.
[107] ibid.

and generate a pressure on the Croats, this issue was linked to the exchange of POW (prisoners of war), most of them Croats. Both listings were to be presented to the ICRC (International Committee of the Red Cross) by 13 May 1993, at 1200 hours.

In the return of displaced persons, both sides committed themselves to provide assistance in restoring the displaced people to their own properties or places of residence, under the guarantee of safety and security. Everyone around the table was aware that contrary to the European culture and tradition of peace arrangements in which those agreements were concluded, in Bosnia the expectations arising therefrom would never be realized. Quite the reverse, each party would be obviously invited to settle the uprooted population elsewhere, and only a slight minority of the displaced would ever be allowed to return to their homes. Anyone who was familiar with the permanent Palestinian claim for the "right of return" and with the continued festering of their problem knew that displaced people in time of war stood very little chance of repatriation.

Deployment of UNPROFOR, SPABAT was restricted to Medjugorje, located in the suburbs of Mostar. The Croats opposed any attempt of patrolling any part of the city of Mostar (East or West) by any UN forces. The Spaniards seemingly manifested an "understanding" of the needs of the fellow Catholic Croats, and they decided to deploy and accommodate one company of their Spanish Battalion in Mostar. The Croats, relying on the "understanding" of the Spanish, ignored that stipulation of the agreement for many months[108].

---

[108] See various reports reflecting this problematic approach including testimonies at the ICTY court in the Hague. Indeed, General Morillon manifested more than once his impatience vis-à-vis the Spanish Battalion acting as "new comers" in International missions.

Albert Benabou chaired the opening of those negotiations between the parties at the UN outpost in Kiseljak and their follow-up at the SPABAT headquarters in Medjugorje. Newly appointed as the UNPROFOR civil affairs officer coordinator in the region of Mostar, he was requested to assist in the negotiations between the Croatian and Muslim parties. Victor Andreev, the UNPROFOR civil affairs chief coordinator in Bosnia-Herzegovina, considered that the newly arrived Israeli official was the appropriate UN officer to stand by the deputy commander of the UNPROFOR forces, the Spanish Lieutenant General Luis Feliu, who launched the talks. For the first time in history, Spain also was participating in a UN peace keeping mission. Its military group, *Agrupacion Tactica Canarias*, which was a battle group of legionnaires, was detached to UNPROFOR—the United Nations Protection Force assigned to protect the civil population during the armed conflict in Former Yugoslavia. SPABAT's zone of responsibility covered the city of Mostar and its surroundings. Mostar is the county town of Herzegovina, recognized for its multicultural and historic heritage, where Muslims, Croats, and Serbs reached, during many periods of time, a fragile equilibrium beyond their everlasting mutual hatred. This spectacularly beautiful region, crossed by the restless water flow of the Neretva River, offers a dazzling scenery of majestic nature in the midst of the mountain chain of the Dinaric Alps, which abound in flora and fauna. While projecting the illusion of a serene and unperturbed nature, this enchanting area turned out to be the theater of one of the most violent confrontations during the war in Bosnia-Herzegovina. The stunning landscape could not hide the fact that Mostar, where Croats and Muslims were now slaughtering each other, stood out for being a strategic crossroads in southern Herzegovina, connecting vital routes from Sarajevo to the Adriatic Sea passing by Travnik and central Bosnia. Colonel

Angel Morales, chief officer of SPABAT, and Albert Benabou, the civil affair officer, were both novices in the corridors of power in the UN peace keeping forces and in charge of this highly sensitive area. But it would take a very brief time for both of them to realize that the ground rules in the terrain reflected the complexity of the conflicting interests of each participating European nation in UNPROFOR.

The first lesson was offered upon the landing in Medjugorje, on 9 May 1993, of General Philippe Morillon, commander of the UN forces in former Yugoslavia. He decided to take over the lead of the negotiations and to handle personally the discussions between the parties. At that point, the ball rolling between the parties was not commensurate with the lofty goals spelled out by the terms of the "comprehensive agreement[109]" between Croats and Muslims for the "demilitarization of Bosnia-Herzegovina[110]." Marching into the dining room, which was to serve as the meeting hall as well, General Morillon announced, in a spectacular entrance, "Here, I am the chief[111]." Albert Benabou felt pushed aside. Getting closer to his newly found friend, the SPABAT Commander Colonel Angel Morales, he whispered in his ears, "Where are the Indians, his troops[112]?" Morillon was in fact repeating the same error he had committed in the past when signing with the Serbian General, Ratko Mladic, the accords for the evacuation of Srebrenica. Rushing to get to the end results, he had not been attentive to the military developments on the ground in Srebrenica and to the manipulations at the time of the shrewd Serbian officer. Indeed, though Mladic did evacuate his forces from the city, as he had

---

[109] See Agreement on the demilitarization of Bosnia and Herzegovina concluded between General Milivoj Petkovic and General Sefer Hallilovic on the 12th of May 1993 in the presence of Lt. General Phillipe Morillon.
[110] ibid.
[111] Recorded in the personal memoirs of Albert Benabou of the War in Bosnia.
[112] ibid.

pledged in the agreement, he redeployed them on the "Opstina," the suburb area dominating and totally controlling access to the city (see map in pictures). In other words, there was no connection between the signed documents and their application in the field, neither with the Serbs in Srebrenica nor with the Croats in Mostar. All of them were declaring in the meeting room whatever pleased Morillon's ears and were signing without any intention to implement. They were both pursuing their hostilities in the terrain with a view of realizing what they had concretely envisaged and planned, particularly concerning the ethnic cleansing of "unwanted populations," i.e. Muslims from Srebrenica and Mostar.

This attitude derived from the firm belief among all war participants that they could still hold on or even reverse the situation on the battlefield. In West Mostar, the Croats were planning to intensify the military operations and the ethnic

Among the UN Spanish Officers: Colonel Angel Morales praising with a wide smile the achievement of his Battalion to General Philippe Morillon. Morillon listens politely more concerned by his negotiations between the warring parties: Muslims and Croats

cleansing of Muslims. In East Mostar, the Muslims were determined to reinforce their defensive positions and gain terrain. Benabou learned about these plans directly from his ongoing contacts with the warring parties. The Defense Information Staff of BRITFOR (British Forces), positioned on the Adriatic coast in Divulje barracks, reaffirmed this state of mind and tendency among the military and political decision makers in its accurate intelligence reports. In the framework of UNPROFOR, the member countries of the western European Union shared and exchanged, on a permanent basis, military information and evaluations. Therefore, General Morillon was updated from reliable sources and should have realized that none of the signatories of the agreements, neither the Croats nor the Muslims (nor the Serbs for that matter) intended to apply them in the real world. Each party was in fact pulling to his side, aiming for "the largest possible piece of the blanket[113]" to cover his strategic intentions and uncover the counterpart plans. Basically, they were pursuing the same objective, weakening as much as possible the terms of the agreement and applying some sort of a vague accord that could facilitate their troop movement and/or justify their redeployment in the future. Their obvious respective goals in those negotiations were to improve their immediate tactical positions, something that they could not do under Tito in federal Yugoslavia but could ironically try to advance under the UN "peace keeping" umbrella. General Milivoj Petkovic had been just appointed by Franjo Tudjman, the Croatian president, as the top military man in Zagreb. Petkovic manifested a hands-off approach, acting as a maestro in military strategy who was trusted with pulling off magic solutions that would assure the victory of the Croats. Apart from his bosses in Zagreb, whom he updated regularly, he frequently

---

[113] ibid.

informed also Mate Boban, the Croatian president of Herzeg-Bosnia, who operated in West Mostar where Prime Minister Jadranko Prlic managed the business of the area, gathering around him local leaders and decision makers.

Prior to the agreement, on 7 May, Benabou had reported in a SITREP (Situation Report) that the tension between Croats and Muslims had reached a new high. Due to the recorded military pressure exercised by the HVO forces in the zone, the military had anticipated a conflagration in the region, and both the British and Spanish analysts recognized the same state of affairs. Nor could the Muslim BiH Armija afford a defeat for, due to the dwindling resources which economically strained most of Bosnia- Herzegovina, a military collapse would doom the future of the Bosnian state altogether and precipitate its disintegration. However, among the Croatian military and political leadership of Herzeg-Bosnia, it was evident that violence between HVO and BiH Forces had become inevitable. It was only a question of choosing the appropriate pretext, circumstances, and timing to trigger the military clashes. Mr. Vladislav Pogarcic, the adviser for International Affairs to Mate Boban, the president of the self-declared Herzeg- Bosnia, confirmed that the only way to avoid bloodshed consisted of compelling the three sides to sit around a negotiation table and agree on the implementation of the Vance-Owen Plan, after it had been rejected and declared dead by all sides! However, before the ink dried on the signatures of the agreement, Petkovic made it clear that nothing would come out of this paper. He had just arrived to the arena, determined to crush the Muslims of Mostar, military and civilians, more effectively than the Croatian military chiefs who had preceded him. In addition, Hallilovic, the Muslim military chief, was the wrong person in the wrong place, for he revealed flexibility when assertiveness and self-confidence were expected from him. This poorly trained negotiator hoped, nearly beyond all hope, to relieve the Muslim population caught in the infernal siege in East Mostar, but in spite of being choked by the Croatian state of siege, the besieged were more determined than him to resist and to hold on. In fact, Hallilovic estimated that the pressure of the French on the Croats would help him to obtain results, and that allowed him to persist in his diplomatic expectations at a time when a swift military approach was needed.

Ultimately, ignoring the contribution of Benabou to the negotiations, Morillon excluded him from cosigning the final document of the agreement, for his personal pride and that of France and Europe was at stake. In addition to changing the terms of the agreement and modifying the direction of the talks, he preferred to honor his French compatriot, Jean-Pierre Thebault, in the ratification of the agreement. The latter indeed represented the EUM (European Union Monitoring) and considered his participation as a high prize; therefore, he hurried to sign without even verifying the content or the viability of the agreement, or even raising essential questions. That was how personal vanity and conflicts of interests took priority over issues of fairness, durability, credibility, and conflict resolution. Indeed, the differences between the terms of the finalized agreement and the process that had been initiated by Benabou were flagrant. Irritated by what he thought was the wrong approach of Morillon, Benabou kept silent. He initiated a consultation with Victor Andreev, the chief civil coordinator for Bosnia-Herzegovina via INMARSAT (International Maritime Satellite Telecommunication, a UN body set up for the purpose of establishing a satellite communications network for the maritime community, but the UN capitalized on it and used it for all terrestrial communication in the war in former Yugoslavia). Benabou clarified his opinion and transmitted on the same day a detailed report to the headquarters in Zagreb and Kiseljak. In any event, there was no time to spend arguing about the end results of those negotiations, for Benabou intended to act concretely on the ground with a view to protecting the Muslim populations that were abandoned to their fate for certain massacre, contrary to the core of the UN-PROFOR mandate in former Yugoslavia. But for this Israeli officer, this mission went without saying, beyond any doubt, ambiguity, or hesitation, something which could hardly be said of UN bureaucrats in general.

All parties admitted that, on the same day of its ratification, the document became null, void, and irrelevant, since no one intended to apply it or enforce its fulfillment. The main concern of Benabou focused on regaining, as soon as possible, in partnership with Spanish Colonel Morales, the confidence of the belligerents and leading to a specific dialogue between them on a restricted mutually agreed agenda, instead of sinking into formulas, wide-ranging agreements and pompous ceremonies, which brought much temporary glory and glamour to their signatories, all right, but there was no substance to them. Reviewing the stages to be followed, Benabou took advantage of the fact that his signature as the new UNPROFOR civil affairs officer in the region did not figure in the agreement, because he had not been allowed by Morillon to participate. In the consultations between Benabou, Andreev, and Morales, it was decided to ignore this last document and notify the Croats and the Muslims that the newly appointed civil affairs officer was not fooled by their signatures, for the only seemingly "agreed" upon item therein was the implied ongoing rampage, destruction, and carnage. The Spanish Colonel, Angel Morales, adopted the same attitude and had also abstained from cosigning the document. As a course of action, Benabou was resolute to target limited but realizable objectives. Namely, since these people, Croats and Muslims alike, had lived not long ago as one peaceful community, he banked on their former relations and aspired to install a constructive mechanism based on the human contacts between the leaders for the benefit of the noncombatant civilians who had been drawn into the war and become its victims. This courageous and out-of-the-box approach, however, would not spare Benabou his share of naive errors.

**Friday, 14 May, 1993**

Benabou spent the night of 13 to 14 May negotiating and shuttling between the headquarters of the Bosnian Armija forces and the Croatian Military Organization (HVO). His objective was to obtain an immediate agreement for a food convoy towards the eastern part of Mostar, for famine had become rampant in the besieged city, and there was an urgent need for emergency medical supplies. Due to the lack of basic hygiene, the civil affairs officer and his staff even feared the beginning of an epidemic. Late in the night of 13 May, Benabou requested a reconnaissance patrol to the war zone. Accompanied by Colonel Morales and Captain Acuña, the SPABAT intelligence officer, they moved deep into the bombed area in a Spanish APC (armored personnel carrier), which, though easy to maneuver, had suffered from accidents due to instability in slippery terrain. Colonel Morales insisted to verify the planned track for the convoy before allowing its entrance to the city in the morning of November 14. The UN officials were all astounded by the violence which was revealed to them. The streets of Mostar and particularly the "Boulevard," which was used as a line of demarcation between Croats and Muslims, were devastated by fires of the mutual bombardments. The trees and the buildings burning in the flames offered a glowing light of hell. A multitude of questions leaped to mind: Where are the people? Where is the city? Where has the cultural, intellectual, and social harmony of this community gone? Where did the softness of living along the banks of the Neretva disappear? Did it ever exist? It was as if everything was suddenly smashed, pulverized, banalized. At a time of profound divisions and yawning enmities, everyone seemed united by the shortage of electricity and running water, and everyone was starved for bread and other foods. Deep misery, a shared anxiety, and an overwhelming uncertainty seemed to unite these people across the divide in this torn apart country. Devastation and brutality reigned supreme, making recognizable a graffiti on one of the carbonized walls, which poignantly implored, "Please Tito, come back[114]." Another unfortunate victim, who could not contain his bitter sense of humor, responded for Tito, "Do you think that I've lost my mind?![115]"

The UN convoys of provisions, which were becoming more and more infrequent, had set the new tempo of life in this besieged city in ruin. Following that night of negotiations, at last, the military units of both parties received, at dawn in the early morning of Friday 14 May, the order from their respective headquarters to ceasefire during the day of 14 May, 1993, between 0500h and 1700h. This pause in the battlefield was calculated to facilitate and ensure the safe passage of the convoy. The relevant military ordinances were simultaneously addressed to the troops deployed on the line of confrontation on each of the two banks of the Neretva. The Croatian General Petkovic and the Bosnian General Hallilovic had confirmed that they would guarantee the passage of the convoy of food and medicine as well as the international personnel which took part in this operation, i.e. the representatives of the UNHCR, of the International

---
[114] ibid.
[115] ibid.

Committee of the Red Cross, the International Military Observers, the Committee for the Refugees, the Military Forces of SPABAT (Spanish Battalion) as well as the delegates of the European Union. "We started to breathe with relief and perceive the light at the end of the tunnel after working many hours on maps and on aerial and panoramic photographs of reconnaissance," Benabou noted in his Journal. The procedures were duly established and finalized with the Croatian and Bosnian generals, as well as with the international organizations.

At the last minute before departure, startled by the last-minute request of Benabou, Colonel Morales was speechless. He was visibly embarrassed by the demand that Albert Benabou presented to the Croatian and Muslim generals, inviting both of them to join him in his APC till the crossing of the last Croatian military checkpoint was completed. In other words, he requested their presence at each roadblock and implied that they were sort of hostage-guarantors of the safe passage of the entire convoy, something the UN troops were not accustomed to require. The chief of information of the Spanish Battalion, Commander Carlos Murillo de Salas, tried to convince Benabou to renounce this, explaining that the situation was already complicated enough and that there was little chance that the generals would consent to play this unexpected game. He tried to persuade recalcitrant Benabou that there were enough elements in place to secure the success of the operation, even without implementing what seemed an unusual demand. Adamant, Benabou refused to let go, though he knew that his obstinacy, which often served him well, might turn against him in a delicate and flimsy situation like this. He feared a failure of the operation, replicating the situation where General Morillon had been trapped in Srebrenica. Although the convoy was well prepared, Benabou insisted he did not intend to move without the presence of the two enemy generals in his Spanish armored vehicle. This incident highlighted a state of affairs which did not exist within a regular army hierarchy, in which orders were carried out without question, and if they were not, then court-martial awaited the violators. In the mix of nationalities, sensitivities, interests and semi-autonomy of the various UN units, it turned out that orders could be negotiated, strict rules made flexible and almost democratic debates could take place.

One hour and a half passed, awaiting the denouement of this last minute snag and the final order to roll the convoy, but all the efforts, negotiations, and explanations appeared to drive towards a dead end. A heavy rain started to fall, which not only did not cool the spirits but became an additional obstacle, which harassed all day and stopped only at night. At dawn, fourteen heavy trucks loaded with all the relief and goodies one could offer to a starving civil population, which had been besieged for more than a month, were already assembled and parked along the fence by the gate of the base. A dozen of those Spanish APCs, loaded with medicine and sensitive equipment, were also ready to accompany the trucks. The soldiers had been waiting for the order to move since 4:00 a.m. Their bodies were half numbed by the long wait on their armored vehicles, but no man moved a muscle. All the attention was fixed on the stubbornness of Benabou. The Commander Carlos de Salas sermonized to him, "We hold the guarantee for a successful operation. If we ask for too much, we are likely to lose all of it[116]." Or as he put it, "*Alberto, eso es demasiado*[117]," (Albert, that is too much). Benabou looked deep in the eyes of de Salas and explained, "It is not a question of chivalry or of a word of honor. Those are chiefs of war. We must have them permanently with

---
[116] ibid.
[117] ibid.

us during the movement of the convoy[118]." He thought that even though they had committed themselves to a momentary ceasefire, he could hardly rely on their declarations, because the war did not only unfold between the parties but also between factions on the same side, and he feared lest the instructions transmitted through the regular chain of command would not be respected by all units. Suddenly Colonel Morales popped out of his office, walked in a firm step towards Benabou, and announced with a radiant face, on the tone of an order, "*Ya esta. ¡Los dos vienen!*[119]" (There it is. Those two are coming). Morales had just received the confirmation that both generals would be accompanying the convoy. They had received the authorization from their respective political leadership (Zagreb and Sarajevo) to join the humanitarian convoy up to the crossing of the last military roadblocks.

Secured by the Spanish Battalion, Albert Benabou is in the lead of a food convoy in the War Zone. He insisted having the Croat and the Muslim Generals accompanying the UN troops.

---

[118] ibid.
[119] ibid.

At last, the convoy was ready to leave. Close to three hundred tons of food and medical materials stood to be distributed between the Croatian part (Western) and Muslim part (Eastern) of the town of Mostar. Approaching the first Croatian military checkpoint, Sasha, the faithful interpreter of Albert Benabou all along his mission in Bosnia, sensed fear pressuring her guts. She caught the furtive glance of Benabou, who was scrutinizing from the turret of the APC the surroundings of the first military roadblock. Soldiers of the HVO (*Hrvatske Vojne Organizatsje*—Croatian Military Organization) were ducking in the woods, behind each poplar, along the straight road that sliced through the forest. Armed with automatic machine guns, they were in a shooting position, the barrel of their guns pointing to the trail of the convoy. Serbs, Croats, or Muslims, all of them had been trained in the former Yugoslav Army. Determined to achieve their goal, they shared the same military culture. Excellent artillery officers, they would not hesitate to pound the city and massacre the population, even in the presence of the representatives of the international community. Therefore, unless the commanding generals were there, there was no telling what might happen. Taking a deep breath, Sasha succeeded to silence her inner anxieties and started doing her job. Standing by Albert Benabou, she acted as the precious linguistic bond translating and interpreting from Serbo-Croatian into English and back. Born to a Serbian father and a Croatian mother, she would be often accused by each side for assisting the United Nations and was perceived as a traitor to the cause of her people. The Croatian commander of the checkpoint, his fair hair tied into a ponytail with a leather cord and two meters (seven feet) tall, appeared to Albert Benabou like a player from the Jugoplastika Split basketball team in a game against Maccabi Tel Aviv competing for the European Cup. Casually carrying his gun over his shoulder, the giant stopped the convoy, looking down with contempt at Albert Benabou and Alexandra Milankovic (Sasha) and walked to their encounter. Sasha did her job, translating the tense dialogue between Albert and the Croat. She avoided a direct look at either of the two men clashing through her because she had never been trained for such a situation. She spoke quickly, weighing her words, in an effort to retransmit the most precisely possible terms of Albert in Serbo-Croat. Now, the very life of thousands of inhabitants, besieged within Mostar, depended on her translation. But whatever she said or did, her people would consider her as a turncoat at the service of the United Nations, and in that capacity, she became the articulated voice of Benabou since he had chosen her for the job in their first meeting in Kiseljak. She became the "alter voice" of Albert Benabou and formed one bloc with the Israeli, who had invited her to be his interpreter in their first meeting in Kiseljak, not far from Sarajevo.

Whatever ideological camp one chooses, civil war can distort any sense of compassion and humanism. In the village of Kiseljak, located some ten kilometers from Sarajevo, Alexandra Milankovic, nicknamed Sasha, had been introduced to Albert Benabou by Victor Andreev, coordinator of the civil affairs of UPROFOR for Bosnia-Herzegovina. The meeting was held in a former Yugoslav military base, in one of the old offices hardly illuminated by a shy ray of sun. Sasha was desperately looking for a job, for she had to survive the hardships of war and support her mother and her brother, who were trapped in Sarajevo. Not very inclined to recruit a woman under the circumstances of a war in which no code of honor seemed to function, Albert was hesitant. On the other hand, Sasha projected a force of will that seemed able to overcome any difficulty. Watching her sitting on her bench, she projected firmness and strength of will, though she appeared frail. He decided to recruit her and push on with her help with his initial curiosity to grasp the reasons of this Bosnian War, the underlying volcano of savagery, which he and others had believed had been deadened forever after World War II.

On that day of Friday, 14 May, which incidentally coincided with Israel's first Independence Day, when the fledgling state of Israel was declared on 14 May, 1948, amidst war, Albert and Sasha, his interpreter, faced that giant Croatian guard in the first roadblock, while the entire humanitarian convoy trailed them, waiting for permission to cross, consisting of fourteen heavy trucks of UNHCR, the Red Cross, and other humanitarian agencies. A heavy silence and atmosphere of expectation reigned, for any ill calculated move, any uncautious tone of speech, and any smallest inattention to detail could easily burst into an act of murder. The UN personnel were sheltered in their armored cars, and no one was willing to make the first move. The trucks were surrounded on all sides by the Spanish armored vehicles for protection, under the command of Colonel Morales (nicknamed by some bad mouths in the UNPROFOR Headquarters as "Colonel More-or Less"), who sported his green neckerchief in the fashion of the ancient Spanish warriors. In the middle of the convoy there were five armored cars that Benabou had demanded to project power, in spite of the total absence of weapons in its midst. Ignoring the threat of the guns, which were hidden behind the huge poplars that overshadowed the scene, Benabou pursued his negotiations with the giant guard, who in fact held the key for any access to Mostar. Albert, using his Sasha intermediary, was striving to gain access, but the guard did not seem persuaded to give way. He held his Kalashnikov in a way signaling that the law was made at that roadblock by him, and ignoring the long convoy behind them, he addressed Albert and Sasha, who were rushing towards him. *"Nema Passage"* (No passage), he uttered, while Sasha was asked by Albert to submit the proper documentation, signed by the political and military chiefs of both Croats and Muslims, to the effect that the passage should be open. This was one of the supreme absurdities of the war, in which the United Nations and its members were in fact supplicating to extend assistance to the warring parties and their starving civilians whom no one else cared for, while the parties themselves were "doing a favor to the world[120]" for allowing aid to come, instead of begging for it themselves, for their starving people.

"This is worth nothing,[121]" replied the guard after a quick glance at the documents, and he ordered the five soldiers stationed with him on the roadblock to load their weapons. Facing this situation, Albert reiterated that he, "the Israeli," as he was called and known in the Mostar area, would insist on the passage of the convoy even if Presidents Tudjman and Boban should have to be alerted personally. He was self-assured due to the presence of the two "hostage" generals of the rival forces, Petkovic and Hallilovic, whom he sheltered in one of the Spanish armored cars of the convoy. Perspiring profusely, the two generals observed the arena from the interior of their armored car, evidently dumbfounded by the new civil affairs officer who had arrived on the scene only ten days earlier and seemed already in command of the local agenda, undeterred by the war, bloodshed, violence, and brutality that were unfolding before his eyes. Most of the participants in the convoy had not taken a rest for about sixty hours in a row, the drivers of the heavy trucks had been at the wheel all night, and the Spanish personnel had been on alert to join their convoy since 4:00 a.m. It was already Friday afternoon, which for Albert meant the approaching Sabbath. His thoughts wandered to his family, whom he had left in

---

[120] ibid.
[121] ibid.

Jerusalem behind him. He was almost itching to call his wife and remind her that the time had come to kindle the Sabbath candles, and, imagining that had he been at home, it would have been time soon to go to the synagogue of his neighborhood in Jerusalem.

During the preceding sixty hours, Benabou had led exhausting talks, with all parties participating: Muslims and Croats, civil and military, UN and humanitarian NGOs, all attending the meeting at the Spanish headquarters in Medjugorje. Spanish Captain Carlos de Salas labored through maps to identify exactly the itinerary of the convoy which Benabou was to lead. The latter had been trained in the hostile deserts of Sinai and the Negev where no prominent features existed to facilitate navigation, therefore having to follow compass and stars in clear summer nights. In Bosnia, he found pleasure in orienting himself on the mountains, rivers, valleys, and forests which characterized the landscape where he was operating. Still facing the guard and uncertain about the access he was seeking, Benabou began worrying that the European troops and personnel, who were waiting for his breakthrough, might get to the limits of their patience, endurance, and nerves, especially those originating from places which had not witnessed acts of war in the past half century. He sensed that the gun barrel of the guard was directed at him, and he ordered Sasha to translate, "What are you up to now?[122]" He pushed away the threatening gun and asked Sasha to translate, "Call Vladislav Pogarcic, who is at President Mate Boban's office.[123]" The guard reluctantly did, and finally the roadblock was lifted. Delighted by this development, the personnel began smiling, and the trucks started off one after the other. They were elated to cross this last segment of the road, which linked the airport to the besieged and starved city.

---

[122] ibid.
[123] ibid.

Albert also was relieved, though no sign of his emotions could be seen on his stoic face. Thoughts quickly tumbled in his head, and his heart was beating at an accelerated pace. He was trying to practice in those tense moments the lessons he had learned at the Israeli officers school, where he had been trained years back, namely to act rapidly and slowly at the same time, that is to review deliberately, one by one, all the necessary steps to be taken, but at the same time to grasp the whole picture and not to lose sight of the desired results. Sasha, who found her place in the first vehicle of the convoy, was already far away as Albert was reviewing all vehicles, to the last, to make sure that they had all crossed the roadblock. Finally, he took his seat near the driver of the last car in the convoy, somewhat relieving the tensions from his aching body, and his vehicle plunged behind all others into the thick of the forest.

During a brief moment of a pause, Benabou regained the head of the convoy. His Spanish colleagues, Morales and de Salas, were waiting for him at the head of the procession, while Generals Petkovic and Hallilovic were elated to leave their UN-marked armored car after it had crossed the last roadblock. Between Benabou and the Spanish officers a complicity born out of the camaraderie of warriors began to take shape and to be articulated through the sparks in the eyes of the accomplices, who said little, but understood it all. Suddenly, the enormous explosion of a shell hit the rear of the convoy, soon followed by another in the front. Understanding that the Croats were dispatching to him a signal of intimidation, Benabou ordered his driver to pursue his trajectory at the same pace, even as the shelling of the convoy did not relent. Shells continued to fall in front and from behind, on the right and the left, but far enough away so as not to cause any casualties among the UN personnel. Benabou thought that a small distance was yet to be covered before the convoy could complete its mission without yielding to the Croatian menace. The shelling continued, forming a "guard of honor" in fire accompanying the convoy in its slow advance.

"We are here!" clamored Sasha, indicating that the convoy had reached the entrance to Mostar. As an echo to her jubilant clamor, it was possible to hear the deafening rain of shells and bombs, which landed on the town, covered by the yet stronger human shouts of the destitute refugees, who must have been exhilarated to have perceived the convoy of redemption approaching. But the bombs and the shells, insensitive to the human suffering of the starving people, did not recede. Without regard to the projectiles which fell constantly around them, the people of Mostar also seemed insensitive to the menace that was being showered on them, God (or Allah) knew where from. In any case, the bread and water brought in by the United Nations, at great risk, seemed much rarer than the abundance of bombs which descended on them, for it always seemed that the regularity with which the bomb supply was assured and punctuated the rhythm of life of those unfortunate people on both sides of the divide, took much precedence upon milk for the starving children, or bread and water for the desperate victims of the war. The Boulevard, a sort of natural divide between the Muslim and the Croatian parts of the town, was devastated and in ruins. The streets were burned and destroyed, while human phantoms were running along the last vestiges of the large Ottoman public buildings to dodge the bombs and avoid injury. A spectacle of apocalypse reigned throughout the remnants of this town, which threatened at any moment to pulverize in the air into dust without leaving a trace.

For the entire duration of the humanitarian operation, the bombardment of the Muslim part of the city did not recede. Nonetheless, the Spanish Battalion managed to connect with the Muslim population, under the constant fire of the Croatian artillery. Petkovic, who maintained his contacts with the United Nations, routinely threw the burden of responsibility on the Croatian political leaders, whom he accused of not respecting their own pledges, for they sought to impress upon the Muslim population that it was still at the mercy of Croatia in spite of the presence of the United Nations, meaning that the United Nations were incapable of offering them protection. However, despite the fires which broke out in East Mostar, the population felt that it could be helped from the outside, and in spite of the unrelenting attacks and bombardments on them, the issue of obtaining new provisions and drinking water was paramount in their minds. They felt encouraged from the outside to hold on, and some of them even began to see the light at the end of the tunnel. "*Voda, kruch*!!!" (water, bread!), were the words one heard most. Occasionally, emerging out of nowhere, a crowd of miserable destitutes demanded the right to live or to survive. Men and women, hardly dressed in rags and shredded clothes, ran after the UN convoy, incessantly crying for water and bread, and that heart-tearing long litany of supplications, born out of extreme suffering and of living on the brink, never left Albert and the others during the duration of their mission.

At Benabou's instigation, the convoy stopped at a subterranean depot in order to unload part of the provisions there: water, flour, and dry and non-perishable grains, which restocked the desperately empty storage space. Out of the blue, a well dressed man in a faded gray uniform and meticulously groomed moustache approached him, offered a handshake, and asked:

"Mr. Benabou! I am Tzakan Alikadic, the person you contacted by radio prior to the departure of the convoy from Medjugorje."

"*Doberdan*! (Good day!)," responded Benabou in the local language.

*"Dobro docli Mostaru,* (Welcome to Mostar)," answered Alya Alikadic, nicknamed Tzakan, his eyes smiling in delight.

This brief introduction sufficed for Tzakan to invite Benabou to follow him to the Mostar hospital. The two men walked to the premises, surrounded by hundreds of children, who otherwise wandered in idleness in those empty streets conquered by war and death. A deep and lasting relationship had just been born between Benabou and Tzakan when they firmly shook hands amidst the rain of bombs and shells which enveloped them. Benabou reflected upon the strange state of affairs in war, where people are allowed to spare their sentimentality and to spend their emotions only on worthwhile matters, for the perennial feeling of danger and urgency and the truth which looked one in the face did not let one trivialize one's existence. So, when he was looking Tzakan in his penetrating eyes, that cultivated Muslim inhabitant of Mostar, who was an admirer of Israel, was being motivated by almost the same thoughts and ideas as his visiting interlocutor. Hence the total confidence that they placed in each other and the mutual trust and understanding they developed in the coming months. Jewish Benabou and Muslim Alikadic did in fact transcend their religious and cultural biases to distill from them an exemplary relationship between them, founded on a limitless belief that brotherhood between them facilitated their common walk, hand in hand, to a common destiny, be it in paradise or in hell. Ultimately, while the American Edward Joseph affectionately imputed the title, "the Star of Mostar" to Benabou, sober and down-to-earth Tzakan, followed by his entire Mostar community, clung to his, "Brother from the Orient[124]" epithet.

The two new friends got to the "hospital," the only improvised one in Mostar under siege. That was an old building,

---

[124] ibid.

whose roof had been damaged by artillery shells. In the nearby alley, Albert Benabou met Dr. Dragan Milavic, the director of this facility of fortune that was deprived of the most basic equipment and of medicine. Without being much concerned about niceties and courtesy, the doctor rushed to the convoy to try to lay his hands urgently on what he could, of all the requirements that he had listed, ordered, and hoped for, but only a fraction of which he could hope to receive. For better protection, the medical supplies were placed in one of the armored vehicles of the convoy. Under the hurried and confused directions of the doctor, the armored car backed up to unload its precious cargo, and the Spanish soldiers carried out that mission swiftly and effectively. The doctor was frantically opening the boxes to verify their contents, finally admitting in despair that his installation, which could hardly be called a clinic, was again facing catastrophe, since it was no longer capable of treating the civilians wounded in the war zone. He decried in his language his situation, lamenting the total depletion of anesthetics, which forced him to chain-operate on civilians, both children and adults, using alcoholic drinks that were manufactured locally by the besieged inhabitants. "Did you ever hear the cries of a child screaming from pain as he is amputated without anesthesia[125]?" he explained by questioning. Benabou was consternated by this drama, and he sought a moment when the doctor came back to his senses and could again reason rationally to ask him to evaluate the needs and let him try to resolve the problem urgently.

In basic English, the doctor decried, "I must anesthesia, I must, I must, much and fast[126]!" He also tried to explain that he needed a respiratory unit to equip a room which he wanted to turn into an operation theater. Dismayed by the doctor's despair, Benabou promised to transmit the request

---

[125] ibid.
[126] ibid.

urgently to the highest authorities of the United Nations and of the other international medical and humanitarian organizations. The doctor also explained that since his "hospital" was not recognized as a "war hospital," it was in fact abandoned to the shooting and shelling of the Croatian forces. Later, Victor Andreev would explain to Benabou that recognition as a "war hospital" depended on the Security Council of the United Nations, and such recognition would not happen until the end of kidnapping of UN forces by the desperate people of Mostar. For now, Albert and the doctor shook hands, with the former realizing that he actually held in hand the only chance for a rescue operation of the unfortunate Muslims of Mostar, especially for the hundreds of children, who would henceforth accompany him in each of his coming visits to the city that was teetering between life and death, poignantly shouting "*Videmose Albertu!*" (We shall see you, Albert). To paraphrase Churchill on an equally critical war situation, never did so many innocent Muslim civilians owe so much and so critically to the goodwill and dedication of a single Jew. It was sad to observe that, since the kids were so hopeful and enthusiastic about Albert's mission, they disregarded the permanent danger of snipers, who did not distinguish between civilian and military, child and adult. Many of them fell while engaging in their games in the border area and were to never see Albert again.

    Those experiences impacted thenceforth upon Benabou's state of mind, and rescuing children in any way he could became a haunting obsession for him. He was in permanent contact with the branches of UNICEF and of the World Health Organization (WHO) in Zagreb. For him, meeting, talking to, reassuring, and comforting the besieged population of eastern Mostar, and trying to justify the trust, hope, and expectations of those unfortunate and forlorn victims of the war in his capacity to help, became the motto of his mission. He could not

*Savagery in the Heart of Europe*

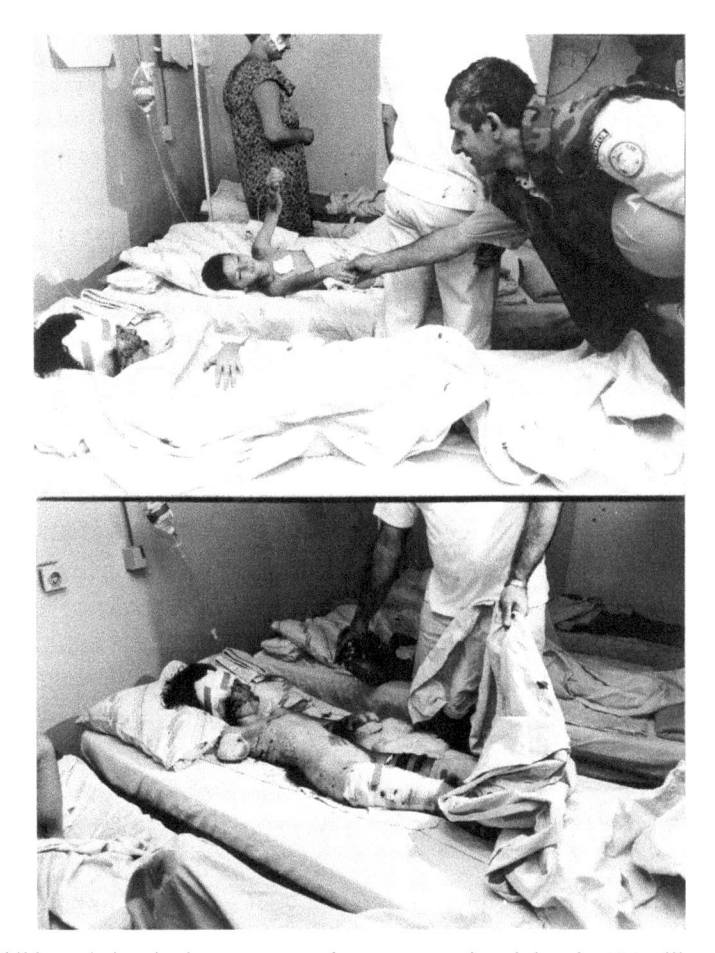

Children victims in the war zone—they were convinced that the UN will save them...

help reminiscing about the 1982 Battle of Beirut, during the Israeli incursion into Lebanon, where he had served as a liaison officer trying to facilitate the contacts between the rival Christian and Muslim factions. Now, as then, he was involved in diplomatic mediation in the midst of his military service, but he was asking himself whether the military job he had fulfilled then as a major in the IDF could facilitate his civil affairs job in the ethnic and religious confrontation of Mostar. In his report to Zagreb and New York, Benabou rendered homage to the Spanish Battalion, citing a line from Rimbaud's poetry, as was his wont whenever he was in danger and had to formulate a report on the sad events he was managing, "At dawn, armed with a burning passion [for peace], we entered into the splendid towns[127]."

The military base at Medjugorje was home to both the Spanish Battalion and to the civil affairs office of the area. The camp was located on the border of a forest and controlled the roads leading from Mostar westwards to the Adriatic Sea and eastwards towards Sarajevo via central Bosnia, which was under the responsibility of the British and Canadian units, which were quite experienced in international peace missions, while the Spaniards were facing such a situation for the first time. Whenever Benabou returned from the field, he rapidly retired to his office, which was equipped with the most modern and updated communication systems, though the furnishings were primeval in that complex which included an office, an adjacent bedroom, and a large meeting space. Once disengaged from his bulletproof vest and from his helmet (working for the United Nations was no guarantee to one's safety), he put himself to writing all the reports he owed to the UN institutions, as well as to the humanitarian NGOs and agencies at Kiseljak and Zagreb and on to New York. He worked scrupulously on every detail to make his reports realistic, precise, and credible.

A close collaborator of Benabou during his mission was Captain David Belmonte, a Dutch career officer, who became a vital element in the UN bureaucracy in dismantled Yugoslavia, where the system of communications had altogether collapsed and could no longer be counted on.

---

[127] Doc. 002 17 May 1993, SITREP (situation Report) Mostar (see the post scriptum).

Belmonte was in charge of DUTCHCOM, the signals unit of the Dutch military in NATO, which was attached to the United Nations and positioned in Medjugorje. Thus, he became the wizard of the communications system, both on the base and beyond. He assured regular communications with the UN headquarters in Zagreb, Sarajevo, Belgrade, and New York, and when needed, with other European capitals, as well as with the entire territory of former Yugoslavia, including even besieged Mostar. In his thirties, wearing black hair which lent to him a firm and confidence-inspiring air, he was fast to share with Benabou any incoming piece of relevant information. Tall and energetic, always on the move, he briskly and repeatedly combed with his fingers his abundant hair, and he covered the distance between his offices and the civil affairs office with long strides. His smile showed his perfectly white and impeccably aligned teeth, and his hands, like those of an artist, were stylized and aesthetic. He projected at all times a sense of relaxation and easygoing, imposing an atmosphere of calm and sobriety.

For Benabou, DUTCHCOM was the nervous center where things happened. Due to his close relationship with Belmonte, his messages to New York and Zagreb enjoyed a certain degree of high priority, and every message Benabou wished to send was taken care of expeditiously and by the quickest means, including satellites. Belmonte had originated from a Jewish-Portuguese family, who had immigrated to Holland during and due to the Inquisition, which tormented Iberian Jewry in the early modern era. During his service for the United Nations, this young officer had the revelation of a colleague, Andrea de Valenci, who also worked for the United Nations, however on the other side of the Atlantic, in New York. A love story developed between the two that came to engulf the entire essence of their lives. Benabou wrote his regular reports, and on one occasion, he asked for an important and urgent message to be transmitted to the UN headquarters in Kiseljak, with a copy to Zagreb. Its nature harked back to the persistent and perennial problem of besieged Mostar and demanded an early delivery of the anesthetics and other medical substances requested by Dr. Milavic. Since no early response had arrived, Belmonte decided to refer the matter to the Office of the Peace Missions of the UN, which was at the time directed by Kofi Anan, who entertained the ambition to replace the job of Secretary General Boutros-Ghali, who was edging towards the end of his term.

The story began in New York on a wintery and cold day, though spring was already in the offing. Andrea was taking her habitual morning walk to work at the glass building of the United Nations, where she was in charge of the new recruits to UN missions in Bosnia, and she was curious and intrigued by the prospect of interviewing new candidates who came forward to be dispatched to that war zone. She could not suspect that on that day she would not only be put face-to-face with these intrepid volunteers, who were ready to put their lives on the line, but she would also put her well organized and predictable life upside down and revolutionize her physical and emotional being. Satellite and electronic communications were only at their debut then and about to generate e-mail, which would proclaim the advent of the era of the Internet. It was these reduced distances by instant communication around the globe, but where privacy and intimacy could be somewhat preserved nevertheless, which threw these two young people into the throes of love in the midst of this ambience of war. On 18 May, 1993, Belmonte, comfortably installed in his communication office in Medjugorje, read a message on his computer screen, dispatched from the UN HQ in New York, signed by Andrea Valenci. It read:

From Andrea Valenci

To: David Belmonte
Dispatched from New York, 17 May, 1993, 17:56h

Subject: Mostar-Materials for Medical Anesthetics

Benabou's report on the breakthrough of the aid convoy to Mostar, which you transmitted urgently, by chance landed on my desk and captivated my attention. I am not employed by the Office of Peace Missions, but from my position at the personnel department, I will follow his appeal to rescue the population of Mostar as rapidly as possible from the horrors of this carnage. *Que Dios te Jade* [not being certain of Belmonte's origins, Andrea tried a Sephardic Jewish blessing: May God preserve you, in Judeo-Spanish, or Ladino, thus revealing her own origin[128]].

David responded without delay:

Benabou was happy to learn that his appeal was at long last affected by a sensitive soul at the Glass Building . . . I would like to know, who is Andrea Valenci . . .
*Que dios te bendiga* (May God bless you).

DB

The correspondence continued. Andrea answered by hinting that since she was already treated as a "soul," there was no need to say more, prompting David to observe that they were then two souls at the service of the United Nations. He added that since technology in the middle of hell allowed two distant souls to dialogue, he also hoped that henceforth the wounded of Mostar would undergo surgery under

---

[128] Recorded on Benabou's personal journal of the War. All the following private correspondence, names and profiles have been altered in order to protect the personal privacy of the people involved in the love part of the book.

anesthetics, thanks to her enlightened help to Benabou. Once awakened, the transatlantic attraction between these two young and idealistic people, lovers of fortune around a situation of war and destruction, increasingly grew and intriguingly drew them closer. The correspondence continued; Andrea hinted that being a soul did not preclude her from being also a woman. David picked up the hint and began to tell about his origin in the "flat country," but also referred to the "exile of his people" from the "city that bathes in gold and encompasses the basic knowledge of humanity. To that city, people address their prayers." He asked Andrea to guess his origin. The game between the two became more intimate and gradually more daring. They were intrigued by each other but delicately and cautiously explored their mutual revelation and were very careful not to precipitate things.

Soon Andrea avowed that for her, too, Jerusalem lay at the base of her identity and sentiment, something which prompted an immediate unity of dream, reality, and ambition. Little did they know that in their extraordinary encounter (for now by correspondence only) they were joining hands, as Jews of Sephardic extraction, to assist Muslim victims in a God-forsaken place where even their own kin did not care much for them. And they took their humanitarian concern, as Benabou did, as a matter of course, without any regard to politics or to the suffering of their own people. Andrea originated from a Marano family, whose ancestors were forced to convert to Christianity, but when they could, they returned to their original faith. It was ironic, and humanly heartwarming, that in a land where Christians and Muslims battled to the finish, it was these three Jews (Albert, David, and Andrea), who met by coincidence, who took upon themselves to rescue the unfortunate Muslim victims of an alien war, at a time when their Jewish kin were being murdered, delegitimized, demonized, and hated, especially by the Muslim world of today.

Andrea's family had been expelled from Spain, together with other Maranos who had been forced to convert to Catholicism, but continued to practice their faith in secret. The Jewish communities in the Iberian Peninsula were numerous, prosperous, and influential in all domains: political, economic, scholarly, and scientific, especially during the rule of the Spanish Umayyad Dynasty, which recognized the worth of its Jews and catered to them, despite their officially inferior status of "dhimmis." Some of the greatest Jewish thinkers, like Maimonides, grew up in Cordova and the other political, economic, and cultural centers of Muslim Spain, where Jews attained high government and societal positions until the fanatic Muslim dynasties of North Africa, the Almoravids and the Almohads, took over and destroyed the harmonious and prosperous existence of the Jews there. The Christian reconquest made things even worse, when the Iberian Jews were expelled, and they had to flee to either North Africa, to place themselves once again under Islam, or to the Ottoman Empire in Anatolia Proper or in the Balkans, where Jewish settlement of Ladino speakers spread. Andrea's family of bankers had to escape from the prosperous Jewish city of Toledo and kept wandering throughout Europe, but in the eighteenth century, they embarked from Amsterdam to the New World and settled in New Port, Rhode Island.

The success of the 14 May convoy to Mostar immediately posed the question, "Where do we go from here?" At the Medjugorje base, Benabou arranged for a meeting on 15 May with Generals Petkovic and Hallilovic, the respective commanders of the rival forces, not to debrief them on what had happened the day before but rather to ignore the shelling and bombardments during the UN operation on the previous day, where no victim fell, and try instead to plan for the future. Benabou sensed an immense breakthrough in the fact that despite the ill feelings of the rival generals towards each other, they were talking directly for the first time, probably a lesson that Benabou had learned from Israeli experiences in the past, where UN mediation sometimes aggravated the issues between Israelis and Arabs, instead of resolving them.[129] He suggested nightly talks between the parties on his idea to remove all the roadblocks on the way from Metkovic on the Adriatic to Sarajevo, passing through Mostar, Jablanica, Kostanjica, Konjic, and Tarcin. His idea was to force the generals to deal with their common problems via their face-to-face meetings. They knew each other since they had served together in Tito's army, and it was essential to lead both of them to act for their common benefit.

The two generals looked at each other with visible contempt, in that part of the world where the ethnic groups grew up loving to hate each other. Benabou exerted efforts to penetrate the reasoning of those rivals and to study the attitudes of those leaders who held in their hands the destinies of entire nations and the fate of multitudes of common people, who were swept by the fortunes of the war and subjected to the violence and brutality which civilized Europe had once again generated, half a century after the horrors of World War II. Petkovic indeed was reluctant to acquiesce to the demands advanced by Hallilovic and distanced himself all the time from any commitment that, in any case, he had no intention to respect. He was loath to undertake any responsibility, and as far as he was concerned, the Muslims had to be evacuated/expelled/cleansed from Mostar. Hallilovic was not assertive enough, and he constantly sought Benabou's support for each one of his demands and requests. He did not realize that it was up to him to draw the perimeters of his dialogue with his enemy. Finally, the two men were agreed on the need to remove all the roadblocks from the Metkovic

---

[129] Raphael Israeli, *Jerusalem Divided: the Armistice Regime (1947-1967)*, Frank Cass, London, 2003.

road, where the main storage points of UN humanitarian aid were located, on the road to Sarajevo. Serbs and Muslims were struggling in the entire open space in between, hence the slow progress of the talks between the parties, which permitted to tackle only the most urgent humanitarian cases.

Benabou was frustrated by these limited achievements, and in consequence, he was constantly striving to achieve more tangible and far-reaching results. Action was needed to open up the isolated enclaves around Konjic, where massacres and rapes had become everyday occurrences, without evidence being collected or investigations being conducted to deter further violations. At dawn, the parties got to the issue of opening the Jablanica crossroads, with the two generals mentioning the necessity to repair the Bila Bridge that had been destroyed during the battle. Benabou, who was striving for such an outcome, immediately consented and announced that the UN unit of British engineers attached to BRITFOR, which was stationed at Divulje on the Adriatic coast, was ready to install in place a Bailey bridge, under the following conditions:

- The bridge would be open to everybody under a permanent patrol of UN troops;
- Free traffic should be guaranteed to everyone and respected by all parties all along the route marked on the map;
- A document should be signed by all the political groups of each party, who would undertake to commit themselves to it[130].

Having little faith in the signatures on the agreement document, Albert incessantly emphasized that the direct interest of the parties entailed the reparation of the bridge. A few days later, Hallilovic, sensing that circumstances had moved to the Muslims' favor in both Sarajevo and Mostar, dared to

---

[130] See doc. 002 paragraph 3 in the chapter concerning open roads.

submit more demands and put the choking siege of Sarajevo at the top of the agenda. During the fighting at Konjic, located on the main axis leading to Sarajevo, a high intensity electric cable had been burned. The situation was that sixty percent of the power needs of Sarajevo were supplied by the hydroelectric plants of Kostanjica and Konjic, while the rest of the consumption was provided by coal operated power plants in the Karanj area, but the coal production had been paralyzed since the onset of the war. In consequence, Sarajevo was practically cut off from the electric grid and came to depend on generators that were spread in various locations of the city. Hallilovic seemed to get interested in this topic, and Benabou explained to him that the British engineers attached to the United Nations had taken charge of this issue, and that within days a solution would be suggested for both the power and water problems in town.

UNCIVPOL (the UN civil police) now came up with the idea to position fifty policemen in Mostar in order to "control the disarmament of the Mostar population.[131]" That unit also demanded that Mostar be patrolled jointly by a mixed Croatian, Muslim, and UN civil police unit. Easier said than done, for the unending red tape of the UN bureaucracy was taking over and obstructing the efficiency and the speed of decisions which were warranted in war time. As Benabou was raising the issue of the mixed police in Mostar, with UN participation, with his superior, Victor Andreev, he referred to the required lengthy procedures by citing what he had heard before in this regard: "One would need a mandate of the Security Council in New York to provide this measure, because it would be up to the contributing members of the force to recruit those troops.[132]" Engaged on this

---

[131] ibid see chapter UNCIVPOL.
[132] See report sent by Albert Benabou on 6 June 1993 to Victor Andreev, Kiseljak UN Headquarters concerning United Nations Civil Police operation in Mostar.

matter, General Petkovic would have no choice but to cooperate, thought the UN civil affairs officer, for otherwise he would have to account before the international community. Benabou had directed his appeal to the Security Council via Andreev, the coordinator for civil affairs of the Bosnia and Herzegovina command located at Kiseljak. Andreev, the Ukrainian, had worked for the United Nations for many years, and he was familiar with all UN mechanisms. He had accepted Benabou's service with apprehension from the outset, and he seemed reserved from his novice junior colleague's independence of mind and surplus of energy, which were articulated in many languages under his command.

Originally, Andreev had accepted Benabou's appointment only under pressure from Cedric Thornberry, head of the UN mission for civil affairs and an Irishman who had served in the United Nations in Jerusalem and was more familiar with the free spirit and savoir faire of the Israelis. Apparently, Andreev sought the understanding of the identity and spirit of Israel, which he did not know, in the Russian stereotypes. On one occasion, when functionaries of all nationalities were assembled for briefing by Andreev, he whispered in Benabou's ears, "Come to think of it, you and I are Bolsheviks.[133]" Far from Bolshevik convictions, Albert smiled to himself at this oversimplification of the Israeli complex national character, formed of a mosaic of Jews from all over the world.

## Saturday, 29 May, 1993

Without early notice or early coordination, the first French ambassador in Bosnia and Herzegovina, Henry Jacolin, arrived at Medjugorje, the headquarters of the Spanish Battalion. He was accompanied by Isumi Nakamitsu, the

---

[133] Recorded in personal memoirs of the War in Bosnia of Albert Benabou.

representative of the UNHCR at the UN office in Zagreb. Surprised by this unexpected visit, Colonel Morales asked Major de Salas to summon Benabou to the offices of the force, at a moment when he was busy recapitulating and analyzing the events of the previous week. That day, it rained dogs and cats, with only short intervals between the storms, so the mood was rather gloomy, and the prospects to cheer it up by the visit of the ambassador did not appear too promising. De Salas arrived at Benabou's office out of breath, asking him to rally to Morales urgently, but Benabou lingered a bit on his paperwork before joining the colonel's office, for he had learned from his fourteen years of work with Foreign Minister David Levy that even the most urgent affairs of this sort could take a few moments of reflection before they were undertaken. He was wondering whether the visit was calculated to jump-start a new initiative of France, what Morales had in mind, and to what extent he had to take with him any documents needed to make his case.

De Salas urged Benabou to hurry up, and after a few minutes, the two men, dripping with rain, crossed the threshold of Morales's office. The introductions were brief and skipped the customary niceties, and Nakamitsu declared with an openness untypical of the Japanese that she had been literally kidnapped by the French ambassador, who presented himself without warning to the UN office in Zagreb. Jacolin had been urged by the Quai d'Orsay to visit the field, and since he was very perturbed by the siege of Mostar, he wished to visit the town without delay, in order to verify on the ground the reports on the ethnic cleansing that was unfolding in that war zone. The ambassador whispered in Benabou's ear that all those horrors were happening under the Spaniards' noses, something that in his eyes might mean their tacit consent to this reprehensible procedure. Albert could not help acquiescing in that evaluation

*Savagery in the Heart of Europe*

of the events. Nakamitsu emphasized that she had engaged in discussions with the leaders of the HVO, Tadic and Prlic, who had "admitted that the Croats were engaged in some movements of Muslim populations in the area of Mostar and on the banks of the Neretva[134]," which amounted in reality to ethnic cleansing. She also referred to the positions taken by Mate Boban, the president of the HVO, who declared his readiness to transfer the Croatian population of Zenica in exchange for the Muslims of Mostar. In fact, Boban had expressed his will to execute that detailed plan of population exchange in one of his encounters with Benabou.

Ambassador Jacolin was assigned the clear mission to throw light on the situation. The French were demanding an immediate and unequivocal response on this affair. Targeting a precise investigation in the area under Spanish supervision, Benabou launched an inquiry, comparing his data with those of Major Acuña, who was in charge of Spanish intelligence in place, but key issues had remained open to further investigations with the Croats and the Muslims. Benabou began even to suspect that some Muslims were collaborating with Croatian leaders on this issue. Thus, another visit on the ground was absolutely necessary to authenticate the data, for Benabou was not satisfied with the superficial answers he had received until then. Similarly, the French ambassador was fed more by "tranquillizers" than by intelligent and thorough data. As a result, Benabou decided to expand the distribution of his messages and reports to more agencies that were involved in the war, for example the British and American representatives at the headquarters in Kiseljak, Zagreb, and New York, in order to ensure that when necessary, action could be undertaken on the ground. He

---

[134] See doc. 003, report sent by Albert Benabou on the 30th of may 1993 to the UN Headquarters, updating on the current issues and Jacolin unexpected visit to Meddjugorje.

was particularly dismayed by Colonel Castro, the second in command of the Spanish forces, who used to, as a Catholic, attend services on Sundays at the Croatian Church in West Mostar, often expressing in public his desire to "enter one day [Muslim] East Mostar, simultaneously waving the flags of both the Spaniards and the Croats.[135]" It goes without saying that he was expressing his personal views, not those of his battalion or of his country, but his obtuse sensitivities in this delicate situation, which betrayed his lack of international and diplomatic experience, amounted to less than what was expected of an impartial UN officer in a war zone.

In the meantime, David Belmonte of DUTCHCOM, attached to the Spanish Battalion, transmitted regularly, swiftly, and with great precision the messages, in this and other regards, that Benabou was dispatching to Victor Andreev at the UN command in Kiseljak and to Cedric Thornberry at the headquarters in Zagreb. He also widened the distribution of the messages to New York, among others via his correspondence with Andrea de Valenci, with their words of burning love lending meaning to those otherwise routine, stale, cold, and boring business messages. And so, their post scripts at the end of their messages, because like those of Benabou who was in the custom of sprinkling his letters with poetry and words of wisdom were strained by the long and impatient wait to consummate their love. Passion is impatient.

**Sunday, 30 May, 1993**

At dawn of this day, at 5:25 in the morning, Benabou was back to Mostar, after he obtained safe passage without difficulty from both parties. He took in his company the British General Veer de Hayes, who was quite astonished by the

---

[135] Recorded in personal memoirs of the War in Bosnia of Albert Benabou.

facility of communication between Benabou and the rival field forces on the ground. De Hayes had arrived without warning the night before from the headquarters in Kiseljak, since he wanted to take stock by himself of what was happening on the terrain, mainly on the question of whether the Croats were indeed conducting ethnic cleansing in the Muslim area in that region. Benabou had established a good working relationship with de Hayes, a tall and resolute man, who represented a typical British officer with whom Benabou found an easy way of communication and much in common in terms of military culture. They could easily understand each other, even when speaking in hints and allusions. Morales also joined the visiting mission in order to ascertain and show to his officers, de Salas and Acuña, that no war crime was being perpetrated in this sector. To avoid differences of view, it was agreed between the Spaniards and the British that Benabou would write and dispatch the report of the visit to Zagreb and New York.

At the end of the afternoon, the entire delegation was retreating for the night to the headquarters in Medjugorje. Now, the balance sheet had to be drawn of what was taking place in the two rival camps of Mostar. The Croats, pretending that the entire turmoil around that visit was alien to them, raised their heads to heaven in apparent confusion, acting as if that entire business of "population movements" was not familiar to them. The Muslims, on their part, began to realize that the joint commission established to manage situations of emergency was in fact used to impose a permanent separation between the two communities and to move the Muslims of West Mostar to the East. The Muslims had been pushed to the eastern part of the river, which ran along the Boulevard divide between the two parts. That magnificent thoroughfare, which had symbolized the historical and harmonious coexistence between Muslims and Christians in the times of Tito, had become the demarcation line between the warring parties, along which Croats and Muslims were massacring each other with religious fervor and abysmal hatred, leaving behind them and in front of them a scarred landscape not worthy of habitation. Women, children, and adult Muslims were piled up on top of each other in the eastern part of town, which was besieged and constantly bombarded by the Croatian artillery.

On the night of 30 May, the Muslims lodged an official protest and announced that they would no longer cooperate with the mixed commission, since it dawned on them that the Croats sought to implement via its intermediary what they could not achieve in the battlefield, i.e. push back the entire Muslim population, and in fact, build a ghetto for the Muslims in the eastern part of the city, where the Muslims would be at worse massacred, at best expelled from the city. As a result, the HVO declared that the commission was to cease its activities until further notice. But the rumor lingered in town regarding the group of Muslim men and young adults whom the Croats had assembled in the field of the Heliodrom and surrounded with barbed wire. Access to that concentration camp had been denied to outsiders, but the Spaniards did not insist on our right to visit, and that was the one topic that continued to preoccupy Albert and to cause tension between him and the Spanish Battalion. As a result, though when he was writing his reports he usually kept balance between all points of view and tried to distill all accounts into their pure state, without sullying them with biases and estimates, his instincts and upbringing as an intelligence officer motivated him to always add at the end of each report his evaluations and political analysis.

During his multifaceted contacts with Croats and Muslims, Benabou understood that many of his reports were being regularly transmitted to the Croatian authorities in Grude and in Zagreb. He also learned that in his talks with

*Savagery in the Heart of Europe*

Carlos de Salas, he had established such a close relationship that they could often extricate themselves from embarrassing situations, without, however, totally avoiding inevitable clashes. For example, in one of his messages to the UN headquarters, he reported that a large number of cars were constantly busy loading and unloading entire families with their luggage from West Mostar towards the Adriatic coast and in other directions. Benabou rejected the explanation that the departing families were "going on vacation,[136]" since the travelers appeared tired and harassed, and their luggage was piled up in disorder or their packages rested on the bus benches near them, which raised the suspicion that it was an ethnic cleansing operation. No proof was evident at that point, since there was no direct and systematic evacuation of a certain ethnic group from a certain area, but a big question mark reigned on the "movement of population, and it was necessary to continue to track the buses departing from Mostar for other destinations with their loads of suitcases and bundles. In one of his reports to Zagreb, Benabou cited Stefan Zweig who had written in another context, "I smile when I turn these pages, because everything is true, though the essential is missing. This book describes me, it does not express me. It talks about me, but does not reveal me.[137]" Benabou was determined to dig up the deep motivations and passions of the population under his jurisdiction, and he mentioned in his reports that more investigative messages of this sort would follow, and that his inquiry into the matter had just started and must be pursued.

---

[136] See doc. 011, dated 21 June 1993, concerning the assistance and protection of refugees in Medugorje and attached correspondence with UNHCR, the Italian Ministry of Foreign affairs, and Isabella Oriani, representing the Italian Consortium of Solidarity, assuring the safe movement of population.

[137] Stefan Zweig is quoted in Doc. 003 (dated 30th of May 1993). Benabou felt that the occurring ethnic cleansing around him was familiar to the Jewish People history part of expulsion and rejection from country to country.

## Monday, 31 May, 1993, 10:00 a.m.

Benabou thought/hoped that the intervention of the UN-CIVPOL in Mostar would block, or at least reduce, brutal measures against civilians. On 31 May, 10:00 a.m., he organized a working session with O'Reilly, the UN high commissioner for civilian police, with the participation of HVO officials, Brigadier General Milijenko Lasic and Ilja Filipovic, and General Pasalic and Ramo Mascesa as well as other military and civilian officials of both parties. The commissioner, who was borrowed from the Canadian Mounted Police, was an experienced police officer in criminal affairs, tall and imposing by his presence, the type who would not let the situation slip through his fingers. At first he clarified the rules of the game, insisting that he strove to establish a mixed police force of Croats and Muslims, for any other composition would fall short of protecting civilians, and would result, on the contrary, in chaos even if it was done under the questionable "blessing" of the United Nations. Andrea also received the same messages in New York, and she understood the underlying fears and risks that transpired from underneath those reports. For her, there was no doubt that Benabou, despite his bluntness, did not in fact dare to put his finger openly on the problem and to pursue his devastating conclusions to their ultimate logic. There was no doubt in her mind that ethnic cleansing existed, in spite of the absence of conclusive evidence. But the absence of evidence was not evidence of absence. What was particularly disturbing was the brutality and inhumanity towards civilians, just because they were different, something that her Jewish experience revolted against.

Overwhelmed by the evil conduct of people on the ground, whose only concern was to mark points against their enemies, Andrea sought refuge in her love with David. She gradually discovered that her lover was the owner of a great, generous, and concerned soul, with whom she constantly dialogued. Though she could guess the amount of violence and cruelty which governed the activities of those people, she understood that since Benabou lacked clear evidence, he would not push forward to come to final conclusions. She wrote to David on 31 May:

> I recognize the racist source of the hatred which pushed those people to action, to which Benabou referred in his last message about ethnic cleansing. Do not worry, for not only do I make sure to transmit his messages to UNHCR, but I have also collected a secret selection, to use one day to pursue those bastards in justice. Beyond the evil which has been pouring out in front of your eyes, I would like to stress what the love of a woman can express, here is the miracle which makes men live a permanent wonder. This is the secret and the divine key for the self, which women offer to themselves, not knowing that a treasure is hidden there which permits women to conceive and bear children and works of art. The womb is *rehem* in Hebrew, as I had learned in Sunday school. This is how my grandmother used to explain to me this concept, in accordance with our tradition. This Hebrew word also signifies tenderness and proximity, and refers to the 248 actions that one is encouraged to perform in order to open oneself up. The woman's womb is replete with affection, for it encounters the person with whom she lives in love, and opens up in all her dimensions . . . She sleeps on your bosom, exactly as you sleep on hers . . .

**Tuesday,1 June, 1993, 11:00 a.m. –UNCIVPOL**

On Albert's initiative, the local police commanders met at Mostar, Ilija Filipovic and Mate Pehar, the chief of the Mostar police, for the Croats, and Ramo Mascesa, the representative of the Ministry of the Interior, and Zuljevic Salko, chief of the Mostar police, for the Muslims. Albert Benabou presided over the meeting, while O'Reilley, Leo Bang Sorenson, and Agner Skjold took notes of the meeting. Benabou had introduced the order of the day as aiming to establish a plan of cooperation between the two police forces, leaving open the possibility that they might patrol together in the company of UN police forces. Filipovic stated that as far as he was concerned, one police force was sufficient for Mostar, and that was the Croatian police. For him, the Muslim BiH Armija in fact did not comprise any civilian police force, but Mascesa insisted that he belonged to the sole legitimate police force recognized by Bosnia and Herzegovina. But he stressed that he agreed with the joint patrols that were mentioned in the 12 May, 1993 agreement between the parties. For O'Reilley, UNCIVPOL would be ready to contribute its part to the envisaged international forces that were to form part of the joint patrols.

These vain discussions between rivals who hated each other and were hardly prepared to exchange a few words, and when they did, they did it only out of necessity, and when they could, they dismissed their interlocutors' arguments and ignored their concerns, naturally generated prolonged discussions, which often did not lead anywhere, for the meetings were held for the sake of meetings only, creating the false impression that when people talked, they did not fight. In this instance, the talks broke up as the Croats insisted on retaining their uniforms during the joint patrols, while the Bosniaks complained that they had none at all. Ritually, for lack of better, the parties reiterated their commitment to the 12 May Accords. In search of a compromise, Benabou suggested that the joint patrols be done in common with each party sporting his own uniform. The Muslims, who had no uniform and no money to manufacture or purchase new ones, promptly agreed; the Croats stressed that they could not watch Muslims patrolling West Mostar, which was under Croat control. After much haggling and protracted talks, Benabou finally reached an "agreement," which again taught every participant that nothing comes easily with the United Nations, and that when it comes, it remains flimsy, fragile, and under the threat of violation by either party. The "agreed" accords stipulated:

> That they were valid for the town of Mostar only;
> 
> That the United Nations and Major O'Reilly of UN-CIVPOL would guarantee the terms of the agreement, to make sure that the officers participating in the joint patrols were trained strictly in civilian police duties and would mediate between the parties in case of misinterpretations or other misunderstandings;
> 
> The uniforms to be worn by both parties should be distinctly and clearly civilian and different from military uniforms;
> 
> Detailed regulations would be worked out governing the operation of the patrols;
> 
> Filipovic must confirm the support of his Croatian party, especially of the Minister of Defense, Bruno Stojic, to the agreement;
> 
> The agreement of the political leaders of BiH would be obtained by Benabou; and
> 
> The patrols should start their operation as soon as possible[138].

At 1445h the same day, O'Reilley, the officers of UN-CIVPOL, and Benabou convened a consultation with the Croats Stojic, Petkovic, and Filipovic. Benabou presented the details of the accord and demanded that they confirm its terms. O'Reilley explained professionally the principles

---

[138] See report sent by Albert Benabou on 6 June 1993 to Victor Andreev, Kiseljak UN Headquarters concerning United Nations Civil Police operation in Mostar.

involving UNCIVPOL's missions and again reiterated the obligation to honor the agreement of 12 May, 1993. This impressive show of professionalism and initiative left Stojic speechless. He attempted to preserve good appearances in front of the Canadian and Israeli officials and remarked that only when the withdrawal of troops was achieved after the war would UNCIVPOL be able to patrol the area and ensure security. During his recurring visits to Grude, Benabou heard Pogarcic reiterate that it was Bruno Stojic who obstructed all measures of rapprochement, arguing that if left to his devices, he would, "deliver Mostar clean of Muslims by the end of June.[139]"

## Tuesday, 1 June, 1993

Three Irish drivers were arrested in Mostar by the Croatian police of the HVO. On 31 May, 1993, they were driving three trucks carrying food and humanitarian aid, but their movement had not been coordinated with any UN agency or Spanish unit which controlled the area. Benabou was wondering whether this "humanitarian" assistance did not cover up an attempt by Britain to patrol the area and collect data on the Croatian and Muslim military deployment, as well as on the acts of ethnic cleansing against the Muslim population. At any rate, Benabou wished to release them as soon as feasible. He summoned General de Hayes to form a delegation comprising himself, Morales, and Benabou, to present to the Croatian chief of police in Mostar a demand to release the arrested drivers. Benabou had promised to the local head of police that, if released, the Irish drivers would return the next day to deposit before the Croats their bona fide intentions when they entered the zone and let themselves be

---

[139] See report sent by Albert Benabou on 6 June 1993 to Victor Andreev, Kiseljak UN Headquarters concerning United Nations Civil Police operation in Mostar.

interrogated by the police. Finally, without having to bring the Irish drivers back for investigation, the entire affair was settled in less than twenty-four hours.

**Thursday, 3 June, 1993**

According to Benabou's thinking, UNPROFOR (the Protection Forces of the UN) strategic objective was to secure the opening of the humanitarian aid from the Adriatic coast to Sarajevo. He thought that at that actual stage of the war, it was redundant to discuss a peace solution, for it served no other purpose than to perpetuate conflict, because the time had not come yet. He reasoned that since that route crossed Mostar and then via tortuous mountain paths into the key cities of Konjic, Kostanjica, Tarcin, and Jablanica, and the forested landscape did not allow much flexibility of movement, and due to the scarcity of traffic and the rainy and muddy nature of the road much of the time, it became an ideal spot for ambushes against civilians, without risk of being found out by outsiders. He collected many complaints by women in the surrounding villages who had been kidnapped, and in effect, submitted to slavery, raped, and abused during many months. On 1 June, 1993, the following document was distributed by Benabou at the UN headquarters in Kiseljak, aimed at creating some understanding between the parties in order to relax the situation on the ground, even if partially, by arranging a meeting he coordinated in Konjic between General Hallilovic and General Petkovic:

> We have coordinated a meeting between General Petkovic and General Hallilovic for Thursday, 3 June, in Konjic. We were asked by the generals to invite to this meeting the regional brigadiers from the following areas: Mostar, Konjic, Kostanjica, Tarcin, and Jablanica. The agenda, already discussed with the two generals,

was elimination of the check points along the road Metkovic-Mostar-Jablanica-Konjic-Tarcin; cessation of hostilities between all parties in the mentioned areas; free movement for all parties along the road and patrols of SPABAT—UNCIVPOL; and terms of agreement among all sides for the installation and opening of the Bijela Bridge.

The presence of the regional brigadiers in this meeting should ensure that all concerned factors are aware of the achieved agreement in several domains:

Since the last humanitarian convoy to Mostar on Friday, 14 May, 1993, only two minor convoys have entered the city. Benabou has repeatedly insisted that there must be continuity of humanitarian convoys and presence on a regular basis.

The legal adviser was asked to formulate a draft legal document stipulating the terms for the operation of the Bijela Bridge, showing that access on the bridge will be open to all parties and patrolled by UNPROFOR/UNCIVPOL; at all times there will be freedom of movement for all parties all along the mentioned road (Metkovic-Mostar-Jablanica-Konjic-Tarcin); all existing checkpoints and barrages on this road will be eliminated and will not be replaced at any time; only UNPROFOR/UNCIVPOL will have full authority over the bridge.

The agreement will be ratified by the concerned political entities, and each side will take upon itself full responsibility for damages caused to other parties.

In addition to the actual manpower in SPABAT, three more interpreters were required for this forty-eight hours operation (beginning on Thursday, 3 June, 1993 in Konjic). They were to be equipped with two laptops and portable printers, which would be returned to Kiseljak after the meeting.

An early reconnaissance trip along that axis was effected by Benabou down to Jablanica and Konjic, during which he encountered the Croatian and Muslim commanders in the area, while the summit conference between Hallilovic and Petkovic was postponed to a later date, due to the decision to coordinate a high-level meeting between the parties. On 1 June, the International Conference on ex-Yugoslavia, presided by Cyrus Vance and Lord Owen, presented a draft proposal for a law to establish an ombudsman, or defender of rights, to be independent of executive and judicial powers in the Republic of Bosnia and Herzegovina. That law project would facilitate the appointment of four ombudsmen, representing each of the entities (Croatians, Serbs, Muslims, and others), which would sit in Sarajevo and would swear allegiance to the president of the Republic, namely Alija Izetbegovic.

Cedric Thornberry, who headed the civil affairs office in Zagreb, transmitted the document in English and Serbian to Benabou, who was designated by the UN HQ in Zagreb to deal with the affairs of Bosnia and Herzegovina, apparently anticipating the misunderstanding that would arise between him and Victor Andreev, the UNPROFOR coordinator. Benabou maintained excellent working relationships with all actors in the field, for he was keen not to let personal tensions harm the UN humanitarian work. Already in September 1991, the Vance-Owen Plan had suggested the subdivision of Bosnia-Herzegovina into ten provinces, with Sarajevo being demilitarized. Thornberry's intention was to study the Croat position in this regard and try to persuade them, especially Mate Boban, their leader in Bosnia, to accept the plan. Thus, according to directives from Zagreb, Benabou coordinated that Friday, 4 June, a meeting in Kiseljak between the UN representatives to include David Owen and Thorvald Stoltenberg, the co-presidents of the conference for ex-Yugoslavia, General Lars-Erik Wahlgren, the commander of UNPROFOR, and the highest civil and military Croatian representatives, including President Boban, Prime Minister Jadranko Prlic, the Speaker of Parliament Mile Akmadic, and the chief military, General Milivoj Petkovic. All participants agreed to meet at the British base in Divulje, near Split, in a fascinating Adriatic site amidst that war-torn country. Summing up his impressions from his peace work thus far under the UN mission, Benabou could not help concluding that while the United Nations could provide a degree of provisory maintenance work to prevent matters from further deteriorating, it was utterly incapable of devising permanent solutions in the long haul, due to the many built-in inadequacies in its structure and the infighting between its standing bureaucracy, which protected its continuous self-interest, and the appointed generals who represented the interests of their respective countries and the shifting whims of their leaders.

# Chapter Five

## *Generals and Bureaucrats in the Service of the United Nations*[140]

The impossible mix between bureaucrats originating from various nations, who provide continuity and symbolize the self-interest of the United Nations, and make possible the election of Syria, the Sudan, and Libya to its various human rights commissions, and permit the repeated condemnation of Israel many times over, despite the fact that it surpasses them beyond measure in her record on human rights, and generals who are dispatched by their countries to represent their own interest and the changing moods of their leaders in temporary "peace keeping" missions, are the stuff which makes the UN missions of all sorts abortive by definition and explains why the United Nations has never solved the major problems of the world like the Vietnam War, the Arab-Israeli dispute, the Afghani and Iraqi wars, and the Iran-Iraq War or the nuclearization of Iran and world terrorism. To have any effect on warring parties and to achieve any decision in a world conflict, it is necessary, like in the

---

[140] This chapter is all based principally on:
1. Albert Benabou's war journal, personal experiences, field reports, and UN-PROFOR documents.
2. Lengthy discussions with, as well as direct citations from, papers of and on Generals Philippe Morillon and Jean Cot, as they were preserved in the French National Assemby Archives, and the texts of their hearings at the National Assembly dated 25 January and 22 November, 2001, respectively.
3. Extensive and recurring meetings with other UN officials, military and civilian, as well as the main actors in the fields of all three belligerent parties.
4. Recurrent field visits to the capitals Zagreb and Sarajevo, as well as other regional and local centers of action, such as Mostar and Split.

case of Bosnia, to involve great powers, which can pressure the parties and force on them a solution, temporary as it may be. Moreover, because of the long-term self-interest of the UN bureaucracy, where the secretary general's main concern is to be reelected by satisfying all his prospective electors, no matter how evil they are, and where ensuring permanent jobs and self-advancement of its officials always takes precedence over justice, equity, fairness, and truth, a member state like Iran can threaten in public the annihilation of another member state like Israel, but nothing happens to redress the situation.

In the Bosnian War, many things were said and done, as we have seen above, which are not commensurate with the UN ideals and principles, by reason of the incompatibility between the borrowed generals from donor armies which had never waged war and therefore do not have a clue how to "keep peace," and the entrenched UN officials, or borrowed diplomats and professionals from various nations, who usually have no respect for the generals, and even contempt for them at times. It is especially so, since neither the civil officials nor the military brass in the service of the United Nations usually originate from the most distinguished layers of their societies. Gone are the days when a towering figure like Dag Hammarskjold managed UN affairs, took initiatives to interfere in all places and at all times and in all affairs which required his involvement, and was even killed on duty in Congo. Today, second-rate officials in their second-rate and often authoritarian countries are elected to the top post not for their strength of character and power of decision, but for their weaknesses and docility in toeing the line of the powers that voted for them. And when elected, they pretend to preach to others about democracy, which they had never experienced themselves, or morality while they were Nazi collaborators in their youth, or belong to an authoritarian oppressive regime themselves. Naturally, when they get the lucrative top job, they tend to choose subordinates of their caliber, who share their values or promise their own reelection in time.

Similarly, many generals who are appointed to pacify a country or a region come from the retired or lower layers of their military officialdom at home, because their superior colleagues are usually kept at home. Some can sport a full chest of medals, but they never heard a gun shooting in battle, much less have they had any experience dealing with civilian affairs, alien cultures which they ignore or despise, or processes which take time and patience to develop and cannot be decided on the strength of a brisk military order. We are not talking here of war heroes like McArthur, Patton, or Montgomery, who distinguished themselves in great battles and would have no patience for nonsense. The military tasks have changed since those days, too. While in old days, their mandate was clear cut, crush the enemy and come back home with victory, nowadays, we do not expect brilliant battles but acts of pacification. In the asymmetrical wars, it is the terrorists who determine the time and space of the battlefield, and then they melt into the civilian population, so that the generals cannot respond by bringing to bear their massive armies and their advanced weaponry. Thus, service under the United Nations can only undermine their capabilities and confront them with novel situations they were not trained for, as in former Yugoslavia. This situation was not unlike the generals who headed UNTSO (United Nations Truce Supervision Organization), like Generals Von Horn or Odd Bull, the one Swedish, the other Norwegian, who had never had either battle or diplomatic experience.

Another aspect that put to the test those generals in UN service in "peace keeping" missions has been the fact that while they were usually trained in highly sophisticated technological environments, with ballistic missiles and nuclear arsenals, advanced gunnery and efficient logistics, with high care for human lives and top priority for rescue operations, putting food supplies and medical services at the head of their humanitarian concerns, they were faced in Bosnia with another culture of war, shockingly different from what they were trained to expect in the modern era. To put it directly and bluntly, the brutal style of the war in Bosnia reminded them of the massacres in Africa and of the massive killings and executions that they had been witnessing in past decades in the Arab and Muslim worlds, where human existence counted as little as dust, fanaticism and hatred drove individuals and ethnic and religious groups out of their minds, and while Europe was cementing its unity, the warriors in former Yugoslavia seemed to delight in shattering it into smithereens. While the West was bent on construction, development, and advancement, Bosnia and its surroundings seemed to sink into orgies of killing, utter destruction of the others, and annihilation of their cultures. This was a war where definitions and differentiation between good guys and bad guys were totally blurred, since scenes of mass murder, ethnic cleansing, burning of entire villages, and roaming, uprooted refugees were ubiquitous, total, and apocalyptic. The alien military personnel who tried to establish order, pacify the country, and reinstitute a similitude of civility found itself faced with an utter savagery that it could neither comprehend nor tame.

French General Jean Cot, commander of the UNPROFOR forces in former Yugoslavia in 1993, for instance, demanded authorization to use force in order to carry out his mission, as he understood it. He was constantly claiming that it was a joke to lead a battle while hoisting a white banner that symbolized the United Nations. He wanted his units to wear khaki uniforms as befit his mission and as required in a real battlefield. His mission was, in fact, ended due to his argument with the UN

Secretary General, Boutros Boutros-Ghali, the representative of another totalitarian regime, who had to conform to the wimpy conduct of the UN secretaries since Hammarskjold's death. Conversely, another French general, Philippe Morillon, the commander of UN forces in Bosnia-Herzegovina, acted with assertiveness for the protection of civilians, more as a diplomat than as military. His attitude and lack of resolve resulted in the carnage of Srebrenica, which occurred under the UN flag. The Belgian general who succeeded him, Francis Briquemont, who was squeezed and manipulated by the UN bureaucrats, did not succeed to accomplish any concrete move and resigned in frustration. On the other hand, the Nordic officers, who were veterans of previous international assignments, like General Lars-Erik Wahlgren, former commander of the UNPROFOR forces, who arrived to his mission without expectations, concluded his mission in apathy, born out of his attitude towards the situation of "hopeless and déjà vu." In other words, in this quick sample of various modes of conduct of senior European officers in the service of the United Nations, Europe discovered that it did not possess the tools to respond adequately to violent conflicts of this sort and scale.

When General Philippe Morillon faced the strategic objectives proclaimed by the secessionist Bosnian-Serb presidency, including the creation of a border separating the Serb people from Bosnia's other ethnic communities and the abolition of the border along the celebrated Drina River that divides Serbia from the Bosnian Republika Srpska, the Muslim majority population of the Drina Valley, including Srebrenica and its environs, posed a major obstacle to the implementation of these objectives. That Muslim population has constituted the majority in that area since it was under Ottoman occupation, as masterfully described by Nobel Prize Laureate in Literature, Ivo Andric, in his historical novel, *A Bridge on the River Drina*. In the early days of the campaign of population transfer (alias, ethnic cleansing) that followed the outbreak of the Bosnian War in April 1992, the town of Srebrenica was occupied by Serbian forces. It was retaken by the Muslims under the command of Naser Oric, who would become a renowned Muslim commander due to his post at the head of the remnants of the once infamous Hanjar Division that had collaborated with the Nazis in World War II, during the Ustasha state. Muslim refugees, expelled from towns and villages across the central Drina Valley, sought shelter in Srebrenica, swelling the town's population, thus turning the city and its surroundings into an enclave under Oric's command, surrounded by Serbian forces. That twenty-six-year-old corporal, who had served in a special unit for atomic and chemical defense in the former Yugoslav Army, succeeded with his personal charisma to outmaneuver European generals.

On the sacred night of Orthodox Christmas of January 1993, Naser Oric led, from the besieged town, raids which resulted in the massacre of the Serbian population of the nearby villages. After that slaughter, and bearing the burden of the memory of the Ustasha outrage half a century earlier, the Serbs wouldn't forgive, and they targeted Oric[141] as "public enemy number one." In the spring of 1993, when the Serbs launched the offensive in this region, General Philippe Morillon was called on the scene to observe and recognize the exhumed mass graves of the massacred Serbs. From the Serbian point of view, that was a conclusive and irreversible international testimony. In the "good tradition" of hatred in the Balkans, frustration, bitterness, and resentment

---

[141] The International Criminal Tribunal for the former Yugoslavia (ICTY) in the Netherlands sentenced Oric in 2006 for two years' imprisonment for failing to prevent the deaths of five and the mistreatment of eleven Bosnian Serb detainees, during the period from late 1992 to early 1993 on the grounds of "superior criminal responsibility." On 3 July, 2008, the Appeals Chamber of the ICTY reversed the conviction and acquitted Oric of all charges brought against him.

built up in the Serb's minds, and retaliation kept brewing, ready to explode. The prospects of a forthcoming revenge were brought up again and again in various forums, and it was only a question of time before it happened. It took two years, when in July 1995, the Serbs committed, under the responsibility of their war hero, General Ratko Mladic, the worst massacre Europe had known since the end of the Second World War in which seven to eight thousand Muslims, including children, men, and women, were exterminated in a massive and systematic mad orgy of human slaughter.

On 11 March 1993, General Philippe Morillon,[142] commander of the UN Protection Force in Bosnia-Herzegovina, had led a UN medical and reconnaissance team to assess the condition of the population trapped in Srebrenica. The situation had deteriorated rapidly and went out of control. Thousands of Muslims, including women and children, encircled the UN vehicles and raised roadblocks, preventing the general and his team from departure. Albert Benabou would also venture during his mission, in August 1993, into the same pattern of obstruction by the enraged and desperate populace. At that time, he was captured, together with the UN Spanish Battalion, by the Muslims in East Mostar. This modus operandi of the frustrated Muslim population (which was often manipulated by its leadership) was calling for an urgent injection of humanitarian aid and military protection from the outside. This mode of action meant that once inside the enclave, the UN forces were used as hostages by the Muslims, as a way to call for international attention and proclaim, "You cannot leave, for if you leave, we will be

---

[142] General Philippe Morillon, Commander of UNPROFOR from October 1992 to July 1993, appeared on Thursday, 25 January 2001 at the National Assembly of France at the hearing concerning Srebrenica, chaired by François Loncle, member of the Socialist Party. Loncle was well informed about the events in former Yugoslavia, since he followed personally the operation of UNPROFOR during the drama at Srebrenica in 1993.

slaughtered.[143]" Invariably, the international community carried its responsibility, thus vindicating this mode of action.

Morillon considered that he was mandated, as part and parcel of his mission, to provide assistance to any person in danger. He proceeded as entrusted by the international conference for peace in Yugoslavia and the mission of Cyrus Vance and Lord Owen. In fact, he believed that the tens of thousands of refugees in the town of Srebrenica were in danger of dying of hunger, cold, or massacres ignited by the desire for revenge of the infuriated Serbs. On Saturday, 13 March, 1993, the general went on amateur radio to reassure the people of Srebrenica, but also to address the outside world, that he was "compelled to remain on duty[144]" in the besieged town. Fully conscious that a major tragedy was about to take place, he mentioned that he deliberately came to Srebrenica and had decided to stay in order to calm the anguish of the population and to save them, or at least to attempt to do so. Morillon declared to the population of Srebrenica his version of Kennedy's *"Ich bin ein Berliner."* He told them, "I shall be with you.[145]" Morillon wished to project the classic awe-inspiring profile of a heroic soldier of

---

[143] Source: Benabou's personal memoirs of War in Bosnia. On 25 August 1993, Benabou stood on top of the Spanish APC trying to calm an enraged crowd, instigated by the local leadership in East Mostar, and shouting: "If you leave, we will be slaughtered." Starting 8 August 2013, Benabou was pressuring to attract the attention of the UN Headquarters in New York and Zagreb to the lamentable situation in Mostar. Following intensive weeks of negotiations, Benabou brokered a temporary cease-fire between the HVO and the Muslim leaders in East Mostar and after three months of closure, a humanitarian relief convoy entered East Mostar on 25 August. Large numbers of local civilian prevented the vehicles from leaving, lying down in front of the wheels and straddling buses and other vehicles across the road. 120 United Nations personnel both military and civilian were trapped in the blockade and released only on 29 August.

[144] Published by The British Newspaper :*The Independent* on Sunday 21 March 1993.

[145] ibid.

honor and of a respectable and credible diplomat. But since he had no authority to use force in the realization of his mission, being constrained by the limited UN diplomacy, he had to rely on the short-term power of the international media to put his message of compassion across. To the astonishment of his UN colleagues on the ground, the French general had in a certain manner fallen in captivity in the battlefield, and Paris kept silent for days, not knowing how to react, or whether he could be retrieved through a diplomatic effort, coaxing, or by paying ransom, or an audacious attempt should be made to rescue him militarily. A puzzling question arose, was Morillon acting according to his UN mandate? The French authorities, who had just been lobbying in the UN corridors for the nomination of another French general at the head of a UN peace keeping mission, and won their bid, were now simply not sure how to react, and whether they could do anything to preserve their general's life and honor and at the same time enhance France's badly beaten sense of grandeur.

Morillon was confronted by the Serb commander, General Ratko Mladic, an experienced military officer familiar with the terrain and the population, who knew how to exploit to his convenience all opportunities and favorable factors, including the evident weaknesses of the UN forces. Morillon was over relying on Mladic's word of honor. It is true that Mladic had a word of honor, and when Morillon talked about him, he often said:

> There is only one address where you could go to conclude a deal; it is Mladic—he kept his word while others did not. In Srebrenica, he expected resistance [on the part of Muslims]. There was none. He did not anticipate the massacres . . . but then he had completely underestimated the accumulated hatred [in his camp]. I

do not think it was he who had ordered [the massacres] . . .[146]

At any rate, Mladic never disclosed his cards, and Morillon had to do with the partial information he had, since he did not command a competent military intelligence unit, which was sorely missing in the UN structure. The strong-minded Slavic Mladic, who was often described as "crazy in his operations,[147]" was not about to renounce revenge. He was a talented officer from the JNA (the former Yugoslav National Army), the son of Nedja Mladic, member of the Yugoslav Partisans, who had been killed in 1945 while leading a Partisan attack on the home village of Ante Pavelic, the founder and leader of the pro-Nazi Ustasha regime in Croatia. This was the cultural legacy and memory that he grew up with. Upon his arrival to the town of Kiseljak, where the UN Forward headquarters in Bosnia-Herzegovina was located, Albert Benabou participated in May 1993 in a meeting at the airport of Sarajevo, in the presence of the UN Generals Wahlgren and Morillon, the Muslim General Safet Hallilovic, and the Serb General Ratko Mladic. Srebrenica was, of course, on the agenda. Mladic manifested his curiosity and initiated a discussion with the Israeli newcomer, remarking that, "General Ariel Sharon is a remarkable military leader.[148]" Benabou

---

[146] Today, as these lines are written, General Ratko Mladic is confronted with justice at the Tribunal at The Hague. Reviewing and comparing the case of Srebrenica with the Sabra and Shatilla massacre committed by Maronite Christians against Palestinian Muslims, during the war in Lebanon in 1982, we might acknowledge the relevance of elements of "indirect responsibility" that Ariel Sharon was accused of by the Israeli Kahn Commission of inquiry, without whatsoever connection to the real perpetrators of the crime.

[147] Often used by the UN Officers describing Mladic's ability to improvise and resolve tactical issues in the terrain. Source: Memoirs of War in Bosnia of Albert Benabou.

[148] This dialogue took place on 17 April 1993 in the Airport of Sarajevo during the negotiations concerning the siege of Srebrenica. This was the first meeting between Benabou and Mladic. Source: Benabou's memoirs of War in Bosnia.

responded, specifying that Arik (as he was popularly known in Israel) originated from a Russian family, who immigrated to Israel (Palestine at the time) at the beginning of the twentieth century, adding that, "for his people, he is as determined and dedicated as you are.[149]" That did it, and an instant tacit communication was established between the two. Mladic sent to Benabou a shrewd smile with a twinkle in his eye, insinuating that he was going to "trick the French general.[150]"

At the beginning of the dinner hosted by Morillon, Mladic picked up a loaf of bread in a dramatic gesture. He wanted to demonstrate that, no matter who was invited, he was the master of that land. As a deep-rooted farmer of the countryside, and without any ceremony, he broke the bread with his large, bare hands and started distributing the pieces, offering the first one to Victor Andreev, the UN civil affairs coordinator in Bosnia-Herzegovina, a Ukrainian Christian Orthodox like him, the second to the newfound Israeli friend, Albert Benabou, the third to General Philippe Morillon, with whom he would have to handle his military operations. After a playful hesitation, raising a loud laugh around the table, he offered a smaller piece to the Muslim General Safet Hallilovic. Having made his point, he ignored the ten other military and UN representatives seated at the table. At the conclusion of the meeting/dinner, Mladic committed himself to pulling his forces from Srebrenica. He would indeed do so, with a slight twist, however. As he had guaranteed, he withdrew his units from inside the town and simply repositioned them on top of the hills, dominating the locality and its surroundings. The UNPROFOR negotiators should have insisted in the agreement that the evacuation of the Serb units should include "Srebrenica Opstina," i.e. the town and the nearby controlling mountains. The small difference was between

---

[149] ibid.
[150] ibid.

evacuating solely the town of Srebrenica and maintaining the besieged enclave or releasing the closure altogether and depriving the Serbian units from their obvious military advantage. The bottom line was the usual UN compromise; Mladic improved the deployment of his units, at the same time continuing to dominate the town and its environs, and avoided needless friction with and exposure to the Muslims who, in their rage, constantly initiated skirmishes. Morillon did not think about this detail and did not insist on it. He probably was convinced that he would succeed in obtaining a demilitarization of the region from the UN Security Council. But all he could achieve was a resolution on protected areas, the famous so-called "safe havens," which turned out to become "safe bases for launching attacks[151]" by the Muslims, and for the irritated Serbs a convenient space for holding the packed civilians who remained enclosed under hermetic siege.

On the same evening, returning to the Kiseljak HQ, Albert Benabou asked the G2 Branch (intelligence & security unit) to provide a map of Opstina Srebrenica that clearly reflected the critical topographic situation around Srebrenica (see picture of the original map on next page).

In effect, Kofi Annan, the peace keeping commissioner for the United Nations, noted on paragraph fifty-nine of his report on the fall of Srebrenica:

While the Security Council was speaking out strongly against the action of the Bosnian Serbs, UNPROFOR was

---

[151] United Nations Safe Areas (UN Safe Areas) were humanitarian corridors established in 1993 in the territory of Bosnia and Herzegovina during the Bosnian War by several resolutions (819, 824, 836) of the United Nations Security Council. In 1995 the situation in UN Safe Areas was deteriorating, and it led to a diplomatic crisis which culminated in the Srebrenica massacre; one of the worst atrocities in Europe since WWII. The other declared safe areas knew the same fate and became "safe areas for launching attacks" for the Muslims who benefited from UN protection.

*Savagery in the Heart of Europe*

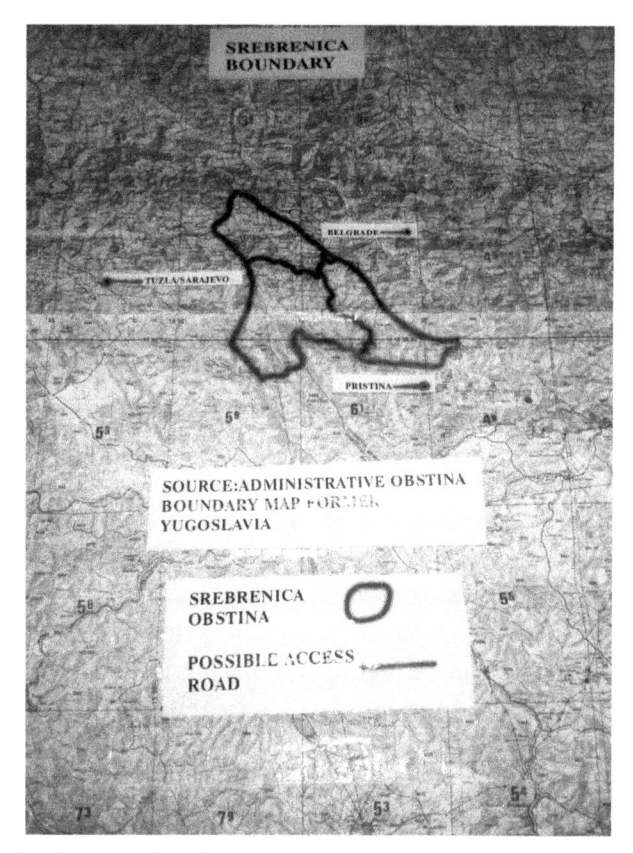

This original map produced during negotiations at the Airport of Sarajevo with Serbs clarifying to Morillon that the Serb General, Ratko Mladic was referring to the retreat of his forces from the town of Srebrenica and position them on top of the controlling hills which were "Srebrenica Obstina" (larger Srebrenica)

confronted with the reality that the Serbs were in a position of complete dominance around Srebrenica.[152]

This was a recognition that not merely the town of Srebrenica, but all its surroundings, were part of the challenge presented to the United Nations by the Bosnian Serbs. Morillon

---

[152] See report of Kofi Annan, the Secretary-General, pursuant to General Assembly of the United Nations Resolution 53/35, the Fall of Srebrenica. Fifty Fourth Session, Agenda Item 42, concerning the Situation in Bosnia and Herzegovina.

succeeded in attracting the international attention to the situation, but did not dwell on this topographic dimension, which was at the core of the complete military picture. Moreover, both parties, Muslims and Serbs, were anyway not interested in halting their belligerent activities. Reading the will of the fighting parties and their deployment in the war theater, one could conclude that it was more valuable for them to insist on an appropriate accord or renounce it altogether, so as to avoid weaving false illusions at the headquarters in New York.

As a result of the international alarm on Srebrenica, the Security Council of the United Nations adopted on 16 April 1993 Resolution 819, followed by Resolution 824, creating the protected areas extending to all enclaves (except Mostar where Benabou operated), for unexplained reasons, at times attributed to the strong Croatian lobby in the West and at the United Nations, which apparently worked on the assumption that a "safe haven" in Mostar would scuttle Zagreb's designs to "cleanse" it from Muslims. Acting under Chapter Seven of the United Nations Charter, the council went on demanding that all parties, and others concerned, should treat Srebrenica and its surroundings as a safe area, which should be free from any armed attack or any other hostile act, and further demanded the cessation of all hostilities and the withdrawal of Bosnian Serb paramilitary forces from Srebrenica. That was the first instance of a civilian "safe area" that was proclaimed to the world. It also demanded that the Federal Republic of Yugoslavia cease supplying weapons, military equipment, and other services to the Bosnian Serb paramilitary units in Bosnia-Herzegovina. Close to one hundred and fifty peace-keepers were later deployed to reassure Bosnian Serb General Ratko Mladic that the town would not be used as a base to attack his forces. But he was not persuaded by these measures, and a month later the concept of a "safe zone" would be extended to other towns including Tuzla,

*Savagery in the Heart of Europe*

Zepa, Bihac, Gorazde, and Sarajevo (but not Mostar) as part of Resolution 824.[153]

However, the UN peace-keepers did not prevent the Muslim forces from utilizing the safe areas as a base of continuing attacks against the Serbian population and its militias. And despite its cautionary wording, Resolution 819 failed to prevent the Srebrenica massacre performed by the Serbs in July 1995, as the United Nations controlled the territory and was supposed to protect it from such horrors. These occurrences ran counter to the naïve understanding of the Secretary General Boutros Boutros-Ghali, who was convinced that UNPROFOR's major strength consisted of its mere presence on the ground and was not to be measured by the might of its deployed units and their weaponry. In fact, the Srebrenica tragedy was triggered when the UN secretariat referred to the relevant UN resolutions as "a positive example where success of this approach [namely resulting from Morillon's and the secretary general's application of their philosophy of engagement and "moral authority" rather than confrontation and the threat of force] has been demonstrated.[154]" In fact, the secretary informed UNPROFOR that none of the sponsors were willing to contribute any additional troops to police the peace in Bosnia, and that none of them, in any case, seemed to envisage a force capable of effectively defending those areas. Moreover, he signaled that deterring attacks against the safe areas should not be construed as signifying deployment in sufficient strength to repel actual attacks by military force, should they occur.[155] The illusion

---

[153] See maps of the UNPAs, United Nations Protected Areas.

[154] In his address to enlarge the "safe areas" in Bosnia (resolutions 824 & 836), prior to the massacre in Srebrenica, and in his argumentation with General Jean Cot, Boutros Boutros Ghali sustained the approach claiming that the morality of the United Nations was demonstrated by those resolutions and stands above the use of force.

[155] See footnote 152.

and the lacuna were there; first, that there was no tight-proof arrangement between Serbs and Muslims in Srebrenica; and secondly, the Resolution 819 was void of any sense if it was not accompanied by the allocation of more troops to back their ability to use force when needed. General Jean Cot, the force commander in 1994 who firmly voiced his reservations about this approach, would have been appalled by this state of affairs, as others have been appalled by the United Nations and others' impotence in the face of thugs, like Ahmadinejad in Iran, Saddam Hussein in Iraq, Omar Bashir in the Sudan, and Assad in Syria, who had been defying the entire world community, which had been instead pathetically insisting on "engaging" them instead of defeating them.

Morillon had unrealistically expected to obtain a resolution calling to demilitarize those "safe areas." He probably wished to withdraw the Muslim fighters from the Srebrenica enclave and send them to join other forces deployed in Bosnian areas like Tuzla, Zepa, or elsewhere, prevailing on those who wanted to stay to surrender their weapons. Morillon expected to convince Mladic to phase out the siege of the surrounding villages, because he was well aware that the population of Srebrenica could not continue to live packed in the enclave and threatened day in and day out. Unfortunately, his plan could not be applied, since the protected areas maintained the potential of being exploited as Muslim launching pads for further raids against the Serbs. Consequently, Mladic opposed their implementation. There were six of them: Bihac, Sarajevo, Gorazde, Zepa, Srebrenica, and Tuzla, but each one of the actors, Serbs and Muslims, was aware of the fact that the resolution was inapplicable, and none of the warring parties intended to respect it. They were only working to ameliorate their military deployment, accusing each other of committing crimes or violating agreements. Obviously, the UN forces and its representatives in the terrain could not stick to Resolutions 819 and 824 of the Security Council because they did not contain the vital military resources that could assure the realization of the mission, thus leading to the tragedy of 1995 in Srebrenica. Not for the first or last time, the decision makers in the glass building in New York were denounced by the field officers as disconnected from the realities in the war zone. They were simply wrong to imagine that the mere presence of forces of peace, without the wherewithal they needed, could ensure the success of their mission. In order to establish safe havens and to make them safe, the UNPROFOR force commander had estimated an additional troop requirement of approximately thirty-four thousand men to obtain a minimal deterrence through strength. But the secretary general stated that it was possible to start implementing the resolution under a "light option," with a minimal troop reinforcement of around seven thousand six hundred. That option had limited objectives and assumed the consent and cooperation of the warring parties. But both assumptions turned out to be unrealistic and wrong enough estimates to lead to disaster.

Kofi Annan, later the secretary general of the United Nations and at that time the head of the UN peace keeping operations, recognized this disastrous lacuna in his report concerning the fall of Srebrenica that was distributed to the General Assembly.[156] Moreover, in a candid interview to Alec Russell, the correspondent of *Financial Times*,[157] Kofi Annan disclosed the fundamental problem of the functioning of the member states of the United Nations. Relating to the perennial UN dilemma concerning the decision to grant protection in a war zone, which was particularly relevant to

---

[156] Report of the secretary general pursuant to General Assembly Resolution 53/35, The fall of Srebrenica, distributed on 15 November 1999.
[157] Alec Russell, UK *Financial Times*, May 16, 2011. Selection from the full transcript.

Resolutions 819 and 824 that dealt with the "protected areas and safe havens," Annan noted:

> The question is where you draw the line. Was every possible action taken by the coalition designed to protect helpless civilians or, in some cases, to support the weak, rebellious militias? And how far do you go? And does it fit with the [UN] Security Council resolution and its mandate? Your hands are tied.[158]

He summed up the dilemma that any UN bureaucrat is living with, at any echelon, taking into consideration the fact that nearly no decision can reflect the opposite or diverse interests of all the member states, even if it was adopted unanimously. In our case, the decision not only was not unanimous, but the council was divided and even major countries, like Russia, abstained in the vote. So, the UN representative in action in the field was all the time reminded to respect the mandate, lest the resolution lose its viability. In Bosnia, the troops on the ground were supplied by the member states. Consequently, the risks one was allowed to take were determined by the member states. In some situations some governments even dictated the locations where they didn't want their troops deployed because they were "considered dangerous." Kofi Annan recognized, "obviously, we made mistakes and there probably are situations where perhaps we could have been more assertive.[159]" The UNPROFOR was unable (or perhaps unwilling) to prevent the action of the Bosnian forces themselves within those protected areas. This explains the rage of the Serbs, and Mladic in particular, against that adopted decision. What followed was the gradual reduction to impotence of UN troops and the drama of taking them hostage in Sarajevo and elsewhere. The UN

---
[158] ibid.
[159] ibid.

soldiers were then drawn unwillingly into a conflict when they were the least equipped possible and strictly forbidden to use force, except when their own lives were in danger. This was obviously a mistake, since while that could be perfectly possible for the functioning of peace keeping forces, it was inapplicable to the tasks that were assigned from the beginning to the UN force. One must admit that the UN generals were inept, unprepared, and unequipped to stop Mladic on the path of his attack on the enclave of Srebrenica, Zepa, and Gorazde. Their hands were firmly tied by an impotent and toothless UN mandate. So big was their frustration.

Morillon described the concept of air force strikes against villains in the war as an "illusion to think that it could block the bad guys.[160]" On the other hand, he also explained that the terrain in Bosnia-Herzegovina, and particularly the area of Srebrenica, did not fit to the deployment of armored units. So, what could be done? In that sense, General Jean Cot, the replacing UNPROFOR force commander, called for concrete, political, and specific instructions to the military. He demanded to have the authority to use the air force strikes as an answer to the misbehaving bad guys, whoever they were. We can then tentatively conclude that the UN headquarters in New York failed to provide adequate answers and support to its representatives in the war zone. On the other hand, the Muslims, looking for international support by playing up their victimization, did not cooperate with Morillon when he was ready to evacuate the people who asked to move to Tuzla, which was under Muslim control. Izetbegovic refused Morillon's request to assist those willing to move, and there were thousands of them. Morillon could not do it without Izetbegovic's agreement; otherwise he would be accused of collaborating with the ethnic cleansing policy of the Serbs.

---

[160] See footnote 140.

The most surprising move in 1995 was that Naser Oric withdrew his soldiers from Srebrenica, leaving the way open to Mladic's forces, which entered the city without any resistance. Oric did not even sabotage the access roads to the town. Morillon was a witness when that order was given to Oric by Sarajevo, i.e. the presidency who deliberately caused the tragedy. Naser Oric was only obeying his superiors in Sarajevo. Morillon considered that Mladic fell into a trap, and that trap was intentionally set by Sarajevo. In his opinion, "Izetbegovic should not be criticized either, for he had no other way to obtain what he wanted, that is, to position the international community on the Muslim side[161]."

That was a very serious accusation by a UN official against the Muslim president, for it meant that seven thousand or more human beings were intentionally sacrificed in a Bosnian ploy to achieve the support of public opinion to his cause. With regard to the Dutch Battalion, which was posted in town to protect the Muslims, its personnel found itself in a terribly impossible situation. First and foremost, they were few in number (four hundred troops); secondly, they saw the Muslim fighters abandon the town; and thirdly, and most importantly, they did not have the authority to open fire except when their lives were in danger. This was the unbearable ground rule imposed on the UN forces of "Zero Deaths," which Annan himself deplored after he quit his post as secretary general as "going to a UN mission with your hands tied.[162]" This often happens in war circumstances, when the will to save casualties ultimately causes more of them. For example, those who opposed the nuclear bomb on Hiroshima could have caused many more casualties to the Americans if they had been obliged to land in Honshu without the bomb.

---

[161] See footnote 140.
[162] Alec Russell, *UK Financial Times*, May 16, 2011. Selection from the full transcript.

Conversely, if the Americans had used the nuclear bomb on Haiphong at the outset of the Vietnam War, they would have killed hundreds of thousands, but perhaps ended the war in the bud. Instead, in order to "save life" and avoid the nuclear holocaust, they bombed with napalm and other explosives and caused the much greater horror of millions of innocent civilians who perished.

The Serbian General Ratko Mladic had one objective, to provoke the withdrawal of the UN force from the war zone. He was convinced that he could beat his enemies without firing a shot. The UN forces were for him troublemakers, intruding into his private domain. The same reaction could be gauged on the part of the Croats in the battle of Mostar. There, Croatian General Milivoj Petkovic[163] had the same attitude towards the besieged Muslims in East Mostar. In both cases, Serbs and Croats, possessing heavy weapons, were confident of their capacity to crush the Muslims, but the latter, though missing the firepower on the field, excelled in manipulating the international opinion to their side. It was decisive in this asymmetrical war. The tradition of "Franco-Serbian friendship" did also play a role in some ways, but the terrible tragedy of Srebrenica, which could not be foreseen, caused fear to prevail. The Serbs, who lived in the mountains around Sarajevo, were told that if they did not participate in the war their wives would be made to wear the Islamic veil. While Tito had succeeded

---

[163] Milivoj Petkovic (born 11 October, 1949) was a Bosnian Croat, a career military officer who graduated from the Yugoslav People's Army military academy. In July, 1991 he left the JNA to join the new Croatian Army as a general. In 1992, he was ordered to take over the Croatian Army's forward command center in the town of Grude, in Bosnia-Herzegovina, and this force would later become the HVO armed forces. He held the title of chief of the HVO general staff until August 1994. He was indicted and charged of war crimes by the International Criminal Tribunal for the former Yugoslavia (ICTY), in the context of the role of the Croatian Republic of Herzeg-Bosnia during the Bosnian War. Albert Benabou's testimony in closed doors at the court in 2008 was crucial in this trial.

in establishing a seeming reconciliation between the various ethnic communities, which was shattered during this war, the Europeans believed in the capacity of the southern Slavs to restore it, and their involvement in the peace making efforts was geared towards reestablishing the illusory harmony that had prevailed before.

## General Jean Cot

In July 1993, General Jean Cot was appointed commander of UNPROFOR, replacing the Swedish General Lars-Erik Wahlgren. Two weeks before ending his mission, General Philippe Morillon came under his command as the subordinate commander of the UN force in Bosnia-Herzegovina. Unlike Morillon, Cot was by nature a military man who followed rules and clear-cut procedures, while the grey areas of diplomacy, which permitted avoidance of duty through debates and contradictory interpretations of guidelines, were not to his liking. Born in 1934, General Jean Cot pursued a long military career, specializing in close air support to ground forces. In childhood, in 1944, he lost his father, who was shot by the Germans. In many aspects, General Jean Cot reminded many of the boldness of Israeli General Meir Dagan, the legendary head of the Mossad (2002-2010), whom Albert Benabou had met during the 1982 Lebanon War, and he remembered this devoted and courageous Israeli military as acting with firmness in the battle around Beirut, when he commanded an armored brigade. Neither Cot nor Dagan would take an ambiguous guideline as an order. Both were ready to carry the burden of responsibility, but they expected to operate under a definite and clear mandate, vested with a full authority that was delegated to them. Dagan kept in his office a picture of his maternal grandfather, who had been murdered in the Holocaust by Nazi soldiers, as Cot treasured his father's. That made both men the product of the painful memoirs of the Second World War.

Cot encountered significant difficulties when he took over the command of UNPROFOR. He inherited from his predecessors an inapplicable mandate, in the vein of Security Council Resolutions, which could state one thing and its reverse, in the disastrous tradition developed by Henry Kissinger and his likes, who professed that "constructive ambiguity" could bring the parties to accept a document or a resolution if they were given the leeway to interpret it their way. Little did they know that when the moment of truth arrived, and those papers had to be implemented, the differences erupted and scuttled any solution, as it has happened with SC Resolution 242 of November 1967, about which no consensus can be secured to this day, in spite of the fact that it was seemingly "adopted" by everyone concerned. Similarly, while the UN secretariat in New York was satisfied with its resolutions (819 and 824) and was convinced that the situation in the terrain was manageable and under control, that imposed formula, which was designed to ensure the protection of the "safe areas," especially in Srebrenica, with a symbolic UN presence, which would be sufficient to "deter any hostile military initiative" among Serbs and Muslims, ended up in the most horrific massacre of the war. Cot met with Naser Oric, who was the commander of the Srebrenica enclave before the massacre. In retrospect, for Cot also, the disturbing question stays open: why were the Muslim basic defenses of Srebrenica removed before the massacre took place in July 1995? In fact, the Muslim military commander, Naser Oric himself, had left town with some of his immediate subordinates. It is quite disturbing to learn that the British General Rupert Smith, who commanded the UN troops in Bosnia and Herzegovina at the time, had gone on leave, then he was summoned to a meeting in Geneva, then he "disappeared" from sight and did not reappear on the stage until 13 July, after the massacre had been perpetrated. The question marks concerning that conduct continue to haunt all concerned to this day.

A Canadian company had been detached to Srebrenica, but its two hundred men were unable to fulfill their overbearing mission, for their presence was less than symbolic. For an enclave the size of approximately fifteen by fifteen square kilometers, that meant they could maintain an average of an observation post every ten kilometers, which obviously fell far short of what might be called the "defense of the enclave." Thus, the Dutch Battalion was assigned to deploy in Srebrenica in January 1994, relieving the Canadian company, whose troops were already "on their knees[164]" from sheer exhaustion. Cot tried to find a temporary intermediate alternative. In order to provide that instant solution, he issued an order to the large Nordic Battalion (NORDBAT) located in Tuzla to provide at least one reinforced company to the Srebrenica enclave to fill the gap between the Canadians and the Dutch. But the commanding Swedish colonel refused to oblige, and Cot had to summon him to explain his disobedience. The Swede, who was accustomed to military discipline, burst in tears, saying, "I am ashamed as an officer, but my government forbids me to execute your order.[165]" Cot thereupon informed the secretariat on 25 September that he had ordered elements of the Nordic Battalion to replace the Canadians to allow for their scheduled rotation out of the enclave, but that the commander, acting on instructions from the government of Sweden, had refused to conform. The Canadians therefore had to remain in Srebrenica until elements of a Dutch Battalion were able to deploy there in January 1994, this timing due to the repeated delays caused by Serbian obstruction. So much for military discipline, which is

---

[164] See Footnote 140.
[165] See Footnote 140.

essential to fulfill military operations but was so sorely lacking in the abnormal structure of the UN forces.

But the saga did not end there, as Cot received from New York, on 15 October, a threatening message asking him to withdraw his order to the Nordic company. The essence of the message was "I hope that such an incident will never happen again," implying that Cot had acted wrongly and that he should never again assume the audacity of fulfilling his job correctly. New York also clarified that every soldier under UN service functioned in two circuits simultaneously, namely under two chains of command at the same time: the UN system and the circuit of his nationality. In other words, when the UN chain of command conflicted with the chain of command of his own country, the commanding officer was put in an impossible situation. But true to its "constructive ambiguity" instinct, the United Nations never clarified who retained the authority to decide, and worst of all, how could a superior commander make any operational decision in the heat of hostilities if he could expect his subordinates to declare at any time his orders "inapplicable?" Cot was not the sort of person to accept unjustifiable scolding, nor remain silent in the face of this chaotic, demoralizing, and destructive conduct of the glass building in New York. He immediately retorted to the secretary general:

> I cannot accept the last sentence of your message. This is not an incident, but a matter of fundamental principle. I will react in exactly the same fashion for any act of disobedience. There cannot be two kinds of troops: those on whom I can rely [he meant the French units] and those who do not obey[166].

This firm reaction did not improve Cot's relations with Secretary General Boutros Boutros-Ghali. The difference of

---
[166] See footnote 140.

opinion and of understanding between those two men about the respective roles of the civilian hierarchy and the military in UN service, especially in peace keeping missions, ultimately would lead Cot to conclude his mission earlier than planned. Nor did this explosion help improve the standard of discipline among the troops of various nationalities during their mission. Asked about a hypothetical case of contradictory directives between an order from the UN headquarters to act and instructions from the French president to disobey, General Jean Cot answered, "It's always easy to say, I would have done this or that.[167]" But, he added, that if he should face such a dilemma, the only way out was to resign his job, unless his conscience indicated otherwise, one way or the other. Those conflicting situations of conscience were common in UN troops in various battlefields. For example, Albert Benabou was often caught in the midst of a bombardment in Muslim East Mostar. In some cases, civilians, among them children and elders, were severely wounded. In such instances, he gave orders to evacuate them in his UN vehicle to the nearby hospital. He was reprimanded by Victor Andreev for acting against the rules of neutrality and for interfering in the battle between the parties. But he was ready to take the responsibility for instructing the UN vehicles to stop and collect the wounded to the field hospital in the city. The British officers who were accompanying him did not argue. Conscience prevailed sometimes over UN regulations.

But Cot was just unaware that his president, Jacques Chirac, was against taking any risk in a UN operation. Kofi Annan reported in an interview to this effect: "My good friend, Jacques Chirac, didn't want to expose his troops. But he stressed, that he was prepared to put in more soldiers on the ground, rather than risk using air power that may further

---
[167] See footnote 140.

*Savagery in the Heart of Europe*

complicate the situation[168]." It is noteworthy that Chirac was even against the use of air strikes, as advocated and required by General Jean Cot. One must also understand that Jean Cot was conscious of the fact that while the Nordics, who counted forty-four thousand troops on the ground, would not agree to risk the lives of their soldiers without investigating first the terms of engagement and obtaining clearance from their government in Stockholm, the French units from all branches of the army would follow orders without any hesitation or question. Moreover, the UN Security Council resolutions (in this case 819 and 824) suffered from intrinsic contradictions, as already indicated above. Specifically, these relevant resolutions provided that UNPROFOR should "take immediate steps to increase its presence in Srebrenica and its surroundings, in order to monitor the humanitarian situation in the security zone[169];" but in the same text, in another paragraph, it is made clear that no more resources would be allocated to that enlarged mission. Then, how, and by whom was that added resolution, which required an addition of troops, to be enforced? Simply stated, the same UN secretariat who demanded the extension of UN action within the Srebrenica enclave, due to the dire needs on the ground, also confirmed that it was short of resources to implement the resolution, implying that the warring parties themselves, who had different axes to grind, different priorities to follow, and different needs to attend, should take certain actions themselves and relieve UNPROFOR from its obligation to establish and protect such safe areas. This was an exercise in futility in the full sense of that expression.

General Jean Cot was familiar with UN resolutions that said "yes and no" in the same breath, without recognizing

---

[168] Alec Russell, UK *Financial Times*, May 16, 2011. Selection from the full transcript.
[169] See footnote 140.

any inconsistency. He analyzed this situation as follows: "We never had the desire to truly defend the safe areas. It was the evil aspect of the Security Council, to set unattainable targets and never admit that it did.[170]" In his view, the attitude of the general secretariat of the United Nations reflected the perversity of its member states. And he thought that while regretting the absence of sufficient resources, the secretary general and the people around him endorsed without scruples the concept that the quality of deterrence was not a function of effective power. As regards the United States, Cot believed that while refusing to commit troops on the ground in the Balkans, where they could be killed, it had always preferred to dispatch NATO air power for such a mission as it had recently done in Libya too during the "Arab Spring" crisis of 2011. At the thirteenth NATO summit, which took place in Brussels in January 1994, the United States indeed presented air strikes as the panacea that was supposed to resolve the need to use force in Bosnia-Herzegovina. The major European troop contributors adopted then the American proposal without debate, in spite of the fact that they contributed all the peace keeping forces via the United Nations. Cot was also expertly aware that close air support, of which he was a recognized specialist, required an extraordinarily complicated cooperation between the troops on the ground and their air support. For that reason, in the overall military strategy of modern warfare, the concept of close air support has been diminishing in importance. Moreover, since it required a wide-ranging and frequent joint training with the users, which was not available on this instance, it made sense to resort instead to amplified use of air power in depth, especially on fixed or semi-fixed targets, as was the case with the NATO air strikes on

---

[170] See footnote 140.

Mount Igman in 1995[171] or later in Kosovo. This kind of air operation was impossible in Srebrenica or Gorazde, where the ground forces were extremely dispersed and diluted in the restrained space of the war theater.

Beyond this technical difficulty, UN Secretary General Boutros Boutros-Ghali had decided to keep exclusively in his hands the decision to use air power in Bosnia. During six months, General Jean Cot tried to convince him that it was clumsy, ineffective, and counterproductive to maintain this lengthy chain of command, when in moments of urgent need decisions had to be made without delay. Finally, the authority to permit air strikes was delegated to the secretary's special representative in former Yugoslavia, Yasushi Akashi, who was also instructed to consult New York and obtain its approval before action, thus effectively tying his hands. Foreseeing the sensitivities of this matter, General Jean Cot, the UNPROFOR commander, had already kicked off the first full air support exercise in Bosnia-Herzegovina on 8 August 1993 in the Bihac pocket. The training was to simulate weapon delivery by NATO aircraft to ground forces, and the exercise was carried out as part of the ongoing training to develop the command, control, and communications links between the UNPROFOR forward air controllers on the ground and NATO aircraft, and to test the UN decision making chain of command. Cot expressed full satisfaction that optimal command and control techniques had been tested over all aspects of the system, stating that the exercises went indeed very smoothly.

However, as predicted by Cot, when the air strikes were needed in the real world the system did not work. For, following the severe Serbian acts against the civil population

---

[171] Mount Igman is the mountain directly controlling from the southwest of the airport and the access to Sarajevo. This was the largest NATO operation to date, which put an end to the war in Bosnia-Herzegovina.

in Bihac, General Jean Cot prepared on the night of 13 to 14 March 1994, in conjunction with US Admiral Jeremy Boorda, an air strike with fifty planes from the AFSOUTH[172] force. The endless exchange of harsh messages with Serb General Ratko Mladic did not help to stop the criminal activities of his militias, so Cot asked Akashi for clearance to use air power. The procedures lasted for hours, because hand shackled Akashi was continuously asking for additional clarifications. When the UN consent was finally given, after five hours of nerve-wrecking waiting and arguing, the sky was covered, and the attack had to be put off. It was, in all evidence, this insistent persistence on the part of Cot which led the secretary general to ask for his recall. Cot inspired reliability and firmness, and he was regarded as the authoritative military address to move forward such operations as the Peace Initiative in Mostar. Though the UNPROFOR civil affairs officials in Zagreb were reluctant, Albert Benabou insisted that involving the military in the process was a sine qua non to its success, for without UN military participation there was no chance to create a constructive dynamism between the warring Croats and Muslims there. Thus, in spite of his personal antipathy to the general, Cedric Thornberry agreed to such a meeting, which was scheduled for 28 December, 1993 in Zagreb.

Colonel Roger Duburg, who served as chief of staff of the sector of Sarajevo, was at that time posted with the personal staff of the commander of UNPROFOR. Duburg, who was put in charge of military negotiations between the warring factions, held a preliminary meeting with Benabou, where he grasped immediately the importance of the initiative. In that spirit, he briefed the general prior to the set meeting. Benabou exposed the initiative to General Cot, elaborating

---

[172] Air Forces Southern: the air force component of United States Southern Command.

on the details of the different stages of his initiative and emphasizing the difficulties he was encountering inside the UN structure due to bureaucratic politicking. The time was just after Christmas of December 1993. Zagreb was under a heavy carpet of snow, which proffered a hapless and helpless general impression of powerlessness at a time when general winter took over that country at war. Benabou was preoccupied by how to elicit and confirm the support of both the military and political decision makers in the United Nations, and that was the purpose of his visit to the headquarters in Zagreb. He recapitulated to the UNPROFOR chief the main outline of his initiative, and at the conclusion of the presentation, General Cot approved Benabou's political and military analysis and pledged that, the same evening, he would exchange views on the initiative with the commander of UNPROFOR forces in Bosnia-Herzegovina, General Francis Briquemont, who had replaced Morillon. He also asked Benabou to set, as soon as possible, a meeting with General Briquemont. Benabou emphasized that he had already tried, on three occasions, to meet with General Briquemont, but without success, and he was afraid the general was avoiding him for some unclear reason. Nonetheless, he promised that he would firmly insist on such a meeting during his next trip to Sarajevo.

At the conclusion of the Zagreb meeting, Benabou noted that new complications might arise from the Muslim party concerning the initiative, because their recent military achievements might encourage them to further advance militarily before they responded to any new peace plan. He added that since on the other hand, the Croatian military forces were still at the level of a militia, and their chances to achieve major military objectives in the field were quite limited, their ability to bargain a political deal was considerably diminished. He thus thought that the moment was adequate to impose a peaceful interim arrangement for Mostar. He also mentioned to the participants that he had shared this assessment of the situation with the Croatian authorities in Zagreb, Grude, and Mostar. Thereupon, General Cot instructed Colonel Duburg to continue to accompany the project and to oversee the necessary preparations of its military aspect. The entire meeting took place in a business-like and cordial spirit of goodwill and cooperation, and General Cot ended up inquiring about Benabou's evaluation of the chances that the donated South African hospital be authorized by the Croats to cross into their territory en route to Muslim East Mostar. Benabou explained that at that period of time, as the Croats were seeking a political settlement, they would not permit any reinforcement to the war effort of the Muslims and to their endurance on the ground.

## General Francis Briquemont

Belgian Lieutenant General Francis Briquemont replaced French General Philippe Morillon as the UN commander in Bosnia-Herzegovina. He declared upon taking office that UN resolutions permitted commanders to define rules of engagement for their troops, adding that "this does not mean that the military chief on the spot is committed to fight to attain any particular objective,[173]" whatever that meant. Briquemont, whose country posted eight hundred troops in former Yugoslavia, dismissed the speculation that he would adopt a more aggressive policy in Bosnia-Herzegovina and announced that he would try to reach a lasting ceasefire. He, like the military and politicians on all sides, including UN bureaucrats, grasped the distress of the civilian population that was abandoned in Mostar while their leaders were playing

---

[173] DOC. 026: Field report from Benabou to UN headquarters reporting in the meeting between General Francis Briquemont and President Mate Boban, dated: 20 July 1993.

war. On Monday, 21 June, 1993, following Croatian leaders' and UNPROFOR officials' urgings, a press conference was convened in Medjugorje at the SPABAT headquarters. General Briquemont was accompanied by his deputy, Spanish General Prado Navarro and the commander of SPABAT, Colonel Angel Morales. The UN civilian participants were the coordinator of civil affairs for Bosnia-Herzegovina, Victor Andreev, and for the region, Albert Benabou. At the head of the Croatian delegation stood their president, Mate Boban, and at his side, the minister of defense, Bruno Stojic, the advisor for international affairs, Vladislav Pogarcic, and the commander of the HVO, General Milivoj Petkovic.

Nothing concrete came out of that stale encounter, not even one topic of substance that could draw the media attention. Every participant was happy to have spoken for himself and for his limited constituency, but the crucial voice which could make the difference was absent and silent, for no representative from Muslim East Mostar was invited or present. General Briquemont preached his obligation to neutrality, insisting that UNPROFOR was not favoring any party in that unfortunate war. He commented on the UNPROFOR mission, stressing that it was committed to benefit all people regardless of their nationality or ethnicity. As a protagonist of an increased presence of the UN forces in Bosnia, Briquemont indeed constantly implored New York to augment the number of posted UN peace keeping forces in former Yugoslavia. That UN message by its military chief in the war zone meant in effect that there were no yardsticks of right and wrong to abide by, and that no matter what one did, the troops charged with keeping that evasive "peace" would remain "neutral." Moreover, Briquemont could not accomplish any concrete move on the field, for unlike Morillon, whom he replaced, he did not grasp the essence of his mission, which was to maintain the equilibrium which nourished permanent contacts and negotiations between the warring ethnic factions in Bosnia-Herzegovina, with a view to providing humanitarian assistance to the civilian population and making sure that it reached them, something that French General Philippe Morillon had placed at the top of his agenda. Being neutral and passive, rather than initiating and prompting the parties to respond, did not serve realizing UPROFOR's goal.

Boban, on his part, was proud to announce that the UN personnel were welcome in Croatian territory, as long as their activities were not undertaken "at the expense of the Croatian national interest,[174]" whatever that meant. This sounded very much like General Ratko Mladic, who was eager to continually demonstrate that he still was the master of the land. Both of those rival Slavic commanders considered as a real threat the prospect that their respective countries, which were overrun by war and half devastated, might become an easy prey for usurpation and domination by foreigners. That state of mind, among leaders at war, certainly deserves a psychological investigation, but in the meantime, Boban claimed that in the future he would facilitate freedom of movement in his territory, and he rejected the charge that Croatian checkpoints were unjustifiably blocking the passage of humanitarian convoys to Muslim enclaves. Those assurances notwithstanding, nothing would change on the ground. In fact, the situation would deteriorate for future humanitarian convoys, as will be explained in the following pages. Briquemont and Boban agreed that the war could only be resolved politically, through negotiations between politicians. All those well-meaning people, Briquemont, Boban, and Colonel Morales, found a way to congratulate each other for the "dedication of UNHCR, the civil affairs office and SPABAT to the Croatian People[175]" during the war.

---

[174] DOC. 026: Field report from Benabou to UN Headquarters reporting in the meeting between General Francis Briquemont and President Mate Boban, dated: 20 July 1993.
[175] ibid.

They all cynically ignored, at the same time, the distress of the civilians who were being directly bombarded in East and West Mostar. Benabou disapproved of the discreet, informal consultation, conducted on the margin of that meeting between the "three Christian leaders" (Briquemont, Boban, and Morales), and sensed that among the three of them the plot was mounted to neutralize his own activity in the field (the interim Mostar Peace initiative).

Referring to that morning's meeting in Medjugorje with Briquemont and the UN officials as vain, Boban decided to transmit his message systematically and informally to the outside world. He invited Albert Benabou, who arrived to the meeting accompanied by Captain Molina (from G2 military branch in charge of intelligence and security) and Captain Pita (from G5 military branch in charge of military cooperation and the media) of the Spanish Battalion. It was clear that Boban wished to transmit personally his informal message. Vladislav Pogarcic, Boban's adviser for international affairs, was also present at that meeting, where Boban spent over two hours stating his fundamental views on the situation. He was primarily concerned about the resolutions that might be generated by the Geneva Conference, which was scheduled for 23 June. He had not been invited to its opening session because the Zagreb officials, who had set up that conference and determined its agenda, were reluctant to afford him too much international exposure. They preferred to prevent an international display of his opinions and of his attitude on the diplomatic scene. At the end, Boban was invited to attend and participate, in spite of his angry rejection of the restrictions Zagreb had attempted to impose on him. He also contemptuously refuted the awkward reputation that was projected on him as a "brute" in Croatian political circles, for his actions and statements vis-à-vis the Muslims of East Mostar.

Boban felt misunderstood. He wanted to demonstrate and prove to Washington that he was in fact, contrary to his image, contributing to stability in the Balkans in the long-term, and he was convinced that the Americans would be persuaded by his analysis. He also realized that the Croats were facing a political situation which was not in their favor during the Bosnian War. He also believed that a major Croatian military operation could gain legitimacy in the eyes of the international community, and he let it be known that the military option remained the most concrete and beneficial, something that proved right in retrospect. Thus, though he expressed his desire to see UNPROFOR outside the Croatian area of the war, he was loath to be later accused of having driven the international forces out of his territory. Be it as it may, the Croatian HVO soldiers continued to paralyze the UNPROFOR movement in Mostar and Central Bosnia. Thus, unless other Croatian military leaders such as Brigadier General Milijenko Lasic, commander of Croatian Mostar, took over, the policy adopted by Boban was as follows:

(a) To maintain a constant pressure on the Muslims in central Bosnia, without initiating any decisive action on the battlefield. Meanwhile, to keep an international policy of dialogue that pleased the United Nations and the international community and to simultaneously coordinate his measures with the military and politician Serbs, in order to create confusion and chaos among the Muslim leadership.

(b) Since the question raised by the Croatian population of Bosnia was, "What did the Croats gain from this war?" Boban saw himself obliged to demonstrate to his constituency, as soon as possible, a political or military gain. This thesis was increasingly discussed among the people in the streets of Mostar and in other towns and neighboring villages of the region. Prlic

*Savagery in the Heart of Europe*

added to the uncertainty by claiming to have effective and subtle solutions that would "eliminate the Muslim presence in Mostar[176]," whatever be his ominous intentions.

(c) The key strategic goal for Boban remained the city of Mostar, which ironically would slip out of Croatian control in the post-war settlement and revert to Bosnian sovereignty. To that end, Croatian military operations in the area of Jablanica and Konjic in central Bosnia were carried out jointly with Serbian forces, in order to liberate the Croat HVO forces to focus their efforts on the battle for Mostar, but to no avail ultimately.

(d) It transpired from Boban's strategy and conduct that he was profoundly traumatized by the prospect that his Croatian territory might be taken over, or at least encircled, by expanding Islam, which was being visibly aided by international Islamic movements like al-Qa'ida, the Chechens, and Islamic countries like Iran, with western connivance.

Thus, upon concluding the meeting, Boban openly stated what sounded as his radical positions, complaining that there was a lack of coordination within the UN mission to Bosnia. He broke the "news" that was hardly news, that Briquemont and Morales were the personification of the intrinsic weakness of their organization, namely, their inability to lead and apply a concerted policy. Further hardening his previous positions, he let all his emotions erupt in devastating volcanic lava. He lashed out at:

---

[176] By the end of July 1993, Bruno Stojic, Boban's Minister of Defense, did not achieve the military objective of taking over East Mostar. Prlic, the political adversary to Boban started to voice louder his ability to be the replacing leader and repeated in closed circles that he was able to do a better job than Mate Boban. Source: recorded on the personal memoirs of war of Albert Benabou out of conversations with Vladislav Pogarcic.

The Vance-Owen Plan, which had been previously agreed upon, was suddenly demanded by Boban to be altered with amendments acceptable to the Croats. Until that eruption, the Croats had affirmed that it was the only viable framework for an agreement between the warring parties.

With regard to Alija Izetbegovic, the President of Bosnia-Herzegovina, Boban stated that he should abandon the idea of a Muslim state in Europe, loudly stressing, "I would never accept the establishment of a Muslim state.[177]"

Pogarcic went even further, suggesting that Izetbegovic should be replaced. Boban bluntly concluded, "Alija Izetbegovic is my enemy, and his statements in Ankara, Paris, and Madrid are part of his rejection of the peace process.[178]"

He accused UNPROFOR of "helping only the Muslims and disrupting Croatian operations.[179]" Boban also declared that the Croats were the only ones accepting the permanence in place of the UN forces, but since they were installed neither in Muslim territory nor in Serbian areas, UNPROFOR had become, in Boban's opinion, an "obstacle to the implementation of the aspirations of his people.[180]" Benabou remarked that this accusation was groundless, since the Croats benefited economically from the presence of UNPROFOR, and they also controlled any movement of Muslims and Serbs.

Benabou quoted in the post scriptum of his report about this meeting a line from Raymond Aron written in his book, *War and Peace among Nations*, that "The primacy of

---

[177] DOC. 012, dated 22 June 1993. Report distributed by Albert Benabou from the field to the UN Headquarters concerning Boban's approach to the Geneva's agenda.
[178] ibid.
[179] ibid.
[180] ibid.

politics permits control of the ascent of the extremes, thus preventing animosity from exploding into pure passion and unrestricted brutality.[181]" He expressed his hope that Boban, the politician, was successful in controlling the zeal of his generals and of Stojic, who sought to unjustifiably radicalize Croatian military actions against the Muslim civilian population, in spite of their vanity to date. Pogarcic indeed informed Benabou that thus far the Croatian military appeared to boast of their feats to not much avail. On one occasion, he confided in Benabou's ear that those fanatics were "braggers who did not gain anything.

Briquemont, was convinced that all topics of contention could be settled around a table with a good meal, which could facilitate dialogue. He was just unaware that Boban was of a neurotic character and ate lightly. Benabou consulted Andreev, who suggested to set up a firm substantial agenda for that meeting with the Croats at the SPABAT headquarters, and to invite to it also Muslim representatives from East Mostar. But that approach was not accepted by the general, who wished to explore the matter with the Croats only. Andreev viewed the Croats and Muslims with the same suspicion, for he regarded both of them as a continuity of the zealous Ustasha pro-Nazi collaborators of World War II, which encompassed Croatia and Bosnia.

The first signs of deterioration on the ground were not late to come. The convoy of enriched milk to six thousand children in Mostar (East and West), due to be delivered on 15 July, was blocked, although Pogarcic informed Benabou in an official memo dated 14 July that Boban had ordered all military units of the HVO to respect four hours of absolute ceasefire, to allow the crossing of the milk convoy. He added that the convoy would go through provided the Muslim part

---

[181] ibid.

of Mostar committed to the same. Benabou cabled the HVO commander in West Mostar, Brigadier General Milijenko Lasic, appending the official pledge issued by Boban that authorized the distribution of enriched milk to Mostar children (Croats and Muslims). The outlines of the operation were also appended:

1. The UNHCR would need a four-hour ceasefire to distribute the milk simultaneously to both sides of Mostar to Muslims and Croats.
2. The Croatian HVO police would verify beforehand the loading of the milk on the Spanish armored vehicles.
3. The HVO police would accompany the convoy to the separation point on the line of confrontation between the Muslim and Croatian forces.
4. Before entering the city, the convoy would wait at an agreed time and place for the clearance of movement from a Spanish reconnaissance patrol, which would confirm that the ceasefire was abided by.
5. The milk would be unloaded from the armored vehicles by the HVO and BiH Armija forces, respectively[182].

As was his wont, Benabou concluded his message by quoting a line from the American poet Carl Sandburg, who had volunteered during the Spanish-American War in 1898: "Babies are the expression of God's intention that the world should continue to exist[183]." This time, Benabou tried to reach Brigadier General Milijenko Lasic, who was unwilling to let the convoy through, but to no avail. In spite of the instructions to the military in a letter[184] of the Presidency

---

[182] DOC. 023, dated 17 July 1993, concerning the milk convoy to babies, distributed by Albert Benabou to the UN, Croat and Muslim military headquarters and decision makers.
[183] ibid.
[184] The letter of instructions was issued by the President's assistant, Vlado Pogarcic. See Ref No: 0082 /93, dated 16 July 1993, addressed to Albert Benabou.

from Mate Boban, to co-operate with UNPROFOR, Lasic justified verbally the blockade with the routine platitude that "circumstances on the ground do not facilitate, for the moment, such activity"[185]. In other words, within the Croatian hierarchical lineup, there was a distribution of labor between those who allowed and others who forbade the passage of the convoy. Never mind that children in both parts of Mostar were again the victims of these inhuman tactics. But Benabou would not easily give in, and he decided to ignore Lasic's response and established a radio communication with the Muslim military and civilian leaders of East Mostar, via the technical prowess of the Dutch Communications Center, on Saturday, 17 July, 1993. The two interlocutors exchanged their concerns:

1. The BiH Armija stood behind the agreement concerning the milk convoy and was anxiously expecting that convoy. Colonel Sulejman Budakovic sent an official fax to this effect through his HQ command in Jablanica, because at that time the Muslim part of Mostar was under a barrage of Croatian heavy artillery and cut off from any outside contact.
2. Smail Klaric, chairman of the civil authority in East Mostar, expressed in the most bitter terms his humiliation and despair at this situation. With a voice saturated with anguish, he exclaimed that (a) due to the HVO blockade, thirty-five thousand civilians living on the East bank of Mostar were cut of electricity, water, and basic health services. He warned that the eruption of an epidemic was imminent in all that part of the city; (b) the hospital was short of essential medical supplies, and he begged UNPROFOR to give top pri-

---

[185] Recorded in the personal memoirs of war in Bosnia of Albert Benabou and noted as evidence in his the testimony in the Hague.

ority to this issue; and (c) that in eastern Mostar there prevailed a sentiment of abandon by the international community.

Benabou consulted with Major Carlos de Salas, and they both concluded that the situation in East Mostar was aggravating. On Saturday, 17 July, 1993 at 2000h, Benabou initiated a communication with Bruno Stojic, the minister of defense of the Croatian community in Bosnia. De Salas was present. The UNPROFOR representatives refrained from comments and listened patiently to the Croatian official announcing that the following topics would be signed on Monday, 19 July, 1993 during the coming visit of Briquemont:

1. Following Boban's instructions, the commander of the HVO, General Milivoj Petkovic, would take charge of the various agencies concerned with the milk convoy.
2. Stojic suggested extending the ongoing operation of the temporary evacuation of Croatian children aged six and seven years to Split till the end of hostilities to the entire civilian population. Stojic also asked Benabou to launch the negotiations for POW exchange, specifying that four pregnant women were among the prisoners held by the BiH Armija.
3. Stojic also insisted on the implementation of the agreement he had concluded a month earlier, between the United Nations and the commander of the HVO in the pocket of Konjic, during the liberation of the imprisoned interpreters of the UNHCR from Croatian custody. Stojic and Benabou had indeed promised to lead a humanitarian convoy to the population that was surrounded in the pocket of Konjic. To accomplish this mission, UNHCR had to confirm its participation in the operation under Benabou and obtain clearance for crossing the territory controlled by the Serbs.

During that radio exchange, Stojic spoke with self-confidence and projected power, for the Croatian authorities in Zagreb and in Grude had mandated him to undertake the HVO military operations in the areas of Mostar, Jablanica, and Kostanjica. Pogarcic had informed Benabou that Stojic was leading a tireless campaign to convince Croatian President Franjo Tudjman and Mate Boban that by late July he would achieve a sweeping victory over Mostar. Stojic believed that his operations with the HVO were wisely calibrated, namely at focusing first on Mostar and Jablanica and leaving Kostanjica for a second stage of the operation. It appears that while his military calculations were well-founded on military maps, he was grossly underestimating the tenacity and endurance of Muslims in East Mostar. All means seemed good to him for convincing UNPROFOR of the need to evacuate the Muslim civilians from East Mostar to an outside region. Their lives, he explained, were in danger, and UNPROFOR would bear the responsibility for the consequences. Pogarcic was busy eliciting the help of various UN institutions in this endeavor, and Benabou made every effort to convey through Pogarcic that nothing could come out of that initiative except more massacres on both sides. He considered that the interests of Croats and Muslims in that war were, at that point, to establish a working understanding or a truce between the parties.

The most recent HVO offensive had been launched against the southern part of Mostar with the objective of causing a withdrawal to the BiH Armija units in the region. Stojic's calculation was to let the Muslims control the Bijelo Polje Bridge, to afford them that way an escape route north from the massacre that he was concocting. But none of that was accomplished since the Muslims of East Mostar stood firm, while unperturbed Stojic was reaffirming to anyone who wished to listen, "It might last another twenty days, but at the end it will be either they or we,[186]" and he succeeded in imprinting his conviction on the military and policymakers in Grude, as well as on the Croatian leaders in Zagreb. His "concern" for the Muslim civilians, that he ostensibly wished to let escape, was not genuine, for in his estimate he would catch two birds with one stone, first permanently evacuate from Mostar the Muslim population without any hope of repatriation, and second, once the women, children, and elders were gone, he would launch a decisive attack to the finish against Mostar, without any restrictions and with full force. Benabou's evaluations of the situation were circulated in the Kiseljak command where Victor Andreev, Brigadier General Veer De Hayes, General Francis Briquemont, the G3 military operations, and G5 civil military operations were stationed; in Zagreb, where the G2 military intelligence, the G3 military operations, the G5 civil operations, civil affairs, Cedric Thornberry, and Hussein Al Alfi were posted; in Divulje, where General Searby, of BRITFOR held his command; and in the New York headquarters, and all through DUTCHCOM. As usual by now, Benabou once again cited Raymond Aron in his post script: "In this confrontation, we are now at the stage where some want to win and others do not want to lose, some are motivated by the desire to emerge victorious, while others just do not want to be exterminated.[187]" Everyone understood who was who in this parable, where the Croats stood and what was the corner to which the Muslims were being pushed.

As the civil affairs coordinator of the Mostar area, Albert Benabou, together with the G5 branch commander of the Spanish Battalion, Major Carlos de Salas, formulated the

---

[186] DOC. 024, dated 18 July 1993, report concerning meeting with Bruno Stojic, Minister Croatian Community Herzeg-Bosnia (chapter two) distributed by Albert Benabou to UN Headquarters.
[187] ibid.

agenda of the meeting called by Briquemont for Monday, 19 July, 1993 in Medjugorje that was attended by larger than expected delegations. For UNPROFOR, those present were Victor Andreev, coordinator of civil affairs for Bosnia-Herzegovina, Albert Benabou, civil affairs regional coordinator, General Francis Briquemont, commander of the United Nations forces in Bosnia-Herzegovina, Colonel Cole, aide de camp of the general, General Prado Navarro, deputy force commander, Colonel Morales, SPABAT, Major Salafranca Alvarez, ACOS, Major Carlos de Salas, G5 commander military civilian operations, Major Alfredo Ramirez, G6 commander information systems, Captain Gerardo Molina, G2 commander intelligence, Commodore Barry Frewer, press information officer from Sarajevo, and Izumi Nakamitsu, UNHCR representative. Representing the Croatian community of Herzeg-Bosnia were Mate Boban, the president, Bruno Stojic, minister of defense, General Milivoj Petkovic, HVO commander, Vladislav Pogarcic, director of international affairs, Slobodan Lovrenovic, press director, and Rudman Jude, a young Croat who lived in Australia and had just arrived in Bosnia, eagerly offering his services to the Croatian war effort as a personal adviser to the president. The following points of interest were meticulously prepared for that August meeting. Benabou again suggested that a draft resolution should be tabled at the Security Council declaring Mostar a demilitarized zone, and its airport put to the service of UNPROFOR, to facilitate the movement of humanitarian aid along the Mostar—Sarajevo axis. He emphasize that the airport would serve all and concluded by quoting the prophet Ezekiel, "whose vision affects multitudes of people.[188]" At that point, the common people in East and West Mostar had

---

[188] DOC.025, dated 19 July 1993 concerning the agenda of the Meeting between Boban and the UNPROFOR responsible, distributed to UN, British, Spanish Headquarters by Albert Benabou.

realized that neither of them would achieve a decisive victory, and therefore, the war and its sacrifices were no longer worth pursuing. Their pleas, and Benabou's, to open that road was to permit mere survival in that cruel and merciless war and regain a modicum of normalcy.

At the scheduled time, the delegations arrived to the SP-ABAT base, some through the chaotic road system, others landing in a UN helicopter from Sarajevo. After brief formalities, a copious lunch was offered for starts, with wines from the finest Spanish wineries and the dishes served elegantly by the Spanish legionnaires, their coarse masculine hands sporting delicately elegant and feminine white gloves, which stood in sharp contrast to their battle uniforms, as the menu stood in eye-poking contrast to the starved populations the UN personnel were supposed to rescue. It was not necessarily a UN binge in the midst of surrounding misery, but a noblesse oblige gesture that fit so well with the host, Colonel Morales, who felt obliged to receive his guests with the pomp and ceremony honoring the kingdom of Spain. But this was also a display of obtuseness and tactlessness, to let the unfortunate belligerents among the guests to discover for themselves where the priorities of the United Nations were, when quality wines were hauled on the non-existing roads of Bosnia, and sparkling white gloves were available in the midst of the muddy and miserable environment where this unrealistic, even grotesque, scene unfolded under the envious eyes of the Croatian top hierarchy in the land.

Unimpressed, Boban, as expected, ate lightly. His mind was elsewhere, and from his point of view the presence of the UNPROFOR general mattered little. By the end of lunch, when Briquemont suggested enjoying the coffee under the trees, in the courtyard of the base, taking advantage of the shiny weather outside, Boban, perhaps piqued by the nonchalant luxury around, ignored him. He spotted, instead, a large clean table in the back of the dining room and moved there, followed by his men and all the rest. Pogarcic, proud of the démarche of his boss, sent to Benabou a smile from ear to ear signaling, "look, how we handle them!" for Boban felt at home and at liberty to behave as he saw fit. That was apparently a shared sentiment among Croats, Serbs, and Muslims of Bosnia, in a country at war where all parties feared that the foreigners invited to save them from their mutual destructive conflict "might steal their country and deprive them of their homeland.[189]" After all were seated, Benabou opened the session, offering the floor to the official host, General Briquemont, who eagerly desired to speak. He ceremoniously made his points:

1. The UNPROFOR is neutral and will act impartially and from an egalitarian viewpoint towards all parties. Briquemont wanted on that occasion to comfort the Croats, who were subject to pressures and demands by Benabou during the previous week. For the first time, Benabou felt directly targeted, pondering on whether he might have gone too far and too harshly with the Croats. At any rate, Briquemont arrived from Zagreb with a UN agenda that sought to accord with Croatian interests, following the Spaniards who had already been there. It seemed that without articulating this wish, all present seemed to believe that the Croats would conclude the war with a victory over East Mostar.
2. Freedom of movement to all was imperative both for UNPROFOR and for humanitarian relief, and the UN forces could not accept any obstacles or traffic

---

[189] DOC. 026, dated 20 July 1993, concerning the outcome of the meeting and reported by Albert Benabou to the UN, British and Spanish Headquarters.

limitation in that territory, as it was unacceptable to target and shoot the UN units. All this should stop categorically, insisted the general.
3. He was prepared to introduce a plan, to be implemented before the winter, providing recovery and maintenance of the roads servicing UNPROFOR troops. Benabou considered that it was not the appropriate moment for such activity, for he believed that road construction would primarily facilitate the movement of the troops of the warring parties. Moreover, he felt that it was precisely this difficulty of traffic in the muddy and rocky terrain which prevented troops from practicing ethnic cleansing from remote villages. Therefore, to his mind, it was not a great idea to restore at this time the road network in the region.
4. In conclusion, the general noted that the resolution of this war was in the hands of politicians. He did not grasp that the decision makers were in Zagreb rather than in Grude.

Then, Boban took the floor and responded in an intonation of arrogance, signifying that he was the master in his homeland and that the general could not hope to be treated as equal under those conditions. From their point of view, the Croats had always considered UNPROFOR as unnecessary and superfluous in their territory, and if it was tolerated it was only for the purpose of preserving stability in the region. At any rate, the UN forces were welcome on Croatian territory only as long as the latter's national interests were not sacrificed. On that occasion, Boban elected to forget that it was the Croats who had required UN presence, in order to gain international recognition and to benefit from the economic advantages of UN activities in former Yugoslavia. He also argued that the Croats had never obstructed the freedom of movement of UNPROFOR, and that if there was a claim of such incidents, he required convincing evidence to that effect. Complete silence fell on the audience, and no one tweeted, not even Colonel Morales, who could not make one step outside the base with his troops without prior coordination, which amounted to obtaining permission. Boban further complimented SPABAT, the civil affairs office, and UNHCR for their assistance to the Croatian population when and where it was required. But regarding the Geneva process, he was vague, stating that he had committed himself "to accept what the others would agree upon.[190]" He concluded by recognizing that "soldiers can be defeated, and I am myself a soldier in the service of my nation.[191]" Those words were obviously addressed to his HVO servicemen seated around the table, for he wanted his people to internalize that he too would fight to the end, though knowing that he could be beaten. In effect, his press attaché was present and sure to convey those messages and their significance to the local media.

Benabou did not let go, and he insisted on raising the issue of access to the besieged Muslims in East Mostar. That was the appropriate occasion to do it, while he was sitting face to face with the Croatian leadership that held the key to the solution of this sore issue, at a time when the Muslim population was starving to death. He took the matter up with General Petkovic and Vladislav Pogarcic, arguing that:

1. The Muslim part of the city of Mostar was sealed for more than three weeks, under constant military attacks and bombings, and snipers were shooting all over the city, within and beyond the military line of confrontation. He said that he had been himself targeted, but once again the snipers had missed him. He stressed

---

[190] ibid.
[191] ibid.

that SPABAT and all international organizations were prevented from crossing to the Muslim side, which was hermetically isolated.
2. He stressed that all efforts he and others had made to ensure access to besieged East Mostar had led nowhere, and even the enriched milk convoy, which was geared to serve the children of both parts of the city, in partnership with UNICEF, was scuttled. Pogarcic and Petkovic reaffirmed the necessity to allow the convoy passing through, alright, but Petkovic repeated that at the time heavy combat had taken place on the site, and that it would have been impossible to cease the military operations, even temporarily. He nevertheless promised to consider alternative routes and offer a solution within twenty-four hours, yet another pledge that would never materialize.

Petkovic rejected Benabou's proposal to open a hot line between Croats and Muslims for emergency communications, and the latter was reduced to sum up his frustration from the Croatian system in yet another report, which included this time General R.V. Searby in the distribution list. In his conclusion, he reverted to a line of Yeshayahu Leibowitz, a celebrated Israeli biologist and philosopher, who detected the "positive aspect of democracy in its ability to lay bare the downsides of dictatorships.[192]" That was in effect what the western educated UN troops were discovering in their contacts with Communist-grown bureaucrats, in both former Yugoslavia and the other regimes of eastern Europe which had recently joined, as novices-in-training, the international club of democracy. In a letter to General Philippe Morillon, the commander of UNPROFOR, Boban virulently attacked the "barbaric devastation and desecration

---
[192] ibid.

of Catholic holy places that Muslims had perpetrated," and he complained that "over one hundred thousand Croats in central Bosnia are at risk and subject to eviction and starvation.[193]" He requested the immediate passage of humanitarian aid to the Croats living in the towns of Vares, Kiseljak, Kresevo, Vitez, Novi Travnik, and elsewhere, but now he was orchestrating exactly the same deprivations, in the reverse direction, against the Muslims of Mostar.

In that letter, Boban wished to ensure the release and free movement of the Croatian population in the regions of Sarajevo, Vares, Bugojno, Zenica, Zepce, and Tuzla. Pogarcic had in effect affirmed, more than once, that the Herzeg-Bosnian government was prepared to offer shelter and care to those Croats as soon as they could exit those areas, and he implied that such process of absorption of displaced populations should be also implemented for the Muslims of Mostar to be absorbed by the Muslims of Bosnia. In his words though a movement of population is not easy to realize, it was still the only feasible arrangement, for there must be a separation between different peoples.[194]" He added in a threatening undertone that if UNPROFOR did not cooperate in this matter, the present course of events could lead to disaster, and the Croats were exonerated from any responsibility. He further intimated that General Morillon was expected to be clairvoyant and convince Muslims to participate in a team of four representatives (two Croats and two Muslims) who would handle this situation in a civilized manner. This language referring to "civilization" put Benabou ill at ease, for he recognized the use of this terminology "civilized Europe" in the recent past when justifying the ethnic cleansing of Jews led by Nazis and their other European collaborators.

---
[193] See letter Ref No 0050/93, dated Mostar, 22 June 1993.
[194] ibid.

On his own initiative, Boban offered to demilitarize twenty kilometers on either side of the road from Mostar to Sarajevo via Jablanica, Konjic, and Tarcin. Benabou replied that the proposal would be studied and brought up to the Muslim side, though he personally doubted the innocent intentions of the Croats and wanted to investigate the application of the proposal on the topography of the suggested axis to be demilitarized, for he was well reminded of General Philippe Morillon being trapped in Srebrenica by the Serbian General Ratko Mladic. Incidentally, despite Boban's and his assistants' public statements concerning their common interests and firm relations with Radovan Karadzic and Ratko Mladic, one could understand the Croats' concerns about the price they would be required to pay for the military aid offered by the Serbs, such as access to the Adriatic. Nevertheless, Boban was determined to pay what it took to achieve his immediate military objectives because his political position and stature were at stake.

## Colonel Angel Morales

Colonel Angel Morales was a dedicated soldier to his country, Spain, and to his battalion, *Agrupacion Tactica Canarias*. His mission as part of the peace keeping forces in former Yugoslavia was the first international UN assignment for the Spanish Army and for himself. He belonged to the first generation which acquired English language education, which often turned out to be a verbalization of Spanglish. The same linguistic aptitude could be said of the soldiers and the officers of the Spanish Battalion, among whom knowledge of foreign languages was practically nonexistent. Receiving Albert Benabou at SPABAT, in May 1993, who was newly nominated as civil affairs officer for the region, an Israeli of Sephardic origin, was revolutionary for the Spaniards, not only for his facility to communicate with them comfortably in Spanish, but also for sharing a common cultural and historic background with them. In their first meeting, as he was reviewing the battalion units and visiting the base, Benabou was assured by Morales that their common job was *"trabajamos por la paz"* (we work for peace), which sounded like "we are going to war for the cause of peace!" This short and flamboyant Spanish colonel, who was moving about with a scarf around his neck blowing in the wind, indeed gave the impression of an aggressive and assertive activist, especially when his jubilant smile could in a split second take on the most serious face of an angry commander with a wrinkled forehead. He reminded one of a matador in a bullfight. A fervent Catholic, though educated under fascist Franco, he believed in his mission for peace from the bottom of his heart. He had more presence than any general or other higher ranking Spanish officers. If confronted between the interests of the Croat Catholics and those of the Muslims, he would be more understanding and lenient towards his brothers from the Catholic church.

Colonel Morales could not accept that, in his zone of responsibility, anyone could be credited with any operation or achievement unless that was his Spanish Battalion. Later, he would realize that it was a joint international operation, in which cooperation was sine qua non between the various national battalions and units, who acted on several levels and in various fashions in the different regions of torn apart former Yugoslavia. He had initially wrongly thought that the honor of Spain was at stake, but he later discovered that, on the contrary, the more there was coordination and cooperation between different units, the more Spain could find its place recognized in any worthwhile operation, like rescuing the gravely sick from the danger of death, evacuating causalities of war, or mounting a joint operation with the British troops in Operation Angel. He was suspicious about any relation that Albert Benabou wove with the British forces located in the Divulje base, close to Split. British General Veer de Hayes, posted at the UN HQ in Kiseljak, also established professional and effective working relations with Benabou, who also generated in August 1993 an ongoing contact with BRITFOR General Robin Searby. Actually, most of the British personnel in former Yugoslavia, starting with the lowest level of humanitarian lorry drivers, and ending with the highest ranking officer, were doubling up as sources of intelligence gathering and analysis, and Albert Benabou, himself a former intelligence officer of the Israel Defense Forces, was pleased to offer and receive valuable information from the British concerning his AOR (area of responsibility) and on the overall developments in former Yugoslavia.

## British Officers

From the moment that link was established, BRITFOR was regularly placed on the open distribution list of messages and reports produced by Benabou. To crown that close relationship, the commander of the British forces in Divulje, General John Reith, assigned Captain Peter Loghan[195], seconded by Sergeant Sean O'Brien, to Medjugorje, in the position of military attaché to Benabou. He operated also as coordinator with the Spaniards, who had become an additional source of information for the British. Loghan acted as a conscientious, committed, and professional soldier and was a reliable resource for evaluation in the decision making process. He reflected in fact the closest spirit of enterprise and ingeniousness to what the Israeli officer was educated to be in the Israeli Defense Forces (TSAHAL). By the end of Loghan's service in Mostar,

---

[195] Names changed for maintaining privacy.

Benabou wrote the recommendation for his promotion to the rank of major. It was the extraordinarily tortuous conditions of war, which created the unusual opportunity for an Israeli Officer, in the service of the United Nations, to recommend for promotion a military officer of an alien army. His recommendation tells the whole story:

> Dear Brigadier Reith, Shalom!
>
> For the last six months, Captain Peter Loghan has served in the capacity of military liaison officer for my civil affairs office in Southern BiH, Mostar. Captain Loghan has coordinated and accomplished complex missions with excellence and high commitment. His camaraderie with his military and civilian peers has been exemplary.
>
> During this period of time, he has manifested a permanent readiness to act and assist others facing dangers and difficulties in the field. Captain Loghan has been a remarkable representative of the British Army. My colleagues and the military officers that have operated with him wish him every success in all his future endeavors.
>
> Best regards and warm shalom,
>
> ABA[196].

On Monday, 3 January 1994, Loghan produced, in conjunction with Albert Benabou, a document evaluating and analyzing the options and the approaches of the various UNPROFOR military units, including a pertinent SITREP (situation report) that encompassed major political trends and sensitivities. The document was forwarded to General Reith, the commanding officer in BRITFOR, Divulje. The report was not an official document of SPABAT but a collation of data from different sources, including conversations

---

[196] See personal recommendation dated Mostar, Thursday 3 March 1994 kept in Albert Benabou private documents.

with various Spanish and Croatian officers. At issue were then the positions adopted by the respective United Nations state members, which participated in the UNPROFOR mission in former Yugoslavia, concerning the establishment of a southern UN brigade command in Chapljina, located in the zone of responsibility of the Spanish Battalion. This analysis is cited here to illustrate the enormous complexity of the process of decision making at the international level, even when units of friendly nations were on a joint assignment.

SPABAT had been for a long time against the establishment of a southern UN brigade for various reasons, but with the growing number of operations, which involved both British forces and Spanish forces, the advantages of such a Brigade HQ had grown apparent, and SPABAT staff officers recognized this fact. In the two largest such joint operations, namely Operation Angel and Operation Nightingale, which involved sending medical supplies to a war theater, and evacuation of the wounded from Mostar, respectively, there arose a large amount of confusion over the division of responsibilities, due also to the lack of clear direction from General Briquemont's headquarters at UNPROFOR BiH Command. A SPABAT staff officer involved in these operations ought to have been given overall command, therefore the lack of central control was felt. This did not only result in various decisions being taken separately and simultaneously by the different parties, but a potential danger of involuntary clashing between them developed in the war zone, which could have been avoided had an overall coordinator been appointed. SPABAT officers also felt that BiH Command was too loosely connected with that area due to its lack of detailed knowledge of its AOR (area of responsibility). At times, this engendered the absence of a thorough appreciation by the Bosnia-Herzegovina command of the situation and entailed SPABAT's having to seek permission to change the concept of operations as issued from the Kiseljak United Nations Headquarters, their superior in the chain of command. At that point, it was agreed that the establishment of a southern brigade would actually reduce the amount of staff work undertaken by SPABAT in the field of communications to and from Kiseljak general headquarters.

SPABAT had also expressed severe reservations about the competence and attitude of MALBAT (Malaysian Battalion). They considered that MALBAT, located in Jablanica, would have to be closely monitored, since that war zone was politically highly sensitive. Moreover, the Spanish reported on various occasions the apprehension of the indigenous population in Jablanica regarding the expected arrival of MALBAT, because the Croatian population had voiced protests over the planned insertion of a Muslim battalion into Croatian territory. At last, when the Malaysian Battalion joined the UNPROFOR mission in 1993, their fifteen hundred forces were effectively deployed to Jablanica. Thus, having in place a southern brigade headquarters monitoring the future arrival of MALBAT would be an enormous advantage for the UN forces. But, in spite of that, the Spaniards expressed serious reservations over the establishment of the brigade HQ, the weightiest of which was that they would lose the power to take decisions which affected their own troops in the areas, which have always been within their AOR.

This fear expressed by SPABAT resulted from the fact that no other unit on the ground had as specialized knowledge of Mostar and its environs as they did. They were concerned that the trust that they had built up with leaders of the warring factions might be destroyed, and the long process of confidence building between Brigade South and the various factions might have to be undertaken from scratch, before it could gain the normal level of acceptance that the Spaniards currently enjoyed in their AOR. SPABAT also truly feared a potential shortfall in the amount of staff appointments they would gain if the brigade HQ were established, due to their suspicion that BRITFOR could then boast the existence of a brigade HQ, well run and well organized, with all key appointments already filled by their own appointees, thus lending to the Brigade HQ a distinct British flavor to it, with a totally new and exemplary modus operandi being forced upon them. That would have left them with little choice but to alter well established SOP (Standard Operational Procedure), which their troops had been long accustomed to, something that could endanger their troops in complex situations in the future.

These petty considerations seem silly to the outside world when one considers the yawning gap between the lofty principles under which the UN forces pretended to operate and the trivial debates that erupted between the participating members, who cared more about personal and national prestige than about those unfortunate populations which were being exterminated under their eyes. An obvious disadvantage of the UN regime in such situations, which was already referred to above, was the language barrier that prevented direct communication between the protectors and the protégés, even among the multinational protectors themselves. Whilst some of the Spanish officers spoke some English, other key staff members did not, and evidently even fewer British officers spoke Spanish. Thus, the suspicious Spaniards concluded that as English would be the primary language and the lingua franca of the UN operations, this would further dissipate their share of power. It had also been suggested that establishing the Brigade HQ would necessarily generate a great deal of upheaval and extra work, and SPABAT did not have the resources or the manpower to effectively put their imprint on the new headquarters, or to maintain their regular level of operations within their AOR, for this would further reduce the amount of influence they could wield on decisions taken in the early planning stages of any UN move. And most of all, they did not feel that a southern brigade was operationally necessary since they had worked alone, quite successfully, in that same area, for a number of months now. Whilst they admitted that a Brigade South would constitute an advantage in joint operations, due to its acknowledged coordination capacities, they considered that, all in all, it might only give rise to confusion in isolated operations and end up causing more damage than good.

Due to their vast reservations about the competence and aptitude of MALBAT to operate in this conflict, the Spaniards also feared the potentially embarrassing situation which might arise if MALBAT were to be entrusted with the overall command in certain instances, and their own troops would find themselves subordinated to the Malaysians in a given operation, a situation they would be reluctant to accept. Comparing the numbers of various national troops (for example, British against Spaniards) in the war theater was an obvious factor in the distribution of command and staff appointments. They fully realized that the British had double the number of troops, and therefore, they regarded this as the greatest single threat against their primacy in the command and influence in the newly envisaged brigade organization. The Spanish had a well-founded respect for the British army as a whole, and all joint operations carried out thus far in conjunction with them had only served to reinforce the good relations between them and to develop a mutual respect between the two forces and their commanders. The Spaniards recognized the professionalism of the British officers and troops and acknowledged their vast experience within NATO. They did, however, consider their own officers as equally competent and well trained as the British officers, while they grudgingly admitted that their soldiers might lack the diverse and long operational experience that British soldiers enjoyed.

It must also be remembered that this was the first conflict that the Spanish military had been involved in since their own civil war almost sixty years previously. They considered themselves under examination from the rest of the forces in the war theater, and they missed no opportunity to advertise their military successes, especially through the United Nations and world media. This was also the first occasion that Spain had been acting on an international arena for many years, while it was still struggling to overcome its backwardness compared to western Europe and to integrate fully into the enlarged European Union, especially militarily. Therefore, they were very cautious with every decision made for fear of making a faux pas that could thrust them backwards. This reticence had tremendously restricted their audacity, creativity, and initiatives, which necessarily became detrimental to the success of various operations and demanded courage, daring, and out-of-the-box thinking. Given these fundamental characteristics, they were concerned about the erosion of their power if and when their military competence was put in doubt, especially as the Brigade South was shaping up as essentially British.

Another element in the negative Spanish attitude towards the new southern brigade headquarters being established was that if they indeed lost a large amount of the power they currently held, that might in itself be regarded as a reflection of their capabilities and a slight against their military competence. However, due to the universal recognition of the potential advantages of such an HQ, the Spanish government had for a long time put this item for deliberation on its agenda, an indication that SPABAT considered it a very real possibility, in spite of its utter opposition to it. On 24, February 1994, Albert Benabou dispatched a message from

Sarajevo in which he elucidated the issue of the installation of the southern brigade HQ in Chapljina, which was to begin in the first week of March, 1994, a proposition that also imposed the streamlining of his own civil affairs office to suit that change. In Benabou's estimate, the civil affairs services and the regional political evaluation should henceforth be made out of one office, which should be appended to the brigade HQ in Chapljina, because there was no justification to deploy further offices in the region and could only hamper the smooth operation of that unit. He considered that since Mostar was the political core of the South, for both Croats and Muslims, it was imperative, for the sake of comprehending any event unfolding in Mostar, Tomislavgrad, Konjic, or Jablanica, to take the area as a whole, as the military command had done. He also thought that the southern sector of his civil affairs office now had a strong and valid case to put forward a request to obtain three more large armored vehicles, to accommodate the enlarged activity in view of the augmented sphere of activity in an arena that was constantly exposed to shelling and bombardments. Moreover, the continuous development of the interrelations between the warring parties required meetings to be convened between them at short notice, while it had become wholly inadequate to have to obtain a military escort into Mostar or Jablanica, only when a prior forty-eight hours' notice was given. Benabou was in fact looking to affirm his freedom of movement, independently of the military, for the armored cars would provide a greater degree of movement, with increased efficiency, and permit the better functioning of his unit.

**Yasushi Akashi, A UN bureaucrat**

On Saturday, 26, February, 1994, Benabou was informed by the headquarters of UNPROFOR in Zagreb that Yasushi

Akashi, the new representative of the secretary general in former Yugoslavia, decided to pay a visit to Mostar on Monday, 28, February 1994. He wished to meet with the local leadership and the UN commanders in Medjugorje. The first reaction in place was that there was no sense to such a visit in the war zone, unless the new envoy was just intent on visiting the area to satisfy his tourist curiosity. Benabou indeed clarified that the Croatian decision makers such as Kresimir Zubak (chairman of the presidential council) and Mile Akmadzic (member of the presidency for international affairs) were and would be during all the following week taking part at the negotiations with the Muslims in Washington. Vladislav Pogarcic, the secretary of the presidency, was also absent. He was following up the talks out of the Croatian Ministry of Foreign Affairs in Zagreb. Even Mate Boban, who became a minor figure in the process, was out of the region. Accordingly, the Croats recommended postponing the visit to another date, between 7 and 10 of March, upon their return from Washington. Moreover, following the talks in Zagreb, a demilitarization of Mostar was already being discussed at the same period of time. Benabou also emphasized that an appropriate visit to the Mostar area would require two days.

In the following telecommunications, Benabou realized that due to the fact that Akashi was neither well informed nor invited to attend the ongoing discussions and negotiations in Washington and in Geneva, he decided to hold a visit to the Mostar area. In other words, it was more a political move than a useful act. It did not matter for him if there was no one to visit in the streets of Mostar, for the most important was for that UN bureaucrat to show his presence on the ground, so as not to be totally ignored. He was also, at the time, one of the front runners for the post of UN secretary general, and he needed to appear as achieving something, or at least to be recognized as trying. Once again, political cynicism took the lead in setting the agenda of the United Nations, rather than the needs of the besieged and starved populations of Bosnia, who were supposed to be under UN protection. Under those circumstances, Benabou forwarded to Akashi a collated agenda made up of meetings with irrelevant leaders from the Mostar region. The program was coordinated and set up with the warring parties in Mostar and Medjugorje and scheduled for Monday, 28 February 1994. The UNHCR Medjugorje coordinator, Jerry Hulme, volunteered to offer a briefing concerning the food supply in the region in order to add some substance to the visit. In East Mostar, meetings took place with the local Muslim leadership, Smajil Klaric (president of the war presidency in Mostar), Safet Orucevic (deputy Cmdr. of the Mostar Brigade and political representative of Izetbegovic), Alija Alikadic (director for international organizations and chairman of the delegation for negotiations on Mostar). After a gloomy visit to the hospital, the program continued during the afternoon, first at the Croatian presidency of West Mostar, to meet with the Croatian leadership, Ivan Bender (speaker of the Croatian House of Representatives), Jadranko Prlic (Prime Minister, Croatian Republic of Herzeg-Bosnia), Slobodan Bozic (director for UNPROFOR affairs), Ivan Tomic (chairman of the Croatian delegation for the negotiations on Mostar), General Ante Roso (HVO Cmdr.), and finally a visit to the Croatian refugee center.

While the truly substantive discussions were taking place in Geneva and in Washington, far from the war zone, the Muslims were concurrently very busy lobbying in the US congress and among the Jewish community in the United States, appealing to public opinion in order to obtain free supply of water, electricity, and food in East Mostar, which was not at that point at its worst, due to the relative ceasefire that was maintained in Mostar. None of the parties wished to be caught in an act of belligerence, for fear of being accused of sabotaging the ongoing talks. Although on the ground exchanges of fires and artillery attacks over East Mostar did take place, the decrease in shelling and sniper activity was considerable. And while the Croats maintained their artillery advantage, the Muslims still benefited from their larger infantry units, therefore the decrease in artillery activity could be exploited by the Muslims for improving their infantry positions. During Akashi's visit, each one of the parties expressed suspicions and doubts concerning the outcome of the talks in Washington, and they declared to the UN representative their readiness to pursue hostilities, insisting on their endurance and reiterating their well-known positions:

The Muslims maintained their refusal to be included in a Croatian political entity, whether a union or otherwise.

The Croats insisted on controlling at least one city, Mostar, without which they would have no capacity to establish a separate, political entity in Bosnia.

During the visit, Benabou initiated collateral dialogues between Akashi and each of the parties, in privacy with a limited audience and no press. On those occasions, the parties announced their readiness to consider a solution based upon the status quo of the line of confrontation in the city, which reflected the reality on the ground, in spite of all their respective public declarations to the contrary. The Muslims pleaded for a constant and large presence of UNPROFOR and other international organizations in both parts of Mostar, so as to guarantee their separate viability, a position not vigorously contended by the Croats. Victor Andreev, the veteran UN employee who was familiar with the mechanism of the organization ," was very cautious in his proceedings, always taking care not to get frontally involved or implicated in any risky venture. He had his loyal people positioned around him, and if one was not one of them, one would always be suspiciously considered an outsider. Andreev avoided participating in Akashi's visit, which he regarded as an informal rather than a business act. Only later would Andreev realize that he had been manipulated and sidetracked by the Irish element in the United Nations, personified by Cedric Thornberry, who was also an international professional with seventeen years of missions for the United Nations, including Israel, and worked discreetly to isolate Andreev in his confrontation with General Jean Cot. Andreev did not position himself in favor of Cedric, ostensibly his friend and partner, and would find himself ultimately rejected.

**The Serbian Actors**

Boban invited Benabou to initiate a meeting with the Serbs in order to elicit their position concerning the proposed demilitarization of Mostar. Since General Radovan Grubac, commander of Herzegovina Corps of the Bosnian-Serbian Army, headquartered in Gacko, had expressed his willingness to meet the Israeli civil affairs officer, they met on Thursday, November 11, 1993, for more than two hours in Jazina on the crossing line between Montenegro and the Serbian territory in eastern Herzegovina. Other high ranking Serbian officers and UN military officials also participated in the encounter. All along the meeting, Grubac projected his determination to implement what he was declaring. During the war, Grubac described Dubrovnik as the headquarters of "terrorist organizations threatening Serbian Herzegovina,[197] prompting the Croatian authorities to charge him of war crimes, allegedly perpetrated in the region of Dubrovnik in October 1992. During the talks, General Grubac stated

---

[197] Source: *Balkan Transitional Justice* published on 9 June 2010 from the indictment issued by The Dubrovnik County Prosecutor's Office.

that the Serbian party was content to stay out of the local peace initiative for Mostar, though observing the developments without interfering in their course. Benabou reassured the general that the Serbs would not be ignored and would not be excluded from the process. Grubac brought up his analysis of events stressing that the BSA (Bosnian-Serbian Army) did not initiate any military action, and that it honored the ceasefire along the confrontation lines, but complained about the infiltration of BiH Armija soldiers, who perpetrated acts of sabotage and provocation in the areas of Gorazde, Trinova, and Konjic.

Grubac made clear that as the Serbs were observing the military clashes between the BiH Armija and the HVO in the central zone (Vares, Bugojno, and Vitez), he assumed that the Armija would not give up the battle for Vitez. He also claimed that the accusations hurled against the Serbs for the recent brutal shelling of Sarajevo were groundless, since he was in possession of conclusive proofs that this was an operation of the HVO using their artillery from their base in Kiseljak. To his mind, this was revenge by Cmdr. Rajic against the BiH Armija, which had ejected the Croatian Brigade from Sarajevo. Grubac's view could not be totally excluded, since the Croatian units often acted on their own local initiative, disregarding their chain of command. Grubac also stated that Izetbegovic was concentrating all his efforts to prepare for the winter military offensive and estimated that the hostilities would continue primarily in the southern part of the country, where climatic conditions permitted such activities. In this case the international community must understand that the Serbs, like the Muslims and the Croats, considered the stretch of territory in eastern Herzegovina up to the Neretva River as Serbian territory. His Slavic willpower overtook the configuration of the face of this determined thirty-five-year-old officer when he declared without the slightest hesitation, "We are fighting for it.[198]" The Serbs considered the free access to the sea to be their inalienable right, therefore they were intent and ready to exercise that right, possibly through the area of Dubrovnik, where there was a military buildup on the part of both Croats and Serbs. Grubac also stated that all the decisions and orders were made and issued by Supreme BSA Army Commander Radovan Karadzic, who was respected and obeyed. He asserted that the Serbian Army was a disciplined organization, unlike the Muslims and Croats who were constantly changing their attitudes, due to the lack of obedience and coordination between their field commanders and their politicians.

On the political level, the Serbs were the only belligerents who had declared their clear political goals and were pursuing them from the beginning of the conflict in BiH. They viewed the Sarajevo government as militant and hardliner, especially since the nomination of Harris Silajdzic to the post of prime minister. For the Serbs, the Croatian Mate Boban was considered more reasonable and a more reliable partner for negotiations for any eventual deal than the Muslims, who were equally resented and hated by the Croats, as the confrontations in Mostar proved. Grubac noted that Boban took firmer and clearer political positions, although he was significantly restricted by the directives of Zagreb. He described the Serbian present ambition to be the pursuit of peace rather than the continuation of the war. He expressed a strong determination for such an arrangement, although the military option was not off the table in case everything else failed. When asked about his preferable partner in peace negotiations, he divulged that tripartite negotiations were more advantageous for him, for in his opinion, the prospects

---

[198] DOC. 114, dated Saturday, 13 November 1993, concerning field report, distributed by Albert Benabou to the UN, British and Spanish Headquarters.

of a possible political solution might include certain local, autonomous arrangements for the Serbs within the BiH held territories. He remarked that East Mostar, for example, might in the future attempt to achieve an autonomous status, but he viewed the Sarajevo government as a serious obstacle to such a solution.

Grubac explained that Karadzic had rejected the Franco-German proposals, which had ignored the cardinal matters involved. He thought that the major stumbling block was the three percent of territory that the Serbs were required to give up, not so much for its area as for its high quality. He reiterated that if the Muslims agreed to concede one percent of a certain area, the Serbs would be ready to offer them in exchange up to five percent in other areas. In other words, Grubac was expressing the will of the Serbs (and so did the Croats in Herzegovina) to disrupt a continuous Muslim territorial control. A Croatian-Muslim alliance, according to General Grubac, was "unnatural," and therefore would not be constructed on sound grounds, even if such an alliance could be achieved under the pressure of the international community, and that had become evident in their latest clashes in central Bosnia and the Neretva Valley. He stated that, due to their ongoing conflict, both Muslims and Croats were experiencing, for the first time, unlike the Serbs, the threat of annihilation of their own populations, something that evoked the religious underpinnings of this war. The Serbian colonel, who attended the meeting, denied the allegations that there was any military activity coordinated between Serbs and the BiH Armija in Mostar. He recognized having met officials from East Mostar, but that the only agenda accepted by BSA in those meetings consisted of humanitarian matters. He volunteered to make general remarks about the Muslims, stressing that "we have made an agreement on POW exchange with them, which they have not honored. This is typical of Muslims, who have no central authority, and therefore you cannot rely on them.[199]"

That summer the crops were meager, and that had caused the critical situation in food supply for the local population to further deteriorate. Grubac demanded the reimbursement of the costs (preferably in fuel), which he undertook when extending humanitarian aid to all the populations across his territory. The problem of the Gacko thermal power plant was raised again, and the Serbian general invited Benabou to hold a meeting on Tuesday, November 16, 1993, in Gacko with the mayor and Colonel Milosevic to tackle the issue. In that context, a proposal for a new humanitarian supply route was brought up along the axis of Stolac-Gacko-Miljevina-Trnovo-Sarajevo. The UNMO team in the area had already been collecting data about humanitarian needs and forwarding them to international organizations. It was the UNMO team in the area which facilitated the meeting and offered overnight hospitality in their premises in Bileca to its participants.

Since the previous meeting, General Grubac and Colonel Milosevic had been expressing a more favorable approach towards the Croats. It seemed that they were getting closer to the Croatian position and distancing themselves from the Muslims, who were described as "unreliable and disrespectful[200]" of any agreements. Thereupon, with the assistance of United Nations observers, a meeting between Serbs and Croats was arranged in Stolac, a small village in Herzegovina located some thirty kilometers south of Mostar. Stolac's population in the pre-war period was composed of one-third Croats, one-third Muslims, and one-third Serbs. But on Friday, 25 June, 1993, which was designated for the meeting, the town was deserted, and the UN armored vehicles which

---

[199] ibid.
[200] ibid.

conveyed the negotiators were under the appalling feeling that the town had been thoroughly "cleansed." The eerie silence of absent life resounded loud and clear from the red tile rooftops of the abandoned homes that lined the narrow streets. Wild vegetation and thorns started invading the forlorn space left behind by the escapees of the horrors that had taken place there, God knows when and by whom. No one was left, no trace of any survivor to give a clue as to what had unfolded there. Passing by the cemetery, only devastation and signs of violence could be imagined amidst the placid quiet. Yugoslavia was indeed plunged in civil war, and the ancient tombs of the Bogomils (a Christian sect, affiliated with the Albigensians of southern France, who wandered to Bosnia during the first Bulgarian Empire in the tenth century) were lying side by side with the latest victims of the war. It seemed that human life had been trivialized in this cruel and unremitting conflict, and the blood of Muslims, Croats, and Serbs was equally flowing and absorbed by this unfortunate land.

Throughout its long history, Stolac had been an outstanding cradle of culture where intellectuals, artists, poets, and leaders had emerged, among them, the well-known Ahmed al-Jazzar (the Butcher), born in 1720 in Stolac, who became, under the Ottoman Empire, the famous Jazzar Pasha, ruler of Acre and the Galilee from 1775 till his death in 1804. His followers during the Bosnian War seemed to be engaged with an equal zeal in butchering their fellow men, as did their infamous predecessor. Mehmedalija Mak Dizdar, by contrast, who was one of the greatest Bosnian and Yugoslav poets, was also born in Stolac in 1917. He spent his World War II years as a Communist partisan, moving frequently from place to place to escape the Ustasha-Nazi persecutions. Asaf Durakovic, a Croatian physician and expert in nuclear medicine, who was also recognized for his poetry and verse, was born, similarly, in Stolac in 1940. He is a founder and medical research director of the Toronto based Uranium Medical Research Center. Zdravko Sotra, born in Stolac in 1933, is a Bosnian Serb who grew to become a renowned film director and scriptwriter. Those were the children who had grown up in that town on the banks of the Bregava River, and it is easy to imagine the pride they inspired in the many generations who succeeded them in that once blessed historical site. But on the early hours of that gloomy day, as many singing birds and the sound of rushing waters were accompanying the arrival of the UN convoy, directed by Benabou in the small town of Stolac, he inserted in his record player the cassette of Gustav Mahler's *The Song of the Earth* and opened to maximum volume the exterior loudspeakers of his Jeep Cherokee.

In that early morning, UNMOs (United Nations military observers) put up an Indian tent in a clear area of the no man's land separating Croats and Serbs. The commanders of both parties, in charge of operations in the war zone, were present, with General Milivoj Petkovic heading the Croatian delegation and General Radovan Grubac his Serbian counterpart. They had decided to meet, in order to assist the Croatian populations in the Konjic pocket, which had been besieged by the Serbs and the Muslims. In fact, the Croats were trapped in central Bosnia, in the midst of the battles between Serbs and Muslims, and except for the UNHCR convoy of 2 June, they did not receive, during the preceding three months, either food or vital medicine. A previous agreement had been achieved between the Croats and the Serbs through the hot lines established for coordinating emergency matters between the two parties, without the involvement of either UNPROFOR or any other international organization. Serbs and Croats used the United Nations as a subterfuge to hide their discreet contacts and secret agreements. This time

Benabou, as the civil affairs officer, and Major Acuña (SP-ABAT) presided over the meeting. The five points of accord were suggested by Benabou and ratified by both generals:

1. A humanitarian corridor would be opened along the road: Stolac-Nevesinje-Luka-Borci-Turija or alternatively: Stolac-Ljubinje-Nevesinje-Bijela.
2. The HVO would provide ten trucks to transport food and medicine to the affected areas. These trucks would also be used for MEDEVAC (medical evacuation) of the wounded and needy population (approximately thirteen hundred people). Given the difficulties in the terrain, the operation would be performed over the following fifteen days.
3. This mode of operation would be extended for MEDEVAC and medical assistance in the future.
4. The HVO would cover all expenses.
5. The open line of communication between the parties would remain permanently so, to be used for solving other emerging problems.

At the closure of the session, Benabou asked if there were any other matters to raise such as violation of the ceasefire, which could be resolved around that table, on that occasion. Both sides were resolute in their reaction: "No, the violations are sporadic, and we will continue to resolve them between us in the field.[201]" They also asked to keep the meeting secret. They were right, for their cooperation on the ground in that region was pragmatic and effective, apparently beyond what Zagreb and Belgrade could agree between them, and they wished to keep it that way. In fact, oddly and unexpectedly enough, those generals were neither trigger happy

---

[201] DOC. 015, dated 25 June 1993, concerning the meeting between Croat and Serb Commanders in Stolac, distributed by Albert Benabou to UN and Spanish Headquarters.

nor seeking confrontations. Finally realizing that there was nothing heroic to be gained from a war against civilians, they elected to handle their affairs through diplomatic channels and pragmatic encounters on the ground, for practice had shown that by discussing directly with each other in the field, they had succeeded on imposing their will on the politicians in Belgrade and Zagreb without any burdensome and tortuous diplomatic process. The UN apparatus was happy to facilitate the meeting, by having the Spanish canteen serve excellent paella for lunch that was appreciated by all.

## The Great Romance in the Midst of War

In the middle of the unfolding drama, in the Mostar human cauldron, the anxieties and the rhythm of war were broken by the poetry of love that was being written, as if war never existed. While the harsh and brink-of-death reality of the city probably interrupted many untold and unrequited love stories, and broke countless hearts as lovers had to place sheer survival over the luxury of loving, the relative safety of UN officials in their protected barracks afforded the personnel the possibility of finding refuge in the world of reverie, fantasy, and love. The passionate love that was building up between David in the SPABAT camp and Andrea in the glass building in New York, against all odds, was burning their hearts, prompting David to invite her to choose between being an eagle or a butterfly. And Andrea chose. She knew that eagles flew high in the sky, were majestic, powerful, free, and independent, searching for prey from a distance, and then rapaciously glided, with their sharp claws ready to capture their victim, all the while fiercely defending their offspring and nourishing them patiently and assiduously, until they acquired the same qualities that would make them independent in their turn. Butterflies, by contrast, were beautiful and magical, but short-lived, fragile, and ephemeral. Their flimsy existence did not seem to be purposeful or follow any logic, and before it came to any peak of its existence, it was ready to die. Unlike the alienation between man and the eagle, due to their separate existence, humans seem to be caught up by the ravishing beauty of the butterfly, which is eternalized in mummies pinned in place in a collector's box, to be admired and enjoyed for posterity. Andrea chose the butterfly, while admitting her folly in doing so. She wrote to David:

> Take me to travel, make me fly on the wings of desire and the unexpected. Make me laugh, blush, and desire! Here I am, very close, and you respond, "Come closer and enfold me." Yes, yearning for you, and at the same time, hesitating between the good and the evil in you . . . I fear that this would be a sweet mirage born of a lack of emotion and lack of altitude. The emotion and altitude that you made me discover anew even while I did not know you. Maybe an imaginary silhouette and a tone of voice, here's where all of my crazy and forbidden thoughts are running.
>
> I'm not hungry anymore; I do not want anything, just to know, who is the man who stole my imagination and nervous connections? Loving this revival that has suddenly splashed into my life, freshened and beautiful, sensing a soft skin, bright eyes, and laughter. The heart beats, legs and hands are wavering, seeking to be embraced. Daring, going beyond the limits; violate the prohibitions and plunge with delight into the abyss of desire; free, free at last from the shackles imposed by our castrating society.
>
> I am a stream of fresh air, you're the sirocco. I desire you, and when I escape, you wait for me. I'm ahead, you know, I invent you, we explore each other. You

lie, I speak the truth, I lie, you say the truth. We play hide and seek, we hope that we never find the object of our love. You'll laugh, as I read my horoscope (what a mystical nonsense), they say your sexuality will be exacerbated by your moon, you will even risk an extramarital adventure . . . And here we are, in the middle of it, isn't that a blow in the face?

Each call leaves me breathless. You repeat again and again that I do not; I cannot extract myself from my moral refuge that I built at the cost of so many sacrifices and pain. I left behind me the garment of light that attracted butterflies of the night; I removed the glass slippers that led me to the balls once forbidden. Now I come before midnight, and I smile at my mirror image reminding myself of a mellowed teenager. This choice weighs on me, as painful barriers I hurt my hands. But I'm trapped alone and I deliberately threw away the keys of freedom beyond retrieval. I was afraid of myself and of my unlimited desires. It was the prison that protected me. Like a freedom-loving bird that is locked into a shelter from oil spills on a safe shore. I am like that bird, sometimes unconscious of the iron bars of my cage, sometimes curled up at the bottom of the enclosure, sad and unable to fly. Do not open my cage, I would kill myself. Never go too far away, now I need the breath of your soul over mine. With you, wherever you are,

   In kneading the dough, I thought of you
   In mixing the ingredients, I thought of you
   In perfuming myself, I thought of you
   In smearing cream, I thought of you
   In falling asleep, I thought of you
   In waking up, I thought of you
   In drinking water, I thought of you
   In combing my hair, I thought you
   And you?

I watch you in silence and wait patiently until you lift your face and look at me if it takes too long, I will come onto you slowly, I would catch your hands and would pass them over my eyes, my mouth, and we will discover each one. I dreamed of a story in which I fell madly in love of a tall, thin man, born in the Netherlands, descendant of a long line of these Spanish Jews, noble and distinguished. I dreamed of a man who encouraged me to pleasure without limits. I dreamed of a naked man lying in the shadows of a large, empty room. I dreamed of a man whose laughter provoked in me spasms of pleasure. I dreamed of a man with secret powers in the civil society (no more an army man). I heard the sweet words he whispered in my enchanted ears. I tried constantly to wake up, release myself from the clutches of the magnetic, hot, and delicious dream. Impossible. I repeated incessantly the lineup of my virtual conversation with the man. The price of this insane battle was that listening to you, I lost (in every sense of the world).

I acknowledge that what is happening is already quite hard. Writing becomes a torment. I constantly tell myself again and again, "Just a little more and I stop." What an exhilarating moment of life—is there anything stronger than what you have raised in me and excited my being . . . do not try to answer. I, the one confronting the most difficult challenges in the course of my life, I lost all my senses and I do not get saturated by you or get drunk with the pleasure of feeling you inside me, hearing you, reading you, and doing everything with you . . . Tell me to stop. I've never been in this spot in my life. When I told you that I had made love with him thinking about you, what did you sense? Why is our love so strong? I'm afraid not to fit your ideal. Swear that we will remain friends whatever happens.

## Savagery in the Heart of Europe

What would you say of taking a long journey, you and I, in the footsteps of our memory? We will start in Cordoba, move to Montpellier, then go to Bruges, then pass by Amsterdam on our way to Rotterdam to cross the Ocean to the shores of Rhode Island . . .

Total voids, lack of oxygen, I cannot breathe, call me soon. Making love will destroy what unites us today, but we will do it for what unites us today even if it will bring us to our destruction. I like it, thinking of you, imagining me naked without any artifice, when I look in the mirror, I learn to love myself as I am, with my qualities and my defects, as you would see me, protected and embellished by your love.

I love the smell of love,

I love the body jilted by the lover

I love that you are looking at me getting lost in pleasure,

I love that your hands never leave me,

I love that we are intermingled, fused, and you talk to me gently

Guiding me to the enjoyment

I do not have a special spot; my spot is my whole body,

Do not caress me first, just simply in the darkness of the room come deep within me. This is how I would recognize you. I never wanted so much to be possessed by a dream and you are in me even before I have known you. This is absolutely amazing.

On them, my wonder offspring, I have no doubt and no fear . . . Yes, a huge desire of mutual love grabbed me, it leads me, and imposes its laws, and maybe it is the narcissism that we love? I love you. That's it, I said it, and does it hurt you? It is said, "What is the manual of 'perfect love' in ten lessons?" I've never remembered it. Since you're me, then you must know all about me. You are right now; there is no reason to fear death. As you have known, you have fulfilled me to completion, nothing stronger is possible, and I reached the top of the world, so it was you that I was missing! And you offered it to me . . . And when days come, *«You will record your war journal... I will write our happiness diary…»*[202]

---

[202] For maintaining privacy, names have been changed and the source is kept in the confidential documents of memoirs of the war in Bosnia of Albert Benabou.

## Chapter Six

## The UN Impasse Gets the Conflict Nowhere

While officially the enmity and savagery on the part of all participants in the Bosnian War precluded any advance towards a solution, and every party tried to grab what it could and to impose its will on the others, many practical arrangements were being made on the ground, at times with UN help, at times without it, or in spite of it. It was becoming evident to all, during the three years of that most cruel conflict, that not only was the UN impotent, due to its intrinsic weaknesses and self-interests, to produce any solution acceptable to the belligerents, but the most it could offer was an upkeep of the status quo, with a view to preventing it from sliding into some uncontrollable free-for-all and chaotic war to the finish. The parties did take advantage of the UN presence to get protection, to channel aid to their civilians, and to arrange for some practical accommodations among the parties, but when they sensed that they could manage on their own, they did not hesitate to circumvent that entire apparatus, and sometimes even wish, or even act, for its departure. However, while expecting some great power, like the United States, to intervene and impose a settlement, the United Nations continued to limp along and even expand its activity, depending more on the initiative and ingenuity of its officers in the field, who often rather represented their country's interest, than on any centrally guided master blueprint to bring peace.

Benabou was one of those officers, detached to the problematic area of Mostar, which was the major flaring point of Muslim-Croatian hostility. In one of his assignments, on a summer day of June 1993, he arrived with an overland UN convoy from the Mostar war zone to the coastal city of Split, where DETALAT, a French airborne unit detached to the UN mission, was stationed. From there, the participants, in yet another one of those endless UN meetings, set out to Kiseljak on board of two Puma helicopters, which were dispatched by their commander, Lieutenant Colonel Rossignol. A radiant sun was trying to pierce its way through a scattering of clouds, which were too scant to block the blue sky. It was as if summer insisted on manifesting itself, amidst the brief drizzles which showered the ground occasionally, leaving in their wake puddles of muddled waters on the uneven asphalt road. It was 7:00 a.m. in the morning, and Albert was snoozing in one corner of the helicopter, which he shared with Boban and Petkovic, to make up for the almost sleepless night he had endured, because he had to leave Mostar overland at 4:00 a.m. in that early morning to make it to the helicopter flight. It was convenient for him to exhibit his fatigue, since he was reluctant to engage the two Croatian officials before the general meeting began in Kiseljak, with United Nations and Muslim representatives attending. He sensed that the Croats would be ill at ease when their Muslim rivals would hurl at them their harsh grievances about the ethnic cleansing that was being perpetrated or concocted against them.

At precisely 11:00 a.m., Benabou's and the Croats' helicopter was violently shaken by a direct hit, and the French copilot explained that their vehicle was targeted from the ground. Albert stressed that he had felt two impacts from his seat, but as long as the aircraft could fly, they should continue on their way undeterred, because they had been allowed to use that air corridor that was coordinated and approved by all three contenders, Croats, Muslims, and Serbs. Expectedly, General Petkovic commented that the area was under the control of the Muslim Armija, which signified that it was their forces which tried to shoot down the UN transport choppers, but anyone who understood and knew the cynicism of that cruel war could not tell for sure who had attempted to down the aircraft. In any case, the shooting was not massive and consisted of only two bullets or rockets, which meant that there was no determined premeditation to take the vehicle out of the sky. For Albert, it could therefore be any one of the three rivals, who were posted at a few hundred meters apart in that area. Therefore, he thought that it might have been only an attempt to frighten the passengers, so as to force them to return to their base in Split and thus scuttle the planned meeting. This kind of dirty tactic, which could have been pursued by any one of the three rivals, only illustrated their boundless mutual hatred and loathing, which in their eyes justified any measure.

Boban was pale and only inquired whether the flight would go on as scheduled. Benabou confirmed yes, for he was even more loathe to emergency land on that spot. But at twenty kilometers from the destination, the pilot announced that weather conditions would not allow him to land in Kiseljak. After consultation, the two pilots decided to return to base and to safely unload their passengers. Benabou's official report[203] to Andreev and to Zagreb on this matter is quite instructive. He recounted that the initial flight from Split had been postponed from 7:00 a.m. to 10:30 a.m. due to weather conditions, and that the helicopter was hit over the area of Kruscica by two bullets, one hitting close to the gasoline tank, and the other at its tail. In that report, Benabou stressed that it was on Boban's request that it was decided to pursue the flight, something that may indicate that

---

[203] UN Document 005, from 4 June, 1993 reporting from British Headquarters to UN Commanders in the Region and in Zagreb.

it was more important to him than to the other participants to hold the meeting as planned, and that the French pilot had informed him that he would have to call off all other flights for the next thirty-six hours to ensure the air corridor flight safety. His routine citations in conclusion of his messages and reports now brought up an ancient Jewish saying that "messengers in the service of good deeds are sheltered from any harm.[204]" Little did he remember that the most, and perhaps the last, capable, diligent man devoted to peace, UN Secretary General Dag Hammarskjold, had been killed in an air accident over the skies of Congo, thirty years earlier, on a similar mission. Biblical sayings, just like the UN white banner, did not indeed guarantee the safety of their users. Benabou's report was this time signed ABA (Albert Ben Abou), which in Hebrew also meant "Daddy," as if it reflected Albert's acting as the benevolent father of all the belligerents, but it was also reminiscent of the celebrated Swedish music band of that name, which in normal times would have been more welcome in Bosnia than the Nordic Battalion.

Benabou also reported to the headquarters of the United Nations in Zagreb and New York that the multilateral encounters that were canceled would be held on 4 June at Divulje with the Croats only, this time without the participation of Muslims, who remained stranded in Kiseljak, so as to learn at least the Croatian position with regard to the proposals that were being discussed in Geneva.

While the major issues of the war and peace in Bosnia were negotiated between the parties elsewhere, with the involvement of major powers and the United Nations, the private affairs of individuals were naturally either sidetracked or left for each person to manage, for the better or the worse. But the United Nations in Bosnia could not ignore the

---

[204] ibid.

burning love affair that kept gaining in intensity and vigor between the Dutch David Belmonte in Medjugorje and the American Andrea Valenci in New York, despite the remote controls by which its manifestations were constantly transmitted between them, regardless of the war atmosphere and the burden of death, destruction, and bureaucratic incompetence that were impinging on it. On 5 June, 1993, Belmonte wrote to his beloved woman, whom he still had not met and did not know:

> This weekend, during which Benabou almost fell victim to the [helicopter] incident, I felt myself seized by this marvelous star of happiness that you represent . . . I have constantly talked about you around me, without mentioning either your name or your position, you whom I have bumped into, in this war where human cowardice reigns supreme. I subtract myself for some moments from all this, to seek refuge, and find a warm spot next to you, imagining you reading my messages and listening to me, while I watch your body, your skin, and your eyes which I do not know. Everything is passing in procession before my eyes, but I prefer to delete the rest and to leave you to imagine and feel for yourself. My dear Dona Valenci, my darling, give me a sign of life.
> 
> David Belmonte [205]

Andrea responded on 7 June, the delay caused by the different time zones, in the same terms of desire and longing:

> Good morning, when you read the message after you wake up, you who causes me a seismic fault. I had decided not to write to you today, but I cannot help responding to your advances, for I am so thoroughly seduced that I must let

---

[205] For maintaining privacy, names have been changed and the source is kept in the confidential documents of memoirs of the war in Bosnia of Albert Benabou.

my fingers play on this keyboard, as an extension of my soul and spirit, to respond to you. To you, a prince from remote Spain, call me,

Andrea Valenci[206]

David called Andrea in New York, but their discussion was constantly interrupted by minutes of silence, when each one of them listened attentively to the beating pulse of the other. David could no longer contain his desire, and he let it prevail over the geographic distance, provoking a no less impassioned reaction from Andrea. She exploded in an uncontrollable gush of sentiments and yearning:

> Your call has left me breathless. I must repeat, once and again, that I did not want, indeed could not, disengage from the moral shelter that I had built around myself, at the price of many concessions and much pain. But I have now left behind me that luminous garb which used to attract so many night butterflies, and I have removed my glass sandals, which used to take me to forbidden balls. Nowadays, I return home before midnight and sit in front of my mirror which reminds me of the image of an innocent adolescent. This choice that I have made, burdens me heavily, like heavy shackles which injure my wrists.
>
> I had incarcerated myself out of my own volition, and then purposely thrown away the keys of my dungeon, because I was afraid of myself and of my unrestricted desires, so I needed a prison to protect me, the way one protects a freedom-loving bird in a cage, to shelter it from black tides. I feel like that bird, sometimes unaware of the iron bars that surround me, sometimes I keep to my corner, saddened by my incapacity to fly. Please do not open that cage for me, for that could kill

---
[206] ibid.

me. But, please, do not stay too far either, for I definitely need to feel the breath of your soul on mine. Feel in my place like if it were yours.

Andrea[207]

In a few days, under the mysterious power of love, of which she had deprived herself, Andrea was undergoing a metamorphosis. The walls surrounding her painful reluctance were crumbling under the insistence of David's unlimited passion and turned into an irresistible attraction that needed to be consummated without delay. She wrote to him on 9 May, under the headline, I am crazy, following your call:

I, my total deprivation, I lacked oxygen and I was suffocating . . . And then you called . . . You talk like me, you think like me, and your lyrical propensity suits the level of my hopes. You do not disappoint me, you are handsome. Make the arrangements to come to New York. Are we going to meet? Are you ready?

Andrea[208]

David Belmonte called Andrea again. He certainly wished to see her, to touch her, to cover her body with his, for she suddenly became concrete and attainable. The master architect of the universe was offering him the crowning act that every human being could hope for, that is, to let their latent love explode into a torrent of passion that their souls were yearning for, for the magic moment of their union had come. Thoughts were now precipitated on each other's minds in a mad succession of questions. How would he reach New York, he was asking himself? How would he justify his departure from the war zone? Andrea was married and a mother of two! How would he maintain his moral stature in the face

---
[207] ibid.
[208] ibid.

of that betrayed family and of his own, which counted three children that he had left behind in the Netherlands? What could he say? How would she reveal the story to her partner of a lifetime and he to his? How would they justify their act to their respective spouses, who had shared their pillow with them for so many years? How would they desecrate their long kept fidelity to their respective better halves? Maybe it was a mere sexual attraction to an unknown lover of fantasy that they both felt, just a passing love affair by remote control, born out of their intimate email exchanges, one from the battle front, the other in her attempt to respond to his urgent pleadings for relief to the unfortunate victims he had in his purview? In short, maybe it was the product of their feverish imaginations that only war situations could create? They suddenly realized that they were scared by the welling sentiments that they suddenly discovered gushing within and out of themselves. They were afraid, yet David explicitly asked her to describe to him how she envisaged the moment he would be making love to her.

Andrea now responded without equivocation, on 9 and 10 June under the enticing heading, "Warm and Humid:"

> I touch virtually this love that unites us. I love the smell of love; I love to imagine your sweat dripping down your forehead, your back, and your chest. I love the moisture of the bodies which entwine to the point of total immersion. I love to see you watching me merging with my supreme pleasure, I love to sense your hands which never keep away from me, I love our being entirely mixed into each other, I love hearing you talk to me slowly, guiding me towards my pleasure. I do not have any sensitive points, for my entire body is. Do not caress me in our first meeting; simply come into me the most deeply possible, because only in that condition will I become aware of your presence . . .

Since you are me, you must know everything about me . . . An immense wave of love has taken me over. It may be our narcissism which has permitted us to love. But I love you, and that is all, even if it hurts. I am tired, exhausted from your invisible presence. Your hands, which I do not know yet, are running down my body constantly, and your mouth, the contours of which still escape me, is becoming more and more demanding. What is happening to us? I would like to wake up and then be anesthetized by you, never again to be aware of your existence, to forget everything you have bestowed upon me, and never trembling again when I see David Belmonte on my computer messages.

Andrea[209]

On Friday, 4 June, 1993, Benabou spent ten consecutive hours at the Divulje base, in an informal discussion with the top level Croatian leadership of BiH, who were waging without respite a cruel war against the Muslims of Mostar and laying an unforgiving siege against them. Mate Boban, the president of BiH, was there, as well as his prime minister, Jadranko Prlic, the speaker of Parliament, Mile Akmadic, and the commander of the HVO (Hrvatske Vojne Organizatsje), General Milivoj Petkovic. But Bruno Stojic was absent, a reflection of the mounting tension and rivalry between him and the prime minister, who suspected that Stojic was taking over some political and international authorities that lay beyond his mandate. They were all strolling in the vast park surrounding the base, where Tito used to take long walks in the heyday of his rule. Tortuous alleys cut through the immense gardens where a huge variety of colorful flowers, dripping with rain, were resplendent under the occasional rays of sun, which pierced through the

---
[209] ibid.

covered sky and scattered among the giant cypress, poplar, and oak trees, which dominated and cast long shadows on the scene. Those marvelously structured and pleasantly conceived gardens were totally oblivious of the human drama brewing in their hearts, as those leaders of an emerging new entity were debating their next steps. Each one of them was trying to leave behind the helicopter incident and prepare for attending the conference on former Yugoslavia, to discuss with its joint chairs its future, without Muslim participation. While delighting in that stroll, they vented their thoughts, which Benabou noted carefully. As far as Boban and company were concerned, BiH did not really exist as a state, for seventy percent of its territory was controlled or threatened by the Serbs, while the other thirty percent was a war zone, where Croats were also claiming their rights. They called attention to the fact that Alija Izetbegovic had not succeeded in keeping together that torn apart country.

Boban was determined to pursue his policy of assuring the protection of the rights of Croats. In other words, he was affirming that the war would be pursued, though he recognized that they had been late to join the conflict.

He opined that there was need for calm and for a process of mediation. Both he and his colleagues were of the firm view that the country was unable to resolve its problems on its own without international input.

Boban referred to the agreement that had been obtained in Mostar on 2 May, 1993, which stipulated the creation of a mixed international police in Mostar, but Benabou knew that a complete cessation of hostilities was a prerequisite to the realization of this project, and that was not about to happen.

Boban also referred to the proposal advanced by his minister of defense, who was not present, which had suggested that units of UNPROFOR be incorporated within HVO units. Benabou promised that he would transmit the idea to the headquarters of the United Nations, even though he considered that the idea had not been proposed seriously.

Boban said that he had agreed to the meeting scheduled for 9 June at Konjic, between Croatian and Muslim military commanders of the Mostar war zone, including Konjic, Kostanjica, Jablanica, and Tarcin. Their agenda for discussion would be:

To eliminate the roadblocks on the road Metkovic-Mostar-Jablanica-Konjic-Tarcin, which served as the axis for the delivery of food aid from the Adriatic coast to the inland areas that were cut off by the war.

To cease the hostilities between all warring parties along that route.

To allow permanent freedom of passage for everyone and permit patrols by SPABAT and the UN civil police (UN-CIVPOL).

To work out an agreement between the parties for the opening of the Bijela Bridge for all.

In that informal exchange, Benabou remarked how pleasant it was to discuss in that beautifully awesome and relaxed atmosphere, which permitted a candid and open hammering of the most sensitive and intimate issues. Thereupon, Boban, who was carried away by the circumstances, suggested that a prolonged tripartite conference of all belligerents should be held, following the pattern of Camp David that had generated the peace accords between Israel and Egypt. Little could they all know how a change of regime in Egypt in 2012, following the Arab Spring, could put question marks on those hard-won agreements signed merely thirty-five years earlier. Boban indeed thought at that time that the Vance-Owen Plan was the only avenue still open for negotiations. Benabou, reporting on that informal meeting with Croatian leaders, which revealed much more of their candid thinking than they would allow under the constraints of official and press covered conferences, invoked the saying of Emerson that "in the art of conversation, man finds himself competing against the rest of humanity.[210]" In any case, Boban thought that the situation was still at the stage of pure talk, and he foresaw nothing concrete to come out of it, especially as long as the talks did not constrain the parties to agree on anything. Benabou thought that the cochairmen of the conference on former Yugoslavia, Owen and Stoltenberg, would certainly have expected much more commitment on the part of the participants.

Later in the afternoon of that Friday, 4 June, the time for the formal meeting came, with the full UN team engaging the Croatian leadership. But in contrast to the relaxed atmosphere of the outdoor encounter, in the indoor conference room a freezing cold ambience reigned, for its walls were barren, and from the ceiling hung a series of pale white neon lights, which far from welcoming the convened parties to cuddle under them, on the contrary repulsed them to take leave. An atmosphere of a large and impersonal hangar enveloped the place where a fateful international conference was to take place. The Britons, who had chosen the site, wished to impose an air of firmness, in order to project the gravity of the agenda under discussion, about which Benabou, based on his earlier stroll with the Croatian chiefs, had reported to the cochairmen of the meeting. He intimated to David Owen that Boban seemed determined to pursue the war, while Muslim civilians, including women and children, still endured the siege and constant bombardment in East Mostar.

No preliminary introduction of the participants was done when David Owen presented on a neutral tone of fait

---

[210] DOC. 007, dated 8 June 1993, reporting on the meetings held on Friday 4 June 1993 with Herzeg-Bosnia officials in Divulje Base, distributed by Albert Benabou.

accompli, the position of the president of Bosnia and Herzegovina, Alija Izetbegovic, and he suggested to accept the legislative act that he had accomplished, with possibly minor amendments. He also demanded that Boban and his party cooperate with the provisional government of BiH. There was one brief moment of silent consternation, quick glances between the Croatian participants, and a momentarily shock-stricken Boban, who for the second time that day lost his balance (the first was during the flight incident). But after a brief but calculated pause, Boban put up his best act, for he could perfectly gloss over the most embarrassing situations and convincingly put up an innocent face to handle it. Without any transition or preface, he opened up: "I defy the legality of that government and its authority to lead, in view of the fact that seventy percent of this land has been under Serbian control and the other thirty percent has been contested in war between all parties.[211]"

Stoltenberg understood that the talks were facing a deadlock, and he suggested pausing for half an hour for consultations, after which he reconvened the session with dinner at the British base. Thus, the issue of the Bosnian legislation, which had aimed at appointing the four ombudsmen of BiH, which had triggered the Croatian wrath, was sidestepped. The entire concept of the ombudsmen, on which that legislative initiative had been founded, was the exact antithesis of that ongoing war, where fundamental human rights, as spelled out by the United Nations, were being trampled upon by civil conflict and ethnic cleansing. Boban had no say in that matter, because the authority that those laws vested in the ombudsmen not only permitted stopping the process of ethnic cleansing, but reversed it, wherever it was already perpetrated in BiH. Benabou had understood, since the onset

---

[211] ibid.

of his mission in the Mostar area, that Boban was under the directives of Zagreb in this domain, and he acted under a tacit agreement with President Franjo Tudjman. Therefore, he thought that the UN mediation effort ought to be directed directly to Tudjman rather than to Boban. Thus, Benabou would initiate in 1994, via the Israeli government, a contact with Tudjman on this affair.

In the second session of the conference, Lord Owen clarified as firmly as in the first session that ethnic cleansing, the question of UNCIVPOL (UN civil police) operation in Mostar, and especially the incarceration of civilians in detention camps was the top preoccupation of the international community. Expectedly, Boban furiously rejected all the accusations, screaming, "There is no truth in all that![212]" Thereupon, Owen asked Benabou, in his capacity as the UN civil affairs officer in the Mostar region, to share with the audience his views on the topics under discussion, which he did promptly. He said that with regard to the operation of UNCIVPOL, he had held a meeting on 2 May, 1993, with the participation of Croatian and Muslim authorities and representatives of the UN force, and that it had been concluded to form a structure of joint patrols, composed of twelve policemen from each party who had the authority to operate in all parts of the city, and that they would wear distinct uniforms so as to avoid any confusion with military uniforms. That agreement had been ratified by Croatian Minister of Defense Bruno Stojic, by Commander of the HVO General Milivoj Petkovic, as well as by Boban himself. So, there should have been no equivocation or misunderstanding, and everybody involved took the necessary measures, including the routes to be patrolled and the arrangements of rotation between the participating personnel. In consequence, at the request of Petkovic and of the

---

[212] ibid.

commander of the BiH Armija, General Safet Hallilovic, a session was held on 8 June, 1993, at the president's house of the Konjic region, with the participation of the brigade commanders of the two parties in the area of Mostar, Jablanica, Konjic, Kostanjica, and Tarcin, where the agenda had been agreed and coordinated, to wit, to discuss the elimination of the roadblocks on the entire axis linking between those localities, to halt the hostilities, to assure the freedom of movement on that route, to set up the joint patrols, and to arrive at an accord on the operation of the Bijela Bridge.

As to the inspectors of UNPROFOR, Boban had confirmed his accord to have them integrated in the units of the HVO, at whatever level they choose, as well as in the units of BiH Armija, which meant that Boban began insisting for the first time that UN participation in the local rival units was to be conducted on an equal basis with the Croats and the Muslims and that they become part of the respective units of each side rather than independent inspectors. To sum up the testimony given by Benabou, General Lars-Erik Wahlgren, the commander of UNPROFOR, stressed that he was very pleased with the suggestion to incorporate UN inspectors within the envisaged joint force. Both Stoltenberg and Owen recognized the importance of the meeting at Konjic and announced that a next meeting had been decided upon. Benabou thought to himself that good intentions and great statements were made, but that things were back to the stage of pure talk. He feared that, in practice, massacres would go on undisturbed in Mostar. In the midst of his pessimism and of his feelings about the vain efforts of the UN intervention, which amounted to nothing, he was somehow cheered and thrilled that the Belmonte-Valenci love affair was reaching the boiling point and lending some meaning to the otherwise gloomy UN existence in Medjugorje. To David's total immersion in the rhythm of his passion and imagination, in which every feeling, thought, deed, desire, and instinct were focused on and about Andrea, she enthusiastically responded that she lived her days and hours with him and for him. She wrote on 8 June:

> I feel like a wild steed, which is enclosed in a barn, does not stop jumping and kicking, in order to avoid the lasso of the one who wants to possess me and become my master. But, am I able to escape now? . . . We are together all the time, we talk, we interrogate each other, we laugh and pray together. You shake me to my most profound being, my heartbeats accelerate, and my legs shake. Please stop reducing me to nothing at every moment, let me revert to what I had never truly been, namely to my mundane denials, to my outside peel, to that exterior envelope which had been built up by tradition, education, and the pretenses that have surrounded me. I yearn to throw all that into the void and let my natural violence prevail between you and me.[213]

To which David immediately retorted:

> I am so proud of having stolen part of your heart, your soul, and your body, for everything in you is appealing to me . . . You too have stolen me and hidden me in the depths of your being, exactly as what was done to me; and I hide you here, where nobody knows that you exist. Just being aware of what is going on, is painful enough, and even more so, to write about it, to the point that I am telling myself that very soon I would have to desist . . . There is no more exciting moment in my life than the one when you have planted so many emotions in me . . . Do not try to answer that, because I am in the middle of trying to confront the toughest moments of

---

[213] For maintaining privacy, names have been changed and the source is kept in the confidential documents of memoirs of the war in Bosnia of Albert Benabou.

my life, but I find reassurance and comfort when I feel you in me, hear you, and read you, and do everything in conjunction with you. Please take cognizance of my tenacity, which makes both my strength and weakness. Please tell me that I have to stop, for I have never known this feeling . . .

**Saturday, 12 June, 1993**

On that day, a working session was held at the headquarters of SPABAT in Medjugorje. Present there were Bruno Stojic, the Croatian minister of defense, Colonel Angel Morales, commander of the Spanish Battalion, and Albert Benabou, the civil affairs officer for the center and south of BiH. Spanish Lieutenant Francisco Jesús Aguilar Fernandez had been killed the day before by a bullet in his back when he was leading a patrol on the Tito Bridge in Mostar. Benabou conducted an investigation and confidentially circulated his report in which he concluded that it was it was a 7.90 mm bullet of an automatic weapon, which was in all evidence fired by a sharpshooter from the bank of the Neretva River, which was under the HVO control. Four BIH Armija soldiers were also wounded at the same moment and were transported, together with the fatally injured officer, to hospital. Thereupon, in conjunction with Croatian and Muslim officials, it was decided to conduct a joint investigation, on both sides of the demarcation line between the two parts of town. Morales was enraged, for he kept losing his men during his mission of peace, and he was at the edge of his incapacity to explain to Madrid his embarrassment. The chiefs of the civil police, the Croatian Ilija Filipovic, and the Muslim Ramo Mascesa, as well as the UN officer in charge of police, Leo Sorensen, were in charge of the official inquiry and expected to hear directives from the chief of UNCIVPOL in former Yugoslavia, Canadian

Commissioner O'Reilley. SPABAT, HVO, and BiH Armija had also appointed their own liaison officers to the team. At that point, Benabou felt that Morales would not press the investigation too far because he would rather avoid embarrassing the Croats, as was his wont. In spite of the Spanish victim of that incident, SPABAT, the Spanish Battalion, pursued its set program of action as if nothing had happened. The chief inspector of UNCIVPOL in the Mostar region, Leo Bang Sorensen, who was leading the investigation regarding the death of Spanish Lieutenant Francisco Jesús Aguilar Fernandez was a firearms ballistic expert, and his term of service under UNCIVPOL was coming to its end. Thus, assessing the enormous political and diplomatic implications of that investigation, Benabou pleaded on the 7th of July for the extension of Sorensen's mandate. In an official letter addressed to Andreev, Benabou explained the necessity to pursue the investigation to its conclusion with the Danish expert, giving full details of the progress made so far of the Croatian and Muslim representatives and insisting, in the Biblical spirit, that "when one does a laudable job, he is invited to bring it to completion,[237]" so Sorenson would be allowed to finish his job. Andreev duly turned to the UNCIVPOL command in Zagreb and obtained the extension of Sorenson's contract by two more months.

On that 12 June, twenty-seven people, including one doctor, three mothers, and four of their children, had been evacuated by ambulance from the hospital of BiH Armija in Mostar towards Medjugorje, and from there on by helicopter to Split on their way to Turkey. That medical evacuation (MEDEVAC) was carried out as a result of an accord achieved between Zagreb and Ankara. That same day, another meeting had taken place on the Medjugorje base, with Zdravko Sancevic, Croatia's ambassador to Bosnia and

---

[237] Doc. 018, dated 7 July 1993, concerning documents related to the death of First Lieutenant Aguilar, Distributed by Albert Benabou to UN Headquarters.

Herzegovina, Colonel Miguel Castro, the commanding officer of the Spanish Battalion, and Albert Benabou attending. The ambassador came to show the generosity of his country towards the Muslim medical evacuees and to present his condolences for the death of the Spanish officer. Benabou vigorously protested and expressed his indignation that UN officers were targeted by sharpshooters on both sides of the conflict and asked the ambassador to exert all his influence in order to reinstitute a measure of confidence with the Spanish Battalion, which had suffered the loss of one of its officers. The ambassador did present his heartfelt condolences, announced that he maintained excellent relations with President Tudjman, and promised to use all his contacts in order to restore peace and quiet, and to call to order "those who had overstepped their boundaries.[214]" The next day, Bruno Stojic, the minister of defense of the Bosnian Croats, arrived at the Spanish base, accompanied by Salko Zuljevic, the chief of police in Mostar, in order to also present his condolences. That happened no doubt as a result of the visit of the ambassador. On that occasion, the Croats wished to prove, at any price, that the shooting did not originate from the area under their control, contrary to the officers of the United Nations and Benabou, who demonstrated, with the aid of their maps, that the deadly shooting had definitely come from the HVO zone of domination. However, the Croats insisted, all the same, to offer their condolences and to compensate for the death of the Spanish officer. So, Stojic announced that humanitarian convoys could be directed to Mostar, Jablanica, Konjic, Busovaca, Vitez, Kiseljak, and even to Sarajevo. Morales retorted with great emotion: "I am personally ready to lead such a convoy, in association

---

[214] Source: Confidential UNPROFOR report, dated Sunday 13 June 1993, concerning the follow up on the incident in Mostar where the SPABAT Lieutenant fell in action, distributed by Albert Benabou to Headquarters in Kiseljak.

with the commanders of HVO and the BiH Armija; and this convoy will bear the name of Lieutenant Aguilar, who fell in the cause of peace.[215]"

On the morning of 14 June, the UNHCR office in Medjugorje informed the military and civil affairs officials on the base that a convoy was being prepared to be launched on that agreed itinerary. UNHCR also announced that the details of the operation were being worked out and finalized the moment their three truck drivers, who were blocked in Sarajevo by the artillery barrages of HVO, could make the trip back to the UN food depots in Metkovic on the Adriatic coast. Thereupon, Benabou left for Sarajevo in order to ensure the passage of these drivers, who were essential for this traffic on the dangerous Bosnian roads. Unfortunately, that much talked about convoy would never set out on its way, and instead a limited transport of sixty tons of provisions would make its way to East Mostar, led by Jerry Hume, who was in charge of that area of the UNHCR and by perennial Benabou. The latter reflected that it would be perhaps necessary to remind the rival generals what war theoretician Carl von Clausewitz had said, that war was the prolongation of diplomacy by other means and never a goal unto itself. In fact, Colonel Morales had let Bruno Stojic temporarily forget that UNPROFOR had strategically positioned itself in former Yugoslavia in order to provide protection for civilians against the military adventures that were geared to achieve political goals. In his classified report, Benabou cited Montesquieu's eternal adage: "The world nations ought to do the most possible good to each other in times of peace and the most possible evil in times of war.[216]" That had been indeed the pattern of behavior of nations as exemplified by the atrocities of the two world wars.

---

[215] ibid.
[216] ibid.

## Wednesday, 16 June, 1993

The Croats had finally started to understand that they were losing ground in the world public opinion and in international organizations, and they were intent on redeeming themselves. Vladislav Pogarcic, nicknamed Vlado, the man in charge of human resources and a close confidant of Mate Boban, was also responsible for managing relations with international organizations. He called Benabou and invited him to Grude, the seat of the president of the Croats in BiH. Benabou, dressed up for the occasion, mounted his Jeep and drove to Grude all by himself. He crossed the entire distance covered by intermittent Muslim and Croatian roadblocks without problems, all the way encountering goodwill and cooperation with the now known figure of the "Israeli." The Croatian presidency was located in an old metallurgic factory that had been managed by Mate Boban in the past. At his arrival, the guards indicated to Albert his parking place, in the open air and under giant trees which projected a thick shade, side by side with luxurious, black Mercedes sedans. Military officers, carrying the short version of the famous Israeli Uzi submachine gun, welcomed him and showed him into Vlado's office, which was modest, almost ascetic, in its subdued paint color, where all the military managers and their assistants were piled up in the same room. Vlado, a tall forty-year-old, with wide shoulders, and wearing a frame of round glasses, which lent to him an air of vivacity and intelligence, welcomed him with a smile. He also sported a nice and refined tie, ornamented in green and gold colors, against the background of an immaculate white shirt with sleeves partly rolled up, being probably aware and proud of the fact that ties had been invented in Croatia (hence cravat).

Vlado immediately announced that there were many topics to discuss, auguring a cordial relationship between the two men which would last as long as they worked together.

Vlado spoke perfect English, generously sprinkling "however" at the beginning of his every second or third sentence, with a very pronounced British intonation. He was surrounded with piles of dossiers, giving the impression of a very busy man. His secretary, Gordana Vlašić, occupied a tiny adjoining room, and with her short haircut framing her pleasant face, and her abundant and elevated chest, and her glances of complicity and dedication to her boss, seemed in love with or in full awe from him. It immediately transpired from the talk that Boban was intent at that point on expanding his responsibility beyond the zone of Mostar, thus betraying his ambition to become the authoritative address for all Croats of BiH. He would have preferred to face British or Canadian troops, who had more responsible units in CANBAT and BRITBAT, than to confront the SPABAT forces who were responsible for the Mostar area. For the Canadians and the Britons had accumulated years of experience with UN peacemaking forces and were more actively engaged in their duties than others, while the Spaniards were novices in that job. However, being Catholics, they felt closer to the Croats. Because the Muslims felt that Boban manipulated them at will, he thought that if attention could be deviated from Mostar he would no longer be accused of besieging the Muslims there or that the Spaniards were his accomplices.

The message that Vlado wished to transmit to Benabou, which was worded in Serbo-Croatian language and signed by Drs. Ivan Bagaric and Toni Kolak, was that they were concerned about the condition of the Croatian population, which was being persecuted and victimized in central Bosnia. They illustrated their anxiety by claiming that the HVO war hospital, which had been moved to the protected area of Nova Bila, had already absorbed more than one hundred and fifty gravely injured patients and that the situation was worsening by the day. In consequence, they demanded the urgent evacuation of those wounded to Split in the Republic of Croatia. When asked, Vlado could not tell where those injured had come from and when they were hospitalized. So, Benabou inquired whether there were any serious incidents in central Bosnia unknown to him, which could justify Boban's new ambitions, but he received no satisfactory response. He then asked himself what hid behind Boban's desire to expand his purview beyond Mostar, and in any case, since his area of responsibility remained primarily Mostar, he would not be able to accord to central Bosnia any particular attention unless he received UN reinforcements.

## Friday, 18 June, 1993

At three o'clock in the morning of that day, a convoy of three light vehicles arrived at the Spanish base in Medjugorje from the armed confrontation theater among Croats, Muslims, and Serbs, in the isolated and inaccessible enclave of Konjic, some two hundred kilometers away, where everyone acted as one pleased. The drivers hardly made their way through the muddy and slippery road, taking many detours to avoid the exchanges of fire and mutual bombardments which had become routine, despite the persistent drizzle of a nagging rain, which accompanied them all along. The Spanish soldiers were transporting a precious cargo that had to be sheltered in a security zone, namely four Muslim interpreters who had just been freed at 8:00 p.m., a few hours earlier, from a Croatian prison of the HVO. Three of them, Mr. Feda Jelskovic, Miss Sadeta Bektasevic, and Miss Amra Hadizukic, were employed by the United Nations, and the fourth, Mr. Samir Osmanovic, by the EU observers. On Wednesday, 16 June, they were taken hostage until Benabou, who negotiated their release, convinced the Croats that the local personnel employed by the international organizations enjoyed

UN protection. In fact, neither the presence nor the activity of those interpreters had been either known or coordinated with the Spanish forces. It was DUTCHCOM in Medjugorje which had received the message on Wednesday the sixteenth about the kidnapping of those four hostages by the Croatian forces of Konjic and immediately informed the Spanish HQ as well as the civil affairs officer. Benabou contacted Bruno Stojic, the Croatian minister of defense, and set a meeting with him for early the next day, 17 June. Spanish majors Carlos de Salas and Juan Coloma, as well as UNHCR representative Izumi Nakamitsu, joined him, and they all appeared at the gate of the HVO HQ in Mostar before 7:00 a.m. that early morning.

Under Benabou's urging, Stojic immediately contacted the Croatian commander of the HVO unit in Konjic, using the facilities of DUTCHCOM, and he used his authority to prevail on him to release the hostages. The commander asked for some time for consultations and finally communicated his agreement under the condition that a convoy of food provisions and medicines be delivered to his unit. Stojic promised that within three days he, together with Benabou, would personally deliver the goods, but asked that the event should be kept under wraps, so as not to create the impression that in the confrontation with the BiH Armija kidnapping could become the favorite avenue to obtain food aid. Thereupon, all UN units in the area were advised of the incident and warned not to circulate in the area of SPABAT without previous notice to the Spanish unit. Notwithstanding those precautions, there was a feeling that the kidnapping event would certainly become a precedent, and that the ransom for release would probably keep mounting every time such an incident occurred. On the way back to their base, Major Carlos de Salas, who was at the wheel, expressed to Benabou, who was sitting at his side, his appreciation for the rapidity and efficacy with which the civil affairs officer had acted without delay and enlisted the immediate intervention of the defense minister, admitting that, "We, the Spaniards, act much more rationally and focus on our target, rather than be prepared to reveal ourselves outwardly; you, Sephardic Jews, also have this trait of character innate in you.[217]" After that outburst of cultural affinity and friendship, de Salas, with a smile on his lips, added, *"Non obstante, no te equivoques, si mi colonel me lo manda, yo te mato, Alberto* (But make no mistake, Albert, if my colonel should give me the order, I would shoot you")[218]. A chill ran down Albert's spine at that chillingly candid and gratuitous admission, but he absorbed it painfully without reacting, and he only thought to himself that if an Israeli soldier received such an order, he would certainly go into a Talmudic debate with his superior instead of executing it, and he congratulated himself for this cultural difference with his interlocutor.

David Belmonte, the head of DUTCHCOM, was also assigned to join the team negotiating the release of the interpreters. His expertise in SATMAR (satellite communication) was vital to ensure the rapidity of the operation. That was another fascinating paradox in action, how the media had become vital to achieve immediacy. David's presence had indeed made the whole difference in the achievement of the rapid result, though his preoccupation led him elsewhere, for he had been cut off from Andrea for the past eight days, because he was far from her in central Bosnia, in his rescue mission of the Muslim interpreters, and had no clue of the suffering she was going through. He had no way to contact her, so he turned all his attention, effort, and energy to the rescue operation, while his love for Andrea was constantly

---

[217] Source: personal memoirs of the war in Bosnia of Albert Benabou.
[218] ibid.

knocking on the doors of his consciousness and being. After he arrived back to base, he took a pause to try again to contact her. It was 7:00 a.m. in the morning in New York, when he imagined she was on her way to work. She received the call on her mobile phone, while rushing between two trains in the chaotic and overcrowded New York subway system. She took a few strides to the side to escape the smashing flow of the noisy crowds, but could hardly hear David's desperate words. She raised her voice in hysteria, "David, my love, I hate you . . . where are you?[219]" And amidst that whirlpool of that mad and chaotic crowd, which she ignored as if she were there all alone on the stage with her beloved David, the communication was cut off. Andrea emerged frustrated from the tunnels of the subway into a resplendent sky of summery New York and rushed to her office on the thirty-second floor of the glass building. No sooner had she set her eyes on the magnificent site of the ocean, which extended to the east, than the phone rang. Without waiting for the caller to identify himself, she burst at him, "Tell me, why this long silence? It has been ten days.[220]"

It had been "only" an eight-day recess, but he understood her frustration, which led to exaggeration. He meekly retorted, "I have been for all those days in central Bosnia. I think I am coming soon to New York. I cannot speak much more.[221]"

"Read my messages and answer quickly,[222]" she concluded and hung up.

But the amorous correspondence continued uninterrupted, many times a day, every message dwarfing the intensity and passion of the previous one, she finding no interest in the

---

[219] For maintaining privacy, names have been changed and the source is kept in the confidential documents of memoirs of the war in Bosnia of Albert Benabou.
[220] ibid.
[221] ibid.
[222] ibid.

people surrounding her, who seemed tasteless, stale, and irrelevant as if they were sleepwalking, while her mind was floating far away to the hills of south Bosnia, trying to imagine at every moment what he was doing and trying to guess why he had forgotten her. Proclaiming herself as his missing rib, of which she was made up, she cried out her impatience to give herself all up to him. In one of those messages, of 14 June, she brought up the idea that she yearned to meet him in the dark, where he would be groping to find her and touch her. On 18 June, he responded that, being constantly obsessed by her, he had already arranged to be in New York for work, but he was concerned about how to detach himself from the people who would be surrounding him in order to find his way to the dark room, where she was resolute to reach out and find him. She was worried that he might arrive in New York without previous notice, and she wanted to be notified of his arrival, so as to prepare "to protect you from ourselves,[223]" because she feared causing harm to him. She wanted him to know (be warned?) that exactly as she could easily become addicted to him, she could also be driven by an urge for an obsessive independence, which in the past had left her loved ones devastated and desperate. And despite those fears and warnings, she swore to have never felt such a perfect harmony with anyone....

## Saturday, 19 June, 1993

On that day, weekend or not, in a war arena that knew no let-up or pause, both Croats and Muslims submitted urgent requests to SPABAT and to the civil affairs office, asking for humanitarian convoys of food and medicine for their respective populations, which were on the verge of disaster. Some of their leaders were speaking of human catastrophes on an

---
[223] ibid.

African scale, implying that while those misfortunes may have become "acceptable" for Africans, they remained unthinkable for Europeans. Colonel Angel Morales, the commander of SPABAT, and civil affairs coordinator for that region, Albert Benabou, dispatched an urgent message to the advanced UN HQ in Kiseljak, where British General Veer de Hayes was exploring access routes between Jablanica and Konjic, for it was believed that such convoys would help to reduce tensions in that area where the civil war had already transcended the zones of authority and control of Croatian and Muslim leaders, and where local military commanders did as they pleased. So, though no one believed that the requested convoys would put an end to hostilities, the United Nations thought that their very presence in the states of ex-Yugoslavia would be justified by the real assistance they brought to the unfortunate civilian populations.

The idea was that SPABAT would provide the security of the convoys, in coordination with each party to the conflict in its zone of control, while the distribution of the emergency goods would be negotiated between the humanitarian organizations and each locality separately, so as to guarantee that the supplies reached the needy civilian populations. One hundred trucks were envisaged to constitute the convoy, with a view to satisfying the needs along the agreed itinerary.[224] Actually, that route was planned very close to the already existing path of humanitarian aid, where a safe passage was authorized only to forces of SPABAT and UNPROFOR. The good working relations that were established between SPABAT and the warring factions of the HVO and BiH Armija allowed the planners a certain degree of assurance that the convoy could go through. The assumption at the headquarters in Medjugorje

---

[224]The agreed number of trucks for each locality was as follows: Mostar-ten, Dreznica-five, Jablanica-ten, Kostajnica-ten, Ljiubina-ten, Konjic-ten, Vitez-ten, Busovaca-five, Sarajevo-ten.

was that the success of the convoy would create a psychological reduction of the animosity between the parties, among those populations which had been isolated and starved for too long. Until then, Colonel Morales felt frustrated by the deterioration of the situation within the civil population in that war zone, due to the inaction of the international bodies, therefore, he was constantly in search of new ways to ease the living conditions of the population, while the Croatian and Muslim leaders wanted to obtain what assistance they could while preserving the military gains they had made on the ground. Again Raymond Aron's saying came to Benabou's mind: "In a situation of civil war, which is the worst that can happen to any country, the best way out is to call for outside intervention in order to resolve the conflict.[225]" It is doubtful whether Abraham Lincoln would have concurred with this conclusion during the American Civil War that he had to tame in his own country, but it was certainly a way to rationalize the United Nations, American, Islamic, and European meddling in the Bosnian War.

**Sunday, 20 June, 1993**

At 6:00 a.m. that day, one hundred and four Muslim refugees came to knock on the door of the SPABAT base to ask for asylum, since they had been expelled by local authorities from Posušje under the excuse that they were being sent out for their safety, after six HVO soldiers who lived in the town had been murdered. That agglomeration, which was ninety-eight percent Croatian, had registered a strong support during World War II for the Ustasha regime. In the bus which brought those refugees to the base was Isabella Oriani, a representative of the Italian Consortium of Solidarity, which had taken charge of sheltering

---

[225] DOC. 010, dated 19 June 1993, concerning requirements for special survival convoys distributed by Albert Benabou to UN Headquarters.

them in Italy, with SPABAT helping coordinate the deal with international organizations. Spanish soldiers, posted aboard their light Pegasus armored vehicles, prevented access from the bus, which was being pursued by Croatian private cars whose passengers clamored for vengeance. The clock indicated 2:30 p.m., and temperatures were augmenting in that early summer day, and the Spaniards wanted the bus out of their zone of control forthwith. It was the inescapable siesta time, which Colonel Miguel de Castro, who would have had to deal with those unfortunate expellees, could not miss. Thus, Captain Molina of the SPABAT G5 operations, accompanied by Benabou and Oriani, addressed the UNHCR office in Medjugorje, with a view of resolving the fate of the passengers and in the meantime settling the question of their accommodation. It was Sunday, and it was difficult to find a decision maker, especially on that sunny day. Rita, who was in the office of UNHCR in Jablanica, offered a rapid and efficient way out, assuring the movement of those refugees towards Split, where they would be embarked for Italy. The Italian permits and documentation for this human transfer were also arranged.

Back on the bus, the three found a Croatian HVO officer, who demanded that all men disembark so that he could interrogate them. So Benabou and Oriani, in concert, decided to invent a story in order to avoid what seemed to them as a superfluous exercise that could only frighten and jeopardize those unfortunate people. They told the officer that NATO forces had already taken stock of all the passengers of the bus under their protection, and that they would monitor anyone who came into contact with them. Therefore, Benabou "advised" him in a "friendly" tone, "We do not want to know your name, just go away as quickly as you can, before you are designated as a war criminal.[226]" The Croat retreated towards

---

[226] Source: personal memoirs of the war in Bosnia of Albert Benabou.

his people. Benabou had just witnessed another manifestation of that hatred, and he expressed the wish and the prayer that someday it could be said that Andric had exaggerated.

**Tuesday, 22 June, 1993**

Boban was in full swing preparing for the Geneva Conference, in concert with Zagreb, which excluded him from the opening session. Early that Tuesday morning, Vlado called Benabou and transmitted to him many messages that were directed to international organizations. The messages were written under the letterhead of The Republic of Bosnia and Herzegovina, and in subtitle, the Croatian national emblem and the scripture, *Hrvatska Zajednica Herzeg Bosnia*, (The Croatian community of Herzeg-Bosnia), corrected into *Hrvatska Republika Herzeg Bosnia* (the Croatian Republic of Herzeg-Bosnia, following the February 1994 Washington Agreement), Office of the Presidency. The main issues raised in those messages were to the joint presidents of the conference on ex-Yugoslavia in Geneva, Thorvald Stoltenberg and Lord David Owen, with copies to Secretary General of the UN, Boutros Boutros-Ghali, the President of the US William Clinton, the members of the Security Council and to the EU presidency. Boban wrote that the sole solution to the conflict consisted of creating a union of the three major component people of Bosnia, with equal rights, in the territory of Bosnia and Herzegovina. He specified that, "We regard the boundaries of BiH as nonnegotiable and inviolable, while the internal frontiers between the various entities of the Republic are open to discussion.[228]" That was the

---

[228] See Letters signed Mate Boban, dated Mostar, 22 June 1993, addressed to Co-Chairmen of the International Conference on Former Yugoslavia, Mr, Thorvald Stoltenberg and Lord David Owen (Ref.: 0049/93), to General Philipe Morillon, UNPROFOR Commander for Bosnia & Herzegovina ( Ref.: 0050/93) distributed by Albert Benabou to UN Headquarters in Zagreb & New York.

summary of his concept of one united, umbrella state above the three separate entities.

Lord Owen had declared in an interview to the BBC: "The Muslims must get a guaranteed exit to the sea, and it is possible that Mostar should be apportioned to them.[229]" But Mostar is located on the main highway leading from Sarajevo to the Adriatic Sea, and Boban now reacted by claiming that the Croatian majority in multinational Mostar had been maintained during the past century and that the Serbs recognized this fact. Boban emphasized that Mostar was strategically, economically, culturally, and educationally important, and in the name of fairness demanded that since the Muslims were offered four major urban centers (Sarajevo, Tuzla, Zenica, Doboj and Bihac), and the Croats and Serbs combined only two centers (Banja Luka and Mostar), Owen's proposal, which was done under pressure of interested parties, was unacceptable.

In his message to General Morillon, the commander of UNPROFOR, Boban violently accused the Muslims of the "barbaric devastation and desecration of Catholic holy places.[230]" He added that over two hundred thousand Croats in central Bosnia were in danger and subjected to famine and expulsions, and demanded that immediate humanitarian aid to the Croats trapped in the towns of Vares, Kiseljak, Kresevo, Vitez, Novi Travnik, and elsewhere. Boban also insinuated that if UNPROFOR were unable to protect the Croats, he would resort to the right of self-defense provided

---

[229] See letter signed Mate Boban, dated 22 June 1993, addressed to Lord David Owen (Ref.: 0051/93) distributed by Albert Benabou to UN Headquarters in Zagreb & New York.

[230] See Letter signed Mate Boban, dated Mostar, 22 June 1993, addressed to General Philippe Morillon, UNPROFOR Commander for Bosnia & Herzegovina ( Ref.: 0050/93) distributed by Albert Benabou to UN Headquarters in Zagreb & New York.

in the UN charter. He also demanded to receive an answer within twenty-four hours.

Boban also transmitted a document composed of legally formulated clauses that could constitute a permanent accord among all three parties in BiH. This proposal was widely distributed on the eve of the Geneva Conference that was to convene on 23 June. Generally speaking, it recapitulated his main idea of a confederation among the three quasi-independent entities under a united umbrella state, where the specific legislative, executive, and juridical powers would be determined by each entity on its own. He suggested that the presidency of the state would be occupied in rotation by each of the three presidents of the confederated entities. Thus, he argued, no excessive power was given to the federal president, who would be constrained by his limited authority and have no leverage over the constituent entities.

Benabou, who had much doubt about Boban's good intentions when putting forward those proposals, wrote at the end of his report, citing Daniel Webster: "The concept of justice is a thread which links together civilized beings and civilized nations.[231]" In Boban's case, he thought that only political considerations lay at the base of his démarche, rather than a desire to do justice to Croatian and Muslim populations. He had to make his point before Geneva, and he did so loud and clear, in front of all those whose positions counted to world public opinion. He was seeking by the same measure to justify his intensified attacks on Muslim East Mostar.

## Wednesday, 23 June, 1993

Finally, Boban got to Geneva, but his festival of declarations went on in Grude, the capital of the Croats of BiH. Vlado

---

[231] DOC. 013, dated 23 June 1993, concerning Boban's Correspondence, distributed by Albert Benabou to UN Headquarters in Zagreb and New York.

Pogarcic, in charge of international affairs in Boban's office, invited Benabou for a four-hour, in-depth discussion of his boss's ideas and the meaning of his campaign. He went to the meeting, accompanied by Captains Molina and Pita, who represented SPABAT (G5 operations and G2 intelligence, respectively). In that encounter, the obvious items were raised:

The Geneva Conference constituted a new phase for the Croats, for Pogarcic thought that Boban's initiative to establish a limited confederation ought to be taken seriously as the most practical. He emphasized that prior to the launching of that initiative consultations had taken place among all parties to the conflict, with whom the Croatian leadership had maintained good relations, even with some Muslims (not including Alija Izetbegovic and his team). Benabou had suspected indeed that Boban could boast some Muslim collaborators in East Mostar.

The "population movement" (the euphemism for ethnic cleansing) issue that Boban raised in his message to Morillon was in fact geared to ensure the free movement of the Croats in the areas of Sarajevo, Vares, Bugojno, Zenica, Zepce, and Tuzla. Pogarcic had pledged that his government would take care of those populations the moment they moved out of those zones where they were trapped. He thought that a similar process should be suggested to the Muslims regarding their displaced kin, hinting to the fate of Mostar Muslims, whom Boban had envisaged to move elsewhere, so as to leave the city which he regarded as vital to the Croatian entity, *Muslimfrei* (free of Muslims). He emphasized indeed that movements of populations should not be difficult to apply, they being the only way to obtain a "separation of the peoples.[232]" He added that if UNPROFOR did not cooperate in that enterprise, the present trends would inevitably

---

[232] DOC. 014, dated 24 June 1993 Concerning meeting with Vlado Pogarcic, Croat Responsible for International Relations, distributed by Albert Benabou to UN Headquarters in Kiseljak, Divulje, Zagreb & New York.

lead to catastrophe, of which the Croats were washing their hands clean, even before it occurred. He stressed that Morillon should foresee what was coming and convince the Muslims to participate in a quartet, made of two Croats and two Muslims, who would undertake to resolve the problem in a "civilized fashion," something that reminded Benabou of the "civilized fashion" with which Europeans had "solved" the problem with their Jews half a century earlier.

Neither Boban nor any other party to the conflict wished at that point to indicate the exact desired boundaries he was striving to attain. But Pogarcic pointed out to certain elements which hinted at Boban's aspirations:

(a) The Muslims would be allowed to keep the central Bosnian valley, which constituted the richest in resources area of BiH, Bihac, which was indisputably their territory, and Sarajevo, which was destined to become their political and cultural center. Their access to the sea, in the direction of the port of Neum, was to be considered during the upcoming negotiations.

(b) The Serbs should keep Banja Luka as their political and cultural center, while east Bosnia and the other territories under their control would be the object of negotiations.

(c) The Croats claimed the area of northern Bosnia as part of their historical patrimony, and the Croatian people would be open to negotiations in order to acquire that territory in a political deal. As claimed by Boban in his letter to Owen, Mostar was incontestably a historical, political, and cultural Croatian center and therefore would stay in Croatian hands. Therefore, Muslims dwelling there would have to move out in the direction of Muslim areas, namely an ethnic cleansing should be enforced there by agreement (an oxymoron of sorts).

With regard to the existing political leaders of the parties, several interesting points were made:

Concerning the Muslims, since Alija Izetbegovic and his team were not adequate partners for discussion, being dishonest since the outset and acting dishonestly since they took office, replacements like Fikret Abdic and Franjo Boras ought to be considered.

A certain level of understanding had been established with the Serbs, who were recognized as "good merchants." Serbian representatives in the Bosnian government, Mirko Pejanovic and Sasha Lujic-Mijatovic, were viewed as servants of Alija Izetbegovic; therefore, they should not be taken seriously. Benabou noted that the Croats expressed their desire to know the Serbian and Muslim leaders with whom they would have to work.

For the Croats, Boban was their undisputed representative. He was appreciated and admired as the "father of the nation," by all levels of the officers of HVO. But Benabou noted that in his estimate there was lately an erosion in Boban's stature among the Croatian leaders originating from Mostar, like Prlic, Stojic, and Petkovic.

The military top brass of the parties was also submitted to criticism. It was said that:

Among the Muslims, even though General Rasim Delic had been appointed as the chief of the joint forces of the BiH Armija, it was General Safet Hallilovic who continued to hold the supreme responsibility in the chain of command;

The Serbian units operated within a strict discipline, like a professional army;

For the Croats, Petkovic was definitely the commander of HVO, but improvements ought to be adopted on the ground, especially among the young officers who were called to serve. Pogarcic added that at the onset of the war the HVO brigades could have saved Sarajevo, but Hallilovic had

*Savagery in the Heart of Europe*

prevented them from doing so, and he abandoned the city to the Serbs, who then dismissed him. This latter information was also confirmed by Captain Pita of SPABAT, who had captured it from other sources; and

As concerns UNPROFOR, their mandate ought to be revised, maybe in Geneva, with a view to limiting their field of activity, for it was not their fault, but rather that of the United Nations, that UNPROFOR was facing the embarrassing situations on the ground. Pogarcic emphasized that all parties shared this view, but it was the Croats who dared to raise their voice for now.

With regard to UNHCR, Pogarcic denounced their attitude towards the Croats, stressing that "if they had placed their stores in the Muslim areas, we would have seen what could happen,[233]" hinting that they would have been robbed by Muslims. In any case, he said, nobody needed those stores. He informed Benabou that a meeting was going to take place between him and a special representative of UNHCR, and he invited Benabou to take part. The latter, based on past experience and on his instincts, saw there an attempt by the Croats to manipulate international agencies, therefore he declined the invitation, explaining that the attending UNHCR officer would handle the issue highhandedly, making Benabou's presence redundant.

Concluding his report on this meeting, Benabou noted that one ought to understand that in Pogarcic's review of the war situation, he signaled disarray and impasse, both on the domestic and international levels, and that Zagreb's intervention was necessary to redress things to their proper place, something that would occur only later, maybe too late. In this and other contexts, Benabou was reminded of Alexis de Tocqueville's famous adage that "in normal times, as few as possible generals, and when the guns speak, as little as

---

[233] ibid.

possible diplomatic refinement.[234]" He sensed that he was constantly imbued by both, with a very fine and indiscernible line in between, as the generals around him, both UN and local, were trying to make diplomacy, and politicians, again UN and local, were trying to run military affairs.

**Wednesday, 30 June, 1993**

The logistic support that Benabou needed for his operations leaned totally on the Spanish Battalion, but since the scope of his activities had considerably grown both in the space covered and in the intensity of humanitarian operations and diplomatic contacts, he applied to Victor Andreev, who was the coordinator for the entire area of BiH, for more personnel and equipment to meet his obligations, but Andreev was not quick to respond, apparently not satisfied with the importance that the area of Mostar was taking in the eyes of both Zagreb and New York. Indeed, save for the Serbo-Croatian interpreter, Sasha Milankovic, Andreev had refused for a long time to accord to Benabou the reinforcements he considered necessary for the fulfillment of his growing duty. In the long run, this attitude would have a negative effect on the relations between the civil affairs office and the SPABAT, which found itself under increasing demands to widen its base of support. This was strange, in a way, because at the bottom line all these operations were financed by the United Nations and drew funds from the same pocket.

**Friday, 2 July, 1993**

Under the repeated recommendations of the Zagreb UNPROFOR HQ, the operational concept of security zones (colored in pink on the UN maps) in BiH finally came up to

---

[234] DOC. 015 dated 25 June 1993, concerning meeting between Croat and Serbs Commanders in Stolac, Distributed to UN Headquarters by Albert Benabou.

the vote at the Security Council on 2 July, 1993. The tabled resolution was based on the situation reports from the field, particularly those submitted by the advanced headquarters in Kiseljak. That Security Council Resolution 838 also extended the mandate of UNPROFOR, based on the security zones mentioned in SCR 824, which comprised Srebrenica, Zepa, Gorazde, Sarajevo, Tuzla, and Bihac. The new resolution affirmed the authority of the civil affairs office and added more obligations to it, while defining the present and future role of UNPROFOR in Bosnia and Herzegovina. But on the other hand, the renewed mandate, like its precedent in Resolution 824, only included the area of conflict between Serbs and Muslims, excluding the zone of Mostar where Croats and Muslims were warring and where Benabou was active. That was the consequence of Benabou's failure to convince Victor Andreev, who was the coordinator at Kiseljak for the entire country, to also include Mostar in the new resolution which delineated the security zones. But Benabou continued to press, claiming that in order to provide for the urgent needs of the distressed Croatian and Muslim populations in his zone, Mostar too ought to be included in the pink zone, exactly like Sarajevo and other places, because the Mostar area was too much given to the mercy and good will of SPABAT. Benabou was striving to achieve, by a direct mandate from New York, a degree of independence and a regularized direct cooperation with other bodies. Benabou's insistence displeased Andreev, who reacted by opposing the idea, as if the issue were a personal test of forces between them, probably due to Benabou's insensitivity when going to high tones in his arguments with his boss, and the latter's quick tendency to feel insulted by what he must have seen as his subordinate's insolence. It would take them some time to learn to communicate between them.

The mission of the civil affairs office in BiH, as newly defined by the mandate of the Security Council, was worded in these terms:

- To serve as political advisers to UNPROFOR, both civil and military;
- To take part in negotiations with the local military and civil governmental authorities regarding the welfare of the population;
- To participate in the meetings of international agencies and NGOs;
- To provide information regarding the activities of UNPROFOR;
- To collect information on other organizations with a view of better dealing with the humanitarian aspects of the operation;
- To advise and formulate solutions to unforeseen problems as they arose;
- To establish an ongoing relationship with the Center of Human Rights at the United Nations regarding abuses and violations of those rights;
- To submit a weekly situation report (SITREP), which should sum up the recent developments, identify new trends, analyze them, and propose a line of action;
- To act as a liaison officer with the G5 (operations) regarding civil affairs, which required contact with the local authorities, like police, local mayors, and local commanders;
- To serve as the office of accreditation of the press and distribute information.

All considered, the new mandate (SCR 838) added the following tasks to the existing ones, making the UN presence that was supposed by nature and definition to be temporary look and sound as if digging in for the long haul. It now said that it would:

Supervise the application on the ground of the zones of security, in coordination with the forces of UNPROFOR, and pursue permanent negotiations so as to ensure that all parties kept their obligations, namely: demilitarization, freedom of movement, repatriation of displaced persons to their homes, and the supply of unlimited humanitarian aid.

Undertake the construction and upkeep of all utility systems (water, electricity, collection of garbage, sewer), which would constitute great challenges in the security zones. Since a large number of international agencies were presently involved in rehabilitating these systems in urban centers, the civil affairs office would be able to participate in their efforts.

The Center for Human Rights in Zagreb had formulated guidelines for reports on violations of human rights. This document was distributed to all civil affairs offices and would also guide officers of CIVPOL (civil police), UNMO (UN military observers), UNHCR (UN humanitarian aid), and ECLO (EU observers), who would be collecting data on the ground.

Civil affairs offices would also take charge of identifying socio-economic problems which impacted the well-being of the local populations. Even though these instruments did not possess the necessary tools to provide concrete results towards the solution of these issues, they could play an important role in forwarding such solutions.

The Security Council resolution assigned specific tasks to the various offices of civilian affairs and also invested them with a special status vis-à-vis local authorities and the military units of UNPROFOR. But Mostar remained for now outside the privileged circle of security zones, something which would prove cumbersome for Benabou's activities in that zone. That was a typically UN bureaucratic approach of perfectly pushing forward resolutions in the Security Council while sometimes ignoring necessities on the terrain. Benabou did not let go and would raise the issue again and again at every opportunity.

## Sunday, 4 July, 1993

Relentless, Benabou now attempted to achieve by administrative means what he failed to attain by mandate of the Security Council. He applied to Andreev again and asked him to realize what he had himself said during a visit in Mostar, on 13 June, to the effect that "Benabou needed an assistant for international affairs, who could back him up during his high-level meetings, since a local assistant would be unable to respond to such needs.[235]" Andreev had also expressed his desire to accord to the new help the necessary space and furnishings to allow him to operate. Benabou had also complained that even the vehicle put at his disposition, a Jeep Cherokee deluxe, could no longer negotiate the devastated and constantly bombarded muddy roads in the war zone. He quipped that the car being "deluxe" was more fitting for the UN bureaucrats in Zagreb than for field observers like him. Ultimately, he continued to depend on SPABAT for both transportation and communications. To detach himself from this crippling dependence, he created special relationships with the British HQ and the Dutch communications center, which allowed him to act more effectively and to lend more flexibility to his movements on the ground. In the conclusion of his report on this matter, he complained about the Kafkaesque situation where he found himself: "Between Kafka and the theater of the absurd which we encounter in war situations, we should at least try to avoid creating a new breed of "papivores" (paper-guzzlers) who could end up dominating the carnivores and the herbivores of our planet.[236]" That was indeed the feeling he got from Zagreb bureaucrats, who kept asking for and expecting more and more papers, as if

---

[235] See letter, dated 4 July 1993, addressed from the war zone by Albert Benabou to Victor Andreev, UN Headquarters in Kiseljak, concerning Administration requirements.
[236] ibid.

to justify their helplessness in the face of complex demands from the war zone they could not handle. They were not versed in the spirit of operational flexibility and improvisation that he had been brought up during his IDF years.

## Monday, 5 July, 1993

At Andreev's request, from his headquarters at Kiseljak, Benabou asked for an urgent meeting with President Boban in Grude on 5 July. Participating on the Croatian side was also Vladislav Pogarcic, the adviser for international affairs, and in Benabou's company were Captain Julio Salom (whom Benabou thought to be a Marano, as his name derived from the Hebrew Shalom) from the G5 office of SPABAT. Under discussion was the siege that the Croatian HVO troops had laid around the UNPROFOR HQ at Kiseljak. The warring parties had indeed discovered that the chaotic environment, where troops behaved like armed gangs of criminals, laying siege against the UN forces and taking their personnel hostage, could bear the best fruits if they wished to achieve anything on the ground. Benabou, who had to submit to the UN culture of surrendering to the gangs if he wished to save the lives of its officers, launched the negotiations on the telephone, with British Brigadier General Veer de Hayes in Kiseljak at the other end of the line. Albert liked the man and delighted in working with him. By midnight, an "agreement," namely a surrender to the kidnappers, had been concluded, to wit:

That de Hayes guaranteed the free passage of two HVO officers who were surrounded by BiH Armija troops in the area of Visoko, which was under CANBAT (Canadian Battalion) responsibility.

The Canadians, who had accumulated a considerable UN experience, felt that there was a connection between the siege of Kiseljak and the Croatian officers who were blocked by the Muslims in their area of operation. They were now waiting for Hayes's orders.

On his part, Boban undertook to order personally Colonel Blaskic to lift the siege on the UNPROFOR command at Kiseljak and release the four Muslim prisoners whom he held in the HVO camp in town. This showed that Boban was in charge and could have prevented the siege and the arrest in the first place, if there were any civility in that mode of thinking with which the UN was collaborating.

Close to midnight, Pogarcic informed Benabou that the orders were issued and that Blaskic would implement his part of the deal, and this led to the simultaneous realization of both parties' commitments so as not to leave any one of them with temporary advantage over his rival.

**Thursday, 8 July, 1993**

Since the beginning of that week, Benabou had met Mate Boban and his team on three occasions. Many topics of interest were raised:

1. On the territorial level, and following the meeting of minds between the Serbs and the Croats in Geneva, an agreement seemed to emerge between them on the issue of the partition of BiH, with the tentative borders delineated on maps.
2. Despite the fact that the Croats had suffered severe military setbacks in the area of Mostar, Kostanjica, and south Jablanica, they were envisaging to launch at the end of the month new military offensives, which would permit them to regain some of their strategic position, or at the very least to stabilize their situation in the Mostar area. Benabou interpreted that statement as a Croatian threat to widen their siege around the city and to pursue the massacre of its Muslim population.

*Savagery in the Heart of Europe*

3. The Croatian immediate objective was to ensure the HVO control of the axis Mostar- Jablanica-Konjic, and they would have to act rapidly in order to prevent the BiH Armija from consolidating its territorial acquisitions since it had obtained some military successes.
4. Boban declared that he was ready to allow the deployment of SPABAT forces and other UN troops in the area of the Mostar airport, and this could be carried out as part of the military stabilization in the city of Mostar, within one month. For Boban was hoping to achieve, by the end of July, an HVO victory around the airport where he had suffered some humiliating defeats.
5. Boban also raised his proposal to demilitarize the entire road from Mostar to Sarajevo, passing by Jablanica, Konjic, and Tarcin, over an extent of twenty kilometers on either side. Benabou retorted that the proposal would be analyzed and submitted to the Muslims for their reaction. In truth, he was suspicious of the ultimate motives of Boban, but he wanted to verify on the ground the topographical implications of the proposal. He kept in mind the encounter between Morillon and Mladic[238].
6. In spite of Boban and his team's proclamations regarding their firm relations with Radovan Karadzic and Ratko Mladic, one could discern the concern of the Croats regarding the price they would be called to pay to the Serbs, like an access to the Adriatic. However, Boban seemed determined to pay what it took in order to achieve his strategic goal in the short run, so high were the stakes in his eyes.
7. Benabou concluded in his report on the meeting that due to the recent military victories of BiH Armija, and,

---

[238] See above Morillon's error when signing with the Serbian General Ratko Mladic, the accords for the evacuation of Srebrenica.

conversely, to the decisive routs of HVO, it was now impossible to initiate any discussions of the raised issues or a truce. The civilian populations would have to endure suffering before that war ended around the negotiation table, citing the famous verse from La Fontaine's *Le Lievre et la Tortue* (*The Rabbit and the Tortoise*), "Patience and time can do much more than force and rage.[239]"

With the help of Belmonte at the Dutch communications center, Benabou also transmitted the message to Brigadier R.V. Searby, commander of BRITFOR at the base of Divulje, near Split, in addition to the regular distribution to the HQ of Morales, Kiseljak, Zagreb, and New York. He wished to ensure that NATO forces too were well informed, and at the same time, open a channel with the British. From that day on, all of Benabou's messages were regularly transmitted to the Britons and via them to the Americans.

**Tuesday, 13 July, 1993**

A meeting took place at Grude, the Croatian HQ, with the participation of Prime Minister Jadranko Prlic and Vladislav Pogarcic, Boban's aide and adviser. UNPROFOR was represented by Albert Benabou, Carlos de Salas of G5 (operations) and Major Angel Ramirez of G6 (communications) of SPABAT. The topics discussed included:

1. The SPABAT and other units of UNPROFOR, which were deployed at Jablanica, Dracevo, and Medjugorje, would redeploy to the airport of Mostar, but the operation of relocation would not be carried out before three or four weeks. Actually, the move would never

---

[239] DOC. 020, dated 9 July 1993, concerning meeting with Boban and assistant team, distributed by Albert Benabou to UN Headquarters.

*Savagery in the Heart of Europe*

take place. It seemed to Benabou that Prlic was simply playing master of the place and of the situation. UNPROFOR was invited to submit a redeployment plan of its units and of its functioning at the airport to cover the humanitarian and civil missions of the UN troops. UNPROFOR undertook to submit a plan that could win the approval of all parties (Croats, Muslims, and Serbs).

2. Those issues had already been taken up by Boban on various occasions. However, Benabou detected for the first time an undertone of competition between Prlic and Boban, but he retorted that the proposal would be studied by the UN authorities in place, and their answer would be delivered at the earliest possible time. At that point, Benabou and Pogarcic exchanged a significant smile, accompanied by a nod of complicity, which attested that they understood what was going on.

3. Prlic confirmed that Croats and Muslims had met on Saturday, 10 July, at Makarska, forty kilometers southeast of Split on the Adriatic coast. Prlic claimed that the parties reached an agreement on humanitarian convoys on various routes to Sarajevo. Prlic also transmitted to Benabou the full original text of that accord, in which handwritten amendments by Mate Granic, the foreign minister of Zagreb, had been introduced, as the Croatian authorities had been at the source of this initiative due to their embarrassment from the brutal activities of the Bosnian Croats against the Muslim civil population of Mostar. As a result, Muslims and Croats had decided to form a bilateral commission, which, as of 15 July, would decide upon the destination, the route, and the volume of each convoy, according to the needs of each locality. Prlic suggested that the Serbs too should be sitting in that commission and expressed

his readiness to convene at the earliest possible a meeting at Divulje or Makarska, with a view of preparing a tripartite humanitarian project. He suggested that these people should take part: Jadranko Prlic for HVO and the Croats, Hazdo Efendic for the Muslims and the BiH Armija, and Vladimir Lukic for the Serbs.

4. Prlic also solicited UNPROFOR sponsorship of that encounter and asked the UN authorities to invite the Serbs to the talks. He specified that the Muslims had already accepted the principle of Serbian participation. Benabou suggested that his boss, Andreev, would take care of that request. It was suggested that SPABAT, UNICEF, and the civil affairs office would go forthwith with a convoy of enriched milk to six thousand needy children of Mostar, both Croatian and Muslim, and Prlic pledged his support to such an operation. But ultimately, the plan and promises would stay confined to paper, and Benabou would be the subject of derision from his colleagues for fighting so insistently on this noble project. It was thought that the details of the convoy, tentatively scheduled for 15 July, when the parties were supposed to hold fire for two consecutive hours, would be planned by Brigadier General Milijenko Lasic (HVO) and General Pasalic (BiH Armija). Benabou cited in his report the passage from Psalms, which praised God for giving force to the words of the newborn and babies, hinting at the treatment by the Croats of UN officers as if they were children. Or, in other words, he did not believe one word of what they said. In such instances, his diplomatic and military instincts and experience were ringing an internal alarm in his mind, because that was auguring ill for the coming days, as he sensed that all the Croatian measures, initiatives, and smooth talk were calculated as

anesthetics, to numb everyone around while they were preparing to mount a decisive and large scale attack on East Mostar.

Benabou still lived the catastrophic failure of the warning system of the Israeli intelligence, where he had served twenty years earlier during the Yom Kippur War (1973), when his brother, Dany, who commanded an armored unit, was seriously injured (80% burns), and had the impression that a similar stratagem of misleading information was being played once again in front of his eyes. He warned the command in Kiseljak that the Croats in Zagreb and Grude considered them idiots. They had neither the intention to allow UN redeployment, which did not depend only on them anyway, and could only reinforce UN control, which they dislike, nor to implement the passage of convoys. Their only objective for now was to distract our attention and to use to their advantage the features of the terrain in order to maximize their chance in the offensive they were preparing against the Muslims in Mostar.

Benabou could not help reminding the continuation of Carl Sandburg's verse as he was witnessing the horrifying carnage of that war just before the turn of the twentieth century:

> Destroy the cities, shatter the walls into pieces, break the cathedrals and the factories, the stores, and the houses, turn them into piles of stone and wood that are incinerated black and fly with the wind, for you are soldiers and we order you to obey. But also, build the cities, rebuild the walls, put together again the factories, the cathedrals, the stores, and the houses, in buildings intended for the living and the working, for you are all civilians and workers and we order you to do so.[240]

---

[240] Source: personal memoirs of the War in Bosnia of Albert Benabou.

As Benabou was sadly watching the implementation before his eyes of the first destructive part of that poem, he was asking himself when and whether the second, constructive part, might begin. For the moment, he decided to ignore Lasic's negative response to the milk convoy and addressed directly, by wireless communication, the Muslim military and civilian leaders of Mostar via the technical prowess of DUTCHCOM. The exchanges between them on that Saturday, 17 July were poignant.

The BiH Armija was firmly in support of the accords on the milk convoy and was eagerly waiting for its delivery. Colonel Sulejman Budakovic, at the same time, sent an official message by fax, through the command in Jablanica, to the effect that the Muslim part of Mostar was being intensely bombed and cut off from the outside. That may have explained to Benabou the reason why the Croats were so evasive and reluctant to carry out the agreement.

Following intensive consultations with Major Carlos de Salas (SPABAT, G5), Benabou initiated on Saturday, 17 July, another meeting with Bruno Stojic, the defense minister of the Croatian community, where de Salas was present, but the UN representatives abstained from any remark, preferring to listen to the Croatian litany of stories and pledges. Benabou noticed that Stojic seemed self-confident and radiant from his power, probably due to the mandate he had been recently vested with by his authorities, both at Grude and Zagreb, to launch hostilities in the area of Mostar, Kostanjica, and Jablanica. Pogarcic had expressed the idea that Stojic wished to prove to Franjo Tudjman and to Mate Boban that by the end of July he would pull off a victory in Mostar. Stojic was allegedly convinced that his operations with the HVO were wisely calculated, namely to concentrate on Mostar for now and abandon Kostanjica, while leaving Jablanica to a second stage. He considered that objective as solidly anchored in a sound strategy. He thought that the Muslims had evinced more tenacious resistance than he had anticipated, and he was sure that all means were adequate to convince UNPROFOR that it was necessary to displace all the Muslims of East Mostar outside the region. He explained that otherwise their lives would be permanently in jeopardy, and the UNPROFOR would bear the responsibility for that. That was the typical argument advanced by terrorists, who take hostages and threaten to kill them, placing the responsibility on those who refuse to pay the ransom. Pogarcic was busy attempting to enroll the various UN units to participate in the implementation of that vision, but Benabou was equally adamant in showing that such a measure would only cause more massacres between both parties. He firmly believed that, on the contrary, the rivals in that cruel war ought to search for common interests to draw them together, rather than for more hatred, which was bound to augment the misery and the mutual slaughters.

**The Denouement of the Love Story in Filigree**

Reading the report written by Albert Benabou, who required an urgent supply of the anesthesia material for the war hospital of East Mostar, and following the saga of its delivery, love and passion surged between David Belmonte in the war zone and Andrea Valenci at the UN headquarters in New York. The first meeting of David Belmonte, the Dutch officer from DUTCHCOM (Dutch center for communications servicing UNPROFOR) and Andrea Valenci, in charge of the information office at the headquarters of the United Nations in New York, grew out of that official exchange of messages via the virtual, cold, and impersonal computers they worked with and matured into a shaking earthquake in which David Belmonte and Andrea Valenci used the wonderful power of writing, even when they were sometimes limited to laconic messages and were constrained to develop their love story by correspondence until it became embedded in the history of the war. David finally decided to travel to New York and meet Andrea for the first time. They will bring full circle their respective stories as descendants of Sephardic Jews, who escaped the horrors of the Spanish Inquisition, fled to Amsterdam, from where her family wandered to New Amsterdam in the New World. As we will see later, they would meet once more and for the last time in Zagreb and then conclude, like the amorous partners in Clint Eastwood's *Madison Bridge*, to return to their spouses and families from whom they had been tempted by the circumstances to stray temporarily.

That was not the first or only love affair occasioned by the Bosnian War, neither among the local people who strove to survive nor among UN officials and employees who were there to facilitate peace between them. As part of our account of the war, another love story developed at the center of the war zone. Alexandra (Sasha) Milankovic,[241] the faithful interpreter of Albert Benabou, who followed him like his shadow, for she had become his voice among the Serbs, the Croats, and the Muslims he worked with during his term of office, learned and knew more about him than anyone else. Sasha was usually in a serious and often gloomy mood. Nonetheless she brought her vocation of building bridges between Albert Benabou and his interlocutors to the degree of art. She was constantly under the oppressive mood occasioned by the brutal destruction of her country and the massacres, which hardly left alive any hope for a better future. No wonder that anyone could hardly discern a hint of a smile at the corners of her lips. Between two bombings, she asked Albert for an urgent private

---

[241] For maintaining privacy, names and profiles have been altered.

meeting and shyly confided that she was pregnant. Dazzled, he defensively replied, "I do not remember having done it with you." And since she permanently was at his side, and he was not aware of any other relationship she had entertained, he could not understand how it could be.

Sasha remained calm and responded with a fixed smile, "No, I cannot say who the father is, but I have to be evacuated from here, to give birth in a normal place." Arrangements were made immediately by Albert, with the Israeli Minister Yossi Sarid, and Sasha was transported to Israel to give birth to healthy twins in Haifa. This love affair, which had started in the greatest secrecy, was later revealed as having been woven between Sasha and Commander Peter Loghan, the British forces military attaché to Benabou's office. The surprise of it all did not diminish the joy of the new family which was founded as a result.[242]

Back to Andrea and David. As soon as the idea of their encounter in New York was born in Andrea's mind, excitement, confusion, and hardly contained sentiments started to come into play. David wrote to her: Reserve the room as soon as you read this message, in the Plaza in New York. She promptly responded: "How can you come up with such an idea? You realize that you are asking me to appear naked in a cruel manner? How can you wonder, when I am so deeply installed in you forever? I am in you, are you aware of it, do you feel it? I will meet you in the dark.[243] My body is waiting for you, and it is open to your impatience. And, do you want me to add words on the strength you bring into me?"

He retorted: "Close all curtains to make it dark, and then we will express ourselves freely."

---

[242] Sasha, the courageous woman, and her beautiful twin children were transferred to a third country and succeeded to unify with the members of her family.
[243] Not daring to see each other before consuming their love, she was inspired by René Magritte's painting "Les Amants" kissing with their head covered (see picture).

She replied, "I give you all my treasure, gold, and raindrops, emeralds, and the flight of a dove, my open hands, and silver bracelets, go and stay there under my window singing your song of love that delights my soul and my body.[244]"

Referring to her marriage in which she felt she was entrapped, she wrote, as a metaphor to what was happening in the Bosnian War:

> A marriage is not necessarily an equation of love. Here it is, just assembled in a few words, an enlightened truth that nobody wants to admit. Deny it and you sink in quick and opaque sand, admit it and you walk in confidence over sands which would become emotional. But do you think I could tell him the way I write what I feel today? Call me as soon as you can from that hell where you are. Sharing a bed is sharing two souls. How you understood the dirty beast that I am. When you kiss me and my breathing quickens, it is because my soul wants to rush into yours, and absorb you when you are inside me, it is finally the magic of one united soul. There is no history of pleasure, orgasm, or joy and tutti quanti; there is a merger, the absolute, the starry sky. Everything is organized like a magical puzzle. Now I understand why making love with Daniel brought me pleasure and a technical deep malaise at the same time, even before I knew you. My body was happy and my soul suffered being offered as in a rape, I was consumed by incest. With him, there is room for great things, but not in this area. The only thing I want now is that he manages to realize that it was the same for him towards me. Hopefully, he has ever loved me as I love you. My love, the princess and the prince are returning from school and they will be home for the winter break. Maybe we

---

[244] Recorded on Benabou's personal journal of the War. All the following private correspondence, names and profiles have been altered in order to protect the personal privacy of the people involved in the love part of the book.

will be able to talk on the phone during the weekend. And then we will be forced to complete silence till I give you a sign. In the meantime and until Monday, you can communicate from your center anything you desire. Until we find something better, since there is no silence when we write. My love, my man, my light, my sweetest kisses and most burning caresses for you! I love you.
Andrea[245]

David responded with Pablo Neruda's poem, *La Nuestra*:[246]

**A Song in Despair**

The memory of you emerges from the night around me.
The river mingles its stubborn lament with the sea.
Deserted like the wharves at dawn.
It is the hour of departure, oh deserted one!
Cold flower heads are raining over my heart.
Oh pit of debris, fierce cave of the shipwrecked.
In you the wars and the flights accumulated.
From you the wings of the song birds rose.
You swallowed everything, like distance.
Like the sea, like time. In you everything sank!
It was the happy hour of assault and the kiss.
The hour of the spell that blazed like a lighthouse.
Pilot's dread, fury of blind driver,
Turbulent drunkenness of love, in you everything sank!
In the childhood of mist my soul, winged and wounded.
Lost discoverer, in you everything sank!

---

[245] Recorded on Benabou's personal journal of the War. All the following private correspondence, names and profiles have been altered in order to protect the personal privacy of the people involved in the love part of the book.
[246] Pablo Neruda (1904-1973) born in Santiago, Chile. In 1971, Neruda received the Nobel Prize for Literature He was best known for his erotic book, *Twenty Love Poems and a Song of Despair*. The poem was translated as the *Song in Despair* into English by William Merwin.

You girdled sorrow, you clung to desire,
Sadness stunned you, in you everything sank!
I made the wall of shadow drawback,
beyond desire and act, I walked on.
Oh flesh, my own flesh, woman whom I loved and lost,
I summon you in the moist hour, I raise my song to you.
It is the hour of departure. Oh abandoned one!

David

Deeply touched, effervescent Andrea could not help reacting:

Here is what my friend from Brooklyn, Rebecca, wrote to me this morning, "I love you so much, you're not my challenge, not my illusion, you are my soul. My Teshuva,[247] I love you and it is enough. Loving you is my life." God built men and women to love. Some of them, who potentially love tenfold, are those who, I am sure, are the closer to God. I have for you my soul, my belly, and my heart, you're glued to me, and all our childish games tearing one from the other will not help. Repeating to you that you are one of the most beautiful machines the Great Builder ever realized, his most beautiful Lego . . . You enclose within you the rainbow and you shine of the morning dew and the tornadoes—am I the only one in this world blessed with the privilege of watching and admiring you?

Andrea[248]

Against all odds and promises, to put an end to that impossible love, they met again in New York, because she was:

Thinking constantly about you; a special dream that night, I see myself again swallowed by your eyes. I no-

---

[247] *Baal Teshuva* refers to a Jew who turns to embrace Orthodox Judaism. i.e., one who has repented or "returned" to God.

[248] Recorded on Benabou's personal journal of the War. All the following private correspondence, names and profiles have been altered in order to protect the personal privacy of the people involved in the love part of the book.

*Savagery in the Heart of Europe*

ticed that when I make love with Daniel, I feel terrible, betraying, deceiving you. The situation is reversed, and now everything which is not you, is a deception. Only family, friendly partnership is possible with him, love becomes a concept almost obscene, incest with him. While with you, it is the love that dwells in me and nothing else, well, that's all I needed to tell you. I love you. Do not call me this week; I will probably not be on my own.[249]

His retort was prompt and smashing:

Doña Andrea, *tu alma*!
  I yearn again for your kisses, do you?
  Happy with you in this escape in New York
  As for me, if you let me do it, I will kidnap you; I will steal you, laughing and walking for hours in nature with you. I will hide you in the northern lands, making love with you in the snow and warming up by the fire and conceive a baby in whose eyes we will read the wonders of life.[250]

It was Andrea who arrived for a visit to Zagreb, and when back at home, their love knew no respite. She wrote to him:

It's funny, or sad, I do not know. But a minute after hanging up with you, Daniel called me to tell me that the time had come to separate us. He knows everything about us. Voilà. It had to happen. I wanted it, and I was scared of it, I felt a great sorrow for him, in the midst of this lie and betrayal. I believed everything I told you, and when I tried to cut the link, you have ceased to do everything to keep it alive. Unlike you, it becomes im-

---

[249] ibid.
[250] Recorded on Benabou's personal journal of the War. All the following private correspondence, names and profiles have been altered in order to protect the personal privacy of the people involved in the love part of the book.

359

possible for me to manage two stories at the same time, I would stay probably because you will go your way, but that's how the light was too strong, and as I feared (and wrote) at the beginning, I got burned . . .

You know that I can be completely addicted, and at the same time flee to my independence, and leave the people I love lost and devastated. I want to protect you from ourselves. Never before did I drop so totally the barriers surrounding my life. Shhh! Shut up, I must do my work, I love you. The United Nations is waiting for me.

Our dialogue is like a ballet of love, so beautiful that I fear the worst. I like to get into your head that I would like to be with you all the time and with limitless boundaries. You've already owned me by your voice and your words. Your soul is so big and strong and I am writing to you wonders that you have the supreme power to say them, see them, because your heart and soul are bigger and can express the verb. I like when you call me "mi doña." Observe the common greatness of life, the majestic, the simplicity of nature. Observe and you will see the power that holds mountains and valleys, oceans and rivers, plants and animals, stars and galaxies, you and me. Are you confident in our relationship? Remember there is also chaos of the universe.

I love you, my love. My prince of the invisible, impossible love, those big words are for you, but you arrived late, and I do not know how to stop it. Here it is, you simply repeat, every morning, those words and you have learned the basics that will allow you to manage going on a trip to the planet love. Being well with you; doing everything with you; being gentle with you; desiring you; laughing with you; staying profound with you; being complete with you; being intelligent with you; being light with you; in tears with you; heavy with you; comfortable with you; foolish with you; loving you. I miss you tonight, and more forever more. I no longer want only to be with you. I want you to make love to me. I want to work with you day and night. I want to eat pizza with you. I feel that a chip was implanted in my brain that controls my will. I am ordered to call you constantly, write to you, see you, to be kissed by you, to be glorified by you, to be touched, and understood by you.[251]

He wrote to her:

Our electromagnetic reactions ran beyond spatial control bands, they affect and vibrate in unknown areas and cause spasms and violent outbreaks of masses of two magmas (namely beings) in a total infinite—an interesting mathematical equation, worth developing . . . and realizing. You're the one I love. I have chosen you out of the billions of human beings who inhabit the only planet I know. You're my connection, my source of energy, my original rock . . .[252]

## The Bridge of Hope

In early November 1993, Albert Benabou warned Alija Alikadic (Tzakan, member of the Muslim War Presidency) that the Croatian Army was preparing to destroy the old bridge of Mostar, thus dealing a fatal blow to all hopes of intercultural and interethnic reconciliation in the future. Benabou had earned the nickname of "The Star of Mostar" and the esteem of his colleagues at the United Nations. Tzakan, the man with the well-groomed mustache, a Bosnian Muslim with a world culture and admirer of Israel, used to correct the nickname into Benabou—the Brother from the East. On November 9, Benabou noted in a report to the UN

---
[251] ibid.
[252] ibid.

headquarters in Zagreb: "Today I saw the bridge of Mostar die, we are returning to square one in the negotiations between the parties.[253]" Indeed, in a precise gunfire, shells reached in full force the arch of the bridge, penetrating the construction before exploding and blowing into the air all that fine structure that had been "protected" by its designation by UNESCO as part of the "heritage of humanity." The Mostar bridge had been built back in the sixteenth century, even preceding the more famous *A Bridge on the Drina River*, celebrated in and by Ivo Andric's renowned novel bearing that title. The Mostar Bridge was ruined and came to the end of its life symbolically at the same time that the ancient Jewish synagogue of Sarajevo, also an old relic of Jewish culture in the Balkans, was destroyed that very morning. But the Mostar Bridge was reconstructed, stone upon stone, and reopened in July 2008 by Prince Charles of Wales.

## Yom Kippur in Sarajevo

The Jewish community of Sarajevo had arrived to Sarajevo at the end of the 15th century and the beginning of the 16th. After several centuries of prosperity under the Muslim rule, the Jews marched to this land from their Spanish exile, where the Catholic Inquisition had forced them to convert and expelled those who remained loyal to their faith. The refugees had been hosted by the local Turkish Pasha and took root in Bosnia, forming the largest and most influential Sephardic community of the Balkans. *Yom Kippur*, the Day of Atonement of 1993, which marked the height of Jewish High Holidays in the Fall season, in war-torn Sarajevo, will remain imprinted in the memory of Albert Benabou...

---

[253] Albert Benabou noted in his personal memoirs of the war in Bosnia upon receiving letters from Alija Alikadic, Member of the War Presidency in East Mostar addressed to Thornberry and Benabou (DOC. 111, dated 10 November 1993).

*Savagery in the Heart of Europe*

In this first week of September 1993, the City of Sarajevo was already covered with a layer of snow. In the midst of war and massacre of population, nature decided to wear a white mantle of purity. Any part of skin exposed to the air was freezing in this early winter. A sign for the days we lived, thought Benabou. He was at the UN base, located at the entrance of the city, close by the airport, just arriving for a meeting with British military colleagues. They expected a first source report on the situation in the city of Mostar, which was already under siege for more than four months. The debriefing took a few hours, getting to the "finest precise tuning" as usual with the Int Corps (the Intelligence Corps of the British Army, responsible for gathering, analyzing and disseminating military intelligence). An interminable shelling served as background music all along the discussion, in the area surrounding the base. At last, the bombardment stopped and the encounter was over. Benabou moved on to completing his weekly SITREP (situation report) to the Head Quarters in Kiseljak. Andreev eagerly awaited the updating report. This report was meticulously prepared and dispatched through the SATMAR wherever he was roaming in the terrain of Bosnia.

Benabou was focusing in the writing of his document. He raised his head when suddenly a shadow darkened the room. A French officer as large as a wall wardrobe emerged in front of him and required him to come immediately to the gate of the base where two people wanted to see him urgently. "How do you know, they asked for me?" inquired Benabou. "They look for an Israeli and as we know, there is only one in mission for UNPROFOR", responded the Officer. "It is very cold outside. We are eight below zero. So I think we should hurry identifying them and find out what did they want. Anyway, we will not let them in before you do recognize them" clarified bluntly the Officer. Walking on the snow behind the military, Benabou found himself at the gate of the base facing people he had never met. They responded to his hello with a Shalom tinted with a local accent. Benabou introduced himself as Albert Benabou, Civil Affairs Coordinator for UNPROFOR stationed in Mostar. He did not realize that he was embarking himself in an unforgettable saga. The three reacted as in a trained chorus: "We are the leaders of the Jewish community, all the Jewish community. I am Ivica Cerecnjac, President of the community and here are my deputies, Jakov Finci and David Kimche. As you can see, Ashkenazi and Sephardim are represented." "Well gentlemen" said Benabou "With this we are perfectly served and what can I do for you?" They signaled that it was time letting them enter the building. In fact, everyone started feeling the harsh winter wind of Sarajevo blowing in the open space close to the gate. The French soldiers in guard waited patiently for Benabou's clearance. Understanding that they could not stand planted outside in the cold, he gave the OK with a smile at the corner of his lips. The gate wide opened. In order to warm up; they climbed to full speed the staircase leading to the large reception room of the base.

Well curled in a sofa situated close to a burning chimney, Ivica Cerecnjac immediately pushed the conversation to the core of the issue: "we need you; the Jewish community needs your help. We are close to the celebration of Yom Kippur (the Day of Atonement) and we need a rabbi, a rabbi who can conduct the prayers." Benabou reacted immediately and promised to invest all his efforts to find a Rabbi, from wherever it will be… Ivica interrupted the response and made clear that it was himself they were designating as the Rabbi and that they expected from him full assistance. Confused and stunned by the declaration, Benabou mumbled that he is not and has never officiated as Rabbi or even conducted a religious service. Moreover, being a Moroccan Jew, it was the community prayer mode he was acquainted with. The three eminent Jews from Sarajevo kept on watching him silently affirming in a persistent look and indicating that he was the only solution and their salvation for this 1993 Yom Kippur in Sarajevo trapped in an infernal War. Their unique alternative was the Israeli who just arrived to Bosnia. Finci observed that there was nobody who could read Hebrew, and the Jewish community counted less than 300 families, gathered mostly in Sarajevo. Others were scattered in Mostar or elsewhere in Bosnia-Herzegovina. The leaders of the Jewish Community of Sarajevo continued, waiting impatiently for instructions from Benabou. They did not leave room for questioning or arguing. It was either Benabou or no one. He finally grasped that there was no choice and that he had to start getting organized the best he could for the most important day in the Jewish calendar.

Benabou commenced verifying his check list: "do you have Yom Kippur prayer books?" The answer was no. "Do you have Talits (prayer shawls)?" The answer was again no. "Do you have a Sefer Torah (torah scrolls)?" No, said Ivica, since the beginning of the War, they are preserved in the museum and you will have to negotiate with the Prime Minister, Silajdzic in order to use them for Yom Kippur. In fact, when the conflagration started, all the Bosnian heritage was hidden underground. This included the Sefer Torah dating from over a century. Benabou finally asked if they had at least a synagogue. Yes they answered. You will see, one of the most beautiful in Europe. The synagogue of Sarajevo over 400 years is a UNESCO world heritage.

From Sarajevo, Benabou called Nessim Benshetrit, the Deputy Director General for Administration at the Israeli Ministry of Foreign Affairs. The reaction to his address to receive the essential articles for the Yom Kippur services was abrupt: "Albert, you have perhaps lost your mind in the middle of a War in Europe. We certainly have nothing to do there and I do not see how I can help you from Jerusalem." The communication ended in a mood of non venue. Benabou felt uncomfortable, questioning himself: "Why, did I even call? It was senseless and useless." Later in the evening, he was trying to figure out an alternative, a concrete solution, when the communication center informed him: "a call for you from Jerusalem." Wondering who it could be, since he was always the one initiating the complicated satellite connection home, his first thought was to his family. Surprised, he discovered Nessim Benshetrit on the line with a reconciling and forthcoming request: "Check out through which European capital, we can dispatch you a palette with the necessary material." The solitary Israeli serving in a remote UN mission launched his verification which turned out to be a magic waltzing through the Jewish History with the nations of the Continent.

Colonel Angel Morales answered with conviction to Benabou: "Spain had always sheltered the Jewish People and we will be pleased to receive from Jerusalem to Madrid the prayer material and transfer it to Split in a Spanish Aircraft." However, this zone of operation is under the British Forces and you will have to discuss with them for the continuing transport. "No problem" responded Brigadier Veer De Hayes, "Great Britain had always protected the Jewish People and helped them to obtain independence—one of our Royal Navy Choppers from her Majesty Ship the Invincible (a light aircraft carrier) will transport the palette from Split to Sarajevo. From here, dear Albert, you have to consult the French Forces controlling this Sector." Here come the declaration of the eternal "Grand Amour of France"—Brigadier Andre Soubirou, announced that not only the French will carry the material from Sarajevo Airport to the Synagogue, an Egyptian Unit commanded by Captain Walid Omar will secure the Yom Kippur Services in the Synagogue. Benabou giving the details to the young Egyptian Captain, explained: "Thanks God the Jewish People benefited here from a discount and unlike Ramadan 30 days, the fast and the service of Yom Kippur are only for one day."

On that Yom Kippur day of 1993, the representatives of the nations of the world assembled under the UN flag, gathered under the roof of the Synagogue, assisted the Jewish people to hold its prayers. In this last magnificent vestige of the local Jewish community who was in the process of extinction since its slaughter in WW II by the Ustasha regime, were packed hundreds of worshipers, among them members of the Bosnian Jewish community, Muslims, Croatian Catholics and Serbian Orthodox, hoping for the end of this war and the salvation of Sarajevo. All of them apparently believed that their city in distress, that was taken hostage and dilapidated by the war, would somehow be rescued. In that very space, Yom Kippur of 400 years before, had been celebrated by marking the arrival of Jews from the exile in Spain to the shelter offered by the Ottomans, and now it was the Catholic Spanish forces who assured the connection with Jerusalem for that very same ceremony. When the time of Kadish was reached, remembering the passed away members of the community, a women stood up in the hall and claimed, addressing Albert Benabou: "I am Sonia Elazar, cousin of Dado, General David Elazar Chief of Staff of the Israel Defence Forces during the Yom Kippur war, born in Sarajevo, he stood where you are for his Bar Mitzvah, can you please recall his name among the dead of our community." So did Benabou stood in honor for his commander during that War. Concerned about the preparation for precisely blowing the Shoffar, announcing the end of the day, David Kimche assured Benabou specifying that he had recorded it on cassette in any case...Nonetheless, Kimche blew perfectly in a Shoffar sent in the palette from Madrid by Rabbi Moshe Ben Dahan. At the conclusion of this moving Yom Kippur services, all the congregation, Jews and non Jews, joined in the singing of "Adios Querrida"—the melody song by the Jews exiled from Spain.

The Synagogue of Sarajevo where took place the Yom Kippur Services conducted by Albert Benabou during the time war in 1993. The Members Nations of UNPROFOR in Bosnia joined efforts and assisted the Jewish community in this realization.

# Chapter Seven

## US Mediation and the Dayton Debacle

When peace treaties are signed, one expects the signatories to express their joy with smiles and a sign of content on their faces, for the meeting of minds their negotiations had produced, which had generated mutual concessions to reach that happy exit from bloodshed, doom, and destruction that any war occasions. But the presidents of Bosnia and Herzegovina, Serbia and Croatia, Alija Izetbegovic, Slobodan Milosevic, and Franjo Tudjman, respectively, who attended and applied their signature to the "General Framework Agreement of Peace in Bosnia-Herzegovina," also known as the "Dayton Accord" or the "Dayton Agreement," or the "Paris Agreement," or the "Dayton-Paris Agreement," on 14 December, 1995 in Paris, did not smile or show any sign of contentment. Because there was no meeting of minds, and their signature was no more than an expression of their forced acceptance of the exit map that was imposed by the United States and its NATO partners, when they could no longer afford to sit idly by while savagery was unfolding under their eyes, and the United Nations was at the height of its impotence to resolve the conflict. The agreement was negotiated in the American Wright-Patterson Air Force Base near Dayton, Ohio and concluded there in November 1995, after three and a half years of war, and signed in Paris, on 14 December, 1995 in the presence of the United States and major European powers.

### Summary of the Dayton Peace Agreement

The Dayton proximity talks culminated in the initialing on November 21, 1995, of a "General Framework Agreement for Peace in Bosnia and Herzegovina." The agreement was initialed by the Republic of Bosnia and Herzegovina, the Republic of Croatia, and the Federal Republic of Yugoslavia. It was witnessed by representatives of the contact group nations—namely the United States, Britain, France, Germany, and Russia—and the European Union Special Negotiator. According to the terms of the agreement, a sovereign state known as the Republic of Bosnia and Herzegovina was "agreed" upon, which would consist of two entities: the Bosnian Serb Republic of Srpska and the Federation of Bosnia. The main terms of the framework were:

Bosnia and Herzegovina, Croatia, and the Federal Republic of Yugoslavia (FRY) agreed to fully respect the sovereign equality of one another and to settle disputes by peaceful means;

The FRY and Bosnia and Herzegovina recognized each other and agreed to discuss further aspects of their mutual recognition;

The parties agreed to fully respect and promote fulfillment of the commitments made in the various annexes, and they obligated themselves to respect human rights and the rights of refugees and displaced persons; and

The parties agreed to cooperate fully with all entities, including those authorized by the United Nations Security Council, in implementing the peace settlement and investigating and prosecuting war crimes and other violations of international humanitarian law.

The details of the accords were summarized in a series of annexes, which together constituted the backbone and the essence of what had been painfully negotiated and "agreed" upon, though no party was totally satisfied with the results:

1. Military Aspects
    The ceasefire that began with the agreement of 5 October, 1995 was intended to continue;

Foreign combatant forces, mainly the Muslim Mujahedeen currently in Bosnia, were to be withdrawn within thirty days;

The parties must complete withdrawal of forces behind a zone of separation of approximately four kilometers within an agreed period. Special provisions would be related to the surrounded enclaves of Sarajevo and Gorazde;

As a confidence-building measure, the parties agreed to withdraw heavy weapons and forces to cantonment/barracks areas within an agreed period, and to demobilize forces which could not be accommodated in those areas;

The agreement invited into Bosnia and Herzegovina a multinational military implementation force, the IFOR, under the command of NATO, with a grant of authority from the United Nations;

The IFOR was to have the right to monitor and help ensure compliance with the agreement on military aspects and fulfill certain supporting tasks. The IFOR was to have the right to carry out its mission vigorously, including with the use of force as necessary. It claimed unimpeded freedom of movement, control over airspace, and status of forces protection;

A joint military commission was established, to be chaired by the IFOR commander. No persons under indictment by the international war crimes tribunal could participate;

Information on mines, military personnel, weaponry, and other items had to be provided to the joint military commission within agreed periods; and

All combatants and civilians must be released and transferred without delay in accordance with a plan to be developed by the International Committee of the Red Cross.

2. Regional Stabilization

Representatives of the Republic of Bosnia and Herzegovina, the Federation of Bosnia, and the Bosnian Serb Republic must begin negotiations within seven days, under the Organization for Security and Cooperation in Europe (OSCE) auspices, with the objective of agreeing on confidence-building measures within forty-five days. These could include, for example, restrictions on military deployments and exercises, notification of military activities, and exchange of data;

The Republic of Bosnia and Herzegovina, the Federation of Bosnia, and the Bosnian Serb Republic, as well as Croatia and the Federal Republic of Yugoslavia, agreed not to import arms for ninety days and not to import any heavy weapons, heavy weapons ammunition, mines, military aircraft, and helicopters for one hundred and eighty days or until an arms control agreement took effect;

All five parties must begin negotiations within thirty days, under OSCE auspices, to agree on numerical limits on holdings of tanks, artillery, armored combat vehicles, combat aircraft, and attack helicopters;

If the parties failed to establish limits on these categories within one hundred and eighty days, the agreement provided for specified limits to come into force for the parties; and

The OSCE was to organize and conduct negotiations to establish a regional balance in and around former Yugoslavia.

3. Inter-Entity Boundary

An inter-entity boundary line between the Federation of Bosnia and the Bosnian Serb Republic was agreed to;

Sarajevo would be reunified within the Federation of Bosnia and would be open to all people of the country;

Gorazde would remain secure and accessible, linked to the Federation of Bosnia by a land corridor; and

The status of Brcko would be determined by arbitration within one year.

4. Elections

Free and fair, internationally supervised elections would be conducted within six to nine months for the presidency and house of representatives of Bosnia and Herzegovina, for the house of representatives of the Federation of Bosnia, and the national assembly and presidency of the Bosnian Serb Republic, and, if feasible, for local offices;

Refugees and persons displaced by the conflict would have the right to vote (including by absentee ballot) in their original place of residence if they chose to do so;

The parties must create conditions in which free and fair elections could be held by protecting the right to vote in secret and ensuring freedom of expression and the press;

The OSCE was requested to supervise the preparation and conduct of these elections; and

All citizens of Bosnia and Herzegovina aged eighteen or older listed on the 1991 Bosnian census were eligible to vote.

5. Constitution

A new constitution for the Republic of Bosnia and Herzegovina, which would be known as "Bosnia and Herzegovina," was to be adopted upon signature at Paris;

Bosnia and Herzegovina would continue as a sovereign state within its present internationally recognized borders. It would consist of two entities: the Federation of Bosnia and the Bosnian Serb Republic;

The constitution provided for the protection of human rights and the free movement of people, goods, capital, and services throughout Bosnia and Herzegovina;

The central government would have a presidency, a two-chamber legislature, and a constitutional court. Direct elections would be held for the presidency and one of the legislative chambers;

There would be a central bank and monetary system, and the central government would also have responsibilities for foreign policy, law enforcement, air traffic control, communications, and other areas to be agreed;

Military coordination would take place through a committee including members of the presidency;

No person who was serving a sentence imposed by the International Tribunal, and no person who was under indictment by the tribunal and who had failed to comply with an order to appear before the tribunal, might stand as a candidate or hold any appointive, elective, or other public office in the territory of Bosnia and Herzegovina.

6. Arbitration

The Federation of Bosnia and the Bosnian Serb Republic agreed to enter into reciprocal commitments to engage in binding arbitration to resolve disputes between them, and they agreed to design and implement a system of arbitration.

7. Human Rights

The agreement guaranteed internationally recognized human rights and fundamental freedoms for all persons within Bosnia and Herzegovina;

A Commission on Human Rights, composed of a human rights ombudsman and a human rights chamber (court), was established;

The ombudsman was authorized to investigate human rights violations, issue findings, and bring and participate in proceedings before the human rights chamber;

The human rights chamber was authorized to hear and decide human rights claims and to issue binding decisions; and

The parties agreed to grant UN human rights agencies, the OSCE, the International Tribunal, and other organizations full access to monitor the human rights situation.

8. Refugees and Displaced Persons

The agreement granted refugees and displaced persons the right to return home safely and either regain lost property or obtain just compensation;

A Commission for Displaced Persons and Refugees would decide on the return of real property or compensation, with the authority to issue final decisions;

All persons were granted the right to move freely throughout the country, without harassment or discrimination; and

The parties committed to cooperate with the ICRC in finding all missing persons.

9. Commission to Preserve National Monuments

A Commission to Preserve National Monuments was established;

The commission was authorized to receive and act upon petitions to designate as national monuments movable or immovable property of great importance to a group of people with a common cultural, historic, religious, or ethnic heritage; and

When property was designated as a national monument, the entities would make every effort to take appropriate legal, technical, financial, and other measures to protect and conserve the national monument and refrain from taking deliberate actions which might damage it.

10. Bosnia and Herzegovina Public Corporations

A Bosnia and Herzegovina Transportation Corporation was established to organize and operate transportation facilities, such as roads, railways, and ports; and

A Commission on Public Corporations was created to examine establishing other Bosnia and Herzegovina public corporations to operate joint public facilities such as utilities and postal service facilities.

11. Civilian Implementation

The parties requested that a high representative be designated, consistent with relevant UN Security Council resolutions, to coordinate and facilitate civilian aspects of the peace settlement, such as humanitarian aid, economic reconstruction, protection of human rights, and the holding of free elections;

The high representative would chair a joint civilian commission comprised of senior political representatives of the parties, the IFOR commander, and representatives of civilian organizations; and

The high representative had no authority over the IFOR.

12. International Police Task Force

The United Nations was requested to establish a UN international police task force (IPTF) to carry out various tasks, including training and advising local law enforcement personnel, as well as monitoring and inspecting law enforcement activities and facilities;

The IPTF would be headed by a commissioner appointed by the UN secretary general; and

IPTF personnel must report any credible information on human rights violations to the Human Rights Commission, the International Tribunal, or other appropriate organizations.

13. Agreement on Initialing the General Framework Agreement

In this agreement, which was signed at Dayton, Bosnia and Herzegovina, Croatia, and the Federal Republic of Yugoslavia agreed that the negotiations had been completed. They and the entities they represented committed themselves to sign the General Framework Agreement and its annexes in Paris.

They also agreed that the initialing of the General Framework Agreement and its annexes in Dayton expressed their consent to be bound by these agreements.

These were the terms of the imposed agreement, most of which were so far implemented, others partly, and still others, for example the return of refugees to their homes and the mutual respect of holy sites, were grossly violated in Kosovo, where most of the Serbian population had irretrievably been uprooted, and many of the ancient Orthodox monasteries and churches had been destroyed or burned. The very process of the negotiations, which were most of the time accompanied by the echoes of the war and of the gains or losses of the parties on the battlefield, was directly influenced both by the military advances in the frontlines and by the pressures the great powers exerted on behalf of their clients who were battling on the grounds. So, though the basic concepts of the Dayton Agreement began to appear in international talks since 1992, the negotiations were initiated following the unsuccessful previous peace efforts and arrangements, or the field operations undertaken by the parties, like the August 1995 Croatian military Operation Storm and its aftermath, or the Bosnian government military offensive against the Republika Srpska, in concert with NATO in Operation Deliberate Force. During September and October 1995, many of the world powers (especially the United States and Russia) gathered in the contact group and applied intense pressure to the leaders of the three sides to attend the negotiations in Dayton, Ohio. The conference took place from November 1 to November 21, 1995. The main participants from the region were Serbian President Slobodan Milosevic (representing the Bosnian Serb interests due to the absence of Karadzic), Croatian President Franjo

Tudjman, and Bosnian President Alija Izetbegovic with Bosnian Foreign Minister Muhamed Sacirbey.

The peace conference was led by US Secretary of State Warren Christopher and negotiator Richard Holbrooke, with two cochairmen in the form of EU Special Representative Carl Bildt and Russia's First Deputy Foreign Minister Igor Ivanov. A key participant in the US delegation was General Wesley Clark (later to become NATO's Supreme Allied Commander Europe [SACEUR] in 1997). The UK military representative was Col. Arundel David Leakey (later to become commander of EUFOR in 2005). Paul Williams, through the Public International Law and Policy Group (PILPG), served as legal counsel to the Bosnian government delegation during the negotiations. The secure site was chosen for several reasons: to remove them from the luxury and media of Europe/Washington, DC and to securely house over eight hundred staff and attendants. Curbing the participants' ability to negotiate via the media was also an important consideration. Richard Holbrooke wanted to stop the posturing and walls that could be built up due to early leaks to the press. After having been initialed in Dayton, Ohio, on November 21, 1995, the full and formal agreement was signed in Paris on 14 December, 1995, also by French President Jacques Chirac, US President Bill Clinton, UK Prime Minister John Major, German Chancellor Helmut Kohl, and Russian Prime Minister Viktor Chernomyrdin. The state of Bosnia- Herzegovina was set as the Federation of Bosnia-Herzegovina and the Republika Srpska. Bosnia and Herzegovina is a complete state, as opposed to a confederation; no entity or entities could ever be separated from Bosnia and Herzegovina unless, of course, through due legal process. Although highly decentralized in its entities, it would still retain a central government with a rotating state presidency, a central bank, and a constitutional court.

The agreement mandated a wide range of international organizations to monitor, oversee, and implement components of the agreement. The NATO-led IFOR (Implementation Force) was responsible for implementing military aspects of the agreement and deployed on 20 December 1995, taking over the forces of the UNPROFOR. The Office of the High Representative was charged with the task of civil implementation. The Organization for Security and Cooperation in Europe was charged with organizing the first free elections in 1996. Before the Dayton Agreement, Bosnian Serbs controlled about forty-six percent of Bosnia and Herzegovina (23,687 square kilometers), Bosniaks twenty-eight percent (14,505 square kilometers) and Bosnian Croats twenty-five percent (12,937 square kilometers). Bosnian Serbs got large tracts of mountainous territories back (four percent of Bosnian Croats and some small amounts from Bosniaks), but they were pressured to surrender Sarajevo and some vital eastern Bosnian/Herzegovinian positions. All in all, by changing quality to quantity, their percentage grew to forty-nine percent (forty-eight percent if excluding the Brcko District, 24,526 square kilometers) from a little bit more than forty-six percent prior to Dayton.

Bosniaks got most of Sarajevo and some important positions in eastern Bosnia and Herzegovina, while they lost only a few locations on Mount Ozren and in western Bosnia. Their percentage grew from twenty-eight percent prior to Dayton to thirty percent, and they greatly upheld the quality of the gotten land. Large tracts of prewar Bosniak (and Bosnian Croat) inhabited lands remained under Bosnian Serb Control. Bosnian Croats gave most (four percent of BiH territories) back to the Bosnian Serbs (nine percent of today's RS), and also retreated from Una-Sana canton as well as Donji Vakuf (in the central Bosnia canton) municipality afterward. Small enlargement of Posavina canton (Odžak and parts of Domaljevac municipality) had not changed the fact that after Dayton Bosnian Croats controlled just twenty-one percent of Bosnia and Herzegovina (10,640 square kilometers) especially when compared to more than twenty-five percent prior to Dayton. It is important to note that one of the most important Bosnian Croat territories (Posavina with Bosanski Brod, Bosanski Šamac, Derventa, and Modrica) was still left out of Bosnian Croat control.

The immediate purpose of the agreement was to freeze the military confrontations and prevent them at all costs from resuming. It was therefore defined as a "construction of necessity." Despite this, the Dayton Agreement proved to be a highly flexible instrument, allowing Bosnia and Herzegovina to move from an early post-conflict phase through reconstruction and consolidation, passing from a contra societal approach to a more integrationist one. Many scholars refer to this process as "the most impressive example of conflict resolution." Wolfgang Petritsch, OHR, has argued that the Dayton framework had allowed the international community to move "from state building via institutions and capacity building to identity building," putting Bosnia "on the road to Brussels." Except that under the present doubts being raised regarding the EU idea in the first place, it is not clear yet what advantages might accrue to Bosnia if she were to join. Nevertheless, Dayton's main shortcomings may be described as:

> Enabling international actors (such as the OHR), unaccountable to BiH's citizens, to shape the agenda of post-war transition, up to enacting punishment over local political actors, leaving each ethnic group discontent with the results; the Bosnian Serbs for the somehow limited results (although strongly favored in statistical terms), such as the arbitration over the Brcko district; the Bosniaks for ignoring the human rights issues such as the

Srebrenica massacre and recognizing Serbian entities such as the Republika Srpska; the Bosnian Croats for the lack of equality, lacking a Croat entity. According to University of Leipzig professor and Bosnian Academy of Sciences and Arts member, Edin Šarčević, the current legal structure of the agreement does not abide by the basic principles of international law and the secular concept of national citizenship, making the Bosnian territorial and political situation continually unstable and fractious since its implementation in 1995.

# Chapter Eight
## Dealing with Domestic and International Islam

The Bosnian War, which began as a civil war between the ethnic and religious components of former Yugoslavia, and ended (at least for now) only through massive intervention of the United Nations, the European Union and the United States, continues to brew under and over the surface, due to the involvement of world Islam both in cultivating Bosnia as a Muslim entity in the heart of Europe and in enhancing Islamic stature in Europe in particular and the West in general. These trends did not begin with the Bosnian War per se, which was a direct product of the dismantling of Yugoslavia, but have deep roots in the long heritage that the Ottoman Empire had left behind when it was compelled to abandon Muslim positions in Europe, for the second time, at the end of the nineteenth century after a rule extending over four centuries in the Balkans. When Bosnia emerged as a separate Muslim entity, various Islamic models competed for prevalence in Bosnia, in order to shape it to their respective tastes, and that too has conditioned the fate of the country, in accordance with the powers that supported this or that model, rightly or wrongly.

The key to understanding the implanting and growth of Islam in Bosnia, which lies at the base of its Islamization in modern times, on the one hand, and its rejection by its Christian neighbors, on the other, must be sought in the heavy heritage that the Ottomans left behind, which turned Slavic Bosnians, who were originally either Croats or Serbs, into enemies of the latter and into a self-conscious separate "ethnic

*Savagery in the Heart of Europe*

group," which was recognized by Tito in the 1960s as a counterpart of the other ethnic groups who made up the Yugoslavian Federation. In the conference on the Turks and Islam at the University of Indiana, Stephen Schwartz[254] offered a brilliant analysis of that heritage. He first found it necessary to recognize the difference in the religious and cultural destinies of the people in the area who were brought under Ottoman rule, beginning in the fourteenth century CE. The main Balkan states to be absorbed early into the empire, i.e. Macedonia after 1371, followed by Bulgaria in 1422, Serbia in 1459, and Greece in 1460, as well as the vassal entities of Wallachia and Moldavia, remained Orthodox Christian in the majorities of their populations. Some members of the autochthonous populations accepted Islam, and these today-indigenous Muslims, including the Macedonian Slav Muslims and Pomaci in Bulgaria, with small numbers in Thrace and other neighboring localities, survived the fall of the empire as significant minorities. They currently number in the tens, and possibly hundreds of thousands. He stresses that Greek and Serbian converts to the faith of Muhammad are both topics of historical controversy. A Greek Muslim community originating in conversions seems to have mainly disappeared from that country, during the population exchanges with Turkey after the First World War, although a new Muslim immigrant community, mainly comprising Albanians and Arabs, has lately revived Islam in Greece. Muslim Albanians in the Greek Epirotic area, known to Albanians as Çamëria, were expelled or have been forcibly assimilated into the Greek state.

The Ottoman state, which reached Vienna at the pinnacle of its expansion, was multiethnic and multireligious, and under its

---

[254] Stephen Schwartz, "The Heritage of Ottoman Islam in the Balkans," Conference on the Turks and Islam, 12 September, 2010. See www.islamicpluralism.org/1663/the-heritage-of-ottoman. Much of the following discussion is based on this lecture.

Muslim-majority dominance Christians, Jews, and others lived side by side for many centuries. However, this coexistence was not born out of a modern concept of tolerance of the other on the basis of acceptance of differences and equality to all, but on a sense of superiority, which tolerated others in spite of their inherent inferiority. Therefore, even though Muslims, or Turks, as they became universally known in European parlance, may have temporarily constituted the minority in the population in some areas of the occupied empire, they reigned supreme by virtue of their Muslim master status, while the various Christian groups (and Jews for that matter) were relegated to the status of "protected people" (*dhimmis*). Christians and others who had integrated into the Ottoman system, by embracing Islam, speaking Ottoman Turkish and going into the government service, soon became part and parcel of the Ottoman culture even when they kept their attachment to their ethnic origin and to their mother tongue. The case in point were the Bosnians, many of whom felt privileged to go into the devşirme system of enrolling their boys to the prestigious Janissary Corps, who in the course of time were Islamized though they preserved their Slavic roots and language.

Schwartz stressed that Serbian historical legend depicts all Slavs who became Muslims as "renegade Serbs" who left their past faith either under compulsion or to avoid the Jizya poll tax on non-Muslims that was imposed by the Muslim Empire and to gain other advantages. There certainly were and are Serb Muslims, although many were driven out of the country during the wars, massacres, and expulsions of Slav and Albanian Muslims during the long southerly expansion of Serbian territory, beginning in 1804. *Muhajirs*[255]

---

[255] Muslim *Muhajirs*—(literally "migrants") have been using that same terminology to designate refugees who were either forced through "population exchanges" (like between Turkey and Greece and later between India and Pakistan) into exile, or were constrained by circumstance to move into an alien land (like Pakistanis in England).

or refugees from persecution for their Muslim faith settled in places as distinct from one another as Kosovo and Turkey. At least three and a half percent of the Serbian population of 7.5 million today is Muslim, concentrated in the southwest, with Slavs, who identify themselves as Bosniaks, living in the northern part of the former Sandjak of Pazar and Novipazar, which was divided between Serbia and Montenegro after the Balkan Wars of 1912-13. The Sandjak, as it is known to Bosniaks today, also includes a significant Albanian Muslim presence at its eastward extremity, bordering on Kosovo. Ottoman emigration to these districts was uneven after their takeover, with some receiving considerable numbers of Turkish colonists and administrators, others fewer. Remnants of Ottoman Turkish communities, sometimes speaking archaic dialects of the language, are to be found today in Kosovo, Macedonia, Bulgaria, and Thrace. In addition, Turkish language *ilahije* and spiritual songs are still sung by Sufis in the region.

The outcome for Bosnia, which was finally subdued in 1463, and Albania, overtaken in 1478, was different than the other formerly Christian lands. Bosnia-Herzegovina had long harbored Catholics in its west, as did the Albanian ethnos in its northern regions, including parts of today's Montenegro, as well as Kosovo and western Macedonia. Both Bosnia-Herzegovina and Albania in its present borders include large Orthodox Christian communities in eastern Bosnia and southern Albania. But the majority of the Bosniak people and the Albanians became Muslim. To consider the Bosnian elite who became Muslims after the victory of the Ottomans in the fifteenth century as "former Serbs" is a popular shibboleth of Serbian and other Christian historians and apologists. Bosniak Muslim intellectuals argue that their community was independent from both Catholic Croatia and Orthodox Serbia and that its mass acceptance of Islam did not represent a betrayal of either of the Bosniaks' neighbors, but, if justified by any political imperative, was a recourse taken to reinforce their separate identity. Certainly, Croats no less than Serbs have attempted to claim the Bosniaks as their "forcibly Islamized" lost sheep. In the late nineteenth century, with the rise of conservative Croatian nationalism, the right-wing political leader Ante Šarčević referred to the Bosnian Muslims as "the flower of the Croatian nation.[256]"

From the Habsburg occupation of Bosnia in 1878 until the end of the First World War, Bosnian Muslims were treated by the Austro-Hungarian authorities as a separate community from both Croats and Serbs. Under monarchist Yugoslavia, between the two world wars, Bosnian Muslims wavered between identification as Muslim Croats and as Muslim Serbs. During the Second World War, the German-installed Ustasha regime united Croatia with Bosnia-Herzegovina, in the Independent State of Croatia (NDH by its Croatian initials). With the help of the Mufti of Jerusalem, Haj Amin al-Husseini, who collaborated with the Nazis, Bosnian Muslims were recruited to fight under German and Croatian command in the Waffen SS, as were Albanians. Worse, the Ustasha regime established the infamous extermination camps of Jasenovac and Jadovno, where some Bosnian Muslims also served, and where hundreds of thousands of Serbs, Jews, and Gypsies were annihilated. Much of the hatred, suspicion, and instinct of revenge evinced by Serbs against Muslims and Croats during the Bosnian War was the fifty-year-old residue of those hostile memories. Bosnian Muslims, or Bosniaks, were not granted a distinct ethnic category by Yugoslav authorities until 1968, when the Tito regime recognized "Muslims by nationality" (not officially called "Bosniaks," although the use of the term is historically established before the twentieth century) as a

---

[256] ibid.

separate census classification. "Yugoslav Muslims" are still self-defined, separately from Bosniaks, in Montenegro and Serbia. Some Bosniak intellectuals today, as in the past, advocate the view that Bosnian Muslims and their forebears were never Slavs, either Croat or Serb, except in adopting their language, and that Bosnians, like Albanians, are descendants of the Illyrian population that inhabited the region prior to the Slavic invasions of the seventh and eighth centuries. Substantial evidence for this theory remains lacking, although Bosnians and Albanians share some cultural markers that could indicate either a common origin or extended contact.

Until the Communist era, Bosnia was rich with Sufi activities, including those of the main *tariqats* (orders) aside from the Naqshbandis and Qadiris, such as the Mevlevis, who are said to have converted a former dignitary of the autonomous Bosnian Church (Bogamil, similar to the heretic Albigensi movement of southern France)) to Islam. On the whole, according to Schwartz, Bosnian Islam has maintained an air of pronounced Sunni "rigor," although its popular culture, as revealed in song traditions, is replete with positive references to rebels. Nevertheless, resentment of the distant authority in Istanbul is found under the surface of many Bosnian Muslim cultural products. For example, two Muslim brothers from the eighteenth century, the Morići, were hanged by the authorities yet are looked upon as beloved symbols of Sarajevo and celebrated in many folk songs, as are the victims of Ottoman Turkey celebrated in Bosnian Andric's, *Bridge on the Drina River.* One of the folk songs proclaimed, "Imperial sultan, you are damned as long as your sword denies justice and the empire stands on evil; Oh, pashas and vezirs will come and go but my Bosnia will never die." These songs became patriotic anthems during the 1992-1995 war in Bosnia-Herzegovina, and the reference to the evil foundation of the Ottoman Empire invariably elicits waves of applause when this ballad is included in public performances in Bosnia.[257]

Muslim Albanians in Kosovo and western Macedonia remained loyal to Sufism, which could not be suppressed in their regions of the former Yugoslavia. By contrast, Sufism was outlawed in Bosnia-Herzegovina in the 1950s. In a certain sense, Bosnian Muslims may be said to have preferred the worldly rewards brought by the Communist system, in the form of artificial industrial development, over the spiritual bounties of the Sufis. The result of this is that Sufism has a rich tradition of local sheikhs and authors in Bosnia, but most of them are figures of the past, although some Sufis fought with distinction in the 1992-1995 war. Today, Sufism has a more abstract, intellectual, and even folkloric quality in Bosnia-Herzegovina than in Kosovo, western Macedonia, and Albania proper. In the former it is but one among many competing cultural trends, Islamic and non-Islamic, but in the latter it maintains a strong presence in public life. Under Titoite Yugoslavia, the non-Bektashi Sufis of Yugoslavia had their headquarters among the Kosovar Albanians of Prizren, while the teaching and clerical institutions of the Yugoslav Islamic community were centered in Sarajevo. Although Bosniaks and Kosovars speak different languages, the Islamic faculty of Sarajevo continues to serve as the main teaching institution for Muslim religious functionaries in the western Balkans, for Kosovar Albanians as well as Bosnians and others.

In April 1998, the State Department published its annual report on global terrorism. Among other things, it referred to the unidentified terrorists who acted against the international presence in Bosnia and especially to the Mujahedeen, who had served in the Bosnian army during the civil war but were

---

[257] ibid.

after it engaged in warrant killings. According to that report, the Bosnian government began arresting some of those loose terrorists, and by November 1997, it had incarcerated twenty of them, who were identified as Arabs or Bosnian Muslims.[258] In that same year of 1998, there were reports that Iranian intelligence agents were mounting extensive operations and had even infiltrated the American program to train the Bosnian Army. According to those reports, more than two hundred Iranian agents were identified as "having insinuated themselves into Bosnian Muslim political and social circles . . . to gather information and to thwart western interests in Bosnia." Those agents, it was believed, could be helpful in planning terrorist attacks against NATO forces or targets.[259] Taken together, these reports did identify the "unidentified terrorists" mentioned above. Moreover, these reports linked together into an Islamic international centered around Iran, where most of the major terrorist activities were carried out by Islamists then, from the Israeli Embassy in Buenos Aires (1992); the international gathering of Islamic terrorist organizations in Teheran (1997); the Hezbollah stepped-up activities against Israel in the late 1990s; the arrest in Israel of Stefan Smirak, a Muslim of |Bosnian origin, a would-be "suicide bomber" for Hezbollah (November 1997); the attacks against American interests in the Gulf, East Africa, and on American soil (throughout the 1990s),[260] to say nothing of the Muslim separatists in northwest China (the Uighurs of Xinjiang) and the Islamic resurgence in Bosnia and Kosovo.

People spoke during the Bosnian War of the clashes between Serbs and Muslims in Bosnia, and Serbs and Albanians in Kosovo, in terms of ethno national conflicts, with the more

---

[258] US Department of State, *Patterns of Global Terrorism,* April 1998.
[259] Author, "Policy Watch" no. 296 (1998):3 The Washington Institute, citing reports by *The New York Times* and *The Washington Times.*
[260] ibid.

numerous Serbs figuring as the oppressors and their rivals as the underdogs and the oppressed. Prima facie, the very usage of the terms Serbs (and Croats for that matter) against Muslims equates the latter (essentially members of a faith and civilization) to the former who clearly belong to religious-ethnic groups. This points out the fact that not only did Yugoslavian statism and universalistic communism fail to obliterate ethnic and kinship identities (real or imagined), but that communal interest overrode the state umbrella, economic interest, or even sheer common sense. But this also raises the question of whether Islam, a universal religion predominant in more than fifty countries around the world, is or can be perceived as a local nationalism that is particularistic by definition.

### Ideological Underpinnings of the Islamic Revival[261]

In 1970, well before the collapse of the Yugoslavian order imposed by Tito and the outburst of communal nationalism, which instigated the process of its disintegration, a political manifesto was written by an unknown at the time Muslim in Bosnia- Alija Izetbegovic (born in 1925), but it was not immediately released to the public. It was, however, duplicated and made available to individual Muslims who circulated it among their coreligionists, apparently to serve as a guide of a Muslim order to replace the godless communist system in Bosnia. That pamphlet is known as the *Islamska Deklaracija* (*The Islamic Declaration*). In 1983, after Tito's death but while the communist state was held together, a trial took place in Sarajevo where the author and some like-minded individuals were prosecuted for subverting the constitutional order and for acting from the standpoint of Islamic fundamentalism and Muslim nationalism. Significantly, after the

---

[261] Much of this chapter is based on R. Israeli, *The Islamic Challenge in Europe*, 'The Re-Islamization of the Balkans," 197-218.

fall of communist power, the accused were publicly rehabilitated, and the declaration was then officially published in Sarajevo (1990). Izetbegovic, at the head of his Democratic Action Party (SDA), won the majority of the Muslim votes in the first free elections in Bosnia-Herzegovina (November 1990), but his pamphlet was obscured and not heard of again. However, judging from the wide appeal of his later book, *Islam Between East and West*, which was published in English in the United States (1984), then in Turkish in Istanbul (1987), and in Serbian in Belgrade (1988), and from the developments in the Bosnian War in the mid-1990s, one might be well-advised to take a look at it.

The declaration, which in many respects sounds and looks like the platforms of Muslim fundamentalists elsewhere (e.g. the Hamas Charter),[262] assumed that its appeal would be heeded by Muslims around the world, not only by its immediate constituency, accused the West of wishing to "keep Muslim nations spiritually weak and materially and politically dependent," and called upon the believers to cast aside inertia and passivity in order to embark on the road of action.[263] And like Muslim radicals such as Sayyid Qutb of Egypt, who urged his followers to reject the world of ignorance around them and transform it on the model of the Prophet of Islam, the Declaration of Izetbegovic also called upon the millions to join the efforts of Muslim individuals who fought against the Jahiliyya (the state of ignorance and godlessness which had preceded the advent of the Prophet),[264] and dedicated the text to the memory of "our brothers who have laid their lives for Islam,"[265] namely the

---

[262] Raphael Israeli, "The Charter of Allah: the Platform of the Hamas," in The Annual of Terrorism, ed. Y. Alexander (The Netherlands: Nijhoff, 1990), 99-134.
[263] ibid., Introduction to the Pamphlet,1-2.
[264] ibid., 2.
[265] ibid.

*shuhada'* (martyrs) of all times and places who had fallen in the cause of Islam.

The manifesto, again like other Muslim radicals' writings, not only addressed itself to the restoration of Islam in private life, in the family, and society, but also expressly shunned local nationalism of any sort and substituted for it the creation of a universal Islamic polity (the traditional umma), "from Morocco to Indonesia."[266] The author awakened his people to the reality in which "a few thousand of true Islamic fighters forced England to withdraw from the Suez Canal in the early 1950s, while the nationalist armies of the Arabs were losing their battles against Israel,[267]" and where "Turkey, an Islamic country, ruled the world," and when it tried to emulate Europe, it dropped to the level of a third-world country. In other words, he claimed, it was not nationalism that makes the force of Muslim nations, but their abidance by Islam in its universal version. Therefore, it does not befit Muslims to fight or die for any other cause but Islam, and it behooves Muslims to die with the name and glory of Allah in their hearts, or totally desert the battlefield.[268] Translated into the Bosnian scene, Muslims ought not take part in, or stand for, any form of government which was not Islamic, and any cause which was not connected to Islam. To the Bosnians, whom Izetbegovic addressed, there were only two options left: either subscribe to Muslim revival and its political requirements, or be doomed to stagnation and oblivion.[269]

The manifesto then went into a long dissertation explaining the reasons and history of "backwardness [of] the Muslim nations.[270]" Basically, it refuted modernists who regarded the notion of the Islamic din as only religion in the European

---
[266] ibid., 3.
[267] ibid
[268] ibid., 4.
[269] ibid.
[270] ibid.

*Savagery in the Heart of Europe*

sense and insisted on viewing it and living by it as an entire religious, cultural, and political way of life, which unified "religion and science, ethics and politics, ideal and interest."[271] In the typically fundamentalist fashion, it attacked established conservative Islam and its "hodjas and sheikhs, who organized themselves as a caste unto itself and arrogated to itself a monopoly over the interpretation of Islam, and placed itself in the position of mediator between the Qur'an and the people."[272] It also mocked the modernists for emulating the West and worshipping its material life, ultimately producing corruption and decadence instead of spiritual uplifting. In this context, the author belittled the role of Mustafa Kemal in modern Turkey because he wrongly thought that by ordering the fez out, the heads, which wore it, would also be transformed.[273] That was the reason, in the author's mind, why modern Turkey and Japan, which began from the same starting point at the turn of the century, grew in totally different directions. Japan, which knew how to integrate its own culture with modernity, but kept its traditional writing system, became a great power, while Turkey, which abolished her Arabic script, which "ranks among the most perfect and the most widely used alphabets," to introduce the Latin script, remained a third-world country.[274]

This total rejection of the Kemalist Turkey's model of course stood in sharp contrast and contradiction to western, especially American, hopes to "sell" that very precedent of modernity, Europeanization and moderation to the emerging Muslim entities in central Asia and the Balkans. As against the perceived failure of Turkey and other Muslim countries due to "the weakening of the influence of Islam in

---

[271] ibid., 5.
[272] ibid., 6.
[273] ibid., 7-8.
[274] ibid., 9.

the practical life of the people," the author posited that "all successes, both political and moral, are the reflection of our acceptance of Islam and its application in life."[275] Therefore, while all defeats, from Uhud Battle at the time of the Prophet (AD 625) to the Sinai War between Israel and Egypt (1956), were due to "apostasy from Islam," while any "rise of the Islamic people, every period of dignity, started with the affirmation of the Qur'an." But in the real world, the Qur'an, complained the author, was being recited instead of practiced. Mosques were "monumental but empty." The form took over from substance, as the Holy Book turned "into a mere sound without intelligible sense and content."[276] This reality was caused, lamented the author, in line with other Muslim fundamentalists, by the western inspired or imposed school system in all Muslim countries.[277]

Secularism and nationalism, the products of that foreign educational trend, took over the minds and hearts of the new generation of Muslims. The masses, who did not submit to these fleeting concepts, which are foreign to Islam, chose indifference, but if they were rightly guided, they could rise to action provided they were spurred by "an idea that corresponded to their profound feelings and that could only be the Islamic idea," instilled by a new intelligentsia, which "thinks and feels Islam" and would ultimately "fly the flag of the Islamic order and together with the Muslim masses initiate action for its realization."[278] This new Islamic order should unite "religion and law, upbringing and force, ideals and interests, the spiritual community and the state, free will, and coercion," for "Islamic society without Islamic rule is incomplete and impotent; Islamic rule without Islamic

---
[275] ibid., 12.
[276] ibid., 14-15.
[277] ibid., 16-17.
[278] ibid., 19.

society is either utopia or violence."[279] This in effect means, in the vein of other Muslim fundamentalist platforms, that the Muslim state ought to enforce ("coerce") the Islamic order, short of which violence would erupt by necessity. For, according to this scheme, and contrary to the European concept of a liberal society where the individual is prized, a Muslim "does not exist as an individual entity," and he must create his Islamic milieu in order to survive, by way of changing the world around him if he does not want to be changed by others.[280]

The manifesto held that there was no point to legislate laws, as has been Western wont, because they end up corrupting society. Better to educate people and teach them to obey the decree of Allah, and that would put an end to corruption and lawlessness.[281] This is the reason for the "incompatibility of Islam with non-Islamic systems;" therefore, "there can be neither peace nor co-existence between the Islamic faith and non-Islamic social and political institutions."[282] This means in effect that Muslims should not submit to a non-Islamic rule and that they should exclusively strive to create and live under an Islamic system, due to the assumption that "Islam clearly rules out any right or possibility of action of any foreign ideology [supposedly including democracy, pluralism, tolerance, freedom, equality, etc.] on its turf." As a result, "there is no room for the lay principle, and the state should be an expression of the moral concepts of [the Islamic] religion and supportive of them."[283] In the light (or rather the obscurity) of these principles, which shun mysticism and stagnation and assume the right of innovation to make things adaptable to

---

[279] ibid., 20.
[280] ibid.
[281] ibid., 21-22.
[282] ibid., 23.
[283] ibid.

every time and place, the pamphlet defined and traced a long series of rules and regulations which ought to guide the individual Muslim[284] in practically all spheres of his societal life. The core of this orientation is that "Islamic society may not be based upon social or economic interest only, or on any other external, technical factor of association. As a community of believers, it is based on a religious and emotional aspect of affiliation. This element is most clearly visible and enshrined in the *jemaat* as the basic unit in Islamic society."[285] This would mean in the Bosnian context that only a religiously based society, on the model of religious associations (jemaat), is viable, and no provision ought to be made for non-Muslims or for a multireligious or multicultural society in its midst. (See the question of minorities below.)

The question of life in such a Muslim community was left unclear. On the one hand, the manifesto assures the "equality of all men"[286] and discards divisions and groupings according to race or class. But, if man's worth is determined according to one's "integrity, and spiritual and ethical values,"[287] and these noble qualities are grounded in Islamic creed and value system, then only if one is a good Muslim can he be considered worthy. This is all the more so when the concept of the unmet, the universal congregation of all Muslims, is taken as the "supra-nationality of the Muslim community," and Islam and Pan-Islamism define its boundaries, "Islam determines its internal and Pan-Islamism its external relations," because "Islam is its ideology and Pan-Islamism its politics."[288] By Islam, the author means certain limitations on private property in order to ensure a fair distribution of wealth based on Qur'an precepts. The restoration of Zekat

---
[284] ibid.
[285] ibid., 25-6.
[286] ibid., 26.
[287] ibid., 27.
[288] ibid., 27-8.

*Savagery in the Heart of Europe*

(paying of alms, one of the Five Pillars of the Faith) to the status of a public obligation as of old, and the enforcement of the Qur'an prohibition of collecting interest, were seen as the instrument to achieve social justice.[289]

Izetbegovic, in intending to establish the "Republican Principle," namely that power should not be inherited, defeated his own purpose by positing at the same time the Qur'an "recognition of the absolute authority of Allah, which means the absolute nonrecognition of any other omnipotent authority," for "any submission to a creature which implies unsubmission to the Creator is not permissible."[290] This, of course, would have a direct ramification on the entire question of sovereignty, democracy, authority, and power. In this scheme, the idea of the inviolability of the individual is totally rejected, as it is made clear that, statements of equality of all men notwithstanding, and "irrespective of man's merits," he must submit to the Islamic order where there is a "synthesis of absolute authority (in terms of its policy and program of action) and of absolute democracy (relative to the individual.")[291] It takes a lot of intellectual acrobatics to extricate the meaning of this "absolute democracy" that is strapped to the "absolute authority" of the divine Qur'an message under which the believer was expected to operate. For, while the author subscribed to the idea that all men, including the Prophet, were fallible, and worshipping them was a "kind of idolatry," he assigned "all glory and praise to Allah alone, because Allah alone can judge the merits of men."[292] This, of course, would render any process of election between men impossible, and anyone who reached a position of authority could only gain legitimacy if he submitted to the "absolute authority" of the Qur'an teachings.

---

[289] ibid., 29-30.
[290] ibid., 30.
[291] ibid., 31.
[292] ibid.

A part of this brand of democracy is insinuated to us when the author suggested that in his envisaged Islamic order, the mass media "should be controlled by people of unquestionable Islamic moral intellectual authority. Perverts and degenerates should not be allowed to lay their hands on these media . . . and use them to transmit the senselessness and emptiness of their own lives to others. What can we expect if people receive one message from the mosque and a totally opposite one from the TV relay?"[293] The author did not spell out the criteria to judge the "emptiness and senselessness" of journalists under his regime, nor did he explain how he, or anyone else, could judge any person when all judgment is left to Allah. But he dared, under the heading of "Freedom of Conscience,"[294] to suggest all those limitations on the media, which would certainly make them anything but free, the protestations of the author notwithstanding.[295]

While the statement that "there can be no Islamic order without independence and freedom" may still sound plausible, in view of the Islamic regimes of Iran, Afghanistan, and Saudi Arabia, and now, gradually, following the "Arab Spring" and the Turkish upheaval, in the rest of the Islamic world, its vice-versa, namely that "there can be no independence and freedom without Islam"[296] seems a bit presumptuous by any stretch of the imagination. For that would mean that the freest and most democratic nations of the world are in fact deprived of freedom and independence as long as they do not see the light of Islam. Unless, of course, he meant that the idea applied only to Muslim people. In that case, the author argued, only if the Muslims asserted Islamic thought in everyday life could they achieve spiritual and political liberation. Moreover, he claimed

---

[293] ibid., 33.
[294] ibid.
[295] ibid., 34.
[296] ibid., 35.

that the legitimacy of the ruler in any Islamic nation will always depend on the extent of the ruler's commitment to Islam, short of which he turned for support to foreigners who maintained him in power.[297] Conversely, if he acted according to Islamic requirements, he thereby achieved the true democracy by consensus, which is inherent in Islam and which alone makes violence redundant.[298] But the road to this utopian state of affairs is not obtained in "peace and tranquility, but in unrest and challenge."[299] That means that like other Muslim fundamentalist movements who promise their constituencies sweat and blood, and they earn credibility and appeal in so doing, the Islamic declaration under discussion treads the same road to contrast with the empty promises of rulers in the Islamic world, who make sweeping pledges of peace and prosperity but are unable to deliver. The author's prediction that the road to Islamic order was paved with violence was to be completely vindicated during the Bosnian War.

Now comes the problematic issue of the relations between the Muslim host culture and minority guest cultures under the Islamic order. The manifesto provided religious freedom and "protection" to the minorities, "provided they are loyal," something that smacks of the traditional Muslim attitude to the *dhimmis* (protected people) under its aegis. The interesting aspect of all this is that when the situation is reversed, namely Muslim minorities dwell in non-Muslim lands, their loyalty is made conditional on their religious freedom, not the other way around. Moreover, even under such conditions, the Muslims are committed to carry out all their obligations to the host community "with the exception of those that are detrimental to the Muslims."[300] The

---
[297] ibid.
[298] ibid., 35-6.
[299] ibid., 37.
[300] ibid., 40.

question remained unanswered as to who was to determine what is detrimental to Islam, when, and where. When he assumed that the status of Muslim minorities would depend on "the strength and reputation of the Islamic world community," this meant two things to the author: that there was a possibility for Izetbegovic that the Muslims of Bosnia would remain a minority. Indeed, their rate is about forty percent of the total population (and growing, due to a higher birthrate), and if the Catholic Croats and Orthodox Serbs of Bosnia should gang up against them (as had happened in the past), this manifesto still provided them with a chance for survival. That was incidentally one of the reasons why the Muslims ended up federating with the Croats, their old-time mortal enemies, so as to create a majority coalition that could stand up to the stronger Serbs.

In either case, the Bosnian Muslims were counting on the intervention of the world Muslim community, something that was to be corroborated during the Bosnian and then the Kosovo wars.

Again, like the Hamas and other branches of the Muslim Brotherhood, this manifesto proclaimed the primacy of education and preaching, in order to conquer the hearts of the people before power, a prerequisite for enforcing the Islamic order, is conquered. "We must be preachers first and then soldiers"[301] is the motto of the manifesto. Force to take over power will be applied, in his words, "as soon as Islam is morally and numerically strong enough, not only to overthrow the non-Islamic rule, but to develop the new Islamic rule," because "to act prematurely is equally dangerous as to be late in taking the required action."[302] The author was confident that this could be done, because "history is not only a story of constant changes, but also of the continual

---
[301] ibid., 45.
[302] ibid., 45-6.

*Savagery in the Heart of Europe*

realization of the impossible and the unexpected."[303] The model for the new Islamic order, which the manifesto put on the pedestal, is Pakistan, the Muslim state which, in spite of its many deficiencies, remained the "great hope" of Izetbegovic[304], contrary to the preferred failed Turkish model, for which the West was squandering its resources in the killing fields of Serbia, Bosnia, and later Kosovo. But his great goal was the unity of the Muslim people, and in the meantime, he urged every Muslim country to be concerned about all the rest; Egypt ought to care for the Muslims of Ethiopia and Kashmir,[305] and by inference, the Muslims of Bosnia and the Balkans should be the business of all the rest of the Islamic world. He felt that the fact that sentiments of affinity for oppressed Muslim brothers everywhere were not translated into action was the fault of the Western-educated Muslims who substituted nationalism for Pan-Islam.[306] Had he lived, Izetbegovic may have been jubilating and feeling vindicated today by the reversal that the "Arab Spring" has been producing these days.

Under the heading, "Christianity and Judaism," the manifesto determined the future relationships of the envisaged new Islamic order with those two faiths, which the author generously considered as "the two foremost religions" and the "major systems and doctrines outside the sphere of Islam."[307] Nonetheless, the author distinguished between Jesus as a persona and the church as an institution. The former, said he, in line with Qur'an teachings, was part of divine revelation, while the latter, as embodied in the Inquisition, was abhorrent to his heart. At the same time, however, as is the normative Islamic wont, he accused Christianity of

---

[303] ibid., 46.
[304] ibid., 48.
[305] ibid., 49-50.
[306] ibid., 51.
[307] ibid., 55-57.

"distorting certain aspects" of the divine message and accused the church of intolerance.[308] Similarly, he differentiated between Jews and their national movement or Zionism, idealizing the times when they lived under Islam, but he totally rejected their plea for independence and nationhood.[309] So, as long as the Jews were submissive and stateless in their dhimmis status within the Islamic state he envisaged, all was well, but to dare to declare independence and stand up to the Islamic world, that was unforgivable. He claimed that Jerusalem was not only a Palestinian city, but first of all, a Muslim one, and therefore he warned the Jews who "have created themselves" the conflict with the Arab regimes (not the Arab or the Muslim people) that a prolonged war would be waged against them by Muslims until they released "every inch of captured land." He threatened that "any trade-offs or compromises which might call into question these elementary rights of our brothers in Palestine will amount to treason, which can destroy even the very system of moral values underpinning our world."[310]

In sum, this passionate message of Izetbegovic, based on the Qur'an and the revival of Islam, addressed the universal congregation of all Muslims, and, like the Muslim Brothers and their many affiliates, strove to establish an Islamic world order (a caliphate) based on Qur'an precepts. The idea of nationalism, any nationalism, was totally rejected in favor of the Islamic Republic, which alone could respond to the challenges of their modern world and restore to Islam its glory and preponderance (as it has been dismally demonstrated in the separate republics of Iran, Pakistan, Taliban Afghanistan, Syria, Algeria, and Turkey in our days, some of which he did not live to see). Like the platform of the Hamas and other

---
[308] ibid., 55-56.
[309] ibid., 56-7.
[310] ibid., 57.

fundamentalists, the text of the Qur'an, rather than the commentaries of the Muslim establishment, provides the rationale for the cultural, social, and political revolution that the author proposed to undertake. Indeed, the profuse citations from the Holy Book that we find interspersed throughout the text of the declaration bear witness to the Qur'an hegemony in the thought and plans of the author. Moreover, by positing the listed principles as deriving from the Holy Scripture, namely the eternal and immutable Word of Allah, the document creates, like the Charter of the Hamas (released in February 1988), the impression of a divinely guided program, which is not given to debate or consideration. The vow insinuated in this declaration that Islam would reconquer its people peacefully if possible, by force if necessary, which might throw some light (or rather obscurity) on some of the events that took place in Bosnia in the 1990s, including Iranian and other Mujahidin, who participated in the battles and gained momentum later in Kosovo and elsewhere, where al-Qa'ida was taking root at the turn of the millennium.

It is said[311] that immediately after World War II, in spring 1946, as a member of the "Young Muslims,"[312] Izetbegovic,[313] together with Omer Behmen (later vice president

---

[311] R. Israeli, one of the coauthors, was repeatedly told this during his talks in Serbia, and was handed the text of this poem, whose authenticity was verified. The lyrics of the poem, "To the Jihad" in its original version were given by Munir Garankapetanović in his autobiographical book, *Mladi će mjesec opet blistati* (Sarajevo,NIPP Ljiljan, 1996). Munir Garankapetanović was born in 1928 in Sarajevo and died in 1999. He joined the "Young Muslim" organization in 1943. He was tried in Sarajevo in 1949 and was sentenced to eight years of prison plus two years of deprivation of civic rights. In 1951, he was released from prison.

[312] Sarajevo "Young Muslims" trial lasted from 1 to 12 August in 1949, and the four main defendants, Hasan Biber, Halid Kajtaz, Omer Stupac, and Nusret Fazlibegovic were sentenced to death by firing squad, and about another two hundred and fifty members were sentenced to penalties between two and twenty years in prison, while the hundreds of other members of "Young Muslims" (among them women and girls) without a court judgment were sent to the so-called "socially useful work" (community service) for a period of several months to two years.

to the SDA party), and Dr. Shachirbay (father of Muhamed Shachirbay,[314] later the Bosnian ambassador to the United Nations) started an illegal magazine, The Mujahidin,[315] in which the following poem was published:

The earth throbs, the mountains quake
Our war cry resounds through the land
Heads held high, men old and young,
In a holy jihad our salvation lies
   Chorus: The time has come, onward brethren
Onward brethren, onward heroes
To the Jihad, to the Jihad let us go.
Proudly the green banner flies,
Close ranks beneath it in steel-like file,

---

[313] Historian Nebojša Malić from Sarajevo wrote in October 2004 about Izetbegović, "His 1983 trial may have been a farce, but he was a member of a Muslim youth organization that recruited for the Waffen SS during World War Two and he did write the "Islamic Declaration" in 1970, in which he argued that:

The exhaustive definition of the Islamic Order is: the unity of religion and law, education and force, ideals and interests, spiritual society and State ... the Muslim does not exist at all as an independent individual ... It is not in fact possible for there to be any peace or coexistence between 'the Islamic Religion' and non-Islamic social and political institutions.

This is as explicit as Islamic fundamentalism gets. Oh, there is also the matter of Muslim soldiers killed in the Bosnian War being called *shahid*, "martyr for the faith," indicating theirs was a Muslim holy war (jihad), not a struggle for some fictitious multiethnic utopia. Izetbegovic requested to be buried at the main *shuhada* cemetery in Sarajevo, next to the holy warriors who died for his vision.

Nebojsa Malic, *The Real Izetbegovic*, 24 October, 2003 http://original.antiwar.com/malic/2003/10/23/the-real-izetbegovic/ ) Incidentally, Zoran Piroćanac attributed the poem, "To the Jihad," to Alija Izetbegović, referring to it as a "non-signed poem of Alija Izetbegović."

After release from prison, young Muslim members wrote under pseudonyms, and their articles were regularly published in *PREPOROD* and *TAKVIM*, the magazines that were official and legal media of the Islamic community in Yugoslavia. An alias of Alia Izetbegović was LSB after the first letters of the names of his children. *PREPOROD* is now the name of the Bosnjak Kultural community and its magazine.

[314] Dr Shachirbay (father of Muhamed Shachirbay, later the Bosnian ambassador to the United Nations)—this surname is in fact Shachirbayovich or Šaćirbegović

Let the brotherhood of Islam bind us,
Let us scorn death and go to the battle
Chorus: The time has come . . .
With our war cry, "Allah Akbar"
Rot the old and corrupt world
For the joy and salvation of mankind
Boldly, heroes, let us go into battle!
Chorus: The time has come . . . [316]

---

in Serbian transcription. Arabic and Turkish transcripts of the name are combined with typical Serbian surname suffixes IĆ and OVIĆ in this surname, a combination which is the trademark of our Yugoslavian Muslims. Nedžib Šaćirbegović was a WW II time friend of Alija Izetbegovic, and his own son, Muhamed Šaćirbegovića, was later BiH ambassador with the United Nations.

[315] The "illegal magazine"—*The Mujahid*—was the forbidden underground magazine of the "Young Muslims." Alija Izetbegović and Nedžib Šaćirbegović were arrested in 1946 under suspicion that they belonged to the "Young Muslims" terrorist organization and that they had founded the illegal Islamist magazine, *Mudžahid*. Alija was sentenced to three years of prison, Nedžib Šaćirbegović to four years. So both of them were in prison at the time of the Sarajevo trial in 1949. What is important is that they were sentenced by the Supreme Military Court of Yugoslavia.

[316] This poem is quoted in the book, Mladi će mjesec opet blistati," (Young Moon Will Shine Again) by Munir Garankapetanović, (Sarajevo: NIPP Ljiljan, 1996), his book of memoirs of one of the "Young Muslim" organization members sentenced in the Sarajevo trial in 1949. This is what he wrote about this poem in the chapter on his trial, "For evidence of terrorism, the article "How Will We Fight," written during the war [WW II], was read at the trial, even though there was no mention of the Communists or terrorism in the article. Finally, they read the lyrics of the song, "To the Jihad." Both were read by Kajtaz Halid. In court it was stated that I wrote that song and Nusret [Fazlibegovic] congratulated me. The song, "To the Jihad" was taken by the court as a physical fight, since they were not knowing and not wanting to know the essence of the meaning of this word. Jihad, in the first place, is a struggle of man against his own passions. Generally, the jihad is a struggle on the path of God, that is, struggle for all the good in this world, but not limited only to the armed struggle. Muhammad (a.s) after he has returned from a battle, he told to his companions (ahbabs), "We came back from the small jihad, now the great jihad is in front of us." Here he was referring to the struggle against their passions and evils that are in man. However, to tell such a thing to the state prosecutor and to the judge would be the same as the talk to the deaf. Here's the text of the poem, "To the Jihad" in Serbian,

Zemlja drhti i brda se tresu,
Prostorom trepti naš borbeni glas!
Čela visoko, stari i mladi,
U svetom džihadu leži naš spas!

Raphael Israeli and Albert Benabou

These themes are strikingly similar to those propagated in cassettes by the Hamas organization[317] to glorify the death for the cause of Islam in the course of Jihad. They also strikingly originate from the same thinking which produced the Islamic Declaration analyzed above. It is not surprising therefore that as early as 1992, at the genesis of the Bosnian War, the Islamic community newspaper in Sarajevo *PREPOROD* (Revival, Renaissance) published the following poem:

> Go into battle with a clear mind and with full confidence
> In Allah. If you survive, you will be a *ghazi* [a Muslim fighter]
> If you die, you will be a *shahid* [martyr]. Otherwise,
> You will not be one or the other, and most surely you will be humiliated.
> Go into battle, if possible with *abdest* [ritual ablution] and, obligatorily,
> With Allah's name in your heart and on your lips.
> On no account must you go unbathed,
> Because any such individual can be the cause of disaster
> Both to himself and to others.
> During the attack on the enemy, or in combat with him,
> Shout the tekbir [Allahu Akbar—Allah is the Greatest].

---

Vrijeme je došlo, naprijed, braćo, naprijed, junaci,
U džihad, u džihad, pođimo svi!

Gordo se vije naš zeleni stijeg,
Zbijmo se pod njim u čelični stroj!
Islamsko bratstvo neka nas veže,
Prezrimo smrt i naprijed u boj!

Vrijeme je došlo, naprijed, braćo, naprijed, junaci,
U džihad, u džihad, pođimo svi!

S našim poklikom "Allahu ekber,"
Rušimo stari i truhli svijet!
Za sreću, za spas čovječanstva,
Smjelo, junaci, naprijed u boj svet!

[317] Raphael Israeli, "Islamikaze and Their Significance," in Terrorism and Political Violence, vol. 9 no. 3 (Autumn 1997):112-3.

If possible, carry the Qur'an with you.
After all this, the Muslim must know that he is fighting
On the side of justice and is following the path of Allah.
Allah promises assistance to such men.
The man on whose side Allah is, no one can defeat.
This and next world are his.[318]

In yet another song, popular among the Muslim fighters, one could hear:

Wake up soldiers, it is dawn, it is time for prayers
We are the army of the Jihad; there is no God but Allah
This is the remedy for every pain; there is no God but Allah
In the Bosnia River Valley, an army corps is being formed
We are brothers like steel, every Chetnik[319] fears us
And every Ustasha,[320] there is no God but Allah.
We are the army of the Jihad; there is no God but Allah.[321]

## The Concept of Greater Albania

During the turmoil, which swept the Balkans on the eve of the Berlin Congress (1878), the Albanians, as an ethnic group, came up with the concept of including within their fledgling national entity all the Albanians of the Balkans, beyond the geographic boundaries of Albania itself. Being Muslims, the

---

[318] Ed. Vesna Hadzivukovic, et all, "The Future Saints," in Chronicle of Announced Death, 1993, 46.
[319] Chetniks were the nationalist Serbs, under pro-Royalist General Mikhailovic, who started by resisting the German occupation, and were aided by the British but ended in being persecuted by both the Germans and the Ustasha regime and shunned by the British for their occasional collaboration with the Nazis.
[320] The Ustasha was the pro-Nazi and ultra Nationalist Croatian regime, which encompassed Bosnia and launched an annihilation program against the Serbs, the Jews, and the Roma.
[321] ibid.

Albanians, like the Islamized Bosnians, enjoyed a privileged status in the Ottoman Empire. In 1878, the Albanian League was established in Prizren, which presented the Greater Albania plan. While the Albanians constituted the majority in the core areas of Albania proper, their proportion in Kosovo did not exceed forty-four percent.[322] Like in the case of Bosnia, where ethnicity was religion bound, namely that there could not exist an Orthodox Croat, nor a Catholic Serb, nor a Bosnian who was not Muslim,[323] so in Albania, Islamized Serbs, Greeks, and Bulgarians became ipso facto Albanians. In 1912, an attempt was made under Austro-Hungarian auspices to implement the idea, followed by another such attempt under the Italian fascists in 1941. The third attempt, initiated at the end of the 1990s as a result of the collapse of the Soviet Union and Yugoslavia, translated into tearing Kosovo, by now predominantly Albanian-Muslim, from Serbian sovereignty, following up on the Bosnian experience which had subtracted that province from Serbian-Yugoslavian hegemony.

The precedent of Bosnia, which had allowed in 1971, ironically under the communist rule, the recognition of Bosnia's nationalism as Muslim, would now propel the ethnic Albanians to revive their Islamic heritage and claim their Muslim identity, which ipso facto would justify their separation from the Serbs. At first, the awakening of the Albanians was undertaken along the ethnonational track. Prior to 1971, the break between Maoist Albania and Yugoslavia had occasioned the Albanian revolt in Kosovo (1968), but after the normalization of their relationships in 1971, the Albanians turned to cultural propaganda by

---

[322] Jovan Canak, ed., Greater Albania: Concepts and Possible Consequences (Belgrade: The Institute of Geo-Political Studies,1998), 8-11.

[323] Jens Reuter, "From Religious Community to Nation: the Ethnogenesis of the Bosnian Muslims," in Tezic (ed.) op. cit. pp. 617-23.

*Savagery in the Heart of Europe*

peaceful, if subversive, means. Interestingly enough, like the Palestinians who were competing with Israel over their ancestral land by conveniently claiming that they were the descendants of the ancient Canaanites who had preceded the Israelites on the land, the Albanians now advanced the claim that they inherited the ancient heritage of the Illyrians, who were the original inhabitants of Kosovo.[324] This resulted in the Albanian Rebellion of 1981, in which they demanded the status of a republic (no longer an autonomous region within Serbia, like Voivodina in the north), but as a Seventh Republic, still within the new seven-republic Yugoslavian Federation. After the fall of Communism in Albania, the new regime recognized, in 1991, the self-declared Republic of Kosovo, and its head, Ibrahim Rugova, opened an office in Tirana.[325]

The disintegration of Yugoslavia by necessity revived the old dreams of Greater Albania, which now eyed not only Kosovo but also parts of Macedonia, Greece, Serbia, and Montenegro, where an Albanian population had settled over the years. The rising of Muslim consciousness in the Balkans, after the Bosnian precedent and the spreading of the Izetbegovic doctrine, now acted as a catalyst to draw together, under the combined banners of Greater Albania and Islam, all the Albanian populations of that region. In 1992, Albania joined the Conference of Islamic Countries, and it has been working to attract support by other Islamic countries to the Greater Albania plan, actually presenting itself as "the shield of Islam" in the Balkans.[326] It has been noted that since the Albanian demographic explosion in Kosovo, which has allowed them to predominate and demand secession, has not taken place in

---

[324] Jovan Canak, Greater Albania: Concepts and Possible Consequences, 42-43, The Institute of Geo-political Studies, Belgrade, 1998, pp 8-11.
[325] ibid.
[326] ibid., 47-48.

Albania itself,[327] perhaps it is an indication, as in Palestine and Bosnia, that the "battle of the womb" heralded by nationalists and Muslim fundamentalists was not merely a process of natural growth, but may be also politically motivated to achieve political domination through a demographic majority.

In more recent developments, there are indications that together with the normalization one can observe in the streets of Sarajevo, and the amazing sights of older women, veiled in part or in total like mobile tents, walking side by side with their young daughters wearing jeans or shorts and provokingly revealing their belly buttons or lovely shaped legs, a form of spread and radicalization of Islam has been taking root in the mosques and in the countryside of the country. That is not only reflected in the massive building of mosques, with their gracefully svelte and elegant pencil shaped minarets, Turkish style, which betray the origin of the benefactors who built them, but also in the increased numbers of worshippers who visit houses of prayer. Most of all, this reflects the apparent victory of the more active and militant Islam, now that Turkey no longer provides the "moderate" model that the West had deluded itself existed, while the Christian (Serbian) and Jewish minority have shrunk to almost insignificance, and Iran is no longer the feared, radicalizing alternative once Turkey had become its ally. Most dramatically, this trend is represented by a Muslim Bosnian neo-Nazi group, which attributes most of the world problems to "a plot aimed at letting the Chosen People control the world."[328]

---

[327] ibid., 49.
[328] We are talking of the BosanskiPokret Nacionalnog Ponosa (Bosnian National Pride Movement), founded in 2010, describing itself as a national socialist (Nazi) movement championing white supremacy and Bosnian national revival. It was founded by, and intended for, Bosnian Muslims. Their Internet site states that ninety-five percent of the group's members are Muslim and that they celebrate the Muslim-Nazi alliance during WW II. It reveres the Muslims who joined the Nazi war effort and sees a role model in their then leader, the Mufti of Jerusalem, Haj aMin, who between 1941 and 1945 collaborated with Nazi leadership and the SS.

Worse yet, a document found by the Italian police at the Islamic Cultural Institute in Milan draws the more general contours of the Muslim struggle in the Balkans:

> We, as Muslims, have been given the task to realize the supremacy of the law of Allah on earth, and of not allowing that any group on earth governs without the law of Allah. We fight whoever refuses that and rejects the obedience [of Allah] . . . The fight is imposed on us to remove the apostate ruler from the land of Islam, to fight those who support them and their laws, to impose the Caliphate, to revenge Palestine, Spain, the Balkans, the Islamic Republics in Russia, and to free the Muslim prisoners. Our enemies are: Christians, Jews, apostates, those who adore the cow and fire, our secular rulers who replace the laws of Islam and the hypocrites . . . Jihad has been introduced to spread Allah's religion and to destroy any ruler that is not subject to the adoration of Allah . . . Fighting the infidels has the purpose of exalting the revelation of Allah.[329]

## Conclusions

While in Serbian national terms, the loss of Kosovo to the Albanians is equivalent in their eyes to Israel losing Jerusalem,[330] in international terms, the importance of this issue lay in the emerging pattern of the re-Islamization of the Balkans. True, the immediate concern of the Serbs is to what extent can a minority which achieves a local majority within their sovereign territory demand the right of secession, especially when that demand is backed up by irredentist claims of a neighboring country. If that should be the case, then

---

[329] Evan Kohlman, Al-Qa'idah's Jihad in Europe: The Afghan-Bosnian Network, 15.
[330] Duro Fuletic, "Consequences of a Possible Creation of 'Greater Albania,'" Review of International Affairs, L, no. 1085-6, (October-November, 1999): 23.

entire areas of the United States populated by Mexican-Americans, or parts of Israel where the local Arab population has achieved the majority, or the Kurdish populations of Turkey, Iraq, Iran, Syria, or Arab enclaves in France, could raise the question of their autonomy and ask for their right to secede. For that matter, the Croats and Serbs of Bosnia could also revert to their initial demand at the outset of the Bosnian crisis to merge with their respective national entities. The larger concern, however, is to what extent the settling patterns of the Albanians can disrupt the physical continuity between the major Christian political entities of the Balkans: Greece, Macedonia, Serbia, Croatia, Bulgaria, Romania; or, more importantly, whether a new continuity of Islamic settlement, from Bosnia through Kosovo and now southern Serbia, can link up with the Muslims of Bulgaria to achieve a geographical continuum with Muslim Turkey. In view of the Islamic Declaration analyzed above, which does not accept the present state of affairs in the Balkans and Turkey and makes provision for an Islamic revolution to redress the situation to its liking, the Bosnia and Kosovo events seem only as an ominous precursor of things to come.

These concerns have been raised due to the perverted link that has been established in real politics between Muslim fundamentalist powers like Saudi Arabia and Iran and now Turkey and the emerging Muslim states (Egypt, Libya, and possibly Syria in the near future), following the "Arab Spring," which seek to further the penetration of Islam into the Balkans, against western interests, and the inexplicable rush of that same West to facilitate that penetration which is already turning against it. From the Muslim point of view, things are easy, and their goals are clear, to ensure the continuity of Muslim presence from Turkey into Europe, namely to revitalize a modern version of the Ottoman Empire. True, until recently, successive civil governments of Ankara were committed to secularism of the Kemalist brand under the guardianship of the military. But as the Erbakan experience has shown (1996-1998), when democracy is allowed to operate, then the Algerian scenario gains the upper hand, and an Islamist government is elected to power that may also opt for the strengthening of the Islamic factor in Europe. Muslim fundamentalists across the world, from the Uighurs of Chinese Turkestan to the Arabs of the Middle East, from the Mujahidin of Afghanistan to the disciples of Izetbegovic in the Balkans, do not hide their designs to act for the realization of this new world order.

A summon by the Saudi scholar Ahmed ibn-Nafi', of Mecca, which was circulated to all centers of the Pan-Islamic Salvation Committee at the outset of the conflict in Bosnia, stated in no uncertain terms:

> Let it be known, brothers, that life in this ephemeral world differs immensely from the life lived in keeping with the principles of Jihad . . . Fortunate is he whom Allah enlightens in this life . . . by waging a Jihad for him. Following Allah's instructions, the Pan-Islamic Salvation Committee has devised a holy plan to clean the world of unbelievers. We entrust you to see to the imminent establishment of the Caliphate in the Balkans, because the Balkans are the path to the conquest of Europe.
>
> Every individual imam in our states, and especially Turkey, is ready to help. Know, therefore, brothers, that time is working for us. Let us help our brothers who are fighting for the holy cause in Bosnia. Let us help them for the sake of Allah, by sending them as much money and weapons as we can, by sending them new Mujahidin. Furthermore, in keeping with this holy plan, all women and children and some men must immediately be given refuge in Europe. And you, brother Muslims,

must care for them as for your own, so they will spread everywhere and preach our religion, for our sake and for the sake of Allah. Brothers, give women and children refuge in each center, collect money and weapons and send them to Bosnia. Gather Mujahidin and send them to Bosnia! This is your obligation. Help them so that Islam will spread as soon as possible . . . With all your heart and soul and everywhere, fight the unbelievers! This is your duty! The Caliphate is at hand! . . . May Allah reward you![331]

This appeal was by no means an isolated case. In the same month of August 1992, a poster was plastered on walls in Sarajevo signed by the spiritual head of the Iranian Revolution, Imam Khamenei, which accused the western nations for not preventing the genocide against the Muslims of Bosnia, due to their innate hostility to Islam, and urged them to clear the way for Iranian Mujahidin and other young Muslims to wage the war and "drive the Serbs from this Islamic country."[332] In Zagreb, at the time the ally of the Muslims against the Serbs, a local journal echoed that call:

"The Muslim nation in Iran began its revolution with 'Allahu Akbar!' and succeeded. On the territory of Yugoslavia, the Serbs could not tolerate a Muslim [Izetbegovic] as the president of Bosnia-Herzegovina. Their only rival is Islam and they fear it. The time is approaching when Islam will be victorious."[333]

While the traces of Iranian and other Muslim volunteers' jihad in Bosnia were rife, Western reactions seemed more and more obtuse. Except for the theory that the United States

---

[331] The handwritten Arabic text of the epistle of 17 August, 1992 appears in Vesna Hadzivukovic, The Future Saints, 52.

[332] The text of the summons, with Khamenei's picture, appears in Serbo-Croat ibid., 54.

[333] Vecernji List, Zagreb, 9 August, 1992.

had to please Saudi Arabia as it had done during the Gulf War (1991-1992) when it desisted from occupying Baghdad, other explanations range from sheer misunderstanding of the dangers that Islamic fundamentalism pose to the West to cold-blooded commercial interests in the short run, which obscure the long-term strategic considerations of the West. If that quandary raised many eyebrows in the West during the Bosnian War, where the United States and European powers supported Bosnia to the detriment of the Serbs, so much more so for the intransigent, costly, and destructive military intervention of NATO in Kosovo. As it is known, war does not determine who is right; it only determines who is left. It is time to draw the balance of who is left and what is left from that war. The "good guys" of NATO had set out, under the cover of a barrage of propaganda, to address the humanitarian problem of "ethnic cleansing," forgetting the "ethnic cleansing" that the Serbs had suffered over centuries in Bosnia and Kosovo. While accusing the Serbs of inflicting collective punishment on the entire Kosovar-Albanian population for the sins of the Kosovo Liberation Army, they have themselves destroyed the lives and livelihoods of millions of innocent Serbs, depriving them of bridges, potable water, supplies, municipal services, broadcasting stations, and whatnot. And all that while they were relentlessly repeating in their harrowing press briefings that they held no grudge against the Serbian people, only against their leader. The real questions for the horrors of that war were never raised by NATO, and certainly never answered; what has caused the mass uprooting of people from Kosovo, including Serbs? Was it only Serbian abuses against the Albanian population, or perhaps also the fear of people who were caught in the crossfire? Why were only the old, women, and children the ones who ran away to safety in refugee camps? Was it only because the Serbs callously imprisoned or exterminated able-bodied men, or perhaps because they were recruited into rebellious KLA troops who aided NATO's designs? Was Serbia encouraging or preventing ethnic cleansing? One day we were told that the refugees were pushed across the borders of Kosovo, another time we were told that they ran away by themselves, and yet another time we were assured that the Kosovars were prevented by the bad Serbs from crossing in order to serve as human shields. Who could take these inconsistencies seriously?

The havoc that was wrecked on Kosovo, far from settling the issue, on the contrary aggravated it. The Serbian population was almost totally forced out of the province, and those who stayed can only do so under the protection of NATO or UN forces. Two months after they had "established order" there, a *New York Times* editorial had this to say about it:

> Kosovo remains lawless and violent. There are no local police, or judges . . . NATO is doing an uneven and unsatisfactory job of preserving order . . . Local thugs, rogue fighters of the Kosovo Liberation Army and Albanian gangs slipping [from Albania] across the unpatrolled borders, have taken advantage of the law enforcement vacuum to terrorize the Serbian and Gypsy minorities and drive them from their homes . . . The same violent elements also prey on Kosovar Albanians subjecting people to extortion, and potential political rivals and suspected collaborators with the previous Serbian authorities, to intimidation and murder . . .
>
> NATO must rethink its overly indulgent attitude towards the KLA, which has been permitted to postpone the deadline for surrendering heavy weapons and expects to see its former fighters included in the new local police forces.[334]

---

[334] The New York Times Editorial, 6 August, 1999.

One year later, in July 2000, things did not seem to have changed much. Chaos seemed to be still prevailing, and the parties determined that the Kosovars wanted independence from Serbia, and the Serbs to prevent it, lest the Greater Albania plan came to be implemented, with the related instability in Macedonia and other areas inhabited by Albanians.[335] The UN troops were supposed to impose a "substantial autonomy" for the Kosovars under Serbian sovereignty, but that was not in the making, while Albanians who lived in Serbia proper wished to draw UN troops across the border, to widen international sponsorship of allegedly Albanian territory. Reports from the spot identified a "Kosovo-wide problem of attacks on [Serbian and other] minorities, harassment, intimidation, and persecution" and the "vicious Albania-based mafia that was spreading crime."[336] The irony in all this is that while the problem of Bosnia remained unsettled, with the Serb and Croat entities there entertaining their hopes to join their mother lands and Kosovo still an open wound, NATO found itself backing, or at least seeming indifferent to, the Islamic takeover in the heart of Europe. In 2007, talk in Europe and the United Nations was of imposing Kosovo independence on the reluctant Serbs, whose new democratic leadership opposed, as vehemently as Milosevic in his time, any separation of Kosovo from Belgrade. If it were not for Russian opposition, the West might have foolishly celebrated the severance of Kosovo from its Serbian nexus even earlier than it did. So contradictory attitudes of supporters and deniers of an independent Kosovar entity still linger on.

Robert Cohen-Tanugi, in his series of articles which has drawn world attention,[337] proposed the thesis that the United

---

[335] Therese Raphael, The Wall Street Journal, 7 July, 2000.
[336] Flora Lewis, "The Kosovo Mission of the UN is left to Fail," The Herald Tribune, 10 March, 2000, 8.
[337] Robert Cohen-Tanugi, in Diaspora/Le Lien, no. 112, 30 July, 1999; no. 117, 22 October, 1999; and no. 120, 3 December, 1999.

States was basically interested to promote Islamic states to create the "Green Belt," loyal to it, around Russia and China, and its subsidiary, the "Green Diagonal," designed to link central Europe with Turkey, in order to restore the power and hegemony of this pivot of American strategy to its Ottoman times. That was the reason, he claimed, for the American determination to advance the cause of Islamic revival in Bosnia and Kosovo and, conversely, to eliminate nationalist Serbia, which stands as the major obstacle on that road. However, rising fundamentalist Islam, which is inimical to the United States in particular and Western culture in general, he rightly, precisely predicted would not necessarily play the American game, and may turn against its benefactors sooner and with more vengeance than either the United States or its European allies suspect, just as it did in Afghanistan. The daily flights from Teheran to Sarajevo did not carry nuns or Christian missionaries but Muslims from the Middle East and Asia who converged on Bosnia en route for other European countries. While many of them sought their economic fortunes through the porous borders of Bosnia into the West, there is no telling how many of them might, in the future, become agents of trouble and Islamic revolution when their numbers and local circumstances in Europe permit. The wide-ranging survey of these forces in the making, including al-Qa'ida in Bosnia,[338] ought to be enough of a deterrence to prevent any responsible Western leader from any complacency on this matter.

The elections in Turkey of 2002 brought to power the Muslim party headed by Erdogan, who had been incarcerated several years earlier, when as the mayor of Istanbul he made fiery declarations much in the Izetbegovic style. The previous incarnation of the same party, headed by Necmettin

---

[338] Evan Kohlman, Al-Qa'ida's Jihad in Europe, Berg, N.Y. 2004.

Erbakan, had won the plurality in 1996, and Erbakan became prime minister, but he was ousted by the military in 1998 and his party outlawed. Under those circumstances, the thought about linking moderate Turkey to the Balkans may have had some justification, had it been implemented in time, or under the civil governments of Menderes, Ecevit, Ciller, or Ozal. But in view of the new situation, in which the Islamist party got the majority in Parliament (no longer the plurality as in Erbakan's times), and again in 2006 and 2010, so much so that they could defy their alliance with the Americans and deny them the right to open a northern front in the war against Iraq in 2003, the dreams of a moderate continuity of Islam evaporates. Certainly, Turkey is interested in showing the pretty face in her struggle for access to the European Union, but at the same time, Erdogan was frantically appointing his own men to the upper echelons of the army, and he arrested the top leadership of the military, who were the guarantors of the secular constitution, under a third-world fabricated scenario of a "conspiracy," so that when the day came of shifting demonstratively to Islam, no military, who held themselves as the "curators of Ataturk's heritage," could topple the government as they did to Erbakan.

In that perspective, retaining a Serbian Kosovo and a Christian Macedonia and Sandjak would have at least arrested Islam's advance into the heart of Europe and scuttled the recreation of the similitude of a Muslim Ottoman Empire in the Balkans. But it would take time for the West to awaken and reclaim its Christian heritage, which it had painfully struggled for centuries to maintain within the Ottoman Empire and against it and then to disinherit the Turks from Europe.

# Chapter Nine
## Collecting the Pieces and Adjudicating War Crimes

The three-year Bosnian War, like other preceding Balkans wars, ended in uneasy settlements which were imposed on the parties from the outside, but, perhaps except for Croatia, which emerged independent and seemingly democratic and liberal, to the point of being admitted into the European Union, and seems content with the results of its worthwhile struggle, the other rivals did not quite settle into the new post-war reality and give vent to their frustration from the war and its consequences. True, there prevails now a veneer of civility, which followed the savagery of war, and which all parties wish to forget and to accuse the others of its horrors while they strive to minimize their part in it. There are diplomatic relations between all the warring parties of yesteryear, but when one crosses over the borders separating them, one senses tension and hostility and little grace and hospitality. Especially enervating and symptomatic to the traveler is the crossing of the narrow stretch of Croatian territory along the Adriatic coast between Split and Dubrovnik, which was ceded to Bosnia as part of the peace settlement to serve as its outlet to the sea but thereby severs continuity along the narrow coastal strip between those two important cities. The contrast is great when one comes in from Europe, where road controls hardly exist anywhere among the twenty-seven member states, and it is quite irritating to observe those neighbors who were the citizens of the same country for decades erecting those obstacles between them, which signal hostility, alienation, suspicion, and estrangement.

The big question is, what will be the durability of the present arrangements, in which one can detect all the elements that were mentioned in all the peace plans raised at one time or another, by one party or another? But since the United Nations, under whose mantle all those attempts were made, insisted on its "neutrality," nothing could be enforced on the unwilling parties, which considered the whole game as zero-sum. Maybe Croatia, which gained the most from the war, mainly by subtracting herself from Serbian dominance, would be the most amenable to preserve the general framework of Dayton, and her coming membership into the European Union will provide the needed umbrella of guarantee to that end. But Serbia remains seething with frustration, not only because she lost the hegemony in the larger Yugoslav federation which was led and managed from Belgrade, but because she was also forcibly severed from Kosovo, a historically vital part of her territory, where many monasteries and Orthodox churches were burned, destroyed, or otherwise aggressed or besieged. That feeling of unfinished business is reinforced when one visits Republika Srpska and its sprawling capital of Banja Luka, where dreams of rejoining Serbia did not die, and the feelings of frustration and bitterness against the unfairness of the settlement are rife. Unsatisfactory settlements are the recipe for the next conflagration, and it is only a matter of time and circumstance when the present intermezzo in the Balkan wars will end and hostilities rekindle. The sense of passionate hatred, burning suspicion, and condescending contempt for the Croats and the Bosniaks is perceptible when one digs beneath the veneer of civility.

The character of the settlement does not make for a genuine reconciliation either, since the three parties which fought the Bosnia War got less than they wanted. The Croats did not get Mostar and had to coalesce with the Muslims they had fought against, just to stand the pressures of the much larger and more powerful Serbian population. In other words, they did not join the Muslims out of love or attraction or admiration, but only because their hatred and fear of the Serbs were much greater that their reluctance from Muslims. Under the table, deals that were and are still going on between Croats and Serbs, during the war and after it, point to the basic joint revulsion from Muslims and the fundamental fear from Islam, which unite them. The Serbs got forty-nine percent of the territory of Bosnia, despite their lesser demographic weight in the population, which does not surpass forty percent. That meant that the Muslim-Croatian demographic coalition maintains the majority for its bloc so as to justify its non-Serbian (or anti-Serbian in their eyes) character. Nonetheless, the Serbian part is more prosperous and can continue to claim economic dominance of Bosnia, though in politics, diplomacy, and security matters, they constitute only one-third of the triangular presidency. The whole is a federation, the like of the Helvetic federal state, but where the Cantons determine all the requirements of daily life for the citizens.

Is the present uneasy quiet merely a truce until either circumstances change or a new outburst of hostility flares up, or is it sustainable for the long run? Only time will tell. But in the meantime, all parties prepare for a change, cultivate their separate identities, insist that their common language has in fact splintered into three different tongues, and do not show signs of accepting the new reality indefinitely. Maybe their common quest to gain access to the European Union will be the ultimate remedy to guarantee long-term non-belligerence. But for now, the attempts being made on all sides to whitewash their own past and to splash mud on their rivals; to preserve their own memories of victimhood and blacken the images of their neighbors as the real oppressors; to manufacture a spruced-up history for themselves while obliterating any positive deeds that their rivals may have done; and, worst of all, to revive (on the margins for now, to be sure) bygone manifestations of ultra-nationalism, fascism and anti-Semitism do not augur well for the future. For, if federal Yugoslavia was busy smoothing over differences among the various ethno-religious groups, building a united new Yugoslavian culture and language, and hiding the incriminating past which inflamed the tempers, now the contrary process is in full swing, that is distinguishing oneself from the others, cultivating one's own culture, praising one's own history and condemning the others.' If the previous trends, problematic as they were, suffocated contentiousness and disagreement, the present ones, on the contrary, encourage and inflame them.

One case in point was the malicious vandalizing of the Jadovno Memorial monument, which exposed in public the atrocities done by the Ustasha Croats and their Muslim collaborators against Serbs, Jews, and Gypsies. It now stands in vandalized ruins. Its central pillar has been decapitated, and someone has carefully chiseled away the plaques bearing the victims' names. The entire scene is covered by a weed carpet on the entire isolated site. The journalist, Tracy Wilkinson, who visited the site, said that in the forest behind the monument, which referred to the entire vast Jadovno complex, down a steep path, sits another part of the memorial in equal neglect. It is a deep, black pit tunneled into the hillside, where the bodies of hundreds of Jews and Serbs were dumped in 1941 by Croatian Ustasha, the rulers of Croatia's Nazi puppet state. As she surveyed the scene, right after the Bosnian War fifty years later, she wrote:

> Fifty years later, these same hills around the tense, insular town of Gospic, were used to dispose of more bodies of Serbs and Croatian dissidents that a new generation of Croatian nationalists worked to eradicate. Such gruesome recycling of history might end there, except

that it now appears that some of the same officials in charge of local government during the 1991 killings were restored to power in elections three months ago. They also are probably part of the gang that destroyed the monument to Jewish and Serbian victims. The persistent presence of people, who could qualify as war criminals, contaminates most societies that emerged from the former Yugoslav federation. In Croatia, human rights activists say the government of President Franjo Tudjman—until recently the region's closest United States ally—encourages impunity and cyclical violence by distorting the past and glorifying a nationalist history while overlooking the murderous side. As it attempts to build an ethnically pure state, the government has failed to purge criminals from its ranks, and in fact rewards many. "These people poison the atmosphere for everybody. If we want a better future for this country, we have to get rid of these kinds of people," said Ivo Goldstein, a history professor at Zagreb University and an opposition activist.[339]

This does not certainly sound like a people seeking reconciliation, evincing an acknowledgment of their past and acting to take a distance from what their predecessors did and to mend their historical record. Croatian-Jewish historian Ivo Goldstein's interest is as much personal as historical when he refers to these events. His grandfather was among the Jews slain outside Gospic in 1941 and dumped into a deep, narrow pit. The site, known as Jadovno, in the hills about nine miles west of Gospic, was the first death camp among twenty-six concentration camps created by Croatia's

---

[339] Tracy Wilkinson, "Croatia, Alleged Criminals Thrive While Memorial Fades", Los Angeles Times, published on 14 July, 1997 and based on an interview with Ivo Goldstein, the most prominent Holocaust historian in Croatia and author of the great monograph, Holocaust in Zagreb, among other books.

pro-Nazi World War II regime, with thousands of Jews and Serbs who were rounded up by Ustasha agents and transported in rail cars to the Gospic area, were forced to walk through fields and then knifed to death—all during a three-month period in 1941. The bodies were thrown into the pit. Among the victims, according to today's tiny Croatian Jewish community, were two hundred members of the Maccabi Jewish Sports Club of Zagreb. Goldstein's grandfather, also named Ivo, was a bookshop owner in the central Croatian city of Karlovac when he was taken away. His grandmother also was arrested but released before fleeing, with two young sons, to territory controlled by anti-fascist partisan fighters. At the better-known Jasenovac death camp in north-central Croatia, many more thousands of Serbs, as well as Jews, Gypsies, and others, were killed during World War II. Due to its size, which placed it third among the death camps of Europe, Jasenovac has been the center of international focus while Jadovno has languished ignored, until the June 2011 Jadovno Conference in Banja Luka placed it back on the gruesome map of the Holocaust.

The Jadovno monument, Goldstein and others believe, was destroyed as part of a campaign to eliminate traces of Ustasha atrocities when like-minded fascists began to take charge of parts of Croatia after Tudjman declared the former Yugoslav republic's independence in 1991. Hundreds of large and minor monuments honoring both Partisans, who defeated the Nazis, and the victims of fascism have been destroyed all over the country in a wave of fervent nationalism that equates anti-fascists with Communists, Serbs, and other enemies of the Croatian fatherland. Tudjman has fueled such attitudes by praising the Ustasha's stated goal of independence, even if the regime was guilty, he allowed, of certain "wrongdoings." Thank you for that outburst of generosity and decency. One of the most notorious men who rose to power in the Gospic area in 1991 was Tihomir Oreskovic, a leader of Gospic's "crisis committee," formed amid the Serbo-Croat war that raged at the time. Gospic was a frontline city, a last defense against Yugoslav-backed Serbian militia fighting against Croatian secession. Always a remote, isolated place, Gospic and its Lika Valley surroundings were under siege. In October 1991, thirteen Croats were killed there. In swift retaliation, between one hundred and twenty and two hundred Serbs, including judges and other civilians, were rounded up and murdered, according to human rights researchers. The bodies were concealed in the same hills that fifty years earlier had become the mass graves for other Serbian and Jewish victims. Associates of Oreskovic emerged later to describe in Croatian newspapers the slayings and general reign of terror that swept through Gospic in 1991. Officials and military police conspired to draw up lists of Serbs who were taken away and executed according to these accounts. The record of horrors kept growing, which bridged over a hiatus of fifty years between the Ustasha of yesteryear and the horrendous savagery of the Bosnia War (1992-1995).

During the Yugoslav wars of the 1990s, both the Serbs and the Croats tried to whitewash their Holocaust and WW II track record by presenting anti-Semitism as an alien importation into their otherwise philo-Semitic lands. The existence of Serbian anti-Semitic groups before the war, like the Zbor and others, is well documented, and these became the natural collaborators with the Nazi occupiers. While not directly exterminating Jews, they closed their eyes or even aided the Nazis in carrying out the final solution. Conversely, there were many heroic cases of humanism and decency in which Jewish refugees were absorbed, hidden, and protected, or their lives were saved by their Serbian neighbors at the risk of their own lives. Croatia also is trying to erase its own blemishes of the Ustasha years, not by pretending that no Jews were exterminated in Jadovno and Jasenovac as part of their own genocidal effort, mainly against Serbs but also against Jews and Gypsies, but by claiming that the Serbs were even worse, something that is difficult to back up by hard evidence, and not only because it is hard to imagine anything worse than genocide. On the face of it, shifting the accusation to the Serbs seems to have no leg to stand on, for the Serbs can always argue that they acted under the constraints of the Nazi occupier, who would not let up, but that Serbs themselves never initiated on their own any genocide against anyone, though some anti-Semitic outbursts are admitted among their most extreme groups. By contrast, the Ustasha excelled and even surpassed their Nazi mentors in annihilating Serbs, Jews, and others.[340] Jasenovac and Jadovno are lasting monuments to that dark history.

Contrary to the endorsement and praise showered by other quarters, Dennis Reinhartz, an American historian, said in his review of Philip Cohen's *Serbia's Secret War* that it belonged to the "current popular-historical and journalist literature that seeks to demonize and condemn more than to chronicle and elucidate fairly." He added that the book was in danger of degenerating itself into an irrational conspiracy history by belonging to those histories of the Balkans that contribute little to understanding the past and its impact on the present and future.[341] Indeed, Jasa Almuly, a Belgrade Jewish author, was reported as stating, in the same vein, that he doubted whether an American physician (Cohen is a dermatologist) could write such a "political

---

[340] The very appellation Ustasha was self-appropriated by those in the Croatian nationalist movement of the pre-war era, who swore that the dismantling of the Yugoslavian federal state would facilitate the destruction of Serbdom and of the Orthodox Church, both of which they intensely loathed. See the Nova Hrvatska of May 4, 1941.

[341] Dennis Reinhartz, "Serbia's Secret War: Propaganda and the Deceit of History," in Philip Cohen's, Holocaust and Genocide Studies, February, 2000, 302.

propaganda pamphlet," and he suspected that it came from Franjo Tudjman's kitchen in Zagreb, in the form of some institute specializing in political propaganda. While this sweeping generalization sounds exaggerated and geared to demonize that writer whose work has been considered seminal and pathbreaking, it is nonetheless true that one does not need to be trained in history to be entrusted with writing history. Winston Churchill was not trained as an historian, nor are the contemporary writers on Islamic affairs, Bat Ye'or, the author of *Dhimmi and Eurabia*,[342] and Andrew Bostom, whose medical profession did not prevent him from publishing his two celebrated anthologies, *The Legacy of Jihad* and *The Legacy of Anti-Semitism*.[343]

Dr. Kraus, the president of the Jewish community of Zagreb, suggested that at least the Catholic Church in Croatia should follow the example of Pope John Paul II and apologize for the past sins against the Jews. But Dr. Adalbert Rebic, one of the experts on Judaism and Christianity in Croatia, replied that the crime was not committed by the Catholic Church or on its behalf but was committed by individuals in the name of the ideology that was subordinated to Hitler's Germany. Thus, he said, "the invitation has been delivered to the wrong address, because it is the government, the Croatian president, that should apologize for those crimes, just like German Chancellors [Adenauer and] Brandt did after the war. In addition, the Holy Father has just done that on behalf of the entire Catholic Church." Rebic put a special emphasis on the "role of the blessed Cardinal Stepinac," who in occupied Europe strongly supported the rights of the Jews as well as the Orthodox Serbs. He said that, "Cardinal

---

[342] Both published by Fairleigh Dickinson University Press, London and Toronto, 1985 and 2005, respectively.

[343] Both published by Prometheus Books, Amherst, N.Y, 2005 and 2008, respectively.

*Savagery in the Heart of Europe*

Stepinac condemned the crimes, and his successors need not apologize."[344] But it seems that as long as no clear-cut recognition by present-day Croatia of the crimes of their predecessors is reached to replace the current denials and minimizations started under Tudjman, not much can be expected either from that country or from its church, which had very clearly collaborated with the Ustasha. Even the role of Archbishop Stepinac, while recognized for the Jews he rescued, is nevertheless taken to task for the Jews he failed to save, even when he could.

This kind of attitude, which attempts to diminish the harsh effects of the Ustasha policies and to dissociate today's Croatia from the horrors of its predecessors, is evident in Zagreb not only in the complaints of Jews, who precisely claim that nationalist President Franjo Tudjman had instigated this wave of self-exoneration in his memoirs, and that many of his countrymen were happy to follow him, but also in discussions one holds with influential intellectuals and officials. The trend is clear and admitted in Zagreb, that Croatia must cleanse itself from its past and mend its damaged image to make itself ready to join Europe and to erase the horrible memoirs of Jadovno and Jasenovac. Therefore, much to one's frustration about the inability to get straight talk while on visit to Croatia or holding open discussions of the past and of bold visions of the future, all one hears in talks with officials and intellectuals is an intense endeavor to please the foreigners, to show that all is good, that the nightmares are forgotten and the rosy future looms in the horizon. One cannot say anything that may sound controversial, contradictory, arrogant, or racist, Allah forbid, and let none of those notions be associated with today's Croatia, lest sleeping dogs awaken. Since the Serbs are posing the

---

[344] Veljiko Bulajic, Vecernji List, Zagreb, 13 April, 2000, 39.

most immediate menace to that idyllic landscape by constantly reminding the whole world of their concept and convictions regarding the Ustasha's horrific acts, they are understandably hated and despised, their arguments and data are rejected out of hand, and their innate "aggressive spirit" is constantly blamed for Yugoslavia's problems.

The Serbs, on the contrary, who are accused of the sins of the 1992-1995 Bosnian War, while Croats and Bosnians who suffered at their hands deny their part in the horrors, feel persecuted, hunted, and victims of a Croatian onslaught that has gained impetus since Zagreb associated with the European Union and was promised a part in it in the next round. The Serbs like to compare themselves to Israel, not only as a model of development and national strength, but mainly as a persecuted, despised, and besieged people throughout history, which redeemed itself and set itself on a new course in the forefront of nations. Questions of memory, survival, self-justification, history, and national purpose have been widely discussed, and appeals have been launched to the world to pursue justice and not let the Croats of today efface the abuses of the Ustasha of yesterday. In this endeavor, they regard themselves as a friend and companion of Israel, themselves as the Jewish people, and they let, indeed invite, other Serbs, like those of Srpska and of the Serbian diasporas across the world, to join the same state of mind, to rally around their nation the way Diaspora Jews do around Israel, hoping that their association with the Jewish state, the frequent visits of their leaders, youth, cultural delegations, and Yad Vashem collaborators, would ultimately forge the alliance they hope could affect a renewed rapprochement with the European Union and the United States.

The Muslims, or Bosniaks as they now like to be called, the former being a religious designation (like Orthodox or Catholic) and the latter equivalent to Serbian and Croatian as an ethnic appellation, have gained the independence they were aspiring for under Izetbegovic, who is often compared to Tudjman the Croat, both having fought as ideologues and then as heads of states for the attainment of their peoples' peoplehood and statehood. Except that while Croatia emerged as a modern, democratic state with land continuity, many ports along the Adriatic, and a more or less homogenous population (after the Serbs and many Muslims were successfully "cleansed"), less fortunate Bosnia views itself possessing a truncated country, half of which is dominated by the loathed Serbs and the other half shared with the despised Croats. Worse, they altogether constitute a demographic minority of forty percent in their country, and without their coalition with the Croats they would not have been able to command a governing majority. An unenviable situation, but that is the best deal they could get in the horrible war they underwent in which the horrors done to them in Mostar and Srebrenica would remain main symbols of their struggle for recognition and statehood, and the horrors they committed elsewhere to Serbs and Croats will be gradually whitewashed and condemned to oblivion.

The Muslims of Bosnia will be sustained, on the other hand, by the growing influence and demography of their coreligionists in their immediate neighborhood: in the adjoining state in the making of Kosovo, in Albania, in the Muslim presence in Sanjak and Montenegro, and in Macedonia. Taken together, and in view of international Islam, and principally of Iran, Saudi Arabia and Turkey's direct interest in Islam in the Balkans, Bosniaks view themselves as rescued from their isolation and can proudly imagine themselves as a part of a surrounding Muslim majority. That western powers, especially the Americans, have naively succumbed to the Muslim enticement to encourage the rebuilding of its stature in the Balkans, under the false hope of thereby taming it and rendering it "moderate," is an Allah-sent bonanza that Bosniaks will not reject. But for Croats and Serbs, especially those who share Bosnia with the Muslims and watch with concern radical Islam implanting itself there, faith in the longevity of the present nonfederal arrangement has been dwindling.

With the termination of open hostilities in Bosnia, the war had actually shifted to The Hague, where war crimes were adjudicated. Paradoxically, though, that arena not only calmed some of the emotions of vengeance after criminals were judged, indicted, and convicted, but it also brought up accusations of injustice, as some criminals remained outside the reach of the tribunal, as the testimonies from the bench of the court brought up once again, like the Eichmann trial in Jerusalem of the 1960s, the recapitulation of the horrors of the war on all parts, with Benabou starring as one of the main field witnesses. The Convention on the Prevention and Punishment of the Crime of Genocide adopted by the United Nations on 12 January 1951 was passed in order to outlaw and judge the crimes committed by the Nazis. Articles Two and Three of the Convention defined the term "genocide" and the categories of crimes subject to punishment, but they still fall far short of comprising the various sorts of crimes perpetrated by war criminals. The elaboration of this convention and the adoption of such a scale measuring the various degrees of murder are vital, particularly since, at the turn of the twenty-first century, the international community has been attempting to formulate a new vocabulary to justify its intervention in arenas of conflict like the Yugoslavian wars or those looming in Syria and elsewhere in the Middle East today, where the hopeful "Arab Spring" has grown sour. Indeed, as a lesson from the "Yugoslavian Wars," in the Outcome Document of the high-level plenary meeting of the UN General Assembly in September 2005, heads of states and governments agreed on a text establishing each state's Responsibility to Protect (R2P)[345] its populations "from genocide, war crimes, ethnic cleansing, and crimes against humanity." In the same paragraph, the international community was called upon to assist states to exercise this responsibility and to support the United Nations in establishing an "early warning capability" to this effect. Accordingly, the states hold the prime responsibility to protect their population from mass atrocities, described as genocide, war crimes, crimes against humanity, and ethnic cleansing. The international community carries the responsibility to assist the state if it is unable to protect its population on its own. If the state fails or neglects to protect its citizens, and peaceful measures will have been to no avail, like today in Syria, the international community is called upon to intervene through coercive measures such as economic sanctions, military intervention being considered as the last resort. In this new set of principles, traditional sovereignty is no longer sacrosanct and is displaced by universal responsibility to care for basic human rights.

However, there are still disagreements on the core issue, what is the fatality threshold that must be crossed in order for the international community to legally interfere in a domestic conflict? For the sake of more clarity with regard to the UN (or other international) decision making process, it is necessary also to come to an understanding on the various types of conflict. Such a process, which could be based on the yardstick of numbers of victims that we have suggested above, could facilitate the distinction between the various categories of conflict both in internal and international affairs. A quantitative classification, by number of victims in a

---

[345] The World Summit Outcome Document, UN plenary, September 2005, Paragraphs 138-139.

given time and place, for example in a massive riot, a terrorist attack, a civil war, or a campaign of genocide, would offer a vital tool in the decision process that precedes international intervention. Former US Secretary of State James Baker had questioned the validity of great powers limiting their own freedom of action by giving UN bureaucrats control over their military interventions. Unfortunately, civil wars are and will be a fact of international life in the future and so their recurrence cannot be met with indifference, given their ability to spread beyond others' borders and engulf entire regions. The international community cannot afford to stay on the sidelines during civil wars. The civil war that tore apart former Yugoslavia from the inside out was sometimes dubbed a "total war," because it was not just Croats against Serbs and against Muslims, but one where Europe, the United States, and NATO became deeply involved. Moreover, the belligerents, Croats, Muslims, and Serbs, were engaged in the total mobilization of all their available resources and populations. We have tried above to understand their respective perceptions of the war, its aims, its course, its hoped-for results and its consequences.

Described as Europe's deadliest conflict since World War II, the conflicts in former Yugoslavia have become notorious for the involved war crimes, including mass ethnic cleansing. These were the first conflicts since World War II to be formally judged as genocidal in character. According to the International Center for Transitional Justice,[346] established in New York, the Yugoslav Wars resulted in the deaths of 140,000 people. Based in The Hague, the International Criminal Tribunal for former Yugoslavia was established by Resolution 827 of the United Nations Security Council on 25

---

[346] Transitional justice is an approach to achieving justice in times of transition from conflict and/or state repression, through accountability and redressing victims. Transitional justice provides recognition of the rights of victims, promotes civic trust, and strengthens the democratic rule of law.

*Savagery in the Heart of Europe*

May 1993, at the same time when the worst crimes were being committed in Mostar. This resolution created the desired impact and generated restrictions and concern amongst the perpetrators. ICTY is the first international criminal court ever established by the United Nations Security Council and was mandated to prosecute "persons responsible for serious violations of international humanitarian law committed in the territory of the former Yugoslavia since 1991[347]." The precedent pattern of international justice of this type against war crimes was the Nuremberg Trials, with the difference that those were a series of military tribunals, held by the victorious Allied forces of World War II, most notable for the prosecution of prominent members of the political, military, and economic leadership of the defeated Nazi Germany. The ICTY has been granted jurisdiction over persons who allegedly committed grave breaches of the Geneva Conventions of 1949,[348] violations of the laws or customs of war, genocide, or crimes against humanity on the territory of the former Socialist Federal Republic of Yugoslavia since 1 January 1991. By establishing the ICTY, the Security Council aimed to achieve four principal objectives, namely, to bring to justice those responsible for violations of international humanitarian law, to render justice to the victims, to put an end to the crimes being committed in the former Yugoslavia, and to contribute to the restoration of peace by promoting reconciliation in former Yugoslavia.

---

[347] Dealing with war crimes that took place during the conflicts in the Balkans in the 1990's, the United Nations established in 1993 the International Criminal Tribunal for the former Yugoslavia (ICTY) as a United Nations court. This mandate is defined and in accordance with its Statute. This Tribunal has jurisdiction over the territory of the former Yugoslavia from 1991 onwards.

[348] The Geneva Conventions establishes the standards of international law for the humanitarian treatment of the victims of war. It was negotiated in the aftermath of the Second World War (1939-1945) and ratified by 194 countries. It does not address warfare proper-the use of weapons of war-which is the subject of the Hague Conventions.

This tribunal is operating as an independent and impartial body and is formed of three separate organs: the chambers, the office of the prosecutor, and the registry. The chambers, consisting of three trial chambers and one appeals chamber, are composed of independent judges of different nationalities, none of them coming from former Yugoslavia, representing the mainstream legal systems in the world. (As we will observe in the procedures, Attorney Michael Karnavas, the defense of the accused of war crimes, Jadranko Prlic, will attempt to prove that there are fundamental discrepancies between the judges coming from different nationalities and that they are unable to offer a consistent and fair collegial judgment.) The office of the prosecutor conducts the investigations and the prosecution of persons falling within the ICTY's jurisdiction and acts independently as a separate organ of the ICTY. The registry is responsible for the administration and management of the tribunal, servicing both the chambers and the prosecutor. This includes the provision of assistance and protection to victims and witnesses. The defense of the suspect or accused is not, as such, part of the organization of the tribunal. A suspect or accused has the right to legal assistance of his or her own choosing and to appoint counsel to organize his or her defense before the court. See herewith the structure diagram of the Tribunal.

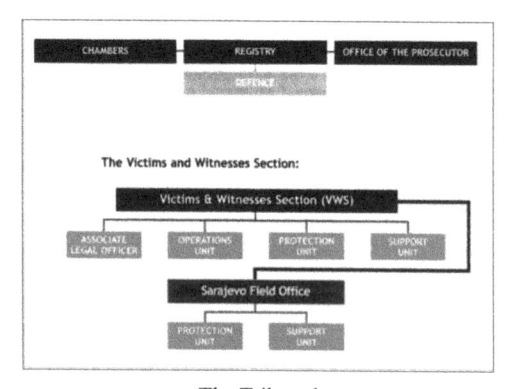

The Tribunal

ICTY has provided victims an opportunity to voice the horrors they witnessed and experienced. In its precedent-setting decisions on genocide, war crimes, and crimes against humanity, the tribunal has shown that an individual's senior position can no longer be immune from prosecution. It has demonstrated that those suspected of bearing the greatest responsibility for atrocities committed can be called to account, as well as that guilt should be individualized, protecting entire communities from being labeled as collectively responsible. This is offering in parallel an open window for reconciliation between the former belligerent ethnic groups, ruling out the trauma of feeling guilt or calling for revenge of an entire community. The tribunal has contributed to an indisputable extent combating against denial and helping populations come to terms with their recent history.

Entrance to Mostar after Breaking the Siege: Albert Benabou Briefing CNN Correspondent, on his right Cedric Thornberry, Zana Dragicevic, and Dr. Dragan Milavic. On the Back Alija Alikadic (Tzakan) The Muslim Admirer of Israel dedicated to Mostar and faithful partner of Albert Benabou.

Raphael Israeli and Albert Benabou

The ICTY's Office of the Prosecutor (OTP) has investigated many of the worst atrocities to have taken place in Europe since the Second World War, such as the 1995 Srebrenica, and prosecuted civilians, military, and paramilitary leaders for their responsibility over such crimes. While the most significant number of cases heard at the tribunal dealt with alleged crimes committed by Serbs and Bosnian Serbs, the tribunal has also investigated and brought charges against persons from every ethnic background. Convictions have been secured against Croats as well as both Bosnian Muslims and Kosovo Albanians for crimes committed against Serbs and others. The judgments demonstrate that all parties in the conflicts committed crimes, and the tribunal regards its fairness and impartiality to be of paramount importance. Evidence is the basis upon which the prosecution presents a case. The judges ensure to their utmost a fair and open trial, assessing the evidence to determine the guilt or innocence of the accused. ICTY has charged over one hundred and sixty persons. Those indicted by the ICTY include heads of state, prime ministers, army chiefs of staff, interior ministers, and many other high- and mid-level political, military, and police leaders from various parties to the Yugoslav conflicts. Its indictments address crimes committed from 1991 to 2001 against members of various ethnic groups in Croatia, Bosnia and Herzegovina, Serbia, Kosovo, and the former Yugoslav Republic of Macedonia.

On 13 August 1999, Albert Benabou received an official invitation from the office of the prosecutor at ICTY and was asked to approve and transmit documents and reports from the time he served as a UN diplomat in Bosnia during the period of 1993 to 1994. He learned from the letter sent by the ICTY that they were preparing the indictment of Croatian leaders from Herzeg-Bosnia and highest officials from Croatia, including President Franjo Tudjman. At the time, serving in the Israeli Ministry of Science in Jerusalem, Benabou cleared with his administration his agreement to contribute documents and assist the prosecutor. He arrived at The Hague on 5 September 1999 and planned to stay over the week till 9 September. Following the request of the tribunal, however, he prolonged his visit until 12 September. Susan L. Somers, a Jewish attorney from New York serving as a legal adviser to the court, was assigned by the tribunal to coordinate his trip to The Hague, ensuring that Benabou would contribute to his upmost for he was viewed as the closest UN official to the Muslims and Croats in the region of Central Bosnia-Herzegovina and Mostar. She imaginatively figured out that a visit to the landmarks of the city where Baruch Spinoza[349] had lived and was buried in the backyard of a church and an invitation to the Shabbat services in the synagogue of The Hague would facilitate the desired cooperation. This move touched Benabou's heart, who blessed once again the existence of the state of Israel which sheltered him and his likes from the times of abandon of the Jewish people in Europe. The Israeli ambassador to the Netherlands, Yossi Gal, informed the security officer about Benabou's visit and scheduled for him meetings in the country. The visit turned out to be efficient and fruitful.

Following that visit, on 22 September 1999, Benabou sent a confidential report, which was distributed to the concerned parties in Israel, to the legal adviser of the government, to the director general of the Ministry of Science, to the director

---

[349] In 1670, Spinoza moved to The Hague, where he lived. He worked on the Ethics, wrote an unfinished Hebrew grammar, and began his Political Treatise and two scientific essays, On the Rainbow and On the Calculation of Chances. Spinoza died on 20 February 1677, at the age of forty-five. His premature death was said to be due to lung illness, possibly silicosis as a result of breathing in glass dust from the lenses he ground. When he died, he was considered a saint by the general Christian population and was buried in holy ground. Later, a shrine was made of his home in The Hague.

general of the Ministry of Foreign Affairs, and to the legal advisor to the Ministry of Foreign Affairs, who would be following personally and closely all the communications and contacts with the ICTY. Benabou summarized the main items raised during his first visit to the tribunal by showing on a diskette documents related to the period of time of his mission in Bosnia in 1993, many of which are cited in this volume for the first time. At first, the office of the prosecutor declared that he could obtain the documents from the various sources in the United Nations, but it turned out that most of Benabou's reports (hundreds of pages) had "disappeared." Moreover, key personalities had passed away, such as Mate Boban, president of Herzeg-Bosnia, General Arif Pasalic, commander of the BiH Army in Mostar (killed in an accident in Sarajevo), and Jerry Hume, head of the UNHCR in the region. Others like Dr. Dragan Milavic, the physician of the hospital in East Mostar, were mentally affected by the war and resting outside Europe. Benabou expressed consternation about the disappearance of the reports that he had distributed from the war zone to all levels of the UN hierarchy in former Yugoslavia, Medjugorje, Divulje, Kiseljak, and Zagreb and up to the UN headquarters in New York. He mentioned that in fact there was nothing to add to those papers, which proved explicitly the responsibility of the actors in the region of Mostar. He clarified that he did not intend to leave his copies of the documents or transmit any of them without specific instructions from the head of the peace keeping forces in New York. The office of the prosecutor promised to obtain and submit the clearance in writing.

Beyond that, Benabou noted in his memoirs that he was surprised to learn that no Israelis were employed at the ICTY. On the recommendation of Susan Somers, he met with the director of human resources, in charge of enrolling interns and trainees working for the tribunal. The director expressed his willingness to accept Israeli candidates with the appropriate skills, namely, "they should have a high capacity of investigating beyond the knowledge of law and of the English language,[350]" he noted. The message was passed on to Israel. On a message sent on 16 December, 1999, Benabou reminded Susan Somers that the Israeli government legal counsel, Elyakim Rubinstein, who was later appointed to the Israeli Supreme Court, had been briefed about the ICTY intern program by phone and mail, and that she could move ahead with screening potential candidates from Israel. During the months of December 1999 and January 2000, Benabou responded to the tribunal with background and contact information for Croatian patriots who could assist the tribunal in establishing its documentation for the Prlic et al trial. Susan Somers was extremely thankful for the help in what she defined as "a much intricate and difficult dossier.[351]" She also maintained a close contact, particularly after some of the Serbian cases, such as Kordic and the Omarska camp, were coming to conclusion. On 18 May 2004, Kenneth Scott, the senior prosecuting attorney, wrote to Albert Benabou concerning the urgency of holding an interview with the prosecution in The Hague. Scott wrote:

> As you know, during the past several months, Chuck Sudetic, Susan Tucker, and I have been in contact with you to arrange an interview with you at a mutually agreeable time. In your role as an important official with UNPROFOR during the Bosnian War, and based on our investigation and information to date, we believe that you are a very important witness concerning large-scale crimes against humanity and other war crimes, committed under the direction of the Bosnian Croatian

---

[350] Personal memoirs of Albert Benabou of the War in Bosnia and correspondence Emails.
[351] ibid.

leadership, against primarily Bosnian Muslim victims during the period 1992 to 1994 in the region of Herzegovina.

I note that I was initially in contact with the Israeli government some months ago, which gave me approval to deal with you directly, concerning these matters. Please consider this email as a further official request from the ICTY Office of the Prosecutor for your assistance, and to the extent necessary or appropriate, this letter shall also serve to request the continuing cooperation of your government, with our continuing appreciation. Based on recent contacts, we have agreed that you will travel from Israel to The Hague on 2 June 2004 and return to Israel from The Hague on 6 June 2004. Because of the status of our work here and the court schedule, it is essential that this interview take place in the immediate future, and there is some urgency that this interview occurs now as planned. We believe that you have important evidence concerning our case. Please further confirm these arrangements by email addressed to me. If you have any questions, please contact Mr. Sudetic, Ms. Tucker, or myself. Once again, thank you for your cooperation.[352]

The following day, 23 May 2004, Benabou required the authorization from his ministry, in coordination with the Ministry of Foreign Affairs, to travel to The Hague again for a written deposition at the International Criminal Tribunal for former Yugoslavia. Benabou attached Scott's message and obtained the clearance for his trip. From 2 to 7 June 2004, Benabou was interviewed by three officers from the prosecution: an expert police investigation officer, Susan

---

[352] See Series of Email dated from January 2004 to February 2008 between Ken Scott leading the case against Prlic on behalf of the Prosecutor at The Hague and Albert Benabou, the main witness.

Tucker, a judge, Josée D'Aoust, and analyst Charles Sudetic. After the standard identification procedures, Benabou deposited his witness statement and agreed to testify in The Hague, if required to do so, though he knew it easier said than done. In the preface, Benabou recalled his arrival to his mission in Bosnia-Herzegovina and his preparation for the assignment, which evoked his participation in the different operations and negotiations in Zagreb, Sarajevo, and Kiseljak before being posted in Medjugorje at the SPABAT headquarters. After a few months, he developed special relationships with BRITFOR (British Forces) located in Divulje, close by the Adriatic, and ended up listing them in the distribution of his reports in order to maximize sharing information. He communicated through the DUTCHCOM (Dutch communication) center cell based in Medjugorje. The British were operating in a trusted and professional fashion.

He stressed that his work as an UNPROFOR civil affairs coordinator in his region revolved around improving the conditions for the civilian population. To fulfill his mandate, he was actively attempting to generate contact and arrange negotiations between the parties. Part of the responsibility was to take steps to create and improve freedom of movement, the delivery of humanitarian assistance, the protection of the civilian population, and the establishment, if possible, of an interim peace. He was convinced that the way to achieve the goals implicit in his mandate was to try to work with both sides towards agreements on specific issues. His concern was to stop the unnecessary and unjustified injury of civilians, actions such as the efforts by the Croatian Defense Council, the HVO, and its leaders to cut supplies of food and medical equipment to the mostly Muslim population of east Mostar, and the HVO efforts to refuse evacuation of wounded and seriously ill civilians. He had brought these issues up all the time with the leaders of the HVO and the Army of the Republic of Bosnia and Herzegovina (BiH Army), with his superiors in UNPROFOR, particularly Andreev and Thornberry, and with officials from the Republic of Croatia, including Mate Granic, Franjo Tudjman, and the leaders of the Republic of Bosnia and Herzegovina, including with Prime Minister Haris Silajdzic. He also worked on helping to improve conditions for refugees. Then he delivered testimonies on some of the major actors in his area and hundreds of documents that he produced during the war which were used as evidence by the tribunal. Excerpts from his deposition, which can be culled from the detailed descriptions above, are summarized here:

Mate Boban—The first meeting with Mate Boban was in early May 1993, soon after Benabou's arrival to Medjugorje. Boban introduced himself as the president of Croatian Herzeg-Bosnia. The image he projected was of a person who had embarked on a mission, and this mission was that the city of Mostar should be controlled totally by the Croats and should be the capital of a Croatian entity. Boban's approach appeared to be guided by his goal and not any other consideration. He did not care what means it would take to achieve his objective. He was acting, directing, and instructing his subordinates accordingly. Boban made it clear to Benabou that he thought the war could end only with the surrender of the Muslims of Mostar. He repeatedly expressed that he felt the international community did not understand the hatred between ethnic communities in former Yugoslavia. Boban expressed to Benabou the view that Bosnia-Herzegovina had to be divided and dismantled in two steps; first, the people of different ethnic groups should form territorially defined areas along ethnic lines, then they should opt for which successor state of Yugoslavia—Serbia or Croatia—they wanted to join. I did not identify any values that Boban would respect in getting at what he wanted to achieve. Boban was not in a fight for survival; he was focused on obtaining the annexation of Mostar and the surrounding region. Benabou learned from Boban that Zagreb stood behind him and that Zagreb was supporting the division of Bosnia and Herzegovina. Boban's assistant, Vladimir Pogarcic, was the intermediary who set up the meetings I sought with Boban and with other leaders of the HVO.

Boban and Benabou had many hours of conversations and many meetings. Everything Boban said would be reflected on the ground. Boban would create obstacles, set impossible conditions, and stand in the way of UNPROFOR missions. Boban and Jadranko Prlic were in constant competition for authority. At the beginning, this competition was concealed, and later on it became flagrant on many occasions. In June 1993, when the Security Council passed the resolution prosecuting war criminals, Zagreb started limiting public appearances of criminal elements among the HVO and its leadership. They were happy to see Boban and Prlic fading out, and Boban lost out the presidency to Kresimir Zubak. Mate Granic notified many times that Boban was a burden, and he wanted to see Boban dismissed. However, Boban held on to power within the HVO military, especially the members from Herzegovina. They were more faithful to Boban than to their superiors, HVO officers, who mostly had come from outside the area, including Croatia.

Jadranko Prlic—Benabou found Prlic to be shrewder and more sophisticated than Boban. He was also better educated and acted as a profiteer. Benabou held many meetings with Prlic in his office in West Mostar. Prlic was more focused on an egocentric agenda in terms of acquiring power and taking advantage of his decisions for as much personal gain as possible. Prlic organized meetings with UNPROFOR and other international agencies. He would invite participants who would present arguments touching upon the moral sensibilities of his interlocutors and insist that the Croats were the victims of Muslims and that the aggressor was in fact the BiH Army. For example, Prlic would stress how terrible the war was for Croatian kids who could not go to school. He also presented the Nova Bila Hospital near Vitez as another example in which the Croats were shown as victims of Muslims. After "convincing" his audience that the Croats were victims, Prlic would proceed to set unrealistic conditions on aid for hard-pressed, predominantly Muslim areas like East Mostar, where the civil population had nothing, no food, no water, and no medication. Prlic would agree in principle for an action of assistance to civilians and then set impossible conditions to realize his consent.

Prlic surrounded himself with luxury. He acted in the same ruthless way as Boban; however, he covered it with a civilized and presentable fashion. In fact, Prlic was crueler than Boban. He backed Stojic, pushing for more brutality on the part of the HVO in order to show results. They played war, and this was not war, not of an army and not of a guerilla—it was a war of starving and butchering civilians. His goal was to remove the Muslims out of the area the HVO, which he had claimed for the Croats, including all of Mostar. The goal of the military action was to frighten the civilian Muslim population by all means, such as forcible transportation and bombarding their homes, in order to evict them from the zone. There was not one place in Mostar that was not affected by those actions. It was infernal. Prlic did not want UNPROFOR's presence in Mostar. Although at one time Benabou obtained Boban's agreement to establish a permanent office of civil affairs in West and East Mostar, Prlic blocked the execution. UNPROFOR's responsibility was to be on the field in Mostar. Benabou wanted the permanent UN presence in order to secure the protection of the civil population. The HVO were taking actions against the civilian population unnecessarily and unjustifiably. Prlic and other leaders did not want an UNPROFOR presence that would witness, report, and record such actions. Prlic was the decision maker. Attempting to coordinate with the Croats an entrance to East Mostar was always denied. Benabou's talks with Prlic, Stojic, Pogarcic, and Boban to obtain access on a daily basis did not help. He could accomplish it only as a fait accompli, arriving to the checkpoints and demanding to pass, at the risk of his life. The Spanish Battalion accepted the Croatian diktat and was cooperative with Benabou only in the first months of the mission.

Prlic was regularly updated of all events or activity going on in the field via HVO reports. During my visits to Prlic's office, he met HVO military officers coming and going. There were always HVO military people around Prlic during meetings, and he tried to prove to Benabou that he was more of a decision maker than Boban himself. There was not one occasion in which Benabou brought up an issue of which Prlic was not already aware. In other words, Prlic was always briefed through his own channels of command, and he insisted to be at the apex of the reports in the top leadership. This applied to both civilian and military issues. On many occasions, Pogarcic referred me to Prlic as the decision maker on military and civilian issues. Concerning HVO troop movements and military authorization for crossing checkpoints, Prlic would give the answers to Benabou. Benabou brought up to Prlic the issue of HVO shelling and sniping in Mostar, including shelling and sniping against himself. Prlic would be aware of the matter and smile. This was just part of the routine for the HVO. Several times this item was the topic of discussions, including with Petkovic and Stojic. The shelling and sniping attacks on civilians were a permanent issue on Benabou's agenda. Prlic even joked about the HVO missing its targets, which implied his regret that I was still alive.

During the summer of 1993, I was trying to force the Croatian leaders to allow convoys, and negotiations were going on for a while. On 21 August 1993, Mate Granic announced, in Medjugorje, that the Croats would allow the crossing to East Mostar of humanitarian aid convoys. Benabou asked Granic to instruct Prlic and Boban on the matter. He confirmed having done so. Anyhow, Prlic and Boban blocked these convoys. Benabou learned from the entourage of Granic that he was pressuring them to allow these convoys, but no change occurred on the ground. Prlic and Stojic held the actual power of decision making in the field. In a meeting in Sarajevo, on 14 December 1993, with Silajdzic, the prime minister of Bosnia-Herzegovina, Benabou claimed that a political vacuum had developed in Mostar. He said the timing was appropriate for change and for introducing a new process, since the HVO realized that it was useless to pursue further military action. He also saw that chaos had developed in West Mostar and that there was terror in the streets. Prlic, as head of the new government, had changed his priorities and was now trying to restore law and order. Since Prlic was the one setting the priorities, he was also the one who would change the priorities. Prlic could have changed these priorities much earlier if he had wanted to do so. At a certain point, Prlic started to realize that the Croats had gone too far. Prlic understood that he was an actor in transforming East Mostar into a concentration camp. The HVO leaders realized that they were going to get into trouble for the criminal acts that were being perpetrated under their eyes, and they were trying to reverse the situation. Boban was located in Grude. Prlic was in Mostar, and he had much more control over the city than Boban. Silajdzic informed Benabou that he was aware of the HVO policy to remove the Muslims from Stolac and Lubushki. He raised the issue with Boban, and the latter did not deny that this cleansing was a part of the HVO policy. Silajdzic said he brought this up with Tudjman, who told Silajdzic that he respected Boban with regard to the idea of Greater Croatia.

Bruno Stojic—Benabou held many meetings with Bruno Stojic on many occasions. He was manipulating both Boban and Prlic. Pogarcic informed Benabou on several occasions during June and July 1993 that Stojic was pushing to complete the expulsion of Muslims from all of Mostar. In June 1993, Stojic had in fact promised Boban that the HVO would finish the job within a matter of weeks. Stojic concentrated his efforts on military action in order to deliver to Boban and Prlic what they wanted, and this was Mostar on its knees. Stojic was effectively the minister of defense, who was permanently surrounded by military brass. He had a good grasp of military affairs and of people in the field. He was the bridge between Petkovic, the military representatives from Zagreb, and the military actors in the field. Petkovic might have been a great general in the Yugoslav National Army, but that did not translate immediately into weight within the HVO in the field. Stojic possessed that weight being part of the triumvirate, which included Prlic and Boban. Stojic was not acting as a subordinate of Prlic or Boban; he was acting as one of the team, initiating and proving that he would do what he was committed to do. Benabou recalled a meeting in a cafe in Medjugorje when Stojic told him that like all other UNPROFOR staff, he (Benabou) had become undesirable. Benabou insisted to get inside East Mostar and made it clear that he was not going to renounce. It seemed that Stojic positioned himself as a bridge between Zagreb and the HVO. However, the moment Zagreb decided to control more the activities in the area and diminish Boban and Prlic's power, Stojic attempted to replace those two actors.

The HVO would open and shut down the city of Mostar at will. Stojic demanded restrictions of UNPROFOR movements in the field. He succeeded to obtain support from Prlic and Boban. Stojic specified clearly that he was closing the access to Mostar. Stojic was cold-blooded and obstinate in his decision to oust the Muslims from Mostar. On one occasion during the summer of 1993, two buses of Muslim refugees expelled by the HVO stopped by the base in Medjugorje. Stojic described them as "nothing, bandits,[353]" being taken out of the war zone. Prlic also was informed about this incident. His purpose in war was only to kill and eliminate people. I often explained to Prlic that the HVO's activities in Mostar were disastrously affecting also Croatian civilians, including children, but Stojic had no room for such scruples. From listening to discussions with HVO who came to SPABAT at night and brag about their activities, one could learn that Stojic ordered the eviction of people from their homes and the burning of their houses. All those were members of HVO, who were accorded free access to SPABAT's base in Medjugorje.

Milivoj Petkovic—Petkovic was a Yugoslavian National Army officer who appeared to be an outsider among the HVO. It seemed that Petkovic acted with arrogance, considering that the HVO's operation in Mostar was a dirty, little job that did not correspond to his perception of his stature as a general. Although he had problems dealing with restriction of movement of civilians in East Mostar, he was ordering the closure and imposition of siege on the city. Petkovic was probably instructed by Zagreb to accomplish the HVO's goal, and when Benabou talked to Petkovic, he couldn't help associating him with the ruthless civilian leaders. Zagreb's main goals were to dismantle Bosnia-Herzegovina and to

---

[353] Source: Doc. 011 concerning: assistance and protection to refugees in Medugorje. Dated 21 June 1993.

establish Herzegovina as part of Croatia. People like Petkovic, Stojic, Prlic, and Boban were the actors in the field. Benabou met several times with Petkovic at the HVO headquarters in West Mostar, close to the Boulevard. In some of the visits, the HVO personnel there would often inform him that Petkovic was in the battlefield. Petkovic's involvement in the theater of operation was concrete and not theoretical. The HVO soldiers were given and drank large amounts of alcohol before they participated in unclean actions, which was often.

Berislav Pusic—Berislav Pusic had no heart, no compassion; he was a macho man and brutal, a guy from the rudest "street level." Pusic was a regular visitor at the HVO headquarters in West Mostar and held power in the streets of the city. He was the handy man of the main three actors, Boban, Prlic, and Stojic, who would follow instructions and collect his benefits on the way. Benabou held meetings in the office of Pusic in West Mostar. He was in charge of exchanges of prisoners and dead bodies and evacuations of wounded, sick, and displaced people. Pusic was also involved in the recruitment of people into the HVO army. The meetings with Pusic were always on a much defined agenda. Pusic was reporting to the main leaders, Boban, Prlic, and others. He had lots of influence on the street in Mostar, Grude, and Citluk with the mob. The report[354] dated 2 October 1993 referred to an agreement on the protection of the civil population in Mostar and other areas. This was one of many attempts to protect civilians. Pusic was mandated and signed this agreement. It was part of his function, since he had the

---

[354] Tribunal document, ERN R015-4052-R015-4055. This document (070) is a memorandum concerning a cease-fire and the protection of the civil population in Mostar and other areas. It was signed by Berislav Pusic for the HVO And Alija Alikadic for the BiH Armija and Witnessed by the Col. Luis Carvajal for SPABAT, Albert Benabou for Civil Affairs (who negotiated the agreement) and Jerrie Hulme for UNHCR.

responsibility to protect the civil population and refrain from acting against them. Part of the agreement referred to steps to be taken, including the cessation of wanton and random shelling and sniping. This included the shelling of hospitals and clinics. This agreement also included references to the articles of the Geneva Convention. The agreement was not implemented. In terms of evacuating wounded and sick persons, Pusic's reaction would be that he didn't want to agree to evacuate wounded Muslim from East Mostar, since he knew that wounded and sick persons were a burden on the besieged Muslims and therefore made their hardship worse. Although this might not have been said outright, it was clear by the actions of Pusic and the others and by their refusal to agree to evacuations or to using UN helicopters to evacuate these unfortunate people.

Franjo Tudjman—The meeting with Tudjman took place in his office in Zagreb at the end of December 1993. Pogarcic organized the meeting in the context of Benabou trying to promote the initiative for an interim arrangement in Mostar. Tudjman did not want to deal with Mostar and was more interested in communicating with Israel via his visitor.

Mostar—The city was permanently under fire and on fire. At night it glowed, especially its buildings in flames along the Boulevard. There were no Muslims in West Mostar any longer, because there was already a separation between the two parts of the city based on ethnicity, and West Mostar had already been cleansed. On one instance, against the UN rules of nonintervention, Benabou collected off the streets of East Mostar wounded people and transported them in the UN vehicle to the clinic. Upon his return to SPABAT, he was warned not to interfere any more in the war zone. The UN convoys were subject to the HVO shelling, which was tracking movements of vehicles in the field.

Joint Commission—The agreement[355] dated 12 May 1993, cosigned by Petkovic and Hallilovic, was the end result of the negotiations conducted by Benabou. This agreement was crucial for improving the situation of the civilian population on both parts of the city. The agreement, expanded by elements introduced by General Philippe Morillon, turned out to be too ambitious since it covered too many issues, such as freedom of movement, joint police patrols, and more. It did not work out. This agreement never had a chance to succeed. It was not implemented because the Croatian leaders were convinced they would succeed taking over Mostar militarily and expelling its Muslim population. Reports[356] dated 6 June 1993 regarding negotiations on the joint police patrols covered the negotiations conducted on 2 June 1993 and 4 June 1993, dealing mainly with the organization of joint police patrols. During the negotiations, talks were held with the participation of police authorities from West Mostar, UNCIVPOL, the Muslim police, as well as military personnel from both sides. As indicated in the report, the agreement was ratified on the 2 June 1993 by Boban, Petkovic, and Stojic. They had to ratify the agreement because they were the decision makers, the competent authorities to allow such actions. This agreement was never implemented. Joint patrols were to include both Croatian and Muslim police under the monitoring of UNCIVPOL. The agreement did not work because Boban and Prlic did not mean to implement it. They did not want an international presence in Mostar, for they could not allow UNCIVPOL to monitor what was going on in Mostar, namely arbitrary arrests and wanton rapes and murders.

---

[355] Tribunal document ERN R000-5042-R000-5045. This agreement concerning the demilitarization of Bosnia and Herzegovina was negotiated by Albert Benabou and concluded on the 12 May 1993 between General Milivoj Petkovic (HVO) and General Sefer Hallilovic (BiH Armija) in the presence of Lt. General Philippe Morillon.

[356] Tribunal documents with numbers R015-3911-R015-3913 and ZA01-8547-ZA01-8550.

Meetings with the HVO Leadership in Divulje, Medjugorje, etc.—On 4 June, Benabou attended a meeting in Divulje. This meeting lasted about ten hours[357] and was referred to above. Boban's party included Prlic, Mile Akmadzic, Petkovic, Pogarcic, and Stojic, but it was Boban and Prlic who led the discussions. They both held the view that Bosnia-Herzegovina was to be divided between the Serbs and the Croats, leaving almost no space for the Muslims. They believed Europe should bless their actions, and they were surprised that Europe did not identify with their views. Boban felt that Owen and Stoltenberg, just like UNPROFOR and the United Nations, were to be put aside and not disturb their plans too much. During the second part of the meeting, the issue of ethnic cleansing of the area in and around Mostar was brought up. By this time West Mostar had already been cleansed of all Muslims, but there were pockets outside of this area where there were still Muslims holding out. Everyone was at that meeting and heard the Croats' reaction that they were the victims, actually denying what was actually happening on the ground. Sometimes the information on ethnic cleansing was passed to the United States ambassador to Croatia, with Benabou raising on the same occasions the issue of the detention of civilians. Nobody could access the Croatian detention center at the heliport. No UNPROFOR elements could see the detainees. But the best weapon against these Croatian machinations was to inform the press. The Croats claimed that the HVO was detaining nobody and that if we had proof to the contrary we should show it. In fact, Prlic, Stojic, Petkovic, and Boban thought that the

---

[357] Tribunal documents numbers R015-3911-R015-3913 and ZA01-8547-ZA01-8550, covering reports on meetings which took place on Friday 4 June 1993 on the Adriatic Coast in Divulje (BRITFOR base) with the Croat Leadership among them Boban, Prlic, Stojic and the Cochairmen of the Geneva Conference (Owen & Stoltenberg) and the UNPROFOR Commander Lars-Erik Wallgren.

United Nations should never have been involved in Bosnia-Herzegovina.

During a break in the talks, in the promenade around Divulje described above, Boban said to Benabou that, in his opinion, the war in that part of Yugoslavia—referring to Mostar and other areas of Bosnia and Herzegovina—should have started earlier in the process of the dismantling of Yugoslavia. He believed this would be a long-term confrontation, and he was ready to pursue it. Boban explained that from his point of view, Bosnia-Herzegovina should no longer exist. The Muslims would be "finished" and expelled out of Mostar, even though this contradicted the Croatian official position of peaceful acceptance of all ethnic groups. Later on, in his office, he showed Benabou a map of Mostar and clarified that the city and its surroundings would be cleansed of Muslims. Another meeting[358] was held in Medjugorje on 10 June 1993. General Morillon attended the meeting. Boban, Prlic, and Granic attended. Boban expressed the view that there were three constituent people in Bosnia-Herzegovina and that they simply could not live together. This was the view expressed by of all of them. Boban stated that the truth was that they were involved in a war over territory and borders. The intention was to cleanse the territory, to "have a clean border and clean territory.[359]" During this meeting Boban also requested the assistance of the international community to evacuate Croats from areas in Bosnia and Herzegovina where they were threatened, especially from Sarajevo and Tuzla, insisting that they were victims. Boban stated that the HVO was ready to receive them and protect them.

---

[358] Tribunal document number ZA01-8539-ZA01-8539 More citation information is needed.

[359] See DOC. 012 dated 22 June 1993, covering the issues brought up in a two hours meeting with Boban concerning his position on the Geneva's Agenda. The report was distributed by Albert Benabou to UN headquarters in Zagreb and Kiseljak.

The report[360] of 21 June 1993 covered a meeting with Boban and Vladislav Pogarcic. Boban clearly stated that he would never allow a Muslim state to be created in Bosnia-Herzegovina and that Izetbegovic was his enemy. In the meeting, Boban also reported about meetings that he had had with Karadzic. He did not say when these meetings occurred or where. Boban was always interested in concluding a deal with the Serbs in Bosnia-Herzegovina. Serbs and Croats were friendly in Herzegovina; they had a common enemy—the Muslims. Boban also restated that one condition to achieve peace was to establish a loose confederation in which the three ethnic groups were completely separate from one another in a defined territory. This was his vision. Boban was eager to see a wide recognition of his positions in order to facilitate the dismantling of the country. In another report,[361] Benabou also mentioned that Boban had to show success in the political and military fields, because question marks were arising in public about what benefit the Croats had gained from the war. Boban was showering the Croats with promises but not delivering. He needed to receive more help from outside Mostar in order to deliver on his fantasies, but the Croatian population was getting tired of the sacrifices and of the terrible image of themselves that the pursuit of the war effort was creating in the world.

The letter[362] from Boban dated 22 June 1993 and transited by Benabou to General Morillon was brought up in the interrogation that Benabou was undergoing in The Hague. Boban was trying to divert attention from his unsuccessful actions in Mostar by requesting assistance in moving the Croatian population from other parts of Bosnia to Herzegovina. Boban

---

[360] Tribunal document ERN number R015-3917-R015-3920.
[361] Tribunal document R015-3920-R015-3920. At this stage, Stojic did not stand by his commitment to "deliver Mostar cleaned of Muslims."
[362] Tribunal document number R012-2358-R012-2359.

referred to an agreement from 10 June 1993 in Medjugorje, but no agreement was ever made by Morillon to move some fifty thousand Croats from the areas where they were trapped. Maybe it was discussed between them in privacy, and Boban interpreted that talk the way he did. The report[363] dated 24 June 1993 covered a meeting from 23 June 1993 with Vladislav Pogarcic, described above in detail. Benabou was accompanied by Captain Pita and Captain Molina from SPABAT. The most important part of the report was about the failure to deliver humanitarian aid. Concerning Pogarcic, the real issue was the animosity existing among the three sides. In this report, Benabou referred also to elements mentioned in the letter that Boban wrote to Morillon, which was cited by Pogarcic, i.e., if UNPROFOR didn't cooperate in moving the Croatian population, a catastrophic situation would develop, for which the Croats would wash their hands clean of any responsibility. Boban insisted on those declarations, because the Croats were then desperate, with Stojic promising victory in Mostar to the Croats by June but unable to deliver. Boban claimed that even the UNPROFOR personnel in Medjugorje had to be "purified from unclean people in the area.[364]" Benabou asked with a smile if it included the Jew who he was. Prlic simply indicated that it was Stojic who was working out the plan to "cleanse" Mostar.

During the encounter of 23 June 1993, Pogarcic brought up again the issue of the "large movement of populations." He was articulating the idea expressed by Boban, Prlic, and Stojic that they were ready to absorb the Croatian population from other areas of Bosnia-Herzegovina into a Croatian entity, and that Muslim leaders should do the same by taking

---

[363] Tribunal document R015-3921-R015-3924.
[364] Source: recorded on the personal memoirs of the war of Albert Benabou on 23 July 1993 following a private meeting with Mate Boban in presence of Clado Pogarcic.

Muslims into a Muslim entity. The Croats did not really expect the UNPROFOR cooperation in that operation, for they were trying to divert attention from their failures in Mostar. To these men, it was clear that Mostar had to be Croat, to be attained by relocation of the population, though in that meeting they were asking for assistance of the international community to move this population. Benabou reminisced that he was present in the Croatian Grude headquarters when they were formulating the plan to end the presence of Muslims in Mostar. This was about two weeks after the convoy of 14 May 1993 went through. The meeting[365] in Stolac was an attempt to strengthen relations on the local level between Serbs and Croats, though it was not agreed by Zagreb. Granic later told Benabou that Boban had been doing too many things on his own, for that meeting fit his concept of splitting Bosnia between the Serbs and Croats without including the Muslims. The meeting was organized by the UNMOs and took place in a tent. Benabou traveled to the meeting location in Stolac from Medjugorje. Both sides explained that they had ongoing wire communications with each other. Petkovic represented the HVO, and General Grubac and Col. Milosevic represented the Serbian side. Both sides declared they did not need to work out a ceasefire between them, for there was no need, both the Croats and the Serbs being dedicated at point to pound the Muslims in concert.

This report,[366] dated 18 July 1993, covered Benabou's communication with the BiH Army and a meeting he held with Bruno Stojic on 17 July 1993, where Benabou was accompanied by Major Carlos De Salas. In addition to his interpreter, another SPABAT interpreter was present. One of

---

[365] Tribunal document R015-3925-R015-3926. The meeting took place on 26 June and was a clear manifestation of the discreet ongoing contacts between Croats and Serbs at the Military level in Bosnia with the blessing of Boban.
[366] Tribunal document number R014-1248-R014-1252.

the issues in this meeting with Stojic was the milk convoy discussed above. Stojic was urged to back the project and to facilitate for Petkovic its implementation. Benabou initiated the meeting, since SPABAT did not obtain clearance from Petkovic. When things didn't move, Pogarcic recommended addressing Stojic, who was holding greater power of decision making. Stojic required so many conditions on the convoy that it never proceeded, as explained above. On 17 July 1993, Stojic suggested that UNPROFOR evacuate the children from Mostar. Then he proposed to evacuate the entire Muslim civilian population from the Mostar area. Stojic explained that he needed it to be done within twenty days, the needed time to finish the fighting in Mostar. At this time, Stojic was still convinced that HVO could deliver a military victory in Mostar. Stojic's statement reinforced what Pogarcic had quoted from Stojic, "It may take twenty more days, but at the end it will be either us or them,[367]" a pattern of speech ominously and repeatedly heard in the context of the Arab-Israeli dispute.

In the report[368] dated 13 July 1993, Benabou described the meeting in Grude with Prlic, Pogarcic, and de Salas from SPABAT. It was important for UNPROFOR to maintain a presence at the Mostar airport. Prlic accepted the idea and said it would take about three or four weeks. Prlic had the authority to make this decision. Benabou had prepared the working papers for the meeting. Humanitarian issues were also discussed. Prlic mentioned the agreement achieved on 10 July in Makarska regarding freedom of movement and humanitarian matters. Prlic, along with Boban, Stojic, and Petkovic, had the authority to allow humanitarian convoys,

---

[367] DOC. 024, dated 18 July 1993, report concerning meeting with Bruno Stojic, Minister Croatian Community Herzeg-Bosnia (chapter two) distributed by Albert Benabou to UN Headquarters.
[368] Tribunal document number R015-3933-R015-3935.

but to no avail, since during that time the fighting was continuing in Mostar, and access was denied. Benabou visited with the UNMOs, though, to verify the reports on expulsions of populations.

On 8 August 1993, Benabou reported[369] on the meeting in Makarska. Part of that document was a list of the twenty participants in the meeting and the titles they used to describe themselves. Half of the Croatian delegation at this meeting arrived from Zagreb. Benabou was monitoring the meeting, and he mentioned to Prlic and Granic[370] (Point A1) that while they were both claiming that humanitarian aid "was not being used as a weapon of war," they expressed their fears lest that humanitarian aid destined for East Mostar ended up being used by the BiH Army, again a little bit of a reminder of the Israeli siege around Gaza where cement could not go through due to its use by the Hamas to build bunkers, not houses. But Benabou insisted that the humanitarian assistance was distributed to the civilians and was delivered and consumed by civilians, and he warned that the denial of humanitarian aid, via the erection of insurmountable conditions, was used by the Croats as a weapon. He emphasized that the Croatian leaders withheld aid to East Mostar in order to weaken the people and force them to leave the city, for starving the people was an important leverage to remove them. The Croatian and HVO leaders were not always explicit; however, they always insinuated that if the Muslims didn't abide by the rules set by the HVO, the Muslims would not get any humanitarian aid or medical assistance. In fact, in Point A2,[371] Benabou mentioned that Prlic

---

[369] Tribunal document R015-3945-R015-3948.
[370] Tribunal document R015-3945-R015-3948. In this meeting in Makarska, Zagreb was taking more control over Boban and Prlic who were starting to operate too independently in the war zone.
[371] Tribunal document R015-3945-R015-3948.

*Savagery in the Heart of Europe*

and Granic repeatedly said that convoys would be given freedom of movement subject to "routine Croatian checkpoints," which meant that the aid would not get through, because the convoys would be stopped at these checkpoints. Thus, the 12 August convoy mentioned in this report did not take place.

On August 10 1993, a meeting took place in Siroki Brijeg to set the modus operandi for humanitarian relief convoys. The military was supposed to deal with this issue, therefore, the meeting included the HVO and UNPROFOR, and the results were relayed to the BiH Army. Pusic attended the meeting and was in charge of addressing the gathering about the "exchange of people." Pusic spoke vehemently about "criminal Muslims" who were killing Croats. Granic declared that the Croats would respect international rules, but Prlic and Granic were the main actors in this meeting. On 6 September 1993, Benabou described[372] the celebratory dinner that evening in the dining room of SPABAT. Morales, Prlic, Stojic, Pusic, and the Spanish commander from Kiseljak were there. No one from the BiH Army attended. During the meeting, Benabou explained to Stojic his commitment to his mandate and made clear that he intended to accomplish it. A few weeks after this meeting, Prlic started to realize he was losing ground since Zagreb was turning its back on him.

Exchanges of Prisoners—There were three subjects in the negotiations on exchanges of prisoners among the parties: medical evacuations, exchanges of dead bodies, and exchanges of people. The negotiations were not always tit for tat, i.e., prisoner for prisoner or dead body for dead body, for it happened that ten detainees were exchanged for ten dead bodies. The ICRC did not participate in these exchanges because

---

[372] Tribunal document number R015-3992-R015-3993. Benabou noted also in his personal memoirs of the war that the situation was embarrassing: discussing about starvation of people around a table of abundance offered by the UN.

they were not done in compliance with ICRC procedures. However, people were suffering, so something had to be done. Never could the full operation of ICRC be assured, and Benabou realized why the ICRC insisted that the exchanges follow a set procedure, because at one point the exchanges stopped when the Croats refused to cooperate with the agreed procedures. The lists of persons to be exchanged were made based upon pressure applied by the families of persons who were detained or wounded or dead. In all cases, Pusic was the one deciding the listing. Both sides presented lists of prisoners and others to be exchanged. The Muslims wanted to release most of their Croatian detainees, because they didn't have the means to maintain them. Therefore, when the lists were presented, the Muslims required a total exchange, that is all of the inventory of evacuated or exchanged in one stroke. But in fact, they received only what Pusic would agree to, putting Pusic in a position of the sole decision maker in this sensitive humanitarian problem. He was responsible for introducing or deleting names onto the HVO's lists and was not very forthcoming or flexible. Benabou recalled discussing with him whom should be taken, and especially demanding the evacuation of the wounded, since the medical facilities in East Mostar were unbearable, and wounded civilians were piled up in the corridors of the clinic.

A letter[373] dealing with the evacuation of the wounded was addressed by Benabou to the HVO leaders Bruno Stojic, Zarko Tole, and Ivan Bagaric following talks with the participation of two ambassadors, including the ambassador of Germany, to put pressure on the recalcitrant parties. The HVO side was represented by Maric and Raguz, under the leadership of Pusic. People were coming in and leaving during the meeting, which lasted for more than seven hours.

---

[373] Tribunal document 0103-1856-0103-185.

Benabou dispatched, on the twenty-fifth of November 1993, a message[374] referring to the resumption of exchanges of prisoners. The BiH Army requested the intervention of Prlic and Silajdzic, Boban being already practically out. Silajdzic preferred to talk with Prlic. On the same day, Benabou required[375] Prlic's participation at the negotiations. He was tired of Pusic's games and looking for someone with more authority. On November 30, 1993, after twenty-four hours of negotiations, an agreement[376] for exchange was concluded as well as a modus operandi for the operation. Prlic, Jukic, Pogarcic, Pusic, Martin Raguz (head of the Office of Displaced Persons and Refugees), as well as Sergio Mello (from the headquarters in New York) were present. Right away, Benabou realized that once again there would be politics involved. The Croats did not prepare themselves for the technical aspect of the meeting. They were looking for good publicity and no more. This was a meeting of no real value, as far as getting any concrete outcome. Both sides understood that Prlic and Silajdzic were the decision makers in this meeting. In his opening statement, Prlic confirmed that he was the decision maker, but he stressed that he did not come to agree on any procedures. While he recognized that the HVO was holding detainees, he declared that his intention was to close the detention camps and that it was not because of international pressure, although all attending knew that a constant international pressure was building up. When Benabou asked him how he was going to do that, Prlic answered that the minister of defense was going to implement it. Then Jukic announced that the HVO would do it, and it would be according to international law. Prlic was aware of the existence of the camps long before this meeting and

---

[374] Tribunal document number R015-4178-R015-4179.
[375] Tribunal document number ET0151-7075-0151-7075.
[376] Tribunal document number R013-7703-R013-7705.

could have closed them, because Benabou himself had repeatedly raised the question of the detention camps to Prlic on several occasions before.

Negotiations[377] for the release of the impounded UN helicopters by the HVO in Medjugorje took place on 31 October, 1993. Pogarcic had dispatched a letter[378] on this matter to General Ramsay, emphasizing that the detention of the helicopters should not be linked to the conditions on the release of prisoners, though they were linked to the evacuation of patients from the Nova Bila hospital. In fact, there were two or three operations of evacuation from Nova Bila. However, the BiH Army proclaimed that it would not release prisoners without the release of the helicopters first. As mentioned in the 31 October, 1993 report, at one point the process of exchanges of prisoners was stalled by the BiH Army, Pasalic, and Alikadic. The reason was that they held prisoners and wanted humanitarian aid and evacuation of their wounded in exchange. Because they didn't receive this aid, the BiH Army stalled the talks. Both sides were playing this kind of stalling game. Benabou also noted in his diary, on 31 October 1993, that the ICRC wanted to interview prisoners to assess where they wanted to go upon their release from HVO detention centers. This process was not respected, and the ICRC was not able to hold the interviews. Pusic rejected this procedure, while the Muslims agreed. Pusic said they didn't need the ICRC. They were superfluous in their mind, so the Croatian team managed to get the ICRC out of the game. The involvement of the ICRC implied the obligation to respect the Geneva Convention and rules regarding prisoners and civilians, something the Croatian leadership could not envisage. Benabou could not know how the release could be realized and where the people would go once they were

---

[377] Tribunal document number R015-4089-R015-4099.
[378] Tribunal document number R015-4122-R015-4124.

*Savagery in the Heart of Europe*

freed. He understood at a certain point that third countries had offered to accept refugees; however no international credible organization was involved in that process. That is the way things were guided from Zagreb. A wounded young girl from East Mostar, amputee of legs and hands, for example, was sent to Los Angeles, where an organization offered to take care of her. But currently, UNPROFOR did not have access to detainees; no UN organization was allowed to visit the camps. The BRITFOR did a reconnaissance tour in the area to find out where the detainees were held, but without success.

On 20 September 1993, a meeting[379] concerning the exchange of prisoners took place in Dretelj. Prlic, Pogarcic, and Pusic were present in this meeting. Mate Granic indicated that they wanted to close Dretelj. He also said that he wanted international attention to be focused not only upon the Croatian side's detention centers (whose very existence had been denied by Boban and his ilk) but upon the Croats who were held by the Muslims in Bugojno and Konjic. Granic wanted to stress the great gesture the Croats were making by releasing prisoners. During the meeting, Prlic asked the ICRC if they had been denied access to the detention camps. The ICRC responded that they did not have the list of the other camps, so they could not say whether they had been denied or not. The existence of other camps was mentioned. Prlic ignored it deliberately and didn't respond. Later in Medjugorje, Fatima Leho presented a list of the people detained in detention centers. In the report,[380] dated November 3, 1993, Benabou referred to Pusic as head of the Commission for the Exchange of POWs. The exchanges started in August but were stopped. The Croatian leaders—Boban, Prlic, and Stojic—took the decision to stop the

---

[379] Tribunal document R015-4026-R015-4028.
[380] Tribunal document number R015-4110-R015-4111.

exchanges because they had obtained their share with the first exchanges, and they decided to pursue the war instead.

As regards the UNPROFOR a letter[381] signed by Cedric Thornberry and addressed to Prlic, was composed by Benabou, suggesting the opening of an UNPROFOR office in Mostar. It was addressed to Prlic because he had more to say than Boban in that matter. The issue was discussed with Prlic and Vrljic. Openly, Prlic was positive, but though an appropriate building was identified and agreed upon, the project was never realized. On 2 October 1993, Prlic responded to the letter addressed by Thornberry signing[382] it as "president." He absurdly argued that establishing an office in Mostar at this time would interfere with a former agreement reached between the HVO and BiH Army. On the eighth of November 1993, Benabou reported[383] on a discussion with Kresimir Zubak (a new figure replacing Boban) regarding the civil affairs office in Mostar. He expressed his primary concern for the safety of the office's staff. Zubak said he would raise this issue with Prlic, the decision maker on the matter. On the twenty-fourth of November 1993, Benabou reported[384] again about a meeting with Pogarcic to deal with humanitarian affairs, but the issue of the civil affairs office in West Mostar was also raised. Prlic did not participate. Pogarcic agreed that an office would strengthen relations with UNPROFOR and the international organizations. Prisoner exchange was also discussed. Pogarcic announced to Benabou that the HVO would receive guidelines for the resumption of the humanitarian program.

The August convoy to East Mostar—In August, Benabou called UNPROFOR's spokesperson, Shannon Boyd, and

---

[381] Tribunal document number R015-4035-R015-4035.
[382] Tribunal document number R012-3571-R012-3574.
[383] Tribunal document number R015-4133-R015-4134.
[384] Tribunal document number R015-4173-R015-4174.

asked her to convince Thornberry to accompany a convoy to the area of Mostar. Andreev, Thornberry, and Benabou met in the town of Trogir and discussed this project. Thornberry agreed to go to Medjugorje and participate in meetings with Boban, Prlic, Petkovic, and Stojic. This was toward the end of August. A UNHCR convoy was already prepared to go on. The HVO imposed terms and conditions for the convoy passing to East Mostar. They demanded a visit to West Mostar and to the Nova Bila hospital. Those visits involved a large delegation, including mainly the press. The Croats were eager for international positive media coverage. Another condition was a medical evacuation, an exchange of prisoners, and especially, an exchange of bodies which were rotting and stinking on the frontline between the parties. Once we had gone to Nova Bila, we returned to Medjugorje. Benabou insisted on entering East Mostar and restarted negotiating from ground zero with the Croats and the Muslims. A few days later, the convoy left Medjugorje for East Mostar. The convoy was stopped until the exchange of bodies was completed. This took place in the area of the Mostar airport. The stay over in East Mostar lasted for five days. International representatives, the media, UNPROFOR civil affair officers, and SPABAT were kept as hostages. The way out of town was blocked by civilians in the street. Benabou met with Colonel Budakovic to negotiate the release. Journalists from CNN and the BBC were present, and the people of Mostar wanted the world to see their misery. While the international organizations were caught in East Mostar, the Croats did not stop their strong shelling of the city. The release was obtained by stages. One group was freed, then another. Thanks to this convoy, the issue of Mostar was raised in the United Nations Security Council. After the convoy, SPABAT agreed to maintain a presence in Mostar, however, for only a short period of time. After the release of the convoy, several meetings took place with the HVO and BiH Army for further exchanges and medical evacuations. The discussions were promising and were in good spirit. Nothing was implemented. On 1 September 1993, a meeting[385] was initiated in Sarajevo with General Delic and General Petkovic. The encounter was chaired by Lt. Gen. Briquemont of UNPROFOR. This meeting was called to set out the process for the entry of convoys. It did not produce anything in the field. Pogarcic repeated to Benabou that Petkovic and Stojic were in bad shape politically. They did not succeed to deliver what they pledged, the taking over of Mostar.

On 26 February 1994, Benabou wrote to Special Representative of the Secretary General Yasushi Akashi to cancel his plans to visit Mostar, since negotiations were underway in Washington between the Croats and Muslims. Zagreb was setting the rhythm for everything happening in Mostar. There was no sense for that visit, particularly due to the intensity of battles in the field—reaching as much as possible terrain before the conclusion of the negotiations under the US umbrella. Mate Granic was constantly informed about the events. No one could pretend that Zagreb was not aware of what was going on. Tudjman wanted to lower the profiles, the activities, for a constructive interaction in Washington. Benabou wrote that there was a struggle of power between Zagreb and Herzegovina. The people in the battlefield wanted to push for more military action. It was noted that Albert Benabou acted as an honest broker, honoring all of the parties in conflict: Croats, Muslims, and Serbs. His reports served to clarify the precise intentions of the parties, in order to alert the responsible authorities of UNPROFOR in Zagreb and in New York. In order to maintain the same spirit, Benabou concluded his deposition with the citation from Deuteronomy, "Justice, justice thou shall pursue,[386]"

---

[385] Tribunal document number R015-3980-R015-3985.
[386] Deuteronomy , Chapter XVI, Verse 20.

though he was aware that, like beauty and wisdom, justice was in the eye of the beholder.

Thus, the longest trial ever before the International Criminal Tribunal for former Yugoslavia started on 26 April 2006. Those that were sitting on the dock indicted for crimes against humanity, based on hundreds of documents and testimonies scrupulously assembled during more than ten years were:

| Jadranko Prlic | Bruno Stojic | Slobodan Praljak | Milivoj Petkovic | Berislav Pusic | Valentin Coric |

Each one of them personally and all of them collectively were accused of willful killing; inhuman treatment (including sexual assault); unlawful deportation; transfer and confinement of civilians; extensive destruction of property; appropriation of property, not justified by military necessity and carried out unlawfully and wantonly, in a grave breach of the Geneva Conventions; cruel treatment; unlawful forced labor; wanton destruction of cities, towns or villages, or devastation not justified by military necessity; destruction or willful damage done to institutions dedicated to religion or education; plunder of public or private property; unlawful attack on civilians; unlawful infliction of terror on civilians by violating the laws or customs of war; persecutions on political, racial, or religious grounds; murder; rape; deportation; imprisonment; and inhumane acts which constituted crimes against humanity. They represented the highest ranked leadership in Herzeg-Bosnia responsible for the commitment of those acts, while inducing and instructing others to perpetrate crimes against humanity during the Croatian Muslim war in central Bosnia and in Herzegovina (in the municipalities of Prozor, Gornji Vakuf, Jablanica, Mostar, Lubushki, Stolac, Capljina, Vares, and their surroundings). The prosecution incriminated each one of them personally and all of them collectively for a joint criminal enterprise pursuant to their respective roles and authority as follows:

Jadranko Prlic—The highest political official in the Croatian wartime entity, Herzeg-Bosnia. He was a president of the Croatian community of Herzeg-Bosnia (HZ H-B[387]) and prime minister of the Croatian Republic of Herzeg-Bosnia (HR H-B).

Bruno Stojic—Head of the department of defense of the Croatian Defense Council (HVO[388]), and that body's top political and management official, since he was in charge of the Herzeg-Bosnia/HVO armed forces.

Slobodan Praljak—Major General in the army of the Republic of Croatia. In 1992, he became assistant minister of defense for the Republic of Croatia. From March 1992 to July 1993, he served simultaneously as a senior Croatian army officer, assistant minister of defense and senior representative of the Croatian Ministry of Defense to the Herzeg-Bosnia/HVO Croatian Defense Council, overseeing both government and armed forces, also known as "Brada."

Milivoj Petkovic—Military head of the Herzeg-Bosnia/HVO armed forces, with the title of chief of the HVO general staff. From late July 1993, he was the deputy overall commander of the Herzeg-Bosnia/HVO armed forces.

Berislav Pusic—Held a command position in the military police and was HVO liaison officer to UNPROFOR; head of the Service for the Exchange of Prisoners and Other Persons;

---

[387] Croatian Democratic Union of Bosnia and Herzegovina (HDZBiH) in the Croatian Republic of Herzeg-Bosnia (Croatian: Hrvatska Republika Herceg-Bosna).
[388] The Croatian Defence Council (Croatian: Hrvatsko vije_e obrane, HVO)

*Savagery in the Heart of Europe*

president of the commission in charge of all Herzeg-Bosnia/ HVO prisons and detention facilities holding prisoners of war and detainees; a member of the HVO Commission of Exchange of Prisoners, also known as "Berto" or "Berko."

Valentin Coric—Minister of Interior in the Croatian Republic of Herzeg-Bosnia. In April 1992, he was appointed to the position of deputy for security and commander of the HVO (Croatian Defense Council) military policy. His position was later titled chief of the military police administration.

The Indictment—In the Case Information Sheet[389] prepared by the International Criminal Tribunal for former Yugoslavia were listed examples of the main crimes committed by the indicted, together with other leaders and members of the Herzeg-Bosnia/HVO authorities and forces. They were accused of being engaged in:

Instigation and fomentation of political, ethnic, or religious strife, division, and hatred: Through use of speeches, propaganda, and false information, the Herzeg-Bosnia/HVO authorities created, instigated, and supported a charged anti-Muslim atmosphere, promoted ethnic division, and fostered religious mistrust.

Use of force, intimidation, and terror: Herzeg-Bosnia/ HVO authorities and military and police units used force and the threat of force to dominate, suppress, and persecute Bosnian Muslims. In the course of mass arrests and evictions, Bosnian Muslims were killed, severely injured, sexually assaulted, robbed of their property, and otherwise abused. Identity papers and similar documents were often

---

[389] (IT-04-74) PRLIC et al. Carla delPonte, Prosecutor of the International Criminal Tribunal for the former Yugoslavia, pursuant to her authority under Article 18 of the Statute of the International Tribunal for the former Yugoslavia (the "Tribunal Statute"), charged on 2 March 2004: Jadranko Prlic, Bruno Stojic, Slobodan Praljak, Milivoj Petkovic, Valentin Coric And Berislav Pusic with Crimes Against Humanity, Grave Breaches of the Geneva Conventions and Violations of the Laws or Customs of War.

taken from Muslims, placing them at various risks and limiting their freedom of movement. In attacks on Muslim towns, villages, and areas, and in the siege of East Mostar, there was regular and widespread shelling and sniping of Muslim civilians.

Appropriation and destruction of property: Herzeg-Bosnia/HVO authorities and soldiers forced Bosnian Muslims to abandon their homes or sign them over to the HVO. Money, cars, and personal property were often taken or looted. Muslim dwellings and other buildings, including public buildings and services, were appropriated, destroyed, or severely damaged, together with Muslim buildings, sites, and institutions dedicated to religion or education, including mosques. Much of this destruction was meant to ensure that Muslims could not, or would not, return to their homes and communities.

The Herzeg-Bosnia/HVO authorities appropriated public property belonging to the Republic of Bosnia-Herzegovina. Seized or abandoned Muslim apartments and homes were often given or assigned to HVO members or Croatian refugees.

Detention and Imprisonment: The accused and other members of the joint criminal conduct, together with various members of the Herzeg-Bosnia/HVO authorities and forces, established, supported, and operated a system of ill-treatment, involving a network of prisons, concentration camps, and other detention facilities (including, but not limited to the Heliodrom Camp, Lubushki Prison, Dretelj Prison, Gabela Prison, and Vojne Camp) to arrest, detain, and imprison thousands of Bosnian Muslims, including women, children, and the elderly. Many of the imprisoned and detained Muslims were kept in horrible conditions and deprived of basic human necessities, such as adequate food, water, and medical care. Many suffered inhumane treatment and physical and psychological abuse, including beatings and sexual assaults.

Forcible Transfer and Deportation: The accused and other members of the joint criminal enterprise, together with various members of the Herzeg-Bosnia/HVO authorities and forces, established, supported, and operated a system of ill-treatment to deport Bosnian Muslims to other countries or transfer them to parts of Bosnia and Herzegovina not claimed or controlled by Herzeg-Bosnia.

Many of the transferred or deported Muslims were first imprisoned and detained as described above and only "released" to be transferred or deported. Many persons so transferred or deported were forced to sign over their property to the HVO or to simply abandon their property and leave their belongings.

Forced Labor: Many Bosnian Muslims held by the HVO were forced to engage in physical labor, such as building military fortifications, digging trenches, carrying ammunition, and retrieving bodies, often in combat or dangerous conditions, which resulted in many Bosnian Muslim detainees being killed or severely wounded. Some were used as human shields or to draw fire from enemy positions in order to locate those positions. HVO units and soldiers used Muslim prisoners to plunder and loot Muslim homes and property.

In addition to the accused, the office of the prosecutor alleged that many other officials of Herzeg-Bosnia and the Republic of Croatia participated in the collective criminal acts, like former Croatian President Franjo Tudjman, his Defense Minister Gojko Susak, HV General Janko Bobetko, and the Herzeg-Bosnia President Mate Boban, who were all mentioned by name, but since they had died in the period between 1997 and 2003, they were dropped from the lists of the indicted. The indictment, meticulously prepared by attorney Kenneth Scott and his team, was signed by the Tribunal Prosecutor Carla Del Ponte. The court consisted of three sitting justices, with one of them presiding. They were:

Jean-Claude Antonetti from France, presiding: He had served as President de Chambre (presiding judge) at the Court of Appeals in Paris. He had also filled the position of legal counsel to French President Jacques Chirac (which did not add much to his reputation, when his boss was accused of violation of the law). Since September 2002, Antonetti has also been a member of the Consultative Commission of Human Rights.

Stefan Trechsel from Switzerland: Expert in criminal law and criminal procedure, he served for more than twenty years as a member of the European Commission on Human Rights, including as its president. He has specialized in legal and justice reforms in the former Soviet Union and the Russian Federation countries.

Arpad Prandler from Hungary: A PhD candidate in jurisprudence, he has been an honorary professor in the department of international relations at the University of Economics, Budapest. Among his publications are a monograph on the Security Council and several articles on issues related to United Nations activities, such as peace keeping, disarmament, and human rights.

Patrick Robinson from Jamaica served at the time as the overall president of the Tribunal, to contrast with Antonetti, who only chaired the Croatian case deliberations. He was first elected to the Tribunal in 1998 and has been reelected twice since. He is the recipient of the national award, Order of Jamaica, awarded by the government of Jamaica for services to international law, and honorary doctorate degrees from the University of the West Indies, Jamaica, and the Christian Theological Seminary in Indianapolis. He is the recipient of the award of honorary membership of the American Society of International Law for 2011.

On 11 January 2007, Romeu Ventura, an investigator with the office of the prosecutor at ICTY in The Hague, addressed an email to Albert Benabou, who was at the time serving in Paris as director for the Israeli National Tourism Office. Ventura reminded him of the telephone communication held on 24 October 2006, in which it was clarified that considering that Benabou could not be available for testimony at the court before the end of February 2007, other dates would be suggested. Based on that information, attorney Kenneth Scott, the prosecutor in charge of the Prlic case, was scheduling witnesses for February and March 2007, and he wanted Benabou's presence at the Tribunal at an agreed upon date between the end of February and the eighth of March 2007. The testimony was scheduled for six days: two for the preparation with lawyers and four full days at court, without counting the journey, but to no avail. Benabou could not obtain clearance from his office in Jerusalem to present his testimony until 2008, but the prosecutor who considered it vital to the court proceedings insisted on it. Scott paid a visit to Paris to convince Benabou to appear at the court, but when his permission from the Israeli government was not forthcoming, the Tribunal threatened to prepare a complaint from the UN secretary general to the state of Israel, on account of its lack of cooperation with the ICTY. On the same day, 22 May, Benabou sent a detailed response and also informed the legal advisor at the Ministry of Foreign Affairs in Jerusalem and his counterpart at the legal office at the Ministry of Tourism, who was in charge of the dossier. He mentioned that he served the UN peace keeping forces (as the first Israeli) in Mostar and its environs and stressed that all his original reports, which were formulated and distributed from the war zone, had been distributed to the headquarters of the United Nations in Kiseljak, Zagreb, and New York through the regular channels of area of operations: the Spanish Battalion (SPABAT), the Dutch Communication Center (DUTCHCOM), the British Armed Forces (BRITFOR), and the French units (Sarajevo). Those reports reflected events that unfolded in that area where the population was under siege and subjected to starvation and massacres.

Benabou explained that he had already been summoned to The Hague by the prosecutor's office, in September 1999, and was first interviewed by attorney Susan Somers, who started the preparation of the Prlic case. He was then informed that the documents in possession of the United Nations were erased from the system and had "disappeared." He informed the Tribunal that he had retained copies of these documents, and, in June 2004, he presented some of them in his interviews with the investigator, Susan Tucker, Judge Jose D'Aoust, and the analyst Charles Sudetic, and in conclusion, he had signed his deposition at the court. He thought that he could not contribute anything more to the case. He was incensed at the United Nations, which could not preserve its own archives, and at the same time they could not protect him from the threats to his life that he had received while risking his life in the course of fulfilling his UN duties. On 1 June 2007, the prosecutor in charge of the Prlic case, attorney Scott, wrote to Albert Benabou confirming that, based on his involvement in the war and the available documentation that he had shared with the court, his testimony remained of the utmost importance, and he urged him that in spite of his frustrations with his service at the United Nations he should stand as a key witness in the trial, in order to bring to the world "a little bit more justice" and especially "do justice to the many victims of the Balkan wars." He also dwelt on the issue of documentation, for which he needed Benabou's help:

> As to documentation, my team was able during the past years to assemble quite an extensive collection. We have a number of UN documents authored by you and your colleagues which we will be able to review with

you when you next come to The Hague. At the same time, if you have relevant documentation available to you, we will be happy to receive it. In this regard, we would like to firm up with you as soon as possible, because we must work to court schedules and deadlines, your testimony in The Hague. The judges in our case can have so much flexibility, and we must face in planning for the court to present very important evidence, like yours, to the judges. On behalf of the victims and international justice, we look forward to assisting you in giving your very important evidence in this case.[390]

As to protective measures, ICTY rules provide for a possible range of measures, from testifying using a pseudonym ("Witness R") as opposed to a real name, to having one's face protected from being broadcast outside the courtroom, to possibly testifying in closed session (meaning that nothing goes outside the courtroom). Of course, given the requirements of justice, the defendants themselves will always know the identities of the persons giving evidence in the case in which they are charged. None of these measures are given simply on request, but only when the person requesting them can give adequate justification for the measure requested. The required justifications are stricter given the greater degree of protective measures requested, so that, for example, testifying in closed session is very much the exception and only allowed on the basis of the most extensive justification. Further, the prosecution does not decide or control the granting of such measures, as this is something that only the judges can decide, based on the evidence/justification put before them.

---

[390] See Series of Email dated from January 2004 to February 2008 between Ken Scott leading the case against Prlic on behalf of the Prosecutor at The Hague and Albert Benabou, the main witness.

On 16 July 2007, the legal adviser of the Israeli Foreign Minister sent a message noting that after speaking with the Israeli ambassador in Croatia and Yugoslavia, and in The Hague, he learned from Belgrade and Zagreb that, in the past, there had been problems and threats against those who assisted the Tribunal, and in fact, there was a reported case of murder. (It was in 2000, of a man who had cooperated with the court and had not yet testified—and it is quite possible that he was murdered to prevent him from testifying). In all the cases mentioned, they only touched upon the citizens of the former Yugoslavia, and there were no problems with foreign witnesses. So, in view of the attitude of the governments of Serbia and Croatia, and the good level of their cooperation with the Tribunal, due to the two countries' efforts to move closer to Europe, and their current negotiations with the European Union, he thought that Benabou ran no risk of being attacked because of his testimony. The Israeli embassy's legal adviser in The Hague noted that the court provided protection to those who came to testify, and she advised sharing the information about risks with the security officer of the embassy, so as to ensure that the state of Israel facilitated the work of the Tribunal.

On 21 August 2007, Albert Benabou announced to his colleagues at the Ministry of Tourism and the Ministry of Foreign Affairs that in view of the debates within the Israeli bureaucracy on the advisability of his appearance at the court, he informed the Tribunal that he was cancelling his appearance that was scheduled for the first week of September 2007. He took this decision since he was told that his mission abroad would be scuttled for security reasons. Scott was annoyed by that decision and stated that he would use more "formal procedures," such as resorting to the UN secretary general's intervention and even to a court order if necessary. Attorney Kenneth Scott was determined to check everything that could be done to order Benabou's appearance before the court in the near future. He specified that he personally trusted the Israeli government, and he expressed his wish to obtain a written explanation of this unfortunate lack of cooperation with the court, while seeking positive and constructive suggestions for organizing the testimony. On the same day, following the insistence of the Ministry of Foreign Affairs, Benabou was finally instructed to appear before the court and testify. His appearance at the court was set during the week of 20 to 25 January, 2008, in closed session.

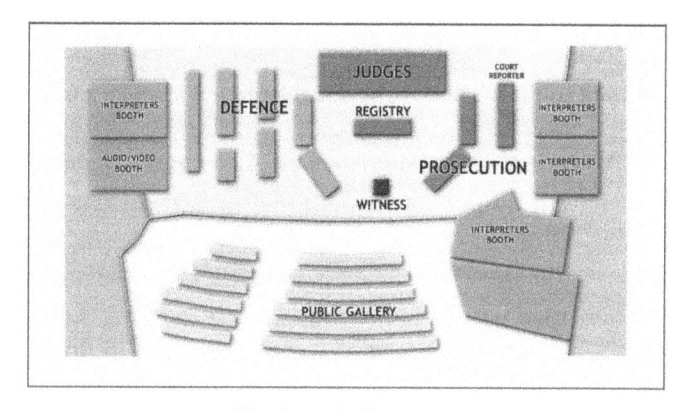

The Court in The Hague

Testimony in Court—Upon his arrival to The Hague, Benabou reviewed his testimony and the documented evidence with the assistance of the investigator and a team of lawyers from the Office of the Prosecution. He was also allowed to review examples of testimonies which preceded Benabou's in order to learn about the ambience and the precedents set by and at the court of a protected witness who had testified a week before. He described the conditions in the HVO prisoner camps in Vitina, in the village of Vrda, and in the Heliodrom. Prisoners were taken to do forced labor and were used as living shields, he said. He was shot in the foot because he didn't know who organized the escape of prisoners from Vrda. After several days of hearings in closed session, the trial of the six former Herzeg-Bosnia leaders was briefly opened to the public for the examination of a witness testifying under the pseudonym EI. A former member of the Territorial Defense, he spent the second half of 1993 in HVO prison camps in the hangar in Vitina, in the village of Vrda, and in the Heliodrom. The prosecutor read out a summary of the statement the witness had given to the Office of the Prosecutor. In it, the witness described the HVO attack on Novi Sehar on 26 June, 1993, his surrender three days later, and his transfer to Vitina, where he spent close to two months. In his words, there were about four hundred and fifty prisoners held in inhumane conditions in a hangar in Vitina. When the prisoners were taken to do forced labor, they were given hot meals. Those who remained in the camp received nothing but a quarter of a loaf of bread, the witness said. They drank rainwater and were allowed to wash once a week. According to the witness, the HVO troops took them to forced labor to the frontlines while threatening to kill them and abusing them verbally and physically. After two months in the Vitina hangar, the witness was taken to the village of Vrda. The prisoners there were used as human shields. During his captivity in Vrda, the witness was shot in the foot. The incident happened after the escape of ten prisoners. The remaining prisoners were interrogated. They were beaten up so badly that he could hardly recognize them, the witness said. The witness didn't know who was responsible for the escape, and the commander put a gun into his mouth, then pressed it to his neck and his ear, and then grabbed his foot and fired a shot. The witness was taken to the Heliodrom in November 1993. The prisoners there were taken to do forced labor on the front lines in Mostar, he said. Many of them were wounded. A man he knew died of his injuries. The defense teams of the six former Bosnian Croatian leaders, charged with HVO crimes in 1993 and 1994 in Herzegovina and central Bosnia, did not contest the witness's claims in their brief cross-examination.

A year before, in January 2007, BBC reporter Jeremy Bowen testified at the trial of the six former Herzeg-Bosnia leaders. In the fall of 1993, he had made *Unfinished Business*, a documentary film about East Mostar, which was shown in the ICTY courtroom in the prosecution case. He described how about sixty thousand inhabitants in East Mostar—most of them Muslims—had faced the choice: to fight or to die. The described situation in East Mostar was worse than that in Gorazde, Sarajevo, and Vukovar. Esad Humo, one of the BiH Army commanders in Mostar, was asked what he was fighting for. His answer was "for survival." Bowen did much of his movie recording on 14 May 1993, when he accompanied Benabou's first convoy to East Mostar that was described above in detail. The film showed the refugees expelled by the HVO from their homes in West Mostar crossing the Neretva River at night, under fire from infantry weapons. Bowen called that "a war crime with a military objective.[391]" He interviewed a rape victim, doctors in the Mostar war hospital, the mother of a wounded daughter who did not live to be evacuated in the first batch of the wounded, a daughter who had lost her father, and a number of other civilians. The film also talked about the practice of using Muslim prisoners as human shields on the frontlines. On the other hand, it also showed the newly acquired cruelty of the Muslim BiH Army soldiers, who took the Croatian prisoners to do forced labor. A soldier explained that it was the law of the jungle in Mostar at the time. Bowen said that the Croatian defense counsel was well organized and that the HVO troops were ready to follow the instructions they

---

[391] See Jeremy Bowen Testimony in ICTY court, in The Hague in January 2007.

received from their superiors. At the time, it seemed to him that the HVO wanted to take over the whole of Mostar and establish full control over the city, with the support and at the instigation of the Croatian government.

At the beginning of the cross-examination, the defense counsel for Jadranko Prlic, Milivoj Petkovic, and Bruno Stojic accused the British journalist of bias, because he only showed one side of the Mostar story. As Bowen explained, before he started filming in East Mostar, his producer had spent several days in Medjugorje, trying to get permission from the Herzeg-Bosnia officials to film in West Mostar, but to no avail. The defense counsel did not accept the explanation proffered by the British journalist, and he accused Bowen of hurling an easy and unfounded accusation against the Croatian authorities for their "participation in the Bosnian Croatian nationalist project,[392]" when he claimed that the siege of East Mostar was done with the support and at the instigation of the Zagreb government. Bowen replied that he could not believe that this allegation came as a surprise to anyone, because it was a notorious fact at the time and was openly and widely discussed.

Another witness, identified as CU, testified in January 2007 and accused the HVO of launching the attack on Mostar on 9 May 1993 and subjecting detainees to physical abuse in prisons in Mostar, Siroki Brijeg, Lubushki, the Heliodrom, and Dretelj. He alleged that the Croatian jailer told him to open his mouth, and after having put out his cigarette on his tongue, he ordered him to swallow it. The witness was detained by the HVO in Siroki Brijeg, following his arrest in Mostar on 10 May 1993. The jailer also forced the witness to hit his head against the wall, as hard as he could, ten times. In 1992, witness CU had been a member of the

---

[392] ibid.

HVO Security Service in Mostar, and in April 1993, he decided to join the BiH Army, having realized that there might be a conflict between Croats and Muslims. He claimed that in the early morning of 9 May, 1993, the HVO launched an artillery attack on Mostar. He heard broadcasts on the Mostar radio station announcing that a large-scale action would follow, aimed at the "liberation of right-bank in Mostar," and calling upon the Muslims to surrender. In the course of his captivity in the HVO prisons in Mostar, Siroki Brijeg, Lubushki, the Heliodrom and Dretelj, the witness, who gave his testimony under protection, was repeatedly physically abused and taken to do forced labor. He recounted how he was transferred to the HVO frontline in Mostar, where he was used as a human shield. The worst experience he had was in Santiceva Street. A HVO soldier forced him to sit on sandbags on the demarcation line and used his shoulder to rest his rifle as he fired at the BiH Army lines. Sitting on the sandbags, the witness pointed to his shoulder, signaling to the BiH Army soldiers to shoot him there to put an end to his misery.

Attorney Kenneth Scott, in charge of the Prlic and other Croatian cases, scheduled the appearances of his witnesses in a consistent and coherent order, geared at building up the case. Once he proved the shocking crimes were perpetrated, it was time to affirm the responsibility of the accused sitting in the dock. The impressions from the tortured victims were still in the air when Benabou entered the chamber. The public gallery was shut down, and at the opening, Michael Karnavas, defense attorney of Jadranko Prlic, accused Albert Benabou of being an agent of the Mossad. Benabou was not caught by surprise, since this accusation had accompanied him all along his mission in Bosnia, which he refuted categorically. Scott intervened immediately and informed the judges that the issue was checked in Israel, and it was confirmed that he was not. During long and interminable successive daily sessions, documents were reviewed, one by one, and Benabou was invited to comment, provide details, elaborate, explain, add, and recall events which had occurred fifteen years previously. The record, kept in order, was precise, and Judge Antonetti was pleased to inquire in French, which suited Benabou just fine. Judge Trechsel insisted on obtaining focused answers, particularly during the cross-examination. Judge Robinson, president of the Tribunal, was present during the testimony.

Scott firmly established the close and day-to-day relations between the accused and Benabou at the time of the latter's mission there, and on one instance, he asked Benabou to spell out the personal phone numbers of the Croats at the time, which were still registered on his cell phone, as a sign of his familiarity with them, which he did at the surprise of the judges. Kenneth Scott then moved to prove unequivocally that those were the decision makers in charge and responsible for the criminal acts against the civilian population in the war zone. In the cross-examination, the defense, counting twelve lawyers and assistants, attempted relentlessly to discredit the testimony, but to no avail. The defense also showed a film presenting Benabou and the accused in an atmosphere of close cooperation, and the court was astounded by Benabou's remark, "I had to dance with the wolves.[393]" They also tried to demonstrate that Prlic, Petkovic, and Stojic were negotiating for peace in Mostar, but Benabou responded that it was true but with a slight difference: they participated in the process to obtain an agreement in Mostar, and in many other negotiations, with one single goal in mind, "to get it all and at any price,[394]" in the process

---

[393] Source: Albert Benabou personal memoirs of the War in Bosnia.
[394] ibid.

unjustifiably crushing the civilian population. "How could a military officer that I respected, like Petkovic, stay indifferent to the killing, shooting, and bombarding of civilians, and prevent any assistance to the wounded and dying children? They were not warriors," said Benabou in disgust. Benabou also said that the accused not only oppressed the Muslim population, but they also betrayed the Croatian people, who expected from them a responsible leadership and an end result for their sacrifice in this merciless war. This was the feeling in the streets of West Mostar, Medjugorje, Citluk, and elsewhere. They even missed the opportunity to obtain an arrangement in Mostar, which would never be offered to the Croats again. The court accepted all the documents and testimony as evidence.

Prosecution: Final Argument—As the prosecution brought on 5 February 2008 its argument at the trial of former Herzeg-Bosnia leaders to a close, prosecutor Kenneth Scott quoted from an HVO military police document in which, at the height of the conflict in Mostar, the Croatian military police reported that on that particular day, "No crimes were registered, just the ethnic cleansing of the Muslims[395]." According to Kenneth Scott, senior trial attorney in the case, this and other evidence clearly indicated that the Bosnian Croatian leaders saw ethnic cleansing not as a crime but as a means to accomplish their main objective—an ethnically cleansed Herzeg-Bosnia, which would be part of a Greater Croatia. The accused were well aware of the "ethnically colored policy" that was run from both western Mostar and from Zagreb. They encountered it every day during the Muslim-Croatian conflict in 1993 and 1994, and instead of investigating the crimes to identify and punish

---

[395] Source: based on a series of validated documents presented by the prosecution and registered on court on page 27119.

the perpetrators, the Croatian military police was involved in some of the gravest crimes in Prozor, Gornji Vakuf, Capljina, and Mostar. Pusic and Coric were issuing orders that certain prisoners be released, provided they had documents needed to leave for third countries. The prisons and camps in Mostar, Capljina, Dretelj, and the Heliodrom were used as temporary accommodation for the civilian population before it was expelled from the Herzeg-Bosnia territory. Noting that the HVO removed its own population from central Bosnia, in order to populate the now empty towns of Stolac and Capljina in Herzegovina, the prosecutor cited the testimony of Peter Galbraith, former US ambassador to Croatia, that former President Mate Boban had admitted to him that there was a plan to transfer as many ethnic Croats from central Bosnia to the territory of Herzeg-Bosnia as possible. Indeed, instead of protecting the Croats in the territory where they lived, Boban asked the international community to help with the evacuation of Croats from Vares.

The defense for the accused former Herzeg-Bosnia leaders argued that the prosecution had failed to prove their responsibility for the crimes they were charged with. In his reply on 4 February 2008 to the defense, the prosecutor quoted at length from President Tudjman's transcripts. The quotes showed that the operation aimed at establishing a Greater Croatia, whose borders would correspond to those of the former Banovina (one of the subdivisions of the kingdom of Yugoslavia from 1929 to 1941) and "was run both from Zagreb and from Mostar,[396]" the prosecutor contended. According to him, the key players who made all the decisions were the Croatian president, Franjo Tudjman, and Defense Minister Gojko Susak, together with the president of the HZ HB, Mate Boban, and its Prime Minister, Jadranko Prlic. In

---

[396] ibid.

a conversation from September 1993, Praljak told Tudjman and Susak about the problem of "an increasing number of Muslim refugees. It is better we take care of them now, as it will be difficult to expel them later . . . If we don't expel them, we won't have a Croatian majority,[397]" Praljak said. Soon after that meeting, the HVO attacked Prozor. In the prosecutor's view, the Vance-Owen Peace Plan accommodated Tudjman's aspirations to have the Croatian nation within the broadest possible borders. Croats rushed to sign this plan, because the borders of the Croatian provinces it envisaged corresponded to the Banovina borders. Croats believed that the international community would support their actions; therefore, they launched the implementation of their plan despite the fact that the other two sides—Bosnian Muslims and Serbs—had not signed it. The Vance-Owen Plan was implemented prematurely, the prosecutor explained, because the Bosnian Croats wrongly concluded that the plan called for the subordination of the BiH Army to the HVO in the three Herzegovina districts envisaged by the plan. A few days after the plan was accepted, in mid-January 1993, Prlic gave the BiH Army five days to either leave the Croatian territory or to be subordinated to the HVO. The BiH Army interpreted the Vance-Owen Plan differently, and the ultimatum resulted in a violent attempt by the HVO to take over power. The conflict had broken out first in Gornji Vakuf and Travnik and then spread to other parts of central Bosnia-Herzegovina.

On 10 February 2011, the prosecution asked for long prison sentences for the former Herzeg-Bosnia leaders, ranging from twenty-five to forty years for the six accused who were charged with the HVO crimes against Bosnian Muslims in 1993 and 1994 in central Bosnia and western

---

[397] ibid.

Herzegovina. Concluding his closing arguments, prosecutor Kenneth Scott noted that the six people in the dock may look "like regular Sunday churchgoers,[398]" but during the conflict— when they instigated, ordered, and abetted the ethnic cleansing in the Herzeg-Bosnia area—they were just nothing but bullies. "This is your best chance to say—never again,[399]" the prosecutor told the judges. He reminded them of the victims. The Tribunal was established for their sake, yet their voices were growing weaker. "Our task is to seek justice on their behalf, as those who help the helpless,[400]" the prosecutor noted. In the first part of the hearing in that day, prosecutor Douglas Stringer talked about the roles of Valentin Coric and Berislav Pusic and their contributions to the joint criminal enterprise aimed at creating Herzeg-Bosnia. As Stringer said, Coric "is hiding behind his office desk,[401]" claiming he was just a bureaucrat, as Eichmann and his ilk had repeated in Jerusalem and their bosses had stated before them to the Nuremberg Court. He claimed that he didn't have any control over the military police and that he didn't know about the crimes—although he was the head of the HVO military police. According to the prosecutor, the evidence showed that Coric regularly received reports about the situation in the field and that he was well aware of the mass expulsion of Muslims from western to eastern Mostar. Coric knew very well that they were detained and abused in Dretelj, Lubushki, the Heliodrom and Gabela. Coric also knew about the poor conditions in the HVO prisons and prison camps, and he knew that prisoners were taken to do forced labor at the front lines.

    The prosecutor also argued that Pusic was not just a cog in the HVO machinery, as his lawyers claimed in the final

---

[398] ibid.
[399] ibid.
[400] ibid.
[401] ibid.

*Savagery in the Heart of Europe*

brief. Prosecutor Pieter Kruger noted that as the head of the Commission for the Exchange of Prisoners, Pusic had actively participated in high-level meetings, and he illustrated the claim with the recordings from those meetings and documents that confirmed his contacts with the then Croatian foreign minister, Mate Granic. The prosecutor stressed that Pusic's claims that he "had lied about his powers[402]" in his previous interviews should not be believed. If Pusic lied earlier, why should he be trusted now, the prosecutor asked, noting also Pusic's notorious reputation at the time of the conflict when he thought he was forever immune from punishment. According to the documents produced by the intelligence service, the SIS,[403] Pusic was known in 1992 as Berko Pusic aka Two Hundred Deutschmarks because of the amount he charged the Serb detainees for their liberty. As time went by, the amount went up, and in 1993, Pusic could earn up to eight thousand German marks per Muslim detainee. Continuing the closing arguments on 8 February 2011, the prosecution focused on the contributions of the accused to the joint criminal enterprise, claiming that Prlic controlled all the levers of power in the HVO, that Stojic was responsible for HVO prisons and prison camps, and that Praljak's only interest was winning the war. The crimes in Herzeg-Bosnia were widespread and systemic, prosecutor Kenneth Scott added, for those crimes were not isolated incidents perpetrated by out of control people, "after a bad night's sleep," but they followed a coherent pattern of behavior from October 1992 to the end of 1993 in the entire territory of Herzeg-Bosnia.

All this did not mean that only Croats were accused of all war crimes, or that Serbs and Muslims were saints. The

---

[402] ibid.
[403] The Secret Intelligence Service (SIS) commonly known as MI6 (Military Intelligence, Section 6) supplies Her Majesty's government with foreign intelligence.

Croatian cases cited here were simply connected to the area of Mostar, where Benabou served and was familiar with. But Serbian and Muslim leaders too, from Milosevic to Mladic, were also arrested, judged, and convicted, and nothing that is attributed here to the Croatian leadership reduces one iota of their own crimes. In fact, on 12 July 2010, the prosecution in the case of the former Herzeg-Bosnia leaders had filed a motion to use relevant parts of General Ratko Mladic's war diaries as evidence. The prosecution claimed that the diaries corroborated the allegations in the indictment on the joint criminal enterprise of the Croats to annex parts of BiH to Croatia. The prosecution had asked that some fifteen excerpts from Mladic's diaries be accepted, which dealt with the meetings between the Bosnian Serb political and military leadership and Jadranko Prlic, Slobodan Praljak, Bruno Stojic, and Milivoj Petkovic from October 1992 to February 1994. The prosecution alleged that those notes showed that the Croatian and Herzeg-Bosnia leadership engaged in secret negotiations with the highest ranking representatives of Serbia and Republika Srpska. The prosecution quoted Mladic's entry from a meeting with the delegations from Croatia and Herzeg-Bosnia in Pec on 5 October 1992, where Praljak allegedly stated that, "The goal is the Banovina of 1939; if not, we'll continue the war.[404]" Praljak added that, "The agreement between Tudjman and Izetbegovic does not contain anything—it is formal and has been made at the insistence of the Americans.[405]"

Noting that the Croatian President Franjo Tudjman had discussed the division of BiH with the highest ranking representatives of the rump Yugoslavia, the prosecution quoted

---

[404] Source: based on a series of validated documents presented by the prosecution and registered on court on page 27119.
[405] Source: based on a series of validated documents presented by the prosecution and registered on court on page 27119.

an entry from a meeting with Dobrica Cosic[406] on 21 October 1992, where, "Tudjman and I agreed on the division, Vance and Owen rejected it,[407]" said Cosic unequivocally, adding that he told Tudjman that he should not bring his troops and not threaten eastern Herzegovina. At the time, eastern Herzegovina was under Bosnian Serb control, and, "We're on a good path to compel Alija to divide Bosnia,[408]" were Praljak's words at a meeting in Njivice on 26 October 1992. "It is in our interest that the Muslims get their own canton so they have somewhere to move to,[409]" Praljak went on to say. The prosecution alleged that those words confirmed the desire to remove Muslims from parts of Bosnia and Herzegovina that the Croats claimed as their own, and to establish Croatia's borders in BiH in order to form a Greater Croatia. "The Croatian state borders are obvious, but in BiH they are yet to be established,[410]" Praljak said. The prosecution claimed that this quote illustrated the point. Mladic went on to note in his diaries that at a meeting attended by Tudjman, Boban, Karadzic, Owen, and others in Geneva on 4 January 1993, Izetbegovic said he was ready to accept the agreed principles of the peace plan, but not the proposed map. Owen then told Tudjman, "One cannot count on having a state within a state.[411]" Nevertheless, some days later, the Croats issued an ultimatum to the BiH Army to force it to accept the agreement it didn't want. At a later meeting on 23 January 1993, Izetbegovic repeated, "We didn't approve the map either then or now, we had five objections . . .[412]" The prosecution

---

[406] First president of the Federal Republic of Yugoslavia from 1992 to 1993. Admirers often refer to him as the "Father of the Nation."
[407] Source: based on a series of validated documents presented by the prosecution and registered on court on page 27119.
[408] ibid.
[409] ibid.
[410] ibid.
[411] ibid.
[412] ibid.

maintained that this confirmed that Izetbegovic didn't accept the Vance-Owen Plan of January 1993 and that the warring sides knew it. The entries from Mladic's diaries corroborated the contents of some documents that were already in evidence as prosecution exhibits, including the correspondence between Milivoj Petkovic and Ivica Rajic, about the contacts between the HVO and the 'XY' side, i.e., Bosnian Serbs. There were also documents about the HVO's debt to the VRS (*Vojna Republika Srpska*, VRS, namely the Bosnian Serbian Army, BSA) reaching DEM Five, seven million with which the purchase of ammunition was arranged.

According to Mladic's diaries, on 8 July 1993, Karadzic said to his generals, "Help the Croats in order to force the Muslims to agree on a division of Bosnia.[413]" Mladic also claimed that Milosevic offered to hand the Muslims over to Tudjman, but Tudjman didn't want them. The diaries also contain an entry from a meeting between Petkovic and Mladic in Njivice on 8 July 1993. The commanders of the HVO and the VRS negotiated their joint combat operations against the BiH Army in Mostar. "I would like first to defend Fojnica, Kresevo, and Kiseljak and to link up with Busovaca,[414]" Petkovic told Mladic. At a meeting with Karadzic, Mladic, and Krajisnik on 3 February, 1994, Mate Boban said that, "the most important task was to destroy the legitimacy of BiH. We said long ago how to stop the war, by stopping humanitarian aid to Muslims, because *begluk* (feudal tax revenue) is their way of life.[415]" Jadranko Prlic remarked that, "Muslims are the common enemy. There are two or three ways to keep them down, first militarily by breaking their backbone . . . and secondly, to destroy the legitimacy of BiH because the world has recognized Izetbegovic and his

---

[413] ibid.
[414] ibid.
[415] ibid.

government.[416]" At those meetings, the Croatian and Serbian leaders talked about the restoration of Croatian Banovina from 1939, denied the legitimacy of Izetbegovic's government, and considered joint actions against the BiH Army. The fact that the accused men knowingly cooperated with Mladic and other Bosnian Serbian leaders responsible for widespread crimes, perpetrated to establish a Greater Serbia showed, as the prosecution contended, that the Bosnian Croatian leaders intended to commit other crimes to implement their goal—namely the establishment of Herzeg-Bosnia under Croatian dominance. The prosecution argued that admitting parts of Mladic's diaries as evidence would not affect the right of the accused to a fair trial. The prosecutor noted that the evidentiary value of the documents was significant in relation to the small number of documents submitted to the court. The prosecution did not intend to call any new witnesses, and it was left to the Trial Chamber to decide if it would allow the defense teams of the accused to call any more witnesses.

Amazingly, admitting some of the guilt they were accused of, while they denied any wrongdoing, Prlic declared in the court on 2 March 2011 that, "Those who suffered deserve compassion and justice.[417]" Like the other five Bosnian Croatian leaders in the dock, Prlic denied any responsibility for the crimes committed in Herzeg-Bosnia in 1993 and 1994. Reexamining his behavior in the war, Prlic concluded that he hadn't done anything he would not do again in the same circumstances. Addressing the judges in English, Prlic said that he didn't perpetrate or instigate any crimes in his capacity as a "provisional executive body." He "didn't know" if any other members of the HVO were "involved in something

---

[416] ibid.
[417] Source: ICTY, Prlic defense, court transcript, dated 2 March 2011, page 52922 - 52976.

like that. We did everything we could to alleviate the consequences of the war and destruction and took all the required measures to punish the perpetrators of those crimes,[418]" lied Prlic. Addressing the judges, former president of the Herzeg-Bosnia's department of defense, Stojic, pleaded that he sincerely sympathized, from the bottom of his soul, with the victims of the war, especially with the Muslim victims. As he heard the victims' testimony in court, Stojic said he, "realized that there were crimes," and that those were the "most difficult moments of his life.[419]" Nevertheless, like Prlic, Stojic said that he didn't instigate or order those crimes. "Your honors," he supplicated, "I never wanted any crimes to happen. I never ever plotted or arranged any crimes.[420]" General Milivoj Petkovic was the only one accused to apologize to the victims of HVO crimes. After his thirty-minute closing argument, General Slobodan Praljak left it to his defense counsel to address the judges. Denying the accusations that Croatia and the HVO occupied parts of BiH territory, the defense said that Praljak was an officer who served on the frontline to prevent mass expulsions of Croats.

The ICTY was due to deliver verdicts in these cases in 2012, but due to their complexity, the appeals proceedings in the Prlic et al.[421] cases are unlikely to be completed by the end of 2014, when the Hague based court is to close its doors. Appeals proceedings in the case of Prlic et al. are expected to run into 2016. While operating in full capacity, the Tribunal is working towards the completion of its mandate.

---

[418] ibid.
[419] Source: ICTY, Stojic defense, court transcript, dated March 2011.
[420] ibid.
[421] Et al. is the abbreviation for et alii in Latin, which means "and others."

# Summing Up: Epilogue and Conclusions

On Wednesday, 16 March 1994, a few weeks before the Jewish Passover, Benabou began to take leave from his one-year mission in Mostar. He released a farewell message to the leaders of Mostar and to his colleagues at the UN headquarters in New York and Zagreb. In this final report, he reviewed the positions and expectations from each of the parties involved in the conflict. Remaining faithful to the standards of fairness, impartiality, openness, and direct language which were reflected in his field reports, he addressed the same text to all three parties— Serbs, Croats, and Muslims:

> On 7 April 1994, I will be concluding my mission with UNPROFOR, where I served as coordinator of civil affairs for southern Bosnia and Herzegovina. I had the honor and privilege to serve in this position as the first Israeli in any UN peace keeping forces.
> My farewell is addressed to all of you, leaders and people of Mostar, who have been the focus of my attention, and where I have invested my heart and soul during this past year. In this period of time, I have sensed your hopes and sorrows, your pains and reliefs, your humiliations and exaltations. I believe that, after the Washington agreement and the negotiations in Vienna, Mostar is facing a new beginning. It is a turning point in this hostile confrontation—which will hopefully end with defining through a federation, a canton system, or any other political formulas, the desired modus vivendi for a new dawn.
> Each one of you preserves in a corner of his heart the dream that he wished to see realized. Mostar, located over the Neretva River, which is dominated by turbulent wa-

ters running between majestic mountains in this florescent and fertile valley, used to be the metropolitan model of coexistence between Croats, Muslims, Serbs, and Jews—an ideal which has crumbled during the conflict. We are now in a new phase, where each one aches and expects to affirm his autonomy and respect for his way of life. I have witnessed the aspiration of those who struggled for Mostar, a place so tied in with their identity, that they would consider themselves non-existent if they were to be uprooted from it. I have observed your fighting for the proud survival of your respective cultures and for the continuation of your presence in this area, hence your tenacity in holding on to the turf against all odds.

Altogether, with your leaders of Mostar, we have searched for and constructed, at times, that small bridge which connects between human beings, away from the perpetual shelling and the daily carnage. This has enabled us to achieve the release of prisoners and detainees, the evacuation of wounded from the war zone, the supplies in food and medicine, and even conceiving a peace plan for Mostar. According to the heritage that I bring from my people and my country, Israel, I have internalized your concerns and preoccupations as mine. It will be my honor to assist you, in the immediate future, in a joint project for the reconstruction of the Stari Most, the old bridge, that symbolizes the unity of Mostar.

Please, accept my sincere wishes that your peaceful endeavors and your coordinated actions for the benefit of the Croats, Muslims, Serbs, and the other ethnic communities in the beloved city of Mostar, bears fruit.

With a strong hand shake & a warm shalom,
Albert Benabou[422]

---

[422] See DOC. 202, dated 16 of March 1994, concerning Farewell to Mostar, distributed by Albert Benabou to UN Headquarters in Zagreb and New York, and to the leadership in Croatia, Bosnia and Serbia.

*Savagery in the Heart of Europe*

On Thursday, 17 April 1994, three hours before his departure flight from Zagreb to Jerusalem, Benabou released his end of mission report. It was mainly destined to the UN headquarters in New York, where decisions were to be made for the future of this unstable region of the world. The document was addressed to the Secretary General Mr. Boutros Boutros-Ghali, former Egyptian Minister of Foreign Affairs who had participated and contributed to the peace agreement achieved in Camp David in 1978 between President Anwar Sadat of Egypt and Prime Minister of Israel Menachem Begin. It read:

Dear Mr. Ghali, Shalom Wa-salam!

I had the honor and privilege to serve as the first Israeli in the UN peace keeping forces. As you have notified the premier of Israel, Mr. Yitzhak Rabin, the idea occurred to you, one of the artisans of the peace treaty between Israel and Egypt (1979) took up the position of secretary general of the United Nations Organization. I conclude today a year of mission in UNPROFOR. It was a year of challenges and extraordinary encounters, particularly when participating in Egyptian peace keeping forces who secured and assisted me in the Yom Kippur services in the Jewish community in Sarajevo that I was invited to conduct in the thick of the war. Please find attached my end of mission report in which you might find interest. Looking forward to future peace keeping missions, please accept my warmest shalom wa-salam for you and all my mission colleagues, who have offered support and cooperation throughout[423].

For those who are fascinated or amused by historical fortunes, ironies, improbabilities, and strange turns of events, we reserve the tale of several odd developments. The Hanjar

---
[423] ibid.

SS Division formed by the Nazis in Bosnia during World War II, in collaboration with the Jerusalem Mufti, Haj Amin al-Husseini, was revived during the Bosnia War (1992-1995), and Nasser Oric was appointed its head when surrounded by the Serbs in the Srebrenica enclave in eastern Bosnia, where the tragedy of Muslim extermination unfolded. In 1994, all units under Oric's command were named "The Eighth Operative Group," and he was promoted to Brigadier General. In November 2000, he was indicted for possessing illegal weapons, and he was convicted for "extortion," but the verdict was later reversed. In 2006, he was convicted by the International Court in The Hague for failing to prevent the killing and torturing of Serbs in the area under his command. The perpetrators of violence belonged to ethnic groups, but while hatred persisted from WW II through the Bosnian War of the 1990s, the postwar political settlement, incorporated in the Dayton Accords, has at least limited the scope of hostilities and violence ever since.

The eruption of the Arab Spring in early 2011, in which the Arab world, which had suffered under various forms of oppression since it reconstituted itself in nation states after World War I and the collapse of the Ottoman Empire, has revived the idea of the Turkish model as the panacea of the current turmoil. Indeed, from practically all the Arab countries which experienced the unrest, namely, Tunisia, Egypt, Libya, the Yemen, Syria, and Bahrain, only in the first two did the dust seem to settle on the "Muslim option," until merely one year later (summer 2013) when thost alternatives were reversed by violent popular counter revolution. Many brands of liberals, pro-democrats, champions of civil rights, and the like, stood in the forefront of that public debate and proclaimed the solution that they advocated for the future of their country. But they soon realized that it was much easier to remove a dictator from power than to build a consensus around an alternative program of action. Many ideas contended for supremacy in the public square, which is reminiscent of the 1918, 4 May Movement in Republican China, where the fall of the imperial Confucian system forced the public debate about the new way to choose: liberalism, conservative republicanism, a new autocracy of some sort, communism, and the like. After years of civil war, communism had prevailed for the subsequent decades. No wonder then that in the only two Arab countries, Tunisia and Egypt, where the national army took things in hand and presided over the transitional period of transferring power to elected institutions, did Islam emerge as the first choice.

Why Islam and of what sort? In practically all Arab countries that were shaken by the spring that turned into winter, there is a strong presence of the Muslim Brotherhood and its affiliates, who are often overtaken on the right by one kind of radical Islamic movement or another, be it dubbed Salafi, al-Qa'ida, Islamic Jihad, and the like. What they all have in common is their commitment to install in their societies an Islamic regime, governed by the Shari'a law, where the sacred law of Islam becomes the sole source of legitimacy and of legislation of the state. Theoretically, that should be an ideal solution, because the democratic elections, which have led to the new Muslim majorities in the respective parliaments of Tunisia and Egypt so far, lend the optimal means of legitimacy to the new regime. However, the radical Islamic movements accept democracy only as the best way to accede to power and then deny the workability of western style democracy in an Islamic regime, where the law of Allah reigns supreme, because it rejects the notion of the people's sovereignty, in a democracy as a system that represents the will of the people. Moreover, since no Arab autocrat has so far acquired legitimacy from his electorate by free elections, they all sought legitimacy through Islamic symbols: the king of

Saudi Arabia as "the Curator of the two Shrines," the king of Jordan as the "Curator of al-Aqsa Mosque," and the king of Morocco as a descendant of the Prophet Muhammed. In any non-monarchical Arab regime now in the making, legitimacy will be acquired through elections. Monarchies in Morocco, Jordan, Saudi Arabia, and the Gulf have so far resisted any reform or spring, sanctioning Libya and then Syria for not responding to their peoples' demands, but making it clear that they would neither need nor tolerate nor succumb to any changes or reforms in the absolute rule of the sheikhs. Their solidarity with each other on that score suggests to Morocco and Jordan to join the Gulf Cooperation Organization, which has turned from a regional security alliance to a UPAM (Union for the Preservation of Absolute Monarchies). In the meantime, while they continue to "dance sheikh to sheikh," they have drawn the attention away from the "Arab Spring" and centered it on the "Iranian Peril."

For a long time, the West has promoted the idea of the Turkish model, believing that the Kemalist successor of the Ottoman Empire had firmly established a civil society, paradoxically accepting the hegemony of the military as the guarantor of the Kemal Ataturk's republican and secular heritage. That worked for eight years (1922-2002) under the civilian democratic systems of Menderes, Ecevit, Ozal, and Ciller, but once Erbakan's Islamic party was allowed to rule for less than two years (1996-98), before it was removed and outlawed by the military as undermining the Kemalist patrimony, everyone realized that the patient field work undertaken by the Islamists in the last decades had slowly reversed the trend of de-Islamization of Turkey, especially in the countryside. That new development came full bloom when the disciples of Erbakan, Teyyip Erdogan, and Abdullah Gul, led their revived Islamic party to a stunning victory in December 2002 and again in 2006 and 2010, and brought re-Islamization of the country full circle, with the military dethroned from their privileged position and tamed and subjected to the authority of the Islamic party and government.

That domestic reversal, which provides the opportune platform for Erdogan to spread lies, like the flotilla against Israel, and the "killing of Palestinian children by Israel," to imprison journalists, to behave like a thug towards foreign dignitaries, and to incite masses, while the emasculated military no longer threatened to intervene, as they had on four occasions since the 1960s, has also occasioned a dramatic turn in Turkey's international orientation and foreign relations, engineered and implemented by a bad professor turned at worse into diplomat, Davotoglu. Disillusioned from the dream of joining the European Union and of reinforcing its cultural orientation towards the West, Erdogan's Turkey has turned eastwards, towards the emerging Muslim republics of central Asia, trying to become, according to the old Jewish adage, "the head of foxes, rather than remain the tail of lions." This policy turnaround has alienated Turkey from the United States and Israel, now that there is no longer a military lobby to that trend, and pushed it to throw its lot with the Arab and Muslim world, in an attempt to become its leader and dominant model. It encountered some pitfalls on the way, like nuclearizing Iran, which is feared by the rest of the Sunni world, or a recalcitrant Syria in which Assad, the newly adopted friend of Erdogan, who later turned into an enemy, persists in the slaughtering of his own people. So much so that despite Turkey's record of the massacre of the Armenians, which they continue to deny, and their relentless campaigns against the Kurds, domestically and externally, they elect to draw the attention of the world to "Israel's ravages against the Palestinians" and to withdraw silently their sponsorship of Assad, for fear that their own image might be irretrievably tarnished.

The West, which is desperate to keep Turkey within NATO, especially with the renewed rise of the authoritarian regime of Putin in Russia and his aspiration to retrieve from oblivion Russia's primary standing in the Mediterranean, still needs the Turks to its side, and therefore, while it has publicly desisted from hailing the Turkish model, it has not openly denounced it or distanced themselves from it as yet. But the emerging regimes in the spring-swept Arab world do hold on to that image, suggesting that Turkey has become a democratic and modern Islamic state, not necessarily inimical to the West, which they will strive to emulate, so as not to lose western support while they re-Islamize their societies. This is the quandary now facing the Bosniaks, the Albanians, and the Kosovars, who would like to tread the same pattern, except that their neighbors and partners in Serbia, Croatia, and federated Bosnia stand alert and ready to oppose any such development, by the very fact that they are part of the structure of the government as envisaged in the settlements that put an end to the Bosnian War, for now. The vast sympathy and deep friendship that the Serbs and Croats, and as result, even Bosnia of the three-partite federation, feel towards Israel will also constitute a certain guarantee in the short run against Bosnia drifting too much towards Iran or Turkey.

During his year of service with UNPRFOR in former Yugoslavia, Albert Benabou was constantly reminded by the Serbs that they were the real historical allies of the Jewish people and Israel. Moreover, Ratko Mladic, the much demonized Serbian leader of the Serbs in Croatia during the war, had laid out, in his own terms, his feelings and thinking on this matter when the two met at first in the Sarajevo Airport in May 1993. He specifically emphasized that the "Judeo-Christian civilization was under the threat of a totalitarian Islam, which was an extension of fascism.[424]" That

---

[424] Source: Albert Benabou Personal Memoirs of the war in Bosnia notes on his meeting with General Ratko Mladic in Sarajevo Airport in May 1993.

did not deflect Benabou from his humanitarian mission and from his many daring attempts, at the risk of his life, when he was caught in the crossfire between BiH, the HVO, and the people of Mostar, to extend assistance equally to all warring forces. Indeed, in spite of the high tensions and the sensitive tempers which prevailed during the war, he was universally liked, welcomed, highly appreciated, and resorted to by all parties, who considered him as the "Israeli" officer who was there to help, had no ax to grind, and was not there to protect or represent any Israeli interest. That unusually disinterested UN official, with which the international organization was not familiar, and who so dramatically and demonstrably acted "out of the box," took risks and initiatives, and held human life above any other consideration, was in all probability just too much for the UN peace keeping forces, which never again accepted to repeat such an experience with another Israeli after Benabou's departure.

What happens next? The Hague International Court held the trials of war criminals in 2008, where Benabou was summoned as a major witness, and many of his field reports were taken as conclusive evidence by the judges. When one looks backwards at the suffering and the flow of tears and blood suffered by all parties, one asks oneself about the significance of war, about the human adamancy to resort repeatedly to it, in spite of the horror, criticism, and condemnation that it invokes across the board. The rivals in the war still try to rationalize their participation in it by claiming that they were dragged into it against their will. Both Croats and Serbs continue to claim that the Bosniaks are in fact their own kin who had been forcibly Islamized by the Ottoman occupiers, hence their wish that they could undo that history, so as to have perhaps avoided that war in the first place. In this vein, late nineteenth century conservative Croatian nationalist right-wing political leader Ante Šarčević referred to the Bosnian Muslims as "the flower of the Croatian nation." From the Habsburg occupation of Bosnia in 1878, following the Berlin Congress, until the end of the First World War, Bosnian Muslims were treated by the Austro-Hungarian authorities as a separate community from both Croats and Serbs. Under monarchist Yugoslavia, between the world wars, Bosnian Muslims wavered between identification as Muslim Croats and as Muslim Serbs. During the Second World War, the German-installed Ustasha regime united Croatia with Bosnia-Herzegovina, in the Independent State of Croatia (NDH by its Croatian initials), and in a chapter of Bosnian history much discussed, but little elaborated by historians outside the region, Bosnian Muslims were recruited to fight under German and Croatian command in the Waffen SS, as were Albanians. Bosnian Muslims, or Bosniaks, were not granted a distinct ethnic category by Yugoslav authorities until 1968, when the Tito regime recognized "Muslims by nationality" (not officially called "Bosniaks," although the use of the term was historically established before the twentieth century) as a separate census classification. "Yugoslav Muslims" are still self-defined, separately from Bosniaks, in Montenegro and Serbia.

But the Bosnian War, which has sharpened the differentiation between these rivals, despite their previous joint cultural and linguistic background under Communism, had the lasting effect of marking the boundaries between them in blood and making the divide indelible. True, a "peaceful" settlement imposed from the outside has forced them into a much loathed and despised coexistence, sharing common borders and even joint institutions in the country of Bosnia. But it was exactly that unfinished business, which had compressed the genie into the bottle, which may also pave the way in the future for eruptions of hatred and hostility, if the cork of international containment can no longer stand the pressures coming from within. The involvement of Islam in such a potential eruption, which in Kosovo, Bosnia, Macedonia, and the Sandjak has been already brewing and will certainly gain the support of Muslim countries and institutions when the time comes, in itself augurs ill for the future of that region. And then, people there might regret not having embraced the solution of the transfer of populations, which should have homogenized and uniformed the human compositions of those countries once and for all, in spite of the temporary suffering of that one generation. After all, if much of the Jewish plight around the world could not be resolved before an independent state of Israel could offer them a sovereign existence, why would the fate of Kurds, Gypsies, Druze, and for that matter, the countries of the Balkans, be different?[425] There, the major determinant for the transfer of populations was the choice that decision makers had to make between a temporary disruption in one generation of a minority people, however harsh it may be, and the permanent hell that both majority and minority would suffer for eternity if they are not separated. Mixtures of different cultures, languages, religions, and ethnicities have worked in some places but have failed dismally elsewhere, and there is no point trying to force the impossible even if it appears meeting the loftiest human ideals.

**Towards a Model of Conflict Management**

By definition of its mandate, UNPROFOR was in charge of the protection of the civil populations, whoever they were, Serbs, Croats, or Muslims, and wherever they were, in cities, villages, towns, hamlets, or in tiny rural communities,

---

[425] Joseph Schechtman, Postwar Population Transfers in Europe (1945-55), Univ of Pennsylvania Press, Philadelphia, 1962. See also Raphael Israeli, Palestinians Between Israel and Jordan, Praeger, NY, 1991, especially Chapter 9 157-176.

who were victims of crime or exposed to a risk to their lives. This was its mission, and UNPROFOR was accountable for it as the envoy of the international community. Where did it fail and why? There will always be voices claiming that the organization did its utmost within the constraints and the limitation imposed by the UN member states mandate. Why didn't they follow the voices, like that of General Jean Cot, who asserted loudly that it was impossible to assure the protection of the civil population in that structure? The headquarters in New York were constantly explaining that the UN mandate was by definition toothless, but the officers in the field had to accept it and operate according to it. But then stood the question of who should be invited to the court in The Hague and required to give an explanation for collaborating stoically with this state of affairs? It sounds like calling for justice for the victims of an incompetent system, striving to survive as a cold and detached bureaucracy caught in unbending indifference. Apparently, UNPROFOR, instead of focusing on its mandate, attempted to respond to the agendas of the desperate former communist politicians in former Yugoslavia, who sought to imitate Tito. Those politicians started a war and were inapt to terminate one way or another, while pretending to express the voice of their "democratically butchered" people.

The UN member states are called upon to pay attention to an honest and fair introspection into their organization, where thugs and criminals can today be elected to chair many of its institutions, and invited to revise its modus operandi, particularly the peace keeping administration. Yes, there was another option to deal substantially with the UNPROFOR mandate, even in its restricted definition, responding to the grassroots level with the local leaders held responsible to their populations. There was no chance trying to resolve the conflict in which only the great powers had a word to say and were the only ones able to finalize an adequate solution. The United Nations is not conceived to respond to that challenge, which is reserved for the great powers, and should not try to achieve the impossible where it had never succeeded before. UNPROFOR was set to please politicians and could not offer the required administrative support according to the task at hand and to the essence of the proposals brought up at the local level from the field, like in Mostar where the local leadership was expecting the United Nations to extend its hand instead of imposing solutions.

Maybe what is needed is an entire overhaul of the UN system, by creating a new Union of Democratic Countries (UDC), to be founded by western powers and joined only by countries who meet those standards in the eyes of the founders. The rest, that is most countries of the world, which are ruled by tyrants of monarchs, will be left to manage their old, outdated, and turned-insignificant UN, which will also become the Union of Tyrannies (UT). Nothing will serve as a better incentive to develop regimes into democracies than a coveted membership of UDC, as nothing will discourage war as that very membership. For UDC will exclude from its midst any member and reject any candidate for membership who wages war or threatens war against any member of the union. Similarly, members of the union will enjoy not only peace, development, and security, guaranteed by its membership, but also support to stand against any outside aggression.

However, the experience accumulated in the exercise of the interim arrangement at the local level in Mostar may perhaps serve as a model in the conflict management, pending the conflict's resolution. The International Accords signed in the aftermath of the Cold War, particularly in the Balkans, the Mediterranean basin, and between the nations of the Middle East and North Africa, have provided only partial security and stability in the region. The achieved agreements, such as Israel and the Palestinian Authority, the Dayton Agreement in Bosnia, and even with Sin Fein in northern Ireland, did not generate the expected grassroots cooperation between the parties in conflict. In fact, those agreements are still encountering frustration, antagonism, resistance, and terror from different opposing sources, rather than their full and faithful implementation. But, in the meantime, local and grassroots affairs have also to be addressed in the vein of that Lebanese farmer who, in the thick of the repeated Lebanese wars asked, *"Et les affaires de mon village?"* (And how about my village business?) A model has been developed to deal with situations of this sort:

The national level of each country or entity involved in a project would offer a tacit support to the local initiative (at the regional, local, municipal, community level).

Domestic factors among civil society (UN/NGO/municipal/universities/media) engage in identified concrete projects servicing parties in conflict.

A third party (from the United States, Canada, or a European country) assists and participates in the project as a reasonable broker and partner.

The state of affairs of any peace process at the national level is put aside and not dealt with in this context.

In a pending political process, the international community should strive to invest and serve as a catalyst in regional cooperation between local entities in conflict. This defined model is conceived to reinforce the achieved international accords in a slow, cautious, and long process, which builds confidence through cooperative steps in regional and neighboring communities. Discretion between parties is imperative, and a mutual understanding of confidentiality, including no publicity without consensus, is encouraged during the course of establishing a project. A sample of issues selected and agreed upon by parties engaged in promoting stability can be conceived to promote collaboration among the parties, taking into account that at times the hatred and hostility can be so intense as to sacrifice self-interest for ideological goals. This model can serve civil society, the local authorities, and the public sector. It includes in its structure members of the public and private sectors representing various municipalities from international institutions and out of the region involved in concrete projects. The prime objectives are to facilitate grassroots projects through public and private partnerships for investments in sustainable economic, educational, social, and technological development in the region. DOSSIA (Domestic Support System in International Accords) is such a model, which addresses the problem of achieved agreements on the international/national level between entities in conflict, who are encountering escalating resistance and difficulties in the implementation of their accords from varied sources at the domestic/local level.

It is estimated that in parallel to agreements negotiated and reached on an international/national level, it is imperative to negotiate at the domestic/local level supporting micro-political systems which assert the successful implementation from the grassroots. DOSSIA offers, after examination at the domestic/local level set-up, a framework engendering between neighboring communities in conflict interaction and accountability between the leaderships and their communities. It affords evolution of solutions to upcoming problems at the start of this century in international relations, specifically in the field of models and theories of negotiations. Specific programs are to be identified in the assessments of needs, elaborated in cooperation with the municipalities and for the benefit of their citizens. Examples of such projects and applied programs are provided below:

1. The development of cultural and educational programs through formal and informal institutions (schools and community centers);
2. Innovating programs with employment opportunities, including training and mobility;
3. Mutual action against civil crime, terror, and drug abuse, through exchange of information and centers of assistance;
4. Creation of a shared mechanism (modus operandi) between the municipalities/regions for controlling and managing emerging crises; and
5. Establish and encourage cooperation between the emergency departments of both municipalities (such as hospitals, police, and firemen).

Until it is replaced by some fair and reasonably operating institution, the United Nations can serve as a platform for basic ground operation offering preventive diplomacy and solutions to countries and groups that cannot ignore the animosities between the ethnic groups forming the states, all over the world, not only Europe or the Balkans. To reinforce tranquility and stability in the Balkans (and in the Middle East for that matter), an entente is required. Simultaneously, with the establishment of the federation/confederation process that was initiated in Bosnia by Washington, an arrangement on a political and economic basis was necessary and even inevitable for the Balkan countries. Confusion mixed with apprehensions exists among the region's leadership, which is delighted to abandon the ancient regime but does not possess the guidelines for a new system. Maybe some steps and measures will be necessary to provide those guidelines.

    A. The activation of an equitable judiciary system, which should be mandated to:

1. Monitor the local legal system, including the reestablishment of police functions, courts and prisons;
2. Provide all necessary assistance to the War Crimes Tribunal in The Hague, in order to avoid settling scores between the warring parties and creating social chaos;
3. Establish and protect free market economic transitions.

B. Launching free, regional, and national elections based on the status quo of the confrontation lines and ethnic identity and supervised by the United Nations.

C. Initiating and encouraging economic projects from the Western world on a private and national basis.

# Acronyms and Abbreviations

These explanations of the abbreviations and acronyms, both civilian and military, used by the United Nations bodies, international forces and local institutions in former Yugoslavia, are presented in alphabetic order to facilitate access to the reader.

**A**

ACOS—Assistant Chief of Staff.
ADC (O)—Assistant Division Commander (Operations) is in charge of the battle formations in his unit: infantry, armor, field artillery, cavalry, engineering, air defense artillery, and aviation assets. He also controls the medical company.
ADC (S)—Assistant Division Commander (Support) is in charge of all the combat support, combat service, and maintenance elements of the division.
AFSOUTH—Air force Component of the American Southern Command.
AOR—Area of Responsibility—zone under control of a military unit.
APC—Armored Personnel Carrier.
ARMIJE—The Bosnian-Muslim Army.

**B**

BiH—Bosnia and Herzegovina.
BRITFOR—British Forces—Headquarters in Divulje, close to Split.
BSA—Bosnian Serb Army, under the Command of General Ratko Mladic.

**C**

CAC—United Nations Civil Affairs Coordinator (on a regional basis).
CANBAT—Canadian Battalion—United Nations military unit located in the area of Visoko and Srebrenica.
CAO—United Nations Civil Affairs Officer.
CASEVAC—Casualties Evacuation, usually supervised by the Red Cross.

Cmdr.—Commander- Usually a General (or Brigadier) who commands the military formation.
CO—Commanding Officer.
COS—Chief of Staff—Officer who runs the headquarters on a day-to-day basis and who often acts as a second-in-command.

**D**

DETALAT—a French airborne unit, detached to the UN mission in Bosnia, was stationed near the coastal city of Split.
DUTCHCOM—Dutch Communication in charge of communications between all the United Nations Protection Forces units in former Yugoslavia.

**E**

ECLO—Embargo Control Liaison Officer manned be EU (European Union) Observers.
ECMM—European Community Monitor Mission (now European Union Monitoring Mission; diplomatic mission to Bosnia and Herzegovina starting 1991).

**F**

FMSO—Foreign Military Studies Office, a research and analysis center for the United States Army, which does not necessarily represent the official policy or position of the Department of the Army, Department of Defense, or the US government.
FREBAT—French Battalion—United Nations military unit covering the area of Sarajevo.
FRY—Federal Republic of Yugoslavia.

**G**

G1 Branch—Responsible for personnel matters including manning, discipline, and personnel services. Serves under the command of the COS—Chief of Staff.
G2 Branch—Responsible for intelligence and security. He or she controls two other officers: assistant G2 for security and assistant G2 for intelligence. Serves under the command of the COS—Chief of Staff.
G3 Branch—Responsible for operations, including staff duties, exercise planning, training, operational requirements, combat development, and tactical doctrine. Serves under the command of the COS—Chief of Staff.

G4 Branch—Logistics and quartering. He or she is in charge of all supplies except ammunition. Serves under the command of the COS—Chief of Staff.

G5 Branch—Civil and military cooperation and media. Serves under the command of the COS—Chief of Staff.

G6—(relatively new unit) Information Systems. Serves under the command of the COS—Chief of Staff.

G8—The eight major economies of the world: United States, Russia, Britain, France, Germany, Italy, Japan, and Canada.

## H

HCA—Head Civil Affairs—in charge of all civilian operations in former Yugoslavia.

HCC—Head of Coordinating Center, particularly for distribution of UN humanitarian assistance.

HDZ—*Hrvatska Demokratska Zajednica* (The Croatian Democratic Union—Largest Croatian Party in Bosnia).

HOO—Head of Operations.

HOS—the Croat-Bosnian faction which supported, together with the Muslims, the territorial integrity of the Bosnian state, contrary to the position taken by Mate Boban.

HQ—Headquarters.

HV—*Hrvatska Vojska* (Croatian Army).

HVO—*Hrvatsko Vijece Obrane*—Croatian Defense Council, military formation of the self-proclaimed Croatian Republic of Herzeg-Bosnia during the Bosnian War.

## I

ICRC—International Committee of the Red Cross.

ICTY—International Criminal Tribunal for former Yugoslavia located in The Hague, Netherland.

IDF- Israel Defense Forces.

IFOR—Implementation Forces, which replaced the UN Forces (UNPROFOR) after the signing of the Dayton Agreement

INMARSAT—International Maritime Satellite Telecommunication, a UN body set up for the purpose of establishing a satellite communications network for the maritime community. The United Nations capitalized on it and used it for terrestrial communication in the war in former Yugoslavia.

IPTF—UN International Police Task Force.

IRC—International Rescue Committee.

## J
JMO—Muslim Party of Bosnia.

## K
KFOR—the Kosovo Force, mandated by the Security Council of the United Nations to bring peace to Kosovo.
KLA—Kosovo Liberation Army.

## L
LDK—Democratic League of Kosovo, headed by Ibrahim Rugova.

## M
MALBAT—Malaysian Battalion, located in the area of Jablanica.
MDM—Médecins du Monde (Doctors of the World) French non governmental organisation of medical doctors serving for rescue all over the world (founded by Bernard Kouchner).
MEDEVAC—Medical Evacuation usually supervised by the Red Cross.
MoD—Ministry of Defense.
MOU—Memorandum of Understanding.
MSF—Médecins Sans Frontières or Doctors Without Borders, is a secular humanitarian-aid non-governmental organization best known for its projects in war-torn regions and developing countries facing endemic diseases.

## N
NATO—North Atlantic Treaty Organization.
NDH—Independent State of Croatia (by its Croatian initials).
NGO—Non-Governmental Organization.
NORDBAT—Nordic Battalion made out of troops from Scandinavian countries and located in Tuzla.
NORMOVCOM—Norwegian Movement Communication in charge of the air transport to and from Sarajevo.

## O
OHR—The High Representative for Bosnia and Herzegovina, with the Office of the High Representative (OHR) in Bosnia and Herzegovina, was created in 1995 immediately after the Dayton Peace Agreement to oversee the civilian implementation of this agreement.

OSCE—Organization for Security and Cooperation in Europe. It sent two thousand unarmed "verifiers" to Kosovo.

## P

PILPG—Public International Law & Policy Group.

POW—Prisoners of War. The exchange of prisoners of war is usually supervised by the Red Cross.

## Q

QRF- Multinational Quick Reaction Force. Is a military unit, generally Platoon-sized in the US Army, that is capable of rapid response to developing situations. They are to have equipment ready, to respond to any type of emergency, typically within ten minutes or less, although this is based on unit Standard Operating Procedures (SOPs). This model has been copied with a multinational participation in former Yugoslavia.

## R

R2P or RtoP—State Responsibility to Protect its populations from genocide, war crimes, ethnic cleansing, and crimes against humanity, adopted in the Outcome Document of the high-level plenary meeting of the UN General Assembly in September 2005.

*Republika Srpska* (or simply Srpska)—the half of Bosnia where the local Serbian majority established its own autonomous political entity, which remains part and parcel of the new independent Bosnian state.

## S

SACEUR—(NATO's) Supreme Allied Commander in Europe.

SALW—Small Arms and Light Weapons, a term used in arms control protocols to refer to two main classes of weapons: (a) small arms, including hand-held small caliber firearms, usually consisting of handguns, rifles, shotguns, manual, semi-automatic, and fully automatic weapons and man-portable machine guns, (b) light weapons, including a wide range of medium caliber and explosive ordnance: man-portable and vehicle-mounted antipersonnel, antitank, and antiaircraft rockets, missiles, grenade launchers, rocket launchers, landmines, antiaircraft guns, mortars, hand grenades, and rocket propelled grenades (RPGs), and so on.

SATMAR—Satellite Communication.

SCR—Security Council Resolution.

SDA—*Stranka Demokratske Akcije* (Muslim Party for Democratic Action), the main Muslim party in Bosnia and Herzegovina.

SDS—*Srpska Demokratska Stranka* (Serb Democratic Party in Bosnia and Herzegovina). The main Serbian Party in Bosnia, whose head served as a vice president and a member of the presidency council under the Dayton Agreements.
SITREP—Situation Report, usually transmitted from the field to the headquarters.
SOP -Standard Operational Procedure.
SPABAT—Spanish Battalion, United Nation unit responsible for the area of Mostar, stationed in Medjugorje.
SRGS—Special Representative for the General Secretary of the United Nations.
Staff Levels:
C staff—Combined staff. Any time two or more nations' militaries work together, a C staff coordinates them.
G staff—Division and Corps levels.
J staff—Joint staff. Any time two or more services work together, a J staff is used to coordinate them (for instance an Airborne Corps and Army Ground Special Operations Command).
S staff—Battalion and Brigade levels.

## U

UCK—the Albanian acronym of KLA (Kosovo Liberation Army).
UN—United Nations.
UNESCO—United Nations Educational, Scientific, and Cultural Organization.
UNHCR—Office of the United Nations High Commissioner for Refugees, leading humanitarian agency during the Yugoslav wars.
UNICEF—The UN Children's Education Fund.
UNCIVPOL—the UN Civil Police.
UNMO—United Nations Military Officers, often described as the "eyes and ears" of the UN Security Council.
UNPA—United Nations Protected Area, as defined by the UN Security Council resolution. That means enclaves in the war zone which deserved humanitarian protection, like hospitals, besieged populations, or bases of the UN Peace Missions in Bosnia.
UNPROFOR—United Nations Protection Forces.

## W

WHO—World Health Organization.
WW I—World War One (1914-18).

WW II—World War Two (1939-45).

**Y**
YFA—Yugoslav Federal Army.

# List of Officials and Key Functionaries (Local and International)

Many names referred to in the text, some of them unfamiliar to Western ears, are listed below to assist the reader to find his way through this volume. The most prominent names at the service of the United Nations were included in some detail in Chapter Five, so they will only be listed here as part of the complete picture. Others who were introduced in the text, but without much elaboration, are made more familiar to the reader in the following lines. At time, several names are stated as filling the same position, for example, the Commander of the UN forces in Bosnia. This is due to the frequent rotation of officials, especially in the military, who were sent by their countries for a one-year tour of duty and then replaced by others (e.g. Cot, Morillon, Briquemont, and others who served successively as commanders of the UN troops in former Yugoslavia).

### A

Abdic, Fikret—A Muslim leader in Bosnia, whom the Croats suggested as a possible replacement to Alija Izetbegovic.
Acuña, Captain—The SPABAT Intelligence Officer.
Ahtisaari, Martti—A former Finnish president, became a mediator for the United Nations in the Bosnian War and its aftermath.
Akmadic, Mile—Speaker of Bosnian-Croatian Parliament.
Al Alfi, Hussein—Posted as a UN official at Cedric Thornberry's HQ in Zagreb.
Alikadic, Alija (nicknamed Tzakan)—A Muslim leader in Bosnia, led his besieged people in East (Muslim) Mostar. He also was director for International Organizations and chairman of the Delegation for Negotiations on Mostar.

Alispahic, Bakir—Minister of Internal Affairs, BiH. He was born in 1958. He graduated from the school of political science, Department of National Defense. From 1985, he was appointed to several responsible positions in the Ministry of Internal Affairs of BiH. In June 1993, he was appointed as Minister of the Internal Affairs of BiH.

Ahlstrom, Colonel John—Assistant Chief of Staff.

Almuly, Jasa—A Belgrade Jewish author who was reported as stating that he doubted whether an American physician (Philippe Cohen is a dermatologist) could write such a "political propaganda pamphlet," and he suspected that it came from Franjo Tudjman's kitchen in Zagreb.

Andreev, Victor—A Ukrainian diplomat, in charge of civil affairs for the United Nations in Bosnia and Herzegovina.

Andric, Ivo—A celebrated Bosnian writer, Nobel Prize in Literature.

Annan, Kofi—A UN diplomat who started as the UN officer in charge of humanitarian issues in Bosnia. When Boutros-Ghali ended his mandate, Annan took over as the secretary general of the United Nations.

Arbour, Louise—Prosecutor of the ICTY, played a role in prosecuting and bringing to justice in The Hague the war criminals of the Yugoslavian wars.

## B

Bagaric, Dr. Ivan—A Croatian leader in Bosnia.

Baker, Secretary James—A former American Secretary of State under the first Bush administration. He made some annoying remarks during the Bosnian War.

Beganovic, Prof. Mustafa—Minister of Health, BiH. He was born in Cracanica in 1929. He graduated from the school of dental medicine in Sarajevo. He got his master's degree in 1972, completed his specialization in 1973, and got his PhD degree in 1978. Since 1968, he has been working in the school of dental medicine in Sarajevo. He started to work for his professorate in 1981. He was the president of the association of the dentists of BiH, and the vice president and the president of the association of the dentists in Yugoslavia. He is a member of the European committee for dental education. He published more than ten scientific and specialized papers in domestic and foreign magazines. In 1992, he was appointed the minister of health. He speaks German.

Bektasevic, Miss Sadeta—A Muslim interpreter for the United Nations, taken into captivity by the Croats in a HVO prison and later released.

Belmonte, Captain David—A Dutch career officer, who became a vital element in UN bureaucracy in dismantled Yugoslavia, where the system of communications had altogether collapsed and could no longer be counted on. Belmonte was in charge of DUTCHCOM, the signals unit of the Dutch military in NATO, which was posted near Mostar.

Bender, Ivan—Speaker of the Croat House of Representatives in Bosnia.

Bildt, Swedish Prime Minister Carl—He was involved in negotiating the terms of the truce and then the peace agreement between all factions in 1995. He worked closely with Richard Holbrooke.

Blaskic, Colonel—He was personally ordered by Boban to lift the siege on the UNPROFOR command at Kiseljak and to release the Muslim interpreters he had taken prisoners.

Boban, Mate—A Croat and Christian, the president of the self-declared independent Herzeg-Bosnia during the Bosnian War. He was tough and held almost fanatic views of the "others," namely the Muslims who opposed him, whom he wished either to eliminate or to evacuate from the Croatian part of Bosnia-Herzegovina.

Boorda, Admiral Jeremy—Commander of the Air component of the American Southern Command. He prepared on the night of 13-14 March, 1994, in conjunction with General Jean Cot, an air strike with fifty planes on Bosnian targets.

Boras, Franjo—A Muslim leader in Bosnia, whom the Croats suggested as a possible replacement to Alija Izetbegovic.

Boutros-Ghali, Secretary General Boutros—Secretary General of the United Nations during the Bosnian War. He was very much involved in the strategy and deployment of UN forces, and he interfered with daily decisions in the field via his special representative in Bosnia, Mr. Akashi, to whom he lent his strong support, and repeatedly ruled out any consideration of firing him during clashes between him and the international commanders of the UN forces on the ground.

Bozic, Slobodan—Director for UNPROFOR affairs for the Croats in Bosnia.

Briquemont, General Francis—Belgian commander of UN troops in Bosnia, succeeded to General Morillon.

Budakovic, Colonel Sulejman—An HVO officer who took part in the siege around Muslim East Mostar.

Bukvic, Edib—Deputy Prime Minister of BiH. He was born in Sarajevo in 1957. He graduated from the school of economics, department for marketing, there. From 1982 until 1991, he worked in the corporation Energo Invest. In October 1991, he was appointed as assistant to the

Minister of Finance (Republic's Budget Office) in the BiH government. In March 1992, he was elected to the secretariat general of the government auditing office of BiH.

Bulatovic, Momir—A Milosevic faithful follower in Montenegro, who was handily defeated in the first elections by independent and more liberal Milo Djukanovic.

## C

Chernomyrdin, Viktor—A Russian diplomat and prime minister. Together with Martti Ahtisaari they presented on 2 June 1999 to Yugoslavian President Milosevic the requirements of the G8 to end the conflict in Kosovo. This plan included the main objectives of the West for the deployment of an international force, the withdrawal of Serbian forces, and the return of refugees.

Chirac, French President Jacques—Jacques René Chirac; born 29 November 1932) is a French politician who served as President of France from 1995 to 2007. He previously served as Prime Minister of France from 1974 to 1976 and from 1986 to 1988 (making him the only person to hold the position of Prime Minister twice under the Fifth Republic), and as Mayor of Paris from 1977 to 1995.

Clark, General Wesley—He served in the American delegation in the peace negotiations in Bosnia and was later to become NATO's Supreme Allied Commander Europe SACEUR in 1997.

Clinton, American President Bill—William Jefferson "Bill" Clinton (born William Jefferson Blythe III; 19 August, 1946) is an American politician who served as the 42nd President of the United States from 1993 to 2001. Inaugurated at age 46, he was the third-youngest president. He took office at the end of the Cold War, and was the first president of the baby boomer generation. Clinton has been described as a New Democrat. Many of his policies have been attributed to a centrist Third Way philosophy of governance. Before becoming president he was the Governor of Arkansas serving two non-consecutive terms from 1979 to 1981 and from 1983 to 1992.

Cohen, Philip—An American dermatologist, author of the controversial *Serbia's Secret War*.

Cohen-Tanugi, Robert—In his series of articles, which has drawn world attention, he proposed the thesis that the United States was basically interested in promoting Islamic states to create the "Green Belt," loyal to it, around Russia and China and its subsidiary, the "Green Diagonal," designed to link central Europe with Turkey, in order to restore the power and hegemony of this pivot of American strategy to its Ottoman times.

Cole, Colonel—Aide de camp of General Francis Briquemont, commander of the United Nations Forces in Bosnia-Herzegovina. Often participated in negotiations between the parties.

Coloma, Major Juan—An officer with the Spanish Battalion.

Cot, General Jean—Commander of the UNPROFOR forces in former Yugoslavia in 1993.

## D

De Castro, Colonel Miguel—Second in command of the Spanish forces in Bosnia, under the command of Colonel Morales.

De Hayes, General Veer—British General in the British forces in Bosnia.

De Salas, Carlos—G5 Commander, military-civilian operations in the SPABAT forces.

Delic, General Rasim—The commander of the Muslim forces in Bosnia.

Despotovic, Nedjeljke—Minister without portfolio, BiH. He was born in Tuzla in 1948. Since 1948, he has been living in Sarajevo. He graduated from the school of law in Sarajevo. He was the president of the executive board of the community assembly of the municipality center and executive board of the city assembly. He was the director of the trade company Marketi and stock company Business Systems—UPI Sarajevo. He is a member of the European chamber of commerce, finance, and industry, in Brussels. He speaks English.

Dizdar, Mehmedalija Mak—He was one of the greatest Bosnian and Yugoslav poets and was born in Stolac, in 1917. He spent his World War II years as a Communist Partisan, moving frequently from place to place to escape the Ustasha-Nazi persecutions.

Djukanovic, Milo—An advocate of liberalization and greater autonomy of his republic, Montenegro, from Serbia and the Federation. He got a landslide victory against Momir Bulatovic, the Milosevic faithful follower.

Drekovic, General Ramiz—The Fourth Corps Commander of the Muslim Armija in Mostar.

Duburg, Colonel Roger—He served as chief of staff of the sector of Sarajevo in the UN forces, counted among the personal staff of the commander of UNPROFOR. He was put in charge of military negotiations between the warring factions.

Durakovic, Asaf—A Croatian physician and expert in nuclear medicine, who was also recognized for his poetry and verse. He was born in

Stolac in 1940. He is a founder and medical research director of the Toronto based Uranium Medical Research Centre.

Durakovic, Prof. Enes—Minister of education, science, culture, and sport, BiH. He was born in Derventa in 1947. He is a professor at the school of philosophy in Sarajevo and the president of the Muslim cultural society *Preporod*. He is the author of the monograph on great BiH poets, *Mak Dizdar and Skender Kulenovic* and of the book, *Rijec i Svijet, The Word and the World* on BiH poets of the twentieth century. Together with Alija Isakovic, he was the editor of the project *Bosnian Literature,* in one hundred volumes.

Dzabic, Professor Nadjija—He was designated to participate in a UNICEF seminar in Israel, dealing, among others, with the situation of traumatized children in East Mostar. Amela Pedisa was designated to bring up the life conditions of the children in Mostar.

Dzidic, Fuad—Minister for Coordination for Zenica-Doboj region, BiH. He was born in Zenica in 1954. He graduated from the school of philosophy, department of philosophy and sociology. He got his master's degree in the field of philosophy and European humanism. From 1979 until 1981, he was professionally engaged as the member of the editorial staff of the magazine, *Nasa Rijec*, from Zenica, and then as a teacher in high school. He published specialized articles in a large number of magazines. He published two books, *Robija Sutnje* (about the suffering of Muslims in the period 1945-1987), and together with Esad Hecimovic the book, *Dan Iskona: Vdera-Nacija-Politika (A Day out of Mind: the Vdera-Nation Policy)*. He speaks English.

**F**

Filipovic, Ilja—An HVO official.

Finn, Ruder—President of the public relations firm of Global Public Affairs, based in Washington, DC, to which Muslims and Croats turned to improve their image in the United States.

Frewer, Commodore Barry—Press Information Officer in the UN headquarters in Sarajevo.

**G**

Ganic, Vice President Ejup—Vice President to President Izetbegovic of Bosnia during the war. He feigned "surprise and shock" when Muslim troops opened fire on a Danish detachment which was securing the Sarajevo Airport, in preparation for the papal visit there, and claimed that UNPROFOR falsely accused a Muslim unit due to their anti-Muslim biased attitude. Subsequent to this incident, the papal visit was cancelled. President Izetbegovic promptly blamed UN Special Envoy Yasushi Akashi for "deceiving" the Vatican by exaggerating security concerns.

Gojer, Gradimir—Minister without portfolio, BiH. He was born in Mostar in 1951. He graduated from the faculty of philosophy, comparative literature with theater. He was the director of the theater in Sarajevo, then artistic director of the youth theater in Mostar, and director and artistic director of the youth theater in Sarajevo. He was the member of the editorial board of *Kamerni Teatar* in Sarajevo. He was a member of the editorial staff of the magazine, *Pozoriste*, from Tuzla and *Bastina* from Sarajevo. He was one of the founders of the Sarajevo war theater. He is the vice president of the association of the theatrical and movie worker of the Croatian cultural society, *Napredak*. He directed plays in all BiH theaters and most Yugoslavian theaters. He was awarded numerous theatrical awards and the "April 6" award of Sarajevo.

Gore, Vice President Al – He served under President Clinton and got his hand in Bosnian affairs. Some Bosnians felt that it would have been worthwhile if the vice president had concentrated on human rights. Indeed, in a conversation with Silajdzic, Gore had proffered the opinion that this "conflict was both immoral and cowardly treated.[426]"

Granic, Mate—Croatian Foreign Minister from 1993-2002. One of the most moderate associates of Tudjman in Zagreb.

Grubac, General Radovan—A Serbian general. He commanded the Herzegovina Corps of the Bosnian Serb Army, headquartered in Gacko.

## H

Hadizukic, Miss Amra—A Muslim interpreter for the United Nations who was captive in a HVO prison and then released.

Hadzihasanovic, Hamdo—Minister of Defense of BiH. He was born in Rogatica in 1942. He graduated from the school of mechanical engineering in Sarajevo. He worked as constructor and manager in the factory of filters in Rogatica, and finally as a manager of the factory's department of transmissions and as director of the research and development department of the corporation, Famos, in Sarajevo. From 1985 he was employed in the Ministry of Defense in the logistical sector.

---

[426] Source: Memo No 13—notes from the meeting in Sarajevo between Albert Benabou and Haris Silajxic, Bosnian Prime Minister.

Hammerskjold, Dag—Secretary General of the UN, in the 1950s, who died on duty in Congo.

Holbrooke, Richard—An American diplomat, whose advice on the Balkans determined the course and the outcome of the Clinton administration policy there. The Dayton Accords, which ostensibly ended the conflict, were said to have been his brainchild.

Hulme, Jerry—UNHCR Medjugorje coordinator.

Husseini, Haj Amin al—The Mufti of Jerusalem since the 1920s, a violent opponent of both the British Mandate in Palestine and of Zionists, whom he combated militarily and politically. During WW II, he associated with the Nazis against the British and the Jews, who were perceived as the sworn enemies of both, and subscribed to the Nazi "final solution." As the German ranks were depleted during the war, they sent him to Bosnia to recruit Muslims there for the infamous Handjar SS Division, and he continued to support the pro-Nazi Muslim propaganda from Berlin until the end of the war.

# I

Imamovic, Munever—Minister of Restoration and Construction of BiH. He was born in Gradacac in 1943. He graduated from the school of civil engineering. From 1965 until 1986, he worked in the company, *Energoprojekt-hidroinzinjering*. From 1986 until 1990, he was the leading engineer in the hydro electrical plant on Drina in the company, *Elektroprivreda*. He was a member of the BiH. Since 1990, he has been employed as the manager of the hydro construction engineering sector, in the corporation *Energoinvest-enebgoinzenjering*. He speaks English.

Ivanov, Igor—First Deputy Foreign Minister of Russia who participated in the peace settlement in Bosnia.

Izetbegovic, President Alija—President of Bosnia-Herzegovina. In 1970, well before the collapse of the Yugoslavian order imposed by Tito and the outburst of communal nationalism which instigated the process of its disintegration, a political manifesto was written by a then unknown Muslim in Bosnia, Alija Izetbegovic (born in 1925), but not immediately released to the public. It was, however, duplicated and made available to individual Muslims, who circulated it among their coreligionists, apparently to serve as a guide of a Muslim order to replace the godless communist system in Bosnia. That pamphlet was known as the *Islamska Deklaracija* and became in fact the platform of his Democratic Action Party (SDA), which won the majority of the Muslim votes in the first free elections in Bosnia-Herzegovina (November 1990). Otherwise, that pamphlet maintained a low profile due to the controversy it created and was not heard of again. However, judging from the wide appeal of Izetbegovic's later book, *Islam Between East and West*, which was published in English in the United States (1984), then in Turkish in Istanbul (1987), and in Serbian in Belgrade (1988), where his Islamic dreams were laid out, and then from his election as president of Bosnia in the first free elections, he had remained quite popular among the Muslims of Bosnia.

## J

Jazzar (the Butcher), Ahmed al—He was born in 1720 in Stolac, Bosnia and became, under the Ottoman Empire, the famous Jazzar Pasha ruler of Acre and Galilee from 1775 till his death in 1804.

Jacolin, Ambassador Henry—French ambassador in Bosnia and Herzegovina.

Jelskovic, Feda—A Muslim interpreter for the United Nations, taken in captivity by the Croats, in an HVO prison, then released. Four Muslim interpreters had just been freed at 8:00 p.m., a few hours earlier, from a Croatian prison of the HVO. Three of them, Mr. Feda Jelskovic, Miss Sadeta Bektasevic, and Miss Amra Hadizukic, were employed by the United Nations, and the fourth, Mr. Samir Osmanovic, by the European Union.

Jude, Rudman—A young Croat who lived in Australia and had just arrived in Bosnia, eagerly offering his service to the Croatian war effort as a personal adviser to the president.

## K

Karadzic, Radovan—The political leader of the Bosnian Serbs. He was later persecuted as a war criminal by the Hague.

Klaric, Smail—Chairman of the Civil Authority in besieged Muslim East Mostar. He often expressed in the most bitter terms his humiliation and despair at this situation.

Knezevic, Ivo—Minister of Information, BiH. He was born in Vienna in 1943. He graduated from the school of philosophy, department of philosophy and sociology. He got his master's degree at the University of Sarajevo. He was a teacher of philosophy and sociology in high school in Konjic. From 1971 until 1982, he was a research fellow and the head of the department for culture and information in the city committee of the Communist Party of Sarajevo. From 1977

until 1987, he was the assistant professor (course on sociology) at the school of economics at the University of Sarajevo. From 1982 until 1986, he was first executive secretary and then secretary of the municipal committee of the Communist Party of the Sarajevo municipality. From 1986 until 1987, he was the executive secretary of the city committee of the Communist Party of Sarajevo. After these functions, he spent four years in Egypt. From 1991 until 1993, he was a professional member of the Social Democratic Party of BiH. In March 1993, he was appointed the minister of information. He speaks French and English.
Kohl, German Chancellor Helmut
Kolak, Dr. Toni—A Croatian leader from Bosnia.
Koluder, Ibrahim—Minister of Coordination for Mostar region, BiH. He was born in Mostar in 1943. He graduated from the school of electrical engineering in 1968. He has been the general manager of the company, PTT, in Mostar since 1988. He speaks German.
Kostunica, Vojislav—Leader of the Serbian Democratic Party, who opposed the policy of Milosevic, the head of the Yugoslav Federation, but he was also a nationalist and hostile to the West. He served as a prime minister after the fall of Milosevic.
Kouchner, Bernard—A French diplomat and human rights activist who was appointed by Secretary General Kofi Annan as the administrator for the civil peace in Kosovo.
Krajisnik, Momcilo—(SDS) A Serb who was elected to serve as the vice president under Izetbegovic in the Presidency Council of Bosnia, in accordance with the new accords.
Kraljevic, Blaz—Leader of HOS, the Croat-Bosnian faction which supported, together with the Muslims, the territorial integrity of the Bosnian state, contrary to the position taken by Mate Boban.
Kraus, Dr.—The president of the Jewish community of Zagreb. He suggested that at least the Catholic Church in Croatia should follow the example of Pope John Paul II and apologize for the past sins against the Jews.
Kreso, Dr. Sead—Minister of Finance of BiH. He was born in Sarajevo in 1954. He graduated from the school of economics in Sarajevo. He got his master's degree in 1984 (his master's thesis was "The World Inflation") and PhD degree in 1990 at the University of Zagreb. He was assistant professor at the school of economics in Sarajevo, of the course "Finances." He was also the advisor for finances in the na-

tional bank of BiH. He published numerous scientific and specialized articles. He speaks English and French.

Kulenovic, Dr. Salih—Minister for Coordination for Tuzla-Drina region, BiH. He was born in Jajce in 1944. He graduated from the school of natural sciences and mathematics in Sarajevo. His PhD dissertation was on "Antropogeographical and Ethnological Characteristics of the Population of Gracanica." From 1971, he was employed in the museum of eastern Bosnia, and then the regional museum for northeastern Bosnia. In 1991, he was appointed the assistant of the director of the Republic's Bureau of Statistics in Tuzla. Since the beginning of the war in BiH, he was engaged at first as the assistant to the commander for morale and then as the assistant to the commander of the Second Corps of the BiH Army.

## L

Labus, Miroljub—Deputy Prime Minister in the Zizic government, a member of the coalition with Vojislav Kostunica.

Lasic, Brigadier General Milijenko—An HVO commander of the area of West Mostar.

Leakey, Colonel Arundell David -The UK military representative in the peace negotiations in Bosnia, later to become commander of EUFOR in 2005.

Levinsohn, Florence Hamlish—A Chicago journalist, who noted in her book about that war that Muslims and Croats had paid thirty thousand dollars monthly in fees to the American public relations firm, Ruder Finn, based in Washington, to tell their story to the world.

Ljubljankic, Dr. Irfan—Minister of Foreign Affairs, BiH. He was born in Bihac in 1952. He graduated from medical school, got his master's degree and completed his specialized training. He published a large number of scientific articles in the field of medicine and general culture. He speaks English and Russian.

Loghan, Captain Peter—A British intelligence officer who served as Benabou's military attaché in the war zone.

Lovrenovic, Slobodan—Press director for the Bosnian Croat entity.

## M

Mahmutcehajic, Prof. Rusmir—Minister of Specialized Production of BiH. He was born in Stolac in 1948. He has a PhD degree in the field of electro-technical sciences. He was a professor at the University of

Osijek. He is the minister of energy and industry in BiH. He speaks English.
Major, British Prime Minister John
Mascesa, Ramo—An HVO official and representative of the Ministry of the Interior.
Mihailovic, General—A royalist supporter of the king of Yugoslavia, who continued to oppose the German occupation at the head of the Chetniks after the king fled to London. Occasionally he collaborated with the Germans, and that made him a controversial figure of wartime Yugoslavia, since he was at first supported by the British and then abandoned by them when they realized his double game.
Milankovic, Alexandra (Sasha)—Benabou's translator.
Milosevic, Slobodan—Leader of the Serbian Nationalist Movement in Serbia. He reorganized all the powers under his authority in 1987. Following a general strike and violent clashes in March 1989, he declared a state of emergency and sent the army to Kosovo. One year later, the chauvinistic spirit gained in crescendo, upsetting the West, who used NATO to bomb Belgrade and other cities to submission. Later, he was caught and tried in the Hague for war crimes. He died in captivity before the verdict was delivered.
Milutinovic, Milan—A Milosevic faithful partisan, who became president of Serbia after the fall of his patron in 1996.
Mladic, General Ratko—The senior Serbian commander in Bosnia who was involved in the Srebrenica Affair and later surrendered to the Hague for war crimes that he was alleged to have committed.
Molina, Captain Gerardo—G2 commander branch in charge of intelligence and security in SPABAT.
Morales, Colonel Angel—CO of SPABAT, with HQ in the Mostar area.
Morillon, General Philippe Morillon—Commander of the UN forces in former Yugoslavia.
Muratovic, Hasan—Minister without portfolio, BiH. He was born in Olovo in 1940. He got his PhD degree in the field of organizational sciences and is a professor of economics at the school of electrical engineering. From 1965 until 1975, he was the director in the corporation, Famos, in Sarajevo. From 1975 until 1978, he was a technical director in the United Bus Company of Zambia. From 1978 until 1988, he was a research fellow and technical advisor at the Institute for Organization and Economy in Sarajevo. From 1988 until 1992, he was appointed the minister of forestry and industry of processing of

lumber in BiH government. He published three books and more than eighty articles. He speaks English.

## N

Nakamitsu, Izumi—Representative of the UNHCR at the UN office in Zagreb.
Navarro, General Prado—Deputy Force Commander, of the UN forces in BiH.

## O

O'Brien, Sergeant Sean—He was sent by BRITFOR to Medjugorje to assist Captain (then Major) Logan as a military attaché to Benabou.
O'Reilly, General—The UN High Commissioner for Civilian Police. He was borrowed from the Canadian Mounted Police and was an experienced police officer in criminal affairs.
Oriani, Isabella—A representative of the Italian Consortium of Solidarity, which had taken charge of sheltering Bosnian refugees in Italy.
Oric, General Nasser—A famous Muslim warrior during the Bosnian War. He commanded the Muslim fighters in the Srebrenica enclave in eastern Bosnia, which was surrounded by Serbs, and he was reputed for having led the unit, which prided itself as the descendant of the pro-Nazi Handjar SS Division of WW II.
Orucevic, Safet—Deputy Cmdr. of the Mostar Brigade and Political Representative of Izetbegovic in Muslim East Mostar.
Osmanovic, Mr. Samir—A Muslim interpreter, employed by the European Union, who was taken prisoner by HVO Croats and then released.
Owen, David—Former British Foreign Minister, who worked with others in a UN commission to mediate a cessation of hostilities in the Bosnian War. Among others, he served as cochairman of the commission together with Cyrus Vance.

## P

Pasalic, General—An HVO official.
Pedisa, Prof. Amela—She was designated to participate in a UNICEF seminar in Israel, dealing, among others, with the situation of traumatized children in East Mostar.
Pehar, Mate—The chief of the Mostar police, for the Croats.

Pejanovic, Mirko—Serbian representative in the Bosnian government, who was viewed by the Croats as a servant of Alija Izetbegovic, and therefore they opposed him.

Petkovic, General Milivoj—Commander of the HVO and member of Croatian Defense Council, the separatist Croatian Forces in Bosnia. He was appointed by Franjo Tudjman, the Croat president, as the top military man in Zagreb. Petkovic manifested a hands-off approach, acting as a maestro in military strategy who was trusted with pulling off magic solutions that would assure the victory of the Croats.

Pesic, Dragisa—A Montenegrin politician, a member of the Socialist People's Party of Montenegro, and a former ally of the ex-president, who succeeded him as head of government.

Petritsch, Wolfgang – (OHR Office of the High Representative) Wolfgang Petritsch (born 26 August 1947) is an Austrian diplomat of Slovene ethnicity. Petritsch served between August 1999 and May 2002 as the High Representative for Bosnia and Herzegovina. In this role, Petritsch was the final authority on civilian implementation of the 1995 Dayton Peace Agreement. While living in Bosnia and Herzegovina – one of the most mine-infested countries in the world – Petritsch witnessed firsthand the humanitarian impact of anti-personnel mines.

Pita, Captain—From G5, the military branch in charge of military cooperation and the media of the Spanish Battalion.

Pogarcic, Vladislav (nicknamed Vlado)—a Croatian leader who counseled President Boban on international affairs.

Prlic, Prime Minister Jadranko—Of the Herzeg Republic, which was the Croatian part of Bosnia, who managed the business of the area, gathering around him local leaders and decision makers

# R

Rajic, Ivica—A Croatian field commander in Bosnia, who was accused by Serbian General Grubac of having bombarded Sarajevo in revenge against the BiH Armija, which had ejected the Croat Brigade from Sarajevo. Grubac's view could not be totally excluded, since the Croatian units often acted on their own local initiative.

Ramirez, Alfredo—G6 Commander, Information Systems of SPABAT.

Ramsey, Brigadier General Angus—Chief of Staff. Major-General Angus Iain Ramsay (born 1946) is a former senior British Army officer. He served as Chief of Staff of the United Nations Force in Bosnia in

1993 and Commander of the Multi-National Division (South-West) in Bosnia in 1997.

Rebic, Dr. Adalbert—One of the experts on Judaism and Christianity in Croatia. He asserted that the crime was not committed by the Catholic Church or on its behalf but was committed by individuals in the name of the ideology that was subordinated to Hitler's Germany.

Reith, General John—Commander of BRITFOR in Divulje near Split.

Rose, General Sir Michael—UN Force Commander, Kiseljak.

Roso, General Ante—HVO Commander.

Rugova, President Ibrahim—A Muslim Albanian leader from Kosovo who was elected as its first president at the issue of the Yugoslavian wars.

## S

Sacirbey, Muhamed—Bosnian Foreign Minister.

Salafranca, Major Alvarez—ACOS to the SPABAT.

Salom, Captain Julio—Served at the G5 office of SPABAT.

Sancevic, Zdravko—Croatia's ambassador to Bosnia and Herzegovina.

Šarčević, Professor Edin—University of Leipzig professor and Bosnian Academy of Sciences and Arts member.

Sarid, Minister Yossi—He arranged for Sasha, Benabou's interpreter, who had a secret love affair with the British officer, Peter Loghan, to be transported to Israel to deliver her twins, the fruit of her love, in a Haifa hospital.

Searby, General Robin—Posted in Divulje, the HQ of BRITFOR.

Silajdzic, Dr. Haris—Prime Minister of BiH. Born in Sarajevo in 1945. He graduated and got his master's degree at the University of Bengasi. His doctoral dissertation was on the relations between the United States and Albania. He published several articles in the field of international relations. He was professor at the University of Pristina. From 1990, he was the BiH foreign minister. He speaks English, Arabic, and French.

Skjold, Agner—UN official in Bosnia.

Smailbegovic, Faruk—Minister of Economy. He was born in 1941. He graduated from the school of mechanical engineering and has a master of science degree. He held responsible positions in the company, *Unis Pobjeda*, from 1968 until 1992. He was the member of the business office of the company. In July 1993, he was appointed the general manager of the Unis-holding. He speaks German and Russian.

Smajkic, Prof. Arif—Minister for Refugees and Social Welfare of BiH. He was born in Mostar in 1933. He graduated from the medical school in Sarajevo and got his master's degree at the University of Zagreb (field radiological protection). His PhD dissertation was "Social and Health Consequences of the Migration of Population." In 1973, he became a research fellow at the post graduate studies at the School of Health in London and of Caroline's Institute for Social Medicine in Stockholm. Since 1963, he has been working in the Institute for Social Medicine, Organization and Economy of Health care of the medical school in Sarajevo. In March 1990, he was appointed the director of the BiH public health institute. Since 1980, he has been the advisor of the World Health Organization in the field of organizing health care and medical education. He published 240 scientific and specialized papers. He was the founder and editor of the international magazine, *Substance Socio-medical*. He speaks English and Russian.

Smith, General Rupert—A British officer who commanded the troops at Bosnia and Herzegovina at one time.

Solana, Javier—The Secretary General of NATO who announced on 23 March 1999 the "launching of air operations over the Federal Republic of Yugoslavia".He continued to be involved in Bosnian and Kosovo affairs after he was elected the representative of the European Union, in charge of foreign affairs.

Sorenson, Leo Bang—A UN official in Bosnia.

Sotra, Zdravko—Born in Stolac in 1933, he is a Bosnian Serb who grew to become a renowned film director and scriptwriter.

Sray, Lieutenant Colonel John E.—From the US Army, an analyst at the FMSO (Foreign Military Studies Office). He issued in 1995 papers reevaluating the American policy in the aftermath of the Bosnian civil war.

Šarčević, Ante—Nineteenth century conservative Croatian nationalist who termed the Muslims "the Flower of Croatia."

Stepinac, Cardinal—The Controversial head of the Catholic Church in WW II Ustasha Croatia, who on the one hand is claimed as having supported the rights of the Jews as well as the Orthodox Serbs. But, on the other hand, he is accused of having looked the other way while Serbs, Gypsies, and Jews were being annihilated.

Stojanov, Prof. Dragoljub—Minister of External Trade of BiH. He was born in Sombor in 1946. Since 1947, he has been living in Sarajevo. He got his PhD degree from the school of economics at the University of Sarajevo in 1975. Since 1985, he has been a full professor in the school of economics of the University of Sarajevo. From 1977/1978 he studied in the United States as the holder of a Fulbright scholarship, and in 1985 he was a guest professor in the organization of the Fulbright Foundation. He is the member of the board for economic relations in BiH and the president of the scientific section of the association of the economists of BiH. He was a member of the center for strategic studies in Belgrade, a member of the executive board of Unis-Komerc. During 1990, he was a member of the expert group of the presidency of the Social Federative Republic of Yugoslavia. He was a member of the expert group of the BiH Presidential London and Geneva Conference. In 1992, he attended the summit of the nonaligned countries as a member of the BiH delegation. He published numerous books, essays, and papers in scientific and specialized magazines.

Stojic, Bruno—Croatian Minister of Defense in Bosnia.

## T

Thornberry, Cedric – An Irish diplomat in charge of civil affairs at the UN HQ in Zagreb.

Tito, General Josip Broz—A Croat at birth, he rose as a Communist in prewar Yugoslavia, who during World War II created the Partisan forces, which relentlessly fought the German occupation and caused it enormous losses and damages, at a high price. He ensured British support, financial, political, and military, after Britain had abandoned the Chetniks, and by the end of the war, he became the predominant power in Yugoslavia, which welcomed the Soviets into Belgrade in 1944. He reunited the prewar federation under his communist regime, of which he became the prevailing power until his death.

Tomic, Ivan—Chairman of the Croat delegation for the negotiations on Mostar.

Trnka, Prof. Kasim—Minister of Justice of BiH. He was born in Sarajevo in 1939. He got his PhD degree in the field of law. From 1962 until 1976, he was the advisor for the political system in the central committee of the Communist Party of BiH. Since 1985, he was a professor at the law school in Mostar. Since March 1985, he has also been the president of the constitutional court of BiH. He speaks French.

Tudjman, President Franjo—President of Croatia who was a member of the Partisans under Tito during WW II. When Croatia separated from Yugoslavia in 1992, he became its president. His books caused much controversy due to his attempts to diminish the numbers of Serbs and Jews eliminated under the Ustasha regime. Even more controversy was generated by his attempts to hide his nationalistic propensities and put up moderate face to gain western, especially American, favor.

## V

Valenci, Andrea—A UN employee at the UN HQ in New York.

Vance, Cyrus—Former American Secretary of State. He was dispatched by the Clinton administration to work out a ceasefire in the incessantly growing open hostility between the belligerents in Bosnia since the opening of the war in 1992. He mediated one of the first cessation of hostilities as cochairman, together with David Owen, of a UN commission.

Veladzic, Mirsad—Minister of Coordination for Bihac-Banja Luka region, BiH. He was born in Bosanska Krupa in 1956. He graduated from the faculty of agriculture and got his master's degree at the school of chemical engineering in Novi Sad. From 1982, he has been at different managerial positions. He was the president of the executive board of the community assembly of Velika Kladusa and Bihac.

## W

Wahlgren, General Lars-Erik—The Commander of UNPROFOR.

Williams, Paul—Through the Public International Law & Policy Group (PILPG), he served as legal counsel to the Bosnian government delegation during the peace negotiations.

## Y

Yasushi, Akashi—The chief UN official in Bosnia. According to the Washington Post (7 May, 1993), the Clinton administration reprimanded him for letting Serb tanks traverse a zone near Sarajevo prohibited to heavy weapons by UN order. State Department spokesperson, Christine Shelly, called on him "to do a better job. We would not like to see him acquiesce in actions which violate the exclusion zone," she said.

## Z

Zimmermann, Ambassador Allen—He served as the last American ambassador in Yugoslavia and was involved in negotiations among the parties during the war.

Zizic, Zoran—A Montenegrin politician, in accordance with the constitution. He was elected as prime minister to succeed Milosevic. A member of the Popular Socialist Party, he was seconded by Deputy

Prime Minister Miroljub Labus, a member of the coalition with Vojislav Kostunica.

Zubak, Kresimir—Head of the HDZ, the main Croatian party in Bosnia, who served as vice president and member of the presidency council of Bosnia after the first elections.

Zuljevic, Salko—Chief of the Mostar police, for the Muslims.

# Bibliography

Documents
Owen-Vance Peace Plan
The Dayton Accords
Security Council Resolutions on Bosnia
Secretary General's Reports
Field Reports by Benabou and others
Newspapers, Magazines and Websites
Debatte: Review of Contemporary German Affairs
Encyclopedia Britannica
Financial Times
Foreign Affairs
Herald Tribune
Holocaust and Genocide Studies
Los Angeles Times
Mediterranean Quarterly
New York Times
Newsday
Nova Hrvatska
Religion in Eastern Europe
Revue des Deux Mondes
Patterns of Global Terrorism, US Department of State
Policy Watch, The Washington Institute
Terrorism and Political Violence
Vecernji List, Zagreb
Wall Street Journal,
Washington Times
www.britannica.com/EBchecked/topic/1365562/Bosnian-conflict
www.islamicpluralism.org/1663/the-heritage-of-ottoman
http://original.antiwar.com/malic/2003/10/23/the-real-izetbegovic/

Anzulovic, Branimir. *Heavenly Serbia: From Myth to Genocide*. London: Hurst and Co., 1999.
Bat, Ye'or. *The Decline of Eastern Christianity Under Islam: From Jihad to Dhimmitude*. Madison: Fairley Dickinson University Press,1996.

———. *The Dhimmi*. Madison: Fairley Dickinson University Press, 1985.

———. *Eurabia*. Madison: Fairley Dickinson University Press, 2005.

Bostom, Andrew. *The Legacy of Antisemitism*. New York: Prometheus, 2008.

———. *The Legacy of Jihad*. New York: Prometheus, 2004.

Canak, Jovan, ed. *Greater Albania: Concepts and Possible Consequences*. Belgrade: The Institute of Geo-Political Studies, 1998.

Cohen-Tanugi, Robert. "The Green Line," in Diaspora/Le Lien, No. 112 of 30 July, 1999; No 117 of 22 October, 1999; and No 120 of 3 December, 1999.

Covic, Boze, ed. *Roots of Serbian Aggression*. Zagreb: Center for Foreign Languages, 1993.

Charuel, Marc and Gaston Besson. *Une Vie en Ligne de Mire (A French Volunteer in the Croatian War of Independence)*. Zagreb: Studeni, 2011.

Garankapetanović, Munir. *Mladi c_e mjesec opet blistati*. Sarajevo: NIPP Ljiljan, 1996.

Gitman, Esther. *When Courage Prevailed: Rescue and Survival of Jews in the Independent State of Croatia, 1941-5*. St. Paul: Paragon House, 2011.

Goldstein, Ivo. *Croatia: A History*. London: Hurst and Co., 1999.

Goldstein, Ivo. *Holocaust in Zagreb*. Zagreb:

Israeli, Raphael. *The Death Camps in Croatia: Visions and Revisions*. City: Transaction, 2013.

———. *The Islamic Challenge in Europe*. New Brunswick: Transaction, 2008.

———. *Jerusalem Divided: the Armistice Regime (1947-1967)*. London: Frank Cass, 2003.

———. *Palestinians Between Israel and Jordan*. New York: Praeger, 1991.

Kohlman, Evan. *Al-Qa'ida's Jihad in Europe: the Afghan-Bosnian Network*. New York/Oxford: Berg, 2004.

Krestic, Vasilije. *Through Genocide to a Greater Croatia*. Belgrade: Svet Knjige, 2009.

Levinsohn, Florence Hamlish. *Belgrade, Among the Serbs*.

Marijan, Davor. *Storm*. Zagreb: 2010.

Marijanovic, Jovan ed. *The Collaboration of Mijailovic's Cetniks with the Enemy Forces of Occupation (1941-44)*. Beograd: Arhivski Pregled, 1976.

Miller, William. *The Balkans: Romania, Bulgaria, Serbia, and Montenegro*. London: Fisher Unwin, 1923.
Novak, Viktor. *Magnum Crimen: Half a Century of Clericalism in Croatia*. Belgrade.
Reinhartz, Dennis. "Serbia's Secret War: Propaganda and the Deceit of History," in *Holocaust and Genocide Studies* by Philip Cohen, February 2000.
Shatzmiller, M. ed. *Islam and Bosnia: Conflict Resolution and Foreign Policy*. McGill University Press, 2002.
Schechtman, Joseph. *Postwar Population Transfers in Europe (1945-55)*. Philadelphia: University of Pennsylvania Press, 1962.
Skoro, Gojko. *Genocide over the Serbs in the Independent State of Croatia: Be Catholic or Die*. Beograd: Institute of Contemporary History, 1995.
Svob, Melita. *Jews in Croatia: Holocaust Victims and Survivors*. Zagreb: Jewish Community in Zagreb, 2000.
Terzic, Slavenko ed. *Islam, the Balkans and the Great powers XIV -XX Century, Proceedings of the Conference held in Belgrade, 11-13 December, 1996*. Belgrade, Historical Institute of Serbian Acadmey of Sciences and Arts, 1997.
Todorov, Vrban. "The Federalist Idea as a Means for Preserving the Integrity of the Ottoman Empire."
Umeljic, Vladimir. *Definitionism Theory and the Phenomenon of Genocide*. Beograd, 2010.
Zerjavic, Vladimir. *Population Losses in Yugoslavia 1941-5*. Zagreb, 1997.

## Articles

Alec Russell,UK *Financial Times*, 16 May, 2011.
Bardos, G.N. "Balkan Blowback? Osama Bin-Laden in Southeastern Europe." *Mediterranean Quarterly* 13.1 (2002).
Batakovic, Dusan "La Bosnie-Herzegovine: le System des Alliances." in Terzic, op. cit. pp 335- 343.
Bled, Jean Paul. "La Question de Bosnie-Hercegovine." *Revue des Deux Mondes*, Paris, 1876, Vol II, No 1, 237-254.
Brown, M.B. "Slobodan Milosevic and How the US Used al-Qa'ida in the Balkans", Debatte: Review of Contemporary German Affairs, 14.2:161-165
Gompert, David, "How to Defeat Serbia», Foreign Affairs, July/August 94, Vol. 73, No.4, 30 – 47

Hadzivukovic, Vesna (and others), "The Future Saints": in Vesna Hadzivukovic and others (edts), Chronicle of Announced Death, 1993. 46.
Israeli, . Raphael "The Charter of Allah: the Platform of the Hamas", in Y. Alexander (ed), The Annual of Terrorism, 1988-9, Nijhoff, the Netherlands, 1990, 99-134
Israeli, Raphael, "From Bosnia to Kosovo: the Reislamization of the Balkans", Palestinians Between Nationalism and Islam, Vallentine-Mitchell, 2008, London, 75-102
Israeli, Raphael , "Islamikaze and their Significance", in Terrorism and Political Violence, Vol. 9 No 3 (Autumn 1997) 112-3.
Karcic, H. "Alija Izetbegovic and the Myth of the Islamic State: Separating Fact from Fiction", Religion in Eastern Europe 29.4:32-39, November, 2009
Lewis, Flora, "The Kosovo Mission of the UN is left to Fail", The Herald Tribune, 10 March, 2000, 8.
Malcolm, N.R., "Bosnian Conflict", Encyclopaedia Britannica, retrieved from :www.britannica.com/EBchecked/topic/1365562/Bosnian-conflict]
Malic, Nebojsa, The Real Izetbegovic, 24 October, 2003
http://original.antiwar.com/malic/2003/10/23/the-real-izetbegovic/
Pena, C.V. "Al-Qa'ida:the Balkans Connection", Mediterranean Quarterly, 16.4: 65-76, 2005
Raphael, Therese, "Kosovo", The Wall Street Journal, 7 July, 2000.
Reuter,.Jens , "From Religious Community to Nation: the Ethnogenesis of the Bosnian Muslims", in Terzic (ed. ) op. cit. 617-23.
Riedlmayer, A.L. "From the Ashes:the Past and Future of Bosnia's Cultural; Heritage", in Shatzmiller, M. (ed), Islam and Bosnia: Conflict Resolution and Foreign Policy Mc Gill University Press, 2002, 98-135
Russell, Alec, "Interview with the UN Secretary General, Kofi Annan" , Financial Times, 16 May, 2011
Schwartz, . Stephen "The Heritage of Ottoman Islam in the Balkans", Indiana University, Bloomington , Conference on The Turks and Islam, 12 September, 2010. See www.islamicpluralism.org/1663/the-heritage-of-ottoman. Much of the following discussion is based on this lecture
Wilkinson, Tracy, "Croatia, Alleged Criminals Thrive While Memorial Fades" Los Angeles Times published on 14 July, 1997 and based on an interview with Ivo Goldstein, the most prominent Holocaust historian in Croatia, author of the great monograph Holocaust in Zagreb, among other books.

# List of illustrations

1. The Vance Owen Peace plan (map): 83
2. The Union of Three Republics Plan (map): 86
3. Meeting with the Bosnian Prime Minister Harris Silajdzic (picture): 88
4. Mate Boban at the UN negotiating table (picture): 99
5. "Maybe Airlines" stamping (UN Passport copy): 170
6. Among the Spanish Officers with Morillon and Morales (picture): 178
7. Leading of a food convoy in the War Zone (picture): 187
8. Children, victims in the war zone (picture): 199
9. Map produced during negotiations with Morillon and Mladic (copy): 237
10. The Synagogue of Sarajevo, Yom Kippur Services (picture): 368
11. Diagram of the International Tribunal in The Hague (illustration): page 436
12. Entrance to Mostar after the UN broke the Siege (picture): 437
13. Indicted and Convicted of war crimes (pictures): 469
14. Setting of the Court in The Hague (illustration): 479

# Index of Names, Locations, Institutions, Key Words

**A**

Abbasid: 2
Abdic, Fikret: 29, 36, 338, 519
Aborigines: xii
AbuZayd, Karen Koning: 53
Acuña, Major: 183, 211, 213, 296, 519
Adios Querrida (song concluding the Yom Kippur Services in Sarajevo during the War: 368
Adriatic: Muslim & Croat on the race for access to the Sea: 80, 113, 114, 176, 200, 206, 221, 276, 313, 322, 324, 347, 349, 454; British Forces Headquarters on the Coast: 179, 207; deportation through the Sea: 215; meeting in a British Warship: 129, 224; strategic locations along the Coast: 420, 431
Afghanistan: vi, xiii, 1, 398, 402, 413, 418
Africa: x, xi, xiv, 24, 82, 228, 330, 389
AFSOUTH, Air Force Southern Command (US): 254, 512
Agreements: Carrington-Cutileiro agreement: 84; Civil Police agreement for Mostar: 218, 219, 220, 222, 312, 313; convoys and ceasefires: 65, 76, 157, 183, 207, 265, 266, 326, 349, 352, 451-453, 459, 463; Croats and Serbs arrangements: 295, 293; Dayton: 3, 89, 118, 369-381, 508; DOSSIA model (agreement at the local level): 509; evacuation of casualties: 72, 173; Élysée agreement (Serbia – Bosnia): 91; Graz agreement ( (Tudjman – Milosevic): 64; internal Muslim disagreements: 58; Israel-Arab models: 497, 508; Kosovo agreement: 92, 93; Mostar Interim: 72, 74, 87, 88, 89, 96, 102, 104, 110, 113, 117, 118, 122, 124, 126, 129, 131-137, 140-145, 154, 171, 443, 484; Mostar demilitarization: 173, 174, 175, 177, 179, 180, 181, 182; Moving populations: 457; POW exchange: 37, 97, 102, 292, 345; Serbia & Montenegro: 22, 94; Srebrenica agreement: 177, 178, 235, 240, 243; violations: 48, 51, 52 ; VOPP, Vance Owen Peace Plan: 83, 262, 313; Washington Agreement between Muslim & Croats & Geneva preparations: 21, 58, 62, 64, 76, 79, 80, 86, 117, 158, 160, 164, 333, 346; at the court in The Hague: 490, 495; relevant abbreviations / official names: 515, 517, 532
Agrupacion Tactica Canarias (Spanish Battalion): 176, 276

Ahmadinejad: vii, 240
Ahmici: 67
Ahtisaari, Martti: 89, 92, 519, 522
Air corridor: 304, 306
Air Force: 39, 89, 151, 243, 254, 369, 512
Air strike: 93, 251, 252, 253, 254, 521
Airport Mostar: 126, 154, 155, 156, 164, 192, 269, 347, 347, 348, 349, 363, 459, 467,
Airport Sarajevo: 234, 237, 253, 366, 502, 524
Airport Split: 152
Akashi, UN Special Envoy to Bosnia, Yasushi: approach to Mostar: 159, 286, 287, 288, 289, 468; relations with the US administration: 49, 50, 521, 525, 536; relations with the Military: 50, 253, 254;
Akmadzic, Mile: 224, 311, 519
Al Alfi, Hussein: 268, 519
Alaman, COS of SPABAT, Lt. Col.: 53, 101
Albania: Greater Albania: 407-412; Islamization: 5, 383-389; relations with Kosovo: 10, 22, 90, 91, 92, 415,-417, 431, 438, 502, 504, 517, 533; relevant abbreviations / official names: 539
Albigensians (members of a religious sect of southern France in the 12th and 13th centuries): 294, 387
Albright, Madeleine: 50, 158
Algeria: vi, 402, 413
Al-Husseini, Haj Amin: 386, 498
Alikadic, Alija, Tzakan: Muslim political heritage: 40; humanitarian action and refugees in East Mostar: 53-57, 195, 196, 287; Vis-à-vis the Serbs: 57, 58; Mostar Interim Agreement: 59, 60, 95, 105, 106, 111, 124,125, 131, 132, 146-149, 152-155, 158, 161-165; destruction of Mostar Bridge: 361, 362, 437, 451, 464; relevant abbreviations / official names: 519
Alispaho, Zulfikar (Zuka): 56
Al-Jazzar, Ahmed (the Butcher): 57, 294
Allah: 16, 194, 391, 392, 395, 397, 398, 403, 405, 406, 407, 411, 413, 414, 429, 432, 499
Almohad: 205
Almoravid: 205
Almuly, Jasa: 427, 520
Al-Qa'ida: 261, 403, 411, 418, 499, 539, 540, 541
Alvarez, Major Salafranca: 269, 533
American Jewish Committee: 44

American Jewish Congress: 44

American: Civil War: x, xi, xii, 28, 29, 331; involvement In Bosnia: xiii, 39, 46, 75, 82-89, 100, 138, 152, 196, 211, 244, 245, 252, 260, 264, 307, 348; imposing the Washington and Dayton Agreement: 369, 389, 393, 412, 418, 419, 427, 431, 474, 490; Jewish lobby supporting the Muslims: 42-46; lobby for the Croats: 77; relevant abbreviations / official names: 512, 520-523, 526, 529, 534, 536

Amsterdam: 205, 301, 354

Anatolia: 2, 205

Ancona: 152

Andreev, Victor: approach to Mostar: 72, 77-79, 444, 467; contact with the terrain: 112, 113; supporting Benabou on the field: 152, 161-163, 168, 176, 181, 182, 189, 340, 341, 344, 345, 350, 363; expertise on UN procedures: 198, 208, 209, 212, 219, 220, 223, 235, 250, 257, 263, 268, 269, 288, 289, 305, 320; relevant abbreviations / official names: 520

Andric, Ivo: 13, 229, 333, 362, 387, 520

Andric, representing the HVO, Colonel: 68

Ankara: 262, 320, 412

Annan, Kofi: on Kosovo: 93; on Srebrenica: 236, 237, 241; the inherent problematic of the UN mandate: 242, 244, 250; relevant abbreviations / official names: 520, 528

Antisemitism: 423, 426, 428

Antonetti, Jean-Claude: 474, 484

AOR, Area of Responsibility: 278, 280, 281, 282, 283, 497

APC, Armored Personnel Carrier: 183, 185, 186, 188, 232;

Arab: Arab-Israeli conflict (comparatives to Bosnia): vi, vii, x, xii, xiii, 1, 145, 206, 225, 412, 413, 459, 498, 499, 500, 501, 502; Arab Spring: 252, 313, 398, 401, 402, 432; Arabic in the Turkish culture: 393; Muslim internal confrontations: 228; The Muslim Nations enrolling for Bosnia: 29, 39, 41, 383, 389, 392, 414, 415

Arbour, Louise: 92, 520

Armenian: x, xi, xii, 2, 501

Aron, Raymond: 262, 268, 331

Artillery: Serb & Croat superiority over the Muslims in material: 34, 51, 52, 68, 69, 70, 89, 122, 168; professional equality in ability between Croats, Muslims and Serbs: 88, 195, 288, 290, 322, 372; indiscriminate use of artillery on civil targets by all parties: 197, 214, 265, 483; relevant abbreviations / official names: 512

Ashton, Katherine: 10

Assad, Bashar: 240, 501
Attorney General: 170
Australia: xii, 31, 269, 527
Austria: 4, 8, 64, 532
Austro-Hungarian: 7, 9, 11, 386, 408, 504
Autonomy: 17, 18, 21, 36, 90, 92, 113, 186, 412, 417, 496, 523

**B**
B'nai B'rith, Anti-Defamation League: 44
Bagaric, Dr. Ivan: 324, 462, 520
Baghdad: 415
Balkans: Albania claiming Kosovo: 388, 390, 407, 409; disagreement between Generals and Bureaucrats in the battlefield: 252; Islamization and inference of the Muslim countries: vii, xiv, xv, 2, 3, 401; involvement of the Great Powers and gaps of evaluation: 5, 7-9, 24, 42, 44, 49, 82, 84, 90, 94, 119, 120, 260, 289; maintaining the States cohesion: 22; The Ottoman legacy: 110, 205, 230, 362, 382, 383, 385, 393; Summing up chapters in the Balkans history: 411, 412, 413, 419-421, 427, 431, 435, 476, 505, 507, 510
Banja Luka: 30, 31, 85, 117, 334, 337, 421, 425, 536
Banovina: 63, 486, 487, 490, 493
Bar Mitzvah: 367
Bashi-Bazouks: 4
Bashir, Omar: 240
Bat Ye'or, Gisèle Littman: 1, 2, 4, 428, 538
BBC: 92, 334, 467, 481
Behmen, Omer: 403
Beirut: 199, 246
Bektasevic, Miss Sadeta: 325, 520, 527
Bektashi: 388
Belgian: 50, 229, 256, 421
Belgrade: alienation & resistance: xiii, 5, 8, 9, 16, 17; at the court in The Hague: 478; conflict of interest with the Bosnian Serbs: 62, 77, 83, 85, 91, 92; Croats and Serbs in Bosnia cooperate without consent from Belgrade: 296, 297; facing the separation from Kosovo: 408, 409, 417, 421, 427; past glory: 13, 14, 18; supporting the Serbs in Bosnia and Kosovo: 20, 22, 33, 42, 59; relevant abbreviations / official names: 520, 527, 530, 535
Belmonte, Captain David: 200, 201, 202, 203, 212, 307, 309, 311, 317, 327, 348, 353, 353, 521

Ben Dahan, Rabbi Moshe: 367
Benabou, Dany: 351
Bender, Ivan: 116, 287, 521
Benshetrit, Nessim: 365, 366
Berlin: 7, 232, 407, 504, 526
BiH Armija: acting for normalization of life in East Mostar: 218, 264, 265, 266, 267; actions against Serbs: 34; benefiting from international support: 97, 98, 101, 102, 111, 113, 124-138, 163; Confident Armija commanders preparing military offensive : 48, 50, 51, 52; cooperating for evacuation of casualties, food convoys and installing civil police in Mostar: 320, 322, 330, 338, 345, 347, 350, 352, 451, 453; dismantling Croat units: 35;   local Commanders in Mostar: 55, 67, 70, 71, 74, 80; worthless mutual slaughter between Muslims and Croats: 173, 180, 181, 183; sabotage activities against Serbs, Croats and UN units: 290, 292, 305, 317, 319, 326; Serbs deny coordination with Muslims in Mostar: 37; relevant abbreviations / official names: 523, 532
Bihac: 104, 116, 172, 239, 240, 253, 254, 334, 337, 341, 529, 536
Bijela (bridge): 222, 313, 317, 296
Bijelo Polje: 58, 70, 267
Bila Bridge: 207
Bildt, Carl: 89, 378, 521
Blagaj: 57, 71
Blaskic, Tihomir: 68, 346, 521
Boban, Mate: against the Muslims in a total war and for cooperation with the Serbs: 24, 36, 59; proclaiming free Croatian community of Herzeg-Bosnia: 62-70; relations with UNPROFOR: 73; pushed aside by the Pope and the US: 76, 80, 84, 86; warning against the cooperation of the Muslim states and the Muslims in Bosnia: 99; supporting the interim agreement with the local Muslim leadership in Mostar: 102, 103, 108, 121, 125-135, 139, 141, 142, 155, 156, 169, 180; Condemning the illusionist attitude of the West: 112-116; meeting with Owen & Stoltenberg in British barracks: 223, 224, 256-259; Boban analysis of the conflict and adopted strategy: 260-269; meeting with UNPROFOR leadership in Spanish barracks 270-276, 311-317; position towards the Geneva Conference: 286, 289, 291, 304, 305; losing ground and evinced from power: 323-325, 333-338, 345-349, 352, 440, 444-467, 473, 486, 491, 492; relevant abbreviations / official names: 514, 521, 528, 532
Bobetko, Janko: 473

Bodiroga, Milan: 163
Boers: xi
Bogomils (religious political sect founded in the first Bulgarian Empire by the priest Bogomil during the reign of Tsar Petar I in the 10th century): 294, 387
Bonn: 117, 157, 161, 162
Boorda, Admiral Jeremy: 254, 521
Boras, Franjo: 338, 521
Borci: 296
Bosanski Brod: 380
Bosanski Šamac: 380
Bosnian Serb Army (BSA): capabilities and military moves: 34, 35, 37, 38, 39; The US protecting the Muslims is counterproductive: 48, 50 51, 52; relations with the Muslims in Mostar: 57, 58, 60, 113, 289, 290, 291; BSA following orders of the political leadership: 292, 492; relevant abbreviations / official names: 512, 525
Bostom, Andrew: 428, 539
Boulevard (confrontation line between East and West Mostar): 70, 183, 194, 213, 451, 452
Bowen, Jeremy: 481, 482
Boyd, Shannon: 466
Bozic, Slobodan: 79, 287, 521
Braggers (Croat militaries accused by the political level): 263
Brajkovic, Miso: 163
Brcko: 373, 379, 380
Bregava River: 295
Bridge (Stari Most /Mostar) destroyed by the Croats: 69, 71, 110, 111, 361, 362, 496
Brigade South (UNPROFOR redeployment in Bosnia): 281, 283, 284
Briquemont, General Francis: challenged by the Croats: 114, 255; General Cot instructs involving Briquemont in the Mostar interim agreement: 143; Briquemont manipulated in the terrain: 229, 256-261, 263, 266, 268-271, 280; unachieved humanitarian convoys for Mostar: 468; relevant abbreviations / official names: 519, 521, 523
BRITBAT (British brigade deployed in center Bosnia): 68, 70, 324
BRITFOR, British Forces: 112, 171, 179, 207, 268, 278, 279, 280, 282, 348, 355, 366, 443, 454, 465, 475; relevant abbreviations / official names: 512, 531, 533
British / Britons: historic involvement in the region: 3, 4, 9, 10; entry in the conflict: 43, 49, 78, 79, 82, 87; efficient military support: 111,

112, 122, 124; negotiating and settings for Mostar interim agreement: 129, 141, 152, 153, 155, 156, 160, 168, 171, 179, 180; engineering & deployment in central Bosnia: 200, 207, 208, 211; competent military leadership: 212-224, 232, 247, 250, 269, 271, 278, 279-284, 291; hosting negotiations in Divulje British barracks: 305, 314, 315, 324; terrain analysis: 330, 344, 345, 348; assistance for Yom Kippur Services & British romance: 355, 363, 366; testimonies in The Hague: 407, 443, 475, 482; relevant abbreviations / official names: 512, 523, 526, 529-535
Bruges: 301
Brussels: 149, 150, 158, 252, 380, 523
Budakovic, General Sulejman: in command: 56, 98; leading the military talks for East Mostar: 131, 132, 133, 134; supporting the interim agreement for Mostar: 146, 148, 149, 153, 154; dealing with humanitarian convoys to East Mostar: 265, 352, 467; relevant abbreviations / official names: 521
Buenos Aires: 389
Bugojno: 34, 68, 275, 290, 336, 465
Bugojno: 34, 68, 275, 336, 465
Bulatovic, Momir: 21, 91, 522, 523
Bulgaria: 5, 13, 294, 383, 385, 408, 412
Bull, General Odd: 227
Buna: 70
Bureaucrats (the mechanism of UN Bureaucracy): 72, 87, 142, 182, 225, 229, 242, 255, 256, 274, 285, 286, 307, 343, 344, 434, 488
Busovaca: 108, 109, 112, 116, 321, 330

## C

Caliphate: 402, 411, 413, 414
Çamëria: s 383
Camp David: 82, 313, 497
Canaanites: 409
Canadian / Canada: xii, 31, 72, 200, 216, 220, 248, 319, 324, 345, 508, 512, 514, 531
Canadian Mounted Police: 216, 531
CANBAT, Canadian Battalion: 72, 324, 345, 512
Canton: 33, 76, 379, 422, 491, 495
Carrington, Lord Peter: 82, 84, 105
CASEVAC, casualties evacuation: 172, 512
Castro, Colonel Miguel: 212, 321, 332, 523

Catastrophe: 71, 93, 111, 197, 329, 337, 351, 457

Catholic: allying with the Muslims against the Serbs: 6; Serbs allying with the Muslims against the Catholics: 7; Croat Catholic Church during WWII: 13; ongoing mutual hatred: 14; Austro-Hungarian conquest: 24; Croat relations with the Spanish Battalion: 106, 175, 205, 212, 275, 277, 324, 362, 367, 385; the rationale behind uniting with the Muslims: 400, 408; apologies for crimes during WWII: 428, 430; relevant abbreviations / official names: 528, 533, 534, 540

Census: 32, 373, 387, 504

Central Bosnia: confronting historic genocide: 37; Armija attacks in the region: 52; mujahidin from Arab countries siding with Bosnian Muslims: 67; Croats counter attack: 68, 69; convoys to the region: 70, 80; UN casualties: 109-113; Croat political activities supported by the UN: 120, 176, 200, 260, 261, 275, 292, 295, 324, 325, 327, 328, 334, 337, 379, 439, 470, 481, 486, 487

Cerecnjac, Ivica: 364

Ceylonese: xii

Chain of command: 56, 74, 161, 187, 249, 253, 281, 290, 338

Chaplina / Caplijna: 56, 65, 101, 470, 486

Chechnya: 41, 261

Chernomyrdin, Viktor: 93, 378, 522

Chetnik: 10, 13, 407, 530, 535

Chicago: 42, 77, 529

Chinese / China: xii, xv, 389, 413, 418, 499, 522

Chirac, Jacques: 250, 251, 378, 474, 522

Chosen People (referring to the Jews): 410

Christian: under the Ottoman rule: xiv, 2-5, 41; division between East (Muslims) and West (Christians) Mostar: 57, 97; Christians and Muslims in a total war in Mostar: 199; Jews in Spain between Christianity and Islam: 204, 205; meeting Mladic in Sarajevo: 213, 234, 235; among Christian military officers: 259, 294; remnants of antique Christianity in Stolac and the Region: 382-385; confrontation with Islam: 401, 410, 411, 412, 418, 419, 428, 439, 474; relevant abbreviations / official names: 502, 521, 533, 538

Christmas: 149, 150, 239, 255

Christopher, Warren: 378,

Church: 13, 24, 198, 212, 277, 377, 387, 401, 402, 421, 427, 428, 429, 439, 488, 528, 533, 534

Churchill, Winston: 10, 198, 428

CIA: 83, 86

Cibo, Safet: 56
Ciller, Tansu: 419, 500
Citizen: 32, 57, 78, 96, 122, 136, 147, 158, 164, 373, 380, 381, 420, 422, 433, 478, 509
Citluk: 106, 107, 451, 485
Civil Affairs (United Nations Unit): enquiring on the Serb positions: 34; meeting the Muslim leadership: 40, 54; cooperating with UN agencies: 71; UN engineer corps on the field: 78, 79; installing headquarters: 100, 101, 106, 108; initiating an interim agreement in Mostar: 112, 113, 119, 123, 133, 135, 149, 151, 153, 161; involving the headquarters in Zagreb: 163, 166; First Israeli serving in the peace keeping forces: 168, 169, 171, 176; at the negotiating table with the warring parties: 182, 183, 189, 191, 200; the Dutch communication center assisting Civil Affairs: 201, 209, 223, 227, 235, 254, 257, 258; cooperation with the British forces and the Spanish battalion: 268, 269, 273, 276, 279, 285, 289, 296, 316, 319, 322, 326-330, 340-343, 350, 364, 443, 446, 451, 466, 495; relevant abbreviations / official names: 512, 514, 520, 535
Clark, General Wesley: 378, 522
Clausewitz, Carl von: 322
Cleansing (ethnic cleanse): relevance of the international law: 26, 29, 46, 67, 68, 89, 90, 91, 137, 150, 174, 178, 179, 206; Paris and London alarmed by the ethnic cleansing in the Spanish AOR: 210, 211, 213, 215, 216; the Jewish consciousness is reacting: 217; releasing innocent civilian prisoners: 220; the dilemma between moving civil populations or exposing them to slaughter : 228, 230, 238, 243, 272, 275, 294, 304; Boban does not like the idea of an ombudsman: 315, 316; Lord David Owen calling for supervision and action against violations and crimes: 336, 337; cleansing the Serbs in Kosovo: 415, 416, 429; responsibility of a government to protect its population: 431, 433, 434; the trauma of the Nazi past and at the court in The Hague: 449, 452, 454, 455, 457, 485, 488; relevant abbreviations / official names: 516
Clinton, Bill: 19, 43, 49, 83, 84, 333, 378, 522, 525, 526, 536
CNN: s 437, 467
Cohen, Philip: 427, 520, 522, 540
Cohen-Tanugi, Robert: 417, 522, 539
Cold War: 25, 507, 522
Cole, Colonel (aide de camp of General Navarro): 269, 523
Collective: xi, 17, 84, 157, 415, 437, 469, 470, 473

Coloma, Major Juan: 326, 523
Communist: post war Yugoslavia: 13, 15; Serbian domination: 18; the Muslims empowered as an entity by Tito: 41; Boban member of the Communist League: 63, 84; the American commitment to Bosnia: 130; the communist cultural legacy: 274, 294, 387, 388, 390, 391, 405, 408, 425, 506; relevant abbreviations / official names: 523, 526, 527, 528, 535
Congo: xi, 226, 306, 526
Constructive ambiguity: 247, 249
Convoy: under fire: 49; smuggling weapons: 51; humanitarian assistance: 53, 69; convoy drivers killed: 70, 72; blocked convoys: 108, 110; UNPROFOR escorting convoys: 112, 122, 157, 168, 174; forcing the way through blockades: 183-197, 203, 205, 222, 232, 258; the milk convoy: 263-266, 274; facilitating military encounters in Stolac: 295, 304; humanitarian convoy as compensation: 321, 322, 325, 326; exploring access routes: 329, 330, 331; renewing the milk convoy: 349-352; Zagreb announces roads opened: 448, 452, 458-461; stopping the siege around East Mostar: 466-468, 481
Coordinator (UN): facing the starving crowd and peace negotiating: 87, 88, 112, 113; shuttling between warring parties: 167, 176, 176; communicating with headquarters: 181, 209, 223, 235, 257, 268, 269, 278, 280, 287; field reconnaissance and evaluation: 330, 340, 341, 364, 443, 495; relevant abbreviations / official names: 512, 526
Cordova: 205
Coric, Valentin: 116, 469, 471, 486, 488
Cot, General Jean: 38, 72, 143, 146, 225, 228, 239-256, 289, 506, 519, 521, 523
Croatian Democratic Union (HDZ): 21, 62, 65, 91, 104, 470, 514, 537
Croatian Kralij Tvertko brigade (Croat military force in Sarajevo dismantled by the Muslims): 35
Custer, General George: xi
Cutileiro, Jorge: 82, 84, 105
Czechoslovakia: 13

**D**
D'Aoust, Judge Jose: 443, 476
Dagan, General Meir: 246
Dalmatia: 11
Dancing with the Wolves (declared at the court in The Hague facing the indicted of war crimes): 171, 484

Danish: 49, 109, 141, 320, 524
Darfur: vi, xi, 29
Darfur: vi, xi, 29
Davotoglu, Ahmet: 501
Delic, General Rasim: 52, 72, 76, 117, 132, 135, 137, 338, 468, 523
Demilitarization: 82, 124, 148, 173, 177, 236, 286, 289, 343, 453
Democratic League of Kosovo (LDK): 22, 91, 515
Deportation (of populations): 29, 469, 473
Derventa: 380, 524
Detainee (civilian): 45, 122, 123, 146, 148, 158, 174, 230, 454, 461, 462, 463, 465, 471, 472, 473, 482, 488, 489, 496
DETALAT, Détachement Léger Aérien de Transport (French unit of choppers): 304, 513
Deuteronomy (Book of): 468
Deutschmark: 489
Dhimmi (lower social status of Jews and Christians under Muslim regime): 2, 3, 4, 110, 205, 384, 399, 402, 428, 538, 539
Dinaric Alps (surrounding Mostar): 176
Displaced: 26, 56, 80, 137, 139, 175, 275, 336, 343, 370, 373, 375, 433, 451, 463
Divulje (on the Adriatic Coast): 171, 179, 207, 224, 268, 278, 279, 306, 311, 314, 336, 348, 350, 440, 443, 454, 455, 512, 533
Dizdar, Mehmedalija Mak: 294, 523, 524
Djukanovic, Milo: 21, 90, 522, 523
Djukanovic, Milo: 90, 522, 523
Doboj: 104, 116, 334, 524
Domaljevac: 380
Donji Vakuf: 379
DOSSIA, Domestic Support System in International Accords (at the local level): 509
Dracevo: 348
Drekovic, Brigadier Ramiz: 163, 165, 523
Drenica: 22, 91
Dretelj: 465, 472, 482, 483, 486, 488
Drina River / Valley: 229, 230, 362, 387, 526, 529
Druze: 505
Dubrovnik: 18, 35, 289, 291, 420
Duburg, Col. Roger: 143, 254, 256, 523
Durakovic, Asaf: 294, 523
DUTCHBAT, Dutch Battalion: 112, 244, 248

DUTCHCOM, Dutch Communication Center: 201, 212, 265, 268, 326, 327, 344, 348, 352, 353, 443, 475, 513, 521
Dzabic, Nadjija: 54, 524
Dziho, Dzevad: 57
Dziho, Sefkija: 124

**E**
Eastern Europe: 5, 11, 13, 14, 130, 274, 541
Eastwood, Clint: 354
Ecevit, Bulent: 419, 500
ECMM, European Community Monitor Mission: 70, 115, 152, 153, 164, 181, 513
Efendic, Hazdo: 350
Egypt: vi, vii, 16, 82, 166, 313, 366, 267, 391, 394, 401, 412, 497-499, 528
Eichmann: 432, 488
Elazar, General David Dado: 367
Elazar, Sonia: 367
Elections: suspects of war crimes surrendered to The Hague: 10; Izetbegovic hiding political agenda: 15; with Tudjman's election started the dismantlement of Yugoslavia: 17, 21, 22; Croats expectations of the new Bosnian federation: 76, 90, 91, 94, 114; municipal elections in the interim agreement for Mostar: 115, 121, 124, 141, 155, 156: the Dayton agreement: 373, 374, 376, 379, 391, 418, 424, 499, 500, 511; relevant abbreviations / official names: 522, 527, 537
Emerson: 314
Enclave / Pocket (areas under military siege): 18, 46, 47, 57, 73, 74, 207, 230, 231, 236, 238, 240, 243, 247, 248, 251, 253, 258, 266, 295, 325, 340, 371, 412, 454, 498, 517, 531
Entity (political, social and cultural): 7, 20, 22, 32, 40, 41, 63, 75, 80, 90, 94, 107, 288, 312, 335, 336, 372, 378, 381, 382, 395, 407, 417, 444, 457, 458, 470, 508, 529
Epirotic: 383
Erbakan, Prof. Necmettin: 413, 419, 500
Ethiopia: 401
Ethnic: historical background and comparatives: x, xiv, 1, 2, 3, 7, 8; Tito plastering all differences: 14, 15, 17, 19, 20; belligerence outburst: 24, 26, 29, 31, 32, 33, 39, 40, 41, 46, 63, 65, 67, 68, 78, 83, 89, 90, 91, 95; the international community requires accountability from the leaders: 105, 113, 120, 121, 122, 133, 137, 145, 150; ethnicity at the

core of the conflict: 169, 174, 178, 200, 206, 210, 211, 213, 215-217; collecting data from the field on ethnic "purification": 220, 228, 229, 230, 243, 246: General Jean Cot demands more UN presence in the terrain: 257, 258, 272, 275, 304, 315, 316, 336, 337, 361, 375, 380, 382, 383, 384, 386, 390, 404; Albania acts for unifying its ethnic group in a territorial continuity: 407, 408, 415, 416, 424, 431, 433, 434, 437, 438, 444, 452, 454, 455, 456; ethnic cleansing judged as crime at the court in The Hague: 471, 485, 486, 488, 496, 498, 504, 505, 510, 511, relevant abbreviations / official names: 516, 532

European Union (EU): France and Germany leadership: 1, 10; Slovenia and Croatia joining: 18; acting for stabilization in the Balkans: 22, 77; establishing a standing Conference on Former Yugoslavia: 82, 84, 88, 94; Mostar to be placed under EU administration: 96, 97, 108, 150, 151, 153, 159, 160, 164, 165, 171; EU member States exchanging intelligence data: 179, 181, 185, 284, 325, 333, 343; witnessing the Dayton agreement: 370, 378, 380, 382; relations between Turkey and the European union: 419, 420, 421, 422, 430, 478, 501; relevant abbreviations / official names: 513, 527, 51, 534

Exile: vi, 204, 362, 367, 368, 384

Ezekiel (Book of): 269

# F

Fascism: 111, 120, 423, 425, 502

Federal Army: 18, 518

Federal Republic of Yugoslavia: (FRY): 20, 21, 30, 90, 92, 93, 94, 238, 370, 372, 376, 435, 491, 513, 534

Federation: historical background: 5, 14; Serbian dominance and dismantlement: 17-22, 26; the "Yugoslav Wars" among the entities: 28, 31-33; confederation between Croats and Muslims: 48, 59, 76, 79, 89, 90, 93, 94, 96, 100; on the eve of the Geneva conference: 335, 336; the Dayton process: 370-374, 378, 383, 400, 421, 422, 424, 456, 474, 495, 502, 510; relevant abbreviations / official names: 523, 528, 535

Feliu, Lieutenant General Luis: 176

Fernandez, Lieutenant Francisco Jesús Aguilar: 319, 320, 322

Filipovic, Ilja: 216-219, 319, 524

Financial Times: 241, 241, 244, 251, 540, 541

Finch, Susan: 146, 148, 149

Finci, Jakov: 364, 365

FMSO, Foreign Military Studies Office: 46, 513, 534

Forced Labor: 469, 473, 479, 480, 481, 483, 488
Fourth Corps: 55, 56, 80, 98, 163, 165, 523
Frankfurt (NATO Headquarters): 152
French / France: historic context: 1; Serbs reject the French-German proposal: 36; the Muslims influences the Western Media: 43, 44, 47, 49, 84, 113; UNPROFOR Commander, General Jean Cot echoes a realistic analysis of the conflict: 143, 155, 156, 167; Hallilovic, The Muslim Commander relies on the French pressure over the Croats: 181; French Ambassador on urgent visit to SPABAT concerning the ethnic cleansing: 209, 210, 211; French generals report to members of the French National Assembly: 225, 228, 229, 231, 233, 235, 249, 250, 251, 256, 258, 294; French helicopter under attack: 304, 306, 363; French assistance for the Yom Kippur services in Sarajevo: 366, 370, 378, 387, 412; French judge at the court in The Hague: 474, 476, 484; relevant abbreviations / official names: 513, 514, 515, 522, 527, 528, 529, 533, 535, 539
Frewer, Commodore Barry: 269, 524

# G

G2 Branch (intelligence and security military unit): 236, 259, 268, 269, 336, 513, 530
G8, (8 Great Powers) foreign ministers: 93, 514, 522
Gabela: 148, 472,488
Gacko: 38, 56, 57, 58, 137, 389, 293, 525
Gal, Yossi: 439
Ganic, Bosnian Vice President Ejup: 49, 58, 98, 524
Gaza: xiii, 460
General Assembly (UN): 166, 237, 241, 432, 516
Geneva: International Humanitarian Law: 25, 28; Conference on Former Yugoslavia: 59, 80, 95, 96; activities of the permanent forum of the Conference: 105, 106, 117, 140; proceeding with the interim agreement for Mostar: 147, 149, 150, 158, 160, 161, 162, 163, 174, 247; Boban aiming at the Geneva Conference: 259, 262, 273; Washington and Geneva forum work jointly for an accord: 286, 287, 306, 333, 335, 336, 339, 346, 435, 452, 454, 455, 464; Geneva conventions serve to inculpate war criminals at The Hague: 469, 471, 49; relevant abbreviations / official names: 535
Genocide: viii-xii, 11, 12, 27-29, 37, 40, 92, 414, 427, 432-437, 516
German / Germany: historic context: viii, x, xii, 1, 10, 12, 13; Germany, first to recognize Independent Croatia in 1991: 19, 22, 29, 36; The

Muslims reject the idea of German administrator for Mostar: 58, 84; German troops participate in the SFOR, Stabilization Force: 91, 113; failure of the multiculturalism in Germany: 155, 165, 246, 292, 370; contribution to the Dayton agreement: 378, 386, 407, 428, 435, 462, 489, 504; relevant abbreviations / official names: 514, 520, 526

Ghali, Secretary General Boutros Boutros: 50, 166, 202, 229, 239, 249, 253, 333, 497, 520, 521

Goldstein, Ivo: vii, 424, 425, 539, 541

Golem: 85

Gorazde: 34, 46, 50, 172, 239, 240, 243, 253, 290, 341, 3711 373, 481

Gorbachev, Mikhail: 5

Gore, Vice President Al: 43, 88, 525

Gornji Vakuf: 66, 68, 101, 174, 470, 486, 487

Gospic: 423, 424, 425, 426

Gotovina, General Ante: 30

Grabovica: 74

Grandes, Lt. General Munoz : 73

Granic, (Croat) Foreign Minister Mate: 73, 99, 142, 143, 156, 158, 349, 444, 445, 448, 455, 458, 460, 461, 465, 468, 489, 525

Graz: 64

Great Britain / United Kingdom / England: 9, 10, 47, 49, 84, 113, 220, 366, 370, 384, 392, 514, 535

Greeks: xii, 408

Green Belt: 418, 522

Grubac, (Serb) General Radovan: 34, 35, 36, 37, 38, 289, 290, 291-295, 458, 525, 532

Grude: interference in Mostar: 57, 59; Boban home town became HVO Headquarters: 62, 65, 80; presentation of the interim agreement for Mostar to Boban: 95, 101, 103, 105, 106, 112, 117, 126, 128, 129, 130, 137, 143, 144, 146, 158; the Spanish transmit Benabou's UN internal reports to Grude: 214, 220, 245, 256, 267, 268; the leadership in Grude subordinated to the Croat government in Zagreb: 272, 323, 335, 345, 348, 351, 352, 448, 451, 458, 459

Guerassev, Vladislav: 159, 160

Gul, Abdullah: 500

Gulf: 389, 415, 500

Gypsies: viii, ix, 11, 12, 13, 63, 386, 423, 425, 427, 505, 534

# H
Habsburg: 386, 504

Hadizukic, Miss Amra: 325, 525, 527
Haiphong: 245
Hallilovic, Chief of Staff of the BiH Army, General Sefer: 55, 173, 177, 180, 181, 184, 191, 193, 205, 206, 207, 208, 221, 223, 234, 235, 317, 338, 453
Hamas: 16, 391, 400, 402, 403, 406, 460, 541
Hammarskjold, Dag: 226, 229, 306
Hanjar Division: 230, 497
Harff, James: 44
Hayes, (posted at Kiseljak UNPRFOR Headquarters) General Veer de: 212, 213, 220, 268, 278, 330, 345, 346, 366, 523
Hebrew: xii, 85, 217, 306, 345, 365, 439
Heliodrom: 146, 214, 472, 479, 480, 482, 483, 486, 488
Helvetic: 422
Herzeg-Bosnia: self-declared community: 24, 30, supported by the Republic of Croatia: 62-69; under attack by the Muslim Armija: 74, 75, 78, 96, 99; warning against the Muslim invasion of Europe: 104, 107-117; operating with political institutions: 121, 125, 127, 142, 145, 164, 180, 245, 268, 269, 275, 287, 314, 333; indictment at The Hague: 438, 440, 444, 459, 469-473, 480, 481, 482, 485-494; relevant abbreviations / official names: 514, 521
Hezbollah: 389
Hiroshima: 244
Hitler, Adolf: 9, 428, 533
HMS Invincible / British Warship (proposed as location for Mostar local negotiations between Muslims and Croats): 129, 366
Holbrooke, Richard: 89, 92, 378, 521, 526
Honshu: 244
Horn, General Von: 227
HQ, Headquarters: Kiseljak UN headquarters for Bosnia Herzegovina: 37, 44; Zagreb UN headquarters for all Former Yugoslavia: 53, 59; Boban headquarters in Grude: 62, 68; Yugoslav forces cooperating with NATO: 93, 97, 98, 101, 102, 106, 108; Spanish headquarters in Medjugorje servicing Mostar and the Southern Region of Bosnia: 111, 112, 130, 140: NATO headquarters controlling from Frankfurt (military Air traffic): 152, 154, 155, 158, 159, 161, 162, 164, 166; reporting to UN headquarters in New York: 168, 171, 172, 176, 182; shuttling negotiations between the Muslim and the Croat headquarters: 183, 184, 190, 192; The DUTCHCOM Center in Medjugorje assuring communication with the UN headquarters in Zagreb, Sara-

jevo, Belgrade, and New York, and when needed, with other European capitals, as well as with the entire territory of former Yugoslavia, including besieged Mostar: 201, 202, 208, 209, 211, 212, 213, 215, 219, 220, 221, 223, 232; UN forward headquarters in Sarajevo: 234, 238, 236, 243, 250, 255, 256, 257, 258, 262-265, 268, 269, 271, 278, 280, 281, 282, 284; Zagreb UN headquarters planning without field coordination: 285, 289, 291, 296, 305; Efficiency in the British headquarters in Divulje: 306, 313, 319, 320, 321, 326, 330, 331, 333-336, 340, 341, 344, 345, 348, 353, 362, 388, 440, 443, 451, 455, 458, 459, 463, 475, 495-497, 506; relevant abbreviations / official names: 512-514, 517, 519, 524, 525, 530, 533, 535,

Hulme, Jerry: 53, 99, 108, 287, 451, 526

Human right: 25, 43, 88, 95, 97, 104, 114, 225, 315, 342, 343, 370, 373, 374, 375, 376, 380, 424, 426, 433, 474, 525, 528

Human shields: 416, 473, 480, 481, 483

Humo, Esad: 481

Hungarian / Hungary: viii, 7, 9, 11, 24, 95, 386, 408, 474, 504

Hussein, Saddam: 39, 240

Huterer, Branimir: 116

HVO, Hrvatsko Vije e Obrane, (Croatian Defence Council): the military branch of the Bosnian Croats operating in central Bosnia: 34, 35, 51, 52, 57; HVO formation: 64-70; Stojic, acting as minister of defense controls all HVO operations: 74, 76, 80, 97, 102, 111-113, 115; the war between Croats and Muslims ends when HVO's General Ante Roso and Armija's General Delic sign the cease fire agreement: 117, 124; HVO does not achieve its main goal, making Mostar the Croat political capital: 126, 127, 130-148, 156, 173, 180; negotiating with HVO for facilitating humanitarian convoys: 183, 188, 211, 214, 216; HVO arrests convoy drivers: 220, 232, 245, 257; the HVO does not deliver Mostar, Boban's key strategic goal: 260-269, 273, 287, 290, 296, 311, 312, 316-326, 330-332, 338, 345-352; the military pressure fails and the Croat miss an opportunity to obtain a stronghold in Mostar through negotiations: 443- 455, 458-473, 479-483, 485-489, 492-494, 503; relevant abbreviations / official names: 514, 520, 521, 524, 525, 527, 529-532

# I

Ibn-Nafi, Ahmed: 413

ICFY, International Conference on Former Yugoslavia (in Geneva): 140, 160, 163, 223, 232, 333

ICRC, International Red Cross Committee: 79, 87, 168, 175, 185, 190, 371, 512, 375, 461, 462, 464, 465, 514, 516
IDF, TSAHAL, Israel Defense Forces: 170, 199, 278, 345, 514
IFOR, Implementation Force: 90, 371, 376, 379, 514
Igman Mountain: 55, 252, 253
Ilahije: 385
Illyrian: 387, 409
Imam: 413, 414
Immigrate / Migrate / Muhajirs (migrants): 31, 201, 235, 384
Inca: xii
Independence Day (Israel): 190
Indian (Amerindians): xi, xiii, 177
Indiana: 383, 541
Indonesia: 392
INMARSAT, IMMARSAT, International Maritime Satellite Telecommunication (used by the UN during the Yugoslav Wars): 78, 181, 514
Intelligentsia: 118, 121, 139, 394
International Center for Transitional Justice: 289, 434
International Criminal Tribunal for former Yugoslavia (ICTY): the tribunal is founded (may 1993) - worst crimes are realized in Mostar: 30, 31, 45, 62, 66, 69; Milosevic is indicted for crimes against humanity: 92; the "bells of the Tribunal" start impacting the actors on the war theater: 123, 175, 230, 245; Benabou called to testify against war criminals: 432, 434, 435, 436, 437, 438, 440, 441; Croat leadership judged for war crimes in Mostar: 442, 469, 471, 474, 475, 477, 481, 493, 494, 494; relevant abbreviations / official names: 514, 520
Interpreter (the UN and the NGO employed a great number of locals as interpreters when the Serbo-Croat language was similarly used by all three entities): 99, 154, 188, 189, 190, 222, 266, 325, 326, 327, 340, 354, 458, 520, 521, 525, 527, 531, 533
IPTF, UN international Police Task Force: 376, 514
Iran (interference): vii, 39, 41, 58, 225, 226, 240, 261, 389, 398, 402, 403, 409, 410, 412, 414, 431, 500, 501, 502
Iraq: vi, 1, 225, 240, 412, 419
IRC, International Rescue Committee: 79, 87, 168, 515,
Israel: the Arab-Israeli confrontation is minor in casualties compared to the Yugoslav wars: vi, vii, ix, x, xiii, xv; cooperation and confidentiality between Alikadic (the Muslim) and Benabou (the Israeli): 40, 42, 51, 54, 55, 72, 82, 120; Silajdzic, Bosnian Prime Minister, recalls the Ottoman Empire benefiting the people of Israel more than the US:

138, 144; the Croats consider being in a parallel situation to Israel facing the Arab World: 145; the first Israeli participating in a UN peace keeping mission: 166, 167; 225, 226, 313, 316, 355, 389, 392; Kosovo for Serbia is like Jerusalem for Israel: 411, 412, 430; the advantage of an Israeli serving in a conflict where Israel is not Involved: 439, 452, 460, 497, 501
Israeli Foreign Ministry: 166, 167, 365, 440, 442, 475, 478, 479
Italian Consortium of Solidarity: 215, 331, 531
Italy / Italian: 13, 18, 152, 215, 231, 332, 414, 408, 411, 531
Ivanov, Igor: 378, 526
Izetbegovic, Alija: publishes the Islamic Declaration: 15, 16, 21; Mostar is not among its priorities: 32, 35, 45; considering the UN at the service of the Muslims: 49; Orucevic, faithful representative in Mostar: 56, 58, 59, 67, 76, 81; aligning his positions with the US: 84, 91, 100; supports the interim agreement for Mostar. The Croats will lose the best deal they could obtain: 103, 104, 106, 117, 126, 127, 129, 141; strengthening relations with Tudjman: 146-148, 156, 157, 161, 162, 163, 165; obtain allegiance from the Bosnian Serbs and Bosnian Coats: 223, 243, 244, 262, 287, 290, 312, 315, 336,338; Boban is evinced, the Dayton process is initiated: 369, 378; Izetbegovic pursues a fervent Muslim agenda following his "Islamic Declaration": 390, 391, 392, 397, 400-405, 409, 413, 414, 418, 431, 456, 490, 491, 492, 493; relevant abbreviations / official names: 519, 521, 524-528, 531, 532, 538, 541

## J

Jablanica (at the core of the confrontation in central Bosnia): 53, 55, 56, 113, 125, 174, 206, 207, 221, 222, 223, 261, 265, 267, 276, 281, 285, 313, 317, 321, 330, 332, 346, 347, 348, 352, 470, 515
Jacolin, Henry: 209, 210, 211, 527
Jadovno: vii, xii, 11, 44, 386, 423, 424, 425, 427, 429
Jahiliyya: 16, 391
Janissary: 3, 384
Janjaweed: xi, xii, 29
Japanese / Japan: xii, 210, 393, 514
Jasenovac: vii, viii, ix, xii, 11, 44, 386, 425, 427, 429
Jazina: 34, 37, 289
Jelskovic, Mr. Feda: 325, 527
Jemaat (associations): 396

Jerusalem: 144, 192, 204, 206, 209, 366, 367, 386, 402, 410, 411, 432, 439, 475, 488, 497, 498, 526
Jesus: ix, 11, 20, 30, 31, 32, 33, 36, 40, 86, 90, 229, 377, 378, 381, 421, 490, 492, 516
Jewish: vi-xii, 2, 4, 11, 12, 13, 27, 29, 37, 44, 53, 55, 63, 85, 138, 144, 196, 198, 201-205, 209, 216, 275, 287, 300, 306, 327, 337, 354, 358, 362, 364, 365, 425-430, 439, 457, 495-502, 505, 520
Jihad: 2, 39, 403, 404, 405, 406, 407, 411, 413, 414, 418, 428, 499, 538, 539
Jizya: 384
JMO (Muslim Party of Bosnia): 8
JNA, former Yugoslav National Army: 22, 51, 188, 230, 234, 245, aa9, 492
Jordan: vi, vii, 500, 539
Joseph, Edward : 95, 409
Jugoplastika Split: 188
Jukic, Perica: 126, 463
Justice: 4, 116, 217, 226, 234, 289, 335, 387, 397, 407, 430, 432, 434, 435, 468, 469, 473, 474, 476, 477, 488, 493, 506, 520, 535

# K
Kafka, Franz: 344
Kakanj: 70
Kalashnikov: 190
Kaluder, Ibrahim: 139
Karadordevo: 64
Karadzic, Radovan: 35, 36, 59, 62, 64, 83, 84, 86, 276, 291, 292, 347, 377, 456, 491, 492, 527
Karlovac: 425
Karnavas, Attorney Michael: 436, 483
Kashmir: 401
Kemal, Mustafa / Kemalist: 393, 413, 500
Kennedy, John: 232
KFOR, Kosovo Force: 93, 515
Khamenei, Imam Ali: 414
Kimche, David: 364, 367
Kiseljak (UNPROFOR Headquarters in Bosnia-Herzegovina) : under Croat HVO artillery attack: 34, 112; Civil Affairs Coordinator in Kiseljak stands by Benabou, when his safety is at risk: 161, 162, 168, 174; chairing the opening of negotiations for Mostar in Kiseljak: 176,

*Savagery in the Heart of Europe*

182, 189, 200, 202, 208, 209, 211, 212, 213; briefing the UN commanders in Kiseljak on Mostar affairs: 219-223, 234, 236, 268, 275, 278, 281, 290, 304-306, 321; with General de Hayes exploring convoy routes for Kiseljak headquarters: 330, 334, 336, 341, 344; HVO forces encircling UNPROFOR headquarters in Kiseljak: 345, 346, 348, 351, 363; reports distributed to Kiseljak HQ during the War disappeared and were not available for the court in The Hague: 440, 443, 455, 461, 475, 492; relevant abbreviations / official names: 521, 533
Kissinger, Henry: 247
KLA, Kosovo Liberation Army: 90, 92, 416, 515, 517
Klaric, Smajil: 56, 88, 95, 96, 97, 139, 152, 161, 162, 163, 164, 165, 265, 287, 527
Knin: 17
Kohl, Helmut: 378, 528
Kolak, Dr. Toni: 324, 528
Konjic (strategic point on the road from the Adriatic to Sarajevo): 34, 51, 53, 55, 56, 206, 207, 208, 221, 222, 223, 261, 266, 276, 285, 290, 295, 313, 317, 321, 325, 326, 330, 347, 465, 527
Kordic, Dario: 62-66, 68, 116, 441
Kosovo: 5, 7, 10, 15, 17, 22, 23, 59, 90-95, 127, 253, 377, 385, 388, 389, 400-421, 431, 438, 505, 515, 516, 517, 522, 528, 530, 533, 534, 541
Kostunica, Vojislav: 93, 94, 528, 529, 537
Kouchner, Bernard: 93, 515, 528
Krajina: 17, 18, 21, 30, 61, 90, 91
Krajisnik, Momcilo: 21, 91, 492, 528
Kraljevic, Blaz: 67, 528
Kraus, Dr. Ognjen: 428, 528
Kresevo: 79, 275, 334, 492
Kruger,: 489
Kruscica: 305
Kupres: 65
Kurds: 501, 505
Kuwait: 39

**L**

La Nuestra (Love poem written by Pablo Neruda): 357
Labor Party: 155
Labus, Miroljub: 94, 529, 537
Lacuna: 240, 241
Ladino: 203, 205

La Fontaine: 348
Lasic, Brigadier General Milijenko: 134, 216, 260, 264, 265, 324, 350, 352, 529
Lasva Valley: 67, 68, 80
Latvian: viii
Leakey, Col. Arundel David: 378, 529
Lebanon: vi, 120, 137, 199, 234, 246,
Leho, Fatima: 154, 156, 163, 465
Leibowitz, Yeshayahu: 274
Leipzig: 381, 533
Lemkin, Raphael: 27
Levisohn, Florence Hamlish: 42
Levy, David: 167, 210
Libya: vi, x, 26, 225, 252, 412, 498, 500
Lika: 17
Lincoln, Abraham: 331
Lithuanian: viii
Livno: 65, 116
Livno: 65, 116
Ljubinje: 296
Log Brigade: 146
Loghan, Captain Peter: 87, 152, 153, 278, 279, 355, 529, 533
Los Angeles: 465
Lovrenovic, Slobodan: 269, 529
Lozancic, Ivo: 116
Lozo, Obren: 154, 163
Lubushki: 65, 449, 470, 472, 482, 483, 488
Lujic-Mijatovic, Sasha: 338
Luka: 296
Lukic, Vladimir : 350

**M**
Maccabi Tel Aviv: 188
Maccabi Zagreb: 425
Macedonia: 8, 18, 19, 23, 383, 385, 388, 409, 412, 417, 419, 431, 438, 505
Madjarevic, Mato: 116
Madrid: 63, 160, 161, 262, 319, 366, 368
Mahler, Gustav: 295
Maimonides: 205

Majer, British Consul: 4
Major, John: 378, 530
Makarska: 349, 350, 459, 460
MALBAT, Malaysian Battalion: 281, 283, 515
Marano: 204, 205, 345
Markovic, Pero : 116
Martinovic, Jozo: 116
Martyrs: xiii, 16, 120, 392, 404, 406
Mascesa, Ramo: 216-218, 319, 530
Massacre (definition and appreciation of criminal acts during the conflict): vi, x, xi, xiii, 8, 27, 28, 29, 74, 102, 134, 170, 182, 188, 207, 214, 228, 230-236, 239, 247, 248, 267, 317, 346, 353, 354, 363, 381, 384, 476, 501
Maya: xii
Maybe Airlines (UN planes renamed due to their unsafe traffic in the war zone): 170
McArthur, Marshal Douglas: 227
MEDEVAC, Medical Evacuation: 172, 296, 320, 515
Mediate: 47, 76, 156, 168, 219, 536
Medjugorje, Civil Affairs, UNHCR, SPABAT HQ: the holy town hosts the UN forces in the region: 53, 54, 97, 106, 107, 108, 111, 117; the warring parties, Muslims and Croats convey in Medjugorje: 122, 123, 130, 158, 161; the town is hosting the international forum preparing the Geneva Conference: 162, 171, 173; SPABAT limited to the perimeter of Medjugorje: 175, 176, 177, 192, 195, 200, 201, 202, 205; emergency meeting in Medjugorje to verify the ethnic cleansing: 209, 213, 257, 259, 269, 278, 286, 287, 307, 317, 319, 320, 322, 325, 326, 330; Medjugorje serving as a transit location for expulsions: 332, 348, 440
Mello, Sergio: 463
Mencken, Henri Louis: 47
Menderes, Adnan: 419, 500
Merlino, Jacques: 44
Metkovic: 125, 174, 206, 222, 313, 322
Mevlevi: 387
Middle East: vii, xi, xiii, xiv, xv, 51, 67, 145, 159, 413, 418, 432, 507, 510
Mihailovic, Draza: 10, 530
Milavic, Dr. Dragan: 57, 197, 202, 437, 440
Miljevina: 38, 293

Milosevic, Col. Novak: 34, 37, 38, 57, 293, 458
Milosevic, Slobodan: 10, 17, 20, 21, 59, 62, 64, 85, 89, 90, 91, 92, 93, 94, 369, 377, 417, 490, 492, 522, 523, 528, 530, 536, 540
Milutinovic, Milan: 21, 90, 530
Mladic, Nedja: 234
Mladic, Ratko: 177, 231-245, 254, 258, 276, 347, 490, 491, 492, 493, 502, 512, 530
Modriča: 380
Moldavia: 383
Molina, Captain Gerardo, G2: 259, 269, 332, 336, 457, 530
Mongol: xi
Montenegro: 8, 9, 20, 21, 22, 23, 31, 34, 64, 90, 93, 94, 289, 385, 387, 409, 431, 504, 522, 523, 532, 540
Montesquieu: 322
Montgomery, Field Marshal Bernard: 227
Montpellier: 301
Moral / morality: xi, xii, 43, 57, 92, 226, 239, 309, 394, 395, 398, 400, 402, 446
Morales, Colonel Angel (Commander of the Spanish Battalion, newcomer in the international scene, accomplishing his national first UN mission with dedication): 71, 73, 177, 178, 182-187, 190, 193, 210, 213, 220, 257-261, 269-273, 276, 277, 319-322, 330, 331, 348, 366, 361, 523, 530
Morillon, General Philippe: taking over the negotiations between Croats and Muslims in Mostar: 173, 175, 177, 178, 179, 181, 182, 185; testimony at the French National Assembly, concerning Srebrenica: 225, 229-240, 243, 244, 246, 255, 256, 257, 258, 274-276; Boban challenges Morillon on the Geneva Conference: 333-337, 347, 453, 455, 456, 457; relevant abbreviations / official names: 519, 521, 530
Morocco / Moroccan: 167, 364, 392, 500
Mosque: 42, 394, 398, 410, 472, 500
Mossad: 246, 483
Mostar: massacres in the city: xiii; the victimization as a burden: 28; Mostar is not in Izetbegovic agenda: 32-37; the Muslim position: 40, 42-45, 51-61, 64; Mostar divided: 69-76, 79; the outcome of military confrontation remains unclear: 84-89; negotiating the Mostar interim agreement: 95-198; Mostar in flames: 200-239, 245, 250, 254-257, 259-269, 273-275, 279-281, 285-297; UNPROFOR leadership and the Geneva Conference forum alerted for Mostar: 303, 304, 311-326, 330, 333- 353, 361,-365; no genuine reconciliation for the people of

Mostar: 421, 431, 435, 437, 439, 440, 443-448, 480-492, 495, 496, 503, 507; relevant abbreviations / official names: 517, 519, 521, 523, 524-531, 533, 535, 537
Mount Ozren: 379
Movement of population: 31, 118, 215, 275, 457
Mufti: 386, 410, 498, 526
Mujahidin / Mujahedeen: 10, 41, 50, 67, 99, 371, 388, 403, 404, 405, 413, 414
Municipal: 22, 67, 69, 70, 78, 91, 101, 103, 104, 124, 145, 167, 379, 380, 415, 470, 508, 509, 510, 523, 528
Muslim brothers: 67, 387, 401, 402
Nakamitsu, Isumi: 209, 210, 211, 269, 326, 531

## N

Namibia: 82,
Naqshbandi: 387
NATO: 9, 22, 38, 47, 50, 52, 86, 91, 91, 92, 93, 98, 152, 201, 252, 253, 283, 332, 348, 369, 371, 377, 378, 379, 389, 415, 416, 417, 434, 502, 516, 522, 530
Navarro, General Prado: 257, 269, 531
Nazi: viii, xi, 11, 12, 13, 19, 29, 44, 63, 226, 230, 234, 246, 263, 275, 294, 386, 407, 410, 423, 425, 426, 427, 432, 435, 498, 523, 526, 531
NDH, Independent State of Croatia: 386, 504, 515
Nedic, Milan: viii
Negev: 192
Neretva Ninety-Three: 74
Neretva River (crossing the city of Mostar): 33, 35, 37, 54, 55, 71, 74, 75, 80, 110, 113, 114, 136, 176, 184, 211, 290, 292, 319, 481, 495
Neruda, Pablo: 357
Netherlands: 123, 230, 300, 310, 391, 439, 514, 541
Neutrality: 45, 85, 145, 250, 257, 258, 259, 271, 314, 421
Nevesinje: 56, 57, 58, 296
New Port: 205
New York Times: 49, 158, 389, 416
New York: Muslim lobby established in New York: 42, 49, 101, 158, 164; at the occasion of the General Assembly, Rabin opens the door for an Israeli candidacy to the Peace Keeping Forces: 166, 168, 172, 200, 201, 202, 203, 208, 211, 212; the romance grows between the staff member at the glass building and the Officer in Medjugorje: 213, 216, 232, 238, 241, 243, 247, 249, 253, 257, 268, 297, 306, 307,

308, 309, 328, 329, 333-336, 340; at last Mostar attracts the attention of the UN in New York: 341, 348, 353-355, 358, 359, 389, 416, 434, 439, 440, 463, 468, 475, 495, 496, 497, 506; relevant abbreviations / official names: 536
New Zealand: xii
Newsday, Long Island newspaper: 44
NGO, Non-Governmental Organization: 53, 192, 200, 342, 508, 515
Ninth Brigade: 74
NORDBAT, Nordic Battalion: 248, 306, 515
NORMOVCOM: 169, 515
North Africa: 67, 167, 205, 507
Northern Slav: 13
Nova Bila: 73, 324, 446, 464, 467
Novi Sehar: 480
Novi Travnik (Travnik): 63, 66, 67, 68, 70, 78, 79, 174, 176, 275, 334, 487
Novipazar: 385
Nuremberg: 435, 488

## O

O'Brien, Sergeant Sean: 278, 531
O'Reilly, UN High Commissioner for Civilian Police: s 216, 219, 531
Oceania: xi
Odžak: 379
Ohio: 89, 369, 377, 378
OHR, Office of the High Representative: 380, 515, 532
Omar, Captain Walid: 366
Omarska: 441
Ombudsman: 223, 315, 374
Opstina (Suburb): 178, 235, 236
Oreskovic, Tihomir: 426
Oriani, Isabella: 215, 331, 332, 531
Oric, Naser: 230 244, 247, 498, 531
Orthodox: 6, 14, 24, 230, 235, 358, 367, 377, 383, 385, 400, 408, 421, 427, 428, 430, 534
Orucevic, Colonel Safet (faithful representative of Izetbegovic in Mostar): 45, 56, 58, 59, 60, 80, 98, 106, 130, 131, 132, 146, 148, 149, 152, 163, 164,165, 287, 531
Orucevic, Zijad: 124

OSCE, Organization for Security and Cooperation in Europe: s 92, 372, 373, 375, 516
Oslo: 166
Oslobobdjenje, Liberation, newspaper in Bosnia-Herzegovina: 165
Osmanovic, Mr. Samir: 325, 527, 531
OTP, ICTY's Office of the Prosecutor: 436, 438, 440, 442, 473, 474, 480
Ottoman: xii, xiv, 2-9, 11, 19, 24, 41, 95, 110, 138, 194, 205, 229, 294, 367, 382-387, 408, 412, 418, 419, 498, 500, 503, 523, 527
Owen, Lord David: 30, 64, 82, 83, 84, 105, 140, 150, 158, 160, 166, 169, 180, 223, 232, 262, 313, 314, 316, 317, 333, 334, 337, 454, 487, 491, 492, 531, 536, 538
Oxford: 9
Ozal, Turgut: 419, 500
13

**P**
Pakistan: 1, 39, 58, 384, 401, 402
Pale: 31, 33, 59, 62, 83, 85, 86, 117
Palestinian: vi, x, 46, 51, 137, 166, 167, 175, 234, 235, 402, 409, 410, 411, 501, 505, 508, 526, 539, 541
Panama Canal Zone: 82
Pan-Islamism: 396
Paris: 92, 167, 233, 262, 369, 373, 377, 378, 474, 475, 522, 540
Partisan: 10, 13, 14, 21, 90, 234, 294, 425, 523, 530, 535
Pasalic, General Arif: 55, 56, 216, 350, 440, 464, 531
Pasha: 294, 362, 387, 527
Pasic, Mugdin: 135
Patton, General George: 56, 227
Pavelic, Ante: viii, 63, 234
Pazar: 385
Peace Initiative (for an interim agreement in Mostar): 43, 84, 87, 88, 95, 104, 142, 146, 147, 148, 149, 254, 259, 290
Pedisa, Amela: 54, 524, 531
Pehar, Mate: 217, 531
Pejanovic, Mirko: 338, 532
Pellnas, General Bo: 105, 106, 107, 162, 163
Peres, Shimon: 144
Perestroika: 5
Perry, Secretary of Defense William: 39
Pesic, Dragisa: 94, 532

Petkovic, General Milivoj: negotiating for POW exchange: 37, 144, 173, 177; Petkovic appointed by Tudjman: 179, 180, 184; facilitating a food convoy to Mostar: 191, 193, 195, 205, 206; the threat of the international court of Justice: 209, 219, 221, 223, 224, 245, 257, 266, 269, 273, 274, 295; in the flight of the helicopter impacted ground: 304, 311, 316, 338, 447; indicted for war crimes at the court in the Hague: 449, 450, 451, 453, 454, 458, 459, 467, 468, 469, 470, 471, 482-494; relevant abbreviations / official names: 532
Petritsch, Wolfgang: 380, 532
PILPG, Public International Law and Policy Group: 378, 516, 536
Pita, Captain, G5: 259, 336, 339, 457, 532
Platform: 16, 391, 395, 402, 501, 510, 526, 541
Plaza, Hotel: 355
Ploce: 125, 158
Pogarcic, Vladislav (Vlado): 59, 60, 80,105, 106, 114, 116, 126, 129, 130, 142, 143, 144, 145, 158, 164, 180, 192, 220, 257-275, 286, 323-325, 333, 336-339, 345, 346, 348-353, 445, 447, 449, 452, 454, 456, 457, 459, 463, 464, 465, 466, 468, 532
Poland / Poles: viii, 13
Pomaci: 383
Ponte, Prosecutor Carla Del: 473
Pope John Paul II: 49, 76, 428, 528
Porte: 5
Portuguese: 82, 105, 201
Posavina: s 116, 379, 380
Posusje: 65, 331
POW, Prisoners Of War: 75, 97, 102, 122, 124, 125, 128, 132, 133, 146, 168, 171, 175, 266, 292, 465, 471, 516
Praljak, Slobodan: 69, 469, 470, 471, 487, 489, 490, 491, 494
Prandler, Arpad: 474
Prizren: 388, 408
Prlic, Jadranko (Prime Minister of Herzeg-Bosnia): extreme member controlling the party in Bosnia: 62, 67, 75, 78, 79, 102, 103, 108; supporting the interim agreement for Mostar: 109, 116, 121-134, 137, 141, 155, 156, 180, 211, 224, 260, 261, 287, 311, 338; the military prospect for a Croat victory: 348, 349; Indicted for war crimes and condemned at the Hague: 350, 436, 441-471, 475-477, 482-494; relevant abbreviations / official names: 532
Prophet: 16, 391, 394, 397, 500
Prosecution: 148, 435, 436, 437, 438, 441, 443, 470, 477-493

Prosecutor (International Tribunal at The Hague): 92, 169, 289, 405, 436, 438-442, 471, 473-477, 480, 485-489, 493, 520
Prozor: 56, 67, 108, 109, 112, 174, 470, 486, 487
Puma: 304
Pusic, Berislav (Berko): 75, 451, 452, 461-465, 469-471, 486, 488, 489

**Q**
Qadiri: 387
QRF, Rapid Reaction Force: 86, 516
Quai d'Orsay: 210
Qur'an: 393, 394, 396, 397, 401, 402, 403, 407
Qutb, Sayyid: 16, 391

**R**
R2P, Responsibility to Protect: 433, 516
Rabbi: 85, 364, 368
Rabin, Yitzhak: 166, 497
Radio Mostar: 69
Raguz, Martin: 462, 463
Rajic, Ivica: 34, 290, 492, 532
Rambouillet: 92
Ramirez, Major Alfredo: 269, 348, 532
Ramsay, General A.I.: 464, 532
Rankovici: 70
Rape: 10, 26, 64, 207, 221, 356, 453, 469, 481
Rebic, Dr. Adalbert: 428, 533
Red Army: 13
Rehem (in Hebrew: woman's womb; original meaning in Aramean: love): 217
Reinhartz, Dennis: 427, 540
Reith, General John: 112, 278, 279, 533
Relief: 37, 38, 109, 112, 119, 158, 160, 185, 186, 232, 271, 310, 461, 495
Religion / Coreligionists: 3, 4, 78, 15, 24, 110, 114, 138, 390, 392-395, 401, 404, 408, 411, 414, 431, 469, 472, 505, 526
Republika Srpska, Serbian Republic:
Resolution (UN SCR): 27, 96, 170, 236-242, 247, 251, 256, 259, 269, 341, 342, 343, 376, 434, 435, 445, 516, 517
Refugee: comparing Bosnians, Jews and Palestinians: vi, xiv; Kosovo Albanians: 22; originating from all over former Yugoslavia: 25, 30,

39, 57; 66; humanitarian assistance for the surviving: 93, 109, 111, 112; influx from villages to the big cities: 118, 119, 123, 128; Silajdzic claims return: 151, 160, 185, 194; uprooted: 215, 228, 230; Morillon for the refugees in Srebrenica: 232; centers for refugees: 287, 331, 332, 362, 370, 373, 375, 373, 385, 415; dispersion of refugees: 416, 426, 444, 450, 463, 465, 472, 481, 487; relevant abbreviations / official names: 517, 522, 531, 533

Revival (Islamic religious and ideological in Bosnia): 298, 390, 392, 402, 406, 410, 418

Rhode Island: 205, 301, 354

Rhodesia: 82

Rimbaud: 200

Robinson, Patrick: 474, 484

Roma: x, 9, 13, 29, 407

Rome: 152

Rose, Lt. Gen. (Sir) Michael: 48, 533

Roso, General Ante: 76, 80, 116, 117, 120, 141, 287, 533

Rossignol, Lieutenant Colonel: 304

Rotterdam: 301

Rubinstein, Elyakim : 441

Ruder Finn: s 42, 44, 77, 524, 529

Rudman, Jude: 99, 269, 527

Rugova, Ibrahim: 22, 91, 92, 409, 515, 533

Rusmir, Cisic: 101, 104

Russell, Alec: 241, 244, 251, 540, 541

Russia: 13, 84, 209, 235, 242, 370, 377, 378, 411, 417, 418, 474, 502, 514, 522, 526, 529, 533, 534

Ryan, John: 80, 126, 132, 149

## S

Sabbath: 85, 191, 192

SACEUR, Supreme Allied Commander Europe: 378, 516, 522

Sacirbey, Muhamed: 378, 533

Safe Areas: / Safe Havens: 172, 236, 238, 239, 240, 241, 242, 247, 251, 252

Salas, Major Carlos de: 185, 186, 192, 193, 210, 213, 215, 266, 268, 269, 326, 327, 348, 352, 458, 459, 523

Salko, Zuljevic: 217, 321, 537

Salom, Captain Julio: 345, 533

SALT II: 82

SALW, small arms and light weapons: 50, 51, 69, 516
Sana River: 31
Sancevic, Zdravko: 320, 533
Sandburg, Carl: 264, 351
Sanjak / Sandjak: 94, 532
Santic, Vlado: 116
Sarajevo: historic context: xiii, 4, 7, 8, 15, 20, 21; Muslim military offensives: 30-36, 38, 41-55, 58-62, 74-76, 79; Sarajevo to be demilitarized according to the Vance-Owen Plan: 80-91, 95, 98, 101-107, 112, 115-118, 126-146, 148; Shuttling between Sarajevo and Zagreb for the Mostar interim agreement: 150, 157, 162, 165, 170, 172, 173, 176, 187, 189; the strategic access to Sarajevo under Serb or Croat control: 200, 201, 206-208, 221, 223, 225, 234, 237, 239, 240, 242, 244: NATO operations putting an end to the War: 245-255, 269, 270; Boban calling UNPROFOR for the protection of Croats in Central Bosnia and Sarajevo: 275, 276, 285, 290-293, 321, 322, 330; Lord David Owen declares that an access to the (Adriatic) Sea is to be guaranteed to Sarajevo: 334, 336-338, 341, 347, 349; Yom Kippur in Sarajevo: 362-368, 371, 372, 379, 387; the Islamic faculty in Sarajevo educates functionaries for the Balkans countries: 388, 390, 391, 403-406, 410, 414, 418, 440; testimony of war time in Sarajevo: 443, 448, 455, 468, 476, 481, 497, 502; relevant abbreviations / official names: 513, 515, 520-536
Šarčević, Ante: 386, 503, 534
Šarčević, Edin: 381, 386, 503, 533
Sarid, Yossi: 355, 533
Sasha, Alexandra Milankovic: 188, 189, 190, 191, 192, 193, 194, 338, 340, 354, 355, 530, 533
SATMAR, Satellite Communication: 327, 363, 516
Saudi Arabia: 39, 41, 398, 412, 415, 431, 500
Sava River: ix, 31
SC, Security Council (mandate & resolutions): 77, 86, 92, 93, 96, 97, 170, 172, 198, 208, 209, 236, 238, 241, 242, 247, 251, 252, 269, 333, 341-344, 370, 376, 434, 435, 445, 467, 474, 515, 516, 517
Schwartz, Stephen: 383, 541
Scott, Kenneth: 441, 442, 473, 475, 476, 478, 483, 484, 485, 488, 489
SDA, Muslim Party of Democratic Action: 15, 21, 91, 391, 404, 516, 526
Searby, General Robin: 268, 274, 278, 348, 533
Secular: 41, 100, 381, 394, 411, 413, 419, 500, 515

Sefer Torah: 365
Sekerija, Luka: 68
Seljic, Sulejman: 135
Serb Democratic Party (SDS): 21, 91, 517, 528
Setka, Dr.Zijo: 57
Seventh Muslim Brigade: 67
SFOR, Stabilization Force: 22, 91
SFOR, Stabilization Force: 22, 91
Sharan, Ram: 149, 150
Shari'a: 42, 499
Sharon, General Ariel: 234, 235
Sheikh: 388, 393, 500
Shelly, Christine: 48, 50, 536
Shitaka, Emma: 159
Sho'a, Holocaust: ix, x, xii, 27, 28245, 246, 424, 425, 426, 427, 538, 539, 540, 541
Shuhada: 16, 392, 404
Sibenik: 18
Silajdzic, Haris (Bosnian Prime Minister): 44, 58, 59, 87, 88, 89, 98, 100, 102, 129-141, 148, 150, 151, 153, 156, 158, 161, 165, 169, 291, 365, 444, 448, 449, 463, 525, 533
Sinai: 192, 394
Siroki Brijeg: 57, 461, 482, 483
SIS, Secret Intelligence Service: 489
SITREP, Situation Report: 180, 200, 279, 342, 363, 517
Skjold, Agner: 218, 533
Slav: s 2, 3, 6, 8, 13, 24, 41, 120, 246, 258, 290, 383, 384, 385, 387
Slavonia: 17, 21, 90, 91
Slovenia: 8, 17, 18, 19, 21, 23, 91
Smith, General Rupert: 247, 534
Solana, Javier: 22, 92, 94, 534
Somers, Susan L.: 439, 440, 441, 476
SOP, Standard Operational Procedures: 152, 282, 516, 517
Sorenson, Leo Bang: 218, 320, 534
Sotra, Zdravko: 295, 534
South Africa: xi, 256
Southern Slav: 8, 13, 24, 120, 246
Soviet: 14, 25, 34, 82, 408, 474, 535
SPABAT, UNPROFOR Spanish Battalion: evaluating the needs of the civilian population: 53, 54, 71; taken as hostages: 86, 97; turning blind

eye: 100, 101, 106, 112, 130; hosting negotiations: 158, 161, 162, 171; opening the city of Mostar: 173, 175, 176, 177, 183, 185, 187; escorting humanitarian assistance: 194, 200, 209, 212, 214, 222, 231, 257, 258, 259, 263; coordinating with civil affairs: 268-277, 279, 280, 281, 282, 284, 296, 297; military record: 313, 319-321, 324, 326, 329, 330, 331, 332, 336, 339; offering logistical support: 340, 341, 344, 345, 347, 348, 350, 352, 443, 447, 450, 451, 452, 457, 458, 459, 461, 467, 475; relevant abbreviations / official names: 517, 519, 523, 530, 532, 533
Spanish-American War: 264
Spinoza, Baruch: 439
Split (city on the Adriatic Coast): 18, 78, 79, 152, 188, 224, 225, 266, 278, 304, 305, 320, 325, 322, 348, 349, 366, 420, 512, 513, 533
Sray, Colonel John E.: 47, 534
Srebrenica: xiii, 24, 29, 58, 89, 172, 177, 178, 185, 229-248, 251, 276, 341, 347, 381, 431, 438, 498, 512, 530, 531
Stalin, Joseph: 14
Stalingrad: 18
Stari Most: 69, 110, 496
State Department: 43, 48, 50, 77, 88, 388, 536
Stefan Smirak: 389
Stepinac, Cardinal Aloysius: 428, 429, 534
Stockholm: 251, 534
Stojic, Bruno (Minister of Defense of Herzeg-Bosnia indicted and convicted in The Hague): 65, 74, 103, 219, 220, 257, 261, 263, 266-269, 311, 316, 319-322, 326, 338, 352, 446-462, 465-471, 482, 484, 489, 490, 494, 535
Stolac: 38, 56, 57, 137, 293-296, 340, 449, 458, 470, 486, 523, 524, 527, 529, 534
Stoltenberg, Thorvald: 30, 82, 84, 89, 105, 112, 113, 140, 141, 142, 143, 146, 149, 150, 158, 159, 223, 314, 315, 317, 333, 454
Sudan: xi, 29, 225, 240
Sudetic, Charles: 441, 442, 443, 476
Suez Canal: 392
Sufi: 385, 387, 388
Suisjbic, Said: 139
Suleiman the Magnificent: 110
Sunni: 387, 501
Susak, Goyko: 65, 473, 486, 487
Swede: 248
Synagogue: 85, 192, 362, 365, 366, 367, 368, 439

Syria: vi, x, 27, 225, 240, 402, 412, 432, 433, 498, 500, 501

**T**
Tadic, Boris: 10
Taliban: 402
Talits: 365
Tanzania: 82
Tarcin: 53, 174, 206, 221, 222, 276, 313, 317, 347
Tariqats (orders): 387
Terror: xiii, xiv, 56, 59, 120, 136, 225, 227, 289, 353, 388, 389, 391, 405, 406, 416, 426, 434, 448, 469, 471, 508, 510
The Convoy of Joy Incident: 69
The Hague: xv, 10, 25, 31, 45, 67, 92, 123, 169, 170, 171, 175, 234, 265, 432, 435, 439, 441, 442, 443, 456, 474, 476, 477, 478, 479, 481, 494, 498, 503, 506, 511, 514, 520, 527, 530
The Song of the Earth (composed by Mahler): 295
Thebault, Jean-Pierre: 181
Thornberry, Cedric (Head of Civil Affairs in Bosnia Herzegovina): 71, 72, 73, 99, 108, 113, 140- 144, 152, 159-161, 168, 169, 209, 212, 223, 254, 268, 289, 362, 437, 444, 466, 467, 519, 535
Thrace: 383, 385
Tirana: 409
Tito, Josip Broz: xiv, 10-16, 19, 71, 179, 184, 206, 214, 245, 311, 319, 383, 386, 388, 390, 504, 506, 526, 535, 535
Tole, Zarko: 462
Toledo: 205
Tomic, Ivan: 106, 107, 163, 287, 535
Toronto: 295, 524
Total War: 24, 434
Trauma: 12, 17, 54, 55, 93, 261, 437, 524, 531
Trechsel, Stefan: 474, 484
Tribunal (International court in The Hague, for against Humanity perpetrated in Former Yugoslavia): 4, 31, 45, 62, 92, 94, 123, 169, 170, 171, 230, 234, 245, 371-376, 432-444, 451-488, 494, 511, 514
Trieste: 18
Triumvirate: 449
Truce: 89, 227, 267, 348, 422, 521
Trvno: 34, 38
Tucker, Susan: 441, 442, 443, 476
Tudjman, Franjo: his election engenders the dismantlement of Yugoslavia:

ix, 17, 62, 64, 65, 66; way of conduct towards his faithful friend, Boban: 75, 103, 117, 130, 142, 143; changing attitude towards Sarajevo: 144, 150, 151, 156, 157, 159, 161, 162, 169, 179, 191; no victory in Mostar: 267; aspiring contact to Israel: 316, 321, 352; the Dayton agreement: 369, 424, 425; minimizing Croat crimes during WWII: 428, 429, 431, 438, 444, 449; meeting Tudjman: 452, 468, 473, 486, 487, 490, 491, 492; relevant abbreviations / official names: 520, 525, 532, 535
Turija: 296
Turkey: vii, 84, 320, 383, 384-387, 392, 393, 402, 410-413, 418, 419, 431, 500, 501, 502, 522
Tuzla: 70, 72, 104, 117, 172, 174, 238, 240, 243, 248, 275, 334, 336, 341, 455, 515, 523, 525, 529

**U**
UDC, Union of Democratic Countries: 507
Uganda: 82
Uhud Battle: 394
Uighurs: 389, 413
Ukrainian: viii, 209, 235
Umayyad Dynasty: 205
UNCIVPOL, United Nations/Serbian/Croatian/ Muslim Civil Police: 22, 60, 91, 150, 208, 216-222, 239, 264, 312, 313, 316, 319, 320, 321, 342, 343, 376, 416, 426, 438, 443, 453, 470, 510, 511, 514, 517, 531, 537
UNESCO: 167, 362, 365, 517
UNHCR - United Nations High Commissioner for Refugees: 32, 53, 78, 79, 87, 99, 108, 109, 149, 152, 168, 184, 190, 210, 215, 217, 258, 264, 266, 269, 273, 287, 295, 322, 326, 339, 343, 440, 451,467, 517, 526, 531
UNICEF: 54, 198, 274, 350, 517, 524, 531
United Nations Protected Area (UNPA): 28, 236, 238, 239, 240, 242, 517
United States of America (USA): American history: x, xi, xii, xiii, 16, 28, 29, 31, 38; US Air force securing areas in Bosnia: 39; Muslim and Croat lobbies: 42, 43, 44-50, 58, 59, 60, 62, 64, 76, 77; switching positions towards Vance-Owen Peace Plan: 84, 87, 89, 92, 96; Silajdzic calling for US intervention: 100, 107, 113, 120, 117, 144, 153, 158, 159, 173; relations with the Allied forces implicated in the ground: 252, 254, 287, 303; the Washington agreement between Muslims and Croats leading to the overall Dayton Peace Treaty: 369, 370, 377,

382, 391, 412, 414, 415, 418, 424, 430, 434, 454, 501, 508 relevant abbreviations / official names: 513, 514, 522, 524 527, 533, 534
UNMO, United Nations Monitoring Officer: s 38, 45, 54, 73, 150, 293, 295, 343, 458, 460, 517
UNTSO, United Nations Truce Supervision Organization: 227
UPAM, Union for the Preservation of Absolute Monarchies: 500
US Care, International Food Organization: 146
US Navy: 47, 48
Ustasha: vii, viii, ix, x, xi, 11, 12, 13, 17, 18, 19, 29, 63, 230, 234, 263, 294, 331, 367, 386, 407, 423-430, 504, 523, 534, 535
UT, Union of Tyrannies: 507

**V**
Valdiness, J.: 152
Valenci, Andrea de: 201, 202, 203, 212, 307, 308, 317, 353, 536
Vance, Cyrus: 19, 30, 64, 82, 83, 84, 105, 160, 166, 180,223, 232, 262, 313, 487, 491, 492, 531, 536
Vares: 34, 111, 112, 275, 290, 334, 336, 470, 486
Varinika, Nouri Aga: 4
Vatican: 49, 525
Venice: 140
Ventura, Romeu: 474, 475
Vezir: 387
Victimization: 77, 243
Vienna: 2, 76, 155, 156, 160, 161, 383, 495, 527
Vietnam: xii, 119, 225, 245
Vietnamese: xii
Visoka: 4
Visoko: 72, 345, 512
Vitez: 34, 68, 70, 73, 78, 79, 108, 109, 111, 112, 275, 290, 321, 330, 334, 446
Vitina: 479, 480
Voivodina: 32, 95, 127, 385, 419, 505, 431
VOPP, Vance-Owen Peace Plan: 82, 83, 90
Vrda: 479, 480
Vrljic, Stojan: 144, 466
Vukovar: xiii, 18, 481

**W**
Waffen SS: 386, 404, 504

Wahlgren, General Lars-Erik: 224, 229, 234, 246, 317, 454, 536
Wales, Prince Charles of: 362
Wallachia: 383
Wannsee Conference: xi, 12
War Crimes: 10, 25, 65, 81, 130, 170, 213, 289, 370, 371, 420, 432, 433, 434, 435, 436, 437, 441, 481, 489, 511, 516, 530
War Presidency: 53, 54, 56, 95, 96, 111, 124, 125, 131, 154, 156, 163, 287, 362
Warsaw: 14
Washington: 21, 33, 41, 42, 48, 58, 62, 64, 75, 76, 79, 85, 86, 87, 100, 103, 105, 110, 117, 118, 125, 158, 159, 160, 164, 260, 286, 287, 288, 333, 378, 389, 468, 495, 510, 524, 529, 536, 538
Watkins, Philip: 152
Webster, Daniel: 335
Western Colonizers: xi
Western Nations: xiii, 1, 9, 10, 14, 29, 31, 39, 41, 45, 46, 47, 77, 89, 93, 98, 99, 113, 114, 179, 261, 274, 284, 379, 389, 394, 395, 401, 412, 414, 418, 431, 499, 502, 507, 511, 519, 536
WHO, World Health Organization: 198, 517, 534
Wilkinson, Tracy: 423, 424, 541
Williams, Paul: s 378, 536
World War I: s x, 7, 11, 498
World War II: vii, viii, xiv, 8, 10, 12, 18, 19, 44, 62, 63, 190, 206, 230, 263, 294, 331, 403, 425, 434, 435, 498, 523, 535
Wright-Patterson (US Air Base): 369

**X**
Xinjiang: 389

**Y**
Yemen: vi, x, 498
Yom Kippur: 351, 362, 364, 365, 367, 368, 497
Yugoslavian Kingdom: 8, 63, 486
Yugoslavian Wars: 25, 27, 28, 432, 520, 533
Yugoslavian Wars: 29, 30, 426, 434, 517

**Z**
Zagreb: the persisting hatred: xiii, 8; in total control of the Croat leadership in Bosnia: 36, 51, 53, 59, 60-65, 74-77; positive approach towards the interim initiative in Mostar: 87, 95, 101, 103; no frictions

with the US broker: 106-108, 112, 117, 118, 126, 130-134, 140-144; last efforts to save the interim peace agreement for Mostar: 150-162, 164; first station for the UN peace keeping mission: 166, 168, 172, 173, 179, 182, 187, 198, 200, 201, 202, 210, 211, 212, 213, 214, 215; UNPROFOR headquarters in Zagreb calling for multilateral talks concerning Mostar: 223, 225, 232, 238, 254, 255, 256, 259, 267, 268, 271, 272, 285, 286, 291, 296, 297, 305, 306, 316, 320, 333, 334, 335, 336, 339, 340, 343, 344, 348, 349, 351, 352, 354; the authorities in Zagreb instructing the military operation of HVO in Bosnia: 359, 362; Washington and Dayton Agreements: 414, 424, 425, 428, 429, 430, 440, 443, 445, 449, 450,452, 455, 458, 460, 461, 465, 468, 475, 478, 482, 485, 486, 495, 496, 497
Zbor: 426
Zekat: 396
Zelic, Slavko : 115
Zenica: 67, 68, 70, 104, 127, 174, 211, 275, 334, 336, 524
Zepa: 89, 172, 239, 240, 243, 341
Zero Deaths: 244
Zero-sum: xiii, 421,
Zimmermann, Warren: 83, 84, 536
Zionism: 167, 402, 526
Zivkovic, Ivo: 116
Zizic, Zoran: 93, 94, 529, 536
Zona Franca: 58
Zubak, Kresimir: 21, 76, 91, 108, 111, 112, 116, 164, 286, 445, 466, 537
Zweig, Stefan: 215

Lightning Source UK Ltd.
Milton Keynes UK
UKHW01f0651221018
330961UK00001B/290/P